CIVIL TAX PROCEDURE

SECOND EDITION

DAVID M. RICHARDSON
Professor of Law
Frederic G. Levin College of Law
University of Florida

JEROME BORISON
Associate Professor of Law
Sturm College of Law
University of Denver

STEVE JOHNSON
E.L. Wiegand Professor of Law
William S. Boyd School of Law
University of Nevada, Las Vegas

GRADUATE TAX SERIES

LexisNexis™

Library of Congress Cataloging-in-Publication Data

Richardson, David M. (David Maurice), 1939-
    Civil tax procedure / David M. Richardson, Jerome Borison, Steve Johnson.
        p. cm.
    Includes index.
    ISBN 978-1-4224-1756-0 (hardbound)
    1. Tax administration and procedure — United States. 2. Taxation — Law
and legislation — United States. 3. Income tax — Law and
legislation — United States. I. Borison, Jerome, 1946- II. Johnson,
Steve, 1949- III. Title.
KF6300.R53 2007
343.7304--dc22   2007038857

Editorial Offices
744 Broad Street, Newark, NJ 07102 (973) 820-2000
201 Mission St., San Francisco, CA 94105-1831 (415) 908-3200
701 East Water Street, Charlottesville, VA 22902-7587 (434) 972-7600
www.lexis.com

(Pub.03639)

LexisNexis
GRADUATE TAX SERIES

PREFACE

The Lexis Graduate Tax Series grew out of the recognition that the goals of a graduate tax program are different than those of J.D. tax courses. J.D. tax courses are introductory in nature. Although many J.D. tax courses provide a good overview of their targeted areas of law, time rarely permits either in-depth analysis of complicated Code or Regulation provisions, or the application of those provisions to real life problems. In essence, J.D. tax courses provide students a foundation in the core statutory and judicial concepts.

LL.M. programs build on, and significantly expand, students' knowledge of the Code, Regulations, and judicial doctrines, and enhance their Code and Regulations reading skills. LL.M. programs require students to concentrate on the primary sources of the law, the Code and Regulations. Students are expected to improve their ability to read, comprehend, and apply the Code and Regulations, and they do so by working on complex fact patterns that raise difficult legal issues.

The different goals of graduate tax programs and J.D. tax courses suggest that the course materials used in those programs should also be different. Students in LL.M. programs need to move away from the standard, J.D., "author tells all," casebooks, which contain extensive quotations from cases and other secondary sources, and toward emphasis on the primary sources of the law. By applying the Code and Regulations to real-life fact patterns, students gain the confidence necessary to rely on the Code and Regulations as their main source of information.

An important, but different, driving force behind the development of specially designed course materials for LL.M. programs is the dramatic expansion of the quantity and complexity of tax law over the past forty or fifty years. The current commercially available versions of the Code and Regulations are roughly four times as large as their 1970 predecessors. Over that period, class time dedicated to tax has grown very little. Covering much more material in the same period of time has led authors to write longer J.D. textbooks, many of which exceed one thousand pages. Such comprehensive coverage leads to extended textbook assignments. This both forces and permits the students to bypass the assigned Code and Regulations provisions and spend their available time answering problems by reference solely to the author's explanation of the law in the textbook. Tax casebooks written primarily for the larger J.D. market that purport to be suitable for both J.D. and LL.M. tax courses, also lean towards comprehensive explanations of the Code and

Regulations, which tend to deflect students away from the primary sources.

Books in the Graduate Tax Series are designed to be read with, and complement, the study of the Code and Regulations. Although some chapters of books in the Series provide detailed explanation of the topic, more frequently the chapters provide a general, normally brief, overview of the topic together with more complete explanations of the applicable portions of the Code and Regulations that are particularly difficult to understand. Also, many of the problems are based on situations encountered in practice or found in decided cases. Although some of the questions either state or disclose the issues and even the applicable statutes, many of them require analysis of a given set of facts to first determine and then resolve the critical issues.

Students need to recognize that shifting the emphasis to primary sources and practice-based problems, which is made possible by reducing the time spent reading and analyzing cases and other secondary sources, increases the responsibility of the student for his or her education. It is harder to master a complex statute or regulation by studying it than it is to have someone explain it. It is also harder to identify the issues and applicable law from a group of facts than it is to answer short problems that identify the issue and the applicable law.

Students in an LL.M. program should be able to handle the higher level of personal responsibility. Furthermore, if one accepts the premise that learning a core set of rules and developing Code and Regulations reading skills are equally important goals, it is clear that students must dedicate a significant portion of their study time to the primary sources of the law.

Like all other areas of law, tax law has both substantive and procedural components. This book addresses the procedures by which taxpayers' liabilities are determined and collected. These procedures include the filing of returns, the administrative and judicial mechanisms for resolving disputes about how much tax is owed, the administrative and judicial mechanisms by which unpaid taxes are collected after the extent of the liability has been determined, and penalties for noncompliance with tax rules. The focus of this book is on civil tax procedure. Although criminal tax rules are occasionally mentioned, this book does not examine them in detail.

A great many of the rules of civil tax procedure were created or significantly revised by the Internal Revenue Service Restructuring and Reform Act of 1998, Pub. L. No. 105-206, 112 Stat. 685. Throughout the book, this legislation is referred to as the 1998 Reform Act. Unless otherwise indicated, references to sections in this book are to the Internal Revenue Code of 1986 as amended through December 31, 2004.

In this course, students should focus on the assigned reading materials, principally sections of the Internal Revenue Code and the Regulations promulgated under it. For additional information and as aids in practice, there are numerous books and articles exploring in greater depth the topics addressed in this book. Some of the best are the current editions of: Jerome Borison (ed.), Effectively Representing Clients Before the "New" IRS (3 volumes); Michael Saltzman, IRS Practice and Procedure; and William D. Elliott, Federal Tax Collections, Liens, and Levies.

David Richardson would like to express his appreciation for the Summer Research Grants provided by the Frederic G. Levin College of Law at the University of Florida that helped make this book possible. He thanks Walter E. Afield, Ashley D. Money, Jacqueline K. Queener, and Ryan M. Schwartz, graduates of the University of Florida tax program, and Daniel A. Wolf, a J.D. student at the University of Michigan Law School, all of whom worked on the book. Most of all, he thanks his wife Regina for putting up with the many distractions associated with the evolution of the Lexis Graduate Tax Series and writing of this book.

Jerome Borison wishes to thank his super family—Meg, Spencer and Georgia—for giving him only a modestly tough time about the hours and hours spent in the basement office working at the computer on this book. Fortunately, he did not have to miss any soccer, baseball, softball, tennis, skiing, basketball, piano or choir activities or performances to do it.

Steve Johnson is grateful for the financial support of the E.L. Wiegand Foundation and the William S. Boyd School of Law, University of Nevada, Las Vegas. He also is grateful to Evelyn Johnson, Susan Stabile, Monica Miller, Cynthia Sawyers, Dick Morgan, Lauren Robel, Bill Popkin, John Sexton, and Lisa Goldberg for their contributions to his growth as a scholar and a person.

ACKNOWLEDGMENTS

Portions of this book are derived from Jerome Borison, Effectively Representing Your Client Before the "New" IRS (3d Ed.). The authors wish to thank the American Bar Association Section of Taxation, which has kindly granted permission for its use.

TABLE OF CONTENTS

Chapter 1

STRUCTURE OF TAX ADMINISTRATION
AND SOURCES OF TAX LAW

IRC:	§§ 6110(a), (b)(1), (c), (k)(3); 6405(a); 7805(a) & (b)
Regs.:	§§ 601.201(l)(1) - (7); 601.601(a) & (d)(2)
Rulings:	Rev. Proc. 2007-1 (or the corresponding revenue procedure in each subsequent year, such as Rev. Proc. 2008-1, etc.) (skim only); Rev. Proc. 64-22.
Forms:	911; 2848

I. INTRODUCTION

Students new to tax will encounter legal authorities familiar to them from other contexts as well as authorities that are unique to tax. It is essential for a tax practitioner to understand what authorities exist in tax practice and their nature, purposes, and uses. Reading descriptions of tax rules in secondary sources can never replace reading those rules in the sources that prescribe them.

This chapter begins with an overview of the roles played by the three branches of the federal government in formulating and applying tax law. It then describes the principal types of administrative sources and authorities in tax. Finally, the chapter addresses prominent issues that arise as to the various kinds of tax authorities.

II. ROLES OF THE THREE BRANCHES

A few cases suggest that the government's power to raise revenue is pre-constitutional, an attribute inherent in the very notion of sovereignty. Nonetheless, it is appropriate to review the main constitutional provisions bearing on taxation. Article I, section 8, clause 1 of the Constitution gives Congress the power to "lay and collect Taxes." Article I, section 9, clause 4 prescribes that so-called direct taxes must be apportioned among the states in proportion to population, but this requirement has little significance currently. In a widely criticized case, the Supreme Court invalidated an earlier version of the federal income tax because it was not so apportioned.[1] That restriction was swept away when the Sixteenth Amendment was ratified in 1913.

---

[1] Pollock v. Farmers' Loan & Trust Co., 158 U.S. 601 (1895).

As discussed in Chapter 4, the Fourth Amendment proscription against illegal searches and seizures and the self-incrimination clause of the Fifth Amendment sometimes are invoked (usually unsuccessfully) against IRS information-gathering efforts.[2] Apart from those provisions, constitutional challenges to tax measures are asserted only rarely and succeed even less often.[3]

An ill-advised 2006 circuit court decision put constitutional limitations on federal taxation in the spotlight. The taxpayer had received damages from her former employer under whistle blower environmental statutes for mental pain and anguish, and injury to her professional reputation. A panel of the D.C. Circuit correctly held that the statutory exclusion in section 104(a)(2) did not apply, but it held the statute unconstitutional on the ground that such compensation for non-physical personal injury is not "income" within the meaning of the Sixteenth Amendment. This decision provoked a storm of controversy, and the court vacated its decision four months later.[4]

A. Congress

The role of Congress is to write the tax statutes. The highest authority in tax is the statute, whether the Internal Revenue Code or an uncodified session law. For a tax lawyer, identifying the relevant statute(s) and carefully reading the statutory language is the starting point in every case.

The ideas ultimately embodied in tax statutes may originate with the Administration, with individual members of Congress, or with industry groups or key constituents. The ideas will be put into legislative language by congressional staffers, the Treasury Department, or private interest groups. Bills (proposed legislation) will be introduced in the House, the Senate, or both.[5]

The bills are then referred to the tax-writing committees: the Ways and Means Committee in the House and the Finance Committee in the Senate. Many bills die in committee. Important bills may receive hearings by the committee, involving testimony by experts and others and submission of written

---

[2] The Fourth Amendment provides in part: "The right of the people to be secure in their persons, houses, papers, and effects, against unreasonable searches and seizures, shall not be violated." The Fifth Amendment provides in part that no person "shall be compelled in any criminal case to be a witness against himself."

[3] *See, e.g.*, United States v. United States Shoe Corp., 523 U.S. 360 (1998) (harbor maintenance tax held in violation of Export Clause); United States v. Carlton, 512 U.S. 26 (1994) (retroactive application of estate tax change held not to violate Due Process Clause).

[4] Murphy v. IRS, 460 F.3d 79 (D.C. Cir. 2006), *judgment vacated* (December 22, 2006).

[5] Under Article I, section 7, clause 1 of the Constitution, tax measures are supposed to originate in the House of Representatives, but this requirement sometimes is finessed. *See, e.g.*, Moore v. U.S. House of Representatives, 733 F.2d 946 (D.C. Cir. 1984) (rejecting challenge to 1982 tax legislation that effectively originated in the Senate), *cert. denied*, 469 U.S. 1106 (1985), abrogated as to standing issue, Chenoweth v. Clinton, 181 F.3d 112 (D.C. Cir. 1999).

statements. The committee may revise the language of bills in "mark up" sessions. Ultimately, the committee votes on the bill.

Bills that pass the committee (often in amended form) go to the full House or Senate. Typically, the House and Senate versions will differ. Differences between tax bills passed by the two chambers are reconciled by conference committees convened for that purpose. The reconciled measure is then returned to the House and the Senate. After being passed by them, the measure goes to the President for his signature or veto.[6]

The Joint Committee on Taxation is also important. It is a standing committee with members drawn from both the majority and minority of the House Ways and Means and the Senate Finance Committees. It has a sizeable staff of economists and attorneys. The Joint Committee provides expertise on a continuing basis, contributing significantly to the tax legislation process. Sections 8021 through 8023 describe the duties and powers of the Joint Committee. In addition, under section 6405(a), the Joint Committee reviews proposed refunds over $2,000,000.

In recent decades, Congress has passed major tax acts every few years and several lesser measures each year. Initially, tax acts are enacted as session laws, such as the Tax Reform Act of 1969 or the Tax Equity and Fiscal Responsibility Act of 1982. The great majority of important items are then codified in the Internal Revenue Code. The IRC is Title 26 of the United States Code. Thus, for instance, 26 U.S.C. section 163 and IRC section 163 are two ways of referring to the same statute. Generalist lawyers and judges tend to use the first styling while tax specialists use the second.

Before 1939, federal tax statutes existed in session law form only. The first codification was the Internal Revenue Code of 1939, which was succeeded by the Internal Revenue Code of 1954. The 1954 version enacted many new sections and changed the section numbers of provisions retained from the 1939 Code. The current version is the Internal Revenue Code of 1986, which largely preserved the numbering of sections retained from the 1954 Code.

The Internal Revenue Code is divided into subtitles, such as Subtitle A (the income tax), Subtitle B (the estate, gift, and generation-skipping transfer taxes), and Subtitle F (procedural and administrative sections applying to the Code generally). The subtitles are subdivided into, successively, chapters, subchapters, parts, subparts, sections, subsections, paragraphs, and subparagraphs.

Codes tend to operate on internal structural logic. Thus, courts sometimes look to where a provision is situated in the Code as a clue to the meaning of the provision. However, this approach runs counter to section 7806(b), which pro-

---

[6] For fuller discussion of the tax legislative process, see Conference Proceedings, *The Tax Legislative Process—A Critical Need*, 10 Amer. J. Tax Pol'y 99 (1992); excerpts from the 1978 FBA Conference on Writing Tax Law, 35 Fed. B.J. 76 (1978).

vides that no "inference, implication or presumption" shall flow from "the location or grouping of any particular provision" within the Code.

The codified version of a tax statute typically omits some features contained in the session law. For example, the effective date of the statute usually is omitted although commercially available compilations provide effective-date information via notation. Also normally omitted are transitional rules, which exempt (permanently or temporarily) particular taxpayers or activities from the reach of a new provision. Such rules, secured by legislators for important constituents, often are the unavoidable price for getting enough votes to pass a measure, but they may be problematic in terms of fairness, transparency, and democracy.[7]

On occasion, Congress will enact a substantive tax measure in a session law but choose not to codify it in the IRC. This has been done, for instance, with respect to filing relief or tax holidays for American embassy workers held captive in Tehran, 9-11 victims, and soldiers and sailors serving in a variety of combat theaters.[8] Also, on occasion, Congress codifies tax measures, or more general measures that affect the tax system, under titles of the United States Code other than Title 26.[9]

The tax legislative process generates committee reports and other documents. The types of legislative documents relied on in tax controversies include (i) reports generated by the Ways and Means, Finance, and conference committees, (ii) General Explanations (the so-called Blue Books) prepared by the staff of the Joint Committee after passage of major tax acts,[10] (iii) occasional committee prints prepared for general informational purposes, (iv) pre-enact-

---

[7] *See, e.g.*, Apache Bend Apts., Ltd. v. United States, 964 F.2d 1556 (5th Cir. 1992), *rev'd*, 987 F.2d 1174 (5th Cir. 1993) (en banc).

[8] Perhaps the most important tax provision not codified in the IRS is section 530 of the Revenue Act of 1978, which provides safe harbors for making "employee versus independent contractor" classifications. Pub. L. No. 95-600, § 530, 92 Stat. 2763, 2885 (as subsequently amended).

[9] Examples are 38 U.S.C. section 5301(a), which provides an income tax exclusion for certain training expense reimbursements provided by the Veterans Administration, and 18 U.S.C. section 1001, which makes it a crime to make false statements or submit false documents to federal officials, including IRS personnel.

[10] Use of the Blue Books has been controversial. Under the influence of Justice Scalia and others, the role of legislative history in statutory construction has been under attack for some years. Technically, the Blue Books are not even legislative history in the way that House Ways and Means and Senate Finance Committee reports are. The Blue Book is produced by the Joint Committee staff after enactment of the new law; it is not signed by any member of Congress; and it is not approved by either chamber of Congress. Concern also exists that lobbyists may succeed in having self-serving material inserted into the Blue Book. On the other hand, because of the professionalism and expertise of the Joint Committee staff and the significant role of the committee in matters of tax policy, the Blue Book commands considerable respect. As a result of these conflicting considerations, some cases advert to Blue Books as useful interpretive resources while other cases reject them. *See generally* Michael Livingston, *What's Blue and White and Not Quite as Good as a Committee Report: General Explanations and the Role of "Subsequent" Tax Legislative History*, 11 Am. J. Tax Pol'y 91 (1994).

ment versions of the bill, (v) testimony and statements during committee hearings, (vi) colloquies, debates, and statements on the floor of each chamber reported in the Congressional Record, and (vii) presidential, Treasury, and other Executive Branch documents.

Finally, the role of the General Accounting Office ("GAO") should be acknowledged. The GAO is an investigative arm of Congress. Upon request by a member of Congress, the GAO prepares reports about the efficiency and effectiveness of federal programs and activities, often including those involved in tax administration. Over the years, the GAO has released many reports on IRS operations, some laudatory but many critical. Such reports are important political facts and can influence tax debates and legislation.[11]

B. Executive Branch

The President proposes many tax changes that ultimately become law, and the White House is usually involved in the negotiations over major tax proposals. Two Executive departments are of primary significance in tax matters: the Treasury Department (including the Internal Revenue Service) and the Justice Department.

1. Treasury Department

Scores of Code sections (for example, sections 446(b) and 482) refer to "the Secretary." Under section 7701(a)(11), those references are to the Secretary of the Treasury.

Treasury is the parent department of the IRS, but other parts of Treasury also are players in tax policy and administration. Within Treasury, tax legislation historically has been the province of so-called "main Treasury," rather than the IRS. The landmark 1998 Reform Act included a "sense of the Congress" measure that the IRS "should provide Congress with an independent view of tax administration" and that front-line IRS technical experts should advise the tax-writing committees as to the administrability of proposed tax law changes.[12] Thus far, that provision appears not to have had significant effect.

The principal technical tax adviser in Treasury is the Assistant Secretary for Tax Policy. The Assistant Secretary is in charge of both the Office of Tax Legislative Counsel and the Office of Tax Analysis. The Tax Legislative Counsel's office has a staff of lawyers who consider technical questions as to tax legislation, rules, and regulations. This office also helps to develop and finalize regulations, and often comments on proposed revenue rulings and other important

---

[11] In general, requests for GAO investigations of the IRS must be reviewed by the Joint Committee. IRC § 8021(e).

[12] 1998 Reform Act § 4021 (not codified in IRC).

administrative positions. The Office of Tax Analysis is staffed by economists who evaluate economic effects and estimate the revenue consequences of tax features and proposals. Estimating revenue effects of tax proposals is called "scoring." Scoring is central to tax legislation, and the quality and limitations of scoring techniques are frequently controversial.

The Treasury Department also administers the few taxes—such as taxes on alcohol, tobacco, and firearms—responsibility for which has not been delegated to the IRS. Treasury has an Office of General Counsel, which sometimes is involved in tax matters. The 1998 Reform Act created the Office of Treasury Inspector General for Tax Administration ("TIGTA"), whose duties partly overlap those of the Office of Inspector General of the Department of the Treasury.[13] TIGTA studies the IRS and sometimes issues reports on its findings.

Each year, the Treasury and the IRS release a Priority Guidance Plan, which typically is revised during the year. The Plan highlights recently completed regulation and ruling projects, describes ongoing projects, and identifies new projects to be undertaken. Tax practitioners are well advised to review the Plan and its revisions in order to both remain current and monitor changing Government priorities.[14]

2. IRS

Most of the Treasury Secretary's authority over day-to-day administration of the tax laws has been delegated to the IRS.[15] The Commissioner of Internal Revenue is appointed by the President, subject to confirmation by the Senate, for a five-year term with the possibility of reappointment (but is removable at will by the President).[16] The IRS National Office formulates policies and programs while field offices throughout the country (and in major foreign business centers) work cases.

The IRS undergoes frequent reorganization. The 1998 Reform Act directed a major reorganization, which began in 1999. Before that reorganization, the field offices were geographically arranged. Four regions each contained a number of districts, there being thirty-three districts in all. Each district had Examination, Collection, and Criminal Investigation divisions. Ten Service Centers had return processing and related responsibilities.

---

[13] *See generally id.* at § 1103; IRC § 7803(d).

[14] *See, e.g., Treasury-IRS First Periodic Update for 2005-2006 Priority Guidance Plan*, Tax Management Weekly (BNA), March 13, 2006, at 414.

[15] The role of the IRS is *not* to exact every possible dollar it can get by any means fair or foul. "[I]t is the duty of the Service to carry out [tax] policy by correctly applying the laws enacted by Congress; to determine the reasonable meaning of various Code provisions in light of the Congressional purpose in enacting them; and to perform this work in a fair and impartial manner, with neither a government nor a taxpayer point of view." Rev. Proc. 64-22, 1964-1 C.B. 689.

[16] IRC § 7803(a)(1).

Based more on faith than solid evidence, the idea gained traction in Washington, D.C. in and around 1998 that tax administration would be improved were the IRS to more closely resemble private-sector enterprises. Taxpayers now are called "customers" of the IRS, and references to "enforcement" of the tax laws were deleted in favor of a "customer service" ethic. The IRS's current mission statement is found early in each edition of the IRS's Cumulative Bulletin.[17] Compared to prior versions of the mission statement,[18] the current version puts greater emphasis on service and less on enforcement and compliance.[19]

In the same spirit, Congress concluded in 1998 that the IRS would understand, and therefore serve, its "customers" better if its geographical structure were replaced by operating units serving particular groups with similar needs.[20] In addition, it was expected that the reorganization would promote accountability and improve the consistency with which similar taxpayers in different parts of the country would be treated.[21]

Under the reorganization, the IRS now consists of a National Headquarters and eleven business units, comprised of:

• Four operating divisions: Wage and Investment, Small Business and Self Employed, Large and Mid-Size Business, and Tax Exempt and Government Entities,

• Two support divisions: Agency-Wide Shared Services and Modernization, Information Technology and Security Services, and

• Five functional business units: Chief Counsel, Appeals, Criminal Investigation, Communications and Liaison, and the Taxpayer Advocate Service.

---

[17] "The IRS Mission: Provide America's taxpayers top quality service by helping them understand and meet their responsibilities and by applying the tax law with integrity and fairness to all." 2002-2 C.B. ii.

[18] "The purpose of the Internal Revenue Service is to collect the proper amount of tax revenue at the least cost; serve the public by continually improving the quality of our products and services; and perform in a manner warranting the highest degree of public confidence in our integrity, efficiency and fairness," 1996-1 C.B. ii; *see also* 1976-1 C.B. ii (stating in part that the IRS should "be vigorous in requiring compliance with law and it should be relentless in its attack on unreal tax devices and fraud").

[19] Congress commanded revision of the mission statement via section 1002 of the 1998 Reform Act (not codified in IRC).

[20] 1998 Reform Act § 1001 (not codified in IRC).

[21] This aspiration has not been fully realized. Despite the reorganization, "inconsistent policies and procedures related to the handling of taxpayer accounts still pervade the campuses. These different and inconsistent procedures include addressing the tax consequences of stolen identities, Automated Collection System . . . , levy release procedures, audit reconsideration, and correction of collection statute expiration dates." National Taxpayer Advocate, 2004 Annual Report to Congress 132.

The service centers were renamed campuses. They retain responsibility for Submission Processing, Accounts Management, and Compliance, although not all campuses will serve all three capacities.

Most IRS personnel serve in one of the four operating divisions. The field personnel of the divisions are organized among area and territory offices. The four divisions are described in greater detail below.

Wage and Investment Division. W&I deals with (or, in the current argot, "serves") the largest number of taxpayers: individuals who have only wage and/or investment income. Monitoring the compliance of those taxpayers is greatly facilitated by extensive third-party information reporting of wages, interest, dividends, and the like via W-2 and 1099 forms. See Chapter 4. W&I is headquartered in Atlanta. Its functions include CARE (Communications, Assistance, and Research), which provides taxpayer education, assistance, and filing support; CAS (Customer Account Services) which processes returns and payments; and Compliance.

Small Business and Self-Employed Division. SB/SE handles both individuals who are self-employed in whole or in part and corporations and partnerships whose assets do not exceed $10,000,000. SB/SE is headquartered in New Carrollton, Maryland. It contains CARE, CAS, and Compliance functions. Responsibility for wealth transfer taxes, employment taxes, and most collection activities also are centralized in SB/SE.

Large and Mid-Size Business Division. LMSB is headquartered in Washington, D.C. It deals with business entities with assets exceeding $10,000,000. Reflecting the notion that similar companies will have common tax issues, LMSB is organized into industry segments, specifically: Communications, Technology, and Media; Financial Services; Heavy Manufacturing and Transportation; Natural Resources and Construction; and Retailers, Food, Pharmaceuticals, and Healthcare. Given the nature of the customers it serves, international tax issues are centralized in LMSB.

Tax Exempt and Governmental Entities Division. TE/GE is also headquartered in Washington, D.C. It includes a CAS component. Its other components are customer segments dealing with Employee Plans (deferred compensation plans), Exempt Organizations (charities, private foundations, and political organizations), and Governmental Entities (including Indian Tribes and issuers of tax-exempt bonds).

In addition to structural reorganization, the IRS frequently revises its technological systems. The IRS uses a number of not-always-compatible information systems. This has inhibited IRS enforcement, undercut taxpayer service, and created friction with Congress. The IRS frequently announces new or revised technological modernization initiatives. The current version is known as the information technology modernization vision and strategy.[22]

---

[22] *See* Allen Kenney, *IRS Introduces New Modernization Strategy*, Tax Notes, Oct. 30, 2006, at 401.

As IRS information retrieval improves, taxpayers and their representatives will have better access to such information. In 2002, the IRS created the Practitioner Priority Service ("PPS"), a nationwide, toll-free accounts service designed specifically for practitioners as a first point-of-contact for account-related issues. PPS offers information and assistance for individual and business account problems, complex refunds, installment agreements, notices, and payment tracers.

Among the functional units, the Office of Chief Counsel is the principal legal arm of the IRS. Chief Counsel's National Office works on matters of policy embodied in regulations, revenue rulings revenue procedures, private letter rulings, and other types of guidance. The National Office also assists field personnel handling cases and sometimes handles high-profile cases directly. Chief Counsel's field offices handle cases in litigation and pre-litigation status. Counsel offices are organized in parallel fashion to the four operating divisions. Communication and Liaison has jurisdiction over confidentiality and disclosure issues. In addition, it deals with Congress, the public, and so called "stakeholder groups," such as private sector tax practitioners.

Like the so-called "Commissioner's side" of the IRS, IRS Counsel frequently reorganizes. In 2006, the Chief Counsel's Office announced a major restructuring based on a "matrix management approach" combining geographical and functional components. The revised structure includes (i) a national Field Leadership Team, (ii) six Area Teams, and (iii) forty-nine Managing Counsel at field offices throughout the country. This reorganization partly discards and partly confirms principles that guided reorganization after RRA 1998. One of the goals of the new structure is to give taxpayers and their representatives contacts in the field offices to resolve problems.[23]

The Criminal Investigation Division ("CID") does what its name suggests. Serious violations of tax responsibilities can lead to the imposition of criminal sanctions. The federal government initiates relatively few criminal tax cases each year: rarely more than 3000, often fewer. These cases are developed by the Special Agents of the CID.[24]

Appeals' mission is to resolve tax disputes short of trial. It has long played this role in the pre-assessment context (*see* Chapter 4), and its role in resolving collection disputes has increased substantially in recent years (*see* Chapter 13).[25] After reorganization, Appeals has a strategic planning function plus three operating units: the Large and Mid-Size Operating Unit, the General Business Unit, and the Tax Exempt and Governmental Entities Unit.

---

[23] Donald L. Korb, *A New Approach to Managing Our Field Resources*, 2006 Tax Notes Today 43-54 (Mar. 3, 2006).

[24] For fuller description of substantive and procedural aspects of the criminal tax function, see Ian M. Comisky, Lawrence S. Feld & Steven M. Harris, Tax Fraud and Evasion (6th ed. 2004).

[25] *See generally* History of Appeals: Appeals at 60 Years (IRS Document No. 7225) (1987).

The Taxpayer Advocate Service is the current iteration of the IRS's problem-solving function.[26] It exists to cut through red tape and resolve taxpayer difficulties that exist despite (or perhaps because of) normal IRS procedures. The 1998 Reform Act reconstituted this function in response to concerns about the office's independence and effectiveness. Currently, the function is headed by the National Taxpayer Advocate. The national office directs field offices which sometimes correspond to IRS operating division field offices. Taxpayer Advocate offices can resolve difficulties informally or via the issuance of a taxpayer assistance order (TAO).[27] The National Taxpayer Advocate also reports to Congress on systemic problems taxpayers confront and on possible solutions to them.[28] Section 7803(c) describes the duties and powers of the Taxpayer Advocate's Office, and section 7811 describes TAOs. A taxpayer requests a TAO by filing a Form 911.[29]

The tax practitioner also should be aware of the Office of Professional Responsibility ("OPR"), which reports to the IRS Deputy Commissioner for Service and Enforcement. Treasury Circular 230[30] governs professional responsibility obligations of attorneys and others who practice before the IRS. Alleged violations of Circular 230 are considered by OPR, with hearing and appeal rights available. Practitioners determined to have violated Circular 230 face a variety of possible sanctions, including suspension or disbarment from practice before the IRS. Legislation in 2004 added censure and monetary penalties to the sanctions that OPR can impose, subject to a variety of special rules.[31] The IRS and OPR have stated their intention to issue proposed regulations in 2007 to reflect the 2004 legislation.

Finally as to the IRS, the Internal Revenue Service Oversight Board deserves mention. As part of the reorganization frenzy that led to the 1998 Reform Act, concerns were expressed about long-term supervision of and planning as to the IRS. Although the IRS is part of the Treasury Department, Treasury traditionally has viewed the IRS as virtually an independent agency. Moreover, the average tenure of Treasury Secretaries and Internal Revenue Commissioners

---

[26] *See* IRC § 7803(c).

[27] Practitioners differ on their views as to the effectiveness of the Taxpayer Advocate function. The function is underutilized. *See* National Taxpayer Advocate, 2004 Annual Report to Congress 7 ("only about four percent of taxpayers who qualify for the services of [the Taxpayer Advocate Service] contact us and only a small percentage of taxpayers who qualify for TAS' services have ever heard of TAS").

[28] The annual reports of the National Taxpayer Advocate are essential reading for those interested in the problems of our tax system and possible solutions to them.

[29] *See* IRC § 7811.

[30] 31 C.F.R. pt. 10.

[31] American Jobs Creation Act of 2004, § 822(a), Pub. L. No. 108-357, 118 Stat. 1586. The IRS has issued guidance as to the imposition of such monetary penalties. IRS Notice 2007-39, 2007-20 I.R.B. 1243.

has been under three years.[32] The IRS had and continues to have a variety of advisory groups including private sector representatives, but they lack power beyond the power to persuade.

To fill the perceived gap, the 1998 Reform Act created the Oversight Board to oversee the IRS's organization, support, and execution of its missions. The nine members of the Board include the Treasury Secretary, the IRS Commissioner, a federal employee representative, and six individuals from the private sector. The non ex-officio members are nominated by the President and confirmed by the Senate. Section 7802 describes how the Board is constituted, what its specific responsibilities are, and what it is supposed not to do. Thus far, it does not appear that the Oversight Board has had a major effect on tax administration.

3. Department of Justice

Justice's role is principally in tax litigation. The general pattern goes back to the Administration of Franklin Roosevelt. With some exceptions, the IRS Chief Counsel's Office represents the IRS in the Tax Court, while Justice represents the IRS or the United States in other courts. In your study of tax law, you will encounter some cases styled as, for example, "Jones v. Commissioner" and others as "Jones v. United States." The former styling usually connotes that the trial court was the Tax Court (or a predecessor court) and that the government was represented by IRS Counsel. The latter styling connotes that the trial court was either a federal District Court or the Court of Federal Claims (or a predecessor court) and that the government was represented by the Department of Justice.

The Tax Division of Justice is led by an Assistant Attorney General. It has four geographically based civil trial sections. They handle refund suits and all other civil tax litigation in the District Courts and in state courts. Litigation in the state courts is rare. The federal government typically has the power to remove cases from state court to federal District Court,[33] and it nearly always exercises that power. A fifth trial section within the Tax Division handles cases in the Court of Federal Claims.

Civil tax cases may be tried by other government lawyers as well. A large part of Justice (though they sometimes think of themselves as semi-autonomous) is the United States Attorneys Offices in all the federal districts. A tax case in Bankruptcy Court will be handled by any of the following: (i) an attorney from the geographically appropriate civil trial section of the Tax Division, (ii) an attorney from the local United States Attorneys Office, or (iii) an IRS Counsel attorney appearing as a Special Assistant United States Attorney (under a joint arrangement commonly called the Houston Plan).

---

[32] A Vision for a New IRS: Report of the National Commission on Restructuring the Internal Revenue Service (June 25, 1997).

[33] 28 U.S.C. §§ 1442, 1444, 1446.

The Tax Division also has a Criminal Section. It reviews potential criminal tax cases referred by the Criminal Investigation Division of the IRS. The Criminal Section may accept those cases for prosecution, decline them, or return them for further development. In criminal cases that actually reach trial, the government is represented by either the Criminal Section or the United States Attorneys Office. The Criminal Section also maintains liaison with the various organized crime and drug enforcement task forces.

There are three other tax-relevant components of the Justice Department. First, the Tax Division's Appellate Section represents the government in federal Circuit Court, regardless of the trial court in which the case originated. Second, the Solicitor General's Office makes the ultimate decision about whether to prosecute or defend tax appeals. It also argues tax cases before the Supreme Court and occasionally before circuit courts. Third, the Office of Review coordinates the Tax Division's settlement policies. It also researches proposed legislation on which the Tax Division has been asked to comment.

There are numerous coordination functions and procedures among the IRS, IRS Counsel, and the various components of the Justice Department. They usually work reasonably well because of mutual respect among the participants and because of a shared understanding of the importance and challenges of tax enforcement. Nonetheless, occasional strains are inevitable. Sometimes, Justice has a different view of the law than the IRS has. This can produce embarrassing disagreements and set the federal agencies working at cross purposes.[34]

C. Judicial Branch

Constitutionally, "judicial branch" refers to the Article III courts: the federal District and Circuit Courts and the Supreme Court. In the tax world, the term is used more broadly to include all federal courts that hear tax cases, Article I as well as Article III courts.[35] The following briefly describes the types of tax cases, the courts which hear them, and the available avenues of appeal.

---

[34] As one example, consider Campbell v. Commissioner, 59 T.C. Memo. (CCH) 236 (1990), *aff'd in part & rev'd in part*, 943 F.2d 815 (8th Cir. 1991) (IRS prevailed at trial on one theory; on appeal, Justice repudiated that theory but sought unsuccessfully to preserve the victory by offering a different theory).

[35] Under Article I, section 8, clause 9 of the Constitution, Congress has the power to create additional courts whose judges do not have Article III life tenure. The Tax Court, the Court of Federal Claims, and the Bankruptcy Court are Article I courts. Article I courts have only that jurisdiction conferred upon them by Congress.

1. Types of Tax Cases

There are seven types of tax cases. This chapter describes them briefly; other chapters develop the most important of them in greater detail.

Deficiency actions. In general, federal income, estate, gift, and generation-skipping transfer taxes (above amounts reported on taxpayers' returns) cannot be assessed until the IRS has issued a formal determination of additional tax owing. That additional tax is called a deficiency. The formal determination is called a statutory notice of deficiency. The notice also is called a Ninety-Day Letter since the taxpayer has ninety days from the date the notice was mailed to file a petition with the Tax Court challenging the determinations in the notice. In the action following the filing of a Tax Court petition, the taxpayer is the petitioner and the Commissioner is the respondent. *See* Chapter 8.

Refund actions. If the taxpayer failed to file a Tax Court petition or if the tax in question was assessable without the need to issue a notice of deficiency, the IRS will assess the tax plus interest and, if applicable, civil penalties. See Chapter 11 for discussion of civil penalties. A taxpayer who nonetheless wishes to challenge an assessed liability must pay it, then file a refund claim with the IRS, and then (after the IRS denies or ignores the claim) file a refund suit in either the Court of Federal Claims or District Court. A taxpayer who concludes, without IRS intervention, that more tax was paid than legally owed also must file a refund claim and, if necessary, bring a refund suit. *See* Chapter 9.

TEFRA actions. As a result of the Tax Equity and Fiscal Responsibility Act of 1982 ("TEFRA"), income tax liabilities arising as a result of partnership operations may be determined and litigated under special rules. The rules are a hybrid of entity-level and partner-level audit, collection, and litigation. TEFRA litigation may involve an analog of either Tax Court deficiency actions or refund actions. *See* Chapter 6.

Collection actions. The three preceding types of cases involve how much tax the taxpayer owes, therefore how much the IRS may properly assess. Collection suits involve post-assessment matters. They may be brought by the IRS in aid of collection, by taxpayers in opposition to collection, or by third parties (such as other creditors of the taxpayer or co-owners of property with the taxpayer) to prevent harm to their interests. Liability issues are sometimes argued in collection contexts, for instance, in post-assessment spousal relief cases, *see* Chapter 3, and in Collection Due Process cases and suits to reduce tax liabilities to judgment, *see* Chapter 13. Most collection cases must be brought in District Court although the Tax Court's jurisdiction has been broadened to include some collection matters.

Miscellaneous civil actions. A variety of special types of civil tax suits may be brought, usually in District Court. Here are some of the more prominent types of suits: (1) the government may seek a writ, order, or injunction to further tax enforcement;[36] (2) the government may request a District Court to enforce a summons issued by the IRS,[37] *see* Chapter 4; (3) the government may ask a District Court to enjoin income tax return preparers who have engaged in misconduct, to enjoin promoters of abusive tax shelters or other schemes, or to enjoin flagrant political expenditures by section 501(c)(3) organizations;[38] (4) taxpayers may seek expedited judicial review of IRS jeopardy or termination assessments, *see* Chapter 7;[39] (5) taxpayers and (sometimes) aggrieved third parties may seek monetary damages as a result of wrongful IRS conduct,[40] *see* Chapter 13; and (6) affected persons may bring actions for declaratory judgment as to, for example, their status as tax-exempt organizations, status as employees versus independent contractors, or status as qualified retirement plans.[41]

Bankruptcy cases. The IRS is a creditor in a large percentage of bankruptcy cases. Thus, numerous tax issues are tried in Bankruptcy Court. They include liability, collection, and procedural bankruptcy issues. If the IRS believes there are unpaid taxes, it will submit a proof of claim to the Bankruptcy Court, and the merits of the claim may then be litigated. The taxpayer/debtor also can initiate the process of liability determination. The Bankruptcy Court has broad powers to determine tax liabilities and penalties.[42] The taxpayer/debtor can trigger such determination by filing a motion with the Bankruptcy Court. Even if the liability is uncontested, there may be litigation in the Bankruptcy Court as to whether and how those liabilities can be collected either within or outside the bankruptcy process.

Criminal tax cases. Egregious tax behavior may be punished criminally.[43] Criminal tax cases are tried in federal District Court. As is usual in criminal cases of all types, the government bears the burden of proof at a "beyond reasonable doubt" standard. The typical rules of criminal procedure apply.

2. Courts

All law students are familiar with District Court. It is the only tax trial forum in which juries may be used,[44] but jury-trial tax cases are not the norm

---

[36] IRC § 7402(a).

[37] IRC § 7402(b).

[38] IRC §§ 7407, 7408, 7409, respectively.

[39] IRC § 7429(b).

[40] *E.g.*, I.R.C. §§ 7431-35.

[41] IRC §§ 7428, 7436, 76, respectively. See IRC sections 7477-79 for additional declaratory judgment possibilities.

[42] 11 U.S.C. § 505(a).

[43] *E.g.*, IRC §§ 7201-17.

[44] *See, e.g.*, Funk v. Commissioner, 687 F.2d 264 (8th Cir. 1982) (neither Seventh Amendment nor statute requires jury trials in Tax Court deficiency actions).

even in District Court. The other three tax trial fora are described below, and further information as to them is contained in Chapters 8 and 9.

Tax Court. The Tax Court is the most important trial court as to liability determination. When the modern income tax began in 1913, the first controversy resolution forum was an office within the agency itself (then called the Internal Revenue Bureau). Complaints of pro-government bias and lack of institutional independence led to the creation in the 1920s of the Board of Tax Appeals (B.T.A.) as an Executive Branch agency independent of the Bureau. The modern Tax Court was shaped by legislation in the 1940s and in 1969.[45]

As an Article I court, the Tax Court has only the jurisdiction conferred upon it by statute. Legislation over the last several decades has often expanded that jurisdiction, but the court's original purpose—deciding deficiency cases— remains its most important purpose. Sections 7441 to 7448 describe the organization and jurisdiction of the Tax Court.

The Tax Court has nineteen regular judges (each judge being called a "division" of the court), each appointed (by the President subject to Senate confirmation) for a fifteen-year term. It has as well a number of special trial judges who act somewhat like magistrate judges in the district courts.[46] In addition, a number of former regular judges continue to hear and decide cases on senior status.

The Tax Court is located in Washington, D.C., where it holds some trials. In addition, Tax Court judges "ride circuit," hearing groups of cases (trial dockets) in scores of cities around the country. Typically, a draft opinion is prepared by the judge who presided over the trial, and the draft opinion is then circulated to the other divisions of the court. Cases of sufficient importance, or as to which the judges are in disagreement, may receive full-court (*en banc*) review. This sometimes results in a complex of plurality, concurring, and dissenting opinions.

The Tax Court issues several types of opinions. In descending order of precedential or influential weight, they are: (1) reviewed opinions (all or most divisions of the court participating), (2) regular opinions (only one division participating but involving an issue not settled by previous decisions), (3) memorandum opinions (only one division and generally involving only the application of settled law), and (4) summary opinions (resolving small-dollar cases and having no precedential value). Reviewed and regular opinions (both iden-

---

[45] The leading history of the Tax Court and its predecessors is Harold Dubroff, The United States Tax Court: An Historical Analysis (1979). *See also* Harold Dubroff & Charles M. Greene, *Recent Developments in the Business and Procedures of the United States Tax Court*, 52 Alb. L. Rev. 33 (1987).

[46] Section 7443A allows the chief judge of the Tax Court to assign trials of cases to special trial judges. Rejecting constitutional challenges, the Supreme Court upheld the assignment of complex cases to special trial judges. Freytag v. Commissioner, 501 U.S. 868 (1993). Part of the Court's rationale was that, to become effective, proposed opinions in such cases must be adopted on behalf of the court by a division of the court, thus causing the decision to be rendered by a judge, not by a special trial judge.

tified as "T.C.") are published in an official reporter: the United States Tax Court Reports. Memorandum opinions (identified as "T.C.M.") are collected in unofficial reporters. In recent years, all Tax Court opinions (including summary opinions) are posted on the Tax Court's website at www.ustaxcourt.gov.

Court of Federal Claims. The current Court of Federal Claims is the culmination of a long period of evolution. For many years, the Court of Claims existed as a forum of national jurisdiction to hear claims against the United States government. It possessed both trial and appellate jurisdiction. In the Federal Courts Improvement Act of 1982, Congress bifurcated the Court of Claims, vesting its trial jurisdiction in a new Claims Court and its appellate jurisdiction (along with appellate jurisdiction over customs and patent cases) in a new Court of Appeals for the Federal Circuit. The Claims Court was an Article I court, while the Federal Circuit is an Article III court. Subsequently, the Claims Court was renamed the Court of Federal Claims. For tax law purposes, the most important aspect of the court is that it and the District Courts possess concurrent original jurisdiction over suits to recover overpayment of federal taxes.[47]

Bankruptcy Court. Bankruptcy cases are commenced by the filing of a petition in Bankruptcy Court. Typically, the debtor files the petition "voluntarily." The most important of the types of bankruptcy cases are Chapter 7 (liquidations), Chapter 11 (reorganizations), and Chapter 13 (adjustments of debts for individuals with regular income). As noted, federal tax issues often arise in the course of such cases.[48]

The Bankruptcy Court has emerged as a forum of choice for some tax litigators. In some instances, there are procedural advantages to handling tax issues in Bankruptcy Court.[49] Some practitioners believe that Bankruptcy Court is a more pro-debtor forum, that its concerns center on rehabilitating the debtor and preserving assets for private unsecured creditors. It would be a mistake, though, to assume that bankruptcy judges are uniformly of pro-debtor stripe.

---

[47] *See* 28 U.S.C. §§ 1346(a)(1), 1491.

[48] In the Bankruptcy Reform Act of 1978, Congress conferred broad jurisdiction on bankruptcy judges to hear cases in which debtors were involved. However, the Supreme Court invalidated the Act as impermissibly delegating Article III powers to non-Article III personnel. Northern Pipeline Constr. Co. v. Marathon Pipe Line Co., 458 U.S. 50 (1982). In 1984 legislation, Congress overcame the problem by providing for delegation (reference) by District Courts of their bankruptcy jurisdiction to the bankruptcy courts. The District Courts can withdraw the reference, however, and take particular cases themselves. Such withdrawal is not the norm, but it occasionally occurs in cases involving complex tax or other issues. *E.g.*, In re G-I Holdings Inc., 218 F.R.D. 428 (D.N.J. 2003).

[49] For description of how tax issues are handled in bankruptcy, see Frances R. Hill, *Toward a Theory of Bankruptcy Tax: A Statutory Coordination Approach*, 50 Tax Law. 103 (1996); Jack F. Williams, *Rethinking Bankruptcy and Tax Policy*, 3 Am. Bankr. Inst. L. Rev. 153 (1995).

3. Appeals

Not all Tax Court decisions can be appealed. The taxpayer, with the concurrence of the Tax Court, may choose to have the case heard under streamlined procedures that provide no right of appeal for the losing party. This option (called the S or small case procedures) is available in cases in which the amount at issue does not exceed $50,000 for any year.[50] *See* Chapter 8.

Tax Court decisions not subject to the S procedures are appealable to a federal Circuit Court. Venue lies in the court for the circuit in which the taxpayer resides or, in the case of a corporation, in which the taxpayer has its principal place of business.[51]

District Court decisions are appealable to the circuit of which the district is a part. Court of Federal Claims decisions are appealable to the Court of Appeals for the Federal Circuit. Bankruptcy Court decisions are appealable to the district court or to the circuit's Bankruptcy Appellate Panel.[52]

The losing party in the Circuit Court may seek Supreme Court review via writ of certiorari. However, the Supreme Court takes few tax cases each year. The two principal reasons for grant of certiorari are (1) administrative importance (principally the amount of revenue at stake nationally as to the issue) and (2) existence of a split between or among the circuit courts as to the issue.

III. ADMINISTRATIVE SOURCES AND AUTHORITIES IN TAX

Tax statutes are interpreted by cases and by administrative positions. The latter may be less familiar to students, so we explore them now. Administrative interpretations of the tax statutes come in numerous forms. Below, the most important are discussed individually, after which others are described more briefly.

A. Regulations

Regulations are the most authoritative administrative pronouncements in tax. They are drafted by IRS and Treasury lawyers. After many stages of review

---

[50] IRC § 7463(a), (b). Before the 1998 Reform Act, the threshold sum was $10,000. The Tax Court denies S designation only rarely, usually when an important legal issue is present.

[51] The government and the taxpayer can select a different circuit by written agreement although this rarely is done. IRC § 7482(b)(1), (2).

[52] Section 1233 of the Bankruptcy Abuse Prevention and Consumer Protection Act of 2005, Pub. L. No. 109-8, 119 Stat. 23, amended 28 U.S.C. section 158 to create a certification process to facilitate appeals of some Bankruptcy Court decisions to Circuit Courts. The new provision is aimed mainly at cases presenting important, unresolved questions of law.

and possible amendment, a regulation becomes final upon approval by the Secretary of the Treasury.[53]

The tax lawyer should be aware of the steps in the regulation issuance process and should monitor the progress of any regulation project of current importance to clients. Word-of-mouth sometimes provides the first warning. More formally, the government signals its work-plan priorities twice a year in the Semiannual Agenda of Regulations (or Priority Guidance Plan).

In some instances, the IRS publishes an Advance Notice of Proposed Rulemaking. It describes the positions the government intends to propose and invites public comment on them. When the government actually proposes a regulation, it announces it in a Notice of Proposed Rulemaking, which invites public comments. Written comments always are permitted, and oral hearings sometimes are scheduled.

After considering comments, the government may withdraw the proposed regulation, re-propose a modified version, or adopt the regulation with or without modification. When a strong need exists for immediate guidance, the government may issue the measure simultaneously as a proposed regulation and as a temporary regulation going into immediate effect. Temporary regulations expire not more than three years after the date of their issuance.[54] Section 7805 sets out rules governing promulgation of regulations.

Recently, the Treasury and the IRS have experimented with reversing the process. Instead of drafting proposed regulations then seeking public comment, they have sometimes solicited comments from affected taxpayers first, including soliciting from interested parties suggested drafts of regulations.[55] This approach is controversial. However, especially as to highly technical matters affecting large companies, the approach may produce efficiencies by bringing industry expertise to bear earlier.

Proposed, temporary, and final regulations are published in the Federal Register and in the IRS's Internal Revenue Bulletin and Cumulative Bulletin. They are accompanied by Treasury Decisions ("TDs"). The preambles of Notices of Proposed Rulemaking and TDs are not printed in the compilations of final regulations. However, they often contain useful explanations. The thorough tax attorney always examines the preamble(s) in every case in which the meaning of a regulation is at issue.

Final regulations are compiled in Title 26 of the Code of Federal Regulations. Thus, as with tax statutes, there are two ways to refer to the same regulation:

---

[53] In addition to the Treasury Regulations, there are a number of internal procedural regulations of the IRS. They describe how IRS functions are performed and the respective roles of taxpayers and IRS personnel in various administrative processes. *See* Proc. Reg. §§ 601.101-801.6. The procedural regulations are issued by the IRS without the necessity of Treasury approval.

[54] IRC § 7805(e)(2).

[55] *See, e.g.*, IRS Notice 2007-17 (Feb. 28, 2007); Henry Ordower, *First Drafts of Technical Guidance: Industry Participation*, Tax Notes, May 21, 2007, at 761.

26 C.F.R. section 1.162-21 and Treas. Reg. section 1.162-21 identify the same regulation. Tax practitioners typically use the latter styling.

As indicated by the above example, there typically are three components of each regulation citation. The prefix to the left of the period identifies the type of tax or equivalent. As prominent instances, "1" refers to income tax; "20" to estate tax; "25" to gift tax; "31" to some employment taxes; and "301" to procedure and administration.[56] The number immediately to the right of the period identifies the Code section under which the regulation was promulgated. Finally, the number to the right of the hyphen indicates the order in which that regulation is placed among the regulations under that Code section. Thus, section 1.162-21 is the twenty-first regulation under section 162 of the income tax. Temporary regulations are identified with a "T" after the last digit.

The prefixes are of limited utility, but they sometimes matter. For instance, some Code sections affect more than one kind of tax. Sections 1.7520-1, 20.7520-1, and 25.7520-1 all are regulations under section 7520. It helps to know which type of tax each of the three deals with, and that's what the prefix tells us.

Two final notes. First, regulations have been written under nearly every Code section. However, because of competing time demands, many of the older regulations have not been updated to reflect subsequent amendment of the statute. Before relying on a regulation, the practitioner must ascertain whether it is current in material respects. Second, the significance of the regulations vary. In some areas—the consolidated return regulations under sections 1501–1504, for instance—the regulations in essence are the law. In contrast—and many regulations under the procedure and tax collection sections are examples—regulations sometimes just paraphrase the statute, adding little or nothing by way of guidance.

B. Revenue Rulings

A revenue ruling applies the law, or what the IRS believes the law to be, to a factual situation. The factual situation may reflect an actual scenario encountered by IRS personnel (usually during audits) or an amalgamation of such scenarios. The idea is to provide guidance to taxpayers and IRS agents as to significant matters that are not clearly resolved by statute, regulations, and settled case law.

Revenue rulings are numbered sequentially by year of issuance. For instance, Rev. Rul. 83-179 was the 179th revenue ruling issued in 1983, and Rev. Rul. 2002-4 was the fourth revenue ruling issued in 2002. (The IRS switched to the full year prefix in 2000.) Revenue rulings are published first in the IRS's weekly publication, the Internal Revenue Bulletin (the "I.R.B."). The I.R.B.s are collected twice yearly in the Cumulative Bulletin (the "C.B."). Thus, for example,

---

[56] "301" refers to procedural regulations finalized by Treasury, as opposed to the "601" IRS procedural regulations described earlier.

Rev. Rul. 2002-45 was first published at 2002-19 I.R.B. 116 (page 116 of the 19th I.R.B. in 2002), then permanently published at 2002-2 C.B. 116 (page 116 of the second C.B. in 2002).

IRS Counsel drafts revenue rulings. Draft rulings are subject to multiple levels of review within IRS, IRS Counsel, and sometimes Treasury. The number of revenue rulings issued has decreased substantially in recent decades. The tax system would benefit from a greater volume of published guidance, but budgetary realities make significant increase unlikely in the foreseeable future.

C. Revenue Procedures

Revenue Procedures also are published in the I.R.B., then the C.B., and also are numbered sequentially. They set forth procedures and practices, such as when and how taxpayers should effect elections permitted by the Code, how they can change accounting methods, etc. In theory, revenue procedures involve only administrative or mechanical matters. Sometimes, though, substantive policy statements slip into revenue procedures.

Certain revenue procedures are reissued each year bearing the same number (except for year) and restating rules in the same area, albeit sometimes with modification from the prior year's rules. For example, Rev. Proc. 200x-1 each year describes how taxpayers are to go about seeking letter rulings, determination letters, information letters, and similar guidance. Rev. Proc. 200x-2 each year describes procedures for furnishing technical advice memoranda. Rev. Proc. 200x-3 identifies areas as to which the IRS will not issue rulings. Rev. Procs. 200x-4 through 200x-7 relate to similar but specialized types of guidance. Rev. Proc. 200x-8 sets out user fee schedules for obtaining various types of guidance.

How closely must a taxpayer adhere to the steps prescribed in revenue procedures? Perfect compliance is desirable but not always necessary. Missteps, omissions, or delinquencies in the taxpayer's performance may be excused under the equitable doctrine of substantial compliance, particularly if the failing involved a minor matter and worked no significant harm or prejudice to the IRS. The doctrine potentially applies to administrative rules, including those set out in revenue procedures and regulations. It does not, however, apply to procedural requirements imposed by statute. Compliance with statutory requirements must be punctilious.[57]

---

[57] *See, e.g.*, Dirks v. Commissioner, 2004 T.C. Memo. (RIA) 2004-138.

D. Notices and Announcements

IRS Notices and Announcements provide guidance, often in advance of regulations and rulings (which take longer to issue). They are less formal than rulings and have lesser stature. These items also are published in the I.R.B.

E. Other Published IRS Positions

The IRS publishes several other types of positions in the I.R.B. They include disbarment notices (of practitioners no longer eligible to practice before the IRS), orders delegating to named offices or officials the power to take certain actions, and acquiescence and nonacquiescence notices. The latter are issued by the IRS as to cases decided adversely to the IRS. An acquiescence signifies that the IRS concedes the correctness of the decision, thus will not continue to litigate the issue. The IRS may acquiesce only in part, or it may "acquiesce in result only," conceding the correctness of the outcome but not of the reasoning on which the court based the outcome. A nonacquiescence means that the IRS disagrees with the result of the case and will continue to set up the issue in other cases.

Acquiescences and non-acquiescences should be distinguished from actions on decision ("AODs"). Acquiescences and non-acquiescences state the IRS's position with respect to a judicial decision but do not explain that position. AODs explain why appeal of an adverse decision is or is not recommended. AODs are publicly released by the IRS, but they are not published in the I.R.B. AODs are prepared by the National Office of the Chief Counsel's Office. They may involve decisions from any court.[58] AODs often are issued more promptly than are acquiescences/non-acquiescences.

F. Private Letter Rulings

Clients have different levels of risk aversion. Usually, the tax attorney's oral statement setting out his level of confidence in the position to be taken suffices. For extra comfort, the client may request that the lawyer prepare an opinion letter as to tax consequences. When the greatest certainty is needed, the attorney may seek a private letter ruling from the IRS. A favorable private letter ruling is akin to an insurance policy.

The process starts when the taxpayer files a ruling request with the IRS National Office. The request sets out the facts of a proposed transaction, the taxpayer's conclusions as to the effects of the transaction, and the reasoning and

---

[58] Other than the United States Supreme Court. The IRS, of course, accepts Supreme Court decisions as conclusive. Post-1992 acquiescences and non-acquiescences also may be addressed to decisions of any trial or appellate court (other than the Supreme Court). Before early 1993, the IRS issued acquiescences and non-acquiescences only as to regular decisions of the Tax Court.

authorities in support of those conclusions. As noted above, the "how" of requesting a letter ruling is given by the first revenue procedure of the year in question. Appendix B to that revenue procedure contains a sample format for requesting a letter ruling.

The IRS will consider the ruling request, sometimes conferring with the taxpayer's representative in person or by telephone. If the IRS appears to disagree with the taxpayer's conclusion, the standard strategy is to withdraw the request before a negative letter is issued. The existence of a negative letter makes it very difficult for an IRS revenue agent or Appeals Officer to accept the taxpayer's treatment of the issue. It is sometimes thought that withdrawal of a ruling request may trigger an audit, but it is unclear that this happens with frequency. Nonetheless, if—based on review of prior IRS rulings and litigating positions—the taxpayer's attorney concludes that the IRS would be unlikely to grant a favorable ruling, the path of wisdom usually is to refrain from filing a ruling request in the first place.

If the National Office agrees with the taxpayer, it will issue a favorable letter ruling. Although letter rulings are not published by the IRS, they are publicly released (in redacted form to preserve the taxpayer's anonymity) and can be researched through private electronic and print media.

Favorable rulings bind the IRS as to the taxpayer who requested the rulings[59] unless there was a material misrepresentation or omission of facts in the ruling request or a significant change of controlling law. Revocation of a letter ruling typically is on a prospective basis. The IRS will retroactively revoke a ruling only "in rare or unusual circumstances."[60]

For many years, letter rulings were identified by seven digits, signifying year and week of issuance and order of issuance within that week. Thus, PLR 9325003 was the third letter ruling issued during the 25th week of 1993. In recent years, styling has gone to the full year, such as PLR 200425003. The IRS usually finalizes a letter ruling within four months of the filing of the request, and the taxpayer may request expedited consideration.

Because of resource limitations, the IRS ruling program has been under pressure for decades. For several decades, one response has been an IRS campaign to limit so called "comfort rulings," *i.e.*, rulings requested as to matters on which the law already is clear. The annual revenue procedure identifying subjects as to which the IRS will not rule, is one attempt to cull such unproductive exercises. In addition, since the late 1980s, the IRS has charged user fees for letter rulings, on a sliding scale ranging from under $100 to thousands of

---

[59] The Code does not command this result. The IRS is statutorily bound only by a section 7121 closing agreement. The conclusive effect of letter rulings is pursuant to administrative decision. Rev. Proc. 2004-1, 2004-1 C.B. 1, § 11.01.

[60] *Id.* at § 11.06.

dollars.[61] The IRS often tinkers with letter ruling procedures in particular areas in order to improve taxpayer service or efficiency.[62]

G. Determination Letters

Determination letters are similar to private letter rulings except they are issued (1) by field offices, (2) on matters covered by settled law, and (3) as to completed transactions, not contemplated transactions. Most determination letters relate to whether an entity qualifies as a retirement plan or as a tax-exempt organization.

H. Technical Advice Memoranda

Technical Advice Memoranda (TAMs) are similar in organization and numbering to PLRs. However, they arise in a different manner. During an audit or administrative appeal, the IRS and the taxpayer may agree on the facts but disagree on the law. The IRS revenue agent or Appeals Officer may then contact the National Office, requesting its view of the law. Although the IRS field employee is nominally the requesting party, the taxpayer often initiates the process by asking the field employee to submit the request. As noted previously, steps in the TAM process are set forth in the second revenue procedure issued by the IRS each year.

In 2002, the IRS announced creation of a fast-track TAM procedure featuring more taxpayer input: Technical Expedited Advice Memoranda ("TEAMs."). Rather few TEAMs were issued, and the medium was eliminated.[63] However, in 2006, the IRS Chief Counsel's Office announced three new vehicles for providing nonprecedential legal advice to field agents: (i) a streamlined procedure for technical advice, (ii) a procedure for strategic case-specific advice, and (iii) a new type of generic legal advice to apply across an industry.[64]

TAMs often receive more careful consideration than PLRs, so many practitioners accord TAMs a slightly higher persuasive status. Before urging that a TAM be sought, the tax practitioner should have considerable confidence in

---

[61] *See, e.g.*, IR-2005-144 (Dec. 19, 2005) (setting out increased user fees for letter rulings, requests for changes in accounting methods, advance pricing agreements, employee plan opinion letters, and exempt organization rulings).

[62] *E.g.*, Rev. Proc. 2005-66, 2005-2 C.B. 509 (new determination letter system for qualified retirement plans); Rev. Proc. 2005-68, 2005-2 C.B. 694, *superseded by* Rev. Proc. 2006-1 C.B. 1; Rev. Proc. 2006-3, 2006-1 C.B. 122 (expedited letter rulings as to tax-free corporate reorganizations and distributions).

[63] Rev. Proc. 2007-2, § 15.06, 2007-1 I.R.B. 88.

[64] Sheryl Stratton, *Korb Provides Policy Overview for New Guidance Procedures*, Tax Notes, May 16, 2006, at 759; Sheryl Stratton, *IRS Announces Streamlined TAM, Case-Specific Guidance Processes*, Tax Notes, May 8, 2006, at 630.

the correctness of the taxpayer's legal position. Issuance of an adverse TAM often eliminates flexibility the field personnel might otherwise have been inclined to show, leaving the taxpayer with only two options: concede the issue or litigate it.

The IRS Chief Counsel's Office also provides guidance to IRS functions through a variety of less formal devices. These devices include both generic legal advice and case-specific advice.[65]

I. Government Manuals

The Internal Revenue Manual (IRM) exists to guide IRS personnel in the performance of their duties. Its text combines command and advice. As one might expect given the multitude of IRS responsibilities, the IRM is massive. It is divided into parts, covering administration, collection, examination, appeals, criminal investigation, etc. The parts are subdivided variously.

Although the IRM is not "law" in the traditional sense, consulting it can be quite useful to the tax practitioner, especially on matters of procedure. IRS personnel are supposed to follow the IRM. When they do not, knowing of the failure and pointing it out can sometimes give the practitioner a powerful argument while the case remains in administrative posture.

The organization of the IRM creates an obstacle to mining the gold in it. Each successive number is a subdivision of the number immediately preceding it. Numbers over 9 are indicated by parentheses. Thus, a number like 86(12)3 means the third division of the twelfth division of the sixth division of part 8 of the IRM. Without the parentheses, the citation would indicate the third division of the second division of the first division of the sixth division of part 8. More recently, IRM citations sometimes are rendered with periods separating subdivisions. For example, 86(12)3 may be given as 8.6.12.3. This newer version is an improvement, and is the format used in this book.

Commercial services provide print versions of the IRM (often with helpful "How to Use the Manual" explanations). Both the IRS website (www.irs.gov) and commercial sites have versions of the IRM. However, the one on the IRS's site is less complete.

Although less important than the IRM, there are many other government manuals, reports, and digests of potential interest to tax lawyers. They include the IRS Chief Counsel Directives Manual, various Chief Counsel bulletins (dealing with criminal tax enforcement, tax litigation, disclosure litigation, and collection, bankruptcy, and summonses), litigation guideline memoranda, compliance officer memoranda, and various Department of Justice manuals. Many, though not all, government manuals and parts of manuals have been publicly

---

[65] *See, e.g.*, Chief Counsel Notice CC-2007-003 (Jan. 19, 2007) (describing procedures by which other functions in the IRS can obtain advice from the National Office technical functions).

released, either as a result of administrative decision or because of successful litigation under the Freedom of Information Act.

J. Other Government Sources

The discussion thus far accounts for the most important types of administrative sources and authorities in tax, but it is far from exhaustive. At times in your practice, you will encounter references to, among many other sources: service center advice, IRS legal memoranda, IRS information letters, field service advice, industry specialization papers, field directives, etc.[66]

The line-up changes over time. Sometimes, modalities are replaced, as when revenue rulings replaced ITs (income tax unit rulings). Other times, like old soldiers, they simply fade away, like GCMs (General Counsel Memoranda), which once were important but ceased being issued in the late 1990s. In addition, forms of guidance are retooled from time to time. For example, in 2002, IRS Chief Counsel announced a project to revamp field service advice (FSAs), renaming them strategic advice memoranda (SAMs), and to create a streamlined TAM known as the technical expedited advice memorandum (TEAM).[67] It is a safe bet that many such changes will occur during your career as a tax attorney.

IV. SOME ISSUES AS TO TAX AUTHORITIES

A number of issues as to the interpretation and weight of tax authorities recur in practice. Some of them are sketched here. You will hear their echo later in this course and in other tax courses you take.

A. Deference to Regulations Generally

Regulations are the highest level of administrative authority in tax, but just how authoritative are they? How much weight do they carry with the courts? There are three major lines of case law. They can be described in reference to a 1984 Supreme Court decision with which all law students should be familiar: *Chevron*.[68]

---

[66] For description of many of the other administrative positions and modalities, see Gail Levin Richmond, Federal Tax Research pt. 3 (6th ed. 2002), U.S. Dep't of Treasury; Understanding IRS Guidance—A Brief Primer (2005); and *Inventory of IRS Guidance Documents—A Draft*, Tax Notes, July 17, 2000, at 305.

[67] *See* Rev. Proc. 2002-30, 2002-1 C.B. 1184, modified by Rev. Proc. 2004-2, 2004-1 I.R.B. 83.

[68] Chevron U.S.A. Inc. v. Natural Resources Defense Council, Inc., 467 U.S. 837 (1984).

First, there was a pre-*Chevron* line of cases mainly dealing with tax regulations. Among the most important cases in that line was *National Muffler*,[69] which adverted to a number of factors:

> In determining whether a particular regulation carries out the congressional mandate in a proper manner, we look to see whether the regulation harmonizes with the plain language of the statute, its origin, and its purposes. A regulation may have particular force if it is a substantially contemporaneous construction of the statute by those presumed to have been aware of congressional intent. If the regulation dates from a later period, the manner in which it evolved merits inquiry. Other relevant considerations are the length of time the regulation has been in effect, the reliance placed on it, the consistency of the Commissioner's interpretation, and the degree of scrutiny Congress has devoted to the regulation during subsequent reenactments of the statute.[70]

The second line of case law comes from *Chevron* itself. Under the famous *Chevron* "two step," a court looks initially to the statute being interpreted. If the intent of Congress is clear, based on the traditional tools of construction, the court gives effect to the meaning regardless of the view of the agency. However, if Congress' intent is not clear, the court looks to the interpretation placed on the statute by the agency charged with its implementation. If the court finds the agency's interpretation to be reasonable, it should follow that interpretation.

Subsequent decisions, however, have established that *Chevron* does not always provide the controlling standard in challenges to agency interpretations. Thus, the "two step" is actually a "three step," the other step being whether *Chevron* applies at all to the particular controversy. Since this step is logically anterior to the other two steps, it has been called "Step Zero."[71] Although courts have applied *Chevron* in many tax cases, they have chosen not to apply it in many others. Both in tax and other areas, Step Zero results are not easy to predict.[72]

The third line, *Skidmore/Mead*, both predates and postdates *Chevron*: the 1944 *Skidmore*[73] doctrine was reaffirmed and revivified in the 2001 *Mead* case.[74] Under that line of authority, the weight accorded an agency position "will depend upon the thoroughness evident in [the agency's] consideration, the validity of its reasoning, its consistency with earlier and later pronouncements, and

---

[69] National Muffler Dealers Ass'n, Inc. v. United States, 440 U.S. 472 (1979).

[70] *Id.* at 477.

[71] Cass R. Sunstein, Chevron *Step Zero*, 92 Va. L. Rev. 187 (2006).

[72] *See, e.g.*, Irving Salem, *Supreme Court Should Clarify Its Deference Standard*, Tax Notes, Sept. 18, 2006, at 1063.

[73] Skidmore v. Swift & Co., 323 U.S. 134 (1944).

[74] United States v. Mead Corp., 533 U.S. 218 (2001).

all those factors which give it power to persuade."[75] Neither *Skidmore* nor *Mead* was a tax case (although they both referred to tax rulings, among others), but this line of authority has been invoked in some tax cases.

It often is hard to predict which line of authority a court will apply in deciding how much weight to accord to a regulation. That difficulty is mitigated by the fact that choice among the lines is seldom outcome determinative. You will already have noticed similarities among the factors in the *National Muffler* and *Skidmore* quotations above. Similarly, the key question under both *Chevron* step 2 and the pre-*Chevron* line of cases is whether the regulation implements the statute in some "reasonable" manner, undoubtedly a deferential standard.[76] Under whichever standard a court employs, regulations are accorded significant weight by the courts and should be by taxpayers as well. Challenges to regulations always are uphill battles, and they fail far more often than they succeed.[77]

B. Deference to Particular Types of Regulations

A distinction often is made between legislative regulations and interpretive regulations. In tax, legislative regulations are those promulgated under a subsection of the specific statute, expressly authorizing Treasury to promulgate regulations. Sections 217(j), 385(a), 469(l), and 1502 are examples. In contrast, an interpretive regulation is one promulgated without express authorization in the specific section but, instead, only under the general authority of section 7805(a).

This departs from the distinction between these terms as they are used in the Administrative Procedures Act. Under that Act, a legislative regulation is one that makes substantive law while an interpretive regulation merely explains the statute.[78] The significance of the difference for APA purposes is that promulgation of legislative regulations must include public notice with opportunity for public comment while promulgation of interpretive regulations need not.[79] Most Treasury Regulations, whether interpretive or legislative (under either by the tax or the APA definition), are submitted for notice-and-comment before they

---

[75] *Skidmore*, 323 U.S. at 164.

[76] *E.g.*, Estate of Bullard v. Commissioner, 87 T.C. 261, 281 (1986). In other words, regulations are presumed to correctly interpret the statute. They must be followed unless it can be established that they are clearly an unreasonable interpretation of the statute.

[77] For examples of successful challenges, see Nicholas Bogos, Rite Aid *and* Straddles, Tax Notes, Mar. 3, 2003, at 1401, 1402.

[78] *See, e.g.*, New York v. Lyng, 829 F.2d 346, 353-54 (2d Cir. 1987).

[79] *See* 5 U.S.C. § 553. For an argument that many tax regulations were not properly promulgated under the APA, see Kristin E. Hickman, *Coloring Outside the Lines: Examining Treasury's (Lack of) Compliance with APA Procedural Requirements*, ___ Notre Dame L. Rev. ___ (forthcoming 2007).

are finalized. The point just considered is part of a larger set of issues: the extent to which APA rules govern tax procedure. Cases and commentary have addressed this class of issues only rarely, but more may be heard about such issues in the future.[80]

In practical terms, does it matter whether a regulation is legislative or interpretive (in the tax sense of those terms)? Many courts have said "yes," that legislative regulations are entitled to greater deference than interpretive regulations.[81] This is standard doctrine, but some think it is more rhetorical than real. It is a challenge to find cases in which interpretive regulations were invalidated but would have been upheld had they been legislative in character.

It is essentially settled that *Chevron* applies to legislative tax regulations. However, there is considerable disagreement among the courts as to whether *Chevron* applies to interpretive tax regulations and whether the different standards actually produce different results when applied in actual cases.[82]

Two other points. First, temporary regulations have the same weight as final regulations.[83] Second, proposed regulations typically carry little or no weight.[84] However, some courts will take proposed regulations into account, especially when there is a dearth of other authority bearing on the issue at hand.

C. Deference to Lower-Level Administrative Authorities

Do sub-regulation IRS pronouncements receive any deference? If so, how much? It matters, of course, what class of pronouncement the item at issue falls into. Nonetheless, the cases are all over the lot, both generally and as to specific classes of authority.[85]

In the cases you will read during your tax studies, you will encounter these views (plus others): the IRS ruling or other position has significant weight, has

---

[80] For one dip into these waters, see Ewing v. Commissioner, 122 T.C. 32 (2004).

[81] *E.g.*, Fife v. Commissioner, 82 T.C. 1, 15 (1984).

[82] The majority and three dissenting opinions in *Swallows Holding, Ltd. v. Commissioner*, 126 T.C. 96 (2006), frame the issues well. Judge Holmes' dissent gives a circuit-by-circuit breakdown of application of *Chevron* to interpretive tax regulations. *Id.* at 180-81. For analysis of *Swallows*, see Steve R. Johnson, Swallows *as It Might Have Been: Regulations Revising Case Law*, Tax Notes, Aug. 28, 2006, at 773; Steve R. Johnson, Swallows' *Holding as It Is: The Distortion of National Muffler*, Tax Notes, July 24, 2006, at 351.

[83] *E.g.*, Peterson Marital Trust v. Commissioner, 102 T.C. 790, 797 (1994), *aff'd*, 78 F.3d 795 (2d Cir. 1996).

[84] *E.g.*, KTA-Tator, Inc. v. Commissioner, 108 T.C. 100, 102-03 (1997); F.W. Woolworth Co. v. Commissioner, 54 T.C. 1233, 1265 (1970).

[85] For discussion and recommendations as to deference to regulations and other administrative pronouncements, see *ABA Section of Taxation Report of the Task Force on Judicial Deference*, 57 Tax Law. 717 (2004).

little or no weight,[86] binds the IRS only, binds both the IRS and the taxpayer, has weight only if of long-standing or only if it was issued near the time Congress enacted the relevant statutory language.[87]

Some courts have accorded *Chevron* deference to sub-regulation IRS positions.[88] However, something like *Skidmore/Mead* (whether in name or in substance) is more likely to attach than *Chevron*. Indeed, *Mead* itself involved Customs letter rulings, which can be likened to some sub-regulation administrative positions in tax.[89] Broadly speaking, it may be that generalist courts are more inclined than the Tax Court to treat deferentially sub-regulation administrative tax authorities.[90]

D. Regulations Changing Case Law

Can the Treasury and the IRS change by regulation interpretations of the Code adopted in previous judicial decisions? This issue has arisen with regard to the "check the box" regulations[91] as to entity classification for tax purposes. Commentators have argued that these regulations contradict Supreme Court and other precedents,[92] and so are invalid. The only decision on this issue

---

[86] The Tax Court has often described revenue rulings as being entitled to no precedential or influential weight. *E.g.*, Rath v. Commissioner, 101 T.C. 196, 205 n.10 (1993) ("petitioner's reliance on [a revenue ruling] is misplaced. Absent special circumstances, revenue rulings merely represent respondent's position with respect to a specific factual situation and are not treated as precedent in this Court. Consequently, we express no opinion regarding the revenue ruling.") (citations omitted). However, the Tax Court seems to have found "special circumstances" with some frequency, and other courts seem more receptive to revenue rulings than the Tax Court proclaims itself to be.

[87] Many of the authorities are noted in a debate between Professors Caron and Galler as to the weight of revenue rulings. *Compare* Paul L. Caron, *Tax Myopia Meets Tax Hyperopia: The Unproven Case for Increased Judicial Deference to Revenue Rulings*, 57 Ohio St. L.J. 637 (1996), *and* Paul L. Caron, *Tax Myopia, Or Mamas Don't Let Your Babies Grow Up To Be Tax Lawyers*, 13 Va. Tax Rev. 517 (1994), *with* Linda Galler, *Judicial Deference to Revenue Rulings: Reconciling Divergent Standards*, 56 Ohio St. L.J. 1037 (1995), *and* Linda Galler, *Emerging Standards for Judicial Review of IRS Revenue Rulings*, 72 B.U.L. Rev. 841 (1992). In addition, see Vitaly Timokhov, *Revenue Rulings as "Official Interpretation of Law": Unanswered Questions About Rev. Rul. 2002-69*, Tax Notes, Oct. 27, 2003, at 529.

[88] *E.g.*, Johnson City Medical Center v. United States, 999 F.2d 973, 977 (6th Cir. 1993).

[89] *See, e.g.*, Aeroquip-Vickers, Inc. v. Commissioner, 347 F.3d 173, 180-82 (6th Cir. 2003) (questioning *Johnson City, supra*, in light of *Mead*); Federal National Mortgage Ass'n v. United States, 56 Fed. Cl. 228 (2003), *rev'd on other grounds*, 379 F.3d 1303 (D.C. Cir. 2004).

[90] *Compare* Solomon Inc. v. United States, 976 F.2d 837, 841 (2d Cir. 1992) (revenue rulings have precedential weight), *with* Benninghoff v. Commissioner, 71 T.C. 216, 222 n.4 (1978), *aff'd on other grounds*, 614 F.2d 398 (5th Cir. 1980) (revenue rulings have no weight).

[91] Reg. § 301.7701-1 to -3.

[92] Brent J. Hellwig & Gregg D. Polsky, *The Employment Tax Challenge to the Check-the-Box Regulations*, Tax Notes May 29, 2006, at 1039; Gregg D. Polsky, *Can Treasury Overrule the Supreme Court?*, 84 B.U. L. Rev. 185 (2004).

thus far, however, accorded the regulations *Chevron* deference and upheld them.[93]

In *Brand X*, an important non-tax decision, the Supreme Court held that "[a] court's prior construction of a statute trumps [a contrary] agency construction otherwise entitled to *Chevron* deference only if the prior court decision holds that its construction follows from the unambiguous terms of the statute and thus leaves no room for agency discretion."[94] There are some cases testing the application of *Brand X* to the tax area,[95] and more cases are likely in the future. Thus far, it is too early to say what form the doctrine will take when it settles.

E. Use of Private Letter Rulings

As noted previously, a PLR typically binds the IRS only as to the taxpayer who requested it. Other taxpayers, even ones situated similarly to the requesting taxpayer, would seem statutorily foreclosed from relying on the PLR since section 6110(k)(3) provides that PLRs "may not be used or cited as precedent."

Does that mean that a taxpayer whose research discloses a favorable PLR issued to another taxpayer, will remain silent as to that PLR? Of course not. First, the taxpayer will, and should, consider the PLR in deciding what return position to take. More often than not, what the IRS thinks in 2000 it will continue to think in 2010, assuming comparable transactions and no significant intervening change in the law. In this regard, the PLR is being used predictively, not as precedent.

Second, the taxpayer will use the PLR during audit and administrative appeals. The revenue agent or appeals officer will assert section 6110(k)(3). Nonetheless, the PLR probably will have some traction, especially if the taxpayer's attorney can credibly argue "based on the PLR, the National Office would find for us if a TAM were sought. We can save ourselves the trouble and delay of going for a TAM if you just give up the adjustment now."

Third, the taxpayer also will try to use the PLR if the case is litigated. Citation of the PLR in the brief will be accompanied by a footnote explaining why the PLR is not really being cited as precedent. Possible doubts about such a tactic are at least partly eased by the fact that courts too sometimes cite PLRs, section 6110(k)(3) notwithstanding.[96] As noted previously, the degree of IRS

---

[93] Littriello v. United States, 95 AFTR 2d (RIA) ¶ 2005-2581 (W.D. Ky. 2005), *reconsideration denied*, 96 AFTR 2d 2005-5764 (W.D. Ky. 2005).

[94] National Cable & Telecommunications Ass'n v. Brand X Internet Services, 545 U.S. 967, 982 (2005).

[95] *E.g.*, Arnett v. Commissioner, 2007 U.S. App. LEXIS 853 (7th Cir. 2007); Estate of Gerson v. Commissioner, 127 T.C. No. 11 (2006); Swallows Holding, Ltd. v. Commissioner, 126 T.C. 96 (2006).

[96] *E.g.*, Wolpaw v. Commissioner, 47 F.3d 787, 792-93 (6th Cir. 1995); Transco Exploration Co. v. Commissioner, 949 F.2d 837, 840 (5th Cir. 1992).

consistency is relevant to several possible tests of deference. Perhaps the most legitimate use in litigation of PLRs issued to other taxpayers is to show IRS inconsistency.[97]

F. Retroactivity and Prospectivity

Under a former version of section 7805(b), tax rulings and regulations were presumed to be retroactive, although Treasury and IRS could choose to give them only prospective effect. In 1996, Congress revised section 7805(b) to give it its current contents. The section generally prohibits retroactive regulations, but with some exceptions.[98]

However, under section 7805(b)(8), a different rule applies to rulings, defined to include "any administrative determination other than [a] regulation." This retains the pre-1996 presumption of retroactivity. Nonetheless, taxpayers may challenge IRS decisions applying positions retroactively. Courts typically review such challenges on an abuse of discretion standard, and a considerable body of case law exists.[99]

Prospective rules have occasioned far less controversy than retroactive rules. However, when a new rule is more favorable than the prior rule, taxpayers sometimes complain—typically without success—about only prospective application of the new rule.[100]

G. Governmental Inconsistency

IRS consistency is highly desirable for many reasons: regularity in government, fairness, protecting reasonable expectations, and facilitating business planning. Encouraging such reliance, each issue of the Cumulative Bulletin, on the introductory IRS Mission statement page, states that revenue rulings and procedures may be used as precedents.

The government usually achieves positional consistency. Indeed, elaborate review processes exist to further it. Nonetheless, given the volume of matters handled by the IRS and the importance and difficulty of the issues often confronted, there have been more than a few cases over the decades in which the

---

[97] Rowan Cos., Inc. v. United States, 452 U.S. 247, 261 n.17 (1981).

[98] For discussion of factors bearing on permissible retroactivity of tax regulations, see *Snap-Drape, Inc. v. Commissioner*, 98 F.3d 194, 202 (5th Cir. 1996); *Klamath Strategic Investment Fund, LLC v. United States*, 440 F. Supp. 2d 608, 623-25 (E.D. Tex. 2006).

[99] *E.g.*, Automobile Club of Michigan v. Commissioner, 353 U.S. 180 (1957); Lesavoy Foundation v. Commissioner, 238 F.2d 589 (3d Cir. 1956).

[100] *E.g.*, Kandi v. United States, 2006 U.S. Dist. LEXIS 2687 (W.D. Wash. 2006) (holding that the IRS did not abuse its discretion in applying pro-taxpayer proposed regulations only prospectively).

government has taken a litigating or other position at odds with a regulation, revenue ruling, manual, or other published authority.

Earlier, we saw that consistency or lack thereof is one of the factors often considered by the courts as part of the deference inquiry. But can the taxpayer get more mileage out of IRS inconsistency? Can inconsistency alone defeat the IRS adjustment on an estoppel, governmental duty of consistency, or other theory?[101]

There have been a few taxpayer victories, but the preponderance of the cases have been to the contrary.[102] Various rationales appear in the cases, including a general reluctance to apply estoppel against the government, the traditional rule that a mistake of law will not give rise to estoppel, a view of IRS manuals and the like as being directory rather than mandatory, and a concern with the disincentive effects of a vigorous rule of preclusion. The courts reason that, if inconsistency with previously published positions could lead to later litigation losses, the government would be tempted to cease publishing positions. Better to have published guidance with occasional inconsistency than not to have published guidance.

One taxpayer victory on the consistency issue is *Rauenhorst v. Commissioner*.[103] In response to that case, the IRS Chief Counsel's office directed its attorneys not to take litigating positions inconsistent with regulations, revenue rulings, revenue procedures, IRS notices, and IRS announcements, and to coordinate litigating positions in tension with other types of guidance issued by the IRS.[104] Nonetheless, it is probable that the consistency issue will continue to arise from time to time.

H. Weight of Tax Court Decisions

Tax cases comprise a minority of the dockets of the District Courts, the Court of Federal Claims, and the Bankruptcy Courts. The Tax Court is our only tax-specialist court. As a result, should Tax Court decisions be viewed as particularly influential?

The Supreme Court and others adopted that view early.[105] But strong pressures were exerted by generalists. Thus, in 1948, Congress enacted section 7482,

---

[101] *See generally* Christopher M. Pietruszkiewicz, *Does the Internal Revenue Service Have a Duty to Treat Similarly Situated Taxpayers Similarly?*, 74 U. Cin. L. Rev. 531 (2005); Lawrence Zelenak, *Should Courts Require the Internal Revenue Service To Be Consistent?*, 40 Tax L. Rev. 411 (1985).

[102] *E.g.*, Florida Power & Light Co. v. United States, 375 F.3d 119 (D.C. Cir. 2004); Riley v. United States, 118 F.3d 1220 (8th Cir. 1997); In re Dewberry, 158 B.R. 979 (Bankr. W.D. Mich. 1993).

[103] 119 T.C. 157 (2002).

[104] Chief Counsel Notice CC-2003-014 (May 8, 2003), *reproduced at* 2003 Tax Notes Today 93-7 (May 14, 2003).

[105] *E.g.*, Dobson v. Commissioner, 320 U.S. 489, 502 (1943).

attempting to subject Tax Court and district court decisions to the same level of scrutiny on appeal. Opinions are divided as to how successful Congress was in that endeavor and as to the wisdom of heightened deference to Tax Court decisions.[106] Despite section 7482, contemporary courts occasionally still speak of Tax Court decisions as unusually influential, and the thought may enter judicial minds more often than it is voiced.

Yet views are far from uniform. Each court has its detractors as well as its supporters. The Tax Court is praised for its expertise, but a view (myth, in the authors' view) persists in some quarters that it has a pro-IRS bias.[107] The Court of Federal Claims is sometimes thought of as being more receptive to equity and, by some, as the best trial tribunal for taxpayers with shaky arguments. Some Bankruptcy Court judges are seen as pro-debtor while others appear to resolve doubts in favor of the government. The District Courts' generalist perspective is seen as a weakness by some, but as a decided strength by others. These and other impressions are widely debated by tax practitioners. Students will no doubt form their own views over the course of their careers.[108]

PROBLEM

A.

You are a law clerk for a judge of the Tax Court. The judge presided over a trial, and the parties have submitted their briefs. The judge asks you to review the record, including the briefs, and be prepared to discuss which party should prevail and why.

The essential facts are not in dispute. The taxpayer is a minister of the gospel within the meaning of IRC section 107. In each of the three tax years involved (1998, 1999, and 2000), the trustees of the church employing the minister designated $80,000 of the minister's $100,000 approved compensation as a "rental allowance." The minister bought a home for $400,000 in 1995. In each of the three years at issue, the expenditures made on the house (including mortgage payments, utilities, furnishings, landscaping, repairs and mainte-

---

[106] *Compare* David F. Shores, *Deferential Review of Tax Court Decisions: Taking Institutional Choices Seriously*, 55 Tax Law. 667 (2002), *and* David F. Shores, *Deferential Review of Tax Court Decisions: Dobson Revisited*, 49 Tax Law. 629 (1996), *with* Steve R. Johnson, *The Phoenix and the Perils of the Second Best: Why Heightened Appellate Deference to Tax Court Decisions Is Undesirable*, 77 Or. L. Rev. 235 (1998).

[107] *See* James Edward Maule, *Instant Replay, Weak Teams, and Disputed Calls: An Empirical Study of Alleged Tax Court Judge Bias*, 66 Tenn. L. Rev. 351 (1999) (disputing the view that the Tax Court is biased in favor of the IRS).

[108] The actual or supposed nature of each court is one of many considerations that skilled counsel takes into account in choosing the forum in which to try a tax case. For discussion of other considerations, see Nina J. Crimm, *Tax Controversies: Choice of Forum*, 9 B.U.J. Tax Law 1 (1991); David B. Porter, *Where Can You Litigate Your Federal Tax Case?*, Tax Notes, Jan. 27, 2003, at 558.

nance, property tax, and insurance) exceeded $80,000. The minister excluded the entire $80,000 allowance from gross income in each of the years in question.

The IRS audited the taxpayer's returns for the three years. The IRS determined that the fair rental value of the home was only $60,000. The taxpayer did not challenge that determination. At the conclusion of the audit, the IRS increased the taxpayer's income in each of the three years by $20,000—the difference between the amount the taxpayer claimed as an exclusion from gross income ($80,000) and the fair rental value of the home ($60,000).

As reflected by his brief, the taxpayer's position is essentially this: "The IRS should read the statute (section 107 as it existed before amendment in 2002). I was expressly given a rental allowance of $80,000 as part of my compensation. I spent more than $80,000 in 'providing' myself a home. The statute is clear, and I meet it. I am entitled to exclude from income the entire $80,000 rental allowance."

As reflected by its brief, the IRS's position is essentially as follows. Before 1954, a minister who was provided a home by the church did not have to include in income the rental value of that home. However, this created a disparity between ministers who were provided homes by their churches and those who had to provide their own homes. The former did not have to include the rental value of the provided home in their gross income, but the latter did have to include in gross income the portion of their salaries that they used to provide housing for themselves.

The IRS argues that Congress added section 107(2) to the Code in 1954 specifically for the purpose of equalizing the treatment of these two groups. In light of this purpose, the IRS maintains, the exclusion available under section 107(2) to ministers who provide their own housing should be limited to the fair rental value of the housing. Allowing them to exclude more would not equalize the treatment of the two groups but instead would favor (under facts like those of the present case) ministers who provide their own housing over ministers whose housing is provided by their churches.

The IRS contends that, in light of the statutory purpose, the phrase "rental allowance" in section 107(2) means "reasonable rental allowance." The reasonable rental allowance for the home in question in this case is its fair rental value: $60,000.

In further support of its position, the IRS's brief cited Rev. Rul. 71-280, 1971-2 C.B. 92. There, on similar facts, the IRS ruled that the section 107(2) exclusion is limited to the fair rental value of the home in question.

As part of your analysis, you consider the Supreme Court's *Skidmore*, *Chevron*, and *Mead* decisions. The facts of those cases are summarized, and parts of the decisions are excerpted, below. Each excerpt has been edited by excising citations, quotation marks, footnotes, and other material.

Skidmore v. Swift & Co., 323 U.S. 134 (1944):

Several employees of a meat packing plant sued their employer under the Fair Labor Standards Act to recover overtime, liquidated damages, and attorneys' fees. What was encompassed by the term "working time" under the Act was central to the controversy. The Supreme Court considered at length how the federal official charged with implementing the Act, called the Administrator, interpreted the statutory term.

The Court made the following observations. "Pursuit of his duties has accumulated [in the Administrator] a considerable experience in the problems of ascertaining working time." *Id.* at 137.

> The rulings of this Administrator are not reached as a result of hearing adversary proceedings in which he finds facts from evidence and reaches conclusions of law from findings of fact. . . . They do not constitute an interpretation of the Act or a standard for judging factual situations which binds a district court's processes, as an authoritative pronouncement of a higher court might do. But the Administrator's policies are made in pursuance of official duty, based upon more specialized experience and broader investigations and information than is likely to come to a judge in a particular case. . . . The fact that the Administrator's policies and standards are not reached by trial in adversary form does not mean that they are not entitled to respect.

Id. at 139-40. The Court amplified that last point by referring to Treasury Regulations. "This Court has long given considerable and in some cases decisive weight to Treasury Decisions and to interpretative regulations of the Treasury and of other bodies that were not of adversary origin." *Id.* at 140. Ultimately, the Court said this about the appropriate level of agency deference in the case:

> We consider that the rulings, interpretations and opinions of the Administrator under this Act, while not controlling upon the courts by reason of their authority, do constitute a body of experience and informed judgment to which courts and litigants may properly resort for guidance. The weight of such a judgment in a particular case will depend upon the thoroughness evident in its consideration, the validity of its reasoning, its consistency with earlier and later pronouncements, and all those factors which give it power to persuade, if lacking power to control.

Id.

Chevron, U.S.A., Inc. v. Natural Resources Defense Council, Inc., 467 U.S. 837 (1984):

The Clean Air Act Amendments of 1977 impose certain requirements on states which fail to attain national air quality standards. Among other requirements, nonattainment states must establish permit programs regulating "new or modified major stationary sources" of air pollution. The Environmental Protection Agency promulgated regulations implementing the permit requirement.

Several private organizations filed suit, asserting that the regulations were contrary to the statute. The statute did not explicitly define the key term, "stationary source."

The Circuit Court invalidated the regulation. The Supreme Court unanimously reversed, saying: "The basic legal error of the Court of Appeals was to adopt a static judicial definition of the term 'stationary source' when it had decided that Congress itself had not commanded that definition." *Id.* at 842. The Supreme Court then described how a court should proceed in reviewing an agency's interpretation:

> When a court reviews an agency's construction of the statute which it administers, it is confronted with two questions. First, always, is the question whether Congress has directly spoken to the precise question at issue. If the intent of Congress is clear, that is the end of the matter, for the court, as well as the agency, must give effect to the unambiguously expressed intent of Congress. If, however, the court determines Congress has not directly addressed the precise question at issue, the court does not simply impose its own construction on the statute, as would be necessary in the absence of an administrative interpretation. Rather, if the statute is silent or ambiguous with respect to the specific issue, the question for the court is whether the agency's answer is based on a permissible construction of the statute.

> * * *

> The power of an administrative agency to administer a congressionally created program necessarily requires the formulation of policy and the making of rules to fill any gap left, implicitly or explicitly, by Congress. If Congress has explicitly left a gap for the agency to fill, there is an express delegation of authority to the agency to elucidate a specific provision of the statute by regulation. Such legislative regulations are given controlling weight unless they are arbitrary, capricious, or manifestly contrary to the statute. Sometimes the legislative delegation to an agency on a particular question is implicit rather than explicit. In such a case, a court may not substitute its own construction of a statutory provision for a reasonable interpretation made by the administrator of an agency.

> * * *

> We have long recognized that considerable weight should be accorded to an executive department's construction of a statutory scheme it is entrusted to administer.

Id. at 842-44.

United States v. Mead Corp., 533 U.S. 218 (2001):

A federal statute, the Harmonized Tariff Schedule, authorizes the United States Customs Service to make classifications setting the rates of customs duties on imported products, pursuant to rules and regulations promulgated by the Treasury Department. Under those regulations, the Customs Service is empowered to issue ruling letters setting the classifications. Such letters may be issued by the Customs Headquarters Office or by any of the 46 port-of-entry Customs offices.

Mead Corp. imports "day planners," which are organizers used to record scheduling and other information. Between 1989 and 1993, Customs classified imported day planners as duty free. In January 1993, however, Customs Headquarters Office issued a short letter changing the classification so that duties now had to be paid on the planners. After Mead protested, that office issued a new letter—carefully reasoned but not generally published—reaffirming the January 1993 position. Mead brought suit.

While Mead's suit was in progress, the Supreme Court held in a different case that Customs regulations are entitled to *Chevron* deference.[109] In Mead's case, though, the Circuit Court held that customs classification letters differ from regulations since the regulations go through the APA notice-and-comment process while the ruling letters do not. That court held that the ruling letters are not entitled to *Chevron* deference or any lesser degree of deference. The Supreme Court agreed that *Chevron* deference should not attach. However, it remanded the case, directing the lower court to consider the *Skidmore* standard. The Court said:

> We granted certiorari in order to consider the limits of *Chevron* deference owed to administrative practice in applying a statute. We hold that administrative implementation of a particular statutory provision qualifies for *Chevron* deference when it appears that Congress delegated authority to the agency generally to make rules carrying the force of law, and that the agency interpretation claiming deference was promulgated in the exercise of that authority. Delegation of such authority may be shown in a variety of ways, as by an agency's power to engage in adjudication or notice-and-comment rulemaking, or by some other indication of a comparable congressional intent. The Customs ruling at issue here fails to qualify, although the possibility that it deserves some deference under *Skidmore* leads us to vacate and remand.

* * *

> When Congress has explicitly left a gap for an agency to fill, there is an express delegation of authority to the agency to elucidate a specific provision of the statute by regulation, and any ensuing regulation is binding in the courts unless procedurally defective, arbitrary or capricious in substance, or manifestly contrary to the statute. But whether or not they enjoy any express delegation of authority on a particular question, agencies charged with applying a statute necessarily make all

---

[109] United States v. Haggar Apparel Co., 526 U.S. 380 (1999).

sorts of interpretive choices, and while not all of those choices bind judges to follow them, they certainly may influence courts facing questions the agencies have already answered. The well-reasoned views of the agencies implementing a statute constitute a body of experience and informed judgment to which courts and litigants may properly resort for guidance.

* * *

The fair measure of deference to an agency administering its own statute has been understood to vary with circumstances, and courts have looked to the degree of the agency's care, its consistency, formality, and relative expertness, and to the persuasiveness of the agency's position, see *Skidmore*. The approach has produced a spectrum of judicial responses, from great respect at one end, to near indifference at the other.

Id. at 226-28.

In deciding whether there is a "delegation meriting *Chevron* treatment," one "very good indicator" is whether the agency's position has been promulgated under formal rulemaking or adjudication procedures, such as those set out in the APA. *Id.* at 229-30. "The overwhelming number of our cases applying *Chevron* deference have reviewed the fruits of notice-and-comment rulemaking or formal adjudication." *Id.* at 230. However, the absence of such procedures "does not decide the case, for we have sometimes found reasons for *Chevron* deference even when no such administrative formality was required and none was afforded." *Id.* at 231.

Mead appears to suggest, if the analysis reaches this stage, that all the facts and circumstances should be sifted in an attempt to determine whether Congress intended to make a delegation to the agency. The presence of such an intent would lead to *Chevron* deference; its absence would consign the matter to no more than *Skidmore* deference.

1. Based on the foregoing, in whose favor should our section 107 case be decided? Why?

2. Had the position in Rev. Rul. 71-280 been stated instead in a regulation, would your analysis be different?

3. Your research also discloses that section 107(2) was amended by the Clergy Housing Allowance Clarification Act of 2002, Pub. L. 107-181, generally effective for tax years beginning after December 31, 2001. Currently, the subsection reads in pertinent part:

In the case of a minister of the gospel, gross income does not include—

    (2)   the rental allowance paid to him as part of his compensation, to the extent used by him to rent or provide a home and to the extent such allowance does not exceed the fair rental value of the home, includ-

ing furnishings and appurtenances such as a garage, plus the cost of utilities.

Prior to that Act, the subsection read in pertinent part:

In the case of a minister of the gospel, gross income does not include—

(2) the rental allowance paid to him as part of his compensation, to the extent used by him to rent or provide a home.

What part, if any, should the current version of section 107(2) play in the resolution of this case? Which side, if either, is helped by that version?

B.

Familiarize yourself with the IRS website at www.irs.gov. Navigate the site to see what kinds of information are available through it. In particular (but without limitation), go to the "Forms and Publications" page. Click on "Publications and Notices," and skim the list of Publications published by the IRS.

Chapter 2

REPORTING OBLIGATIONS

IRC:	§§ 6001 (first sentence); 6011(a), (e), (f); 6012; 6013(a), (b)(1), (2), (d), (g)(1), (h)(1); 6017; 6018(a), (b) (applicable to estates of decedents dying on or before 12/31/2009); 6019(a) (only on or before 12/31/09 version); 6020; 6031(a), (b); skim titles only of 6032–6053 they are listed immediately preceding 6001; 6061–6065; 6071; 6072(a), (b), (c), (e); 6075(a), (b) (only on or before 12/31/2009 version); 6081; 6091; 6103(a); 6107; 6109 (omit (f) & (g)); skim 6111 and 6112; 6151; 6155; 6159(a); 6161(a), (b); 6164(a), (b); 6166(a)(1); 6702; skim 6721–6724; 6903; 7206(2); 7216; 7502(a)–(d), (f); 7503; skim 66
Regs:	§§ 1.451-1(a) (last two sentences); 1.6161-1; 301.7502-1(a), (d); 301.9100-1(a), 301.9100-3(a) - (c)(1)
Assigned Materials:	Skim Forms SS-4; SS-5; 56; 1127; 8275; 8453; 8879; 9465 Florida Bar Rule 4-1.6 Rev. Proc. 2005-70

I. INTRODUCTION

Subtitle F of the Code, entitled "Procedure and Administration," begins with section 6001. That section directs that "[e]very person liable for any tax . . . , or for the collection thereof, shall keep such records, render such statements, make such returns, and comply with such rules and regulations as the IRS may from time to time prescribe." The record keeping and return filing obligations stemming from this grant of authority, and from other provisions that both define and constrain this authority, are the heart of the administration of our federal tax system. Taxpayers are required to maintain records and report to the government both underlying information about, and their computation of, their tax liabilities.[1]

---

[1] This chapter focuses on the record keeping and reporting requirements stemming from Title 26 of the United States Code. There are, however, other federal statutes that contain record keeping and reporting requirements that are germane to the federal tax system. A notable example is the Currency and Foreign Transactions Reporting Act, 84 Stat. 1118, 31 U.S.C. §§ 5311–5332 (2004). This Act requires reports and record keeping "where they have a high degree of usefulness

Persons who have information relating to the tax liabilities of others also have record keeping and reporting obligations. They are required to file "information returns," the contents of which assist both taxpayers in preparing their returns and the government in auditing those returns. There are several types of information returns, the most often encountered are those that report information: (i) concerning persons subject to special provisions in the Code (sections 6031–6040), (ii) concerning transactions with other persons (sections 6041–6050V), and (iii) regarding wages paid to employees (sections 6051–6053).

In connection with both tax returns and information returns, the Code and Regulations provide guidance as to: (i) who is required to file, (ii) how returns are to be signed and verified, (iii) when and where the returns are to be filed, (iv) when and where tax payments are to be made, and (v) whether, and under what circumstances, extensions of time to file or pay are available.

Compliance with the record keeping and reporting obligations is encouraged through a series of penalties that range from relatively minor civil penalties to significant fines and possible imprisonment if the conduct consists of a willful attempt to evade or defeat any tax. The civil penalties for failure to comply with the record keeping, reporting, and taxpaying obligations mentioned in this chapter are discussed in detail in Chapter 11. Tax crimes are left for another course.

The Service has produced hundreds of forms and thousands of pages of related instructions. The individual income tax return, Form 1040, is only two pages long (exclusive of supporting schedules), but there are over fifty documents listed on the IRS's website relating to some version of Form 1040. The instructions to Form 1040 are a mind-numbing, if not mind-boggling, eighty or so pages long. Furthermore, the service has identified 195 other forms that might be used by individual taxpayers. Discussion of all the recordkeeping, reporting and disclosure obligations is well beyond the scope of this book. Consequently, this chapter focuses on some of the principal record keeping, reporting, and disclosure obligations, and even as to those that are covered, the discussion is best described as an overview.

More detailed information about a given form, including who is required to file the form, when and where it should be filed, and, in many cases, a line-by-line explanation of information to be provided on the form, is contained in the

---

in criminal, tax, or regulatory investigations or proceedings, or in the conduct of intelligence or counterintelligence activities, including analysis, to protect against international terrorism." 31 U.S.C. § 5311 (2004). Under the Act, certain persons are required to report and keep records of specified transactions involving U.S. or foreign currency or other, broadly defined, "monetary instruments." Compliance with the Act is enforced through civil and criminal forfeiture provisions (31 U.S.C. § 5317 (2004)) and through civil and criminal penalties (§§ 5321 & 5322).

instructions to the form. Fortunately, most forms, schedules, and attachments required to be filed by taxpayers are readily available on the IRS's website.[2]

II. THE ELECTRONIC FILING INITIATIVE

As a preliminary matter, it is appropriate to note a current, major policy initiative of the government: facilitating and encouraging electronic filing of returns. Although electronic filing of certain tax and information returns has been available, and in some cases required, for a number of years, Congress provided impetus for the shift to "e-filing," in the 1998 Reform Act. Congress announced its policy that:

> (1) paperless filing should be the preferred and most convenient means of filing federal tax and information returns;

> (2) it should be the goal of the Service to have at least 80% of all returns filed electronically by the year 2007; and

> (3) the IRS should cooperate with and encourage the private sector to increase electronic filing of returns.[3]

To assist the IRS in establishing a strategic plan to implement the congressional policy, the Act directed the Secretary to "convene an electronic commerce advisory group." To this end, the Electronic Tax Administration Advisory Committee ("ETAAC") was formed. Among other things, ETAAC was charged with providing an annual report to Congress of progress made in achieving the stated congressional electronic filing goals.[4]

In response to Congress' paperless-filing policy, the IRS established an "e-file Program" under which taxpayers can file their Forms 1040, 1040A, or 1040EZ, either through an Electronic Return Originator (ERO) or by using their personal computer, online access, and commercial preparation software.[5] To compliment electronic filing, the IRS has established two electronic payment options—credit card or electronic funds withdrawal. Also, most states and the District of Columbia participate in a Federal/State e-file program.

In the past several years the availability of e-filing has been dramatically expanded. E-filing is available to C and S corporations (Forms 1120 and 1120S); employment taxes (Forms 940 and 941); estates and trusts (Form 1041); exempt organizations (Forms 990/990EZ, 990PF, 8868, and 1120-POL); information

---

[2] To find forms on the IRS website, as configured in January 2007, go to http://www.irs.gov and click on the "More Forms and Publications" link. On that page, you have several different links that allow you to find and download forms. For example, you may find a form by its number or by searching through a topical index.

[3] 1998 Reform Act, § 2001(a) (not codified in IRC).

[4] *Id.* § 2001(d).

[5] Rev. Proc. 2000-31, 2002-2 C.B. 146.

returns (including Forms 1098 and 1099); and partnership returns (Form 1041). Furthermore, corporations that have an excess of ten million dollars of assets at the end of the taxable year, and are required to file more than 250 returns "of any type" during the calendar year with or within which the corporation's taxable year ends are required to file returns electronically.[6]

The IRS has issued a number of publications and notices that define the role of "Authorized IRS e-file Providers" (including EROs) in the e-file Program.[7] Also, the IRS's website provides a database containing the names of all "Authorized IRS e-file Providers" who are available to taxpayers in preparing and e-filing income tax returns. Finally, the instructions to Form 1040 not only extol the virtues of e-filing, they also contain a strong endorsement of e-filing by the Commissioner.[8]

As it relates to most of the rules regarding filing tax returns and paying taxes, e-filing is treated no differently than paper filing. However, a number of special rules have been necessary to implement, or encourage implementation of, the policy. For instance, the due date for filing information returns concerning transactions with other persons (sections 6041–6050V) and regarding wages paid to employees (sections 6051–6053) has been extended from February 28 to March 31, if they are filed electronically.[9] Also, the Treasury has issued Regulations detailing the extent to which the section 7502 "timely-mailing-is-timely-filing" rules apply to electronic filing.[10] Under these Regulations, a document filed electronically "is deemed to be filed on the date of the electronic postmark . . . given by the authorized electronic return transmitter."[11]

One critical aspect of implementing the e-filing program has been developing a mechanism for signing and verifying e-filed returns. In the 1998 Reform Act, Congress added section 6061(b) which directs the IRS to "develop procedures for the acceptance of signatures in digital or other electronic form." To this end, the IRS was authorized to "waive the requirement of a signature" and develop alternative methods for signing. According to the statute, any such alternative

---

[6] Treas. Reg. § 301.6011-5T.

[7] *See* Publication 1345, Handbook for Authorized IRS e-file Providers of Individual Income Tax Returns; Publication 1345A, Filing Season Supplement for Authorized IRS e-file Providers of Individual Income Tax Returns; Publication 1346, Electronic Return Filing of Individual Income Tax Returns; Publication 3112, The IRS e-file Application Package; Publication 4163, modernized e-file information for authorized IRS e-file providers of forms 1120/11205; IRS e-file for large taxpayers filing their own corporate income tax return Feb. 2006; Postings to the Electronic Filing System Bulletin Board (EFS Bulletin Board). All publications are available at www.irs.gov.

[8] Section 6011(e) grants the IRS the authority, with certain limitations, to prescribe Regulations setting forth "which returns must be filed on magnetic media or in other machine-readable form." That section also prohibits the IRS from requiring individuals, estates, or trusts to file other than on paper forms.

[9] IRC § 6071(b); Reg. § 31.6071(a)-1(a)(3).

[10] Reg. § 301.7502-1(d).

[11] Reg. § 301.7502-1(d)(1).

methods are to be treated for civil and criminal purposes in the same manner as if the return were actually signed.[12]

In the case of individuals, the IRS has responded by requiring that taxpayers file with the ERO a paper copy of Form 8453 (U.S. Individual Tax Declaration for an IRS e-file Return). By filing this form with the ERO, the taxpayer verifies the accuracy of the prepared income tax return. This completed form, signed under penalties of perjury, must be delivered to the ERO before the ERO can transmit the return to the IRS,[13] and the ERO must mail the form to the IRS within three business days after receiving the IRS's acknowledgement that the return has been accepted. In the alternative, the taxpayer may sign the return using his self-selected permit identification number (PIN).

The electronic filing initiative has been somewhat successful. ETAAC's annual report for the 2006 year estimated that 53.2% of all individual returns were filed electronically.[14] However, it went on to say that at the current rate of increase, e-filing would not reach the announced goal of 80% of all returns by the year 2007. The 2006 report contains extensive recommendations that deal primarily with ways to make e-filing more attractive to both return preparers and taxpayers. One recommendation, that top preparers be required to file prepared returns electronically, is based on the fact that preparers file 60% of all 1040 returns but only 60% of those returns are filed electronically.

Free File is a service that provides free tax preparation and electronic filing for millions of taxpayers. The IRS has entered into agreements with tax preparation software companies to provide the free service to taxpayers who meet certain guidelines. *See* Free File Home – Your Link to Free Online Filing, *available at* http://www.irs.gov/efile/article/0,,id=118986,00.html (last visited March 26, 2006).

The IRS is also encouraging the use of e-services. E-services is a suite of web-based products that allow tax professionals and payers to conduct business with the IRS electronically. Registration is required. When first launched in the summer of 2004, the e-Services incentive products were reserved for those who e-filed 100 or more individual returns. IR-2005-33 (March 21, 2005). Now, in order to register a practitioner needs to file at least 5 or more individual or corporate tax returns electronically during one calendar year in order to utilize e-services. There are many useful tools that a practitioner may access after registration including: disclosure authorization, electronic account resolution, and transcript delivery service.

---

[12] IRC § 6061(b)(2).

[13] In the alternative, the individual taxpayer can use Form 8453 (U.S. Individual Income Tax Declaration for an IRS e-file Return) to: (i) authenticate the tax return, (ii) send accompanying paper schedules or statements, (iii) authorize transmission of the return via a third-party transmitter, or (iv) provide consent that payments can be paid electronically or refunds deposited directly.

[14] ETAAC Report to Congress 2006, Executive Summary, p. 3, *available at* http://www.irs.gov/pub/irs-pdf/p3415.pdf (last visited January 17, 2006).

III. RECORD KEEPING

In addition to directing persons liable for any tax to file all applicable returns prescribed by the IRS, section 6001 requires those same persons to "keep such records" as the Service prescribes. The Service has issued Regulations that describe, in brief but encompassing language, the record keeping responsibilities with respect to the various tax and information returns.[15]

These Regulations require taxpayers to keep such records as may be required to substantiate the items shown on the return. In the case of income tax returns, the records must be sufficient to permit the Service to determine the amount of any income tax liability and they must "be retained so long as the contents thereof may become material in the administration of any internal revenue law."[16] For most individuals with straightforward returns, records should be retained for at least three years after the returns are filed.[17] During that period, the IRS can assess additional tax for the year, and the related records would be material to the determination of the tax liability.[18] However, there are numerous exceptions that extend the statute of limitations on assessment, and consequently the record-retention time, beyond the basic three-year period.[19]

The IRS is also encouraging the use of e-services. E-services is a suite of web-based products that allow tax professionals and payers to conduct business with the IRS electronically. Registration is required. When first launched in the summer of 2004, the e-Services incentive products were reserved for those who e-filed 100 or more individual returns. IR-2005-33 (March 21, 2005). Now, in order to register a practitioner needs to file at least 5 or more individual or corporate tax returns electronically during one calendar year in order to utilize e-services. There are many useful tools that a practitioner may access after registration including: disclosure authorization, electronic account resolution, and transcript delivery service.

The general record keeping rules are supplemented by specific requirements in situations in which taxpayer record keeping and reporting has proven problematic. For instance, section 274(d) contains specific record keeping rules for taxpayers who claim deductions under sections 162 or 212 for traveling expenses, entertainment, amusement or recreational expenses, gifts, or with

---

[15] See, for example, Reg. § 1.6001-1(a), (e), relating to income taxes; Reg. § 20.6001-1(a), relating to estate taxes; and Reg. § 25.6001-1(a), relating to gift taxes.

[16] Reg § 1.6001-1(e).

[17] For this purpose, an income tax return filed before the due date prescribed by law (April 15 for calendar year taxpayers) is deemed to be filed on the due date. IRC § 6501(b)(1). Taxpayers should retain records for more than three years if the records relate to ongoing or continuing transactions or tax attributes. The most prominent example is information as to the bases of assets that have not yet been disposed of by the taxpayer. Other examples include records relating to installment sales and accounting under the percentage of completion method.

[18] IRC § 6501(a).

[19] See Chapter 5.

respect to certain "listed property" defined in section 280F(d)(4).[20] To substantiate the deductions, the Regulations under section 162 suggest that taxpayers maintain a daily diary sufficient to establish both the amount and nature of expenditures such as "travel, transportation, entertainment, and similar business expenses."[21]

Another example of specific record keeping requirements, for which the consequences of noncompliance can be costly, is contained in Regulation section 1.170A-13, entitled "Recordkeeping and return requirements for deductions for charitable contributions." Of particular concern are the substantiation requirements for charitable contributions of property, other than money, having a value in excess of $5,000. In such cases, the taxpayer is required to: (i) obtain a "qualified appraisal" made within a specified period of time, by a "qualified appraiser"; (ii) attach an appraisal summary to the tax return; and (iii) maintain extensive records relating to the gift.[22] Compliance with these substantiation requirements is a necessary predicate to taking a deduction for a charitable contribution.[23]

IV. WHO IS REQUIRED TO FILE?

A. Income Tax Returns

1. Filing Thresholds

Section 6012(a) lists nine categories of persons[24] required to file income tax returns. The major categories are: (i) individuals having gross income in excess of the exemption amount, (ii) every corporation subject to the income tax, (iii) every estate that has $600 or more of gross income for the year, and (iv) every trust that has taxable income for the year or that has $600 or more of gross income for the year regardless of the amount of its taxable income.

However, in classic Code fashion, apparent clarity, particularly as it relates to filing by individuals in section 6012(a)(1), fades in a smog of definitions, cross references, exceptions, and exceptions to exceptions. Fortunately, most taxpayers do not have to wade through section 6012(a)(1) because the dollar

---

[20] In connection with these expenses, Regulation section 1.274-5T contains extensive substantiation requirements and specifically precludes deduction for estimated expenditures, superseding *Cohan v. Commissioner*, 39 F.2d 540 (2d Cir. 1930).

[21] Reg. § 1.162-17(d)(2).

[22] Reg. §§ 1.170A-13(c), 1.170A-13(b)(2)(ii).

[23] IRC § 170(a)(1) (stating that a charitable deduction will be allowed "only if verified under Regulations prescribed by the IRS").

[24] Section 7701(a)(1) defines "person" for purposes of the Internal Revenue Code to include "an individual, a trust, estate, partnership, association, company or corporation."

amounts of the filing thresholds are relatively low and the instructions to the individual tax return (Form 1040) do a good job of translating the section.

Nevertheless, section 6012(a)(1) is of interest. By working through the section, one reaches the counterintuitive conclusion that in many cases it is not possible, solely by reference to the Code and Regulations, to determine whether there is an obligation to file an income tax return. This is because critical elements of determining the threshold for filing or, in some situations, calculating the income tax liability itself, depend on dollar amounts that are administratively adjusted for inflation on an annual basis.[25]

More importantly, because of its multiple definitions, cross references, exceptions and exceptions to exceptions, section 6012(a)(1) is one of a number of provisions in federal tax procedure that provide an opportunity to test one's skills at close reading of complicated statutory language. Question one in the Problem provides one such challenge.

2. Joint Returns of Income Tax

Section 6013 permits a husband and wife to file "a single return jointly of income taxes. . . ." Joint returns traditionally have been favored because the tax liability of a married couple is usually less when reported on a joint return than when reported on separate returns.

However, section 6013(d)(3) provides a persuasive reason, at least in some cases, why joint income tax returns should *not* be filed. That section makes each spouse jointly and severally liable for the tax liability, including interest and penalties. This has led to particularly harsh consequences when one spouse fails to report correctly or to pay his or her share of the correct tax liability, and the other "innocent" spouse is required to pay the deficiency. Early case law led to the enactment of provisions protecting innocent spouses, which provisions are currently found in section 6015. Joint return filing and spousal relief under section 6015 are discussed in Chapter 3.

Eligibility for joint return filing is limited to individuals who have the same taxable year and are husband and wife. Marital status is determined as of the close of the year or if one spouse dies during the year as of the date of death.[26] If one spouse dies during the taxable year for which the joint return is filed, the taxable year for the joint return ends on the last day of the surviving spouse's taxable year.[27]

---

[25] The standard deduction is defined in section 63(c) to be the sum of the basic standard deduction and the additional standard deduction. Both of these components of the standard deduction are subject to adjustment for inflation. IRC § 63(c)(4). The exemption amount, defined in section 151(d)(1) is also subject to the adjustment for inflation. IRC § 151(d)(4).

[26] IRC § 6013(d)(1). *See also* IRC § 7703.

[27] IRC § 6013(c).

As a general rule, joint returns cannot be made if either spouse was a non-resident alien during the taxable year.[28] However, there is an exception in section 6013(g), which, at the election of both spouses, treats a nonresident alien married to a citizen or resident of the United States as a resident—thereby permitting them to file a joint return. Also, a person who was a nonresident alien at the beginning of the year, but who became a resident alien before the end of the year and is married to a citizen or resident of the United States at the end of the year may, with his or her spouse, elect to be treated as a resident for the taxable year.[29]

B. Estate and Gift Tax Returns

1. Filing Thresholds—Estate Tax Returns

Subject to applicable threshold amounts, estate tax returns are required to be filed on Form 706 with respect to every decedent who at the time of death:

(a) was a U.S. citizen;[30] or

(b) was not a U.S. citizen but who

   (i)   was domiciled in the United States;[31]

   (ii)   was not domiciled in the United States but some part of whose gross estate was situated in the United States;[32] or

   (iii) had been a citizen and, within the ten-year period ending on the date of death, had expatriated to avoid U.S. income taxes.[33]

In the case of a decedent who, at the time of death, was a U.S. citizen or who was not a U.S. citizen but was domiciled in the United States, the estate tax liability is reported on Form 706. The liability is imposed, and a return is required, only if the date of death value of the gross estate, increased with respect to certain lifetime gifts, exceeds the "applicable exclusion amount."[34] The applicable exclusion amount is: $1,500,000 for estates of decedents dying in 2004 or 2005; $2,000,000 for estates of decedents dying in 2006–2008; and $3,500,000 for estates of decedents dying in 2009.[35] The estate tax is repealed for estates of

---

[28] IRC § 6013(a)(1).

[29] IRC § 6013(h).

[30] IRC § 2001(a).

[31] *Id.*

[32] IRC §§ 2101(a), 2106.

[33] IRC § 2107.

[34] IRC § 6018(a)(1); Reg. § 20.6018-1(a).

[35] IRC § 2010(c).

decedents dying in 2010,[36] but, as the law now stands, it will be resurrected for estates of decedents dying after 2010.[37]

In the case of a decedent who, at the time of death, was not a citizen of the United States and was not domiciled in the United States, the estate tax is reported on Form 706-NA. The tax is imposed only with respect to the portion of the estate "situated in the United States" at that time.[38] There are extensive provisions in the Internal Revenue Code and related Regulations that define both what property is situated within and without the United States and the computation of the taxable estate for such decedents.[39] Estates of such decedents are entitled to a $13,000 credit against the estate tax, an amount under the current tax rate schedule equivalent to an exclusion of $60,000 from the taxable estate[40] A return is required and tax is imposed only if the date of death value of the gross estate situated in the United States exceeds the $60,000 amount covered by the credit.[41]

Gifts made by the decedent during the decedent's lifetime may increase the taxable estate, and therefore affect the filing threshold. For instance, there may be an addition to the taxable estate for gifts made but previously unreported. In the case of gifts made that were reported, there would be an addition to the taxable estate if the value of the gift was greater than the amount reported. However, under section 2001(f), no such increase in value will be permitted if the item was properly reported on a gift tax return and the value of the gift had been "finally determined" under section 2001(f)(2). For this purpose, the value is finally determined if: (i) the statute of limitations on assessing additional gift tax with respect to the gift has expired, (ii) the value is specified by the IRS and not contested by the taxpayer, or (iii) the value is determined by a judicial decision or a settlement agreement.[42]

---

[36] Economic Growth and Tax Relief Reconciliation Act of 2001, § 901(a), Pub. L. 107-16, 115 Stat. 38.

[37] *Id.* at § 901(b).

[38] IRC §§ 2103, 2106.

[39] IRC §§ 2101–08.

[40] IRC §§ 2001(c), 2102(b).

[41] IRC § 6018(a)(2); Reg. § 20.6018-1(b). Regulation section 20.6018-1(b) states that the date of death value above which a return must be filed is $30,000. This Regulation has not been amended to reflect the current $60,000 threshold. For purposes of determining whether the filing thresholds have been exceeded for either estates of U.S. citizens or residents, or estates of persons who are not U.S. citizens and not domiciled in the United States, there is added to the decedent's gross estate (i) the adjusted taxable gifts, determined under section 2001(b), made by the decedent after December 31, 1976, and (ii) the "amount allowed as a specific exemption under section 2521 (as in effect before its repeal by the Tax Reform Act of 1976) with respect to gifts made by the decedent after September 8, 1976."

[42] IRC § 2001(f)(2).

2. Filing Threshold—Gift Tax Returns

Section 6019 imposes a broad reporting requirement on any individual who makes any transfer by gift. The section specifically excludes: (i) the first $12,000 of each gift made during the year to each person,[43] (ii) the amount paid, on behalf of another person, to an educational organization for tuition or to a medical care provider for medical care,[44] (iii) subject to certain limitations, the value of interests in property transferred to a spouse,[45] and (iv) subject to certain limitations, charitable gifts.[46]

C. Information Returns

There are five types of information returns specified in the Internal Revenue Code. Two of them—"Registration of and Information Concerning Pensions, Etc. Plans" (sections 6057-6059) and "Information Concerning Income Tax Return Preparers" (section 6060)—are narrowly targeted. The reporting obligations in the other three types of information returns range from those affecting most individual taxpayers, such as section 6051, which requires employers to provide the government and each employee information about the amounts withheld for FICA and withholding taxes, to those of narrow interest, such as section 6039F, which permits the IRS to require reporting by U.S. persons who receive gifts in excess of $10,000 (as adjusted for inflation) from any person who is not a U.S. person.[47]

The three types of reporting requirements of more general interest are discussed briefly below.

1. Information Concerning Persons Subject to Special Provisions—Sections 6031–6040

There are a number of provisions in the Code that either grant favorable treatment to, or impose additional burdens on, entities or individuals. The Code requires that certain persons (generally businesses), directly or indirectly

---

[43] IRC § 2503(b)(1). The amount of the annual exclusion for each donee ($12,000 for 2006) is adjusted for inflation. IRC § 2503(b)(2).

[44] IRC § 2503(e).

[45] IRC § 2523(a). There are significant limitations, generally precluding a deduction from taxable gifts where the donee's interest in the transferred property is terminable and the donor either retains or has transferred or may transfer to another person an interest in the property that may be enjoyed by that person upon the termination or failure of the donee spouse's interest. IRC § 2503(b).

[46] IRC § 6019(a)(3).

[47] To date, no Regulations or filing requirements have been established by the IRS under section 6039F.

involved in these special provisions provide information to the government through the filing of an information return. Prominent among the nineteen reporting requirements within this type of information return are annual returns filed by three entities: (i) partnerships—section 6031,[48] (ii) exempt organizations—section 6033, and (iii) S corporations—section 6037. Several information reporting requirements of this type are imposed on individuals.[49] Notably, nine of the nineteen reporting obligations in this category deal in some manner with non-U.S. persons.

There are significant civil penalties for failure to comply with the information-reporting obligations. With respect to information-return filing obligations involving persons subject to special provisions, some penalties are found in the section that imposes the filing requirement.[50] Others are found in section 6652, which establishes specific penalties for failure to comply with a number of the information return filing obligations.

2. Information Concerning Transactions with Other Persons—Sections 6041–6050V

The "transactions with other persons" that result in information-reporting obligations under sections 6041–6050V are primarily payments by a business (on whom the reporting obligation is imposed) to another party. These transactions include, among others, payment of dividends[51] and interest, share of proceeds or in-kind share of a commercial fishing venture,[52] and royalties.[53] There are also reporting obligations imposed on some "third parties" involved in transactions who neither make nor receive the payment in question. For instance, in the case of each real estate transaction, the "real estate reporting person"[54] is required to file a statement with the IRS containing information about the

---

[48] However, a partnership which derives its income from tax exempt obligations may not have to file a return. *See* Treas. Reg. § 1.061; Rev. Proc. 2003-84, 2003-48 I.R.B. 1159.

[49] For example, section 6039E requires that individuals applying for a U.S. passport or seeking permanent residency status under the immigration laws file certain information about their status with the application. Section 6039G requires certain individuals who lose their U.S. citizenship to provide information about their status to one of several listed officials of the government who were involved in the loss of citizenship. In both of these cases, the official receiving the information is required to provide a copy to the IRS.

[50] Section 6038(c) imposes a penalty on any U.S. person who controls a foreign business entity and who fails to provide, on an annual basis, certain information about the entity.

[51] IRC § 6042.

[52] IRC § 6050A.

[53] IRC § 6050N.

[54] Real estate reporting persons include, in the following order as set forth in the statute, the attorney or title company responsible for closing the transaction, the mortgage lender, the seller's broker, the buyer's broker, or anyone else designated by the IRS in Regulations. IRC § 6045(e)(2).

transferor of the property, a description of the property, the date of closing, and the "gross proceeds" received or to be received (without reduction by the seller's basis).[55]

Section 6050I is of particular interest to attorneys who may receive significant cash deposits or payments on account of services rendered. Section 6050I imposes reporting obligations on persons who, in the course of their trade or business, receive more than $10,000 in cash in one or more related transactions. For purposes of this section, cash includes U.S. and foreign currencies and certain cashiers checks, bank drafts, traveler's checks or money orders. The report, filed on a Form 8300, must contain the name, address and taxpayer identification number of the person from whom the cash was received.[56]

Attorneys fought an extended, largely unsuccessful, fight to withhold the names of their clients from whom they have received more than the reporting obligation's $10,000 threshold amount. The position advanced was that divulging the name of a client who paid in cash might trigger an investigation of the client and making any such disclosure would violate the attorney's duty of confidentiality.

Structuring transactions to avoid the reporting requirements is unlawful. For example, one may not make two $6,000 payments or deposits rather than a single $12,000 payment or deposit. Section 6050I(f) imposes civil and criminal penalties for failing to file reports, filing false reports, or structuring or assisting in structuring any transaction, if the purpose therefore was to evade the reporting obligation.

A key feature of most types of reporting obligations that involve "information concerning transactions with other parties," is that they require the person filing the return to provide the same information to the person who is the subject of the report. Generally, this information is required to be provided by January 31 of each year.

Of particular importance are the penalties imposed, under sections 6721–6724, for failure to file information returns on time and failure to include all of the required information. The basic penalty is fifty dollars for each such failure during any calendar year, not to exceed $250,000. If the failure is corrected quickly, both the per failure penalties and the annual cap are reduced. The annual cap is further reduced for persons with gross receipts of not more than $5,000,000.[57] No penalty is imposed if it can be shown that the failures were due to reasonable cause and not to willful neglect.[58] For purposes of these

---

[55] IRC § 6045(e); Reg. § 1.6045-4(g); *see also* IRC § 6045(f) (which requires persons, who in the ordinary course of their business make payments to attorneys for services, to report such payments).

[56] Reg. § 1.6050I-1(e)(2).

[57] IRC § 6721(d).

[58] IRC § 6724(a).

penalties, "information returns" is broadly defined, but limited to, the returns listed in section 6724(d).

V. SIGNING AND VERIFYING RETURNS

Section 6061(a) directs that any returns, statements, or documents "made under any provision of the internal revenue laws or Regulations shall be signed in accordance with forms or Regulations prescribed by the IRS." This broad grant of authority to the IRS is consistent with the similar grant of authority in section 6001 to require taxpayers to "keep such records, render such statements, make such returns, and comply with such rules and Regulations as the IRS may from time to time prescribe." Other Code sections and their related Regulations provide additional guidance about signing documents submitted to the IRS. For instance, section 6064 provides that an individual's name signed on the return, is "prima facie evidence for all purposes" that the person actually signed the return. A taxpayer desiring to disclaim a return that is apparently signed by the taxpayer would have to overcome this presumption.[59]

The Code also requires that unless the IRS provides otherwise, every "return, declaration, statement, or other document" required to be filed must be signed under penalties of perjury.[60] Saltzman has pointed out that "the phrase 'under penalties of perjury' in the return jurat is an historical relic from the time when taxpayers were required to make their returns under oath, and were prosecuted under the perjury statute in the general Criminal Code if they made a false statement on the return."[61] Prosecution for false statements is now under the felony statute—section 7206(1). Alternatively, the government might choose to prosecute under the general false-statement section: 18 U.S.C. section 1001. A section 1001 conviction may lead to a stiffer sentence than a section 7206(1) conviction.

There is additional guidance in the Code about electronic signatures[62] and signatures on returns of corporations[63] and partnerships,[64] and in the Regu-

---

[59] One way to overcome the presumption would be to show that the return was signed under duress. For instance, duress is a defense to joint and several liability under section 6013(d)(3). *See* Reg. § 1.6015-3(c)(2)(v). An interesting discussion and successful use of this defense can be found in *In Re Ellen Ann Hinckley*, 256 B.R. 814 (Bankr. N.D. Fla. 2000). Looking at all the facts, the court found that Mrs. Hinckley "could not resist her husband's demands" and that she "would not have willingly signed [the returns in question], but for Mr. Hinckley's constraint on her will." *Id.* at 828 (parenthesis added).

[60] IRC § 6065.

[61] Michael I. Saltzman, IRS Practice and Procedure ¶ 4.03(1)(c) (revised 2d ed. 2002, 2003).

[62] IRC § 6061(b). See the text following note 10 of this chapter.

[63] IRC § 6062.

[64] IRC § 6063. This section provides that the partnership's return may be signed "by any one of the partners." However, the instructions to Form 1065 say that a general partner "must sign the return."

lations about returns made by agents[65] and by minors.[66] The courts have also weighed in on several issues, one of which is addressed below. However, in relation to other issues of the administration of the internal revenue laws, the signing requirements have given rise to little controversy.

Signatures have been an issue in connection with joint returns. As indicated earlier persons who sign joint returns are jointly and severally liable for the tax due for the year.[67] It would seem that a non-signing spouse should not be burdened with joint and several liability if one spouse prepared and filed a joint return either without the non-signing spouse's signature or by signing the return for the non-signing spouse. The non-signing spouse may not even have seen the return. But, whether or not the non-signing spouse has seen the return, the non-signing spouse may be found to be jointly and severally liable. One such situation is when a non-signing spouse, who is physically unable to sign the return, orally consents to the other spouse signing the return for him or her.[68] More interesting is the series of cases in which a non-signing spouse's intent to file a joint return was held sufficient to validate the joint return for purposes of imposing joint and several liability. In *Hanesworth v. United States*,[69] Mrs. Hanesworth filed a Chapter 7 bankruptcy petition when she found out that the IRS was going to seize her home for nonpayment of tax liability for 1978, a year for which a joint return, signed only by her husband, was filed. The Court upheld the lower court's order in favor of the government, noting that: "[t]he failure of one spouse to sign the return does not negate the intent of filing a joint return by the nonsigning spouse."[70] The court said that:

> [her] failure to object to her liability until she realized her home was actually in jeopardy, the established pattern of joint filings both before

---

[65] Regulation section 1.6012-1(a)(5) authorizes the signing of an income tax return by an agent in certain circumstances and requires that a power of attorney authorizing signing of the return be filed with the return. In *Elliott v. Commissioner*, 113 T.C. 125 (1999), the taxpayer's attorney signed and filed an income tax return for the taxpayer, but at the time did not have (and therefore could not submit with the return) a properly signed power of attorney. By the time a power of attorney was filed, the statute of limitations on assessing additional tax had expired. The Tax Court upheld the Service's argument that an asserted deficiency was timely and said: "Failure to satisfy the requirements for filing a return is fatal to the validity and the timeliness of the return." *Id.* at 128 (citation omitted). However, in case a spouse cannot sign a joint return by reason of disease or injury, the other spouse, with the oral consent of the incapacitated spouse, can sign the incapacitated spouse's name. Reg. § 1.6012-1(a)(5). An explanation of the circumstances must be attached to the return. Regulation section 1.6012-1(b)(3) contains similar rules with respect to non-resident aliens' returns signed by an agent. However, under certain circumstances the agency appointment itself may be sufficient proof of the agent's authorization to sign the return.

[66] Reg. § 1.6012-1(a)(4) (directing that returns of a minor be made by the minor or by the minor's "guardian or other person charged with the care of the minor's person or property").

[67] IRC § 6013(d)(3).

[68] Reg. § 1.6012-1(a)(5).

[69] In re Hanesworth, 1991 U.S. App. LEXIS 13886 (10th Cir. 1991) (Reported as Table Case at 936 F.2d 583).

[70] *Id.* at *3-4 (citation omitted).

and after the year in question, and [her] history of acquiescence in her husband's handling of the family's financial affairs, coupled with the facial declarations on the return, lead to the conclusion that [she] tacitly consented to the filing of a joint tax return for 1978.[71]

Such tacit consent was sufficient to impose joint and several liability on Mrs. Hanesworth even though she did not sign the return.

Note, however, that a joint return signed by a tax preparer is invalid if neither spouse signs the return, even if the spouses intended that the return actually filed be a joint return.[72] In *Olpin* a joint return was filed for the 1995 tax year. The only signature on the return was that of the Olpin's tax preparer. The IRS treated the return as filed, processed the return, and accepted payment of the liability shown on the return. In 1996 the parties divorced. Mrs. Olpin then declared bankruptcy in 1997. The IRS asserted a claim against the estate. During her bankruptcy deposition the IRS informed Mrs. Olpin that neither she nor her husband signed the 1995 joint return. The IRS suggested that Mrs. Olpin file a married filing separately return for the 1995 tax year because at least part of the deficiency was attributable to unreported income of Mr. Olpin. The IRS then asserted a deficiency against Mr. Olpin because his tax liability increased for 1995 as a result of not filing a joint return. Mr. Olpin said that the joint return for 1995 was valid and as such, his 1995 tax liability should not have increased. The facts of the case indicate that the spouses' failures to sign the return were inadvertent. The spouses both testified that at the time the return was filed both intended to file a joint return. The court held that that the IRS did not have the power to waive the signature requirement and thus no joint return was filed in 1995.[73]

VI. TIME AND PLACE FOR FILING

The basic rule for timely filing of income tax returns is that they must be filed by the fifteenth day of the fourth month following the end of the taxable year. The "fifteenth day of the fourth month" rule applies to income tax returns filed by: individuals, estates, trusts, political organizations, homeowners associations, individuals who receive advance payment of earned income credit under section 3507, and, estates of individuals under Chapter 7 or Chapter 11 bankruptcy.[74] The "fifteenth day of the fourth month rule," in effect, also applies to the final return of a decedent for the short period ending on the date of death. Regulation section 1.6072-1(b) provides that the return is due on the fifteenth

---

[71] *Id.* at *11-12 (citation omitted).

[72] *See* Olpin v. Commissioner, 270 F.3d 1297 (10th Cir. 2001), aff'g T.C. Memo. 1999-426.

[73] *Cf.* T.A.M. 200429009 (IRS permitted a corporation to ratify a claim for refund where the original claim for refund had a defective signature and the corporation filed a properly signed claim for refund after the expiration of the SOL).

[74] IRC § 6072.

day of the fourth month "following the close of the 12 month period which began with the first day" of the short period.[75]

Domestic "C" corporations, "S corporations" and foreign corporations having an office or place of business in the United States are required to file their returns on or before the fifteenth day of the third month following the close of their taxable year, that is, March 15 for calendar year corporations.[76] Foreign corporations that do not have an office or fixed place of business in the United States but which are required to file income tax returns, have until the fifteenth day of the sixth month following the close of the taxable year to file their returns.[77]

Partnerships are not required to file income tax returns because the partners, not the partnerships, pay tax on the partnership's income. However, every domestic partnership that has income, deductions or credits is required to file a Form 1065 information return reflecting, among other things, its income, gains, losses, deductions, and credits and the names, addresses, and identification numbers of its partners.[78] The basic "fifteenth day of the fourth month" rule applies to the filing of such returns. Foreign partnerships that have gross income that is, or is deemed to be, effectively connected with the conduct of a trade or business within the United States, or that have U.S. source income that is not effectively connected, are also required to file annual information returns.[79] However, certain foreign partnerships otherwise required to file, including those with *de minimis* U.S. source income and U.S. partners with *de minimis* interests in the partnership, are either relieved of the filing requirement or have reduced filing obligations.[80] Generally, partnerships with more than 100 partners are required to file their returns electronically and other partnerships may elect to file electronically.

Section 6698 imposes a potentially expensive penalty on any partnership required to file an information return under section 6031 that either fails to file in a timely manner, i.e., before the due date of the return, including extensions, or files the return but fails to include the required information. The penalty is $50 a month, not to exceed 5 months, for each person who was a partner in the partnership during the year.[81] Section 6698(a) contains a "reasonable

---

[75] Organizations exempt from tax under section 501(a) ("other than an employees' trust[s] described in section 401(a)") follow the "fifteenth day of the fifth month" rule. Reg. § 1.6072-2(c).

[76] *See* IRC § 6072(b); Reg. § 1.6072-2(a).

[77] Reg. § 1.6072-2(b).

[78] IRC § 6031. For this purpose, partnerships include general and limited partnerships, limited liability partnerships (LLPs), limited liability companies that elect partnership status under the "check-the-box" rules, and any other business entity that is not a corporation and that elects partnership status under the check-the-box Regulations.

[79] Reg. § 1.6031(a)-1(b)(1).

[80] Reg. § 1.6031(a)-1(b)(2), (3).

[81] The section 6698 penalty is in addition to any criminal penalty imposed under section 7203 for willful failure to file a return, supply information, or pay tax. IRC § 6698(a).

cause" exception to the penalty. Based on legislative history relating to the penalty, the IRS has not applied this exception to any domestic partnership that has ten or fewer partners, within the meaning of section 6231(a)(1)(B), provided that all the partners have filed timely income tax returns including their respective shares of the partnership's income, gain, loss, deductions, and credits.[82]

Partnerships must also provide each partner a Schedule K-1 that includes the partner's name, address, and identification number, the identification number of the partnership, and the partner's distributive share of the partnership's separately stated items of income, gain, loss, deduction, and credit, as well as the partner's distributive share of the partnership's non-separately stated items of income, gain, loss, deduction, and credit. The Schedule K-1's must be provided to the partners on or before the due date (the fifteenth day of the fourth month), including extensions, for filing the partnership's return. This often creates problems for both corporate and individual partners, because their returns are due on the fifteenth day of the third month, in the case of corporations and the fifteenth day of the fourth month, in the case of individuals.

S Corporations annually report their items of income, gain, loss, deduction, and credit on Form 1120S. Schedule K of Form 1120 S is a summary of the corporation's items of income, gain, loss, deduction, and credit, and Schedule K-1 is used to report to the IRS and to each shareholder the shareholder's share of those items. Form 1120S, including a copy of each K-1, must be filed on or before the "fifteenth day of the third month" following the end of the taxable year (March 15, for calendar-year S corporations). Form 1120S and its related documents can be filed electronically with certain exceptions listed in the instructions.[83]

Form 706 (Form 706-NA for estates of citizens who were neither U.S. citizens nor U.S. residents) is used to report estate and generation-skipping transfer taxes. The form is to be filed by the executor of the estate within nine months of the date of the decedent's death."[84] According to the Regulations, the due date is "the day of the ninth calendar month after the decedent's death numerically corresponding to the day of the calendar month on which death occurred."[85] If there are two or more executors, each must sign the return.

Estate tax returns for U.S. citizens who were residents of the United States and resident aliens are to be filed at the Cincinnati, Ohio Service Center. Estate

---

[82] *See* Rev. Proc. 84-35, 1984-1 C.B. 509.

[83] The exceptions to electronic filing generally involve something unusual that the IRS wants called to its attention. Electronic filing is not permitted for amended returns, bankruptcy returns, final returns, returns with a name change, returns with pre-computed penalty and interest, returns with reasonable cause for failing to file timely, returns with reasonable cause for failing to pay timely, returns with request for overpayment to be applied to another account, short-year returns, and 52 -53 week tax year returns.

[84] IRC § 6075(a).

[85] Reg. § 20.6075-1. However, "if there is no numerically corresponding day in the ninth month, the last day of the ninth month is the due date." *Id.*

tax returns for U.S. citizens who were not residents of the United States at the time of death are filed at the Philadelphia, Pennsylvania Service Center.

Gift tax returns (Form 709) follow the "fifteenth day of the fourth-month" date of filing rule.[86] An extension of time to file an income tax return also serves as an extension of time to file the gift tax return.[87]

VII. TIME AND PLACE FOR PAYING TAX

Taxes are generally due on the last date for filing the return.[88] Thus, in the case of a calendar year individual whose income tax return is due "on or before" April 15 of the year following the close of the calendar year, payment is due on that April 15. The due date is determined without regard to whether the taxpayer has obtained an extension of time for filing the return.[89] Also, the date a return is considered filed or a payment is considered made is generally the date the return or payment is received by the government in the proper office.

There are two rules that often modify the due dates for both filing and paying taxes. Section 7502 provides that a return or payment addressed to the proper office, mailed by U.S. mail, and postmarked on or before its due date, but which is received after such date, is deemed to have been filed or paid as of the date of the postmark. Long lines at post offices on April 15 each year attest to individual taxpayers' awareness of this "timely mailing is timely filing or paying" rule.

In 1996 Congress expanded the "timely mailing is timely filing" rule to include within its scope delivery by private delivery services.[90] To qualify as a designated delivery service, the service must be available to the public, provide regular service comparable to that available through the U.S. mail, and it must record electronically or mark on the envelope in which the item is delivered the date it received the envelope.[91] This recorded or marked date serves as the postmark for section 7502 purposes. IRS periodically issues a notice listing the qualified designated service providers.[92]

---

[86] IRC § 6075(b)(1).

[87] IRC § 6075(b)(2).

[88] IRC § 6151.

[89] In the interest of uniformity in applying the statutes of limitations on the government with respect to assessing additional tax, or on taxpayers with respect to obtaining refunds, early returns filed and early payments made are generally "considered" as filed or made on the last day prescribed by law for filing or paying. *See* IRC §§ 6501(b)(1), 6513(a), (b). See Chapter 5 dealing with statutes of limitations in deficiency cases, and Chapter 9 dealing with claims for refund.

[90] IRC § 7502(f).

[91] IRC § 7502(f)(2).

[92] *See* Notice 2004-83, 2004-52 I.R.B. 1030.

One question that has come up, in connection with the timely mailing is timely filing rule, is how a taxpayer establish the time of filing if the return is lost. Courts have not agreed on whether proof other than a registered or certified receipt received at the time of mailing can be used to prove the time of filing.[93] The service has proposed an amended version of section 301.7502-1 which would resolve the issue.[94] Under proposed section 301.7502-1(e)(1), other than proof of actual delivery, the exclusive means to establish prima facie evidence of delivery of Federal tax documents to the IRS and the Tax Court is to prove the use of registered or certified mail. The regulation has been criticized as unfairly favoring the United States Postal Service over private delivery services.[95] The future of regulation is unclear at this point.[96]

The other rule that often modifies the filing and paying due dates is section 7503—the "Saturday, Sunday, or legal holiday" rule. This rule says that when the last day prescribed for performing any act falls on a Saturday, Sunday or legal holiday, performance of the act on the next day which is not a Saturday, Sunday, or legal holiday shall be considered timely. So, if April 15 falls on a Saturday, application of both section 7502 and section 7503 means that an individual income tax return mailed by U.S. mail, properly addressed, and postmarked on the following Monday, will be considered timely.

With respect to income taxes, there are two significant prepayment requirements. Employers are required to withhold from wages paid to employees a tax "determined in accordance with tables or computational procedures prescribed by the Secretary."[97] This tax is treated as a "refundable credit" that is applied against the taxpayer's income tax liability.[98] If the amount withheld is greater than the employee's income tax liability, the excess is considered an "overpayment,"[99] which, subject to certain offsets,[100] is required to be refunded to the taxpayer, if timely claimed on the taxpayer's income tax return. The employer is required to pay over the amounts withheld to the federal government. This has resulted in a relatively high degree of compliance with the tax laws by

---

[93] *Cf.* Estate of Wood v. Commissioner, 909 F.2d 1155 (8th Cir. 199) (taxpayers can present evidence other than registered or certified mail to prove that a return was filed on a certain date), with Surowka v. United States, 909 F.2d 148 (6th Cir. 1990) (registered or certified receipt only way to prove filing).

[94] REG-138176-02, 69 Fed. Reg. 56377.

[95] *See, e.g.*, Raby and Raby, *Abolishing the Mailbox Rule for Tax Documents*, 2004 TNT 195-58, and Williamson and Staley, *Are the Proposed Timely Mailing/Timely Filing Regulations Timely*, 2005 TNT 147-25.

[96] When the Treasury Department issued its semiannual regulatory agenda on October 31, 2005, the next regulatory action for treatment of 301.7501-1(e) was listed as undetermined. 70 Fed. Reg. 65033 at 65,142

[97] IRC § 3402(a)(1).

[98] *See* IRC § 31(a).

[99] IRC § 6401(b).

[100] IRC § 6402.

wage earners while, at the same time, creating a significant compliance problem with respect to employers that, for one reason or another, withhold but do not pay over.[101]

The other significant prepayment requirement with respect to income taxes is that individuals, corporations, trusts, estates, and tax exempt organizations (with respect to their unrelated business taxable income) must estimate their tax liability for the year and make four installment payments. This prepayment obligation is discussed in Chapter 11.

VIII. EXTENSION OF TIME TO FILE OR PAY

The Code contains rules for the time by which returns are to be filed and the time by which taxes are to be paid. The time for *filing* a particular form is either the time set forth in the Code, or, if the Code is silent, the time established by the IRS in the Regulations.[102] Section 6081(a) authorizes the IRS to "grant a reasonable extension of time for filing any [required] return, declaration, statement or other document. . . ." Similarly, the Code provides the general rule that the time and place for *paying* the tax shown on any return is "the time and place fixed for filing the return (determined without regard to any extension of time for filing the return)."[103]

Obtaining an extension of time to file an income tax return is relatively simple. In fact, Regulation section 1.6081-4 permits an individual taxpayer to obtain an automatic six-month extension of time to file without having to provide any justification for the delay. Form 4868 requesting the automatic six-month extension must be filed (either electronically or on paper) on or before the due date of the return.[104] Form 4868 requires the taxpayer to "properly estimate" the tax liability for the year. If the tax liability on the application for extension does not constitute a bona fide and reasonable estimate based on facts available at the time, the extension may be held invalid, subjecting the taxpayer to a late-filing penalty.[105] If the estimate is bona fide and reasonable, the extension is valid even if the actual liability turns out to differ considerably from the estimated liability. There is a safe harbor: if the total amounts paid (through withholding, estimated tax payments, and the amount paid with the extension application) is within 10% of true liability, the IRS will not assert penalties.[106]

---

[101] See Chapter 14 dealing with the section 6672 "trust fund penalty" imposed on responsible persons who fail to "collect, truthfully account for, and pay over" tax such as the withholding tax.

[102] *See* IRC §§ 6071 (general rule), 6072 (income tax returns), 6075 (estate and gift tax returns).

[103] IRC § 6151(a).

[104] The General Instructions to Form 4868 indicate that it is to be used to obtain a four-month extension to file Forms 1040, 1040A, 1040EZ, 1040NR, or 1040NR-EZ.

[105] *See, e.g.*, Crocker v. Commissioner, 92 T.C. 899 (1989).

[106] Reg. § 301.6651-1(c)(3)(i).

Beyond that safe harbor, there is little certainty. Neither the case law nor rulings define clearly the contours of "proper estimate."

It may be necessary for the taxpayer to get an extension of time to file that is longer than six months. Except in the case of "undue hardship," no extension longer than six months will be granted unless the taxpayer has first obtained the automatic six-month extension.[107] To ask for additional time to file after the automatic six-month extension, the taxpayer must file Form 2688 and provide "a good reason" why additional time is necessary. Any such discretionary extension is limited to two months.[108] As is the case with Form 4868, Form 2688 can be filed electronically or on paper.[109] If the IRS denies a Form 2688 request for extension of time to file, the taxpayer usually has a ten-day grace period during which the taxpayer can file and avoid the section 6651(a)(1) late-filing penalty. However, the specific instructions to Form 2688 say that if the taxpayer has "no important reason [for requesting additional time to file] but only want[s] more time" the request will be denied and no grace period will be given.

The IRS has made it clear that failure to make a good faith estimate of the tax liability for the year when applying for automatic extension, or the making of false or misleading statements on an application for extension, will result in the request being disregarded[110] In this event, the taxpayer will be exposed to both late filing and late payment penalties under section 6651(a)(1) and (2).

It is possible to obtain an extension of time to file an estate tax return by filing a Form 4768. After an estate tax return is filed one can provide supplemental information by filing another Form 706 with "Supplemental Information" written across the top of page 1. After obtaining an extension, the return must be filed before the end of the extended period and the return "cannot be amended after the expiration of the extension period." However, supplemental information may still be provided to the IRS.[111]

An extension of time to file, even if valid, is not an extension of time to pay.[112] Thus, even if penalties are avoided, interest runs on the underpayment from the original due date of the return until the date of full payment.

Finally, there are several provisions in the Code that may alter the due date for payment of certain taxes. Perhaps most important is section 6161 which

---

[107] Reg. § 1.6081-4(a)(5). Form 2688 requires the taxpayer to disclose whether a Form 4868 has been filed for the year and cautions that if the four-month extension had not been requested, then, in the absence of undue hardship, no extension will be granted in response to the Form 2688 request.

[108] IRC § 6081(a).

[109] Form 2688 can be used to obtain an extension of time to file Forms 1040, 1040A, 1040EZ, 1040NR, and 1040NR-EZ.

[110] Rev. Rul. 83-27, 1983-1 C.B. 337.

[111] Reg. § 20.6081-1(d).

[112] Reg. § 1.6081-1(a).

authorizes the IRS to extend the time for *paying* any tax shown or required to be shown on any return "for a reasonable period not to exceed 6 months . . . from the date fixed for payment thereof."[113] The IRS is also authorized to extend the time for payment of any deficiency in income tax for for up to eighteen months and for an additional period, not to exceed twelve months, if payment on the original due date "will result in undue hardship to the taxpayer."[114]

There are several provisions that permit delay of payment of estate taxes either with the permission of the IRS or at the option of the executor. The IRS may extend the time for payment of estate tax for a period not to exceed four years if the estate can demonstrate "reasonable cause" for the delay. The executor may elect to defer payment of estate tax on the value of any reversionary or remainder interest held by the estate until six months after the termination of the precedent interest.[115] A further extension of up to three years may be granted for reasonable cause.[116] Finally, and probably most important, the executor may elect to pay the estate tax imposed on an interest in a closely held business in as many as ten annual installments.[117] The first such installment may be made any time within five years from the due date for payment of the tax.[118]

Finally, if the IRS determines that it will facilitate collection, the IRS is authorized to enter into written agreements for the payment of any tax in installments.[119] The provision is most often utilized in collection proceedings and it is discussed in detail in Chapter 13.

IX. DISCLOSURE OF REPORTABLE TRANSACTIONS

In the American Jobs Creation Act of 2004, Congress sought to strengthen the reporting and disclosure responsibilities of persons who provide, for compensation in excess of a threshold amount,[120] "any material aid, assistance, or advice with respect to organizing, managing, promoting, selling, implementing, insuring, or carrying out any reportable transaction. . . ."[121] Such persons, called "material advisors," are required to file a return identifying and describ-

---

[113] The General Instructions to Form 4868 at page 2 state that an extension of time for filing an income tax return also serves to extend the due date of a gift or generation-skipping transfer tax return (Form 709 or 709-A).

[114] IRC § 6161(b)(1).

[115] IRC § 6163(a).

[116] IRC § 6163(b).

[117] IRC § 6166(a).

[118] *Id.*

[119] IRC § 6159.

[120] The threshold amounts are $50,000 with respect to reportable transactions for natural persons and $250,000 in all other cases. IRC § 6111(b)(1)(B).

[121] IRC § 6111(b)(1)(A).

ing the tax benefits of the plan. Material advisors are also required to maintain lists of persons whom they advised regarding the reportable transaction.[122]

Taxpayers who participate in any reportable transaction also have disclosure responsibilities which are spelled out in Regulation § 1.6011-4. In November 2006, the Service published proposed regulations[123] (the "Proposed Regulations") which, when final, will replace the existing regulations in their entirety. The Proposed Regulations reflect changes in the underlying statutes and add "transactions of interest" as a new reportable transaction.

The Proposed Regulations are only one facet of the government's effort to improve transparency in order to stem the tide of corporate tax shelters. This discussion is limited to the Proposed Regulations and is included to provide some insight into the scope and nature of the new disclosure requirements. The Proposed Regulations will generally be applicable when they become final, however the disclosure responsibilities with respect to the new reportable transaction—transactions of interest—will be effective for transactions entered into on or after November 2, 2006.

As a preliminary matter, it is interesting that the first paragraph of the Instructions for Form 8886, the "Reportable Transaction Disclosure Statement" prominently makes the point that the American Jobs Creation Act of 2004 established penalties for failure to disclose reportable transactions and for understatements attributable to reportable transactions. Section 6707A imposes a penalty for failure to include in a return "any" information required to be included under section 6011 with respect to reportable transaction. The penalty with respect to reportable transactions, other than transactions of interest, is $10,000 for a natural person and $50,000 for any other taxpayer. For transactions of interest, the penalty is $100,000 for a natural person and $200,000 for any other taxpayer.

Also, there is a new accuracy related penalty, under section 6662A, equal to 20% of the amount of the understatement attributable to a reportable transaction. This penalty applies to listed transactions and other reportable transactions "if a significant purpose of such transaction is the avoidance or evasion of Federal income tax."[124] The penalty is increased to 30%, and the otherwise available reasonable cause defense will not apply, if the relevant facts are not disclosed as required under section 6011.[125]

Form 8886 requires the taxpayer to identify the type of reportable transaction, indicate whether it was acquired through a corporation or a pass-through entity, and provide the name and address of any person paid a fee for promot-

---

[122] IRC § 6112.

[123] IRS News Release IR-2006-167, T.D. 9295, REG-103038-05, *published in* BNA Text Supplement, Vol. 12, No. 212 (Nov. 2, 2006).

[124] IRC § 6662A(b)(2).

[125] IRC § 6664(d)(2)(A).

ing, soliciting, or recommending participation in the transaction or providing tax advice with respect to the transaction. In addition, the Form requires a description of the facts relating to the transaction, the kind of tax benefits expected and the estimated amount of the tax benefits.

Under § 1.6011-4 of the Proposed Regulations, reportable transactions include the following.

1. Listed transaction. These are transactions identified by the Service to be tax avoidance transactions, including transactions that are "substantially similar" to any such identified tax avoidance transactions.

2. Confidential transactions. These are transactions "offered under conditions of confidentiality and for which the taxpayer has paid an advisor a minimum fee."

3. Transaction with contractual protection. These are transactions in which the fee paid is refundable (in whole or in part) if the intended tax consequences are not realized or if the fee paid is contingent of the taxpayer receiving the promised tax benefits.[126]

4. Loss transactions. These are transactions in which the taxpayer claims a section 165 loss in excess of a threshold amount. The threshold amount depends on several factors including whether the taxpayer is a corporation (generally $10 million in a single year or $20 million in any combination of years) or an individual (generally $2 million in a single year or $4 million in any combination of years).

5. Transactions of interest. These are transactions that are "the same as or substantially similar to one of the types of transactions that the IRS has identified" by public notice. Generally, they are said to be transactions about which the Service doesn't have sufficient information to ascertain whether they should be characterized as listed or reportable transactions.[127]

6. Transactions involving a brief asset holding period. These are transactions involving a claimed tax credit in excess of $250,000 in which the assets giving rise to the credit are "held by the taxpayer for 45 days or less."

---

[126] For examples of transactions involving refundable or contingent fees that are specifically excepted from the reporting requirements, see Rev. Proc. 2007-20, 2007-7 IRB (Feb. 12, 2007).

[127] Preamble to REG-103038-05, *supra.*

PROBLEM

Question 1. Assume that a married couple (both under 65) had combined gross income of $17,000 (he earned $7,000 and she received $10,000 of interest income) for 2006.

(a) Are they required to file a return or returns?

(b) Under the same facts, except that one spouse had $15,000 of gross income in 2006 and the other spouse had no gross income for the year, would either spouse be required to file?

(c) Would your answer in (a) change if both spouses were both over age 65?

(d) If they filed electronically, what is the filing date?

(e) Suppose that he filed a joint return and signed both his and her names. Would she be liable for any deficiency?

Question 2. Must a corporation with an operating loss file a return?

Question 3. Must a single United States citizen who lives in France and whose only income for the year is $30,000 of earned income, all of which is excluded from gross income under § 911, file a return?

Question 4. What is the reason for the rules in § 6013(b)(2)(B), (C), and (D)?

Question 5. Who is responsible for making a return for a minor?

Question 6. Your client advises you that in 2006 he received a distribution of $100,000 from an annuity contract purchased for him by his employer. At the time, he was advised by his employer's comptroller that he did not have to include the distribution in his income for federal income tax purposes. He therefore did not bother telling his accountant about the distribution, and it was not included in his gross income on his 2006 return which was filed on April 15, 2007. Although the amount was clearly includible in income, you are convinced that your client acted in good faith. Your client asks you whether he should file an amended return and pay the additional tax.

(a) What should you advise your client?

(b) What would your advice be if you had prepared the return and your client now tells you that he knew all along that the distribution was includible and he did not tell you about it in order to avoid paying income tax?

Question 7. Your client is the executor of an estate of a decedent who died on Saturday, November 24, 2006. You have supervised the preparation of the estate tax return. You reviewed the final draft of the return with the executor, and he signed it on Monday, August 26, 2007. You, your client, and your secretary deposited the appropriately addressed return, including the check for the estate tax that is due, in the United States mail slot on your floor of your high-rise office building at 7:00 p.m. In due course, the envelope reaches the Internal Revenue Service, but the postmark is Tuesday, August 27, 2007.

    (a) Is the return timely filed?

    (b) Would your answer be different if the pick-up times reflected on the mail slot showed a final pick up at 8:00 p.m.?

    (c) Suppose that you used Federal Express, and the return was in fact hand-delivered the next day?

    (d) Suppose that you used Federal Express, and the return got lost and was never delivered?

    (e) Would the return be deemed timely if your office had a postage meter and the date stamped on the envelope was Monday, August 26, 2007?

    (f) What if the postage meter date was Monday, August 26, 2007, but the envelope did not reach the Internal Revenue Service until six days later?

Question 8. Under what circumstances can a return be hand-delivered to a local office of the Internal Revenue Service (which office is not a service center)?

Question 9.

    (a) Section 6081 allows the Secretary to grant a reasonable extension of time for filing any return. Can the Secretary grant an extension of time to file after the period for filing has already expired?

    (b) Consider § 6161 and Form 1127 regarding extensions of time to pay. Where does the "undue hardship" requisite come from, and why are extensions of time to pay so limited?

Chapter 3
SPOUSAL RELIEF

IRC:	§§ 6013(d)(3); 6015; 6330(c), (d) & (e); 7463(f)(1)
Regs.:	§§ 1.6013-4(d); 1.6015-1 to -7 (omit 1.6015-3(d)(4)(iii) to end of that section); 301.6343-1(b)(4)
Cases, etc.:	Krock v. Commissioner, T.C. Memo 1983-551 Stanley v. Commissioner, 81 T.C. 634 (1983) King v. Commissioner, 115 T.C. 118 (2000) Rev. Proc. 2003-61
IRS Forms:	8379; 8857

I. INTRODUCTION

Carol Jones has come to you complaining about her predicament. She recently received a notice from the IRS saying she owes taxes relating to a 2004 joint income tax return Form 1040 she filed with her ex-husband, John. Carol is presently divorced, financially strapped, and has custody of the children. The divorce was ugly and traumatizing for all. She and her ex-husband do not talk to each other any more. She is considering marrying Harold Roberts, a very nice man she met recently.

Carol tells you she does not know much about the details of what was on the 2004 return, as John took care of all the family's finances and had the return prepared by his accountant. She wants to know if you can help her avoid some or all of the tax and keep the tax debt from becoming a financial concern of Harold's, in case they marry. The answer to both questions is, "most likely."

The normal rule when a married couple files a joint return is that each spouse is jointly and severally liable for all tax, penalties,[1] and interest due, regardless of to whom the tax liability is attributable.[2] If the joint return was properly filed, an aggrieved spouse may be able to rely on the "innocent spouse" or "proportional liability" provisions of section 6015 to avoid or reduce the liability.[3]

---

[1] However, section 6663(c) provides a basis for relief from joint and several liability with respect to the fraud penalty, as only the perpetrator of the fraud can be held liable.

[2] IRC § 6013(d)(3).

[3] The relief provisions were significantly expanded and simplified by Congress in the 1998 Reform Act. This chapter focuses on the relief rules of general applicability under section 6015. A special rule dealing with liability for income items from community property exists under section

Three opportunities for relief are described in section 6015, each of which has the effect of allowing a joint filer who makes a timely election to be held responsible for only the portion of the amount due that is attributable to him or her. Two forms of relief—sections 6015(b) and (c)—apply to understatements (deficiencies) and are granted automatically if the taxpayer meets the required burden of proof. The third relief provision—section 6015(f)—applies primarily to underpayments, i.e., the balance due on the joint return filed by the couple, and is subject to the discretion of the Service.[4] All are reviewable by the Tax Court.[5]

If successful, one is relieved of liability for tax (including interest, penalties, and other amounts) to the extent the liability is attributable to all or a portion of the understatement or underpayment with respect to which the requesting spouse was innocent. Subject to various limitations, refunds are possible in section 6015(b) and (f) cases, but not in a section 6015(c) one unless paid subsequent to the grant of relief.[6]

Note that throughout this chapter, the spouse seeking relief may be referred to alternatively as the requesting spouse, the electing spouse, or the spouse seeking relief.

II. UNIVERSAL REQUIREMENTS FOR RELIEF

A. Joint Income Tax Return Filed

In order to be held jointly and severally liable under section 6013(d)(3) and, conversely, to be permitted to seek relief therefrom, a joint income tax return must have been filed. An income tax return may be filed jointly only by a man and woman who were legally married on the last day of the taxable year in issue. In addition, both persons must intend to file a joint return.[7] If a taxpayer can establish that either of these conditions is not satisfied, such as the couple never had a marriage ceremony and did not qualify as married under common law rules, or that one spouse signed the return because the other spouse forced him or her to do so, the return in question does not qualify as a joint return.[8] In

---

66(c). It is important to note that even if relief is granted to a requesting spouse, that person may still be liable under the transferee liability rules. This scenario is likely where, for example, one of the spouses died and left significant property to the other before paying the entire tax debt. Reg. § 1.6015-1(j).

[4] IRC § 6015(f).

[5] *See* note 56, *infra*.

[6] Chief Counsel Advice 200606001.

[7] IRC §§ 6013(a), 7701(a)(38); Reg. § 1.6013-4. Joint filing status cannot be revoked once the due date for filing the return, including extensions, has passed. IRM 25.15.1.2. But spouses who file separate returns can, subject to certain limitations, elect to file joint returns at a later time. IRC § 6013(b). Rev. Rul. 2005-59, 2005-37 I.R.B. 505 (returns prepared by the IRS pursuant to its authority under section 6020(b) are not joint income tax returns since they are not signed by both spouses; completion of Form 870, 1902 or 4549 are not joint income tax returns, even if signed by both spouses, because they are not signed under penalty of perjury).

[8] Reg. § 1.6015-1(b). *See* Steve R. Johnson, *The Duress or Deception Defense to Joint and Several Spousal Liability*, Tax Prac. & Proc. 15 (Dec. 2004-Jan. 2005).

this case, joint and several liability never attaches and the taxpayer can escape liability without having to prove each of the elements necessary for relief under section 6015.[9] For a more detailed discussion of the requirements for filing a joint return, see Chapter 2.

B. Amount Due Involves Income Tax

The relief provisions of section 6015 are available only with respect to balances due for income taxes and related penalties, additions to tax, and interest.[10] Section 6015 does not provide relief for other taxes that must be reported on a joint federal income tax return, such as domestic service employment taxes under section 3510.[11]

C. Timely Election

Assuming that a joint return was intended and no fraudulent transfers of assets occurred between the husband and wife,[12] either or both of them may, by filing Form 8857, make an election seeking relief under section 6015.[13] If only one spouse makes the election and relief is granted, the electing spouse is responsible only for the portion of the understatement attributable to his or her adjustments; the other spouse remains jointly and severally liable for the entire understatement. If both spouses make the election and each is granted relief, then each owes only the share of the understatement attributable to him or her.

One makes the election by completing and mailing Form 8857 to the IRS Service Center in Cincinnati, Ohio, or, if the case is presently active, by handing it to the IRS agent assigned to the case. Relief can be sought under any or all of

---

[9] Raymond v. Commissioner, 119 T.C. 191 (2002). For a wife who is terrified of her ex-husband and who would prefer to forgo her legitimate defenses rather than have to confront him, an added advantage of establishing that a joint returns was not intended is the fact that the nonrequesting spouse is not entitled to notice or other rights under section 6015. In this situation, the Service recharacterizes the joint return as two married filing separate returns and assesses the liability associated with them to the proper spouse.

[10] Reg. § 1.6015-2(b). Income tax, for these purposes, includes self-employment tax.

[11] Reg. § 1.6015-1(a)(3).

[12] A spouse may not seek relief if the IRS is able to establish that the spouses fraudulently transferred assets between them to qualify for relief. Reg. § 1.6015-1(d).

[13] One of the most significant advantages to filing a Form 8857 is that, by statute, the IRS suspends collection from the date the election is filed until the matter is finally resolved plus 60 days. Any improper assessment may be enjoined. IRC §§ 6015(e)(1), 6330(e) (with respect to Collection Due Process hearings); Reg. § 1.6015-7(c).

Since the IRS may not pursue collection once a taxpayer requests relief under section 6015(b) or (c), the statute of limitations (SOL) on collection is suspended for the entire period the matter is being considered and then for an additional 60 days. IRC § 6015(e)(2). Neither the SOL on assessment nor the SOL on filing refund claims is affected by a request for relief under section 6015.

the three provisions in section 6015 by checking the appropriate box(es) on the form.[14]

A section 6015 election may be made at any time after receipt of a notification of an audit or a letter or notice from the IRS indicating that there may be an outstanding liability with regard to that year.[15] It can be made while the return is being examined by a revenue agent (called a "deficiency" election), after the taxpayer receives a collection notice from the Service but before a "collection due process" hearing is requested (called a "stand alone" election)[16] or during a "collection due process" hearing (called a "CDP" election).[17]

The election must be made no later than two years after the date on which the IRS began "collection activity" with respect to the electing spouse.[18] Regulation section 1.6015-5(b)(2) explains the term "collection activity." The most frequent collection activities that start the two-year clock[19] are the issuance of a collection due process notice directed to the electing spouse, the application of a refund otherwise due the electing spouse against the joint return liability,[20] and the issuance of a notice of levy against property in which the spouse making the election has an ownership interest.

D. Not Barred by Res Judicata or a Final Administrative Determination

Relief from joint and several liability is not available if a court has rendered a final decision on the requesting spouse's tax liability and if relief under section 6015 was at issue in the prior proceeding, or if the requesting spouse meaningfully participated in the proceeding and did not ask for relief under section 6015.[21] Also, any final decisions rendered by a court of competent jurisdiction regarding issues relevant to section 6015 are conclusive and the requesting spouse may be collaterally estopped from relitigating those issues."[22]

---

[14] Reg. § 1.6015-1(a)(2).

[15] Reg. § 1.6015-5(b)(5).

[16] If the election is filed as part of an offer in compromise, both the Forms 656 and 8857 are submitted. The basis for the offer is that there is doubt as to liability. As such, the matter is transferred to examination personnel for consideration.

[17] This is normally accomplished by filing a Form 12153 and an attached Form 8857, with the local Appeals Office. A unique aspect of making the claim in conjunction with a CDP hearing is that the spousal defenses may be raised whether or not other underlying tax liability issues may be raised. IRC §§ 6330(c)(2), 6330(d). See also IRM 8.7.1.1.9.14.

[18] Reg. § 1.6015-5(b)(3).

[19] Collection activity does *not* include the following actions: issuance of a notice of deficiency, issuance of a demand for payment of tax, issuance of a notice of intent to levy under section 6331(d), or the filing of a Notice of Federal Tax Lien.

[20] IRC § 6402; McGee v. Commissioner, 123 T.C. 314 (2004) (the two-year period does not begin until notice of the right to petition for relief under section 6015 is sent to the spouse).

[21] Reg. § 1.6015-1(e).

[22] *Id.*

A similar rule applies to final administrative determinations, such as a closing agreement or an offer in compromise.[23]

III. ADDITIONAL REQUIREMENTS IMPOSED TO OBTAIN RELIEF UNDER SECTION 6015(b)

Section 6015(b) can be used by any joint filer. However, it is utilized almost exclusively by persons who are not divorced or separated or who seek a refund.[24] A spouse seeking relief under subsection (b) has the burden to prove each of the following elements:

1. A joint income tax return was filed (or deemed to have been filed);

2. A timely election was made;

3. There is an understatement in income tax attributable to erroneous items of the other spouse;

4. In signing the return, the spouse did not know there was an understatement on the return and did not have reason to know of its existence; and

5. Taking into account all the facts and circumstances, it would be inequitable to hold the requesting spouse liable for the tax.

The discussion above covered elements (1) and (2). Elements (3), (4) and (5) are discussed below.

A. There Must Be an Understatement of Income Tax Attributable to the Other Spouse

The innocent spouse rule of section 6015(b) is available only with respect to an understatement of income tax.[25] An understatement[26] is nearly identical to a deficiency. Essentially, it represents the additional amount of tax and related penalties owed as the result of a taxpayer's erroneous treatment of items on a tax return that are discovered during an examination by the IRS. An understatement should be contrasted with an underpayment. An underpayment is the balance of the tax reflected as due on the filed return. Relief from liability for an underpayment is possible only under the discretionary provisions of section 6015(f).

---

[23] Reg. § 1.6015-1(c). *See also* Dutton v. Commissioner, 122 T.C. 133 (2004).

[24] Section 6015(b) is similar to the relief available under section 6013(e) existing prior to the 1998 Reform Act, but with a potpourri of dollar limitations removed. To the extent the two are alike, old case law is instructive.

[25] Reg. § 1.6015-2(b).

[26] IRC § 6662(d)(2)(A).

In order to obtain relief under section 6015(b)(1)(B), the understatement, or the portion for which relief is sought, must be attributable to the other spouse. To whom an item is attributable normally turns on who would have been required to report the item if separate returns had been filed.[27] If the answer points to one spouse, the other spouse may be eligible for relief. If the answer does not point to either spouse, the understatement is normally attributed to the spouse whose decision-making caused the couple to be involved in the transaction that gave rise to the reporting position. For example, if one spouse invested in a venture and was the sole signatory on documents relating to the venture, any erroneous items of the venture would normally be attributed to this spouse.[28]

B. The Spouse Seeking Relief Did Not Have Actual or Constructive Knowledge of the Understatement on the Return

In order for the requesting spouse to obtain relief under section 6015(b), that spouse must be able to establish that he or she had neither actual knowledge nor reason to know of the understatement on the return. Most cases are decided under the "reason to know" standard. Courts struggle with granting relief under this provision since doing so runs counter to two universally held truisms: (1) everyone is responsible for reviewing tax returns before signing them and (2) ignorance of the law is no excuse. Consistent with this, before they are willing to grant relief, courts expect the requesting spouse to have inquired about items on, or missing from, the return when a "reasonably prudent person in the taxpayer's position" would have felt obligated to do so.[29] One cannot merely "bury one's head in the sand like an ostrich"[30] when there are indications of error. In other words, say the courts, section 6015 protects the innocent, not the intentionally ignorant.[31]

In determining whether the spouse seeking relief should have inquired further, courts and the Regulations consider six broad factors:

1. The nature and amount of the item relative to other items;

2. The couple's financial situation and whether the income reported appears low compared to the standard of living of the couple;

3. The requesting spouse's education and business experience;

---

[27] Bokum v. Commissioner, 94 T.C. 126 (1990); Silverman v. Commissioner, T.C. Memo 1996-69.

[28] This is so even if the decision-making spouse believed the items were allowable because of professional advice he received to that effect. Silverman v. Commissioner, T.C. Memo 1996-69.

[29] Price v. Commissioner, 887 F.2d 959, 965 (9th Cir. 1989).

[30] Cohen v. Commissioner, T.C. Memo 1987-537.

[31] Hayes v. Commissioner, T.C. Memo 1989-327.

4. The extent of the requesting spouse's participation in the questioned activity;

5. Whether a reasonable person would have inquired about the item; and

6. Whether the reporting position of the erroneous item on the return represented a departure from reporting positions on previous years' returns.[32]

1. Omitted Income Cases

Relief for understatements due to "omitted income" has been in the Code to varying degrees since 1972. Courts look to whether the spouse requesting relief knew or had reason to know of *either* the omitted income itself or the transaction giving rise to the omitted income. If so, relief is denied.[33] For example, in *Cheshire v. Commissioner*,[34] the court ruled that the actual knowledge standard in omitted income cases was actual and clear awareness. Consequently, Ms. Cheshire, who knew her spouse received retirement distributions that gave rise to the deficiency asserted, was not eligible for relief. The court was not moved by the fact that Ms. Cheshire was unaware that the couple's joint return misstated the tax treatment.

This analysis is often criticized for failing to take into account how reasonably the requesting spouse acted under the circumstances to determine if the position was correct, such as whether he or she made inquiry of the other spouse or a return preparer. It also fails to take into account whether the requesting spouse had any knowledge of the *specific* facts of the transaction resulting in the omission.

2. Deduction Cases

With respect to "deduction" cases, some courts, particularly the Tax Court, appear to take a tougher position before they are willing to grant relief than is true with omitted income cases.[35] These courts seem to believe that since deductions are plainly visible on the return, the spouse seeking relief has a greater duty of inquiry. Thus, if the spouse knew, or through inquiry should have learned, of the transaction giving rise to an erroneous deduction, relief is denied.

---

[32] Reg. § 1.6015-2(c); Friedman v. Commissioner, 53 F.3d 523 (2d Cir. 1995); IRM 25.15.3.6.1.3.1(2).

[33] *See, e.g.*, McCoy v. Commissioner, 57 T.C. 732 (1972) (even though she did not know that the liabilities exceeded assets and that the transaction resulted in income under section 357(c), wife was not afforded relief because she knew that husband transferred assets and liabilities of a business to a corporation).

[34] 115 T.C. 183 (2000), *aff'd*, 282 F.3d 326 (5th Cir. 2002).

[35] *See, e.g.*, Bokum v. Commissioner, 94 T.C. 126 (1990).

Other courts,[36] seeking to fulfill what they believe was a liberalizing intent by Congress in enacting section 6015 in the 1998 Reform Act, look to the actual words of the statute and focus on whether the requesting spouse had reason to know of the *understatement* rather than whether he or she had reason to know of the *transaction*. As the Fifth Circuit said in *Cheshire v. Commissioner:*

> Accordingly, in erroneous deduction cases, this court questions whether the spouse "knew or had reason to know that the *deduction* in question would give rise to a substantial understatement of tax on the joint return." However, if the spouse knows enough about the underlying transaction that her innocent spouse defense rests entirely upon a mistake of law, she has "reason to know" of the tax understatement as a matter of law. . . . If "reason to know" cannot be determined as a matter of law, the proper factual inquiry is "whether a reasonably prudent taxpayer in the spouse's position at the time she signed the return could be expected to know that the stated liability was erroneous or that further investigation was warranted."[37]

If the spouse seeking relief had a duty to inquire about the correctness of a deduction taken on the return and did not do so, relief is denied. But if the requesting spouse can show he or she made inquiries, relief can be obtained if the spouse acted reasonably to be assured that the transaction was reflected on the return correctly. This duty can be satisfied by inquiry of the other spouse or of the couple's return preparer.[38] Relief is denied only if a reasonably prudent person would not have agreed to the return position or if, through inquiring, the requesting spouse became familiar enough with sufficient details of the transaction to put him or her on an equal footing with the other spouse.

C. It Would Be Inequitable to Hold the Innocent Spouse Liable for the Tax

The determinative issue in innocent spouse cases is frequently whether, based upon all the facts and circumstances during the marriage and afterwards, it would be unfair to hold the electing spouse liable for the tax. Though this inquiry is broad, including both financial and non-financial considerations, a critical factor is whether the spouse seeking relief received a significant economic benefit that is, in some manner, traceable to the understatement. The most damaging evidence to an innocent spouse's claim of inequity is that the

---

[36] *See* Reser v. Commissioner, 112 F.3d 1258, 1266 (5th Cir. 1997); Hayman v. Commissioner, 992 F.2d 1256 (2d Cir. 1993); Price v. Commissioner, 887 F.2d 959 (9th Cir. 1989); Erdahl v. Commissioner, 930 F.2d 585 (8th Cir. 1991) (citing Stevens v. Commissioner, 872 F.2d 1499 (11th Cir. 1989)) (citing Sanders v. United States, 509 F.2d 162 (5th Cir. 1975)).

[37] 282 F.3d 326, 334 (5th Cir. 2002) (citations omitted).

[38] It is not clear how extensively a relief-seeking spouse must inquire of the husband or, if the return was prepared by a professional, of that individual. It appears that the mere inquiry is enough to satisfy her obligation.

couple lived a very lavish lifestyle in the year under review. For this purpose, normal support is not considered a significant economic benefit.[39]

Also problematic for requesting spouses is the situation where the couple divorced and the requesting spouse received substantial financial benefit from the other spouse in the property settlement and the property received is traceable to the understatement. However, if the electing spouse can show that his or her current investments, including property, are traceable to years other than the years in issue or to personal funds, relief is possible.[40]

Since the inquiry into whether it is inequitable to hold the spouse liable is not limited to economic benefit, other facts are also germane. They include physical or psychological abuse, extramarital relations, purchase of assets in a manner that did not benefit the innocent spouse, desertion, failure to pay alimony or child support, separation, and divorce.[41]

IV. ADDITIONAL REQUIREMENTS IMPOSED TO OBTAIN RELIEF UNDER SECTION 6015(c)

One of the most dramatic changes to the innocent spouse rules enacted in the 1998 Reform Act was the addition of the right to elect proportionate liability. The section 6015(c) provision is, in a sense, a "no fault" opportunity for relief. Unless the IRS can establish the existence of a condition defeating relief, relief is granted to the extent the spouse seeking relief proves the portion of the understatement that is not attributable to him or her. The electing spouse is not required to establish his or her innocence, the other spouse's guilt or the unfairness of being held liable for the entire tax.

A. IRS Has Burden to Prove the Electing Spouse's Actual Knowledge

A requesting spouse will be denied relief if the IRS establishes that, at the time the return was signed, the requesting spouse had actual knowledge of an erroneous item giving rise to the deficiency.[42] Regulation section 1.6015-3(c)(2)

---

[39] Reg. § 1.6015-2(d).

[40] Silverman v. Commissioner, T.C. Memo 1996-69.

[41] Reg. § 1.6015-2(d); Rev. Proc. 2003-61, 2003-32 I.R.B. 296. *See* Steve R. Johnson, *The Duress or Deception Defense to Joint and Several Spousal Liability*, Tax Prac. & Proc. 15 (Dec. 2004-Jan. 2005).

[42] If the wife signed the return without having inquired due to a history of abuse by the husband, she is treated as not having actual knowledge. Reg. § 1.6015-3(c)(2)(v). The IRS must plead actual knowledge as an affirmative defense in the answer to a section 6015(c) petition. Chief Counsel Notice 2005-011.

makes it clear that actual knowledge is a different standard than "reason to know" and that only actual knowledge disqualifies a spouse from proportional relief under section 6015(c).

Three cases, *Charlton,*[43] *Cheshire,*[44] and *Martin,*[45] have helped shape the jurisprudence with respect to omitted income in section 6015(c) cases. *Charlton* and *Cheshire* are both discussed in the following excerpt from *Martin v. Commissioner:*

> In *Charlton v. Commissioner,* . . . the taxpayer seeking relief was aware that the source of income was his wife's business, but he did not compare records provided him by his wife with other business records to determine whether his wife had accounted for all of the income. Although Mr. Charlton had actual knowledge of income from a particular source and knew generally of his spouse's source of income, he had no knowledge that all income from that source had not been accounted for as reported. We thus held in *Charlton* that "respondent has not shown that Charlton had actual knowledge of the item causing the deficiency, and that Charlton qualifies for relief under section 6015(c)."
>
> In *Cheshire v. Commissioner,* also an omitted income case, petitioner had actual knowledge of the fact of the omitted income, as well as the amount of income, but submitted that she was entitled to relief because she was unaware of the applicable tax laws. Specifically, petitioner "was aware of the amount, the source, and the date of receipt of the retirement distribution and interest" but did not know the tax consequences of the income. In that case we held that "knowledge" for purposes of section 6015(c) relief disqualification does not require actual knowledge on the part of the electing spouse as to whether the entry on the return is or is not correct. Instead, the electing spouse must have "actual knowledge of the disputed item of income * * * as well as the amount thereof, that gave rise to the deficiency." Thus, in *Cheshire v. Commissioner,* we concluded that ignorance of the applicable tax law is no excuse and that respondent had met his burden of proving knowledge of the omitted income.
>
> . . . .
>
> [In the instant case], without petitioner's involvement or knowledge, Mr. Martin and certain professionals devised this complex and somewhat devious transaction consisting of a series of steps and involving several entities. The transaction was primarily intended to deceive State insurance regulators into believing that the asset position or pic-

---

[43] 114 T.C. 333 (2000).

[44] 115 T.C. 183 (2000), *aff'd*, 282 F.3d 326 (5th Cir. 2002).

[45] T.C. Memo 2000-346.

ture of Mr. Martin's insurance company was improved. The transaction was further complicated because it was structured for tax purposes to appear that the transfer of property to the corporation(s) was a non-taxable event under section 351. Ultimately, the desired results were not achieved, Mr. Martin was incarcerated due to his fraudulent deceptions, and petitioner was left penniless and bankrupt.

Petitioner knew that Mr. Martin intended to contribute shares in Primera to another corporation, but she had no actual knowledge of the myriad and complex steps or entities involved in the transaction. Petitioner's uncontroverted testimony revealed that she was, at most, superficially aware of only a small portion of the details in these complex transactions. Because petitioner had only a superficial awareness of the transaction, petitioner did not have actual knowledge of the amount of the financial gain that was misreported, nor of the underlying facts that gave rise to the gain. Based on the facts pertaining to the transactions available to petitioner, she would not have known that the stock transfer was not a section 351 transaction or that the corporate sale of land could have resulted in financial gain or income to her husband. Like the taxpayer in *Charlton v. Commissioner,* petitioner possessed only a part of the information, and the information that she did possess was insufficient to supply her with actual knowledge regarding the amount of the financial gain from the transaction, if any.[46]

Another case, *King v. Commissioner,*[47] addressed the actual knowledge issue in the context of a tax deficiency associated with losses claimed by her husband but disallowed under section 183 because they were not incurred in an activity engaged in with the intent to make a profit.

The question in this case, therefore, is not whether petitioner knew the tax consequences of a not-for-profit activity but whether she knew or believed that her former spouse was not engaged in the activity for the primary purpose of making a profit. Thus, in determining whether petitioner had actual knowledge of an improperly deducted item on the return, more is required than petitioner's knowledge that the deduction appears on the return or that her former spouse operated an activity at a loss. . . . The Court is satisfied that petitioner's knowledge of the activity in question was that it was an activity that she knew was not profitable but that she hoped and expected would become profitable at some point. Respondent presented insufficient evidence to show that petitioner knew that her former spouse did not have a primary objective of making a profit with his cattle-raising activity. Petitioner, therefore, is entitled to relief from the tax liability arising out of this activity under section 6015(c). Since the activity was an activity attributable

---

[46] *Id.* at 16-20.

[47] 116 T.C. 198 (2001).

solely to her former spouse, the relief to petitioner extends to the full amount of the deficiency.[48]

B. Spouse No Longer Married, Separated, or Widowed at Time of Election

Section 6015(c) relief is only available to unmarried and separated spouses. Marital status is determined at the time of the election. Whether one is divorced or legally separated is decided in the same manner as it is determined in connection with the right to file jointly, i.e., state law controls except in the case of sham divorces that have tax avoidance as their principal purpose.[49] Note that even if the spouses are neither legally separated nor divorced, either may make the election after the couple lived apart for an entire 12-month period.

C. Amount of Deficiency Allocated to Other Spouse

Depending on how complicated the adjustments are, the most challenging aspect of section 6015(c) for the electing spouse may be the requirement of proving the portion of the deficiency allocable to him or her.[50] The regulations are particularly instructive here and should be read carefully by the student. The portion of the total deficiency allocated to the electing spouse can be expressed as follows:

$$\frac{\text{Net Amount of Items Taken into Account in Computing the Deficiency that Are } \textit{Allocable to the Electing Spouse}}{\text{Net Amount } \textit{of All Items} \text{ Taken into Account in Computing the Deficiency}} \quad \chi \quad \text{Total Deficiency}$$

Examples of Allocation of Deficiency:

Basic Facts: H and W filed a joint return for 2003. The IRS examines the return and, as the result of $150,000 in net adjustments to their joint taxable income, determines liabilities of $50,000. H and W later divorce. W timely files a proportionate liability election under section 6015(c); H does not. To the extent W can meet her burden of proof, she will be liable only for the portion of the liability properly allocated to her. H remains liable for the entire $50,000 unless he makes an election also.

Example (1): There is only one source for all the adjustments—H did not report all the income from his business and took some unwarranted

---

[48] *Id.* at 205-06. *See* Rowe v. Commissioner, T.C. Memo 2001-325 for an extensive discussion of the Tax Court's approach to analyzing "actual knowledge."

[49] Boyter v. Commissioner, 668 F.2d 1382 (4th Cir. 1981); Reg. § 1.6015-3(b)(1), (2). A widow(er) is treated as not married and may make the election. Reg. § 1.6015-3(a).

[50] IRC § 6015(c)(2); Reg. § 1.6015-3(d). *See* Capehart v. Commissioner, 125 T.C. 211 (2005).

business deductions. The $50,000 of liabilities is made up of $40,000 additional income tax, $8,000 in accuracy-related penalties, and $2,000 in self-employment taxes. The self-employment taxes, being exclusively attributable to H, are taxed to him regardless of what is true as to the remaining $48,000 in income tax and penalty. However, since none of the items of adjustment relate to W, the percentage of the deficiency allocable to her is 0%. The entire remaining $48,000 deficiency is H's liability. W owes no additional tax.

Example (2): There are two sources for the adjustments: H had unreported income of $100,000 from the sale of stock owned by him in his name. W had a $50,000 casualty loss disallowed with respect to property she owned.[51] Assuming both spouses make the election, 2/3 of the liability is H's and 1/3 is W's. The result would be the same even if some of the casualty loss is disallowed due to the 10% of Adjusted Gross Income floor in section 165(h).

Example (3): Same as (2) except that W only had $35,000 in income. In such case, only $35,000 of deductions attributable to W will be allocated to her; the remainder will be allocated to H.

D. Anti-Avoidance Rules

To prevent the inappropriate use of the election under section 6015(c), two special rules are included in the Code. To quote from the Senate Report:

> [I]f the IRS demonstrates that assets were transferred between the spouses in a fraudulent scheme joined in by both spouses, neither spouse is eligible to make the election under the provision (and consequently joint and several liability applies to both spouses).
>
> . . . .
>
> [Also], the limitation on the liability of an electing spouse is increased by the value of any disqualified assets received from the other spouse. Disqualified assets include any property or right to property that was transferred to an electing spouse if the principal purpose of the transfer is the avoidance of tax (including the avoidance of payment of tax). A rebuttable presumption exists that a transfer is made for tax avoidance purposes if the transfer was made less than one year before the earlier of the payment due date or the date of the notice of proposed deficiency. The rebuttable presumption does not apply to transfers pur-

---

[51] The unreported income and casualty loss would be attributed equally to H and W unless there is clear and convincing evidence that the item is attributable to the ownership of the property by one or the other. The example assumes that such evidence is present.

suant to a decree of divorce or separate maintenance. The presumption may be rebutted by a showing that the principal purpose of the transfer was not the avoidance of tax or the payment of tax.[52]

Example (4): Same facts as example (2) above, except that the IRS establishes that H transferred $10,000 of property to W to avoid tax. If the transfer was not part of a fraudulent scheme, whatever W's share of the deficiency is per the calculation in example 2 above, it will be increased by $10,000. By contrast, if the transfer were part of a fraudulent scheme, neither H nor W could make the proportionate election. Alternatively, if the IRS could prove that W had actual knowledge of H's unreported income, W would not be permitted to elect proportionate liability as to the deficiency flowing from that adjustment, unless she can prove she was forced by the other spouse to sign the return against her will.

V. ADDITIONAL REQUIREMENTS IMPOSED TO OBTAIN RELIEF UNDER SECTION 6015(f)

The section 6015(f) election is revolutionary. It expands the availability of relief to underpayments in situations where, taking into consideration all the facts and circumstances, the Service believes it would be inequitable to hold the requesting spouse responsible for more than his or her portion of the unpaid tax. The Conference Committee Report relative to section 6015(f) states:

> The conferees intend that the Secretary will consider using the grant of authority to provide equitable relief in appropriate situations to avoid the inequitable treatment of spouses in such situations. For example, the conferees intend that equitable relief be available to a spouse that does not know, and had no reason to know, that funds intended for the payment of tax were instead taken by the other spouse for such other spouse's benefit.

> The conferees do not intend to limit the use of the Secretary's authority to provide equitable relief to situations where tax is shown on a return but not paid. The conferees intend that such authority be used where, taking into account all the facts and circumstances, it is inequitable to hold an individual liable for all or part of any unpaid tax or deficiency arising from a joint return. The conferees intend that relief be available where there is both an understatement and an underpayment of tax.[53]

---

[52] S. Rpt. No. 174, 105th Cong., 2d Sess. 59 (1998), 1998-3 C.B. 595.

[53] H.R. Conf. Rep. No 599, 105th Cong., 2d Sess. 254-55 (1998), 1998-3 C.B. 1008-09.

In 2003, the IRS issued Rev. Proc. 2003-61 to provide guidance on how section 6015(f) would be analyzed.[54] Under paragraph 4.01 of the revenue procedure, the IRS will consider granting equitable relief under section 6015(f) only if the individual can establish that certain threshold requirements are met. The threshold requirements include such things as a joint return having been filed, that relief is not available under 6015(b) or (c), that the election was made timely, that the item for which relief is sought is attributable to the other spouse, and that no impermissible transfers of assets or fraudulent conduct took place.

If the requesting spouse meets the paragraph 4.01 threshold requirements, the IRS will ordinarily grant equitable relief under section 6015(f) if the requesting spouse also satisfies *all* the conditions in paragraph 4.02 of the revenue procedure. The paragraph 4.02 conditions include that the joint filers no longer live together, that the requesting spouse had no knowledge or reason to know that the nonrequesting spouse would not pay the income tax liability, and that the requesting spouse would suffer economic hardship if relief is not granted. Noteworthy is the fact that paragraph 4.02 only pertains to underpayments; if an understatement is involved, one must turn to paragraph 4.03 to find what the Service will consider.

If the requesting spouse satisfies the threshold requirements but does not meet the paragraph 4.02 conditions for relief or if the tax due is the result of an understatement, the examiner is instructed to consider a group of nonexclusive factors listed in paragraph 4.03.[55] The conditions for relief include whether the requesting spouse:

1. Is still married to the nonrequesting spouse;

2. Would suffer economic hardship if relief is not granted;

3. Did not know and had no reason to know—

   a. in the case of an underpayment, that the nonrequesting spouse would not pay the income tax liability, or

   b. in the case of a deficiency, of the item giving rise to the deficiency;

4. Has a legal obligation to pay the outstanding income tax liability pursuant to a divorce decree or agreement;

5. Received significant benefit (beyond normal support) from the unpaid income tax liability or item giving rise to the deficiency; and

6. Is in compliance with income tax laws.

Other factors may also be considered, such as whether the requesting spouse was abused or was or is in poor mental or physical health.

---

[54] 2003-2 C.B. 296.

[55] *See also* IRM 25.15.3.8.4.2.

VI. APPEALING AN ADVERSE DETERMINATION ADMINISTRATIVELY AND JUDICIALLY

As with all adverse determinations by local or service center personnel, the taxpayer may seek review of a decision denying relief by filing a protest in the Appeals Office of the IRS. If the Appeals Office upholds the denial, either an unfavorable final determination letter or a notice of deficiency is mailed to the taxpayer. Once this letter is received, the requesting spouse can seek judicial review. If he or she wishes to litigate the matter without first paying the asserted deficiency or underpayment,[56] a petition must be filed with the Tax Court within ninety days of the date the IRS mailed the unfavorable final determination letter or notice of deficiency,[57] or if the IRS failed to act on the election, after six months has passed from the date the taxpayer filed the election.[58]

The Tax Court has taken a very liberal approach to the cases that have come before it on spousal relief. Rather than merely reviewing the record on an "abuse of discretion" standard and deferring to the agency's determination unless the IRS acted arbitrarily, capriciously, or without sound basis in fact,[59] the court reviews all the facts of the case on a de novo basis.[60] This approach is often to the benefit of the spouse who was denied relief.

---

[56] Section 6015(e) was amended on December 20, 2006, to grant jurisdiction to the Tax Court to hear appeals of equitable relief determinations made under section 6015(f). The Tax Relief and Health Care Act of 2006, Pub. L. No. 109-432, Tit. IV, § 408, 120 Stat. 3052 (2006). The amendment effectively reversed a line of cases that held the Tax Court lacked jurisdiction in such cases. Bartman v. Commissioner, 446 F.3d 785 (8th Cir. 2006); Billings v. Commissioner, 127 T.C. 7 (2006).

[57] Alternatively, one can pay the tax, penalties, and interest, file a claim for refund, and, if the claim is disallowed, litigate in the U.S. District Court or Court of Federal Claims. IRM 25.15.1.10.3. Some believe these courts are better suited to hear equitable matters and more predisposed to side with the wife than the Tax Court. However, it may be difficult for many divorced wives to get into these courts as the tax asserted by the IRS, including interest and penalties, must be paid in full prior to trial. See Chapter 9 for a discussion of refund actions.

[58] *See* Reg. § 1.6015-7(b).

[59] Butler v. Commissioner, 114 T.C. 276, 292 (2000).

[60] Ewing v. Commissioner, 122 T.C. 32 (2004); Chief Counsel Notice 2004-026. *See* Chapter 1. The Ewing case cited (Ewing II) was preceded by Ewing v. Commissioner (Ewing I), 118 T.C. 494 (2002) in which the Tax Court concluded it had jurisdiction in a request for equitable relief under section 6015(f) despite the absence of an asserted deficiency. The Ninth Circuit disagreed and vacated Ewing I. This mooted the issue raised in Ewing II.

Once a case is filed with the Tax Court, the court will decide the matter and not remand it to the IRS for reconsideration of its determination. Friday v. Commissioner, 124 T.C. 220 (2005).

VII. OTHER MATTERS

A. Rights of the Nonrequesting Spouse

Unless an election is filed by each spouse in his or her own name, the non-filing spouse is considered a "nonrequesting spouse." Nonrequesting spouses are entitled to many, but not all, of the rights available to the requesting spouse.

Upon receipt of an election by a requesting spouse, the Service must send notice of the election to the nonrequesting spouse at his or her last known address.[61] The notice must provide the nonrequesting spouse with an opportunity to submit information for consideration in determining liability. Intervention and participation are optional. The nonrequesting spouse may submit whatever information he or she deems relevant to the issue of the appropriateness of relief for the requesting spouse.[62] The Service can share information received from one spouse with the other spouse, but upon request will omit information disclosing a spouse's location.[63]

The nonrequesting spouse may participate during the administrative phase of the case in much the same way as the requesting spouse. By filing a protest with the Appeals Office within 30 days of the notification letter's mailing date, the non-requesting spouse is even permitted to appeal a preliminary determination granting the requesting spouse partial or full relief.[64]

After hearing the matter, the Appeals Office will render a final determination. At the conclusion of the administrative consideration of the case, both spouses are notified of the Service's determination. Despite the many rights accorded the nonrequesting spouse to have a hearing and to participate in it, the nonrequesting spouse may neither block an administrative settlement offered to the requesting spouse nor petition the Tax Court to review the determination.[65]

---

[61] Reg. § 1.6015-6(a)(1); Chief Counsel Notice 2003-015. Notice is required regardless whether the claim is filed as part of a deficiency proceeding, a CDP hearing, or a "stand-alone" section 6015 request.

[62] Reg. § 1.6015-6(b) has a detailed list of the kinds of information that could be submitted.

[63] Reg. § 1.6015-6(a)(1). A taxpayer who has been the victim of domestic violence and fears that filing a claim for innocent spouse relief will result in retaliation should check the box on the Form 8857 alerting the IRS to this fact. In that manner, the IRS will make every effort to protect the privacy of the requesting spouse and will, among other precautions, centralize all correspondence in one location so that the nonrequesting spouse cannot guess the whereabouts of the domestic abuse victim. *See* Steve R. Johnson, *The Duress or Deception Defense to Joint and Several Spousal Liability*, Tax Prac. & Proc. 15 (Dec. 2004-Jan. 2005).

[64] Rev. Proc. 2003-19, 2003-1 C.B. 371.

[65] Maier v. Commissioner, 119 T.C. 267 (2002), 360 F.3d 361 (2d Cir 2004). *Cf.* King v. Commissioner, 115 T.C. 118 (2000); Corson v. Commissioner, 114 T.C. 354 (2000). As a non-party, the nonrequesting spouse also may not appeal to the circuit courts of appeal a Tax Court decision granting relief to the requesting spouse. Baranowicz v. Commissioner, 432 F.3d 972 (9th Cir. 2005).

If the requesting spouse files a petition in the Tax Court and if the other spouse (or former spouse) is not already a party to the case, the Commissioner must serve the nonrequesting party with notice of the case.[66] The notice advises the nonrequesting spouse of the opportunity to file a notice of intervention for the sole purpose of challenging the other spouse's entitlement to relief from joint liability pursuant to section 6015.[67] As an intervenor, the nonrequesting spouse has the rights of a quasi-party, including the right to be heard and the right to be a signatory to any proposed settlement.[68]

B. Can the IRS Attach a New Spouse's Income or Property to Pay the Purported Innocent Spouse's Prior Tax Debts?

If a person owes taxes from years before marriage, those tax liabilities are her separate debts. These taxes may have arisen from separate returns filed or from joint returns filed with a previous spouse. The concern of many people who are considering (re)marriage is whether the person they are marrying will be obligated to pay pre-existing taxes.[69]

As a general statement, the new spouse's assets cannot be seized to pay the premarital (separate) debts of the remarrying spouse. Subsequently acquired property purchased with the earnings of the new spouse and titled solely in that person's name is not subject to government seizure to pay the separate debts of the other spouse.[70] This assumes, however, the individuals have not commingled their property. If the property of the new couple is commingled, the IRS will seize the property to satisfy any debts owed to it.

Likewise, the separate earnings of the new spouse are not available to the government to pay the other spouse's debts. Practically speaking, to safeguard refunds attributable to the new spouse from being offset by the Service to pay the other spouse's liability, it is better to file separate returns after the marriage until the debts are paid in full, even though it may cause a higher tax bill. Alternatively, the couple could carefully monitor their withholding and estimated tax payments to insure that they do not overpay their taxes, thus avoiding a refund subject to seizure by the IRS.

---

[66] Tax Ct. R. 325. Chief Counsel Notice 2005-011.

[67] Any intervention shall be made in accordance with the provisions of Tax Ct. R. 325(b).

[68] King v. Commissioner, 115 T.C. 118 (2000); Corson v. Commissioner, 114 T.C. 354 (2000); CC-2003-015. This includes the right to introduce evidence in support of the electing spouse's claim for relief under section 6015. Van Arsdalen v. Commissioner, 123 T.C. 135 (2004). The intervening spouse has no greater rights than those of other parties and may be dismissed if he or she fails to prosecute the case. Tipton v. Commissioner, 127 T.C. 214 (2006).

[69] The IRS may intercept refunds to apply against the following debts: federal tax, child support, state income tax or federal non-tax debt (e.g., student loan). See Chapter 9.

[70] See Pate v. United States, 949 F.2d 1059 (10th Cir. 1991).

If a husband and wife file jointly, they should allocate income and deductions between them,[71] using a Form 8379 for this purpose. This helps avoid the "injured spouse" situation where one spouse's refund is intercepted to pay the other spouse's liability. If the form is filed, the IRS is only allowed to withhold the refund attributable to the liable spouse. To be safest, the form should be filed with the tax return. However, one can file the injured spouse form after the return was filed and the improper offset occurred.

C. Disclosure Issues

Section 6103(e)(8) requires the Service, on request, to disclose certain information to one spouse about the other spouse's payments on a joint income tax liability and about the Service's actions to secure those payments. The spouse is entitled to know the status of collection on the joint tax liability, but is not entitled to personal information related to the other spouse.[72]

D. Effect of Divorce Decree Allocation of Responsibility for Understatements

Even when a divorce decree indicates that one spouse has taken responsibility for taxes owed, the IRS, not being a party to the divorce decree, may continue to pursue either spouse until the liability is paid.[73] The IRS reasons that the paying spouse can then get contribution from the other spouse.[74]

---

[71] Rev. Rul. 80-7, 1980-1 C.B. 296. *See also* SCA 199924056 (IRS must pay a spouse his or her separate interest in a joint refund even if the Service erroneously issued the refund check to the other spouse).

[72] Pursuant to IRM 25.15.8.14, the revenue officer *may* disclose the following information, upon request:

- Whether the Service has attempted to collect the deficiency from the other spouse;

- The amount, if any, collected from the other spouse;

- The current collection status (e.g., delinquent status, installment agreement, suspended); and

- The reason for suspension, if applicable (e.g., unable to locate, hardship).

The revenue officer may *not* disclose the following information:

- The other spouse's location or telephone number;

- Any information about the other spouse's employment, income, or assets; or

- The income level at which a suspended account will be reactivated.

[73] IRM 25.15.7.5.2.1(1).

[74] Though the allocation of responsibility in the divorce decree is not controlling, the IRS considers it as a factor in whether to grant equitable relief under section 6015(f). *See* Rev. Proc. 2000-15, ¶ 4.03(1)(e), (2)(f), 2000-1 C.B. 447, *superseded by* Rev. Proc. 2003-61, 2003-2 C.B. 296. Even in cases not controlled by section 6015(f), agents consider an allocation to reflect on the equities of the situation.

E. Collection Activity and Statute of Limitations Are Suspended

If an election is filed under sections 6015(b) or (c),[75] a freeze is placed on the taxpayer's account and collection is suspended by statute from the date the election is filed until the matter is finally resolved, plus 60 days.[76] Any improper assessment may be enjoined.[77] Levies filed before the claim for relief was filed will normally be released as well.

Since the IRS may not pursue collection once a taxpayer requests relief under section 6015(b) or (c), the statute of limitations (SOL) on collection is suspended for the entire period the matter is being considered plus an additional 60 days.[78]

VIII. CONCLUSION

Finding oneself liable for the tax transgressions of one's ex-spouse can be a significant emotional and financial burden to a taxpayer. Fortunately, Congress has sought to alleviate the harsh consequences by enacting section 6015. While far from perfect, the provisions attempt to balance the duty of the taxpayer to review a tax return before signing and filing it with the realities of many situations where it would be unfair to hold the innocent spouse liable.

PROBLEM 1

Hilda Brown was married in 1977. She and her husband Fred had three children, one of whom died of a drug overdose in 1998. Ample evidence is available to the effect that Fred was domineering and abusive and that, because of this, Hilda generally would "go along" with whatever Fred wanted.

For most of the marriage Fred was a poor provider, and they constantly had trouble making ends meet. However, in 2002, Fred started his own financial services business, naming himself as President and Hilda as Secretary. Hilda, though, had nothing to do with the new business, and Fred rarely talked to her about it. Nevertheless, it appeared to Hilda that the business was doing very well as Fred was depositing large sums of money—$55,000 in 2004 and

---

[75] While not required by statute, collection personnel will suspend collection activity with respect to a request for discretionary relief under section 6015(f) where it appears the request is not made frivolously and collection of the tax is not in jeopardy. IRM 25.15.1.7. The statute of limitations (SOL) on collection is not suspended during equitable relief consideration.

[76] IRC § 6015(e)(1); Reg. § 1.6015-7(c)(2)(i); IRM 25.15.2.4.4. However, a Notice of Federal Tax Lien may be filed during this period. Beery v. Commissioner, 122 T.C. 184 (2004).

[77] IRC § 6015(e)(1)(B); Reg. § 1.6015-7(c).

[78] IRC § 6015(e)(2). Neither the SOL on assessment nor the SOL on filing refund claims is affected by a request for relief under section 6015.

$253,000 in 2005—from his financial services' business checking account into Hilda's separate bank account.

Fred directed most of the payments out of her account during this two-year period. They took expensive trips, bought furniture for their home, and otherwise lived an extravagant lifestyle. In addition, they bought an expensive lot in a residential development in Fred's name. Prior to 2004, Fred rarely gave Hilda more than $800 a month for her account and the most she ever had in the account prior to 2004 was about $2,400. Except for several checks in relatively small amounts, Hilda did not know the payees on the checks she wrote at Fred's request while he was clearing out the account.

Fred and Hilda signed joint returns for 2004 and 2005, showing, respectively, $6,029 and $11,871 of tax liability. Hilda did not have any income during either of those years. As to each year, Fred presented the completed returns to Hilda for her signature and directed her to give him a check from her account to cover the reported tax liability. She knew not to question anything for fear of being beaten.

While Fred often said the business was doing incredibly well, Hilda still wondered where Fred got so much money. On more than one occasion she even mentioned to her mother that she was concerned that the money wasn't from a legitimate source. However, the first real clue to wrongdoing was in March 2007, when she read in the newspaper that Fred had been ordered by a court to stop soliciting investments and that he was under investigation in connection with a two million dollar investment fraud! Fred was subsequently arrested, pled guilty to securities fraud, and was imprisoned in November 2007 for five years. He was ordered to make restitution by signing over title to his residential lot to the court.

When the police targeted Fred and the court ordered him to cease his operations, the IRS began an audit of his returns. The tax deficiencies, based on including the income earned in the securities fraud plus a potpourri of improper deductions, turned out to be $260,173 for 2004 and $644,187 for 2005 (in each case, plus penalties and interest). A notice of deficiency addressed to Fred and Hilda for these two years was received by Hilda recently, and she is now in your office asking for advice. It turns out that Hilda recently inherited just about enough money to satisfy the deficiencies including penalties and interest.

Hilda also recently learned that the IRS is considering assessing the "trust fund liability" penalty pursuant to section 6672 against her and Fred for unpaid withholding taxes for the employees of Fred's business.

You have never represented either Fred or Hilda (or, for that matter, any business in which Fred was involved). Also, you have determined that the notice of deficiency was issued in a timely manner so that the statute of limitations provides no defense.

What will you tell Hilda about her liability and the options, if any, available to her to avoid some or all of the liability? Assume they have not yet divorced. Alternatively, assume they are divorced.

PROBLEM 2

Kathryn and David Apollo timely filed a joint return for 2005. During 2005, David terminated his employment with a corporation for which he had worked for fifteen years and started up a consulting business. Upon leaving, David received a distribution from the corporation's retirement plan in the amount of $200,000. This distribution went into David's personal account. Although Kathryn knew that David had received a distribution from the retirement plan, David never told her the exact amount. David used $125,000 of this amount to pay off the mortgage on their home which was held in joint names.

On their joint return for 2005, David included the entire distribution in income and reported the 10% penalty. However, despite telling Kathryn he was going to pay the $75,000 balance due on the tax return from the retirement fund distribution, David used the remaining $75,000 of the retirement plan distribution in his business and to support his involvement with another woman. All subsequent balance due notices from the IRS were intercepted by David, so Kathryn did not know there was a tax problem.

David and Kathryn's marriage ended after David's relationship became known. The divorce was granted in November 2006. Kathryn was awarded title to the family home, and David got the business. The decree stated that David was solely responsible for all tax liabilities for all years prior to 2006.

In December 2006, the IRS sent David and Kathryn notices of the $85,000 balance due ($75,000 tax and $10,000 penalties and interest) for 2005 and offered them a collection due process hearing. This was the first time Kathryn learned of the outstanding tax. She comes to you for help.

1. Is Kathryn entitled to relief under section 6015?

2. Explain to Kathryn what procedures she must follow to get the IRS to consider granting her relief.

3. Assume that Kathryn sought protection from the tax liability under sections 6015(b), (c) & (f), but the Cincinnati Service Center determined that she did not qualify for relief under any of them. Explain to Kathryn what her

administrative and judicial appeal rights are.

4. To what extent could David intervene in the Appeals Office consideration or the Tax Court proceeding to show that granting Kathryn the requested relief would be inappropriate?

Chapter 4

EXAMINATION OF RETURNS

IRC:	§§ 6001; 7210; 7491; 7517; 7521; 7522; 7525; 7602; 7603; 7604; 7605; 7609; 7612
Regs.:	§§ 301.7121-1; 301.7602-1; 301.7605-1(a)-(d); 301.7606-1
Proc. Regs.:	§§ 601.105; 601.106; 601.107
IRS Forms:	866; 870; 870-AD; 886-A; 906
Cases and Rulings:	United States v. Fern, 696 F.2d 1269 (11th Cir. 1983)

I. INTRODUCTION

Ours has often been called a "self assessment" or "voluntary" system of taxation. Tax protesters (those who proclaim, based on spurious constitutional or statutory theories, that they have no obligation to file returns and/or pay taxes) seize on such language to assert that they are not legally required to pay. That notion, however, has been repeatedly and unanimously rejected by the courts.

> The word voluntary is not the equivalent of optional. To the extent that income taxes are said to be voluntary, they are only voluntary in that one files the returns and pays the taxes without the IRS first telling each individual the amount due and then forcing payment of that amount. The payment of income taxes is not optional.[1]

The first step in the process occurs when the taxpayer files a return and pays the tax reported due on that return. For most taxpayers—those whose returns are not audited—the process ends there. However, when a return is examined, a wide array of procedures is engaged. After discussing the tax gap, this chapter discusses those procedures, including: selection of returns for examination, types of examinations, audit strategies and decisions, IRS information gathering, taxpayer discovery of information from the IRS, Appeals Office consideration after audit, and conclusion of the audit or of Appeals consideration.[2]

---

[1] United States v. Middleton, 246 F.3d 825, 840 (6th Cir. 2001). The IRS website (www.irs.gov) contains detailed refutations of the most common tax protestor arguments.

[2] Examination and audit typically are used as synonyms in tax practice. That practice is followed here.

II. TAX GAP

The IRS conducts examinations both to correct inaccuracies that already have occurred and to deter future inaccuracies. The "tax gap" represents the difference between what taxpayers should have paid and what they actually did pay on a timely basis. The IRS estimates that the tax gap has grown over the years, and now stands at approximately $350 billion.[3] Some estimates are higher however.[4]

The IRS-estimated gap represents a noncompliance rate of about 16%—lower than that of most countries but hardly cause for rejoicing. It is estimated that 82% of the tax gap comes from underreporting on filed returns; 8% relates to nonfiling; and 10% involves the nonpayment of reported taxes. Over half is associated with individual income tax; over 10% relates to employment taxes; and the remainder involves corporate income tax, estate and gift taxes, and excise taxes.[5] The size of the tax gap has received considerable congressional and administrative attention.[6]

After years of declines, the IRS claims recently to have increased audit coverage and amounts recovered through enforcement.[7] However, the IRS statistics should not necessarily be taken at face value, and, in any event, current audit coverage remains low by historical standards. The IRS believes that better data will improve targeting of audits.[8] Current areas for enforcement emphasis include underreporting by high-income individuals, nonfilers, corporations, tax shelters, offshore accounts and other international transactions, and abusive trusts. However, the IRS budget is inadequate to cover all areas of need. Thus, as the IRS shifts resources to one area to curb tax underpayment there, tax underpayment tends to rise in the area(s) from which the resources had been taken.[9]

---

[3] *See* Information Release IR-2006-28 (Feb. 14, 2006), *reproduced at* 2006 Tax Notes Today 31-6 (Feb. 15, 2006). "[T]he average compliant taxpayer is paying thousands of dollars in extra tax each year to subsidize noncompliance by others." National Taxpayer Advocate 2006 Annual Report to Congress, Executive Summary I-1 (2007).

[4] *E.g.*, Allen Kenney, *Government Report Shows $1 Trillion Escaped Tax in 2003*, Tax Notes, Dec. 26, 2005, at 1623 (U.S. Dep't of Commerce study).

[5] IRS information cited by Charles P. Rettig, *Nonfilers Beware: Who's That Knocking at Your Door?*, J. Tax Prac. & Proc., Oct.-Nov. 2006, at 15. For slightly different figures, see Mark A. Luscombe, *Tax Protestors: Is the IRS Turning the Corner?*, Taxes, May 2007, at 3.

[6] *See, e.g.*, Staff of Joint Comm. on Taxation, Additional Options to Improve Tax Compliance (Aug. 3, 2006); Staff of Joint Comm. on Taxation, Options to Improve Tax Compliance and Reform Tax Expenditures (JCS-02-05) (Jan. 27, 2005).

[7] *E.g.*, Mark W. Everson, *Enforcement Revenue Reaches Record in 2004*, http://www.irs.gov/newsroom/article/0,,id~= 131282,00.html (Sept. 3, 2006); Treasury Inspector General for Tax Administration, *Trends in Compliance Activities Through Fiscal Year 2005* (2006-30-055), 2006 Tax Notes Today 69-7 (Apr. 11, 2006).

[8] Kathleen David, *New Data Will Permit Better Targeting of Examinations, Brown Tells Lawyers*, Daily Tax Rep., May 25, 2005, at G-10.

[9] See Steve Johnson, *The 1998 Act and the Resources Link Between Tax Compliance and Tax Simplification*, 51 U. Kan. L. Rev. 1013 (2003).

A sufficient level of audit coverage is important to the health of the tax system, both to detect honest error and to deter overly aggressive reporting. The income tax audit rate, as officially measured, has been dropping for decades, and compliance has dropped with it. In the mid-1960s, the announced audit rate was in the 4.5 to 5% range and the announced compliance rate was over 90%. By the mid-1990s, the audit rate had dipped under 1% and the compliance rate had fallen to about 80%. In the 2000s, the audit rate has hovered around ¾ of 1%.

The official audit rate understates coverage because it does not take into account millions of IRS computer-based checks of some items on returns through the IRS's information matching programs: the Automated Underreporter Program ("AUR") and the Information Reporting Program ("IRP"). On the other hand, it overstates coverage because it fails to distinguish qualitatively among the types of audits. By far the largest group of officially counted "audits" consists of examinations conducted by mail by Service Center personnel. Those audits are decidedly inferior both in comprehensiveness and in level of rigor compared to examinations performed personally by revenue agents. Despite these complications, there is consensus that the current audit rate needs to be raised.

III. SELECTION OF RETURNS FOR EXAMINATION

Although the current audit rate is low by historical standards, clients should not be led to believe that they will surely escape being audited. A number of factors raise the likelihood of one's return being examined. Each year, the IRS determines approximately how many returns will be examined, and the total is allocated among the IRS divisions. The IRS does not announce the criteria it uses to select returns for examination, and those criteria change over time. The following are some of the numerous events and conditions that can prompt an audit.

(1) *Discriminate Function ("DIF")*. This is a major source of examinations. The DIF program is a multi-factor computer process. It scores returns by assessing patterns of deviation from expected ranges. Returns are divided into classes reflecting income and other characteristics. The items on each return are then analyzed through formulae designed to detect variations from amounts and relationships normal to the return's class. The scores from these formulae are added to yield a DIF score.[10] The higher the score, the greater the return error potential, thus the greater the chance that the return will be examined. Returns with high DIF scores are examined by IRS personnel who decide whether the return is to be audited and, if so, which type of audit will be used.

---

[10] For many years, the DIF score was based only on deduction and credit items. The IRS has begun developing income components for DIF purposes.

As one would expect, the DIF formulae are secret. By virtue of section 6103(b)(2), neither taxpayers nor other interested persons can force their disclosure under the Freedom of Information Act or otherwise. From time to time, the IRS does publish data as to the typical ranges of deductions for interest, medical and dental expenses, charitable contributions, etc. However, a taxpayer should not assume that his return is audit-proof even if all his deductions are within such ranges.

For many years, a pillar of the DIF scoring process was the Taxpayer Compliance Measurement Program ("TCMP"). A small percentage of returns were randomly selected for the program each year. The returns selected were subject to intensive scrutiny of every line item—a great burden for the taxpayers who had to explain and document every event and transaction that fed into every return line. Because of complaints about those burdens and consequent pressure from Congress, TCMP audits were discontinued after 1988. The result, though, was year-by-year erosion of the reliability of the IRS's compliance measurement tools.

To supply new data for DIF scoring, the IRS developed the National Research Program ("NRP") in the early 2000s. NRP was less onerous than TCMP. Over 40,000 individual income tax returns were randomly selected. They were worked by specially trained examiners using classification measures and structured procedures with limited taxpayer contact in most cases.[11] NRP audits have ended for now, and the data collected is beginning to produce some results. It would be no surprise to see NRP or a similar vehicle used again in the future.

(2) *Information matching.* As described in Chapter 2, third-party payors sometimes are required to file information statements with the IRS, with copies to the taxpayer. For example, wage and salary payors must file W-2 forms indicating how much they paid each employee and how much income tax was withheld; banks, savings and loan associations, and others must file 1099-INT forms indicating interest paid to depositors, as well as any tax withheld under the back-up withholding rules; corporations must file 1099-DIV forms indicating dividends paid to shareholders.[12]

The IRS's computers match or check such reported information with the recipient's tax returns. If there is a discrepancy between the information report and the recipient's return, the IRS (typically the Service Center to which the recipient's return was sent) will send the taxpayer a letter requesting explanation of the discrepancy. A reasonable explanation often will end the matter.

---

[11] For details, see Robert E. Brown & Mark J. Mazur, *The National Research Program: Measuring Taxpayer Compliance Comprehensively,* 51 U. Kan. L. Rev. 1255 (2003); General Accounting Office, New Compliance Research Effort Is on Track, But Important Work Remains (June 2002) (GAO-02-769).

[12] Related mechanisms exist. For instance, a taxpayer who claims an income tax deduction for alimony paid to a former spouse must supply the recipient's tax identification number (Social Security number) on his Form 1040.

However, if the size, number, or pattern of return errors creates suspicion as to the accuracy of the return generally, the return may be pulled for more searching examination.

Comprehensive information reporting and matching greatly improve the accuracy of tax reporting. According to the IRS, amounts subject to withholding—such as wages and salaries—have a net misreporting rate of about 1.2%. Amounts subject to third-party reporting but not withholding—such as interest and dividends—have a net misreporting rate of 4.5%. Amounts subject to partial third-party reporting—such as capital gains—have a net misreporting rate of 8.6%. Misreporting skyrockets—up to a 53.9% rate—for items subject to neither information reporting nor withholding.[13]

Accordingly, there are frequent proposals to expand information reporting. They include proposals to increase reporting as to government payments for goods and services, as to debt and credit card reimbursements paid to certain merchants, and the bases customers of brokerage firms and mutual fund companies have in their investments.[14]

(3) *Economic level of the taxpayer.* In general, the audit rate rises as the taxpayer's economic level rises. The larger the estate, the more likely is an audit of its estate tax return. The larger the net worth of a corporation or the higher the income of an individual, the more likely is an audit of its, his, or her income tax return.

(4) *Return items.* From experience, the IRS knows that there are certain return items as to which taxpayer error is common. Returns claiming or involving such items may be subject to a higher risk of audit. For example, in some years, income tax returns claiming office-in-the-home deductions or deductions for home computers faced a heightened audit risk. Another example is the Earned Income Tax Credit, which has entailed a great deal of tax return error (some honest mistake, some fraud). This has led to the counter-intuitive result that returns of low-income taxpayers sometimes have been audited more frequently than returns of affluent taxpayers.

Returns that reflect attempts at manipulation or tax protester devices face a higher audit risk. Examples include (i) returns on which the jurat (the "under penalties of perjury" language above the signature line) has been struck out, (ii) returns which have been tailored via home computer to resemble a Form 1040 or other return but which depart from the IRS form in some critical respect, and (iii) returns on which line entries are not numbers but a symbol or abbreviation meaning "refuse to answer: Fifth Amendment privilege against self-incrimination" or something comparably worthless.[15]

---

[13] *See* Rettig, *supra*, at 15-16.

[14] *See* Everson, *supra*; Joseph M. Dodge & Jay A. Soled, *Reporting Tax Basis: Dawn of a New Era*, Tax Notes, Feb. 13, 2006, at 784.

[15] It is settled that, in general, the privilege against self-incrimination does not exonerate failure to file complete and accurate tax returns. *See, e.g.*, United States v. Sullivan, 274 U.S. 259, 264 (1927).

(5) *Infection*. Sometimes, a return would not have been examined based on that return taken alone, but is swept into audit because of its relation to other returns that are or were under examination. For example, if audit of a taxpayer's returns for prior years revealed significant deficiencies, the odds increase of his later returns being picked up for examination. Also, audit of an estate tax return raises the likelihood of examination of that estate's income tax returns. Similarly, if a return filed by a closely held corporation is under audit, the returns of the corporation's shareholder(s) may also be drawn into the audit.

(6) *Taxpayer initiation*. Certain actions by a taxpayer may prompt the IRS to examine a return or to accelerate an examination. Examples include the taxpayer's filing an amended return, a refund claim, or a bankruptcy petition.

(7) *Informant*. Third parties sometimes tell the IRS about alleged tax wrongdoing by another taxpayer. Congress has encouraged this by authorizing the payment of tax bounties or rewards under Code section 7623 to informants whose information results in successful adjustments. The most likely informants are disgruntled employees or ex-employees and former spouses or significant others.

(8) *Notoriety*. High visibility of a taxpayer whose affairs suggest a substantial potential for tax cheating may prompt investigation or examination. For instance, if the local newspaper carries a story on the indictment of your client for embezzling from his church's building fund, don't be surprised if the IRS pulls his returns to check whether he reported the embezzlement income.[16] Or, if your firm is defending a prominent drug trafficker at criminal trial, don't be amazed if there is an IRS agent in the gallery, taking notes on the testimony in order to advance a civil tax audit.

IV. TYPES OF EXAMINATIONS

There are three principal types of examinations: correspondence, office, and field. They are described below, after which several specialized types of examinations are discussed. The various audit types differ in their comprehensiveness, rigor, and methods.

A. Principal Audit Types

1. Correspondence Examinations

Correspondence examinations are the most common type of audit. They are conducted by tax examiners at the service centers or in local area offices. The IRS sends the taxpayer a letter inquiring into an apparent delinquency or return anomaly. The taxpayer is asked to respond by mail, explaining the situ-

---

[16] Illegally obtained income is taxable. James v. United States, 366 U.S. 213 (1961).

ation and providing documentation. Typically, the initial interchange is limited to one or a few items that piqued the IRS's interest, but the examination may broaden if other questionable items are identified.

Correspondence exams generally are limited to simple income tax issues, that are covered by established examination programs. If the exam turns up issues beyond those covered in the programs, the case will be transferred to a field office for more intensive investigation. Such transfer also will occur if the taxpayer requests a personal interview or if the taxpayer is deemed unable to communicate effectively in writing.

2. Office Audits

Office audits are conducted at IRS field offices by personnel known as tax auditors. Office exams often involve more complex issues than those present in correspondence exams. They usually entail some face-to-face contact with the taxpayer or the taxpayer's representative. The exam may involve either individual or business taxpayers.

The scope of the office audit usually is limited to one or a few issues, and the goal is to close the exam after the first interview. Again, though, the possibility exists that the exam may be expanded if the initial interview discloses significant information pointing towards other possible adjustments.

3. Field Examinations

Complex individual and business returns are examined by revenue agents, whose training and experience exceed those of office auditors. Although such exams may take place at IRS offices, they usually are conducted at the taxpayer's place of business or, if different, where the taxpayer's books, records, or other source documents are located. Unlike office audits, field exams often involve multiple meetings over weeks or months, sometimes over a year for complex corporate returns.

B. Other Audit Types

There are variations on the audit types described above. Some have been with us for decades; others are temporary. Here are some of the specialized examinations:

Employment tax audits. Employment taxes, such as FICA (Federal Insurance Contribution Act) and FUTA (Federal Unemployment Tax Act) taxes are imposed by the federal government. The central question in employment tax audits often is whether the worker is properly considered an employee or an independent contractor. This question is analyzed under a multi-factoral test derived from non-tax common law,[17] leading to frequent confusion and controversy.

An important feature of employment tax audits is plural potential targets. Employers and employees share liability for employment taxes. The employer is supposed to collect and pay over to the IRS both the employer's and employee's shares. If the employer is a company and it fails to pay, one or more of its so called "responsible persons" may become secondarily liable for the taxes. *See* Chapter 14.

Estate tax audits. Audits of estate tax returns are conducted by estate tax examiners, who typically are attorneys and often have considerable experience. The largest class of issues in such audits involves valuation of assets. The IRS employs a staff of appraisers, called Valuation Engineers, in both the National Office and the field offices. They sometimes are assisted by specialized functions, such as the IRS's Art Advisory Panel which consists of well regarded private sector art experts. In large cases, the IRS may hire non-IRS personnel as valuation consultants or experts. A distinctive feature of estate tax examinations is that section 6501(c)(4)(A) precludes extension of the statute of limitations on assessment of estate taxes by consent of the parties. This imposes an urgency or inflexibility not present in other audits.

Coordinated Examination Program ("CEP") and Limited Issue Focused Examinations ("LIFE"). A substantial percetage of returns filed by large corporations are examined. Very large corporations experience essentially perpetual audit. A team of IRS revenue agents from LMSB (the IRS's Large and Mid-Size Business Division) is assigned to each such corporation. They are given an office at the corporation, and they examine each return. The agents are reassigned periodically.

Large corporate exams are through the CEP. The exams are performed by revenue agents in the highest pay grades. They have the benefit of industry-specific position papers and audit programs developed through and coordinated by the Industry Specialization Program ("ISP") and the Market Segment Specialization Program ("MSSP"). Thus far, ISP covers about two dozen nationwide industries. CEP features early involvement by IRS Chief Counsel attorneys to provide legal analysis. The idea is to weed out bad issues early in the process and to see that potentially good issues receive the development they need during audit. CEP also can entail accelerated Appeals Office consideration.

LIFE was created in the early 2000s as a targeted audit program for very large business. The aims are to improve communications with the taxpayers and to streamline exams when feasible and appropriate, thus improving allocation of the IRS's resources. Using materiality benchmarks, the audit focuses on the most significant issues, eliminating small issues. The revenue agent(s) and the

---

[17] *See, e.g.*, 303 West 42nd St. Enterprises, Inc. v. IRS, 181 F.3d 272 (2d Cir. 1999); Rev. Rul. 87-41, 1987-1 C.B. 296.

taxpayer enter into agreements as to the process to be followed and time frames within which each will respond to the other's requests.

Early resolution mechanisms. A taxpayer within the jurisdiction of LMSB can ask the IRS to examine specific issues before the taxpayer's return for the year is filed or due to be filed. The goal is to resolve the issues promptly and in a cooperative fashion. If such resolution is reached, the taxpayer and the IRS execute a Prefiling Agreement ("PFA"), which operates as a closing agreement. Because of the constricted time frame, the prefiling process is confined to factual issues governed by well settled law. It does not address issues of law, which are better handled via private letter rulings.

It remains to be seen how significant PFAs will become. LMSB has jurisdiction over approximately 150,000 corporations and partnerships with assets over $10 million. In the early years of the program, fewer than fifty PFA requests a year were made. The number of requests has grown slowly in recent years. The price tag for the PFA process is a $50,000 user fee. The IRS has continued the PFA program through the end of 2008.[18]

Advance Pricing Agreements ("APAs") also entail pre-return discussion and, hopefully, agreement, but they are narrower in scope. Section 482 allows the IRS to recast pricing and other terms of transactions between related taxpayers if the terms set by the taxpayers do not clearly reflect the parties' incomes. Usually, section 482 issues account for more dollars at issue in litigation than any other type of tax issue. Unfortunately, section 482 cases are difficult and expensive for both sides because they are fact-intensive.

APAs were developed to resolve section 482 matters early and non-confrontationally. The taxpayer informs the IRS of the related-party transaction before filing the return for the year, and suggests and justifies a given tax treatment of the transaction. The IRS considers the suggested treatment. The parties confer and, hopefully, find a mutually satisfactory treatment. The taxpayer then reports consistently with the agreement; the IRS honors it; and both parties have avoided controversy, cost, and uncertainty.[19]

LMSB has developed the Compliance Assurance Program ("CAP") under which revenue agents and specialists work with taxpayers to identify and resolve substantial, recurring issues. The goals are to decrease audit time and to increase coverage of taxpayers. Under CAP, a corporate taxpayer can seek IRS agreement—on a single issue or the entire return—before the taxpayer files the return.[20]

---

[18] Rev. Proc. 2007-17, 2007-4 I.R.B. 1.

[19] *See* Rev. Proc. 2004-40, 2004-29 I.R.B. 50. The IRS reports annually on the progress of and problems with the APA program. *E.g.*, Ann. 2006-22, 2006-1 C.B. 779.

[20] Harvey Coustan, *The IRS's Compliance Assurance Program*, J. Tax Prac. & Proc., Feb.-Mar. 2006, at 5; Deborah M. Nolan, *The Compliance Assurance Process: A New Approach to Corporate Tax Administration*, J. Tax Prac. & Proc., Apr.-May 2005, at 13.

In addition, the IRS has developed the Industry Issue Resolution Program ("IIRP") to review complex tax issues common to significant numbers of business taxpayers. In choosing issues to include in the IIRP, the IRS seeks input from taxpayers and other interested parties. Taxpayers also may propose issues for inclusion.[21]

In some situations, the taxpayer can compel the IRS to accelerate examination. For example, taxpayers who are debtors in bankruptcy cases can request prompt determination of their tax liabilities.[22] Also, executors can request prompt determination of decedents' gift tax and income tax liabilities. The executor is excused from personal liability for any such taxes beyond amounts the IRS determines within nine months of the request.[23] As a practical matter, the constricted time frame often compels the IRS to streamline the audit.

C. Special Procedures in Aid of Examination

Several special procedures exist to support the audit function in unusual situations. For example, subject to a number of requirements, the IRS is authorized to conduct undercover operations.[24] In addition, section 7623 has long authorized the IRS to pay amounts deemed necessary for enforcing the revenue laws. The Tax Relief and Health Care Act of 2006 added whistleblower provisions to be administered by a new Whistleblower Office in the IRS. A whistleblower may receive an award of between 15% to 30% of amounts collected as a result of information he or she provides.[25]

V. AUDIT STRATEGIES AND CHOICES

A. Generally

"Hope for the best; prepare for the worst." The prudent taxpayer, though hoping there will be no audit, begins preparing for it even before filing the return for the tax period. He does so by taking reasonable return positions and by gathering and retaining documentation supporting them. The following briefly discusses the general features of the audit process and tactical choices that often arise during it.[26]

---

[21] Rev. Proc. 2003-36, 2003-1 C.B. 859; IR-2004-100 (July 29, 2004).

[22] 11 U.S.C. § 505(a).

[23] IRC § 6905(a). *See also* § 6501(d) (permitting requests for prompt assessment of certain taxes by fiduciaries and corporations).

[24] IRC § 7608(c).

[25] IRC § 7623(b). *See* Paul D. Scott, *Tax Whistle-Blowers To Receive Increased Rewards*, Tax Notes, Jan. 29, 2007, at 441.

[26] There are books and articles addressing these matters in greater detail. Two excellent discussions are Jerome Borison (ed.), Effectively Representing Your Client Before the "New" IRS, chs. 2-6 (4th ed. 2004); Barbara T. Kaplan, *Leveling the Playing Field in Federal Income Tax Controversies*, 56 N.Y.U. Inst. Fed. Tax'n ch. 32 (1998).

The audit materializes when the IRS sends the taxpayer an initial contact letter. The letter identifies the IRS office, the tax return(s) or tax period(s) in question, and the IRS contact person and telephone number. The letter typically states the issue(s) the IRS wants the taxpayer to explain or substantiate and sets a date and time for an appointment, or date for response in writing. From these items, it will be apparent which type of audit the IRS intends to conduct.

The taxpayer and the taxpayer's representative should begin preparing for the response and/or the appointment as soon as possible. They should do so by reviewing records, assessing the merits of the taxpayer's return positions identified as issues by the contact letter, ascertaining whether exposure exists as to other return positions for this year and other years should the examination broaden, and planning the audit defense strategy.

Sometimes, clients want to handle the audit alone or with their accountant or bookkeeper only. They reason that the IRS will see an attorney's involvement as smoke, which will cause the agent to look more closely for fire. Or, they reason that they'll pay an attorney if the matter goes to trial but they may be able to save money by leaving the attorney out of the early phases of the matter. In uncomplicated situations, this may be right. In others, not hiring an attorney to save money is "penny wise but pound foolish." From the standpoint of greatest effect for least cost, each phase of the process offers greater opportunity than the one that follows it. In general, audit is more important than administrative appeal, administrative appeal is more important than trial, and trial is more important than judicial appeal. In many cases, particularly those with complicated facts or in which serious problems are present, it is desirable that the attorney represent the taxpayer from the start of the audit.

In most cases, the best approach is to proceed in an audit in a cooperative fashion, complying in timely manner with reasonable requests by the examining agent. Agents dislike delays and unfulfilled promises. If a problem develops, it usually is best to inform the agent early rather than late. However, the touchstone is always the best interests of the taxpayer, consistent with the attorney's own ethical obligations. Balancing the considerations can require considerable skill.

The IRS tries to complete examination of an income tax return within 26-27 months of the time the return was filed. Thus, if the taxpayer has not been contacted about the return within this period, it is probable that the return will not be examined.

There is a statutory goad to the prompt commencement of an audit. With stated exceptions, section 6404(g) provides for the suspension of interest and penalties in the case of an individual who timely files an income tax return. The suspension arises if the IRS fails to notify the taxpayer of his liability and the basis therefor within eighteen months after the later of when the return was filed or was due to be filed. The suspension ceases twenty-one days after the IRS gives the notice.[27]

In responding to questions asked by the IRS agent, the usual strategy is to provide the requested information but not to volunteer additional information. From that perspective, experienced counsel almost always meet with the agent without the taxpayer being present. Unwise disclosures (as well as the other extreme, stonewalling) might cause the IRS to broaden the examination. The attorney should always be alert to any changes in the pace or tenor of the contacts with the agent. An especially worrisome sign is if the agent abruptly and without explanation ceases all contacts. That might mean that the case has been referred for criminal investigation. Clients should be instructed always to ask for the title of any IRS person who contacts them. Contact from a Special Agent (the title of agents working for the IRS's Criminal Investigation function) signifies that the matter has changed from civil to criminal.

Sometimes, it is helpful to retain an economic, valuation, or other expert to assist the taxpayer and the attorney during the examination. This is almost never so in correspondence or office audits, but may be the case in section 482, estate tax, or other complex examinations. The taxpayer will seek to ensure that the work of such experts is not discoverable by the IRS (except as required by court rules of discovery). To preserve the possible applicability of the attorney-client privilege, the expert should be retained by the attorney, not by the client, and communications with the expert should not be outside the circle of confidentiality.[28]

In most instances, examining agents behave courteously and professionally. Taxpayer ("customer") complaints about agents are taken seriously by the IRS. Moreover, IRS agents often are under demanding case management schedules. It is in the agents' self-interest to maintain good relations with taxpayers in order to move cases expeditiously. Nonetheless, instances arise in which the taxpayer thinks the agent is behaving unreasonably or, perhaps more frequently, has an erroneous view of the applicable law. What can be done in such circumstances?

The taxpayer has a right to elevate the matter to the agent's group manager. Some fear that "going over the agent's head" will antagonize the agent, leading to even more adjustments being set up. That fear is misplaced. Supervisory conferences are a routine, accepted part of the system, and agents realize they have more to lose than to gain by engaging in reprisals.[29] More to the point is the possibility of futility. Managers know they will create morale problems if they overrule their agents too often. Nonetheless, managerial meetings sometimes

---

[27] For explanation of the provision, see Chapter 12 and IRS Notice N(35) 000-172 (Mar. 22, 2000).

[28] *See, e.g.*, United States v. Kovel, 296 F.2d 918 (2d Cir. 1961).

[29] One of the "ten deadly sins," according to the 1998 Reform Act, is violating IRS rules and regulations for the purpose of retaliating against or harassing a taxpayer or taxpayer's representative. *See* Act § 1203(b)(6).

are helpful. They should be considered, especially when it is fairly clear that the agent's position is incorrect.

Also, the taxpayer typically has the opportunity for administrative appeal through the IRS Appeals Office, as described in Section VII below. In addition, other steps are available during the examination itself. If the point of contention is the content or application of the law, the taxpayer may consider asking the agent to obtain a TAM or TEAM from the National Office, as described in Chapter 1.

The taxpayer may also consider resort to the local Taxpayer Advocate or the National Taxpayer Advocate. As noted in Chapter 1, the Taxpayer Advocate function will not intervene in a dispute about the law, but it can be useful if a procedural problem arises.

B. Extending the Statute of Limitations

A frequent and difficult decision involves the statute of limitations ("SOL") on assessment. The SOL is discussed in detail in Chapter 5, but some discussion of it is appropriate here because of the important choices it entails.

Under section 6501(a), the normal SOL period—the period within which the IRS must assess tax—is three years from the date the return in question was filed. This period is extended or suspended under a number of conditions, including, under section 6501(c)(4), the execution by the taxpayer and the IRS of an agreement extending the SOL.

If an examination or Appeals Office consideration is underway but completion is not imminent and only 120 days remain in the SOL period, agents are supposed to request that the taxpayer voluntarily agree to extend the SOL. The taxpayer must then decide whether to execute an extension.[30]

It seems counterintuitive to voluntarily enter into an agreement giving the IRS more time to examine the return. However, tax practitioners frequently recommend agreeing to the extension. This is because of burden of proof matters and the cost of resolving matters in court versus doing so administratively.

If the taxpayer does not consent to the extension, the agent is supposed to issue a notice of deficiency based on the information developed to that point. The result may well be an inflated amount of deficiency. Once adjustments are included in a notice of deficiency, the taxpayer usually must overcome the presumption of correctness that attaches to the IRS's determination.[31] This may be difficult, and it can be expensive if trial occurs. It is sometimes better to sign an

---

[30] The IRS is required to give the taxpayer written notice of the right to refuse to execute the consent and the right to limit a consent to specified issues or a specified period of time. IRC § 6501(c)(4)(B).

[31] *See* Chapter 8.

extension and give the agent more time to examine the return, anticipating that the agent will narrow the issues rather than expand them. This is particularly true when the taxpayer is confident the return under examination is, by and large, correct.

However, if there may be significant issues the agent has yet to explore in a meaningful way, giving the agent more time to find them would be a mistake. In this situation, it is best to let the notice be issued based on what the agent has discovered so far. Similarly, one should not execute an extension of the SOL if the IRS is developing a fraud case or if a criminal investigation is ongoing.

If the taxpayer agrees to extend the SOL, the next choice is whether to use Form 872 or Form 872-A. Which to use depends on the facts of the particular situation.

Form 872 is referred to as a "closed-ended" or "fixed period" extension. It extends the SOL to a future date certain. If additional extensions are necessary, another form must be executed by the taxpayer and the IRS. If the IRS assesses even one day after the date specified on the Form 872, the assessment is void.

Form 872-A, on the other hand, is an "open-ended" extension. It extends the SOL until ninety days after either the IRS or the taxpayer takes certain actions. If no such action is taken, the SOL extends indefinitely. Either the taxpayer or the IRS can unilaterally terminate the extension at any time. The Form 872-A is terminated when any of the following actions occur: (1) the IRS office considering the case receives from the taxpayer a properly completed Form 872-T; (2) the IRS mails a notice of deficiency to the taxpayer; or (3) the IRS mails a Form 872-T to the taxpayer. Upon the occurrence of a terminating event, the other party has a ninety-day window in which to act. For example, if the IRS office considering the case receives a Form 872-T on July 17, the IRS has until October 15 to mail a notice of deficiency to the taxpayer. However, if the IRS mails a notice of deficiency on July 17, the taxpayer has until October 15 to petition the Tax Court. Forms 872-A and 872-T both give instructions for terminating the Form 872-A and mailing the Form 872-T. Strict adherence to these rules is required for the termination to be effective.

Some practitioners like the certainty of the Form 872, thinking it gives the agent a gentle nudge to complete the audit more quickly. In addition, many wish to avoid the traps inherent in inadvertently failing to properly terminate a Form 872-A. Other practitioners prefer the Form 872-A because it allows the agent the maximum time to complete the exam and narrow the issues. The Form 872-A also avoids having to go back to the client to explain the need to execute another extension if the agent does not complete the exam by the date listed on the original Form 872.

If the taxpayer is willing to extend the SOL only for the issues already under consideration by the IRS, or is willing to agree to the resolution of some but not all of the issues raised, the taxpayer and the IRS can execute a "restricted consent."[32] However, the IRS may be reluctant to agree to a restricted consent since doing so could preclude the Service from making valid adjustments the agent might later discover.

VI. IRS INFORMATION GATHERING

Audits are about facts. The taxpayer presumably knows the facts that underlie his tax return positions. The IRS needs to learn enough of the facts to confirm or to correct those return positions. Courts have discovery procedures, of course, but developing the needed facts during audit is clearly preferable.

The IRS can develop facts through three main sources: the taxpayer himself, third parties knowledgeable about the particular transactions, and relevant sources of general information. These sources are discussed below. Also discussed below are the special tools for gathering information abroad and the defenses and protections available to taxpayers and others against IRS information gathering.

A. Information From the Taxpayer

Whether the examination is by letter or in person, the audit will begin with the IRS identifying the issues to be explored and requesting the taxpayer to produce the documents or other information relevant to those issues. If the taxpayer refuses outright or procrastinates, the IRS agent often will elevate the formality of the situation by giving the taxpayer a Form 4564 Information Document Request ("IDR"). IDRs should not be used to force a taxpayer to create documents not already in existence.

If the production still is not forthcoming, the agent may simply process the case based on the information at hand. The taxpayer typically bears the burden of proof in civil tax litigation, particularly when the taxpayer fails to honor IRS requests for information.[33] If the taxpayer fails to provide the requested information in support of claimed deductions, the agent may reduce or wholly disallow those deductions. This option will appeal to agents under pressure to move on to other cases.

---

[32] The restricted consent must contain the statement: "The amount of any deficiency assessment is to be limited to that resulting from any adjustment to (description of the area(s) of consideration) including any consequential changes to other items based on such adjustment."

[33] Under § 7491(a)(2), the burden shifts to the IRS only if *inter alia* the taxpayer has complied with substantiation requirements, maintained all required records, and cooperated with reasonable IRS requests "for witnesses, information, documents, meetings, and interviews." For discussion of the burden of proof in tax, see Steve R. Johnson, *The Dangers of Symbolic Legislation: Perceptions and Realities of the New Burden-of-Proof Rules*, 84 Iowa L. Rev. 413 (1999).

However, when the stakes are high or when the adjustment involves possible underreporting of income rather than possible exaggeration of deductions,[34] the IRS may issue a summons to the taxpayer for the information sought. Sections 6201(a) and 7601(a) provide general authority to the IRS to make inquiries to ascertain tax liability. More specifically, under section 7602(a), the IRS is authorized to issue summonses to compel the taxpayer to produce "books, papers, records, or other data," to give testimony under oath, or both. The summons also can be used to compel the target to appear and give a handwriting sample.[35] The summons is the principal coercive mechanism available to the IRS, and the prospect of a summons lies behind all informal information requests by the IRS. However, summonses are not issued in correspondence or office audits.

The summons must be served either by hand-delivering an attested copy to the taxpayer or by leaving an attested copy at the taxpayer's residence. When documents or data are sought, they must be described in the summons "with reasonable certainty."[36] The IRS's general summons form is Form 2039. It also uses Forms 6637, 6638, and 6639, which are summonses used to gather information in aid of collection.

The attorney should impress upon his client the importance of taking seriously any contact with the IRS, particularly a summons. Potentially damaging documents need to be produced if the IRS request, reasonably construed, calls for them. If the taxpayer lies to an IRS agent, that can be an independent crime under Code section 7207 or 18 U.S.C. section 1001. If the taxpayer destroys documents, that can be a crime under 18 U.S.C. sections 1503 and 1505. If the taxpayer's representative does the lying or destroying, the representative is also punishable under the above statutes.[37] If the taxpayer's representative helps the taxpayer in lying or destroying, the representative is punishable criminally under 18 U.S.C. sections 2 (aiding and abetting) or 371 (conspiracy). In addition to criminal considerations, taxpayers' representatives are under an ethical obligation not to mislead IRS personnel.[38] An attorney breaching that duty can be censured, or can be suspended or disbarred from practicing before the IRS. That attorney may face discipline under state law as well.

The IRS summons is broad, but it is not self-enforcing. The IRS has four options in the event of non-compliance with the summons. It may: (i) seek an order of contempt from the district court under section 7604(b), (ii) institute a

---

[34] Although the ultimate burden of persuasion is on the taxpayer in unreported income cases, some courts have imposed a burden on the IRS to make an initial showing. *See, e.g.*, Bradford v. Commissioner, 796 F.2d 303, 305 (9th Cir. 1986).

[35] United States v. Euge, 404 U.S. 707 (1980).

[36] IRC § 7603(a).

[37] *See, e.g.*, United States v. Fern, 696 F.2d 1269 (11th Cir. 1983) (affirming conviction under 18 U.S.C. § 1001 of accountant for making false statement to IRS tax auditor).

[38] *See, e.g.*, 31 C.F.R. § 10.22 (diligence as to accuracy); *see also id.* at §§ 10.20 (information to be furnished to IRS), 10.50-10.52 (sanctions for violations).

criminal prosecution under section 7210, (iii) request the district court to enforce the summons under section 7604,[39] or (iv) forgo enforcement.[40]

In fact, the IRS's most common response is to forgo enforcement—the resource expenditure often would be too great compared to the utility of the information sought. In addition, unlike a designated summons,[41] issuance of a regular summons to the taxpayer does not toll the statute of limitations on assessment. Thus, even "successful" summons enforcement litigation often would result in the IRS receiving the desired information only after expiration of the limitations period. In addition, the very fact that the IRS issued a summons with which the taxpayer did not comply, will help the IRS persuade the Tax Court that it needs and deserves discovery should the case later be litigated.

When the government does proceed, it far more frequently seeks summons enforcement than either contempt or criminal sanctions. Contempt and criminal sanctions will be applied only if the neglect is contumacious; they will not be applied if the taxpayer interposes a good faith challenge to the validity of the summons.[42]

Since summons enforcement actions are in District Court, the matter will be handled by the Department of Justice. The IRS, through IRS Counsel, will ask Justice to bring suit, in the district where the taxpayer resides, to enforce the summons. Suit is commenced by filing a petition accompanied by an affidavit of the revenue agent setting forth the facts.

The key case as to summons enforcement is the Supreme Court's *Powell* decision.[43] Under *Powell*, the government's affirmative case entails four elements: (i) the examination is being conducted for a legitimate purpose; (ii) the information sought may be relevant to that purpose; (iii) the IRS does not already possess the information; and (iv) the administrative steps required by the Code have been followed.[44]

If the revenue agent's affidavit establishes these elements to the satisfaction of the judge, the court will issue an order requiring the taxpayer to appear and show cause why the taxpayer should not be compelled to comply. The burden of going forward now shifts to the taxpayer to negate at least one of the four elements or to establish an affirmative defense. Defenses may include procedural matters (such as objections to the time and place for production called for in the

---

[39] United States v. Riewe, 676 F.2d 418, 420-21 (10th Cir. 1982).

[40] Some courts take the view that a summoned party may not be criminally prosecuted under section 7210 or subject to contempt sanctions under section 7604(b) for failure to comply with an IRS summons until a federal court has issued an order enforcing the summons and the summoned party has failed to comply after reasonable opportunity to do so. Schulz v. IRS, 413 F.3d 297 (2d Cir. 2005).

[41] *See* IRC § 6503(j). *See also* Chapter 5.

[42] Reisman v. Caplin, 375 U.S. 440 (1964).

[43] United States v. Powell, 379 U.S. 48 (1964).

[44] See *United States v. Norwood*, 420 F.3d 888 (8th Cir. 2005), for a good discussion of the elements of and defenses to summons enforcement.

summons) or substantive matters (such as objections that the taxpayer does not possess the documents sought and cannot readily obtain them, that the summons is overly broad and burdensome, or that the information sought is protected by a privilege).[45] In potential criminal cases, the taxpayer may be able to invoke the Fifth Amendment privilege against self-incrimination.

Contesting a summons, though, is difficult, both doctrinally and pragmatically. Doctrinally, affirmative defenses are construed narrowly, and the four *Powell* elements are construed liberally in the government's favor. For example, the courts have upheld IRS summonses for copies of the taxpayer's returns for prior years, rejecting the contention that, since the original returns had been filed with IRS service centers, the information was already in the IRS's possession. Nor does the fact that the IRS had previously seen, but not copied, the information mean that the information is already in the IRS's possession.[46]

Pragmatically, judges may reason that merely allowing the IRS to have information doesn't harm the taxpayer and that the trial judge will have the opportunity to prevent or cure any prejudice during trial of the merits. Moreover, the judge realizes that, if both sides have access to the facts, the case is more likely to be settled without the need for trial.

In the fiscal year ended May 31, 2006, there were 101 decided summons enforcement cases, more than double the number in the preceding year. This increase reflects stepped-up IRS audit and enforcement activity, and such activity may portend additional growth in the future. Of the 101 cases, there were only three outright taxpayer victories plus five split decisions.[47]

One controversial area is issuing a summons to obtain tax accrual workpapers. Such workpapers are prepared by a corporation's financial auditors. They identify and evaluate questionable positions that may have been taken on the corporation's tax returns. They are prepared to ascertain the adequacy of the corporation's reserves for contingent tax liabilities for financial statement purposes. Given their nature, tax accrual workpapers are a virtual roadmap for an IRS audit of the corporation.

It has been clear for decades that the IRS is legally empowered to summon tax accrual workpapers,[48] but the IRS has had a policy of doing so only rarely and with restraint. Recently, however, the IRS has signaled its intention to pursue such workpapers more aggressively, particularly as to corporations engaged in tax shelter transactions.[49]

---

[45] For discussion of summons litigation, see Bryan T. Camp, *Tax Administration as Inquisitorial Process and the Partial Paradigm Shift in the IRS Restructuring and Reform Act of 1998*, 56 Fla. L. Rev. 1 (2004).

[46] United States v. Texas Heart Inst., 755 F.2d 469 (5th Cir. 1985).

[47] National Taxpayer Advocate 2006 Annual Report to Congress, Executive Summary 111-1 (Jan. 2007).

[48] United States v. Arthur Young & Co., 465 U.S. 805 (1984).

[49] *See, e.g.*, IRS Announcement 2002-63, 2002-1 C.B. 27; Christopher M. Netram, *Summons Enforcement Action Filed for Tax Accrual Workpapers*, Tax Notes, May 8, 2006, at 631.

B. Information From Directly Knowledgeable Third Parties

The IRS often must seek information from third parties who have knowledge of the events and transactions relevant to the taxpayer's return. For instance, (i) the taxpayer may not have, or may claim not to have, some information that is material; (ii) the information supplied by the taxpayer may need to be corroborated; or (iii) information earlier supplied by the third party (such as W-2 or 1099 forms) may have been rebutted by the taxpayer, necessitating checking the information further with the third party.

The checking under (iii) above is particularly desirable as a result of enactment of section 6201(d) in 1996. Under that provision, in a court proceeding involving an income adjustment based on an information return, the IRS often cannot rely solely on the information return. The IRS bears "the burden of producing reasonable and probative information" supporting the adjustment "in addition to such information return." This provision operates whenever the taxpayer "asserts a reasonable dispute" as to the adjustment and has "fully cooperated" with the IRS during the audit. This provision reflects the fact that W-2s and 1099s sometimes contain innocent errors. They also may intentionally overstate the payment(s) to the taxpayer, as when an employer wants to inflate section 162 deductions for wages paid and issues wrong W-2s which appear to support the overstatement.

The 1996 legislation also created section 7434(a), which allows the person as to whom the false information return was filed (the employee in a W-2 case) to bring a civil action for damages against "any person [who] willfully files a fraudulent information return." Under section 7434(d), a copy of the complaint in such an action is to be filed with the IRS, so that the IRS can pursue its own remedies against the information reporter. Those remedies may be civil (as under section 6674) or criminal (as under section 7204).

Third parties usually comply with informal IRS information requests. Before 1998, the taxpayer found out that such requests had been made only if the third party or the IRS told her. The 1998 Reform Act added section 7602(c), under which the IRS generally may not contact third parties "without providing reasonable notice in advance to the taxpayer that contacts with persons other than the taxpayer may be made." The IRS routinely does that via a standardized notification. In addition, the IRS must periodically give the taxpayer a record of third parties contacted and also must provide that record upon the taxpayer's request.

It can be useful to the taxpayer to know with whom the IRS has talked. Nonetheless, section 7602(c) usually is of limited significance. It is a notification section only. It does not prevent the IRS from contacting anyone nor does it prevent the third party from providing information in response to the contact.

Moreover, section 7602(c)(3) contains exceptions—consent, jeopardy to collection, prospect of reprisal, and criminal investigation—which permit the IRS to contact third parties without giving notice to the taxpayer.

The Treasury and the IRS have promulgated final regulations under section 7602(c). They attempt to balance the taxpayer's business and reputational interests with third parties' privacy interests and the IRS's duty to administer the tax laws effectively. The regulations provide for pre-contact notice and for reports in response to taxpayer requests. Despite the statute, however, the regulations do not provide for periodic reports absent taxpayer request—because such reports might lead to harm to third parties.[50]

In some cases, the IRS will have to issue a summons to the third party. The third party's refusal to comply with the informal request is an obvious instance. Other times, the third party may be willing to comply but fears being sued by the taxpayer. The third party may then ask the IRS agent to issue a so called "friendly summons," which provides suit protection under section 7609(i)(3).

In general, the enforceability of a third-party summons turns on many of the same factors as govern the enforceability of a summons to the taxpayer, including the *Powell* factors described above.[51] In addition, some special rules apply to third-party summonses. Previously, special rules applied only if the summoned person was a "third party recordkeeper" as defined by the statute. The 1998 Reform Act broadened section 7609 to apply to summonses to all third parties, save those identified in the exceptions in section 7609(c)(2), (f), and (g).

When the IRS issues a summons to a third party calling for testimony or production of documents or computer software source codes, section 7609(a) directs that the IRS notify the taxpayer of the third-party summons, provide a copy of the summons, and inform the taxpayer of the right of intervention. Notice must be given within three days of service of the summons and not less than twenty-three days before the date for compliance stated in the summons. Some deviation from these timing rules may be excused if the taxpayer is not actually prejudiced.[52]

Under section 7609(b), the taxpayer has twenty days to initiate a District Court proceeding to quash the summons. The summoned party may intervene

---

[50] Reg. § 301.7602; T.D. 9028, 2003-1 C.B. 415.

[51] *See, e.g.,* United States v. Monumental Life Insurance Co., 440 F.3d 729 (6th Cir. 2006) (reversing the district court and denying enforcement of a third-party summons because the IRS already had many of the documents in its possession and because some of the documents were too far removed from the investigation to be relevant). The lengthy summons issued to the third party is reproduced at the end of *Monumental*. Students may find it instructive to read or skim the summons.

[52] *See, e.g.,* Sylvestre v. United States, 978 F.2d 25 (1st Cir. 1992).

in the taxpayer's suit. If the summoned party had brought suit, the taxpayer would have the right to intervene in it.

Under section 7609(d), the IRS may not examine the summoned documents (if received) until expiration of the twenty-day suit period or until conclusion of the proceeding if brought (absent consent or court order). Under section 7609(e), the pendency of a proceeding to quash suspends the running of both the civil and criminal statutes of limitations.

The IRS sometimes suspects that a tax liability exists but does not know the identity of the taxpayer. A summons to a third party in this situation is known as a "John Doe" summons. Under section 7609(f), a John Doe summons cannot be issued unless the IRS obtains permission via an ex parte application to a federal District Court. The IRS's application must establish that (1) the summons relates to a tax investigation of a person or group of persons; (2) a reasonable basis exists for believing that the person or group may have failed to comply with the Code; and (3) the information the IRS seeks is not readily available from other sources.[53] A prominent recent example of the IRS's use of this tool is its issuance of John Doe summonses to financial institutions as part of an investigation of unidentified taxpayers who may have used offshore credit cards or bank accounts to evade U.S. income tax.

C. General Information

Plainly, information specific to the taxpayer's actual transactions is of primary relevance. Sometimes, though, such information is unavailable or incomplete. In those situations, the IRS often will seek general information.

In some instances, the information is available from generally accessible reference sources. For example, in unreported income cases, the IRS often must endeavor to approximate the taxpayer's income through indirect methods. Under the expenditures method, the IRS estimates what the taxpayer spent during the tax period at issue. The premise is that such expenditures, to the extent they exceed non-taxable sources of income, must have been defrayed by taxable income. Since it is rarely possible to ascertain how much the taxpayer actually spent on food, entertainment, etc., the IRS often relies for this part of the expenditures calculation on average living standard/living costs statistics compiled and published by the Bureau of Labor Statistics. Under section 7491(b), the IRS bears the burden of proof "with respect to any item of income which was reconstructed by the [IRS] solely through the use of statistical information on unrelated taxpayers." Typically, though, the IRS does not depend on BLS statistics "solely," but uses them as only one element of the reconstruction.

---

[53] *E.g.*, In re Tax Liabilities of: John Does, 96 AFTR 2d 6656 (N.D.N.Y. 2005) (summons to ascertain the identities of holders of putatively tax-exempt bonds issued by the City of New Orleans).

Some general, relevant information is not readily accessible and must be gathered by the examining agent. For instance, another indirect method—one used for approximating business receipts—is the "percentage mark-up" method. The IRS determines the taxpayer's likely mark-up for the tax year(s) in question through a combination of factors. They include the taxpayer's own mark-up in other years (if that can be ascertained), mark-ups used by similar companies in the area, and industry-wide average mark-ups. By combining the estimated mark-up with the taxpayer's volume of sales, the taxpayer's receipts can be ascertained or at least approximated.

Developing some of these types of information requires contacting persons who, although they know nothing of the taxpayer's specific transactions, possess relevant general information. The IRS almost always seeks such information through informal contacts. Summonses typically are not used in this context.

D. International Information Gathering

Business is increasingly becoming transnational. United States persons doing business abroad may have to pay U.S. tax with respect to their earnings abroad,[54] and foreign persons doing business here may be subject to U.S. tax on their U.S.-source earnings.[55] Full discussion of information gathering in the transnational context is beyond the scope of this book. The main points, however, are sketched below.

Audits of taxpayers engaged in international transactions are conducted by IRS personnel known as international examiners. Most such examiners are located in the United States. In addition, the IRS has resident examination agents in a number of foreign cities which are major business centers.

The task of gathering information as to international transactions can be quite challenging. A multinational enterprise may keep records in a number of locations; complex corporate ownership and affiliation arrangements may blur lines of control; and some foreign jurisdictions have laws forbidding or limiting the disclosure of business records.

The IRS has four major sets of tools for gathering information (both documentary and testamentary) abroad. First, particularly as to business located wholly or partly in the United States, the IRS may issue summonses. These are subject to the rules discussed above governing summonses generally, with some modifications to reflect jurisdiction and international comity.[56]

---

[54] The United States generally imposes income tax on the worldwide income of its citizens and resident aliens, and the constitutionality of this practice has been upheld. *E.g.*, Cook v. Tait, 265 U.S. 47 (1924).

[55] *See, e.g.*, IRC §§ 871, 881.

[56] *See, e.g.*, United States v. Bank of Nova Scotia, 691 F.2d 1384 (11th Cir. 1982), *cert. denied*, 462 U.S. 1119 (1983), *further proceedings*, 722 F.2d 657 (11th Cir. 1983), *appeal after remand*, 740 F.2d 817 (11th Cir. 1984), *cert. denied*, 469 U.S. 1106 (1985).

Second, the IRS may use "exchange of information" provisions under treaties and executive agreements. For example, the United States has comprehensive bilateral tax treaties with about sixty countries. Those treaties typically contain provisions for mutual administrative assistance, which can include help in gathering some kinds of information.[57] In addition, the United States has tax information exchange agreements and mutual legal assistance treaties with a number of countries with whom we do not have comprehensive tax treaties. A multilateral agreement, the Hague Evidence Convention, also has proved useful to IRS information-gathering efforts in some instances.

Third, the IRS from time to time has used the centuries-old device of letters rogatory. This is a flexible technique by which one government may ask a foreign government for help of some sort. The foreign government need not accede to the request, but often will for reasons of comity. Using this device, the IRS sometimes has prevailed upon foreign governments to take testimony under oath or to provide documents needed by the IRS.

Fourth, not content with the above devices, Congress in recent decades has enacted a number of statutory means to assist IRS information-gathering in the international context. These include Code sections 982 (formal document requests), 6038A (information as to certain foreign-owned corporations), and 6038C (information with respect to foreign corporations engaged in U.S. business).

In response to increasing tax avoidance and evasion in the international context, LMSB (the IRS's Large and Mid-Size Business Division) has created a section to focus on fostering greater cooperation among revenue authorities throughout the world. In addition, the IRS Commissioner works with a group of revenue agency directors from ten countries. They meet annually to focus on international tax issues. A Joint International Tax Shelter Information Center currently exists to share such information among revenue authorities, and it may be expanded.[58]

E. Taxpayer Protections and Defenses

Some protections available to taxpayers as the IRS gathers information have already been noted. Others include the following:

(1) Section 7605 contains rules dealing with time and place of examinations. Under section 7605(a), the time and place fixed by the IRS must be "reasonable under the circumstances." Under section 7605(b), taxpayers shall not "be subjected to unnecessary examination or investigation, and [generally] only one inspection of a taxpayer's books of account shall be made for each taxable year."

---

[57] Article 26 of the U.S. Model Income Tax Treaty provides for exchange of information and administrative assistance between the IRS and the treaty partner's tax authority.

[58] *See* Sheryl Stratton, *Everson to Tax Bar: You Should Do More*, Tax Notes, Jan. 29, 2007, at 404.

However, the "only one inspection" rule is of limited significance. First, by its terms, it does not prohibit a second examination, only second inspection of the taxpayer's "books of account," which is a narrow concept.[59] For example, the IRS takes the position that its preparing an automated substitute for return under section 6020(b) does not constitute an examination for Code purposes.[60] It also takes the position that asking a taxpayer to respond to a questionnaire and meet informally with an IRS representative as part of a program to evaluate IRS software to better identify returns with high error probability does not constitute an examination for section 7605(b) purposes.[61]

Second, even this limited stricture is fairly easily circumvented. For example, the IRS may be able plausibly to argue that its first inspection had not ended (merely gone on hiatus), thus that there was no second inspection, just a resumption of the first. Third, section 7605(b) states no remedy for violation, and courts have been reluctant to fashion a meaningful remedy.[62] Fourth, section 7605(b) itself provides that a second inspection may occur if the taxpayer so requests or the IRS "after investigation, notifies the taxpayer in writing that an additional inspection is necessary."[63]

(2) Section 7521 contains a number of rules as to IRS interviews of the taxpayer. Under section 7521(a), the taxpayer, upon advance request, may make an audio recording of any interview. The IRS also may record any interview as long as it gives the taxpayer prior notice and, if requested by the taxpayer, provides the taxpayer a copy (at the taxpayer's expense).

Under section 7521(b), the IRS is required, at or before the first meeting to explain the audit process and the taxpayer's rights in it. If, during an interview (other than pursuant to a summons), the taxpayer expresses a desire to consult with a federally authorized advisor,[64] the interview must be suspended. Moreover, unless the taxpayer is directed to testify pursuant to a summons, the taxpayer need not personally meet with an IRS agent but may send an authorized representative instead.

(3) Section 7602 contains two other taxpayer protections. First, under section 7602(d), the IRS may not issue a summons nor may it begin an action to enforce a summons after (i) the case been referred to the Department of Justice for crim-

---

[59] *See, e.g.*, Benjamin v. Commissioner, 66 T.C. 1084, 1097-99 (1976), *aff'd*, 592 F.2d 1259 (5th Cir. 1979).

[60] CCA 200518001 (May 29, 2005).

[61] CCA 200612015 (Feb. 17, 2006).

[62] *See, e.g.*, Council of British Societies in Southern California v. United States, 42 A.F.T.R.2d (P-H) 78-6014 (C.D. Cal. 1978) (denying § 7605(b) relief).

[63] *See* Rev. Proc. 2005-32, 2005-2 C.B. 1206 (setting forth procedures for reopening examinations under section 7605).

[64] Such an advisor is anyone authorized to practice before the IRS pursuant to the rules of Treasury Circular 230. IRC § 7525(a)(3)(A).

inal prosecution or (ii) a disclosure request has been made by Justice to the IRS.[65]

Second, section 7602(e) prohibits a specific audit technique. In the 1990s, the IRS developed a set of several dozen questions—called financial status or economic reality programs—designed to test whether the taxpayer was under-reporting income. It is unclear how widely the IRS intended to use financial status auditing, but there was a hue and cry against it. In response, Congress enacted section 7602(e) in 1998. It prohibits the use of such techniques unless the IRS "has a reasonable indication that there is a likelihood [that the taxpayer has] unreported income."

(4) Under section 7611, special restrictions apply to tax examinations and investigations involving churches.

(5) In proper cases, evidentiary privileges may be asserted against IRS information gathering, including summonses. The relevant privileges may sound in the Constitution (such as the Fifth Amendment privilege against self-incrimination),[66] a statute (such as section 7525), or the common law (such as the attorney-client privilege and the work product doctrine).[67] Privileges have been sharply controverted in the tax shelter wars of the 2000s.[68] Congress enacted section 7525 in 1998 to extend to taxpayer communications with non-attorney tax advisors the same protection as attaches under the attorney-client privilege to taxpayer communications to attorneys. However, the section 7525 privilege attaches only in noncriminal matters before the IRS and noncriminal tax proceedings in court. It does not attach to written communications regarding tax shelters.[69]

(6) The Internal Revenue Manual and IRS policies are other important sources of taxpayer protections. Here are three examples. First, the IRS has a policy against repetitive audits of the same taxpayer, especially as to the same issues. The attorney should review the details of this policy whenever the client has been audited in the recent past. Second, although collectability usually is not considered at the audit stage, the Manual instructs agents to consider indicators of the taxpayer's financial weakness in deciding the scope and depth of the audit. Third, large corporations are audited every year. Over time, animosities (or excessive cordiality) may build up. To minimize this possibility, IRS policy

---

[65] *See* IRC § 6103(h)(3)(B).

[66] *See, e.g.*, Braswell v. United States, 487 U.S. 99 (1988).

[67] *E.g.*, United States v. Rexworthy, 457 F.3d 590 (6th Cir. 2006).

[68] *See generally* Martin J. McMahon, Jr. & Ira B. Shepherd, *Privilege and the Work Product Doctrine in Tax Cases*, 58 Tax Law. 405 (2005).

[69] *See* Danielle M. Smith & David L. Kleinman, *What Remains of the Federal Tax Practitioner Privilege Under Internal Revenue Code Section 7525?*, Daily Tax Report, June 9, 2006, at J-1.

limits the number of consecutive years that IRS examiners and specialists can be involved in audits of the same taxpayer.[70]

VII. INFORMATION GATHERING BY THE TAXPAYER

The IRS usually is the party pursuing information. At times, though, the taxpayer must obtain information from the IRS. In litigation, the taxpayer has the same discovery options as the government plus the benefit of a few special devices authorized by the Code.[71] Our attention now, however, is on other taxpayer attempts to get information from the IRS.

A. Transaction Planning

The taxpayer may need information when it is planning its transactions and considering alternatives. Especially where the tax stakes are considerable and the law unclear, the taxpayer will need to carefully research the IRS's positions and practices in the area. For the most part, this is comparatively easy now. The IRS discloses a great deal of information through the *Internal Revenue Bulletin* and the *Cumulative Bulletin,* and through rulings, memoranda, advisories, and the like which are released to and published by private companies. It was not always thus. Freedom of Information litigation over several decades triggered disclosure of private letter rulings (redacted under section 6110(c) to excise the requesting taxpayer's identity and some other information), large portions of the Internal Revenue Manual, denials and revocations of tax exemptions, and many varieties of internal IRS memoranda.[72] FOIA skirmishes in tax continue.[73]

Nonetheless, taxpayers and their representatives planning transactions sometimes need more detailed or current information than that which has been published. A private letter ruling request, as described in Chapter 1, often is a good option. Sometimes, a telephone call to IRS Counsel's National Office will be productive. How does the practitioner know whom to call? IRS rulings identify the names and telephone numbers of personnel principally responsible for drafting them, and those who drafted topically relevant rulings are good starting contacts. Also, the IRS sometimes publishes lists of persons responsible for

---

[70] *See, e.g., IRS Establishes Five-Year Duration on Continuous Audits of Taxpayers*, Tax Management Weekly Report, Dec. 4, 2006, at 1811.

[71] *See, e.g.,* IRC § 6902(b) (special discovery rule for transferees in Tax Court cases). See Chapter 8 for discovery in Tax Court.

[72] *See, e.g.,* Hawkes v. IRS, 467 F.2d 787 (6th Cir. 1972), *appeal after remand,* 507 F.2d 481 (6th Cir. 1974); Taxation with Representation Fund v. IRS, 485 F. Supp. 263 (D.D.C. 1980), *aff'd in part and remanded in part,* 646 F.2d 666 (D.C. Cir. 1981).

[73] *See, e.g.,* Tax Analysts v. IRS, 350 F.3d 100 (D.C. Cir. 2003); Tax Analysts v. IRS, 97 F. Supp. 2d 13 (D.D.C. 2000).

areas and their contact information. If the practitioner does not have the name of a particular IRS attorney, the inquiry can be directed to the relevant National Office unit. With patience and perseverance, the right person likely will be reached.

This informal approach will not always be satisfactory. The IRS will sometimes be unable or unwilling to address an issue. Accordingly, the taxpayer may have to resort to more formal information demands, using the Freedom of Information Act or other devices.

B. Audit and Administrative Appeal

Taxpayer information gathering has a predictive purpose when done at the planning stage. The goal is to assess the likelihood of the IRS challenging the taxpayer's treatment of an item on a return. By the time the return is audited, the goal has shifted. The taxpayer has taken a return position, and, if the IRS challenges it, the objective now is to vindicate that position or at least to settle the dispute on acceptable terms.

Information gathering may be critical to achieving that objective. In some instances, the aim is to uncover facts not previously available to the taxpayer but useful to the taxpayer's position. In other instances, the quest is to locate prior IRS rulings, announcements, position papers, and the like which directly or inferentially support the taxpayer's return treatment. Discovery of such items might persuade the IRS to drop the matter or, at least, to refrain from asserting a penalty.

C. Means for Compelling Disclosure

Other than through informal requests, by what means can a taxpayer seek information from the IRS? The Freedom of Information Act ("FOIA") and other means are discussed below.

1. FOIA

Congress enacted FOIA in 1966 as a way of opening the actions of federal agencies to the light of public scrutiny. Codified as 5 U.S.C. section 552, FOIA applies to federal agencies generally, including the IRS.[74] Section 552(a) describes agency material that is subject to disclosure, and section 552(b) lists nine categories which are exempt from disclosure. Additional exclusions exist under section 552(c). Since subsection (a) is a broad principle of disclosure, the

---

[74] An important case applying FOIA in the tax context is *United States Dep't of Justice v. Tax Analysts*, 492 U.S. 136 (1989).

"action" in FOIA cases is at the level of the exemptions. The IRS must disclose information fairly within the taxpayer's FOIA request unless one of the nine exemptions applies. The main exemptions in the tax context are section 552(b)(3), (5), and (7). They are described below. FOIA exemptions are narrowly construed in favor of disclosure.[75]

Exemption 3: This exemption permits non-disclosure of information which is specifically shielded by some other, non-FOIA statute. The major Code section declaring tax returns and tax return information to be confidential, section 6103, is such a statute for FOIA purposes.[76] Under section 6103(b)(2), tax return information includes all information collected to determine the taxpayer's liability.

Exemption 5: This exemption permits non-disclosure of internal agency memoranda which the agency could not be compelled to reveal via discovery in litigation. In essence, this reduces to whether a recognized evidentiary privilege applies. The IRS, no less than private parties, may assert the attorney-client privilege and the work product doctrine. In addition, IRS materials sometimes are covered by the governmental deliberative privilege—a limited privilege which protects predecisional, deliberative communications.[77]

Exemption 7: This exemption shields investigatory records compiled for civil or criminal law enforcement purposes. The contours of this exemption have been shaped and reshaped via litigation and amendment. As examples, witness statements, memoranda revealing investigative techniques, and the identities of informants have been held protected.[78]

In addition to the statutory exceptions, the courts have limited FOIA requests when necessary to protect judicial process. Thus, "a FOIA request cannot be used as simply a way to get around the discovery rules, and limitations, of a civil action."[79] The IRS recently announced procedures to improve coordination between IRS disclosure officers and Chief Counsel attorneys. The goal is to prevent FOIA disclosures that would adversely affect the IRS in examination or litigation.[80]

---

[75] *See, e.g.*, Vaughn v. Rosen, 523 F.2d 1136 (D.C. Cir. 1975).

[76] *See, e.g.*, Chamberlain v. Kurtz, 589 F.2d 827 (5th Cir.), *cert. denied*, 444 U.S. 842 (1979).

[77] *See, e.g.*, Marriott Int'l Resorts, L.P. v. United States, 437 F.3d 1302 (Fed. Cir. 2006); Tax Analysts v. IRS, 416 F. Supp. 2d 119 (D.D.C. 2006).

[78] *See, e.g.*, Barney v. IRS, 618 F.2d 1268 (8th Cir. 1980); Kanter v. IRS, 478 F. Supp. 552 (N.D. Ill. 1979).

[79] United States v. Chrein, 368 F. Supp. 2d 278, 284 (S.D.N.Y. 2005).

[80] *See* Dustin Stamper, *IRS Officials Outline Coming Guidance, Defend New FOIA Policy*, Tax Notes, Oct. 30, 2006, at 430.

2. Other Devices

Some provisions of the Code allow taxpayers to discover facts and theories at the pre-litigation stage. For example, section 534(b) authorizes the IRS to notify a corporate taxpayer in writing that it contemplates making an accumulated earnings tax adjustment before issuing the statutory notice of deficiency. Such notification is routine since, under section 534(a), the IRS bears the burden of proof on the issue if it fails to give such notification.

Another such section is section 7517. Under this section, when the IRS makes a determination of the value of an asset for gift, estate, or generation-skipping transfer tax purposes, the IRS must furnish the taxpayer a written statement as to the determination. The statement must explain the basis of the valuation, set forth computations, and include any expert appraisal by or for the IRS. The statement is to be furnished within forty-five days after the taxpayer requests it.

Another relevant statute is the Privacy Act, enacted in 1974 and codified at 5 U.S.C. section 552a. The principal thrust of the Privacy Act is to stop unauthorized disclosure from federal agency files of personal information on individuals (not entities). The Privacy Act also allows individuals the right, upon request, to view the information on them in agency files. Access is not available to third-party records or internal agency documents in those files. Individual taxpayers might consider making Privacy Act requests for access to IRS files on them. If the information therein is inaccurate, the taxpayer can demand its correction.

As a practical matter, however, the Privacy Act adds little to the options available to taxpayers under FOIA. First, under 5 U.S.C. section 552a(b), access is unavailable as to "any information compiled in reasonable anticipation of a civil action proceeding." Second, under section 552a(k)(2), agencies are permitted to issue rules excluding access to categories of information, including investigatory materials compiled for law enforcement ends. The IRS has used this authority to exempt most information gathered on audit or during Appeals consideration. Third, section 7852(e) precludes use of the Privacy Act to attempt to revise the IRS's determination of "any tax, penalty, interest, fine, forfeiture, or other imposition or offense." Fourth, as the more specific section, section 6103 tends to control over the Privacy Act as to tax confidentiality.[81]

VIII. APPEALS OFFICE CONSIDERATION

The Appeals Office has local offices which broadly correspond to the operating divisions of the IRS established pursuant to the reorganization commanded by the 1998 Reform Act. There are two Appeals programs. One deals with large

---

[81] *See, e.g.*, Gardner v. United States, 213 F.3d 735 (D.C. Cir. 2000).

and mid-size businesses, corresponding to the LMSB operating division. The other, called the General Appeals Program, corresponds to the W&I, SB/SE, and TE/GE operating divisions. Appeals also has officers stationed in the service centers. Discussed here are how a case reaches Appeals, how Appeals handles the case, and factors to be weighed in deciding whether to request review by Appeals.[82]

A. Paths to the Appeals Office

Appeals deals with a number of things, including deficiency, refund claim, and collection matters. Our focus here is on its role in reviewing deficiency determinations.[83] A deficiency matter can reach Appeals through any of three routes: the traditional "undocketed" path, the early involvement path, and the docketed path.

1. Traditional Path

If the issues cannot be resolved at the audit stage, the examining agent will write up the proposed adjustments in a Revenue Agent's Report ("RAR") or similar document. That document is also called a Thirty-Day Letter because the taxpayer has thirty days from the issuance date to request Appeals consideration.

The thirty-day period can be extended. The IRS typically grants an additional thirty days, upon taxpayer request, unless a special circumstance is present. Perhaps the most common special circumstance is imminent expiration of the statute of limitations on assessment. If the limitations period will expire within 120 days, the IRS will require the taxpayer to execute a consent extending the limitations period. The IRS is disinclined to extend the thirty-day period beyond an additional thirty days unless the taxpayer advances a strong justification.

The taxpayer invokes Appeals' jurisdiction by filing a Protest. A Protest filed on the taxpayer's behalf by a representative should be accompanied by an executed Form 2848 Power of Attorney. The Protest should set out the taxpayer's view of the facts and the law. The IRS may reject an insufficiently explanatory Protest although this is rare. When the amount at issue in each tax period does not exceed $25,000, the taxpayer, in lieu of a Protest, can file a simple statement saying that Appeals consideration is desired. A Protest will not be needed in correspondence and office audits, and will be needed in only some field audits.

A Protest is simply a letter sent to the IRS Area Director for the relevant operating division. No particular form is required. Many attorneys structure the Protest rather like a brief. The contents that the IRS expects in a Protest are

---

[82] See Chapter 6 for Appeals Office procedures in partnership audit and appeal cases.

[83] See Chapter 8 for discussion of deficiency determinations.

described in Procedural Regulation section 601.106(f)(5) and in IRS Publications 5 "Your Appeal Rights and How To Prepare a Protest If You Don't Agree" and 556 "Examination of Returns, Appeal Rights, and Claims for Refund."

There are two schools of thought as to the Protest. Some attorneys believe that the taxpayer should submit the skimpiest Protest possible. The theory is that the taxpayer thereby preserves maximum space for maneuvering during the ensuing discussions and, perhaps, also that the Appeals Officer will have less time to dissect and prepare to refute the taxpayer's arguments. The other theory (which is more widely held) is that the Protest should be detailed and complete. The notion is that the taxpayer and her representative have greater credibility with the Appeals Office if they aren't perceived as trying to "hide the ball" or spring arguments "in ambush." In addition, there have been cases in which the Appeals Officer has conceded particular issues from the start of the discussion, having been persuaded as to them by a full and careful Protest.

2. Early Involvement

The traditional path to Appeals consideration has been modified to permit earlier Appeals intervention or to move the case faster in Appeals when it gets there. The first major initiative began in the 1990s. Under the traditional path, Appeals consideration occurs after the examining agent has completed the audit and determined adjustments. In the 1990s, the IRS created the Early Referral Program under which, in certain cases, Appeals could consider some issues while the revenue agent was still considering other issues. More recently, this has been broadened to make the Program available to all taxpayers.[84]

The IRS also created the Fast Track Settlement program, with the aim of concluding administrative appeal within 120 days.[85] Originally available to only LMSB taxpayers, the program has been expanded to include small businesses as well.[86] The IRS also has established rapid-settlement mechanisms as part of its efforts to deal with the current rash of corporate tax shelters.[87]

3. Docketed Cases

Under the traditional path, Appeals consideration occurs after audit but before litigation. However, a case may reach Appeals after Tax Court pleadings have been completed.

---

[84] IRC § 7123(a); Rev. Proc. 99-28, 1999-2 C.B. 109.

[85] Rev. Proc. 2003-40, 2003-25 I.R.B. 1044.

[86] Announcement 2006-61, 2006-2 C.B. 390.

[87] *See, e.g.*, Rev. Proc. 2002-67, 2002-2 C.B. 733.

(1) The taxpayer may have done nothing after receiving the Thirty-Day Letter because of strategy or inadvertence. When no Protest or other statement of desire for Appeals consideration is filed within the thirty days, the IRS issues a statutory notice of deficiency (Ninety-Day Letter). When a Tax Court petition contesting the statutory notice is filed, the normal practice of IRS Counsel is to refer the case to Appeals after the pleadings are complete unless there are reasons to believe that Appeals consideration would be unavailing. If Appeals cannot resolve the case, it is then returned to Counsel for trial preparation.

(2) The taxpayer may have requested Appeals consideration after audit but was properly denied it under established policies—for example, if less than 120 days remained on the limitations period and the taxpayer refused to extend that period. In that event too, IRS Counsel will refer the case to Appeals after close of the Tax Court pleadings. The statute of limitations is no longer a concern since, under section 6503(a), issuance of the statutory notice suspends the running of the limitations period.

(3) The taxpayer may have requested Appeals consideration but was improperly denied it before issuance of the statutory notice. This is not common, but it does happen. That is a particularly appropriate circumstance for post-pleadings Appeals consideration. It is settled that the improper initial denial of administrative appeal does not invalidate the statutory notice.[88]

(4) The taxpayer may have gone through Appeals after audit without being able to resolve the case there. Normally, in such instances, IRS Counsel begins trial preparation. However, if the taxpayer, Appeals, and Counsel agree that settlement potential still exists, the case nonetheless can return to Appeals.

Regardless of which path the case takes to reach Appeals, the docketed status imposes some urgency. The timing ultimately is in the hands of the Tax Court, not the parties. If the court calendars the case for trial, the parties must choose between further settlement efforts and trial preparation. The Tax Court often is receptive to continuance if the parties jointly represent that settlement would be probable with more time, but judges differ in their receptivity and one who assumes that a continuance will be granted proceeds at his peril.

4. Unavailability of Appeals Consideration

The Appeals Office is universally recognized as a crucial part of the apparatus of tax administration. It would be impossible, as a practical matter, for the system to try the numerous cases that Appeals resolves. Thus, there is strong desire on the part of the government to make Appeals consideration widely available.

However, there are exceptions, situations in which normal administrative appeal is foreclosed. Typically, these situations are ones in which appeal would

---

[88] *See, e.g.*, Luhring v. Glotzbach, 304 F.2d 560 (4th Cir. 1962).

be fruitless or could disrupt matters requiring special coordination. These include: (i) cases in which criminal prosecution has been recommended or is pending, (ii) tax protester cases, and (iii) cases which have been designated as litigation vehicles, where obtaining a precedent to govern a class of cases is more important than disposing of any given case in that class.

B. Appeals Procedures

When the taxpayer submits the Protest, it will be examined by the revenue agent and the agent's group manager. Then it will go to a specialized function in a local office known as Examination Support and Processing or Quality Assurance (formerly Quality Review or Quality Measurement). This unit will decide whether the Protest is adequate for processing and whether, in light of the points raised by the Protest, the RAR should be modified, the case should be returned to the agent for further factual development, or the opinion of Counsel should be sought on legal questions. If the case then is sent to Appeals, Appeals will conduct a similar initial review.

Once a case has been accepted by Appeals, that office will contact the taxpayer or taxpayer's representative, scheduling a conference. The general view among experienced tax attorneys is that the representative usually should attend the conference without the taxpayer. The representative may be able to speak with greater candor if the client is not present. Moreover, the client may make unnecessary and damaging admissions, appear evasive, or insult or alienate the Appeals Officer.

At the conference, the taxpayer's representative and the Appeals Officer will exchange their views of the facts and the law. Since the purpose of the conference is settlement, the parties can typically expect that, by virtue of Federal Rule of Evidence 408, their remarks during the conference will not be admissible as evidence if the case must be tried.

Appeals conferences are conducted rather informally. Testimony is not taken under oath, and transcripts are not made. Under section 7521, the taxpayer may record the meetings, in which case the Appeals Office will do so as well. All information deemed reliable may be presented by both sides. The rules of evidence do not apply. Theoretically, potential evidence problems would be part of each side's hazards of litigation calculus. However, as a practical matter, such problems rarely loom large in Appeals discussions.

Especially in non-docketed cases in which the taxpayer is prepared to extend the statute of limitations, Appeals consideration may stretch over many months. A case becomes "over age" under Appeals guidelines after a year. If new facts or law develop, the taxpayer should supplement the protest with additional memoranda or letters.

Unless Appeals is persuaded to concede the case, it will expect the taxpayer to make a settlement offer. If that offer is unacceptable, Appeals may make a counter-offer. The offer must reflect the merits, and "nuisance value" typically is disregarded. Many Appeals Officers follow an "80/20" approach. That is, if Appeals believes the IRS has an over 80% chance of prevailing on a given issue, it will expect the taxpayer to concede that issue in full. If Appeals believes the IRS has an under 20% chance of prevailing, it will concede the issue in full.

If Appeals' assessment puts the issue in the range between 20% and 80%, it is empowered to settle the case on a basis reflecting the perceived "hazards of litigation." Examination agents theoretically do not have this power; they are supposed to "write up" each adjustment with merit that they find, even if hazards exist as to it. However, examination agents, especially revenue agents in CEP exams, do engage in hazards-based settlement, in fact though not in name. They do so by trading issues. For example, when there are two potential audit adjustments with significant hazards for both sides, the agent will set up one, which the taxpayer will concede in return for the agent not setting up the other issue. Nonetheless, hazards-based settlement is more common at Appeals than at audit. Formerly, a common settlement strategy was to trade penalty issues for deficiency adjustments. In theory at least, Appeals has ended this practice. It will still settle penalty issues, but only on the merits and not by way of trade-off.[89]

Settlement practice has been significantly affected by the 1998 Reform Act. Under section 7430, the IRS may have to pay the taxpayer's reasonable professional fees and costs incurred during the administrative and judicial phases of a controversy. The 1998 legislation added section 7430(g) dealing with "qualified settlement offers" ("QSO"s). If the taxpayer makes a QSO which the IRS rejects, the taxpayer will be considered the prevailing party if the judgment ultimately entered in the case is for an amount equal to or less than the amount of the taxpayer's offer. The taxpayer will then be entitled to recover fees and costs incurred after the QSO was made.[90] If litigation appears a possible outcome, the taxpayer should seriously consider whether to make a QSO.

Cases taken to Appeals usually are resolved there. Depending on the kind of case and the particular office, Appeals usually resolves 80% to 90% of the cases it takes, whether by full concession by the IRS, full concession by the taxpayer, or compromise.

If settlement appears to be unlikely through normal means, the taxpayer may consider ancillary procedures. If the taxpayer believes the Appeals Officer misunderstands the law, she may request the Officer to seek advice from the National Office via a TAM (described in Chapter 1) or less formally from the local IRS Counsel's Office.

---

[89] Chief Counsel Notice CC-2004-036 (Sept. 22, 2004), *reproduced at* 2004 Tax Notes Today 186-9.

[90] *See generally* Reg. § 301.7430-7; Burgess J.W. Raby & William L. Raby, *Qualified Offers and Settlement of Tax Controversies*, Tax Notes, Oct. 30, 2006, at 455.

Another approach would be to invoke one of several alternative dispute resolution mechanisms created in recent years as adjuncts to Appeals consideration. The 1998 Reform Act created both arbitration and mediation routes. Section 7123(b)(2) directed the IRS to establish a pilot program under which the taxpayer and Appeals may jointly request binding arbitration. After several years of testing, and despite only mixed success during testing, the IRS formally established the Appeals Arbitration Program in 2006. Arbitration is available only by mutual agreement and when all issues have been resolved other than the specific factual issue for which arbitration is requested. Certain types of issues are excepted from the program.[91]

Outside of the Appeals context, arbitration is making limited inroads into tax controversy resolution. Tax Court Rule 124 permits voluntary binding arbitration in docketed cases, but it is rarely used. Also, arbitration provisions have been included in several recent tax treaties to which the United States is a party, and they may play a larger role in future treaties.[92]

Mediation can come early or late in the Appeals process.[93] The Fast Track mediation program allows SB/SE, LMSB, and the taxpayers under their jurisdiction to mediate disputed issues, using an Appeals Officer as the mediator. Most disputes are resolved within forty days, considerably faster than the regular Appeals process.[94]

Section 7123(b)(1) directed the IRS to establish procedures under which the taxpayer or Appeals may request non-binding mediation of any issue unresolved at the conclusion of Appeals consideration. The IRS has established a mediation process in which the mediator may be an outside party or, more often, a specially trained Appeals Officer. Mediation is available as to most types of issues, factual or legal, regardless of amount. However, it is not available as to collection cases, docketed cases, cases designated as litigation vehicles, cases in which the taxpayer asserts frivolous issues or acts in bad faith, or cases in which mediation would be inconsistent with sound tax administration.[95]

Appeals also has finalized an arbitration program for factual issues.[96] Despite the expansion of alternative dispute resolution devices, the great majority of

---

[91] Rev. Proc. 2006-44, 2006-2 C.B. 800.

[92] *See, e.g.,* Michael J. McIntyre, *Comments on the OECD Proposal for Secret and Mandatory Arbitration of International Tax Disputes,* 7 Fla. Tax Rev. 622 (2006); Lee A. Sheppard, *Treasury Talks Up Treaty Arbitration,* Tax Notes, Jan. 15, 2007, at 153.

[93] *See generally* Ronald Stein, *Make the Most of Recently Expanded Mediation Opportunities,* Practical Tax Strategies, Mar. 2003, at 144.

[94] *See* Rev. Proc. 2003-40, 2003-1 C.B. 1044; Rev. Proc. 2003-41, 2003-1 C.B. 1047.

[95] Rev. Proc. 2002-44, 2002-2 C.B. 800.

[96] *See* Announcement 2002-60, 2002-2 C.B. 28; Sarah Hall Ingram, *Considering All the Options: Make Sure You and Your Client Are Considering All the Resolution Opportunities,* J. Tax Prac. & Proc., Oct.-Nov. 2006, at 37.

taxpayers continue to use the traditional appeals processes, not mediation or arbitration.

C. Whether to Seek Appeals Consideration

Taxpayers are not required to avail themselves of the Appeals Office. Most taxpayers choose to do so, and that often is the right choice. Nonetheless, the decision must be made on the circumstances of each case.

1. Possible Benefits

(1) The most important consideration is the prospect of resolving the case efficiently and on a satisfactory basis. As noted above, Appeals has a high resolution rate. Moreover, resolution at Appeals is usually faster and significantly less expensive than litigation.

(2) Appeals resolution may be more comprehensive. The Tax Court typically has jurisdiction only for those tax years as to which the IRS has asserted deficiencies and which are included in the petition. Appeals can take a more holistic approach. Via closing and collateral agreements, Appeals can settle related tax years or periods, such as those in which the same kind of issue arises and those which involve the multi-year effects of a single transaction. Similarly, Appeals can resolve matters involving parties transactionally related to the taxpayer, such as spouses, sellers and their buyers, transferors and their transferees, and fiduciaries and beneficiaries.

(3) Appeals involves less publicity than does litigation. Judicial proceedings typically are open to the public and may be covered by reporters for local media outlets. Appeals proceedings are private and confidential, except insofar as settlement documents in docketed cases are incorporated into Tax Court decision documents.

(4) Appeals consideration often is necessary to the taxpayer's exhaustion of administrative remedies. As described more fully in Chapter 8, if the taxpayer ultimately prevails in litigation, he sometimes is able to receive from the IRS reimbursement of attorneys fees and costs under section 7430. However, under section 7430(b)(1), such reimbursement is possible only if the taxpayer exhausted administrative remedies available within the IRS, which includes the Appeals Office.

On the other end of the spectrum, if the taxpayer loses in the Tax Court, the court is authorized by section 6673 to impose an additional penalty on the taxpayer (or on the taxpayer's attorney) if the taxpayer's position was frivolous or the taxpayer instituted or maintained the action primarily for delay. Section 6673(a)(1)(c) lists the taxpayer's unreasonable failure "to pursue available administrative remedies" as an additional basis for imposition of the penalty.

The Tax Court does not use failure to go through Appeals as an independently sufficient basis on which to impose section 6673 penalties, but it does consider such failure as part of an overall "facts and circumstances" section 6673 inquiry.

2. Possible Drawbacks

Despite the above benefits, there are times when Appeals consideration may be undesirable.

(1) Examining agents occasionally miss possible adjustments that may be larger or stronger than the ones they did set up. In such a circumstance, the taxpayer may do well to forgo Appeals consideration before issuance of the statutory notice of deficiency and perhaps to forgo it entirely. The concern is that the Appeals Officer may find and raise the issue(s) the examining agent missed. This is infrequent. As a matter of policy, Appeals Officers are discouraged from raising new issues unless they are substantial.[97] But, of course, it is precisely those adjustments about which taxpayer would be concerned.

Taxpayers finding themselves in such a situation have several options, depending on the taxpayer's level of risk aversion and the magnitudes and strengths of both the adjustments that already have been raised and the as yet undiscovered adjustment(s). First, the taxpayer could just concede the adjustments that have been raised. As a matter of administrative realities, that would make it highly unlikely that the potential issue ever would surface.

Second, the taxpayer could default both the Thirty-Day Letter and the Ninety-Day Letter. The IRS would then assess the tax, and the taxpayer would pay it. Then, after the section 6501 limitations period for assessments had expired but before the section 6511 limitations period for seeking a refund expired, the taxpayer would file a refund claim with the IRS, then a refund suit if necessary. *See* Chapter 9. The taxpayer would contend in the claim and the suit that the adjustments reflected in the assessment were substantively unfounded. This could prompt the IRS to examine the whole return. In general, though, the IRS could use the new issue (even if found) only as an offset to the claimed refund and, because of the statute of limitations, could not use it as a basis for an additional assessment. Great care must be taken, however, to be sure that no exception to the statute of limitations on assessment applies.[98]

Third, if the taxpayer needs or wants to litigate in Tax Court, the strategy would be to default the Thirty-Day Letter, file a Tax Court petition contesting the Ninety-Day Letter, and go through Appeals in docketed status. If the

---

[97] IRS Policy Statement P-8-49.

[98] *See, e.g.,* Trans Mississippi Corp. v. United States, 494 F.2d 770 (5th Cir. 1974) (taxpayer brought a refund suit for $78,000 but wound up with an additional assessment exceeding $370,000; the new assessment was timely because of the fraud exception of § 6501(c)(1)). See Chapter 5 for discussion of the assessment statute of limitations.

Appeals Officer or the IRS Counsel attorney finds the new issue, it could be raised, but only via the IRS's answer or an amendment to the answer. The IRS would then bear the burden of proof on the new issue under Tax Court Rule 142(a). In contrast, if Appeals discovers the new issue during undocketed consideration, it would be included in the Ninety-Day Letter, with the result that the taxpayer likely would bear the burden of proof as to that issue during ensuing litigation. *See* Chapter 8.

(2) As noted previously, if under four months remain on the limitations period on assessment, the taxpayer usually can get Appeals consideration in undocketed status only by consenting to extend that period, which may be undesirable. Under section 7430(b)(1), refusal to grant such an extension is not tantamount to failure to exhaust administrative remedies.

(3) In some instances, Appeals Officers have little flexibility, little ability to settle on any basis short of concession by the taxpayer. For example, the issue may be an Appeals Coordinated Issue ("ACI"). These are issues (often CEP or ISP) as to which the IRS particularly desires nationwide uniformity of treatment. Proposed settlements must be approved by an ACI or ISP coordinator, who rarely permits deviation from the national settlement position. Or, the case may have been designated by IRS Counsel as a litigation vehicle. Or, the examining agent's adjustment may be supported by an extant TAM or revenue ruling the validity of which has not been called into question by judicial decision.

In instances such as these, there may be little to hope for from Appeals. However, if the case contains other adjustments not subject to such strictures, Appeals consideration may still be worthwhile, to achieve resolution of those other adjustments, even if the controlled issue may have to be litigated.

IX. CONCLUSION OF EXAMINATION OR ADMINISTRATIVE APPEAL

A. No-Change Cases

If the examining agent accepts the return as filed, the IRS will issue a "no change" letter to the taxpayer. The letter is not precedential. If a similar issue arises as to another tax year, the no-change letter does not preclude the adjustment (although it may help to deflect a penalty). Nor is the letter binding even as to the tax period for which it was issued. Assuming other rules (like the statute of limitations) are not traduced, the IRS can reopen the period even after issuing a no-change letter. However, the IRS rarely reopens absent fraud, material misrepresentation, clear error in applying IRS positions, or other unusual condition.[99]

---

[99] Proc. Reg. § 601.105(j).

B. Agreed or Partly Agreed Cases

If the examining agent concludes that adjustments are appropriate and the taxpayer chooses not to contest their assessment (so called "agreed cases"), the IRS and the taxpayer will execute one of several forms. The most common are Forms 870, 870-AD, 866, and 906. The extent to which the parties are bound as to the tax period(s) in question depends on which form was executed.

The key provision in this regard is section 7121. Section 7121(a) authorizes the IRS to enter into written closing agreements as to a taxpayer's liability for any tax for any tax period. Section 7121(b) provides that such closing agreements are "final and conclusive" and may not be reopened, set aside, or modified "except upon a showing of fraud or malfeasance, or misrepresentation of a material fact."

The courts have held that only Forms 866 and 906 are closing agreements under section 7121.[100] Form 866 "Agreement as to Final Determination of Tax Liability" is used to close the total liability of the taxpayer for one or more tax periods ending prior to the date of the agreement. Form 906 "Closing Agreement as to Final Determination Covering Specific Matters" is partial. It is used to close one or several issues affecting the taxpayer's liability for prior tax periods and/or for subsequent periods. It is useful when there is a recurring issue or a transaction with multi-year effects, obviating the need to refight the same battles each year.

Forms 870, 870-AD, and their ilk are not closing agreements. They have effect only as their terms provide under contract, contract-like, or estoppel principles. Form 870 deals with income tax; Form 890 with estate tax; and similar forms with other types of taxes. They are waiver forms. By executing them, the taxpayer consents to the immediate assessment of the tax without further notification. Under sections 6211 through 6213, this has the effect of eliminating the opportunity for Tax Court review. Under section 6601(c), such execution suspends the running of interest on the liability for the period starting on the thirty-first day after the agreement and ending on the date the IRS makes notice and demand for payment. If there is an overpayment, the form operates as a claim for the refund or credit of it.

However, the 870 and its cognates do not foreclose further adjustment and dispute. Nothing on the forms prevents the IRS from asserting an additional deficiency for the covered period(s) (although this is not common) or prevents the taxpayer from filing a refund claim or suit. Indeed, the language of the forms expressly permits both additional assessments and refund claims.

Form 870 and its cognates are used at the audit level. Similar agreement reached at Appeals is memorialized on Forms 870-AD, 890-AD, and their ilk.[101]

---

[100] *See, e.g.*, Maloney v. Commissioner, 51 T.C. Memo. (CCH) 572 (1986) (Form 870 is not a binding closing agreement).

[101] *See generally* IRM 8.8.1.

Their wording differs from the wording of Form 870 and its near kin. The 870-AD states that, if the IRS accepts the offer, "the case shall not be reopened in the absence of fraud." The IRS takes this language seriously. Some taxpayers, however, have filed refund claims even after executing 870-ADs, usually waiting to do so until after the limitations period on further assessment has expired. The courts are split on whether the 870-AD precludes a refund suit.[102]

An assessment based on a closing agreement can be invalid if the taxpayer did not waive restrictions on assessment.[103] The IRS has developed procedures for securing such waivers in connection with closing arrgements.[104]

The agreements discussed above may be supplemented by collateral agreements. A collateral agreement may address a matter not directly at issue but still appropriate for clarification, such as future year effects. Or, a collateral agreement may be with a related taxpayer, in order to forestall the possibility of the IRS being whipsawed by inconsistent positions. For example, the IRS might, as a condition of settling an estate tax valuation issue, demand that the beneficiaries enter into a collateral agreement committing the beneficiaries to using the agreed-upon estate tax valuation for income tax purposes when they dispose of the assets received from the estate. The beneficiaries, of course, are not legally compelled to sign a collateral agreement. Whether to enter into a collateral agreement and on what terms always are matters of strategy and negotiation.

When Appeals settles a docketed case, the agreement will be memorialized in decision documents to be filed with the Tax Court. Theoretically, IRS Counsel may reject the settlement reached by Appeals and litigate the case or settle it on different terms, but this is exceedingly rare. Counsel will review the decision documents, and any technical defects in them will be corrected. Counsel and the taxpayer jointly execute the documents, and they are filed with the Tax Court. In the normal course, they are signed (stamped) by a Tax Court judge, and the stipulated terms become the decision of the court. Again it is theoretically possible for the court to refuse to accept the settlement, and again such refusal is exceedingly rare.

After a case is resolved administratively by execution of one of the forms described above, or after the parties' agreement in a docketed case is entered as a stipulated decision of the Tax Court, the mechanics enter their final phase. The deficiency, interest, and penalties, if any, will be assessed. Within a few months, the taxpayer will receive a bill from the relevant service center for the assessed amounts.

---

[102] *Compare* Uinta Livestock Corp. v. United States, 355 F.2d 761 (10th Cir. 1966) (suit not precluded), *with* Kretchmar v. United States, 9 Cl. Ct. 191 (1985) (suit barred by doctrine of equitable estoppel).

[103] Manko v. Commissioner, 126 T.C. 195 (2006).

[104] Chief Counsel Notice CC-2006-017 (Aug. 17, 2006).

C. Unagreed Cases

If the examining agent and the taxpayer are unable to reach agreement fully resolving the case, the IRS will issue the Thirty-Day Letter. In cases subject to the deficiency procedures of sections 6211 through 6213, if the taxpayer fails to seek Appeals review, the IRS will then issue the Ninety-Day Letter, leading to the opportunity for Tax Court review described in Chapter 8.

If an undocketed case goes to Appeals and less-than-full resolution is achieved there, Appeals will prepare and issue the Ninety-Day Letter. If Appeals receives the case in docketed status and is unable to resolve it, the case is returned to IRS Counsel for trial preparation.

In cases not subject to the deficiency procedures, the IRS will directly assess whatever underpayment it believes exists. Thereafter, the taxpayer may pay the tax and file a refund claim and institute refund litigation, as described in Chapter 9.

PROBLEM

A.

You are an attorney in private practice. You recently were retained by Fred Jones to handle his tax work. Fred resides in Texas, and he owns and operates a small bar or lounge near Dallas, Texas. Fred hasn't bothered to incorporate the business. Each year, he reports on Schedule C of his Form 1040 the tax results of operating the bar. Fred's business has six to ten employees, working various jobs in various shifts. Fred's returns each year are prepared by Ralph Friendly, an accountant who is not an employee of Fred's.

When you return to your office this morning after several hours in court, your secretary tells you that Fred dropped by while you were out. Your secretary says that Fred was very agitated and barely coherent. Your secretary was able to gather that Fred has received a letter from the IRS stating that his 2004 return is going to be examined. Your secretary made an appointment for you and Fred to meet tomorrow afternoon.

Thinking about the upcoming meeting, you ponder whether to contact Fred before the meeting. Would this be a good idea? If you decide to do so, what would you say to Fred? What, if anything, would you ask Fred to do in advance of the meeting tomorrow?

B.

When you meet with Fred, you discover the following additional information. For year 2004, Fred reported on his Schedule C a small net loss as to the bar. The loss arose in part because of very large expenses claimed for business travel and telephone.

Fred acknowledges to you that, throughout 2004, he was romantically involved with Natalie Imber, a resident of Los Angeles. Fred flew to Los Angeles frequently in 2004 to meet Natalie, and he telephoned her often. The costs of such travel and telephone were included in the Schedule C deductions that Fred claimed on his 2004 return.

However, Fred tells you that these deductions were proper, and he is quite adamant on this point. Fred explains that Natalie is an importer and distributor of foreign beer, wine, and alcohol products. Fred and Natalie met for the first time at a trade convention, and Fred considers Natalie an expert on the products she deals in. Fred says that he always is reviewing his product stock and inventory, seeking to add spirits that could be popular with his customers and give his business an edge over the competition. Fred says Natalie was his expert as to new products. He discussed such products at length with her. Fred insists that all of his travel to Los Angeles, and many of the telephone calls, would not have taken place but for his need to consult with Natalie on such matters, thus the costs were legitimate business expenses. Further, Fred says, Ralph Friendly knew about Fred's relationship with Natalie but still included these expenses as Schedule C deductions on the 2004 return, so they must have been proper. Nonetheless, Fred fears that the IRS might misinterpret his contacts with Natalie.

Fred asks you how he should prepare for the IRS examination and what he should do during it. Develop a strategy. Part of your thinking should include these questions: (1) If the IRS becomes interested in the travel and telephone deductions, how might the IRS learn of or develop the facts as to them, including the nature and amounts of the expenses involved? What options are available to the IRS in this regard? (2) How can Fred protect himself? Specifically, if he does not wish to cooperate in the IRS's development of these facts, what can he legally refuse to do and what can affirmatively be done to oppose the IRS's information gathering? What would or could the IRS do in response?

But do not stop with these questions. Think comprehensively. What are all the steps or measures you would recommend in audit defense? In addition, what would be your "end game" strategy? That is, what might you do if the audit does not result in agreement? What options would the taxpayer have? How satisfactory or desirable would the various options be? Speaking practically, what approach would be the best for your client on these facts?

In devising the above strategy, there may be factual omissions or ambiguities that you would need to explore. What additional facts would you want from Fred? Why would they matter and how would they influence your strategy?

Chapter 5
ASSESSMENT PROCEDURES AND MATTERS RELATING TO THE STATUTES OF LIMITATIONS ON ASSESSMENT

IRC:	§§ 6201-6204; 6211-6213; 6501 except (f) and (h)–(n); 6503(a); 7421(a); 7454(a); 7481(a), (b); 7485; 7502; 7503; Skim § 702(c)
Cases, etc.:	The Colony, Inc. v. Commissioner, 357 U.S. 28 (1958) Insulglass v. Comm., 84 T.C. 203 (1985) T.C. Rule 142(a), (b)
IRS Forms:	Skim 23-C; 870; 870-AD; 872; 872-A; 872-T; 4549; 8275; 8275-R; RASC Report-006

I. INTRODUCTION

Before the IRS can start to collect taxes, penalties, and interest, it must post the amounts due in the Service's computer system. This process is called assessment. The government does not have an unlimited time to make an assessment. Generally, the IRS has three years from the date the taxpayer files a return to assess taxes it believes are due.[1] There are, however, many exceptions and circumstances that suspend or extend the running of the statute of limitations (SOL). The principal focus of this chapter is to explore the general rule and the exceptions[2] and to consider what happens if the IRS does not make an assessment timely.

The reason it is critical to know whether an assessment was made timely or not is that, unless one of the judicial or statutory rules overrides the statute of

---

[1] If the assessment is timely, the IRS has ten years from the date of assessment to collect the tax administratively. At the end of ten years, the statute of limitations (SOL) on collection expires (referred to as the Collection Statute Expiration Date (CSED)), unless the government takes appropriate judicial action to extend the collection period. Thus, without even considering exceptions that might extend either the Assessment Statute Expiration Date (ASED) or CSED, it is apparent that the IRS can be involved in a client's life for as much as thirteen years. The SOL relative to collection is discussed in Chapter 13.

[2] As one reads the Internal Revenue Code to identify the exceptions and circumstances causing suspension of the SOL on assessment, it is important to distinguish those sections that affect the ASED from those that affect the ten-year collection statute. For example, the Code suspends the collection statute, but not the assessment statute, when offers in compromise (section 6331(k)(3)(B)), installment agreements (section 6331(k)(3)(B)), collection due process hearings (section 6330(e)(1)) and innocent spouse relief (section 6015(e)(2)) are requested.

limitations,[3] an assessment made beyond the Assessment Statute Expiration Date (ASED) is void and uncollectible. This means that the taxpayer does not owe the tax and associated penalties and interest. In other words, the taxpayer enjoys a complete victory without ever having to litigate the merits of the tax return positions at issue.[4]

Whether an assessment has been made and the date it was done are significant for other reasons also.

- It represents the first step in the collection process.

- It is the start of the 240-day period a taxpayer must wait before filing a petition in bankruptcy in order to be eligible for discharge of assessed income tax liabilities.[5]

- It is the date the tax lien comes into existence.[6]

Before proceeding with a discussion of the SOL on assessment, however, it is important to understand how assessments are made, what the different types of assessments are, and what constitutes an adequate return for purposes of starting the SOL clock.

II. HOW AN ASSESSMENT IS MADE

An assessment is nothing more than the recording of a tax debt on the books of a taxing authority. It is similar to what businesses do every day when they enter an account receivable on their books and records for a sale made on credit. Just as businesses first book sales and corresponding receivables before sending out statements of amounts owed, so does the IRS assess the tax owed before making attempts to collect it. Without an assessment and a balance due, any collection action by the Service is premature and inappropriate.

In the federal context, section 6203 and Regulation section 301.6203-1 establish the methodology for assessment. The regulation requires that an assessment officer sign the summary record of assessment.[7] Upon request, taxpayers are entitled to a copy of the record of assessment.[8] In practice, it is rare that one

---

[3] *See* Chapter 10.

[4] If the SOL has expired by the time an assessment is made or collection activity pursued, the taxpayer has an absolute right to the return of money collected subsequent thereto and to have any liens removed. IRC §§ 6325(b), 6401.

[5] 11 U.S.C §§ 507(a)(8)(a)(ii), 523(a)(1)(A). *See* Chapter 13.

[6] *See* Chapter 13.

[7] Originally, the summary record was a Form 23-C; thus, tax professionals often refer to the assessment date as the "23-C date." More recently, the IRS uses a computer-generated RASC Report-006.

[8] Regulation section 301.6203-1 states that "[i]f the taxpayer requests a copy of the record of assessment, he shall be furnished a copy of the pertinent parts of the assessment which set forth the name of the taxpayer, the date of assessment, the character of the liability assessed, the taxable period, if applicable, and the amounts assessed."

needs to see the record of assessment. Rather, a "transcript (or record) of the tax account information" usually provides one with the information needed, such as the dates and amounts of assessments, payments and lien filings.[9]

III. TYPES OF EXCEPTIONS TO THE GENERAL STATUTE OF LIMITATIONS RULE

There are three main types of assessments: (i) automatic or summary, (ii) deficiency, and (iii) jeopardy or termination. The different types of assessments are based principally on when in the tax process they are made and whether the IRS must comply with certain procedures before making them. However, regardless of the *type* of assessment, the *method* of recording it on Form 23-C or RACS Report-006 is identical. As we will see, while any of the assessment types can run afoul of the SOL, disputes typically arise from deficiency assessments, as they take place later in the taxing process.

A. Summary or Automatic Assessments

Our tax system is primarily one of self-assessment. This means that taxpayers initially determine the amount of the assessment. This may be by filing a tax return or making a payment of tax. Since taxpayers acknowledge the amount of the liability, the Code authorizes the government to automatically assess the liability without first having to comply with additional procedures to safeguard taxpayers' rights.

Most of the situations that give rise to automatic assessments involve either self-assessment or common errors taxpayers make when self-assessing. These situations include:

(1) Taxes determined by the taxpayer on a filed return.[10]

(2) The amount of tax paid by the taxpayer.[11]

(3) The tax resulting from a mathematical or clerical error appearing on a taxpayer's return.[12]

---

[9] IRM 3.5.20.15. The request can be made telephonically or by sending the government a letter to that effect or checking the appropriate box on a Form 4506.

[10] IRC § 6201(a)(1).

[11] IRC § 6213(b)(4).

[12] IRC § 6213(b)(1), (g)(2). The Service must send the taxpayer notice of the error and of the right to request abatement of the assessment. If the taxpayer makes the request, the IRS will send a notice of deficiency so the taxpayer can petition the Tax Court for judicial review. Because math errors are common and taxpayers rarely seek to litigate them, Congress believed it was appropriate to permit assessment of the difference automatically and put the onus on the taxpayer to request a different procedure.

(4) Taxes and penalties the taxpayer consents to have assessed by completing a Waiver of Restrictions on Assessment.[13]

Automatic assessments are also permitted with respect to:

(1) Any additional taxes and penalties the IRS asserts are due for which the deficiency procedures do not apply.[14] These primarily encompass employment and excise taxes and related penalties.

(2) Interest, even if it relates to a deficiency assessment, as it more closely resembles the cost of borrowing money than a tax liability.[15]

Summary assessments rarely run afoul of the ASED, as most are made shortly after a return is filed, payment is received or a waiver is executed. They must be made within the three-year period, unless one of the exceptions applies.

B. Deficiency Assessments

A deficiency assessment is one made with respect to *additional* income taxes, gift or estate taxes, or certain excise taxes the IRS determines are due. In the case of income taxes, this is the result of an increase in taxable income attributable to additional income or disallowed deductions or credits following an examination of the taxpayer's return.[16]

Because the IRS seeks to hold the taxpayer responsible for more taxes than agreed to on the filed return and because there are no exigent circumstances that would justify jeopardy procedures, the taxpayer is provided something akin to due process rights, i.e., notice and an opportunity to be heard in a court of law *prior* to the government having the right to take/seize property. Basically, what this means is that the taxpayer is entitled to a notice of deficiency and the right to request review of the deficiency by the Tax Court.

---

[13] IRC § 6213(d). This is accomplished via one of the 870 forms, such as the Form 870, Form 870-AD, or Form 4549.

[14] IRC § 6201(e). The definition of a deficiency in section 6211(a) includes only income taxes, estate and gift taxes, and certain excise taxes. Automatic assessment of deficiencies in these taxes is prohibited. Also not permitted is automatic assessment of (i) the portion of late filing and late payment penalties that are calculated as a percentage of a deficiency and (ii) underestimated tax penalties if no return was filed for the taxable year. IRC §§ 6665(b), 6671(a).

Despite the fact there is no statutory prohibition to automatic assessment of other taxes the IRS asserts are due, the IRS usually offers some level of administrative review before making the assessment. *See, e.g.*, Proc. Reg. § 601.106.

[15] IRC § 6601(e).

[16] *Id.* The deficiency procedures prior to assessment also apply to penalties calculated as a percentage of the deficiency, such as the accuracy-related penalty of section 6662, the fraud penalty of section 6663 and the portion of the late filing/late payment penalty so calculated. Interest, on the other hand, may be added to any assessed amount without formal process.

How do these rights affect assessment? Unless the taxpayer executes a Form 870 (or related form) agreeing to the automatic assessment of the deficiency,[17] section 6213(a) prohibits the IRS from assessing the proposed amount until these rights are afforded the taxpayer. Consequently, the government may not assess the asserted deficiency unless it properly mails a notice of deficiency to the taxpayer and, until expiration of:[18]

(i) The ninety-day period available to the taxpayer to petition the U.S. Tax Court, and,

(ii) If a timely petition was filed by the taxpayer, until the decision of the U.S. Tax Court becomes final.[19]

Since a deficiency assessment happens late in the tax process, usually several years after the return was filed, it is the type of assessment that most often gives rise to the question whether the SOL expired before the assessment was made. Like all taxes, deficiencies must be assessed within the normal three-year period, unless one of the extensions or suspensions applies. While any of these exceptions or suspensions could apply to a deficiency, the one most often encountered is the suspension of the SOL upon issuance of a notice of deficiency found in section 6503.

C. Jeopardy or Termination Assessments

A jeopardy or termination assessment is primarily a collection tool used by the IRS when it believes collection of the tax is in jeopardy. For example, jeopardy action is appropriate if the IRS ascertains that a taxpayer is in the process of either transferring property out of the country or otherwise concealing it, which would leave nothing for the Service to attach. Under such exigent circumstances, sections 6851 and 6861 authorize the IRS to assess and collect the tax immediately. These sections provide that a notice of deficiency be given to the taxpayer after assessment and collection rather than before.

While the issue of whether the SOL has expired before a jeopardy assessment is made is possible, it is rare because there are many levels of review within the Service before such assessments are made. Rather, other issues tend to take cen-

---

[17] IRC § 6213(d).

[18] If the IRS erroneously assesses the tax during the restricted period, the assessment is void and section 6213(a) allows the taxpayer to seek an injunction.

[19] IRC § 6213(a), (c). See IRC § 7481 for when the decision of the Tax Court becomes final. *See also* IRC §§ 7482(a)(3), 7485 (unless an appropriate amount of bond is posted, the IRS may assess the amount determined by the Tax Court even though the taxpayer appeals to a Circuit Court; however, the taxpayer need not have paid the assessment to be entitled to appellate review). To expedite the assessment of a deficiency agreed upon by the parties in a case before the U.S. Tax Court, the taxpayer can execute a Stipulated Settlement, which waives the restriction imposed on the Service to wait until the decision becomes final.

ter stage. Jeopardy and termination assessments are discussed in detail in Chapter 7.

IV. WHAT IS AN "ADEQUATE RETURN" TO START THE STATUTE OF LIMITATIONS?

Because the SOL does not begin to run until the taxpayer files an "adequate return," determining whether such a return has been filed is important. In order for a return to be adequate for this purpose, it must:

- Be signed under penalties of perjury,
- Be on the proper form,
- Be filed correctly, and
- Have sufficient information on it to allow the IRS to calculate tax liability and represent an honest and reasonable attempt by the taxpayer to satisfy the requirements of the tax law.[20]

A. Signed Under Penalties of Perjury

In order for a return to be treated as such for purposes of starting the limitations period, it must be signed by the taxpayer under penalty of perjury.[21] A return sent to the IRS unsigned, or with the *jurat* "under penalties of perjury" crossed out or otherwise modified, is not a return for this or any other purpose.[22]

If a taxpayer has not filed a return within a reasonable time after the due date, the Service will send a notice requesting that the delinquent return be filed. If the taxpayer does not do so, the IRS will prepare a return pursuant to its authority under section 6020(b), with the proposed increase in taxes treated as a deficiency.[23]

This kind of return is called a Substitute for Return (SFR). It does not start the running of the statute of limitations since it is missing the taxpayer's sig-

---

[20] IRC § 6065. *See, e.g.*, Beard v. Commissioner, 82 T.C. 766 (1984), *aff'd*, 793 F.2d 139 (6th Cir. 1986); Field Serv. Adv. 200235002 (4/30/02); Sloan v. Commissioner, 102 T.C. 137 (1994).

[21] Reg. § 1.6012-1(a)(5).

[22] IRC §§ 6061, 6064, 6065. Frequently, a taxpayer will have inadvertently failed to sign a return, only to have it sent back by the IRS. If that happens, the SOL does not begin to run until the return is refiled. Late filing penalties generally will be waived if the return is refiled with a signature within 30 days, as there is reasonable cause for the lateness.

[23] Any deficiency resulting therefrom is entitled to deficiency procedures, since it represents an amount of tax in excess of that to which the taxpayer self-assessed. Spurlock v. Commissioner, 118 T.C. 155 (2002); CCA 200149032.

nature.[24] Despite the misleading language in section 6020(b)(2) that such a return is "prima facie good and sufficient for all purposes," a SFR is the equivalent of no return for SOL purposes. The SFR-generated deficiency can be assessed at any time unless the taxpayer responds to the SFR with a return of his or her own making,[25] thus starting the three-year SOL.

B. Proper Form

To start the SOL, the document mailed must purport to be a return. The return should be on the official form (including authorized computer-generated forms) and not, for example, on a plain piece of paper or on a tampered form.

As a practical matter, filing on the correct form is rarely a problem as courts look to the good faith of the taxpayer to determine if an honest mistake was made. If an honest mistake was made, the return actually filed will be accepted for the return that should have been filed.[26] On the other hand, where a taxpayer alters the official form or uses homemade forms, the IRS may treat the form as not being in "substantial compliance" if there is insufficient data to calculate the tax liability or the line titles are altered or the *jurat* is obliterated.[27]

C. Proper Filing

To be effective for SOL purposes, returns must be filed by either mailing or hand delivering them to the proper office of the Service.[28] Depending on the type of return involved and the residence of the taxpayer or business, different rules apply for determining the correct IRS Service Center. Mailing a return to the local office or handing it to an agent, while normally acceptable, may be treated as improper mailing until it reaches the proper office.[29]

---

24 IRC § 6501(b)(3). The only information used by the Service as the basis for income and expenses when preparing a SFR is what is reported to it on Forms W-2, 1099, and the like.

25 SFRs are notoriously wrong because the IRS does not calculate any deductions, credits or exclusions when it prepares the SFR. A taxpayer can usually reduce the amount of taxable income calculated on the SFR by filing his or her own return.

26 Knollwood Mem'l Gardens v. Commissioner, 46 T.C. 764 (1966). See IRC § 6501(g) for statutory exceptions.

27 Serv. Ctr. Adv. 200107035 (citing Badaracco v. Commissioner, 464 U.S. 386 (1984) and Columbia Gas Sys., Inc. v. United States, 70 F.3d 1244 (Fed. Cir. 1995)).

28 IRC § 6091(b); Winnett v. Commissioner, 96 T.C. 802 (1991). Hand delivery is especially important with certain returns, such as estate and gift tax returns.

29 O'Bryan Bros., Inc. v. Commissioner, 127 F.2d 645 (6th Cir. 1942).

D. Sufficient Information to Calculate the Tax

When a taxpayer prepares a return in good faith and includes relevant items of income and expense, the return is adequate for SOL purposes even if there are mistakes on it. The test to determine if the return includes enough information is whether the return affords the IRS the ability to calculate *a* tax liability, not necessarily the *correct* tax liability.[30]

Whereas most taxpayers make an honest and genuine effort to satisfy the law, a group of persons known as "tax protesters" do not. These individuals use a plethora of techniques to avoid filing returns or avoid reporting income correctly. Some of the more common approaches they use are: claiming that the Fifth Amendment provides them with complete protection against including anything at all on the return;[31] placing zeroes or asterisks on each line of the return; or asserting constitutional objections to the existence of the tax laws.[32] Taxpayers' creative reasons for not reporting income and paying taxes are limited only by their imaginations. Courts uniformly brush aside these frivolous justifications for not filing tax returns. Such "returns" expose the individuals to civil and criminal failure to file penalties.[33]

V. STATUTE OF LIMITATIONS ON ASSESSMENT— GENERAL RULE

Throughout the legal world, statutes of limitations are arbitrary deadlines meant to provide fairness to the parties by keeping old and stale matters from being litigated. The same is true with respect to taxes.[34] Unless the SOL is

---

[30] Germantown Trust Co. v. Commissioner, 309 U.S. 304 (1940).

[31] Some taxpayers fear completing the return, or portions of it, for justifiable reasons. If it can be established that the taxpayer has a legitimate reason to believe that the information supplied on the return might lead to *criminal* sanctions, courts are willing to grant a limited exception to the completeness requirement. For example, if the taxpayer were a drug dealer, it would be reasonable to be concerned that if income as being from the sale of illegal drugs is voluntarily reported, the admission could be used in a drug dealing prosecution. Therefore, it would be appropriate to claim the Fifth Amendment as to the *source*, but not the amount, of any illegal income. Note, however, that where information on a return might subject a taxpayer to *civil* penalty only, the obligation to file a return complete in all respects cannot be avoided. *See, e.g.*, United States v. Barnes, 604 F.2d 121 (2d Cir. 1979).

[32] United States v. Mosel, 738 F.2d 157 (6th Cir.1984); United States v. Rickman, 638 F.2d 182 (10th Cir.1980); United States v. Moore, 627 F.2d 830 (7th Cir.1980). *Cf.* United States v. Long, 618 F.2d 74 (9th Cir.1980).

[33] In addition, under section 6702, such returns are normally considered to be frivolous and not processible. This means that a $500 penalty is assessed, the statute of limitations on assessment does not begin to run, and no interest accrues in the taxpayer's favor. IRC § 6611(g). *See* Rev. Rul. 2005-17 to 2005-21, 2005-14 I.R.B. 817-824.

[34] In the tax context, the SOL not only eliminates litigating old claims but also establishes a reasonable period during which taxpayers must keep records.

extended or suspended, the last day the IRS may make a timely assessment is three years from the *later* of the return's filing date or its due date. In the case of income tax returns for individuals, the due date is 3½ months after the end of the year, normally April 15th.[35] For corporations, the due date is 2½ months after the end of the year, March 15th for a calendar year taxpayer.[36]

A. Late Filed Returns

For a return filed after the due date, including any extensions that might have been granted, the assessment period runs three years from the date of filing. Consequently, the SOL for a 2006 individual income tax return filed on December 12, 2007, would extend to December 12, 2010.[37]

B. Early Returns

A return filed before the due date is deemed filed on the due date for SOL purposes.[38] Thus, the ASED for a 2006 individual income tax return filed on February 25, 2007, would be April 15, 2010.

C. Due Date on Weekend or Holiday

If the due date for filing a tax return falls on a weekend or holiday, section 7503 extends it until the next business day. This modification of the due date gives taxpayers one or two extra days to file. For example, individual income tax

---

[35] IRC § 6072(a). Where a husband and wife originally did not file a joint return but elect to do so later, sections 6013(b)(3) and (4) establish the date the joint return is deemed filed for purposes of the SOL on assessment and collection. In no event, shall it be less than one year from the date of the joint filing.

[36] IRC § 6072(b). Due dates for other returns are found in sections 6072 and 6075.

[37] When computing time periods for tax purposes, the day on which the event happens is excluded. Burnet v. Willingham Loan & Trust Co., 282 U.S. 437 (1931). The counting begins with the next day. A month is a calendar month and a year is a calendar year. A year means a twelve-month period, regardless whether it contains 365 or 366 days. Rev. Rul. 72-42, 1972-1 C.B. 398.

For example, assume one wished to determine certain time periods following July 17, 2007. In all cases, July 18, 2007, is day #1.

- Thirty days after July 17, 2007, is August 16, 2007.
- One month after July 17, 2007, is August 17, 2007.
- Ninety days after July 17, 2007, is October 15, 2007.
- Three months after July 17, 2007, is October 17, 2007.
- One year after July 17, 2007, is July 17, 2008.
- Three years after July 17, 2007, is July 17, 2010.

[38] IRC § 6501(b)(1).

returns for the 2007 year would be due April 17, 2008, if April 15, 2008 were a Saturday.

Section 7503 does not affect the starting date from which the running of the SOL on assessment is measured, however. The traditional due date and the actual filing date are what control. For example, if a 2007 return were filed on April 1, 2008, the return would be deemed filed early and the Service would only have until April 15, 2011, three years from the "regular" filing date to assess. With respect to a return received by the Service on April 27, 2008, the ASED of April 27, 2011 is likewise unaffected by section 7503.[39]

D. The Mailbox Rule of Section 7502

A return is normally considered filed when it is received by the IRS.[40] As discussed in Chapter 2, a different rule applies when a return is mailed on or before the due date, but not received until after it. Section 7502, which is the statutory embodiment of the common law "mailbox rule,"[41] states that the U.S. Postmark date[42] "shall be deemed to be the date of delivery or the date of payment" when a timely mailed return is received by the government after its due date.[43]

While the principal focus of the "timely-mailed is timely-filed" rule is to consider returns received after the due date as timely filed, thus avoiding the late filing penalty, it also establishes the filing date for purposes of the running of the SOL. For example, if a 2007 return is mailed April 15, 2008, and received by the IRS on April 18, 2008, the mailing date would be deemed the filing date. An assessment on April 18, 2011, three years from the date of receipt, would be untimely.[44]

---

[39] Brown v. United States, 391 F.2d 653 (Ct. Cl., 1968); Rev. Rul. 81-269, 1981-2 C.B. 243.

[40] First Charter Financial Corp. v. United States, 669 F.2d 1342 (9th Cir. 1982).

[41] In some cases, the common law "mailbox rule" may be broader than section 7502. It is not entirely clear whether the common law rule still can be asserted by the taxpayer or whether it has been preempted by section 7502. *See, e.g.*, Sorrentino v. United States, 383 F.3d 1187 (10th Cir. 2004) (holding that the common law rule is not supplanted); Prop. Reg. § 301.7502-1.

[42] Section 7502(f) treats delivery to certain "designated delivery services," such as FedEx, the same as delivery to the U.S. Post Office. In addition, with respect to returns e-filed, Regulation section 301.7502-1(d) provides that the timely mailed/timely filed rule applies as of the date an "authorized electronic return transmitter" electronically postmarks the return.

[43] Taxpayers should be advised to mail their returns by certified or registered mail, return receipt requested, or its designated delivery service equivalent, as doing so provides proof of mailing and is prima facie evidence of delivery.

[44] Hotel Equities Corp. v. Commissioner, 546 F.2d 725 (7th Cir. 1976). Section 7502 also applies if the due date for the tax return was extended to August 15, 2008, and the return was placed in the mail on August 15th but not received until August 17th. However, section 7502 does not apply (and the regular "date-received is date-filed" rule applies) if, in the preceding example, the return was mailed July 10, 2008, and received July 13, 2008.

E. Returns Filed Pursuant to an Extension to File

If a taxpayer requests an extension of time to file a tax return, all the rules discussed above, except the early return rule, apply with equal force. Thus, the three-year statute for a return filed on July 17, 2008, for which an extension was granted to October 15, 2008, would expire on July 17, 2011, not October 15, 2011.

F. Amended Returns

The date the original return is filed establishes the starting date for the running of the SOL. Amended returns, *filed after the due date*,[45] do not affect the statute of limitations.[46] In *Badaracco v. Commissioner*,[47] the taxpayer filed timely but fraudulent returns for the tax years 1965-1969. In 1971, he filed non-fraudulent amended returns and paid the additional taxes. Six years later, the Commissioner issued notices of deficiency for these years. The taxpayer argued that the amended returns started the running of the three-year statute and superseded the application of section 6501(c)(1), which allows assessment at any time in the case of a false or fraudulent return. The Supreme Court disagreed. "Nothing is present in the statute that can be construed to suspend its operation in the light of a fraudulent filer's subsequent repentant conduct. Neither is there anything in the wording of section 6501(a) that itself enables a taxpayer to reinstate the section's general 3-year limitations period by filing an amended return."[48]

G. Penalties and Interest

Penalties and interest are generally assessed and collected in the same manner as the underlying tax.[49] For example, if a certain tax can be assessed automatically, a penalty related to that tax can be assessed automatically also. This rule of symmetry between taxes and their associated penalties and interest extends to the SOL. Thus, if the SOL for a tax expires after three years, the SOL

---

[45] A corrected return filed before the due date is not treated as an amended return for SOL purposes. Instead, such a return is treated as a substitute return and replaces, rather than amends, the original.

[46] Though filing an amended return will not affect the ASED, it may still be wise to file it and pay the tax due for several reasons: it may be deemed a voluntary disclosure for criminal purposes (so long as the IRS has not yet begun its investigation); it may keep the IRS criminal investigative division away from the taxpayer; and, it may be treated as a "qualified amended return" resulting in the elimination of certain accuracy related penalties. *See* Reg. § 1.6664-2(c).

[47] 464 U.S. 386 (1984).

[48] *Id.* at 393.

[49] IRC §§ 6665(a), 6671, 6601(e)(1), 6601(g).

for assessing penalties and interest on that tax likewise expires after three years.[50]

VI. EXCEPTIONS TO THE GENERAL STATUTE OF LIMITATIONS RULE

A. The Taxpayer Agreement/Waiver Exception

The most frequent reason the SOL extends beyond the normal three years is because the taxpayer consents to its extension. This is accomplished by executing a Form 872 or 872-A (or one of its kin).[51] Extensions are available for all taxes, except estate taxes. In order for the extension to be valid, the taxpayer and the IRS must execute the extension agreement within the limitations period.[52] Once validly extended, the assessment SOL can be extended further in the same manner.

The IRS and the taxpayer sometimes disagree about the meaning of language in particular agreements. In the case of agreements that purport to extend the limitations period, courts typically conceptualize such agreements as unilateral waivers, not contracts. However, contract-like principles often are employed in construing the language of such agreements.[53]

Chapter 4 contains a complete discussion of whether to extend the SOL and, if so, which form to sign.

B. The 25% Nonfraudulent Omission of Income Exception

Employing its authority under section 6501(e), the IRS occasionally will assert that a six-year SOL applies to a return. The six-year SOL applies if a taxpayer omits gross income from the return, and the amount of the omission is greater than 25% of the amount of gross income reported on the return.[54] For

---

[50] There is no SOL for assessing penalties under sections 6694(b) (a willful attempt in any manner to understate the liability for tax by a person who is an income tax return preparer), 6700 (promoting abusive tax shelters), and 6701 (aiding and abetting understatement of tax liability). I.R.M. 20.1.6.1.8. There are special rules for the sections 6694(a) and 6695 penalties on return preparers in section 6696(d)(1).

[51] IRC § 6501(c)(4). With respect to partnerships and S corprations, similar agreements are available.

[52] If a taxpayer filed a Chapter 7 bankruptcy petition, the debtor, not the trustee, is the appropriate person to execute a waiver with respect to prepetition tax debts. ILM 200210032.

[53] *See generally* John A. Townsend & Lawrence R. Jones, Jr., *Interpreting Consents to Extend the Statute of Limitations*, 98 Tax Notes Today 16-108 (Jan. 26, 1998).

[54] For estate and gift taxes, the 25% yardstick relates to items that were omitted from the gross estate or total gifts. IRC § 6501(e)(2). For excise taxes, the 25% omission is with respect to tax that should have been reported. IRC § 6501(e)(3).

the six-year statute to apply, it does not matter whether the omission was intentional, negligent, or accidental. The determination is simply mathematical. Of course, if the omission was fraudulent, the unlimited SOL of section 6501(c) applies instead.

1. Avoiding the Extended Statute of Limitations By Adequate Disclosure

Though determination of a 25% omission is initially mathematical, things in tax law are rarely that simple. The IRS is given the extra three years to make an assessment when a substantial amount of income has been omitted because discovering omitted income is more difficult and time-consuming than auditing deductions and credits reflected on the return.

However, if the taxpayer provided enough information on the return to inform the IRS that there might be an omission, the Service is no longer at a disadvantage. Thus, section 6501(e)(1)(A)(ii) states that an item will not be treated as omitted *for purposes of the 25% test*[55] "if such amount is disclosed in the return, or in a statement attached to the return, in a manner adequate to apprise the Secretary of the nature and amount of such item."

Proving adequate disclosure is the taxpayer's burden. The statute requires disclosure of both the nature and amount of the item omitted; it does not require disclosure of all the relevant facts affecting the item's treatment.[56] Each case is unique. Depending on how complicated and detailed the transaction involved was, different levels of disclosure are expected.[57]

The seminal case on what constitutes adequate disclosure is *Colony, Inc. v. Commissioner*.[58] In *Colony*, the taxpayer had understated the gross profits on the sales of certain lots of land as a result of having overstated its basis due to having including in its cost certain unallowable items of development expense. The Court held that inclusion of the amount of income, though incorrect, and disclosure of the source gave the IRS sufficient notice (a "clue") to examine the income item. Though the *Colony* decision preceded enactment of the present dis-

---

[55] While an adequately disclosed omission is not taken into account for purposes of section 6501(e), it is, nevertheless, still part of the deficiency if the taxpayer cannot establish the SOL has expired.

[56] The disclosure required under section 6501(e)(1)(A)(ii) is not identical to the disclosure required to avoid certain accuracy-related penalties under section 6662(d)(2)(B)(ii)(I). Schmidt v. Commissioner, T.C. Memo 1989-188 (holding the disclosure required under section 6501 is less than that required under section 6662, citing staff explanations accompanying the 1982 enactment of the predecessor of section 6662 in Tax Equity and Fiscal Responsibility Act of 1982 (TEFRA)).

[57] *See, e.g.*, CC&F W. Operations, Ltd. P'ship v. Commissioner, T.C. Memo 2000-286, *aff'd*, 273 F.3d 402 (1st Cir. 2001).

[58] 357 U.S. 28 (1958).

closure requirement in section 6501(e)(1)(A)(ii), the "clue" standard continues to apply.

Where the omitted item of gross income relates to a flow-through entity, such as a partnership or S corporation, the entity's return and the disclosure thereon must also be considered.[59] However, for disclosures on the entity's return to be considered adequate vis-à-vis an owner, the owner's Form 1040 must notify the IRS that the owner is an investor in the entity.[60]

2. Avoiding the Extended Statute of Limitations By Referencing the Definition of Gross Income

Gross income is the measuring stick for both what was included on the return and what was omitted. As used in section 6501(e), gross income generally has the same meaning as in section 61. Thus, gross income is not reduced by any above or below the line deductions, such as losses from a business or losses from property transactions or for any other expenses.[61]

The definitions of gross income in section 61 and section 6501(e) part company, however, with respect to how income from an activity that qualifies as a "trade or business" is treated.[62] Under section 61, gross income from a business is computed by reducing gross receipts by the cost of sales or services and proceeds from the sale of business property by its basis.[63] For purposes of section 6501(e)(1)(A)(i), gross income has no such offsets.

> **Example:** Julius has gross receipts and costs from an activity, as follows:

---

[59] IRC § 702(c); Benderoff v. United States, 398 F.2d 132 (8th Cir. 1968).

[60] Reuter v. Commissioner, T.C. Memo 1985-607.

[61] Chief Counsel Notice 200609024.

[62] Insulglass Corp. v. Commissioner, 84 T.C. 203 (1985).

[63] Connelly v. Commissioner, T.C. Memo 1982-644. One should review section 61 to remind oneself what is included in the definition of gross income. Significantly, it only includes *income* from a business and *gains* from dealings in property. Expenses of a business or losses from dealings in property are "above-the-line" deductions per section 62, despite the way they are presented on the tax return for the IRS' convenience. In addition, gains from dealings in property mean that the adjusted basis and expenses of sale reduce the gross proceeds.

Chief Counsel Advice 200537029 (overstating basis for the sale of property used in a trade or business results in an omission of gross income for purposes of the six-year period because gross income is determined after reducing sales proceeds by basis, except in the case of a sale of a good or service; the sale of property used in a trade or business is not a sale of a good or service for such purposes. Also a disclosure is adequate if the omission is apparent from the face of the return to a "reasonable man.").

Gross Receipts Reported on Return	Cost of Sales or Basis Reported on Return	Gross Receipts Omitted from Return	Cost of Sales or Basis Omitted from Return
$1,500,000	$1,200,000	$350,000	$250,000

If the activity does not rise to the level of a trade or business, the amount of gross income reported on the return is $300,000 ($1,500,000 less $1,200,000); gross income omitted is $100,000 ($350,000 less $250,000), or 33%. If the activity qualifies as a trade or business, the gross income (for this purpose, gross receipts without reduction for cost of sales) reported is $1,500,000 and the omission is $350,000, only 23%.

As was true with respect to the disclosure exception, flow-through entities in which the taxpayer is an investor are treated as part of the taxpayer's return. The Code and a variety of cases hold that the taxpayer's pro-rata percentage of the gross receipts from the entity's business is added to both the "included" and "omitted" gross income calculations on the taxpayer's individual tax return.[64]

> **Example:** Assume the facts in the previous example, and that Julius also was a 10% partner in a partnership that reported gross receipts of $100,000,000. Assume further that the partnership did not omit any income on its return. According to the line of cases discussed above, $10,000,000, 10% of the partnership income, would be added to Julius' reported income, bringing the total to $11,500,000. Therefore, before the six-year statute would apply, Julius would have had to omit more than $2,875,000 (25% of $11,500,000) from gross income on his individual return.

C. The Fraud Exception

If a taxpayer[65] files a tax return that is false or fraudulent with the intent to evade tax, no time limit is imposed on when assessment may occur.[66] The IRS

---

64 IRC §§ 702(c) (partnerships), 1366(c) (S corporations); Roschuni v. Commissioner, 44 T.C. 80 (1965); Rev. Rul. 55-415, 1955-1 C.B. 412. *See also* Harlan v. Commissioner, 116 T.C. 31 (2001) (the rule applies to all partnerships, no matter what tier they are).

65 The IRS has also held that fraud committed by one's return preparer can affect the ASED. FSA 200126019.

66 What constitutes fraud and the defenses thereto for purposes of section 6501(c)(1) are the same as those which apply for criminal and civil fraud penalties under sections 6663 and 7201. A discussion of penalties is available in Chapter 11 of this text.

can pursue the taxpayer at any time in the future.[67] The IRS has the burden of affirmatively pleading and proving the existence of fraud by "clear and convincing" evidence (rather than by a "preponderance of the evidence").[68] However, once the IRS meets its burden regarding the fraud, the normal rules apply as to the amount of the tax liability, i.e., the taxpayer has the burden of overcoming the presumption of correctness that attaches to the deficiency determination of the IRS. The student is directed to Chapter 11B for a detailed discussion of what constitutes fraud.

D. Suspended Statute of Limitations Due to the Issuance of a Notice of Deficiency

As a matter of fairness and quasi-due process, the Code provides that before the IRS can assess additional tax, the taxpayer is entitled to a notice of the proposed deficiency.[69] With this "ticket," the taxpayer has ninety days to petition the Tax Court for a hearing on the matter without first having to pay the proposed deficiency amount.

Since the IRS may not make an assessment during this period, fairness dictates that this time should not be counted toward the government's three-year assessment period. Thus, section 6503 provides that the running of the SOL is suspended until either (i) the ninety-day period lapses and no petition is filed or (ii) if a petition is filed, the decision of the court regarding liability becomes final. In addition, the IRS is given a sixty-day window after the expiration of the later of the preceding two events to take whatever assessment action is needed.

> **Example:** Carol filed her 2005 Form 1040 timely on April 15, 2006. On April 15, 2009, the IRS mailed Carol a Notice of Deficiency as required by section 6212. The IRS may not assess the tax at any time earlier than July 14, 2009, as Carol has the right to petition the Tax Court for a pre-assessment redetermination until that time.
>
> If Carol does not petition the Court within the allotted ninety days, the IRS then has sixty days from July 14 to September 12, 2009, to

---

[67] By contrast, if the taxpayer initially failed to file, even if with the intent to defraud, the subsequent filing of a correct return starts the normal three-year period to make an assessment. Rev. Rul. 79-178, 1979-1 C.B. 435 (a case where the taxpayer did not timely file an income tax return in a willful attempt to evade income tax but, after an IRS investigation began, filed a correct, but delinquent, return).

[68] IRC § 7454(a); Christians v. Commissioner, T.C. Memo 2003-130. Once the IRS has met its burden to prove fraud for SOL purposes, it has automatically also met its burden for civil fraud purposes. If the fraudulent intent to evade was evidenced by the non-filing of a return rather than the fraudulent filing of a return, the unlimited nature of the SOL can be cut to three years from the first filing of a late correct return. Bennett v. Commissioner, 30 T.C. 114 (1958).

[69] The taxpayer is entitled to these procedures under section 6211-6213. However, the taxpayer may waive the right to a notice and/or to filing a petition to the Tax Court by executing an appropriate form, like a Form 870, 4549, or 1902-B.

assess the deficiency. If, on the other hand, Carol timely petitions the court and the court's decision is entered November 7, 2010, the IRS is precluded from assessing until February 5, 2011, the day the decision became final. At that point, the sixty-day window begins to run, giving the IRS from February 6 to April 6, 2011 to make a timely assessment.

Example: Assume the same facts as above except that the IRS issued the notice of deficiency on March 31, 2009, when fifteen days remained on the normal three-year SOL. Those fifteen days are added to the sixty-day window for assessment provided in section 6503. Thus, if Carol does not petition the Tax Court, the IRS' window for assessment would begin June 30, 2009 (the day following the ninety days to petition) and end on September 12, 2009 (75 days later).[70]

E. Other Frequent Exceptions/Suspensions

1. The Taxpayer Assistance Order (TAO)

In this era of substantive and procedural tax complexity, it is not uncommon for a taxpayer to find his or her wages unexpectedly levied upon by the IRS. This often creates a hardship for the taxpayer, such as being unable to pay rent or buy food. In such situations, the taxpayer may file a Form 911 (Application for a Taxpayer Assistance Order) asking the Taxpayer Advocate's office to intervene. Doing so suspends all limitations periods from the date the application is received by the Taxpayer Advocate until a decision is reached, plus whatever period is specified in the TAO.[71]

2. Bankruptcy

A debtor/taxpayer who files under Title 11 for bankruptcy relief is entitled to the benefits of the automatic stay provisions. Among other restrictions, prior to October 21, 1994, the IRS could not assess a tax debt until the automatic stay was lifted. Therefore, the SOL on assessment was suspended for the entire period of the stay, plus sixty days.[72] Currently, however, 11 U.S.C. section 362(b)(9)(D) permits the IRS to assess outstanding taxes unrestricted by the automatic stay; consequently, section 6503(h) has little current significance.[73] *See* Chapter 13.

---

[70] Aufleger v. Commissioner, 99 T.C. 109, 117-119 (1992).

[71] IRC § 7811(d).

[72] IRC § 6503(h).

[73] *But see* Rev. Rul. 2003-80, 2003-2 C.B. 83 (IRC § 6503(h) has continued vitality in certain situations where the IRS issued a notice of deficiency).

3. Third-party Summons

An extended statute of limitations might result where the IRS issued a John Doe summons or a third party summons for which the taxpayer is entitled to notice under section 7609.[74] If the taxpayer institutes, or intervenes in, a proceeding with respect to the enforcement of the summons, the SOL on assessment is suspended during the period of the proceeding and appeal regarding the summons.[75]

4. Transferee Liability

The SOL for the assessment of taxes, interest, and penalties against transferees and fiduciaries, as provided in section 6901, is longer than that regarding the taxpayer. According to section 6901(c), the SOL is one year longer for each transferee than it is for the immediately prior transferor, up to an additional three years. *See* Chapter 15.

5. Partnership Items

The statutory scheme for the audit and litigation of partnership tax items was revised by the enactment of the Tax Equity and Fiscal Responsibility Act of 1982, Pub.L. No. 98-248, 96 Stat. 324, 648-671 (1998). It created a single unified procedure for determining the tax treatment of all partnership items at the partnership level, rather than separately at the partner level.

Section 6229 provides that, except as otherwise provided in that section, such as fraud or a 25% omission of gross income on the partnership return, "the period for assessing any tax imposed by subtitle A with respect to any person which is attributable to any partnership item (or affected item) for a partnership taxable year shall not expire before the date which is 3 years after the later of (1) the date on which the partnership return for such taxable year was filed, or (2) the last day for filing such return for such year (determined without regard to extensions)." Courts are in accord that where section 6229 and 6501 both have application because of the timing involved in assessing a partnership item, section 6229 provides a *minimum* period of time for the assessment of any tax attributable to partnership items notwithstanding the period provided for in section 6501, which is ordinarily the *maximum* period for the assessment of any tax. Rhone-Poulene Surfactants & Specialties, L.P. v. Commissioner, 114 T.C.

---

[74] Prop. Reg. § 301.7609-5.

[75] IRC § 7609(e). However, to extend the SOL on assessment, the summons must have been issued to determine a deficiency and have a substantive tax purpose. A challenge to a summons issued for collection purposes only does not extend the SOL on assessment. Chief Counsel Advice 20050001.

533, 542 (2000); Grapevine Imports, Ltd. v. United States, 71 Fed. Cl. 324 (2006).

6. Listed Transactions

Section 814 of the American Jobs Creation Act of 2004[76] amended section 6501(c) by adding a new paragraph (10). Section 6501(c)(10) provides that the limitations period on assessment with respect to a listed transaction that the taxpayer fails to disclose, as required under section 6011 (an "undisclosed listed transaction"), shall not expire before one year after the earlier of (A) the date on which the Secretary is furnished the information required under section 6011, or (B) the date that a material advisor meets the requirements of section 6112 with respect to a request by the Secretary under section 6112 relating to the undisclosed listed transaction. Section 6501(c)(10) is effective for taxable years with respect to which the limitations period on assessment did not expire prior to October 22, 2004.

A "listed transaction" as a reportable transaction that is the same as, or substantially similar to, a transaction identified by the Secretary as a tax avoidance transaction for section 6011. Generally, if a taxpayer is required to disclose information regarding the transaction, the taxpayer must complete Form 8886, Reportable Transaction Disclosure Statement, for each listed transaction and attach the Form 8886 to the taxpayer's return for each year in which the taxpayer participated in the listed transaction.[77] A copy of the disclosure statement must also be sent to the Office of Tax Shelter Analysis (OTSA) at the same time that any disclosure statement is first filed by the taxpayer.[78] The Form 886 must provide the information requested and be completed in accordance with the instructions to the form.[79]

Section 6112 requires material advisors to maintain lists of investors and other information with respect to reportable transactions, including listed transactions, and to furnish that information to the Secretary upon request.

Rev. Proc. 2005-26,[80] provides additional ways for the taxpayer or material advisor to disclose a listed transaction to start the running of the SOL.

---

[76] Pub. L. No. 108-357, 118 Stat. 1418 (2004).

[77] *See* Treas. Reg. § 1.6011-4(e).

[78] *See* Treas. Reg. § 1.6011-4(d), (e).

[79] *See* Treas. Reg. § 1.6011-4(d).

[80] 2005-17 I.R.B. 965.

7. Others

There are at least a dozen Code sections in which the SOL on assessment is suspended until, or shall not expire before, a certain period after, the taxpayer notifies the IRS of the occurrence of an event. For example, in connection with losses from certain activities, section 183(e) provides:

> If a taxpayer makes an election under paragraph (1) with respect to an activity, the statutory period for the assessment of any deficiency attributable to such activity shall not expire before the expiration of 2 years after the date prescribed by law (determined without extensions) for filing the return of tax under chapter 1 for the last taxable year in the period of 5 taxable years (or 7 taxable years) to which the election relates. Such deficiency may be assessed notwithstanding the provisions of any law or rule of law which would otherwise prevent such an assessment.

Similar provisions exist in sections 453(e)(8), 547(f), 860(h), 982(e), 1033, 1042 (f), 2032A(f), 2055(e), 2056(d), 6038A(e), 6501(c)(8) & (10), 6872, 7507(c), and 7611(d).

VII. PLEADING THE STATUTE OF LIMITATIONS AND BURDEN OF PROOF

A. Spotting a Potential Statute of Limitations Issue

The first clue to a possible violation of the ASED is that the government is proposing to make an assessment more than three years beyond the due date of the return in question. For example, if the IRS mailed a notice of deficiency on November 18, 2006, with respect to a 2002 tax return, a SOL issue appears to be present.

The notices of adjustment or deficiency issued by the Service may provide possible answers to why things appear untimely. For example, if the IRS is proposing a late filing penalty in the notice, this would suggest that the return was filed late and that the three-year assessment period was to begin later than the due date. Likewise, if the Service is asserting the omission of a large amount of income, this signals that the six-year ASED for a substantial omission of gross income under section 6501(e) may apply.

B. Pleading the Statute of Limitations

The purported expiration of the SOL is an affirmative defense the taxpayer has to raise. Normally this is done informally with the revenue agent during the examination of the return.[81] However, if the issue cannot be resolved informally and the matter proceeds to trial, the taxpayer must raise it in the pleadings. While the issue of the SOL is typically raised when the petition or complaint is first filed,[82] the taxpayer may amend the pleadings at any time during the proceedings with the court's permission.[83] The SOL is usually decided by a motion for summary judgment or by a motion to dismiss. If the taxpayer fails to timely raise the SOL defense, it will be held to have been waived.

> **Example:** The IRS mails the notice of deficiency to Lauri at an address other than the section 6212-required "last known address." Lauri does not receive the notice within the ninety days required to petition the Tax Court. The first time Lauri learns of the notice of deficiency is during the IRS' collection efforts. By this time, we'll assume, the three-year SOL has expired. Even though the ninety-day period to file a petition has run, Lauri may file a petition raising the expiration of SOL in the pleadings. The IRS typically will file a motion to dismiss claiming the ninety-day filing period expired. Lauri will file a motion to dismiss claiming the SOL expired. Her claim would be that because the notice of deficiency was mailed incorrectly, it was void and did not suspend the SOL. In this situation, the case will never go to trial but will, instead, be decided by the court when it grants the motion to dismiss of one of the parties.

C. Burden of Proof

The burden of proof with respect to SOL issues is with the party raising the affirmative defense, i.e., the taxpayer.[84] As will be seen, while the burden of going forward switches between the parties, the burden of ultimate persuasion never shifts from the party who pleads the bar of the statute of limitations.

The taxpayer has the first burden of going forward. He or she must establish the date of filing and the date the Service assessed the tax or issued the notice of deficiency.[85] If the taxpayer makes a prima facie showing that more than

---

[81] Most often an undeniable violation of the ASED by the IRS can be resolved administratively. A phone call to the responsible IRS employee or to the Taxpayer Advocate's Office is usually sufficient. If that does not resolve the matter, one might have to appeal the case to a supervisor and so forth up the chain of command. Other administrative approaches include filing an offer in compromise or a refund claim, requesting either a refund (if the tax has already been paid) or an abatement (if not).

[82] *See, e.g.*, Tax Ct. R. 39.

[83] Permission to amend the pleadings is typically granted unless the IRS would be unduly prejudiced, such as could happen if inadequate time would exist for needed factual development. Tax Ct. Rule 41 ("leave [to amend the petition] shall be given freely when justice so requires"); Balunas v. Commissioner, 546 F.2d 415 (3d Cir 1976) (Third Circuit suggested that on remand, a pro se taxpayer be permitted to amend his petition to raise the bar of the statute).

[84] Tax Ct. R. 39, 142(a).

[85] Adler v. Commissioner, 85 T.C. 535 (1985).

three years have elapsed between the two events, the burden of going forward shifts to the IRS. The government must plead and prove the application of an exception.[86] The Service might, for example, introduce a timely completed Form 872 signed by the taxpayer evidencing a valid extension of the SOL. Normally, the IRS must prove the application of an exception by a preponderance of the evidence. However, if the government seeks to establish fraud as the basis for the exception, its burden is by the clear and convincing evidence standard.[87]

If the Service succeeds in establishing that an exception applies, the burden of going forward with the evidence returns to the taxpayer to show that the alleged exception is invalid or otherwise not applicable. This might be established, for example, by proving that the Form 872 extending the statute was signed by the taxpayer under duress.

D. Res Judicata and Collateral Estoppel

Res judicata and collateral estoppel[88] sometimes play a role in meeting one's burden of proof in SOL situations. The IRS sometimes invokes them to obviate the need to prove certain facts a second time. For example, assume the government previously won a criminal fraud conviction under section 7201 against the taxpayer. During a civil tax proceeding to gain the section 6663 penalty or the unlimited SOL of section 6501(c), the taxpayer would be collaterally estopped from denying that the tax returns were fraudulent and that he or she did so with the intent to evade tax.[89] The reason is that once having met the higher "beyond a reasonable doubt" standard of proof, the government does not have to present the evidence again in a trial where the standard of proof is lower, i.e., "clear and convincing."

---

[86] Harlan v. Commissioner, 116 T.C. 31, 39 (2001).

[87] IRC § 7454. If the Service meets its burden to establish fraud for purposes of the SOL, it automatically also meets its burden to establish that the fraud penalty under section 6663 should be imposed.

[88] The doctrine of res judicata bars relitigating the same cause of action. The doctrine applies to a claim if it was, or could have been, litigated as part of the cause of action in a prior case. The doctrine of collateral estoppel, or issue preclusion, provides that once an issue of fact or law is "actually and necessarily determined by a court of competent jurisdiction, that determination is conclusive in subsequent suits based on a different cause of action involving a party to the prior litigation." For collateral estoppel to apply, resolution of the disputed issue must have been essential to the prior decision. Morse v. Commissioner, T.C. Memo 2003-332.

[89] Courts unanimously agree with this proposition, so long as apples are compared to apples, i.e., that the elements of the crime proven in the criminal prosecution are the same elements the government must prove in the civil case to establish an exception to the SOL. For example, the elements for fraud under sections 7201 (criminal) and 6663 (civil) and under section 6501(c) (S.O.L.) are the same and therefore satisfy this requirement. The elements to gain a section 7206(1) conviction (criminal perjury) and those for civil fraud, on the other hand, are not alike. Thus the I.R.S cannot rely on res judicata or collateral estoppel based on the perjury conviction and must prove fraud in the civil case. Wright v. Commissioner, 84 T.C. 636 (1985).

The IRS can also invoke collateral estoppel to avoid having to reprove certain facts already adjudicated in another court. For example, if a state court found an individual guilty of embezzlement in the amount of $400,000, the IRS need not prove either the fact of embezzlement or its amount in a civil tax case. The government would, nevertheless, still have to prove that fraud, rather than negligence, caused the non-reporting.[90]

These doctrines are not always available to the parties. For example, a taxpayer might wish to use them as a shield during a civil proceeding where the IRS *unsuccessfully* prosecuted the taxpayer criminally for tax evasion. In such a case, the taxpayer would argue that since the government failed to prove fraud in the criminal tax proceeding, the IRS is precluded from trying to prove fraud during the civil phase of the tax matter. Courts, however, are unanimous in holding that neither res judicata nor collateral estoppel applies in this situation. In a criminal case, the Service must prove fraud "beyond a reasonable doubt," but in the civil proceeding the government's burden is the lower "clear and convincing" standard. Merely because the government could not convince a jury of the taxpayer's *criminal* intent to evade tax does not mean it cannot convince the trier of fact of the fraud in the *civil* matter.

E. Joint Return Filers

Assuming it is decided that one of the exceptions to the SOL on assessment applies, the tax liability for the entire return is open to determination. The liability is not determined on an individual taxpayer basis. Thus, for example, if a couple filed a joint return and one of them committed fraud,[91] the IRS may examine the return positions of both spouses.[92] What this means is that if the IRS ultimately prevails on the SOL issue, both spouses are put to their burden of proof on the underlying tax.

> **Example:** Assume that five years after the joint return was filed, the IRS sought to prove that Claudia fraudulently omitted income. Assume further that the IRS sought to prove that various deductions taken by her husband, Alex, were erroneous. If the IRS cannot establish that Claudia was fraudulent or that one of the other SOL exceptions applies, the SOL for the year under review will have expired and neither Claudia nor Alex would be liable for any of the proposed adjustments. On the other hand, if the IRS were successful in proving Claudia's fraud, the correctness of the entire tax return would be in issue. Therefore, not

---

[90] Allen v. McCurry, 449 U.S. 90 (1980); Meier v. Commissioner, 91 T.C. 273, 286 (1988).

[91] The fraud penalty, rather than the tax itself, attaches only to the person(s) who were fraudulent. IRC § 6663(c).

[92] Benjamin v. Commissioner, 66 T.C. 1084 (1976), *aff'd*, 592 F.2d 1259 (5th Cir. 1979). However, if only one spouse signed an extension agreement, the SOL is extended as to that spouse only, not as to the other (non-signing) spouse as well. Tallal v. Commissioner, 77 T.C. 1291 (1981).

only would the adjustments attributable to Claudia be scrutinized but those solely attributable to Alex would also be swept into the controversy.

PROBLEMS

The following questions raise hypothetical situations dealing with the 2005 income tax return of Mike and Sue Wilson. Unless the question otherwise requests, give the *latest* date on which the Internal Revenue Service may validly assess the tax and/or penalties of Mike and Sue. [In other words, as of what date will the action be untimely and barred by statute?]

a. The Wilson's 2005 tax return Form 1040 was:

   (i)   Mailed to the IRS on March 7, 2006 and received March 10, 2006.

   (ii)   Mailed to the IRS on April 17, 2006, (using a private meter and Post Office box at Sue Wilson's employer) and received by the IRS on April 21, 2006. It should be noted that April 15, 2006, was on a Saturday.

   (iii)   Never filed.

   (iv)   The Wilsons had inserted the words "Denial and Disclaimer attached as part of this form" below the jurat and above their signatures on the Form 1040, and attached a statement entitled "Denial and Disclaimer" in which taxpayers denied liability for income tax. Otherwise the return was complete and correct and the tax shown was paid when the return was filed on April 15, 2006.

b. The return was filed on April 15, 2006.

   (i)   A Form 872 was executed on April 15, 2009 extending the statute of limitations to December 31, 2009.

      (a)   Same as (i), except the Form 872 was executed on April 16, 2009.

   (ii)   A Form 872-A was executed on March 31, 2009. Mike and Sue sent the Internal Revenue Service a notice of termination of the agreement on October 25, 2009, which was received October 27, 2009.

   (iii)   The IRS mailed a notice of deficiency in tax of $5,000 on April 15, 2009.

      (a)   The Wilsons petition the Tax Court July 18, 2009.

      (b)   The Wilsons petition the Tax Court June 22, 2009, an opinion is handed down April 1, 2010, and a decision of the court is entered on May 12, 2010.

(c) The Wilsons receive a notice of deficiency dated April 17, 2009, which day was a Monday. Is the notice timely sent, so as to suspend the running of the SOL? What if April 17 was a Thursday?

c. Ms. Wilson did not report approximately $40,000 of cash she embezzled from her employer in 2005. The embezzlement was discovered in 2008. She was prosecuted in state court for the crime and pled guilty in 2009. The IRS sent the Wilsons a notice of deficiency dated October 24, 2009, including the $40,000 in their income and disallowing certain charitable deductions for lack of substantiation. Ms. Wilson acknowledges that, for obvious reasons, she did not report the embezzlement income on her 2005 tax return even though she had been advised it was taxable and should have been reported. The Wilsons otherwise reported $200,000 of gross income on a timely filed return.

(i) Is the notice of deficiency mailed timely? Assuming it is timely, can the Service also make the adjustment relating to the charitable deduction?

(ii) Would your answer in (i) above change if your client had filed a correct, amended return on December 1, 2007?

(iii) In light of *Badaracco*, do you agree that a person who files a fraudulent return with the intent to evade should never file a correct amended return?

d. The Wilsons' tax return *as filed* (on April 15, 2006) indicated the following:

Salary		$200,000
Gross receipts from	$750,000	
sole proprietorship on Sch. C		
Cost of goods sold	(350,000)	
Expenses from store	(150,000)	250,000
Dividends from X Corp.		40,000
Capital gain from Z stock		
Sales Price	$500,000	
Adjusted Basis	490,000	10,000
Gross income		500,000
Deductions		(100,000)
Taxable income		$400,000

On audit, the Internal Revenue Service proposes the following adjustments:

1. Dividend on X Corp. stock should have been $140,000, rather than the $40,000 reported $100,000

2. Capital gain of $220,000 on sale of Y stock (proceeds = $1,000,000, AB = $780,000) was omitted $220,000

3. Capital loss of $200,000 (proceeds = $100,000, AB = $300,000) on the sale of W stock was omitted   ($200,000)

4. Deductions of $30,000 were negligently taken $ 30,000

Total Adjustments to Taxable Income $150,000

    (i)   If the adjustments are included in a notice of deficiency dated October 2009, can the IRS assess the tax flowing therefrom? Explain how the burden of proof is allocated between the taxpayer and the IRS.

Chapter 6

EXAMINATION OF PARTNERSHIPS

IRC:	§§ 6031(a), (b); 6211(c); 6221-6233 Skim 6234(a) - (c)
Regs.:	§§ 301.6221-1; 301.6222(a)-1(a), -1(b), -1(c) Example 1; 301.6222(a)-2(a), - 2(b); 301.6222(b)-2(a), -2(c); 301-6223(a)-1(a); 301.6223(b)-1(a), -(1)(b)(5), -1(c)(1); 301.6223(c)-1(a), -1(b); 301.6223(e)-1(b)(1), -1(b)(2) Example 1; 301-6223(e)-2; 301.6223(g)-1(a)(1), -1(a)(2), -1(b); 301.6224(a)-1(a); 301.6224(c)-1(a), -1(b)(1), (2) Example; 301.6224(c)-2(a)(1), -2(a)(2) Example; 301.6224(c)-3(a), -3(c); 301.6226(a)-1(a); 301.6226(e)-1(a)(1); 301.6226(f)-1(a); 301.6227(c)-1(a), -(1)(b); 301.6229(f)-1(a); 301.6231(a)(1)-1(a)(1); 301.6231(a)(2)-1(a)(1) through -(3)(i); 301.6231(a)(3)-1(a), -1(b); 301.6231(a)(5)-1(a) through -1(e); 301.6231(a)(6)-1(a), -1(b); 301.6231(c)-3 through -7.

I. INTRODUCTION

A. Overview—TEFRA

The Tax Equity and Fiscal Responsibility Act of 1982 (TEFRA)[1] dramatically changed the manner in which errors in reporting partnership income for federal income tax purposes are corrected. The need for change became apparent with the advent of syndicated tax shelter partnerships in the 1960s and 1970s that resulted in both the administrative and the judicial branches of the government being bogged down in controversies about the correct determination of partnerships' taxable income. The problem under pre-TEFRA law was that error correction had to take place at the partner, not the partnership, level. Consequently, a single syndicated tax shelter with several hundred partners had the potential to produce several hundred separate proceedings. The traditional "audit, deficiency notice, Tax Court" procedure for resolving the disputes could not efficiently handle the volume of cases.

The TEFRA solution shifted the focus of the inquiry from the individual partners to the partnership itself. But this had to be done without depriving each partner of the right to participate in the error correction proceedings. The

---

[1] Pub. L. No. 97-248, 96 Stat. 324 (1982).

solution was to withdraw "partnership items" from the traditional "audit, deficiency notice, Tax Court" procedure and create a similar, but separate, procedure for partnership items. The new procedure is centered on a single, unified, partnership-level proceeding that binds all partners who have not individually resolved their tax liability with the IRS.

Although the impetus for change was the flood of deficiency cases, overpayment cases based on partnership-level errors also generated multiple administrative and judicial proceedings about the same error. Thus, TEFRA also created a procedure, similar to the traditional refund procedure, that again involves a single, partnership-level proceeding that binds all partners who have not individually resolved their tax liability with the IRS. The partnership equivalent of the traditional refund procedure—an administrative adjustment request—is discussed in Chapter 9.

The TEFRA partnership provisions cover four general topics: basic concepts,[2] administrative proceedings,[3] administrative adjustment requests,[4] and litigation regarding partnership items.[5] Two additional sections contain definitions and rules that relate to the three general topics.[6]

Following the TEFRA partnership provisions, sections 6240-6255 contain rules that govern audit procedures involving "electing large partnerships." Congress enacted these rules in 1997 to reduce the inefficiency and complexity of applying TEFRA provisions to audits of large partnerships.[7] These provisions only apply to partnerships that have at least 100 partners and elect application of the rules.[8] Adjustments to an electing large partnership's return "are either reported by the partnership in the year the examination results are determined, or the partnership can elect to pay an imputed underpayment."[9] If a large partnership does not make the election, any audit of that partnership will

---

[2] IRC §§ 6221, 6222.

[3] IRC §§ 6223-25, 6229.

[4] IRC § 6227.

[5] IRC §§ 6226, 6228.

[6] IRC §§ 6230, 6231. Section 6233 extends the TEFRA partnership audit provisions, to the extent determined by Regulations, to entities that file partnership returns but are subsequently determined not to be partnerships, or that are subsequently determined not to be entities. In either case, the Regulations, in effect, respect and apply the TEFRA audit results. Reg. § 301.6233-1. As an example, Regulation section 301.6233-1-1(a) provides that a determination under the TEFRA partnership audit provisions "that an entity that filed a partnership return is an association taxable as a corporation will serve as a basis for a computational adjustment reflecting the disallowance of any loss or credit claimed by a purported partner with respect to that entity." Section 6234 deals with a situation that arises as a result of the separation from the normal deficiency procedures of procedures relating to partnership audits.

[7] H.R. Rep. No. 105-148, § 1222, at 218-28 (1997), 1997-4 C.B. 319, 540-550.

[8] IRC §§ 6255(a), 775(a). Section 775(b)(2) does not allow an election by a partnership if substantially all of its partners perform substantial personal services in connection with the partnership's activities.

[9] IRM 8.19.1.3.

be conducted under the TEFRA provisions.[10]

B. Basic Concepts

1. The Unified Proceeding

The foundation of the TEFRA solution is expressed in section 6221 which provides that "the tax treatment of any partnership item (and the applicability of any penalty, addition to tax, or additional amount which relates to an adjustment to a partnership item) shall be determined at the partnership level." Partnership items include any item relating to the determination of the partnership's taxable income that, under regulations, is more appropriately determined at the partnership level than at the partner level."[11] The Regulations broadly define partnership items as including, among other things, "[i]tems of income, gain, loss, deduction or credit of the partnership."[12]

In this connection, two related points should be noted. First, while the tax treatment of partnership items (whether relating to underpayments or overpayments) is determined through a partnership level proceeding, the tax treatment of nonpartnership items continues to be determined in a traditional, partner-level proceeding. Thus, a taxpayer may be involved in both a *partnership-level* proceeding (or, if more than one partnership is involved, multiple partnership-level proceedings) and a *partner-level* proceeding with respect to the same year.[13] To further complicate matters, there are several situations in

---

[10] *Cf.* IRC § 6240(b)(1).

[11] IRC § 6231(a)(3). In *Weiner v. United States,* 389 F.3d 152 (5th Cir. 2004), *cert. denied*, 125 S. Ct. 2312 (2005), the court held that question of whether the statute of limitations on issuing a final partnership administrative adjustment has expired is a partnership item and must be litigated in a partnership level proceeding.

[12] Reg. § 301.6231(a)(3)-1.

[13] Section 6234, deals with a problem that arose because of the TEFRA requirement that partnership items be dealt with under a procedure different than, and possibly conducted in parallel with, the traditional deficiency procedure. The problem arises in the situation in which a partner's income tax return shows no taxable income and shows a net loss from partnership items. In that case, if an audit produces a deficiency with respect to non-partnership items but which is eliminated by the net loss from partnership items, there would be no deficiency. If a separate TEFRA partnership proceeding were to result in a reduction in the net loss from partnership items sufficient to create an actual deficiency in tax liability from the non-partnership items, then it might happen that the statute of limitations on assessing that deficiency would expire before the TEFRA proceedings were completed. This would prevent the IRS from collecting the deficiency. In such case, the IRS is authorized under section 6234(a) to issue a "notice of adjustment" with respect to the deficiency resulting from the audit of the non-partnership items, and the taxpayer is given the right to seek Tax Court review of the proposed adjustment. When the notice of adjustment procedure is final (whether because no petition was filed with the Tax Court, or there was such a petition and the order of the Tax Court has become final), the results of the notice of adjustment procedure are "taken into account in determining the amount of any computational adjustment that is made in connection with a partnership proceeding." IRC § 6234(g)(1). The results of the notice of adjustment procedure are taken into account notwithstanding the fact that the statute of limitations on making assessments has expired. IRC § 6234(g)(1).

which partnership items "become" nonpartnership items.[14] As will be seen, partnership items that experience this metamorphosis may or may not trigger application of the traditional deficiency notice procedures. Finally, adjustments to partnership items may, in turn, cause changes in other items. Such other items, designated "affected items," are dealt with in the TEFRA provisions.[15]

Second, although penalties arising out of the reporting of a partnership's income are determined in the partnership level proceeding, partner-level defenses[16] can be asserted only in a traditional refund proceeding following assessment and payment of the penalties.[17] Therefore a partnership level proceeding that results in an assertion of a penalty could, itself, result in a traditional partner-level refund proceeding by a partner seeking recovery of the penalty.

2. The Duty of Consistency

The TEFRA provisions require that partnership items be reported on each partner's return in the same manner that they are reported on the partnership's return.[18] This consistency requirement is waived if the partner notifies the IRS of any inconsistency in reporting.[19] If a partner reports inconsistently, but does not notify the IRS of the inconsistency, the IRS may impose consistency without the normal procedures (discussed below) that permit partners to contest an asserted deficiency without first paying it.[20] Furthermore, any partner who does not disclose an inconsistency in reporting may be subject to the section 6662(b)(1) accuracy-related penalty for disregard of the rules. The IRS has in place a matching program to ensure that partners report consistently with the partnership return.[21]

3. The Tax Matters Partner

To facilitate the administrative and judicial proceedings, TEFRA created, and gave certain powers and responsibilities to, the "tax matters partner" (TMP). The TMP is the person the partnership designates who either: "(i) [w]as

---

[14] IRC § 6230(b)(1).

[15] IRC § 6231(a)(5).

[16] Partner-level defenses are "those that are personal to the partner or are dependent upon the partner's separate return and cannot be determined at the partnership level." Reg. § 301.6221-1(d).

[17] The defenses that are personal to a partner may be raised either before payment in a collection due process hearing (under sections 6320 or 6330) or following payment in a refund action. Reg. § 301.6221-1(d).

[18] IRC § 6222(a).

[19] IRC § 6222(b).

[20] IRC § 6222(c).

[21] *See* IR 2003-27.

a general partner in the partnership at some time during the taxable year for which the designation is made, or (ii) [i]s a general partner in the partnership as of the time the designation is made."[22] The Regulations contain an extensive discussion of the designation or selection of the TMP as well as some special rules relating to the designation or selection of the TMP for a limited liability company.[23] However, of particular interest are the TMP's significant responsibilities in connection with administrative and judicial proceedings relating to the determination of the partnership's taxable income.

(a) The TMP is required to notify partners, who are not required to be notified directly by the IRS, about significant developments in partnership administrative and judicial proceedings.[24]

(b) In the case of administrative proceedings initiated by the IRS that result in proposed changes in the partnership's taxable income or loss, the TMP can enter into a settlement agreement with the IRS that other partners will be permitted to adopt and that will be binding on partners that have less than a 1% profits interest in a partnership with more than 100 partners.[25]

(c) The TMP has the power to extend the period of time within which the IRS can make assessments with respect to all partners.[26]

(d) The TMP has the right to seek judicial review of the proposed changes and to determine the court in which to seek such review.[27]

(e) The TMP has the right to request an administrative adjustment of partnership items on behalf of the partnership, to seek judicial review of the requested adjustment if it is denied, in whole or in part, and to determine the court in which to seek such review.[28]

---

[22] Reg. § 301.6231(a)(7)-1(b).

[23] Reg. § 301.6231(a)(7)-2. Regulation section 301.6231(a)(7)-1 provides rules for the designation or selection of a partnership's TMP by the partnership or, in certain circumstances, by the IRS. The Tax Court has held that the Service, when it has the right to select a TMP, is not compelled to act so long as the other partners are provided adequate notice of how to protect their interests through commencing a partnership proceeding. *See* Seneca, Ltd. v. Commissioner, 92 T.C. 363 (1989), *aff'd*, 899 F.2d 1255 (9th Cir. 1990); *see also* Cinema '84 v. Commissioner, 412 F.3d 366 (2d Cir. 2005), *cert. denied*, 126 S. Ct. 631 (IRS has no duty to appoint TMP).

[24] IRC § 6223(g); Reg. § 301.6223(g)-1(a)(1) - (3). However, if the TMP fails to notify a partner (who is *not* entitled to notice by the IRS) of a proceeding, the partner's due process rights are not violated because "TEFRA's notice provisions are 'reasonably calculated' to apprise all partners of tax adjustments and administrative proceedings involving the partnership." Kaplan v. United States, 133 F.3d 469, 475 (7th Cir. 1998).

[25] IRC § 6224(c)(3).

[26] IRC § 6229(b).

[27] IRC § 6226(a).

[28] IRC § 6228(a)(1).

(f) If the IRS mails a notice of beginning of administrative proceeding to the TMP, the TMP is required to provide the IRS the name, address, profits interest, and identification number of any person who was a partner anytime during the year.[29]

The TMP's power to act on behalf of the partnership can terminate in certain circumstances.[30] Upon termination, the TMP cannot act to bind the partners or the IRS.[31] For example, the TMP's authority to extend an assessment period of limitations for a partnership terminates if the TMP is under criminal investigation for violation of the internal revenue laws.[32]

4. Excluded Partnerships

Congress excluded from the reach of the TEFRA provisions partnerships with ten or fewer partners (at any time during the year), whose partners include only: (i) individuals who are not nonresident aliens, (ii) the estates of partners, and (iii) C corporations.[33] However, any such small partnership is permitted to elect to have the TEFRA provisions apply to it. The election is made by attaching a statement, signed by all persons who were partners at any time during the year, to the partnership return for the first year for which the election is to be effective.[34] Also excluded from the TEFRA provisions are partnerships that have validly elected out of partnership status under section 761(a)[35] and publicly traded partnerships treated as corporations under section 7704(a).

---

[29] IRC § 6230(e). Tax Court rules establish additional responsibilities of the TMP. *See* Tax Ct. R. 241(f)(1), 241(g), 248.

[30] Reg. § 301.6231(a)(7)-1(l).

[31] *See* Computer Programs Lambda, Ltd. v. Commissioner, 89 T.C. 198 (1987) (forbidding the TMP to continue as TMP in a partnership proceeding after the TMP entered into bankruptcy).

[32] IRC § 6231(c); Reg. §§ 301.623(c)-5(a), 301.6231(a)(7)-1(l)(1)(iv). Also, the Second Circuit has ruled that the TMP's authority to act on behalf of the partnership can terminate even if the Service fails to inform the TMP that his partnership items have become nonpartnership items. The court, in *Transpac Drilling Venture 1982-12 v. Commissioner*, 147 F.3d 221 (2d Cir. 1998), held that a TMP may not bind the partnership by extending the assessment limitations period if the TMP is under criminal investigation and ultimately cooperates with the IRS regarding the criminal prosecutions of the partnership. When serious conflict of interest exists, the TMP may not be allowed to act on behalf of the partnership because the TMP holds a fiduciary duty to the other partners. *See* River City Ranches #1 Ltd. v. Commissioner, 401 F.3d 1136 (9th Cir. 2005).

[33] IRC § 6231(a)(1)(B)(i). A husband and wife are counted as one partner. "C" corporations were added as permissible partners for purposes of the "small partnership" exception by the Tax Reform Act of 1997, thereby exempting a number of partnerships that were otherwise covered under the TEFRA provisions. An LLC that is a "disregarded entity" under Regulation section 301.7701-3(b)(1)(ii) is nonetheless a partnership. If it holds an interest in a partnership the partnership will not qualify for the small partnership exception from the TEFRA provisons. Rev. Rul. 2004-88.

[34] Reg. § 301.6231(a)(1)-1(b)(2).

[35] IRM 4.31.2.1.2(1).

II. ADMINISTRATIVE PROCEEDINGS

A. The Notice of Beginning

An audit of a partnership's return begins when the IRS mails by certified mail (or hand delivers) to the TMP a notice of the beginning of an administrative proceeding.[36] The date the notice of beginning is issued to the TMP starts a 45-day period within which the revenue agent can determine whether the case will be "No-Changed." If it is determined that the case will be No-Changed, the notice of beginning issued to the TMP will be withdrawn and no notices will be delivered to the notice partners.[37]

If the case is not No-Changed and is still in process sixty days after the notice of beginning was issued to the TMP, the notice of beginning is mailed to all notice partners.[38] The date of this mailing starts a 120-day period which must elapse before an FPAA (final partnership administrative adjustment) can be sent to the partnership.[39]

Partners whose names and addressees are known to the Service (other than partners who have less than a 1% interest in the profits of a partnership that has more than 100 partners) are considered notice partners.[40] Also, for purposes of the TEFRA partnership audit provisions, the word "partner" includes not only actual partners in a partnership, but also "any other person whose income tax liability . . . is determined in whole or in part by taking into account directly or indirectly partnership items of the partnership."[41]

One example is persons who hold an *indirect* interest in a partnership through a "pass-thru" partner such as a partnership, estate, trust, S corporation, or nominee. Such persons are known as "indirect partners."[42] Indirect partners are supposed to be kept informed by the pass-thru partner of developments relating to the administrative proceeding.[43] However, "indirect partners" whose names, addresses, and profits interests are provided to the IRS are entitled to receive the notice of the beginning directly from the IRS.[44]

---

[36] IRC § 6223(a)(1); IRM 4.31.3.3.1(1)(G).

[37] IRM 4.31.2.2.9.1(2)(B).

[38] IRM 4.31.2.2.9.2(1)(B), (C).

[39] *Id.* at (1)(F).

[40] IRC § 6223(b). Partners with less than a 1% interest in partnership profits in a partnership with more than 100 partners can join with other partners to create a "5-percent group." The 5% group is entitled to designate one of its members to serve as a partner who is entitled to notice. IRC § 6223(b)(2).

[41] IRC § 6231(a)(2)(B).

[42] IRC § 6231(a)(9), (10).

[43] IRC § 6223(h); Reg. 301.6223(h)-1(a).

[44] IRC § 6223(c)(3).

Another example of a person who is not an actual partner, but whose income tax liability is determined by taking into account partnership items, is a spouse who signs a joint return with a spouse who is an actual partner. Since the non-partner spouse is jointly and severally liable for the tax shown on the return, the non-partner spouse is subject to the TEFRA partnership audit provisions and entitled to receive the notices that the partner spouse is entitled to receive.

B. Period for Mailing the Notice of Beginning

No specific date is set forth within which the notice of beginning must be mailed to the notice partners. However, the Code directs the IRS *not* to mail the FPAA to the TMP until at least 120 days after the notice of beginning is mailed.[45] As in the case of the traditional notice of deficiency, the FPAA must be mailed before the statute of limitations on assessment expires, and upon its mailing the running of the statute is suspended.[46]

This might lead one to believe that the notice of beginning must always be mailed at least 120 days before the statute of limitations expires. Otherwise, the FPAA would be ineffective, because it could not be mailed until after the period for assessment expired. However, in a case in which both the notice of beginning of the administrative proceeding and the FPAA were mailed within the 120 days before expiration of the statute of limitations, the Tax Court ruled that the FPAA was timely and it suspended the running of the statute of limitations.[47]

In that situation, a partner's only recourse is that set forth in section 6223(e) which describes what happens if the IRS fails to send any notice to a notice partner in a timely manner. If the administrative or judicial proceedings are still in progress, the partner becomes a party to the proceeding, unless the partner elects either to adopt any settlement agreement previously entered into by any other partner, or to have all partnership items of the partner treated as non-partnership items.[48] However, if all administrative and judicial proceedings are finished when the untimely notice is mailed, then the partner's partnership items are treated as nonpartnership items unless the partner elects to adopt any settlement agreement previously entered into by any other partner.[49]

If the FPAA was not mailed prior to the expiration of the statute of limitations on assessment, this fact should be raised in the resulting judicial pro-

---

45 IRC § 6223(d)(1). This awkwardly worded section purports to fix the date for taking the first action (the mailing of the notice of beginning) by reference to the date on which the second action (the mailing of the FPAA) is taken. White & Case v. United States, 22 Cl. Ct. 734 (1991).

46 IRC §§ 6225(a), 6229(a), (d).

47 *See* Wind Energy Tech. Assocs. III v. Commissioner, 94 T.C. 787 (1990).

48 IRC § 6223(e)(3).

49 IRC § 6223(e)(2).

ceeding under section 6226. If the issue is not raised, partners may not be allowed to raise the defense later in a refund suit.[50]

C. The Examination

1. Participation

All partners, including less than 1% profits interest partners in partnerships with more than 100 partners and indirect partners whose names, addresses, and profits interests have been provided to the IRS, have the right to participate in all administrative proceedings.[51] However, any partner who wishes to attend meetings with the revenue agent or otherwise participate in the proceedings must make arrangements with the TMP to obtain notice of the date, time, and place of any such meetings or other steps in the audit process.[52]

2. Summary Reports

At the end of the audit, the revenue agent prepares a summary report which provides "a detailed explanation of each proposed adjustment for each examined year, including facts, law, argument and conclusion for each proposed adjustment. . . ."[53] A separate report for "affected items" is also prepared.[54] A copy of the report(s) is given to the TMP, who, in turn, is required to provide a copy to all partners.[55] The revenue agent then schedules a closing conference, at which the TMP and other participating partners can discuss with the revenue agent the issues spelled out in the summary report. At the conference, the partners will be given the opportunity to settle the matter, including partnership items, penalties, additions to tax, additional amounts, and, if present, affected items. Form 870-PT is used if there is agreement as to partnership items and not to affected items and Form 870-LT is used if there is agreement as to both partnership items and affected items.

If agreement is not reached as to all partners at the conference, the IRS will send the TMP and each unagreed partner a copy of the Revenue Agent's Report (the "RAR") and a sixty-day letter. Any unagreed partner may file a protest within the sixty-day period and ask for an Appeals conference. All unagreed partners are entitled to attend the conference. If any partners remain una-

---

[50] *See* Weiner v. United States, 389 F.3d 152 (5th Cir. 2004); Chimblo v. Commissioner, 177 F.3d 119, 125 (2d. Cir. 1999).

[51] IRC § 6224(a).

[52] Reg. § 301.6224(a)-1.

[53] IRM 4.31.2.2.9.3(1)(D).

[54] *Id.* at (1)(E).

[55] Reg. § 301.6223(g)-1(b)(1)(ii).

greed at the conclusion of the Appeals conference, the IRS will issue an FPAA, in response to which, first the TMP and then the remaining unagreed partners have the right to seek judicial review.

3. Settlement—Partnership Items

Each partner has the right to reach agreement with the government as to the treatment of any partnership item. When a partner enters into a settlement agreement with either the IRS or the Justice Department, that partner's partnership items become nonpartnership items on the date of the settlement.[56] But even though such items have become "nonpartnership items," the traditional deficiency procedures (deficiency notice and opportunity for prepayment judicial redetermination by the Tax Court) are not available. Instead, the IRS can immediately assess and collect any increase in the partner's tax liability that results from the agreed treatment of the partnership items. This increase is referred to in the Code as a "computational adjustment."[57]

The conversion of partnership items into nonpartnership items by reason of an agreement between the IRS or the Justice Department and a partner triggers a special rule regarding the statute of limitations on assessment. In order to give the IRS time to make the assessment, section 6299(f) provides that the statute of limitation on assessment "shall not expire before the date which is one year after the date on which the items become nonpartnership items." This one- year-certain rule also applies to other circumstances, described in section 6231(a), in which partnership items are converted into nonpartnership items.

4. Settlement—Affected Items

A change in the treatment of a partnership item may affect other items on the returns of the partnership or the partners. If the change in tax treatment of such "affected items"[58] does not require a "partner-level determination," the IRS may immediately assess and collect the additional tax due.[59] Immediate assessment is appropriate when the addition to tax is determined solely by a mathematical computation using known amounts. An example might be a change in a partner's tax liability resulting from a change in the threshold amount of the medical expense deduction that is triggered by a change in a partnership item.[60]

However, if the tax liability attributable to the affected item could not be determined without fact-finding at the partner level, a partner-level determi-

---

[56] IRC § 6231(b)(1)(c).

[57] IRC § 6231(a)(6).

[58] IRC § 6231(a)(5).

[59] IRC § 6230(a)(1).

[60] Reg. § 301.6231(a)(6)-1(a)(2).

nation, involving a deficiency notice and opportunity for pre-assessment judicial review in the Tax Court, would be required.[61] An example of a change in an affected item that would require a partner level determination is the determination of "a partner's at-risk amount to the extent it depends upon the source from which the partner obtained the funds that the partner contributed to the partnership."[62]

Whether or not a partner-level determination is required, it is clear that the deficiency procedures are not required with respect to any penalty, addition to tax, or additional amount generated by a partnership item.[63] All such penalties are determined at the partnership level and are treated as computational adjustments that may be assessed and collected without a deficiency notice. Individual taxpayer defenses to any such penalties can be raised only in a traditional refund procedure.

5. Requests for Consistent Treatment

If a settlement agreement is reached with one or more partners *before* the IRS mails the FPAA to the TMP, the other partners can request settlement terms that are consistent with the settlement agreement. To do so, they must file their request for consistent treatment within 150 days after the day the FPAA is mailed to the TMP.[64] The 150-day period coincides with the period within which the partners may seek judicial review of the FPAA.[65] In effect, for those partners who choose to litigate, the option of requesting terms consistent with a settlement agreement entered into before the FPAA is mailed to the TMP is taken off the table. If the partners do not like the terms of the settlement agreement, they can wait for the FPAA and, when it is issued, challenge it in court.

Although the Code expressly imposes a time limit on requests for consistent treatment with respect to settlement agreements entered into *before* the FPAA is issued, no such statutory limitation applies with respect to requests for consistent treatment with settlement agreements entered into *after* the FPAA is issued. However, apparently in the interest of encouraging settlements, the *Regulations* provide that a request for consistent treatment with respect to a settlement agreement entered into *after* the FPAA is mailed to the TMP must be filed by the *later* of the 150th day after the day the FPAA is mailed to the TMP

---

[61] IRC § 6230(a)(2)(A)(i). If, while a partnership-level proceeding is still in progress, the IRS sends a notice of deficiency for an affected item that results from a partnership adjustment, the notice is invalid and the Tax Court lacks jurisdiction over the matter. GAF Corp. v. Commissioner, 114 T.C. 519 (2000).

[62] Reg. § 301.6231(a)(6)-1(a)(3).

[63] IRC § 6221; Reg. § 301.6231(a)(6)-1(a)(1), (3).

[64] IRC § 6224(c)(2).

[65] IRC § 6226(a), (b)(1).

or the sixtieth day after the day on which the settlement agreement is executed.[66]

III. JUDICIAL REVIEW OF AN FPAA

At the conclusion of the partnership administrative proceeding, if a settlement acceptable to *all* partners has not been reached, the IRS is required to mail an FPAA to the TMP and, within sixty days thereafter, to mail a copy of the FPAA to all other partners entitled to receive the notice.[67] After the IRS mails an FPAA to the TMP, the TMP has a period of ninety days within which to file a "petition for a readjustment" of the proposed changes with the Tax Court, a District Court, or the Court of Federal Claims.[68] If the TMP does not file a petition within the ninety-day period, then any notice partner (including the TMP) and any 5% group is permitted to file such a petition with any one of those courts within the next sixty days.[69] The court with which any petition is filed has jurisdiction to determine: all partnership items for the year, the allocation of the items among the partners, and all related penalties, additions to tax, and additional amounts.[70]

As is the case in a traditional deficiency procedure, the Tax Court is generally the choice of forum because payment of the asserted liability is not a jurisdictional requirement.[71] If the petition for review of the FPAA is filed with the District Court or the Court of Federal Claims, the petitioning partner must, as a jurisdictional requirement, deposit the amount of tax that would be due, deter-

---

[66] Reg. § 301.6224(c)-3(c)(3). If a partner fails to accept a consistent settlement offer within the specified time period, the Service is under no duty to extend the time period even if the partner failed to meet the deadline because the TMP failed to provide notice to the partner. Drake Oil Tech. Partners v. Commissioner, 211 F.3d 1277 (10th Cir. 2000); Vulcan Oil Tech. Partners v. Commissioner, 110 T.C. 153 (1998), *aff'd sub nom.* Tucek v. Commissioner, 198 F.3d 259 (10th Cir. 1999).

[67] *See* Section II.A., *supra.*

[68] IRC § 6226(a). If the petition for readjustment is filed in the District Court, it must be filed in "the district in which the partnership's principal place of business is located." IRC § 6226(a)(2).

[69] IRC § 6226(b)(1). Copies of the FPAA mailed to notice partners and to the designated member of any 5% group show the date the FPAA was mailed to the TMP.

[70] IRC § 6226(f).

[71] Trial by jury is not a choice of forum consideration in TEFRA partnership proceedings. In the Court of Federal Claims, jury trials are generally not permitted. McElrath v. United States, 102 U.S. 426, 440 (1880) (holding that the Seventh Amendment does not require the Court of Claims, a predecessor of the Court of federal claims, to conduct jury trials since there is no right at common law to sue the government); *see also* Gerald A. Kafka & Rita A. Cavanaugh, Litigation of Federal Civil Tax Controversies, Vol. 1, §§ 107, 15.06 (2d ed. 1996). In the Court of Federal Claims, jurisdiction over TEFRA cases is under 28 U.S.C. § 1508. In the District Courts, 28 U.S.C. § 2402 precludes a jury trial in cases, like the TEFRA cases, that are brought under 28 U.S.C. § 1346(e). Tax Court trials never involve juries. *See* IRC § 7459(a).

mined as if the adjustments proposed in the FPAA were correct.[72] If the petition in the District Court or the Court of Federal Claims is filed by a 5% group or by a pass-through partner, each member of the group or each indirect partner must make the jurisdictional deposit.[73]

Any amount so deposited is not considered a "payment of tax" except for purposes of interest computations.[74] This treatment permits the IRS to proceed with collection of any deficiency of that partner that is not based on partnership items without taking into consideration, in determining whether there is a deficiency, the amount of the deposit.

If the petition that goes forward is filed in the Tax Court, no assessment of a deficiency attributable to partnership items can be made until the decision of the Tax Court has become final.[75] However, if the petition that goes forward is filed in either a District Court or the Court of Federal Claims, there is no prohibition on assessment during the pendency of the proceeding. Normally, the IRS will commence collection activities against all the partners without waiting for the conclusion of the District Court or Court of Federal Claims case.

Because this approach could easily result in multiple proceedings, the Code establishes an order of priority. First, if the TMP files a petition, the other partners are precluded from doing so because their right to file is conditioned on the TMP not having filed.[76] If the TMP does not file, the first Tax Court petition that is filed goes forward and any other actions are dismissed.[77] If no Tax Court case is filed, the first action filed in either the District Court or the Court of Federal Claims goes forward.[78]

As can be seen, the FPAA serves the same purpose as a notice of deficiency serves in a traditional audit. It staves off assessment and collection action for a period of 150 days, during which the partnership and the partners have an opportunity to seek prepayment judicial review in the Tax Court.[79]

Unlike the traditional notice of deficiency, the FPAA also serves as a key to a post-payment judicial review. In the traditional approach, if the taxpayer does not respond to the notice of deficiency, the tax is assessed and the IRS sends a notice of tax due. The taxpayer has to pay the tax, or collection activi-

---

[72] IRC § 6226(e). The partner is not required to pay other outstanding tax liabilities to satisfy this jurisdictional requirement. Reg. § 301.6226(e)-1(a)(1).

[73] Section 6226(e)(1) permits correction of a shortfall in the jurisdictional deposit provided that the original amount was determined in good faith. *See* Maarten Investerings Partnership v. United States, 2000-1 U.S. Tax Cas. (CCH) ¶ 50,241, 85 A.F.T.R.2d P-H 2000-1086 (S.D.N.Y. 2000).

[74] IRC § 6226(e)(3).

[75] IRC § 6225(a).

[76] IRC § 6226(b).

[77] IRC § 6226(b)(2), (4).

[78] IRC § 6226(b)(3).

[79] IRC §§ 6225(a), 6226.

ties will begin. After paying the tax, the taxpayer has a period of two years within which to file a claim for refund.[80] If the Commissioner denies the claim, the taxpayer has an additional two years to file suit in the District Court or Court of Federal Claims to recover the claimed overpayment.[81]

However, in the partnership context, once the FPAA is mailed to the TMP, if no suit is filed in any court within the 150-day filing period, the IRS assesses the tax due from each partner and sends each partner a notice of tax due.[82] Again, the partners must pay the tax they owe. But, thereafter they have no opportunity to contest the liability because that right can only be exercised pursuant to a timely response to the FPAA.

If any partner files a petition for a readjustment of partnership items, then all partners are treated as parties and are allowed to participate in the proceedings.[83] If the petition that goes forward is filed in a District Court or in the Court of Federal Claims, the partner filing the petition is required to deposit with the IRS an amount equal to the filing partner's tax liability that would result from making the adjustments called for in the FPAA.[84]

IV. STATUTE OF LIMITATIONS ON MAKING ASSESSMENTS

Section 6229(a) provides that the statute of limitations for assessing tax attributable to any partnership item (or affected item) "shall not expire before" the date which is three years from the later of the due date of the return, determined without regard to extensions (for returns filed on or before that due date), or three years from the filing of the return (for returns filed after that due date).[85] The phrase "shall not expire before" in section 6229(a) seems to indicate that the section does not establish a free-standing statute of limitations with respect to partnership items (and affected items), and that its sole function is to extend the period of limitations defined elsewhere.

The only period that might be so modified by section 6229(a) is the general period of limitations in section 6501(a). Section 6501(a) applies to "the amount of any tax imposed by this title," and, subject to a number of exceptions, requires the tax to be assessed "within 3 years after the return was filed." For this pur-

---

[80] IRC § 6511(a).

[81] IRC § 6532(a).

[82] It is possible for either the TMP or a partner to file a "request for an administrative adjustment" (in effect, a claim for refund), but such a request cannot be filed after an FPAA has been mailed to the TMP. IRC § 6227(a)(2).

[83] IRC § 6226(c).

[84] IRC § 6226(e).

[85] IRC §§ 6229(a), 6501(a). The question of whether or not an FPAA was issued within the statute of limitations is a partnership item that must be litigated in a partnership level proceeding. Weiner v. United States, 389 F.2d (5th Cir. 2004), *cert. denied*, 544 U.S. 1050 (2005).

pose, returns filed before the due date (determined without extensions) are treated as filed on the due date.[86]

A competing view of the role of section 6229(a), that it is a free-standing statute of limitations, is supported by the fact that Congress withdrew partnership items (and affected items) from the traditional error-correction provisions and established an entirely separate procedure for correcting such items. This intent is evident in the structure of section 6229, which like section 6501, provides special rules for: (1) extension by agreement,[87] (2) false returns,[88] (3) substantial omission of income,[89] (4) no return,[90] and (5) returns filed by the IRS.[91] As discussed in Chapter 5, section 6501 contains similar rules for each of those situations.[92] One argument, in support of this competing view, is that, if all that section 6229(a) does is extend the section 6501(a) statute of limitations in some cases, it would not have been necessary to duplicate in section 6229 many of the rules already present in section 6501.

When presented with an opportunity to resolve the issue, the Tax Court, describing the TEFRA partnership provisions as "distressingly complex and confusing," adopted the government's position that section 6229 merely extends, in certain cases, the section 6501 statute of limitations period.[93] The majority opinion's lengthy, technical analysis relied heavily on the "shall not expire before" operative language of section 6229(a), the apparently unlimited scope of section 6501 (which applies to "any tax imposed by this title"), and the "Supreme Court's admonition that '[s]tatutes of limitation sought to be applied to rights of the Government, must receive a strict construction in favor of the Government.'"[94] The dissenting opinions, which relied on Congress' intent in setting up a free standing procedure regarding partnership items, are summed up by Judge Foley in his separate opinion. He said that the majority "stretches the applicability of the statute to ensure that the Government prevails. That is

---

[86] Reg. § 301.6501(b)-1(a).

[87] IRC § 6229(b). Included in this special rule is a provision that coordinates agreements under section 6229(b) with similar agreements under section 6501(c)(4). The special rule limits the applicability of any agreement under section 6501(c)(4) to the section 6229 statute of limitations to those section 6501(c)(4) agreements that expressly acknowledge their application to partnership items.

[88] IRC § 6229(c)(1).

[89] IRC § 6229(c)(2).

[90] IRC § 6229(c)(3).

[91] IRC § 6229(c)(4).

[92] IRC §§ 6501(c)(4) (extension by agreement), 6501(c)(1) (false returns), 6501(e) (substantial omission), 6501(c)(3) (no returns), 6501(b)(3) (returns filed by the IRS).

[93] Rhone-Poulenc Surfactants & Specialties, L.P. v. Commissioner, 114 T.C. 533, 540 (2000). *See also* Andantech L.L.C. v. Commissioner, 331 F.3d 972 (D.C. Cir. 2003).

[94] *Rhone-Poulenc Surfactants & Specialties,* 114 T.C. at 540 (quoting E.I. Dupont De Nemours & Co. v. Davis, 264 U.S. 456, 462 (1994)).

reconstruction, not strict construction."[95] The IRS has adopted the Tax Court's limited "extension" role for section 6229(a).[96]

More recently, in *Ad Global Fund, LLC v. United States*,[97] the Court of Federal Claims addressed the question of "whether section 6229(a) is independent of section 6501(a), or whether section 6229(a) merely serves as an extension of section 6501(a)."[98] In a lengthy opinion addressing a myriad of issues raised by the parties, the court adopted the position of the Tax Court and concluded its opinion with the following observation.

> The court finds that the statute has multiple plausible meanings—it is ambiguous. Furthermore, the court holds that the legislative history is not reliable as it is equivocal and does not make clear the understanding of the enacting legislature as to the meaning of section 6229. . . .

> While the court regrets that poor drafting may have concealed Congress' intent, the evidence presented is not certain enough to overcome the strong presumption in favor of allowing the government to collect the taxes owed to it. Therefore, section 6229(a) is held to contain an extension of time, not a separate statute of limitations on partnership items.

Finally, in *Ginsburg v. Commissioner*,[99] the taxpayer asked for summary judgment on the question of whether a deficiency notice, which was mailed within the period set forth in the ninth consecutive Form 872, was timely as it related to certain affected items. The taxpayers had also executed a series of Forms 872-P (extension of the time for assessing tax attributable to partnership items), but, at the time in question, the last of the extended due dates with respect to partnership items had expired. One might think that if section 6229(a), when applicable, merely extends the underlying section 6501 statute of limitations, then the otherwise valid ninth. Form 872 would apply and the deficiency notice would be timely.

But the Tax Court noted the limitation in section 6229(b)(3) that an agreement under 6501(c)(4) (i.e., Form 872) is only applicable to partnership items if the agreement specifically so states. After some preliminary interpretation of the statute to demonstrate that partnership items for this purpose include

---

[95] *Id.* at 570.

[96] "The general assessment provisions of IRC 6501 continue to control the statute of limitations for investors. IRC 6229 enhances the section 6501 statute by setting forth a minimum period for assessment of the tax at the investor level." IRM 8.19.1.6.6.2(1).

[97] 67 Fed. Cl. 657 (2005), *certified for an interlocutory appeal*, 68 Fed. Cl. 663 (2005), *petition granted*, 167 F. Appx. 171 (Fed. Cir. 2006). *See also* Grapevine Imports, Ltd v. United States, 71 Fed. Cl. 324 (2006) (adopting the holding of *Ad Global Fund LLC v. United States*, but basing its conclusion primarily on the "plain meaning" of section 6229).

[98] *Ad Global Fund LLC*, 67 Fed. Cl. at 659.

[99] 127 T.C. No. 5 (2006).

affected items, the court concluded that, because the last executed Form 872 did not specifically refer to partnership items, the statute of limitations on assessing tax with respect to both partnership items and affected items had expired.

Under the limited role view of section 6229, the section's most likely application will be with respect to extension agreements between the IRS and the TMP on behalf of all partners or between the IRS and any partner.[100] This follows because of the limitations in section 6229(b)(3) that an extension of the statute of limitations under the general rule of section 6501 does not extend the statute of limitations on assessment of the tax related to partnership items unless the section 6501 agreement expressly so provides.

An entity-level extension of the statute of limitations on assessment must be made either by the TMP or by a person authorized in writing by the partnership to sign the extension. If a person other than the TMP is authorized to sign the extension, the partnership is required to file a statement confirming the authorization, specifying the years for which the authorization is effective and containing the signature of "all persons who were general partners at any time during the year or years for which the authorization is effective."[101] A Form 2848 Power of Attorney, if signed by all general partners, will normally be sufficient for this purpose.

The forms used for extending the statute for partnership items are Form 872-P for a specific period of time extension and Form 872-O for an indefinite extension. Open-ended extensions may be terminated by either the IRS or the partnership by delivery of Form 872-N. Understandably, the IRS has a strong preference for entity-level extensions of the statute of limitations. However, partner-level extensions, extending the statute only for partners who sign them, are permitted in certain circumstances.[102]

The running of the period of limitations on assessment in TEFRA partnership proceedings is suspended upon the issuance of an FPAA for the period within which a petition for readjustment of partnership items can be filed (a total of 150 days) and, if no petition for readjustment is filed, for one year thereafter. If a petition is filed, the suspension lasts for one year after the court's decision becomes final.[103] Finally, the period for assessing income tax attributable to any partnership item (or affected item) is also suspended, under certain circumstances, with respect to an unidentified partner until one year after the partner is identified to the IRS.[104]

---

[100] IRC § 6229(b)(1).

[101] IRM 8.19.1.6.6.8.1.2(2).

[102] IRM 8.19.1.6.6.8.2.1.

[103] IRC § 6229(d).

[104] IRC § 6229(e).

PROBLEMS

1. Partnership X

M, Inc., a C corporation, is a general partner with a 5% capital and profits interest in Partnership X, a limited partnership. The remaining general partners are three unrelated individuals having capital and profits interests in Partnership X as follows: Jeff 25%, Teri 10%, and Mark 10%. The limited partnership has 6 limited partners, who in the aggregate, have capital and profits interests of 50%. On Partnership X's 2004 (its first) Form 1065 (U.S. Partnership Return of Income), filed April 15, 2005, M, Inc. was designated the Tax Matters Partner ("TMP") for the partnership. All partnership allocations are proportional to each partner's capital and profits interest.

TEFRA PROBLEM #1 — PARTNERSHIP X

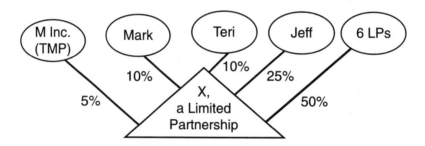

a. Will the partnership be subject to the rules set forth in § 6221-6233?

b. Regardless of how you answered the prior question, for the rest of this problem, assume that the TEFRA partnership provisions apply to this case. If during 2004 M, Inc. filed a petition in bankruptcy under Chapter 11, what, if any, effect would this have on M, Inc.'s designation as the TMP of Partnership X?

c. If M, Inc. ceased to be the TMP, and if the partnership did not designate a successor, which partner would then be deemed to be the TMP?

d. Assume that the TMP is an individual. After the TMP finds out that he is being investigated for criminal tax fraud, he signs a waiver of the three-year statute of limitations on making assessments attributable to any partnership item. After the three-year statute expires, the limited partners in the partnership take the position that the waiver signed by the TMP was invalid since the criminal investigation ended the TMP's right to act on behalf of the partnership. As a consequence, they argue, the statute of limitations has expired with respect to their tax liability arising out of their interest in the partnership. Are the limited partners right?

e. Assume that M, Inc. was the only general partner and that it received an FPAA seven days after it was mailed. On the eighth day, M, Inc. advised Jeff (now a limited partner) that it is not in a position to handle the TMP duties with respect to challenging the FPAA. M, Inc. orally appointed Jeff as the TMP, and Jeff accepted the position solely for the purpose of filing a petition for readjustment. He then filed the petition with the Tax Court within the ninety-day period set forth in § 6226(a). Should the government's motion to dismiss be granted?

2. Partnership B

The Lola Stradford Charitable Trust ("Trust") is a 3% limited partner in Partnership B, a limited partnership consisting of twenty-five partners. The Trust has three equal income beneficiaries to whom all of the Trust's income is required to be distributed no less often than annually. The Trust also has two remaindermen. Partnership B filed Form 1065 (U.S. Partnership Return of Income) for calendar year 2004 on April 15, 2005, and it named M, Inc. (a C corporation) as its TMP.

TEFRA PROBLEM #2 — PARTNERSHIP B

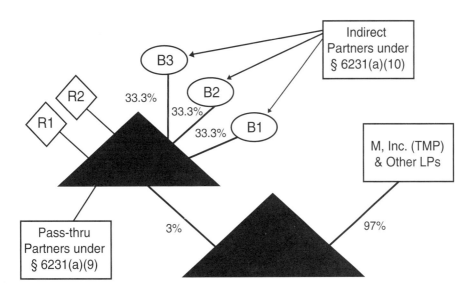

a. To whom among the persons identified in the preceding paragraph would the Service mail a "notice of the beginning of an administrative proceeding" (i.e., a notice of the beginning of an audit of the partnership)?

b. What obligation, if any, does the trustee of the Trust have to its income beneficiaries or to its remaindermen?

c. Which partners, other than the TMP, are permitted to participate in the administrative proceeding?

d. If the Trust does not receive notice of the beginning of a partnership proceeding, what effect does this failure have on the income beneficiaries?

e. During the audit of the partnership return, the agent found one item which he believed should be adjusted and which would increase partnership income for calendar year 2004 by $100,000. The TMP and the trustee agree and enter into a settlement agreement for the partnership with respect to that item. Who is bound by the terms of this agreement?

f. Suppose that the IRS enters into a settlement agreement with one partner of the partnership. Paragraph 1 of the agreement provides a favorable resolution of the partnership items relating to that partner and paragraphs 2 and 3 deal with nonpartnership items. You represent another partner in the partnership. Is your client entitled under the "consistent settlement provisions" in § 6224(c) to the same treatment with respect to your client's partnership items?

g. Within what period of time must the IRS issue the final partnership administrative adjustment ("FPAA")?

h. What effect does the mailing of an FPAA have on the statute of limitations for assessment?

i. What happens in (e) if no settlement agreement is reached?

j. If the Service sends all the partners an FPAA on April 10, 2008, what is the last date on which TMP, M, Inc., can file a timely petition with the Tax Court? Note the following timeline.

TEFRA PROBLEM 2 j & k — TIMELINE

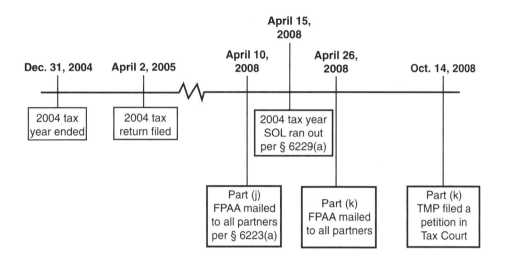

k. If the Service sends the partners an FPAA on April 26, 2008, after the statute of limitations has expired, and the TMP files a petition in Tax Court on October 14, 2008, will the FPAA be considered valid?

l. If the Tax Court precedents are not favorable, what recourse does the TMP have?

m. If the TMP timely petitions the Tax Court for a readjustment of the partnership items for the year, who is bound by the Tax Court decision after it becomes final?

Chapter 7

TERMINATION AND JEOPARDY ASSESSMENTS

IRC:	§§ 6851; 6861-6863; 6867-6873; 7429
Regs.:	§§ 1.6851-1; 301.6861-1; 301.6867-1; 301.7429-2; 301.7429-3

I. INTRODUCTION

As described in Chapter 8, taxpayers typically must be afforded the opportunity for Tax Court review before the IRS can assess deficiencies in income, estate, and gift taxes. Yet audit, administrative appeal, and Tax Court review may consume years. During that time, changes in the taxpayer's financial condition might sharply erode the IRS's ability to collect the deficiencies should the IRS prevail in Tax Court. Furthermore, during that time, some taxpayers with substantial, readily accessible financial resources might attempt to escape responsibility for their tax liabilities by hiding themselves or their assets, or by transferring their assets to relatives, friends, or controlled entities.

There are criminal provisions that can be used to attack such schemes. For example, under section 7201, "[a]ny person who willfully attempts in any manner to evade or defeat any tax . . . or the payment thereof" may be found guilty of a felony. Moreover, under 18 U.S.C. section 371, anyone who cooperates with the taxpayer in a scheme of evasion may be found guilty of criminal conspiracy. However, few such criminal prosecutions are brought each year, and even successful criminal prosecution does not make the IRS whole for revenues lost. Thus, some civil mechanisms must exist by which the IRS can preserve the viability of collection.

Those mechanisms are termination assessment under section 6851, jeopardy assessment under sections 6861 and 6862, and related procedures. When they are invoked, the IRS may assess and collect liabilities immediately, without prior judicial review. Such liabilities include any deficiency for the tax period plus, if appropriate, interest and penalties. The importance of these techniques is underscored by the fact that our system has had expedited means of assessment for as long as it has permitted pre-payment challenge to IRS determinations.

But the peril in expedited assessment is apparent. The deficiency procedures were established for important taxpayer-protection reasons, and their abrogation, even occasionally, is no light matter. Thus, section 7429 provides collateral procedures to afford prompt post-assessment administrative and judicial review to taxpayers subject to expedited assessment. Because they are based on particular need, pose heightened dangers, and entail special procedures, the expedited assessment devices of termination and jeopardy assessments have rightly been called "a singular weapon in the Service's armamentarium."[1]

II. TERMINATION AND JEOPARDY ASSESSMENT AND LEVY

Termination assessments and jeopardy assessments are similar procedures applied to different tax years and sometimes different taxes. These two techniques are applied when the IRS concludes that collection of tax liabilities would be imperiled by allowing the normal processes of assessment and collection to work their course.

A termination assessment under section 6851 is used with respect to income taxes for years that have not yet closed or for which the returns are not yet due. A termination assessment is made during a tax year that has not yet ended, or at any time before the due date (including any extensions) of the taxpayer's return for the preceding year. A termination assessment terminates the year for purposes of computing the tax to be assessed and collected.

A jeopardy assessment is used, typically, for tax periods already closed and for which the return either has been filed or is past due (taking into account properly obtained extensions). Section 6861 authorizes jeopardy assessment of income, estate, gift, and certain excise taxes. Section 6862 authorizes jeopardy assessment of other taxes. Section 6862 assessments are the sole exception to jeopardy assessment being confined to old tax periods. Under section 6862(a), jeopardy assessment may be made "whether or not the time otherwise prescribed by law for making return and paying such tax has expired." The Regulations give this example:

> [A]ssume that a taxpayer incurs on January 18, 1977, liability for tax imposed by section 4061 [the now repealed gas guzzlers' tax], that the last day on which return and payment of such tax is required to be made is May 2, 1977, and that on January 18, 1977, the district director determines that collection of such tax would be jeopardized by delay. In such case, the district director shall immediately assess the tax.[2]

Normally, the IRS uses jeopardy assessments and termination assessments when the taxpayer was engaged in criminal activities, such as illegal drug trafficking, money laundering, illegal gambling, and organized crime. However, the techniques are not confined to those areas. Expedited assessments also are

---

[1] Revis v. United States, 558 F. Supp. 1071 (D.R.I. 1983).

[2] Reg. § 301.6862-1(a). The IRS reorganization mandated by the 1998 Reform Act, § 1001, eliminated the position of district director. The authority formerly vested in district directors has been re-delegated to other IRS officials.

made against legal-source, legal-activity taxpayers who nonetheless meet the conditions justifying expedited assessment.

The expedited assessment techniques of termination and jeopardy assessment should be distinguished from other sorts of rapid or expedited assessment. For example, under section 6213(a), the deficiency procedures described in Chapter 8 apply only to income, estate, gift, generation-skipping transfer, and some excise taxes. Thus, the IRS can immediately assess other types of taxes after audit without issuing a Ninety-Day Letter and without Tax Court review. Moreover, in certain circumstances (such as mathematical or clerical errors on the return), section 6213(b) permits the IRS to immediately assess even those taxes that normally are subject to the deficiency procedures. These direct or immediate assessments are outside sections 6851 and 6861, and related sections, and are not topics of this chapter. The focus of this chapter is only on termination assessment, jeopardy assessment, and related mechanisms.

A. Conditions Justifying Expedited Assessment

The trigger common to termination and jeopardy assessments is also the justification for them: emergency, a state of peril which would compromise ultimate collection of tax if normal processes were allowed to run their course. Section 6851(a)(1) directs the IRS to make a termination assessment if it determines that

> a taxpayer designs quickly to depart from the United States or to remove his property therefrom, or to conceal himself or his property therein, or to do any other act (including in the case of a corporation distributing all or a part of its assets in liquidation or otherwise) tending to prejudice or to render wholly or partially ineffectual proceedings to collect the . . . tax.

Both sections 6861(a) and 6862(a) refer to assessment or collection being "jeopardized by delay," but they do not set out criteria with the specificity of section 6851(a)(1). The section 6851 regulations provide:

> A termination assessment will be made if collection is determined to be in jeopardy because at least one of the following conditions exists.
>
> (i)   The taxpayer is or appears to be designing quickly to depart from the United States or to conceal himself or herself.
>
> (ii)   The taxpayer is or appears to be designing quickly to place his, her, or its property beyond the reach of the Government either by removing it from the United States, by concealing it, by dissipating it, or by transferring it to other persons.

(iii) The taxpayer's financial solvency is or appears to be imperiled.[3]

The sections 6861 and 6862 regulations both refer to the section 6851 regulations. They provide that a state of jeopardy exists when at least one of the these three termination assessment conditions exists.[4] The Government need not show that collection was actually in peril, only that "the circumstances *appear* to jeopardize collection."[5]

It is occasionally argued that, by enumerating these three conditions, the regulations exclude other possible bases for jeopardy or termination assessment. The cases are not entirely consistent, but many decisions look beyond the three grounds in the regulations. In particular, many courts have found that the taxpayer's involvement in criminal activity (especially involving large amounts of cash, as in narcotics trafficking) constitutes strong, sometimes virtually dispositive, support for the appropriateness of expedited assessment.[6]

Another matter of interpretation involves the word "quickly," which appears in the first and second of the three grounds enumerated in the regulations. Just how imminent do the taxpayer's acts have to be? A cramped reading of "quickly" could significantly undercut the utility of the summary device. Recognizing that, the courts have interpreted the word functionally and broadly. If the course of action on which the taxpayer appears to have embarked could significantly erode collection potential before normal procedures have run their course, the "quickly" term will be held to have been satisfied.[7]

The IRS does not make expedited assessments lightly. The expedited assessment procedures are important to the viability of the system. Knowing that, the IRS tends to reserve expedited assessment for clear cases involving substantial dollar amounts.[8] The concern is to avoid creating a body of adverse precedents that could undermine expedited assessment in future cases. Although that is the IRS's usual approach, there are exceptions. The unfortunate fact is that, on occasion, a long, frustrating, and acrimonious course of dealing with a particular taxpayer tips the balance in favor of expedited assessments that might better have been omitted. To minimize such occurrences, expedited assessments

---

[3] Reg. § 1.6851-1(a)(1). The same Regulation clarifies that the insolvency ground "does not include cases where the taxpayer becomes insolvent by virtue of the accrual of the proposed assessment of tax, and penalty, if any." This contrasts with the measurement of insolvency for "in equity" transferee liability cases in which the tax liability is taken into account. *See* Chapter 15.

[4] Reg. §§ 301.6861-1(a), 301.6862-1(a).

[5] Wellek v. United States, 324 F. Supp. 2d 905, 911 (N.D. Ill. 2004) (emphasis in original).

[6] *See, e.g.*, Albury v. United States, 88-2 U.S. Tax Cas. (CCH) ¶ 9511 (S.D. Fla. 1988).

[7] *See, e.g.*, French v. United States, 79-2 U.S. Tax Cas. (CCH) ¶ 9538 (E.D. Okla. 1979).

[8] Restraint is particularly enjoined when the assessment would create public inconvenience, such as when it is against a newspaper, bank, public utility, or other communally important entity. In addition, the IRS sometimes forgoes defensible expedited assessments in order to protect the identity of a confidential informant.

require multiple stages of review and approval within the IRS, including by IRS Counsel.[9]

B. Consequences of Expedited Assessment

1. Termination Assessment

Termination assessment may be made with respect to a given tax year either during that year or before the return for the year is due. Two examples clarify this rule. First, in January 2004, the IRS determines that collection of the taxpayer's income tax for 2003 is in jeopardy. The IRS can make a termination assessment as of December 31, 2003, and collect the determined tax for all of 2003.[10] Second, on May 1, 2004, the IRS determines that collecting the taxpayer's income tax for the current year is in jeopardy. The IRS can make a termination assessment and collect the determined tax for the short period January 1, 2004 through May 1, 2004.[11]

Upon assessment, the tax "shall immediately become due and payable." If a short period was assessed, the year continues until its normal end. The taxpayer is still obligated to file a return for the full year and at the normal time (typically April 15 of the year following the tax year).[12]

The calculation of the tax for the assessed period includes all income the IRS believes pertains to that period. The taxpayer must be allowed all pertinent deductions and credits, including, if a short period is assessed, full personal exemptions.

In conducting an examination which may lead to termination, revenue agents are instructed to make "reasonable" computation of the tax liability, taking into account all known assets, liabilities, income, and expenses of the taxpayer. Additionally, agents are supposed to interview the taxpayer when feasible (preferably before the assessment is made) to give the taxpayer the opportunity to explain the circumstances. When illegal-source income is suspected, agents are supposed to consult non-tax law enforcement officials, when possible, with knowledge of the activities.[13] Estimates of income and expenses are permitted, but they must relate to specific facts and not entail speculative extrapolations.[14]

---

[9] *See, e.g.*, IRC § 7429(a)(1)(A); Rev. Proc. 78-12, 1978-1 C.B. 590.

[10] What if the IRS did not determine the condition of jeopardy until April 16, 2004? Assuming the taxpayer had not obtained a proper extension, the year would be closed and the IRS's remedy would be jeopardy assessment, not termination assessment.

[11] Manual provisions governing termination assessments and jeopardy assessments are set out at IRM 5.1.4.

[12] IRC § 6851(a)(1); Reg. § 1.6851-1(a)(3).

[13] Frequently, federal or state law enforcement officials will inform the IRS about the illegal activity.

[14] *E.g.*, Auth v. United States, 79-2 U.S. Tax Cas. (CCH) ¶ 9726 (D. Utah 1979).

Chapter 13 describes the normal rules dealing with post-assessment collection of tax. Those rules are telescoped following a termination assessment. The IRS sometimes does not rapidly seek to collect after an expedited assessment. When it chooses to, however, it can proceed with such collection within a matter of days, even hours, after the expedited assessment.

The IRS must make demand for payment, and, within five days after making the termination assessment, notify the taxpayer of the assessment and the IRS's basis for it.[15] Notification may be served in person or by certified mail to the taxpayer's last known address.[16] The IRS typically files notices of tax lien immediately. Whether it also levies on the taxpayer's property depends upon how the IRS evaluates the circumstances of the particular case. The taxpayer must be given an opportunity—however brief—to pay before seizure is effected.[17] Section 6331(a) provides that, after notice-and-demand, the IRS may take enforced collection action, including levies, without waiting the usual ten-day period.[18]

After making a termination assessment, the IRS is required to issue a statutory notice of deficiency to the taxpayer. Under section 6851(b), this must be done within sixty days of the later of (i) the due date for the taxpayer's return for the full year (considered with regard to any properly obtained extension) or (ii) the date the return is filed. Section 6851(b) states that the deficiency determined in the notice may be greater than, less than, or the same amount as was assessed. If the assessed amount exceeds the determined deficiency amount, the excess is to be abated. If the excess has already been collected, the IRS will not make a refund until the case is closed. The deficiency is to be calculated on the basis of the full year, not a period shortened as a result of the assessment.

A pitfall exists for unwary taxpayers in this regard. Returns for years for which there was a termination assessment are to be filed with IRS offices identified in the regulations, not with the usual Service Center.[19] If the return is submitted to the wrong office, it is deemed not to have been filed. As a consequence, the sixty-day period for the issuance of the statutory notice of deficiency does not begin to run.

If the return is timely filed and the IRS fails to issue the notice of deficiency within the sixty-day period, the termination assessment is nullified. However, the IRS may make a new termination assessment or a jeopardy assessment, as long as the section 6501 limitations period has not yet expired and a condition of jeopardy continues to exist. Alternatively, the IRS could follow the deficiency

---

[15] IRC §§ 6851(a)(1), 7429(a)(1)(B).

[16] IRM 5.1.4.6.

[17] *See, e.g.*, Mettenbrink v. United States, 71 A.F.T.R. 2d (RIA) ¶ 93-3642 (D. Neb. 1991).

[18] Under section 6330(f), the Collection Due Process protections do not apply in termination or jeopardy situations.

[19] IRC § 6091(b); Reg. § 1.6091-2.

procedures. The failure of the IRS to issue the notice of deficiency within the sixty-day period does not compel the IRS to return any amounts collected pursuant to the now-invalidated termination assessment—as long as the IRS properly makes a new assessment and properly issues a notice of deficiency.[20]

Upon issuance of the notice of deficiency, the taxpayer has the usual options, including filing a petition for redetermination with the Tax Court (with the possibility of Appeals Office consideration once the pleadings are complete). If the taxpayer files a timely petition,[21] the Tax Court has jurisdiction even if the notice of deficiency is filed after the sixty-day period as long as it was timely issued under section 6501.[22] Any amounts collected under the termination assessment are treated as tax payments for the year.[23] However, under section 6211(b)(1), they are not considered payments in computing the deficiency, and therefore do not affect the Tax Court's jurisdiction.

If the IRS eventually concludes that jeopardy to collection did not exist, it may abate the termination assessment. In that event, section 6851(e) directs that the applicable limitations period on normal assessment is determined as if no assessment had been made, except that the running of the period is suspended from the date the assessment was made until ten days after the assessment was abated.

2. Jeopardy Assessment

As noted, jeopardy assessment is the immediate assessment of an "old" tax year. Typically, it is made before a statutory notice of deficiency is issued and Tax Court review is requested. However, if the condition of jeopardy arises after a notice of deficiency was issued and during a Tax Court proceeding, jeopardy assessment still is permitted. However, no jeopardy assessment may be made after any decision by the Tax Court has become final or the taxpayer has filed a petition seeking review of the Tax Court's decision. Usually, the assessment may be greater than, less than, or the same amount as determined in the notice of deficiency. However, if the assessment is made after the Tax Court decision is rendered (but before it becomes final), the assessment "may be made only in respect of the deficiency determined" in the court's decision. Before the decision is rendered, the IRS may abate part or all of the assessment if it believes the assessment was excessive. If the IRS jeopardy assesses during a Tax Court case, it must notify the court of assessed amounts and abated amounts.[24]

---

[20] *See, e.g.,* Estate of McDonald v. United States, 79-1 U.S. Tax Cas. (CCH) ¶ 9182 (N.D. Cal. 1979).

[21] Typically, the petition must be filed with the Tax Court within ninety days after the IRS issues the notice of deficiency. *See* Chapter 8.

[22] *See, e.g.,* Ramirez v. Commissioner, 87 T.C. 643 (1986).

[23] IRC § 6851(a)(3).

[24] IRC § 6861(c)–(g).

Many of the consequences and procedures as to jeopardy assessments resemble those as to termination assessments. The amount assessed becomes immediately due and payable. Computation typically is easier than with respect to jeopardy assessments since completed tax years are involved. Again, notice and demand for payment must be made and, within five days after the assessment, the IRS must notify the taxpayer of it.[25] The IRS may take collection action immediately after making notice and demand, if payment is not made.

Again, the IRS is required to issue a statutory notice of deficiency,[26] but the timing differs from that in the termination assessment context. Section 6861(b) directs the IRS to issue the notice of deficiency within sixty days of making notice and demand. This is so only for section 6861 jeopardy assessments since the taxes subject to section 6862 jeopardy assessments do not involve the deficiency procedures. The cases are split as to whether the failure to meet the sixty-day requirement renders the jeopardy assessment unenforceable.[27]

Occasionally, the IRS makes multiple jeopardy assessments for the same tax year. This might happen, for instance, if the IRS later concludes that its prior jeopardy assessment was inadequate in amount. However, each additional jeopardy assessment requires additional notice and demand and an additional notice of deficiency. Each of the assessments is independent. Thus, for example, a proper second jeopardy assessment will be upheld even if the first jeopardy assessment was defective for some reason.[28]

The IRS has authority to abate improper or excessive jeopardy assessments before finality of Tax Court decision. The normal limitations rules apply, except that the running of the limitations period is suspended from the date the jeopardy assessment was made until ten days after it was abated.[29]

III. SECTION 7429 REVIEW

A. In General

Before 1976, the only judicial recourse available to a taxpayer subject to an expedited assessment was either (i) paying the amount assessed and bringing a normal refund suit or (ii) seeking an injunction under the *Williams Packing*

---

[25] IRC §§ 6861(a), 6862(a), 7429(a)(1)(B).

[26] This requirement is met if the IRS timely sends the notice to the taxpayer's last known address even if the taxpayer does not receive the notice. "The statute does not require receipt of the notice by the taxpayer." Royal Denim for Import & Export, Inc. v. United States, 371 F. Supp. 2d 569, 571 (S.D.N.Y. 2005).

[27] *Compare* United States v. Ball, 326 F.2d 898 (4th Cir. 1964) (yes), *with* Cohen v. United States, 297 F.2d 760 (9th Cir. 1962) (no).

[28] *See, e.g.*, Berry v. Westover, 70 F. Supp. 537 (S.D. Cal. 1947).

[29] IRC § 6861(g).

exception to the Anti-Injunction Act.[30] Neither was satisfactory: the former entailed great delay and burden on the taxpayer and the latter was available only in very limited circumstances.

In response to serious concerns about the fairness and perhaps constitutionality of the expedited assessment regime,[31] Congress in 1976 enacted a considerably better review mechanism: section 7429. Suit under section 7429 is now one of the statutory exceptions to the Anti-Injunction Act. Section 7429(a)(1)(A) reinforces pre-assessment review by requiring approval by IRS Counsel both for jeopardy assessment and for levy within thirty days after notice and demand for payment. More importantly, section 7429 creates an elaborate scheme of expedited post-assessment review. However, section 7429 does not suspend the ability of the IRS to collect the assessed tax. Here are the main aspects of the rather complex section 7429 post-assessment review scheme:

- Within five days after the termination or jeopardy assessment or levy is made, the IRS is required to provide the taxpayer with a written statement of the information upon which the IRS relied in making the assessment or levy.

- Within thirty days after the written statement is provided (or within thirty days after the last date on which it was supposed to have been provided), the taxpayer may request that the IRS review the assessment or levy. This review is conducted by the Appeals Office. The Appeals Office is directed to determine whether the making of the assessment or levy is "reasonable under the circumstances" and whether the amount assessed or demanded is "appropriate under the circumstances."

- If the taxpayer is dissatisfied with the result of this administrative review, he or she may obtain judicial review. Within ninety days after the earlier of (i) the date the Appeals Office notified the taxpayer of its determination or (ii) the sixteenth day after the taxpayer made the request for administrative review, the taxpayer may bring a civil action against the United States in federal District Court challenging the summary assessment or levy. The Tax Court has concurrent jurisdiction, but only in cases in which the IRS jeopardy assessed after the taxpayer petitioned the Tax Court for redetermination of determinations in a statutory notice of deficiency for the same or some of the same tax year(s).

- Within twenty days after the action is commenced, the court is to decide the case. The twenty-day period may be extended up to forty additional days if the taxpayer so requests and establishes reasonable grounds therefor. The government cannot request extension. Saturday, Sunday, or a legal hol-

---

[30] *See* Commissioner v. Shapiro, 424 U.S. 614 (1976); Enochs v. Williams Packing Co., 370 U.S. 1 (1962). For discussion of the Anti-Injunction Act (IRC § 7421) and the *Williams Packing* exception to it, see Chapter 13.

[31] *See, e.g.*, Laing v. United States, 423 U.S. 161 (1976).

iday in the District of Columbia cannot be the last day of any section 7429 period.

• The government bears the burden of proof as to whether it was reasonable to make the expedited assessment or levy. In other words, the government must establish that a condition of jeopardy exists. As to the reasonableness of the amount of the assessment, the government must provide a written statement containing the information on which the IRS's determination of the amount assessed was based. Thereafter, the burden of proof on the amount issue shifts to the taxpayer. The court's review is *de novo*,[32] and the court's decision (at least as to substantive issues) is "final and conclusive and shall not be reviewed by any other court."

The following is a more detailed exploration of the phases of the section 7429 review scheme.

B. Administrative Phase

It is important that the taxpayer properly seek Appeals consideration. Failure to timely request Appeals consideration is viewed as a failure to exhaust administrative remedies, which precludes the taxpayer from obtaining judicial review.[33] Also, if the taxpayer brings suit before expiration of the time prescribed for administrative review, the case will be dismissed as premature.[34]

The Appeals Office, in considering the request for redetermination, may take into account not only information available at the time the assessment was made, but also after-acquired information. This also is true for a court conducting subsequent judicial review.[35]

C. Trial Phase

Venue is determined pursuant to 28 U.S.C. section 1402(a). Thus, in District Court actions, venue for individual taxpayers is in the district where he or she resides; venue for corporate taxpayers is in the district where the corporation has its principal place of business or filed its return; venue is in the District of Columbia district if the previous rules cannot be applied. If the action is filed in the Tax Court but that court concludes that it lacks jurisdiction, the Tax Court may transfer the action to the proper District Court if the interests of justice so require. A transferred case then proceeds as if it had been filed in that District Court on the date it was filed in the Tax Court.

---

[32] *See, e.g.*, Loretto v. United States, 440 F. Supp. 1168 (E.D. Pa. 1977).

[33] *See, e.g.*, Friko Corp. v. United States, 91-1 U.S. Tax Cas. (CCH) ¶ 50,195 (D.D.C. 1991).

[34] *See, e.g.*, Daniels v. United States, 88-1 U.S. Tax Cas. (CCH) ¶ 9196 (N.D. Ga. 1987).

[35] *See, e.g.*, Reg. § 301.7429-2(b); Haskin v. United States, 444 F. Supp. 299 (C.D. Cal. 1977).

As noted, the IRS is directed to furnish to the taxpayer within five days after the expedited assessment a written statement of the information on which it relied in making the assessment. The purpose is to give the taxpayer the opportunity to identify erroneous or incomplete information on which the IRS may have relied. To fulfill that purpose, the IRS's statement should be detailed and comprehensive and it should state specific facts. Sometimes, IRS statements do not fit this description but instead contain only general conclusory language, perhaps merely repeating the predicate language in the Regulations.

Taxpayers sometimes have argued that an excessively general IRS statement should cause invalidation of the assessments. The courts have almost uniformly rejected this argument, usually on a "no harm, no foul" theory. The taxpayer typically gets or has the opportunity to get the detailed information omitted from the statement, by informal communication with the IRS, during Appeals consideration, or via discovery. Thus, the courts reason, the taxpayer is not prejudiced by the generality of the statement and invalidation of the assessment is too drastic a remedy.[36]

A somewhat similar question arises when the court has failed to render its decision within twenty days. Courts usually have rejected taxpayer claims that the assessments should be invalidated on account of such delay.[37] A number of rationales have been offered, including: (1) the taxpayer failed in his or her duty to alert the court to the extraordinary time requirement, (2) the taxpayer suffered no prejudice from the delay, and (3) the statute states no consequence for failure to decide the case within twenty days.

Discovery usually is limited in section 7429 cases, but sometimes can be obtained on a showing of need or other special factors.[38] Both as to the making of assessment or levy and as to the amount assessed, the IRS's determination will be upheld if the court finds it to have been reasonable. The standard of proof has been described as something more than "not arbitrary and capricious" but something less than "substantial evidence."[39] Section 7429 review has been likened to preliminary examination for probable cause in a criminal proceeding but under a different standard: reasonableness. The review is *de novo*.[40] Typically, the courts will admit any information they feel is probative as to the issues, unconstrained by the usual rules of evidence.[41]

Reasonableness as to the making of the assessment always turns on the facts and circumstances of the particular case. Thus, beyond general points,

[36] *See, e.g.*, Evans v. United States, 672 F. Supp. 1118 (S.D. Ind. 1987). *But see* Walker v. United States, 650 F. Supp. 877 (E.D. Tenn. 1987) (invalidating the assessment).

[37] *See, e.g.*, United States v. Doyle, 482 F. Supp. 1227 (E.D. Wis. 1980), *app. dismissed*, 660 F.2d 277 (7th Cir. 1981). *But see* Clarke v. United States, 553 F. Supp. 382 (E.D. Va. 1983).

[38] *See* Steve Johnson, *Discovery in Summary Assessment Proceedings*, 93 Tax Notes , Oct. 10, 2001, at 539.

[39] *See, e.g.*, Harvey v. United States, 730 F. Supp. 1097 (S.D. Fla. 1990).

[40] *E.g.*, Wellek v. United States, 324 F. Supp. 2d 905, 911 (N.D. Ill. 2004).

[41] *See, e.g.*, Daniels v. United States, 88-1 U.S. Tax Cas. (CCH) ¶ 9295 (N.D. Ga. 1988).

cases have limited precedential value. Numerous factors have been noted by courts as part of their discussion of whether the government carried its burden of proof with respect to the existence of a condition of jeopardy. Non-exhaustively, they include the taxpayer's use of multiple names or multiple addresses, use of large amounts of cash, transfer or concealment of assets, failure to provide information, involvement in illegal activities, history of not filing returns or of filing inaccurate returns, insolvency, and unexplained travel, especially foreign travel.[42]

After the IRS explains its basis for the amount assessed, the taxpayer bears the burden of proof on the reasonableness of amount issue. The taxpayer does not satisfy that burden simply by attacking the IRS's computation.[43] There are several reasons for this. First, the taxpayer is closer to the facts and should be encouraged to bring them out rather than simply criticize the IRS's attempts. Second, the circumstances prompting expedited assessment make approximation more typical than precision. Third, the taxpayer sometimes is to blame for any imprecision because of failing to keep or to produce records.[44] Fourth, there will be the opportunity for more detailed consideration of the alleged deficiency in subsequent Tax Court litigation.

The taxpayer sometimes is given the opportunity through discovery to probe the bases of the IRS's computation. Sometimes too, courts have reduced the amount of the assessment, especially when information developed after the assessment clarified liability. However, when a condition of jeopardy exists, it is rare for a reviewing court to entirely invalidate an expedited assessment because of concerns about the amount assessed.

In general, courts have felt themselves constrained as to what they can decide and order in section 7429 cases, limiting themselves to upholding the expedited assessment in full, invalidating it in full, or invalidating it in part and upholding the remainder of it. Rare decisions have gone beyond this, directing the IRS, the taxpayer, or both to undertake broad courses of action or remediation.[45]

---

[42] *See, e.g.*, Varjabedian v. United States, 339 F. Supp. 2d 140, 155-57 (D. Mass. 2004) (upholding the making of an income tax jeopardy assessment against a gas station owner when, among other indicia, the taxpayer maintained large cash hoards, structured postal money order transactions, held numerous assets in his sister's name, and left in his business files specific references to avoiding the IRS).

[43] *See, e.g.*, Robinson v. Boyle, 46 A.F.T.R.2d (P-H) ¶ 80-5078 (E.D. Va. 1980).

[44] *E.g.*, Varjabedian v. United States, 339 F. Supp. 2d 140, 158 (D. Mass. 2004).

[45] As an extreme example, see *Fidelity Equipment Leasing Corp. v. United States*, 462 F. Supp. 845 (N.D. Ga. 1978). The court's attempt at micromanagement predictably failed and was abandoned. *See* 47 A.F.T.R.2d (P-H) ¶ 81-1117 (N.D. Ga. 1981) (vacating the court's previous order in part and entering a new order largely upholding the jeopardy assessment and levy).

D. Post-Trial Phase

Section 7429(f) states: "Any determination made by a court under [section 7429] shall be final and conclusive and shall not be reviewed by any other court." The reason for this rule of non-appealability is that expedited assessment is only a provisional remedy. The idea is to freeze the situation to prevent erosion of collection potential, but not to determine with finality the underlying merits of the case. The merits will be ascertained in a subsequent Tax Court case contesting the statutory notice of deficiency or in a subsequent refund action. The section 7429 proceeding is substantively and procedurally unrelated to a subsequent trial on the merits, and the section 7429 determination has no binding or persuasive effect in the subsequent trial.

Despite the seemingly clear language of section 7429(f), some circuits have held that section 7429 decisions are appealable for limited purposes, such as challenges that the district court exceeded its authority, improperly evaluated the plaintiff's standing to sue, or committed procedural errors.[46] Other circuits do not permit appeal even of such matters. No circuit allows appeal of substantive decisions as to reasonableness of assessment or reasonableness of amount.

IV. OTHER TAXPAYER PROTECTIONS AND OPTIONS

A taxpayer need not seek section 7429 review. A number of other protections are available that may be used instead of or in addition to section 7429. These include (1) administrative abatement, (2) bond in lieu of collection, and (3) judicial review of intended sale of seized property.

A. Abatement

The taxpayer can request the IRS to abate the assessment. The IRS has the power to abate an expedited assessment "in whole or in part, if it is shown to [the IRS's] satisfaction that jeopardy does not exist."[47] An advantage of abatement is that it is not subject to the compressed time frame applicable to Appeals Office consideration under section 7429. The request for abatement may be made at any time before a Tax Court decision is rendered in the case. Section 6404(b) provides that a taxpayer may not file a claim for abatement of income, estate, gift, or generation-skipping transfer tax. Thus, abatement of expedited assessment of such taxes is a matter of administrative discretion. The taxpayer may informally request the IRS to effect abatement. However, if the IRS

---

[46] *See, e.g.*, Morgan v. United States, 958 F.2d 950 (9th Cir. 1992); Schuster v. United States, 765 F.2d 1047 (11th Cir. 1985).

[47] Reg. § 301.6861-1(f)(1).

rejects or ignores the taxpayer's informal request, the taxpayer has no recourse as to abatement.

B. Bond

Under section 6863, the taxpayer may respond to an expedited assessment by filing a bond with the IRS. The purpose is to preempt enforced collection which might prove to be even more disruptive. The bond may be in an amount equal to all or to only part of the assessment, and it should include interest on the portion of the assessment on which collection is to be stayed. The bond may be filed (i) at any time before levy is authorized, (ii) after levy is authorized but before it has been effected, or (iii) in the discretion of the IRS, after levy has been made but before expiration of the collection limitations period.[48]

Additional rules apply in the case of taxes actually or potentially subject to the jurisdiction of the Tax Court. If the bond is given before a Tax Court petition is filed, the bond must contain a condition that, if a Tax Court petition is not timely filed, then the amount whose collection is sought to be stayed, together with interest, will be paid on notice and demand [the section 6863 notice and demand] after expiration of the Tax Court petition period. In addition, the bond must be conditioned on payment of so much of the assessment as is not abated by a final Tax Court decision.[49]

The taxpayer may waive the stay of collection pursuant to the bond in whole or in part at any time. Once the bond has been given, it can be reduced if part or all of the assessment is paid or satisfied by levy, if the IRS abates part or all of the assessment, or if the Tax Court holds that part or all of the assessment exceeded correct tax liability.[50]

Taxpayers rarely avail themselves of the option to file a bond to stay collection on an expedited assessment. Filing such a bond rarely offers substantial advantages over other taxpayer remedies and protections. Moreover, the very conditions that created or appeared to create the condition of jeopardy often render it infeasible to obtain the requisite bond.

C. Stay of Sale

As stated previously, under certain circumstances, the IRS may levy immediately after making an expedited assessment. However, as described below, when non-cash property has been seized, the Code and the regulations limit the IRS's ability to sell that property. The amount the IRS realizes in cash as a

---

[48] IRC § 6863(a); Reg. § 301.6863-1(a). For discussion of the collection statute of limitations, see Chapter 13.

[49] IRC § 6863(b).

[50] IRC § 6863(a), (b)(2).

result of administrative sale of seized property often is considerably less than the true value of the property. The sale-limitation rules protect the taxpayer from such leakage of value in most cases.

In general, sale of property seized pursuant to an expedited assessment is prohibited as long as the taxpayer continues to invoke review rights under section 7429 and subsequent Tax Court adjudication of the merits. Thus, sale typically cannot be effected until after the last of these events occurs: (i) the period for seeking administrative review of the expedited assessment expires without the taxpayer requesting such review; (ii) the period for filing an action to review the expedited assessment expires without the taxpayer filing such an action; or (iii) the court's decision in the action becomes final.[51]

Moreover, property seized pursuant to an expedited assessment may not be sold until after issuance of the required statutory notice of deficiency and either (i) the section 6213(a) period for filing a Tax Court petition challenging that notice expires without the taxpayer filing such a petition or (ii) the decision of the Tax Court in the case resulting from the filing of a petition becomes final. However, these additional limitations on sale with respect to actual or potential Tax Court review do not apply if a termination assessment was made and the taxpayer fails to file a timely return for the terminated year(s), taking properly obtained extensions into account. Moreover, appeal of the decision of the Tax Court does not prevent sale of the seized property unless the taxpayer files a bond as provided under section 7485.[52]

There are exceptions to the above general rules as to stay of sale. The seized property may be sold if the taxpayer consents to the sale, or if the IRS determines that expenses of conserving and maintaining the property will greatly reduce the net proceeds of sale, or if the property consists of perishable goods within the meaning of section 6336. If a Tax Court petition has been filed, the Tax Court has jurisdiction to review the IRS's determination that special circumstances exists. The review is commenced on motion of either the taxpayer or the IRS. The court's order disposing of the motion is appealable in the same manner as other Tax Court decisions.[53]

If a taxpayer submits such a motion, he or she must assert "grounds that are plausible and believable." Thereafter, the IRS must show by a preponderance of the evidence that one of the above exceptions to the stay exists. The Tax Court may consider "affidavits, appraisals, or other appropriate information" in making its decision. The court has authority to issue a temporary stay on sale pending resolution of the motion.[54]

---

[51] IRC § 6863(c).

[52] IRC § 6863(b)(3)(A); Reg. § 301.6863-2(a).

[53] IRC § 6863(b)(3), (c).

[54] Williams v. Commissioner, 92 T.C. 920 (1989).

V. RELATED ASSESSMENT MECHANISMS

The termination and jeopardy assessment mechanisms are the principal means of addressing collection emergencies, but they are not the only means. Here are six others. The characteristic common to them is that they are topical—addressed to highly particular circumstances—rather than general in their application.

A. Departing Aliens

In general, "[n]o alien shall depart from the United States unless he first procures from the [IRS] a certificate that he has complied with all the obligations imposed upon him by the income tax laws."[55] To obtain such a certificate, the departing alien must file certain statements with the IRS, appear before the IRS if required, and pay any tax due.[56]

The departing alien must, at his or her point of departure, present either the above certificate or evidence that he or she is excepted from obtaining one. Failure to satisfy these conditions will subject the departing alien to examination by the IRS at the point of departure and to the necessity of completing returns and statements and paying tax pursuant to a termination assessment.[57]

Some aliens are categorically excepted from the requirement to obtain the certificate. They include employees of foreign governments or international organizations; students, exchange visitors, and industrial trainees admitted under designed visa types and having limited income; tourists, business visitors, and aliens in transit under designated visa types; alien military trainees of the Department of Defense; and residents of Canada or Mexico who frequently commute between their home country and the United States for employment and whose wages are subject to tax withholding.[58]

In considering an application for a certificate of compliance, the IRS will determine whether the intended departure would jeopardize collection of income tax for the current year or the preceding year. If the IRS determines that it would, the tax period will be terminated and the alien will be required to file returns and make payment for the shortened period. If the IRS determines that the departure would not jeopardize collection, the alien may be required to file certain information but will not be required to pay income tax before the usual due date.[59]

---

[55] IRC § 6851(d)(1).

[56] Reg. § 1.6851-2(a)(1).

[57] IRC § 6851(d)(2); Reg. § 1.6851-2(a)(1).

[58] Reg. § 1.6851-2(a)(2).

[59] Reg. § 1.6851-2(b)(1)(i).

If the alien is a United States resident, the intended departure will not lead to termination unless the IRS has information indicating that the alien intends to avoid tax payment through the departure. The intended departure of a non-resident alien will lead to termination unless he or she establishes to the satisfaction of the IRS that return to the United States is intended and that departure will not jeopardize collection. The determination is made based on all facts and circumstances. Evidence tending to negate jeopardy includes "information showing that the alien is engaged in trade or business in the United States or that he leaves sufficient property in the United States to secure payment of his income tax for the taxable year and of any income tax for the preceding year which remains unpaid." If the IRS does make a termination assessment, the departing alien may post a section 6863 bond in order to postpone until the usual time the payment of the determined tax.[60]

B. Tax-Exempt Organizations

An organization otherwise described in section 501(c)(3) can face serious consequences if it makes prohibited political expenditures. The organization may lose its section 501 exemption, and it may be required to pay an excise tax under section 4955. Section 6852 creates a termination assessment remedy to support those taxes.

Under section 6852(a), if the IRS finds that a section 501(c)(3) organization has made political expenditures which "constitute a flagrant violation of the prohibition against making political expenditures," the IRS is directed immediately to determine any income tax payable by the organization for the current and immediately previous tax years. The IRS also is directed immediately to determine any excise tax payable under section 4955 by the organization or any manager of the organization for those years. Those taxes "become immediately due and payable." The IRS is to immediately assess the tax (plus any interest and penalties), give notice of it, and make immediate demand for payment.[61] Since this is a termination assessment, the provision does not apply to a preceding year after the due date of the organization's return, determined with regard to properly obtained extensions.[62]

A section 6852 termination assessment is made only if the flagrant violation results in revocation of the organization's tax exemption. The organization is not liable for income taxes for any period before the effective date of the revocation.[63]

---

[60] Reg. § 1.6851-2(b)(1).

[61] IRC § 6852(a)(1). The key statutory terms have the same meanings as they have under section 4955. IRC § 6852(b)(1).

[62] IRC § 6852(a)(4).

[63] Reg. § 301.6852-1(b).

The protections available as to termination and jeopardy assessments typically also are available as to section 6852 assessments. Specifically, the IRS has administrative abatement authority; a statutory notice must be issued within sixty days, creating the opportunity for Tax Court review; the taxpayer may post a bond to stay collection; and the section 7429 review procedures apply.[64]

C. Corporate NOL Carrybacks

Under section 6164(a), if a corporation files with the IRS a statement with respect to an expected net operating ("NOL") loss carryback for that year, the time for the payment of the corporation's income tax for the immediately preceding tax year is extended. However, if the IRS believes that collection of the amount to which the extension relates is in jeopardy, it is directed to immediately terminate the extension, notify the taxpayer, and demand payment.[65]

D. Passive Foreign Investment Companies

Sections 1291 through 1298 establish a regime of income taxation with respect to passive foreign investment companies ("PFIC"s). Section 1294 provides an election by which the taxpayer may extend the time for payment of tax on undistributed PFIC earnings. However, if the IRS believes that collection is in jeopardy, it is directed to immediately terminate the extension, notify the taxpayer, and demand payment. The amount of undistributed earnings with respect to which the extension is terminated is left to the discretion of the IRS.[66]

E. Receiverships and Bankruptcies

On the appointment of a receiver for the taxpayer in any receivership case, whether state or federal, the IRS is permitted to immediately assess any deficiency (plus interest and penalties) in any of the taxes otherwise subject to the deficiency procedures.[67] Similarly, when a bankruptcy petition has been filed, the IRS may immediately assess any deficiency (plus interest and penalties) in tax otherwise subject to the deficiency procedures. The deficiency to be assessed may be owed by the debtor's estate in the bankruptcy proceeding, or it may be owed by the debtor but (in the latter situation) only if the liability has become *res judicata* in the bankruptcy case.[68]

---

[64] IRC §§ 6852(b)(2), 6863(a), 7429(a), (b); Reg. § 301.6852-1(c).

[65] IRC §§ 6164(h), 6864.

[66] IRC § 1294(c)(3); Reg. § 1.1294-1T(e)(5).

[67] IRC § 6871(a).

[68] IRC § 6871(b).

Typically, the taxpayer's assets are under the control of the court in bankruptcies and receiverships. However, any assets not under such control may be subject to levy after the assessments.[69] The normal protections available with respect to jeopardy assessments, including section 7429 review, do not apply. For example, no subsequent notice of deficiency need be issued. However, the IRS will send a letter "to the taxpayer or to the trustee, receiver, debtor in possession, or other like fiduciary, notifying him in detail how the deficiency was computed." The taxpayer may furnish to the IRS information disputing the deficiency unless a Tax Court petition had been filed before the assessment.[70]

F. Possessors of Large Amounts of Cash

Illegal drug trafficking and other criminal activities often lead to situations in which individuals are found in possession of large amounts of cash, yet they deny they own the cash and deny knowledge of who the owner is. The odds are high that the money represents untaxed income and that one of the conditions of jeopardy exists. However, without an owner, who is the taxpayer and against whom can the IRS make a summary assessment?

Congress responded to these difficulties by enacting section 6867. This section applies when an individual in physical possession of over $10,000 does not claim the cash as his or "as belonging to another person whose identity the [IRS] can readily ascertain and who acknowledges ownership of such cash." In this circumstance, it is presumed for termination and jeopardy assessment purposes that the cash represents income of an unknown single individual for the tax year in which the possession occurs and that collection of tax will be jeopardized by delay.[71] The income is treated as taxable income and is taxed at the highest rate specified in section 1(c).[72]

For this purpose, "cash" includes cash equivalents such as foreign currency, bearer obligations, and, pursuant to regulations, any medium of exchange of a type which frequently has been used in illegal activities. Bearer obligations are taken into account at face amount and other cash equivalents at fair market value. The cash equivalents identified by the regulations include coins, precious metals, jewelry, precious stones, postage stamps, traveler's checks, and certain negotiable instruments, incomplete instruments, and securities.[73]

In general, the possessor of the cash is treated as the taxpayer for purposes of assessment, collection, and the section 7429(a)(1) requirements. Thus, the possessor will receive a statutory notice of deficiency, but solely in his or her

---

[69] Reg. § 301.6871(a)-2(a).

[70] Reg. § 301.6871(b)-1(c).

[71] IRC § 6867(a); Reg. § 301.6867-1(a).

[72] IRC § 6867(b).

[73] IRC § 6867(d); Reg. § 301.6867-1(f).

capacity as possessor of the cash, not in his or her individual capacity. The possessor may file a Tax Court petition contesting the notice of deficiency. Also, the possessor will receive the written statement described in section 7429(a)(1)(B). However, the possessor is not treated as the taxpayer for other section 7429 purposes, so may not seek administrative or judicial review of the expedited assessment. Nor may the possessor file a refund claim or bring a refund suit.[74]

If the expedited assessment later is abated and replaced by an assessment against the true owner of the cash, that replacement assessment is treated for all lien, levy, and collection purposes as relating back to the date of the expedited assessment.[75] The true owner may request administrative and judicial review under section 7429, but any suit must be preceded by a request for administrative review made by the true owner within thirty days after the IRS furnishes the written statement of explanation to the possessor. The true owner, after levy, may bring a section 7426 action to recover the cash within the nine-month period prescribed by section 6532(c). The true owner may, with the permission of the Tax Court, appear in an action brought by the possessor challenging a notice of deficiency issued to the possessor, but the true owner may not bring that action him or herself. However, if the assessment against the possessor is abated and the IRS issues a statutory notice of deficiency to the true owner, the true owner may file a Tax Court petition contesting that notice.[76]

VI. PRACTICAL DIFFICULTY

As a postscript, taxpayers subject to expedited assessment and levy face practical problems. As the foregoing makes clear, there are many complex rules and options in these situations. A taxpayer in such a situation needs a competent attorney.

However, the assessments and levies may leave the taxpayer strapped for the resources to hire an attorney. The IRS does not have to release jeopardy liens so that the taxpayer can pay a lawyer.[77] Occasionally, the obligation to pay attorneys fees is used to help establish that a condition of jeopardy exists (for example, as part of the solvency calculation).[78] Moreover, the expedited assessments and levies may be occurring at the same time as other events (like civil or criminal asset forfeiture, or the pressing of claims by other creditors) that exacerbate the difficulty of paying an attorney.

The attorney accepting one of these cases typically will want payment in advance. Sometimes the taxpayer can make the payment, for example if levy

---

[74] IRC § 6867(b)(3); Reg. § 301.6867-1(d).

[75] IRC § 6867(c).

[76] Reg. § 301.6867-1(e).

[77] See, e.g., Shapiro v. Commissioner, 73 T.C. 313 (1979).

[78] See, e.g., Mesher v. United States, 736 F. Supp. 233 (D. Or. 1990).

has not yet been made or the taxpayer has resources beyond those levied on. Sometimes, the taxpayer can get from a friend or relative the money needed. Sometimes, the attorney thinks that the taxpayer's case is good enough that the attorney is willing to wait for payment until after the victory at Appeals or in court. Sometimes, a lawyer is willing to take such a case on a *pro bono* basis.

PROBLEM

Silas Soleen owns and operates Fins 'N' Feathers, a pet shop formed as an S corporation. The shop used to be owned by Silas' father, Ferdinand. However, Ferdinand had used the shop as a cover for an illegal trade in exotic animals in violation of statutes banning trafficking in protected animal species. Ferdinand spent time in jail for such violations, after which he transferred the shop and related property to Silas. Silas has owned and operated the shop since 2000. He continues to own and profitably operate it today. Law enforcement officials are convinced that some illegal animal trade continues at the shop.

Silas has always filed his Forms 1040 on a timely basis. On his 2002 and 2003 Forms 1040, Silas reported substantial income tax liabilities, but he paid none of them. He attached to those Forms literature from a tax protester group. The literature—insofar as it was decipherable—suggested that the Internal Revenue Code imposes an obligation to file returns but does not impose an obligation to actually pay the tax reported on the returns.

In January 2005, the IRS began an examination of Silas' 2002 and 2003 tax years. The revenue agent determined that delinquency penalties should be imposed as to the liabilities shown on the returns but not paid. Between the two years, the liabilities plus interest and penalties with respect to them total approximately $74,000.

The revenue agent also determined that the 2002 and 2003 returns were inaccurate in two ways. First, she performed a bank-deposits-and-expenditures analysis on the basis of which she concluded that Silas had underreported his income for both 2002 and 2003. The adjustment she made in this regard involves a total of about $40,000 of additional liability (including interest and penalties).

Second, the agent adjusted a deduction appearing on both the returns. Silas says that he conducts a side business as a "neighborhood banker." He has made many transfers over the years which he calls "loans." Some have not been repaid, and Silas took ordinary deductions for them in 2002 and 2003 as "bad debts." The revenue agent disallowed the bulk of these claimed deductions on several grounds: that the transfers were not loans, that the transfers still had repayment potential, and that any bad debts were non-business in nature, so were capital not ordinary. The adjustment involved about $5,000 of additional tax and interest (the revenue agent did not assert penalties as to this adjustment) for the tax years combined.

In 2003, Silas acquired a passport for the first time. Since then, he has made several trips to Southeast Asia and South America, where he has business connections. In February 2005, during the examination, an employee of Fins 'N' Feathers told the revenue agent that Silas often took small suitcases filled with cash with him on these trips.

Concerned by what she uncovered during the examination, the revenue agent received permission from her superiors to expand the examination. Thus, during February and March 2005, the revenue agent considered Silas' 2004 tax year and the first three months of his 2005 tax year. She did this using available records (which were not complete) and extrapolations from her 2002-2003 findings. The agent concluded that Silas had income tax liabilities of $25,000 for 2004 and $5,000 for the first three months of 2005.

Throughout the examination, Silas was uncooperative with the revenue agent. Indeed, in the agent's words, he was "belligerent and verbally abusive" towards her. The agent states that on one occasion Silas told her: "I've always known you were out to get me, but you must really be stupid. Why are you wasting your time? You must know that you'll never get a dime out of me."

On April 1, 2005, on the revenue agent's recommendation and with the requisite approvals, the IRS assessed all of the above liabilities for 2002-2005. Silas had not filed his Form 1040 for 2004 as of April 1, 2005. After the assessments were made, five developments occurred:

(1) The police and FBI brought charges against Silas for illegal trafficking in protected wildlife. Silas was allowed to remain free on his own recognizance pending ultimate disposition of these charges.

(2) Silas developed information which demonstrated that some of the apparent bank deposits in 2002 and 2003 were merely transfers from one account to another. Taking that information into account would reduce the 2002-2003 unreported income adjustment from $40,000 to $35,000.

(3) It was discovered that the employee who had told the revenue agent about the suitcases of cash harbored a strong dislike of Silas because Silas had denied him a promotion he felt he deserved.

(4) The revenue agent analyzed Silas' worth. She concluded that Silas' known assets were worth slightly under $160,000. Those assets did not include any of the cash the employee says Silas took with him on his trips. The known assets consisted of Silas' Fins 'N' Feathers stock (which an IRS valuation engineer opined to be worth $80,000), bank accounts and bearer bonds aggregating to $55,000, and miscellaneous tangible assets (including Silas' 1990 car), a colt that Silas hopes one day to enter as a competitor in horse races, and a quantity of Russian rubles. Silas rents (from Ferdinand) a house in which Silas lives. Silas owed $90,000 to non-IRS creditors.

(5) On April 5, 2005, the IRS levied on Silas' stock, his bank accounts, his bonds, his car, his colt, and his Russian rubles.

Discuss in detail the issues raised by the foregoing facts and events. Among other matters, identify the types of assessments the IRS likely made, the adequacy of the grounds therefor, and the protections and defenses available to Silas. Evaluate the strengths and weaknesses of the partics' cases.

Chapter 8

TAX COURT LITIGATION
OF DEFICIENCY DETERMINATIONS

IRC:	§§ 6211(a); 6212; 6213(a), (b)(4), (c), (d); 6214(a), (b); 6215(a); 6503(a)(1); 6512(b); 6603; 6673; 6703(a); 7422(e); 7430; 7454; 7459; 7463; 7481(a), (b); 7482(c)(4); 7483; 7485; 7491; 7521
Regs.:	§ 301.6212-1, -2
Cases, etc.:	Rev. Proc. 87-24, 1987-1 C.B. 720 Rev. Proc. 2005-18, 2005-13 I.R.B. 798 Abeles v. Commissioner, 91 T.C. 1019 (1988) Est. of Ming v. Commissioner, 62 T.C. 519 (1974)
Forms:	Skim: Form 8822 Thirty-Day Letter Notice of Deficiency Petition to Tax Court for Regular Cases Petition to Tax Court for "S" Cases Decision of the Tax Court

I. INTRODUCTION

Taxpayers seek court review of IRS determinations in many situations in the tax controversy arena. This chapter explores the most common of them, i.e., Tax Court review of a determination that the taxpayer has a deficiency in income, estate, or gift tax. Other situations in which taxpayers seek judicial relief are discussed elsewhere in this book as part of the coverage of a particular subject matter. For example:

- ***Relief from Joint and Several Liability.*** A spouse who seeks relief from joint and several liability under one of the provisions of section 6015 can get Tax Court review if the Service disallows the claim or does not act within six months of the filing of the claim. *See* Chapter 3.

- ***Jeopardy and Termination Assessments.*** When collection is in peril, the IRS is empowered to circumvent the normal assessment and collection procedures by making a jeopardy or termination assessment and levy. Affected taxpayers can obtain expedited review of such assessments in District Court or, less often, in Tax Court. *See* Chapter 7.

- ***Interest Abatements.*** The Tax Court has jurisdiction to determine whether the IRS abused its discretion in not abating interest under section 6404. *See* Chapter 12.

- ***Collection Due Process.*** Regardless of the type of tax involved, one may seek Tax Court review within thirty days of an adverse Appeals Office determination in a collection due process hearing following the issuance of a Notice of Intent to Levy under section 6330 or Notice of the Filing of a Tax Lien under section 6320. *See* Chapter 13.

- ***Trust Fund Recovery Penalty.*** If the IRS assesses the trust fund recovery penalty pursuant to section 6672 against a purported responsible person for willful failure to pay over withheld taxes, review is possible in a District Court or the Court of Federal Claims. *See* Chapter 14.

- ***Transferee and Fiduciary Liability.*** Under certain circumstances, the IRS may seek to collect a taxpayer's liability from recipients of assets of the taxpayer, from representatives of the taxpayer, or from other secondary parties. In such circumstances, the IRS issues notices of transferee or fiduciary liability. The Tax Court and other courts are empowered to hear challenges to such notices. *See* Chapter 15.

II. THE "NOTICE OF DEFICIENCY" AND TAX COURT JURISDICTION

We began the discussion of deficiency determinations in Chapter 4, where we looked at the examination process and a taxpayer's right to appeal the determination administratively. If the matter is not resolved with examination personnel or with the Appeals Office, the IRS is obligated to issue a notice of deficiency. The notice of deficiency, sometimes referred to as the ninety-day letter or statutory notice, is the "ticket to the Tax Court," providing the jurisdictional basis for the court's review.

There are five conditions that must be satisfied for the Tax Court to have jurisdiction to review the Service's determination.

1. The Commissioner must determine a deficiency in tax, as defined in section 6211.

2. The deficiency must relate to the kind of tax specified in section 6211, i.e., income, estate, or gift tax, or certain excise taxes.

3. The IRS must send the taxpayer a notice of the deficiency that conforms to certain form and content specifications identified in section 6212.[1]

4. The IRS must send notice of the deficiency to the taxpayer at the taxpayer's last known address in accordance section 6212.[2]

5. The taxpayer must file a petition with the Tax Court for a redetermination of the deficiency within ninety days (150 days if the notice is addressed to a person outside the United States) after the IRS mailed the notice of deficiency.[3]

A. Meaning of Deficiency

In the typical case, a deficiency is simply the excess of the taxpayer's correct liability over the amount shown on the return, adjusted for other assessments and rebates. Both the correct liability and the tax shown on the return are determined without regard to withholding and quarterly estimated prepayment credits.[4] In the first instance, a deficiency is the additional tax proposed by the IRS in the thirty-day and ninety-day letters. In the end, however, the amount of the deficiency that may be assessed is what the Tax Court decides, or the parties agree, is owed.

> **Example (1):** The Smiths timely filed their tax return reflecting $200,000 in taxable income and $60,000 in tax liability. Since they had prepaid $45,000 through withholding and quarterly estimated tax payments, the Smiths submitted a check for the $15,000 balance when they filed the return. A year later, the IRS examines the Smiths' return, making three adjustments that increase taxable income from $200,000 to $300,000 and tax from $60,000 to $90,000. These amounts are reflected in a ninety-day letter. At this point in the process, the proposed deficiency in tax is $30,000. The Smiths and an Appeals Officer meet and agree to only one adjustment to taxable income of $40,000, resulting in an increase in tax of $12,000. The tax deficiency subject to assessment is $12,000.

> **Example (2):** The facts are the same as example (1), except that the withholding and estimated quarterly payments were $75,000. This resulted in a refund of $15,000 when the Smiths filed their return. The

---

[1] If the IRS issued the ninety-day letter, it can rescind the notice with the taxpayer's consent. IRC § 6212(d); Form 8526. *See also* Rev. Proc. 98-54, 1998-2 C.B. 7. This provides more time for filing a protest with the Appeals Office without first having to file a petition with the Tax Court. In practice, the IRS rarely rescinds ninety-day letters.

[2] IRC § 6212.

[3] IRC § 6213(a).

[4] Reg. § 301.6211-1(a), (b).

amounts of the proposed assessment ($30,000) and assessed deficiency ($12,000) are the same as in the previous example. The deficiency is the difference between the correct amount of tax ($60,000 + $12,000 = $72,000) and the amount shown on the return ($60,000). Withholding and quarterly estimated prepayment credits are disregarded in determining the amount of the deficiency.

B. Types of Tax Subject to Deficiency Determinations

Only certain taxes are entitled to the protections afforded by the deficiency procedures. According to section 6211(a), they include "income, estate, and gift taxes imposed by subtitles A and B and excise taxes imposed by chapters 41, 42, 43, and 44," i.e., those excise taxes associated with qualified plans and private foundations.

Also subject to the deficiency procedures are penalties calculated as a percentage of a deficiency in tax, such as accuracy-related penalties.[5] Employment taxes, consumption-oriented excise taxes, and assessable penalties are not eligible for these procedures. Interest, being merely the cost of borrowing money, is also excluded from the deficiency procedures by section 6601(e)(1).

C. Content and Form of the Notice of Deficiency

If a deficiency is determined, section 6212(a) requires the Commissioner to notify the taxpayer of the determination and to provide the taxpayer with information on how to proceed if he or she disagrees with it. While the IRS has established a series of administrative forms and pattern letters for notices of deficiency, the statute does not mandate any particular form. Since the purpose of the notice of deficiency is "to advise the person who is to pay the deficiency that the Commissioner means to assess him, anything that does this unequivocally is good enough."[6]

Typically, the notice recites that the Commissioner has determined that there is a deficiency in tax and that the letter constitutes notice of the deficiency. The notice also normally contains the following.

1. A statement showing how the IRS computed the deficiency.

2. Notice of the taxpayer's right to review in the Tax Court without having to make payment by filing a petition within ninety days (150 days if addressed to a taxpayer outside of the United States) from the mailing date of the deficiency notice.

---

[5] IRC § 6665(a). *But see* IRC § 6665(b).

[6] Olsen v. Helvering, 88 F.2d 650, 651 (2d Cir. 1937).

3. Notice of the taxpayer's right to utilize the more simplified small tax case procedure for "S" cases, if the tax dispute is not for more than $50,000 for any year.

4. A form for the taxpayer to sign and return in case the taxpayer wishes the IRS to assess the deficiency quickly to limit the accumulation of interest.

5. Notice that the Service will assess and collect the tax if a timely petition is not filed with the Tax Court within the ninety-day (or, if applicable, the 150-day) filing period.

D. Mailing the Notice of Deficiency to the Taxpayer's Last Known Address

The Code states that the IRS must either hand-deliver or mail the notice of deficiency by certified mail to the taxpayer at his or her "last known address."[7] Though the Code uses the term "last known address" in many sections,[8] it fails to define it anywhere. The Code also fails to state what remedies are available for improperly mailed notices. Thus, this has been an area rife with litigation. Courts have generally held,[9] and the Regulations agree,[10] that the taxpayer's last known address is the address on the return most recently filed, not the address on the return under examination. Mailing to this address entitles the IRS to a presumption of correctness.[11] The taxpayer can rebut the presumption with evidence that he or she gave the IRS *clear and concise notification* of a dif-

---

[7] If a husband and wife filed a joint return, the IRS normally sends a single joint notice of deficiency to the two of them at their last known joint address. *See* IRC § 6015(d). However, if either spouse notifies the IRS that they established separate residences, the IRS must, where practicable, send separate notices relating to the joint return to each individual. IRC § 6212(b)(2). *See* Abeles v. Commissioner, 91 T.C. 1019 (1988) (the filing of subsequent year's returns with separate addresses is sufficient notification).

[8] The concept of mailing a notice to the "last known address" is central to a variety of proposed actions. Some of the more important sections include:

- Section 6212(b) – notice of deficiency;
- Section 6303(a) – notice of demand for tax;
- Section 6320(a)(2)(C) – notice of the right to a CDP hearing following filing of a tax lien;
- Section 6330(a)(2)(C) – notice of right to a CDP hearing before levy;
- Section 6331(d)(2)(C) – notice of intent to levy;
- Section 6335(a) and (b) – notices of seizure and sale;
- Section 6672(b) – notice of assertion of so-called 100% penalty;
- Section 6901(g) – notice of liability in transferee case; and,
- Section 7609(a)(2) – notice of third-party summons.

[9] Abeles v. Commissioner, 91 T.C. 1019 (1988).

[10] Reg. § 301.6212-2(a).

[11] *Id.*

ferent address. Courts expect the IRS to exercise reasonable care in ascertaining whether the taxpayer gave the requisite notification.[12]

Whether the taxpayer gave proper notice and whether the IRS properly discharged its duty are questions of fact.[13] A taxpayer can give notice of a change of address in a variety of ways, some boldly declaring themselves notification of a change of address, such as filing a Form 8822,[14] and others less direct.[15]

Normally, giving notification of a change of address to another branch of government is not sufficient notice to the IRS. However, Regulation section 301.6212-2(b)(2) says that a change of address provided to the U.S. Postal Service (USPS) on its official form will satisfy the taxpayer's obligation to provide notice to the IRS. In fact, the cited Regulation says that, until the taxpayer gives

---

[12] Monge v. Commissioner, 93 T.C. 22 (1989). A good example of a situation where the Tax Court found that the taxpayer had given clear and concise notification of a different address is *Hunter v. Commissioner,* T.C. Memo 2004-81. In that case, the taxpayer moved from Gallatin to Hendersonville, Tennessee. After the move he hired new accountants to represent him, filed a power of attorney form with the IRS directing it to send copies of all correspondence to a Nashville office, and listed his new address as Hendersonville. In 1999, the IRS sent deficiency notices to Hunter at his old address, but he never received them. The IRS didn't send duplicates to the new address or to the accountants.

The Tax Court rejected the IRS's argument that the power of attorney form isn't sufficient notice of a change of address. The court also noted that the IRS failed to act on what it knew after the notices were returned as unclaimed, and didn't keep trying to find the correct address. The court noted that the stipulated facts showed no effort was made to redeliver the notices even after the IRS began using Hunter's Hendersonville address in correspondence and meeting with the accountants in settlement talks. The court, noting the IRS can protect itself from those problems by sending a notice to each possible address, concluded that Hunter's inclusion of his Hendersonville address on the power of attorney form provided the IRS with clear and concise notification of the change of address. The court granted Hunter's motion to dismiss for lack of jurisdiction and denied the IRS's motion to dismiss.

[13] Cyclone Drilling Inc. v. Kelley, 769 F.2d 662 (10th Cir. 1985).

[14] If the taxpayer does not use Form 8822 but wishes to clearly notify the Service of a change of address, the following information is required:

- The old address;
- The new address;
- The taxpayer's full name, social security number or employer identification number, and signature; and
- A statement that the notice is a change of address notice.

[15] United States v. Zolla, 724 F.2d 808 (9th Cir. 1984) (knowledge of the change of address by persons in one division cannot be imputed to persons in another division of that same office); Howell v. United States, 69 A.F.T.R.2d (P-H) ¶ 92-313 (D. Kan. 1991) (notice of a new address given relative to a different type of tax does not constitute clear and concise notice with regards to income tax); Pyo v. Commissioner, 83 T.C. 626 (1984) (where the IRS is notified of a new address or establishment of separate residences for a year other than the one at issue and the IRS has corresponded successfully with the taxpayer at the new address, the taxpayer may reasonably expect future notices to come to the new address as well); Berg v. Commissioner, T.C. Memo. 1993-77 (one IRS agent's knowledge of the current address, however obtained, is imputed to all other agents in the same division of that office). *See also* note 12.

clear and concise notification to the contrary, the taxpayer's address in the USPS National Change of Address database is the last known address for section 6212 purposes.

The purpose of the last known address requirement is to ensure that the taxpayer receives a copy of the notice and has time to petition the Tax Court for review of the deficiency determination. If the IRS mails the notice as directed in the statute, the notice is valid irrespective of whether the taxpayer receives it. Taxpayers frequently do not receive validly mailed notices when they move and fail to provide the USPS with a forwarding address or when the USPS erroneously fails to deliver the notice to a forwarded address on file. If this occurs, the taxpayer will not know of the option to petition the Tax Court for review and the IRS will assess the deficiency after the ninety-day restricted period.[16]

A deficiency notice is *not* invalid, however, merely because the Service mailed it to an incorrect address.[17] Since the purpose of the notice of deficiency is to inform the taxpayer of actions the IRS intends to take, a notice of deficiency mailed to the wrong address is still effective if the taxpayer receives it with "ample time" to file a Tax Court petition.[18]

If, however, the IRS *fails* to mail the notice as the statute prescribes *and* the taxpayer does not receive it with ample time remaining on the ninety-day period to petition the Tax Court, subsequent actions by the IRS, e.g., assessments and levy or seizure and sale, are *voidable* by the taxpayer. In order to proceed, the government would have to issue a new notice of deficiency. Since an improperly mailed notice does not suspend the running of the three-year statute of limitations on assessment[19] the government may find itself time-barred from doing so.

If the taxpayer has moved and the IRS has not updated its computer to reflect the new address, the IRS normally will send the thirty and ninety-day letters to the old location. The first time the taxpayer might learn tax is owed is many months or years later when the Service discovers the taxpayer's present address and sends collection notices there. If it turns out the IRS mailed the notice of deficiency to the wrong place, the proper way to proceed is to bring this to the attention of someone at the IRS. If the problem cannot be resolved administratively, the taxpayer should file a petition with the Tax Court even

---

[16] IRC § 6213(a).

[17] Frieling v. Commissioner, 81 T.C. 42 (1983).

[18] Clodfelter v. Commissioner, 527 F.2d 754 (9th Cir. 1975). *Compare* Manos v. Commissioner, T.C. Memo. 1989-442 (38 days left on the ninety-day period was sufficient time to consider what course of action to take, including whether to file a Tax Court petition), *with* Looper v. Commissioner, 73 T.C. 690 (1980) (17 days left was not enough; of importance to the court was the fact that the notice was of transferee liability and not one respecting the taxpayer's own liability about which he would have been aware of a problem).

[19] IRC § 6503(a).

though doing so is well outside the ninety-day period from the issuance of the notice of deficiency. In such case, both parties normally file Motions to Dismiss for Lack of Jurisdiction. The IRS's motion will argue that the Tax Court should dismiss the case because the taxpayer filed the petition untimely. The taxpayer's motion will argue that the Tax Court should dismiss the case because the notice was defective and void due to the improper mailing. The court will decide the case by granting one of the motions and denying the other.

If the court grants the taxpayer's motion, the IRS will have to issue a new notice and do so within the statute of limitations, remembering that the statute of limitations was not suspended from the date of the issuance of the improperly mailed notice. If the court rules in favor of the government, the IRS is entitled to assess the deficiency. If the taxpayer wishes to contest the determination, he or she must pay the deficiency and file a refund claim and, if necessary, a refund suit.

E. Timely Filing the Tax Court Petition

Section 6213(a) requires the taxpayer to file a petition with the Tax Court within ninety days of the date the IRS mails the notice of deficiency.[20] The date the Tax Court receives a document is normally treated as its filing date. However, section 7502 says that documents received after the prescribed period are treated as timely filed if the envelope contains an official United States postmark, or certain designated delivery service marks, dated *on or before* the end of the prescribed filing period.[21] To be treated as timely filed under section 7502, the envelope or outside wrapper must be properly addressed to the Tax Court in Washington, D.C., with sufficient postage. The student is directed to Chapter 2 for a discussion of the "timely mailed is timely filed" rule of section 7502 and the weekend and holiday rule of section 7503.

The ninety-day period is extended in certain situations, the most common being: (1) where the last date for filing specified by the IRS on the notice of deficiency is later than the ninetieth day, (2) where the taxpayer files for bankruptcy relief after the issuance of the notice,[22] or (3) where the notice was addressed to a person who was outside the country, even if temporarily while on vacation.[23] In the latter situation, the taxpayer has 150 days to file the petition.

---

[20] Estate of Cerrito v. Commissioner, 73 T.C. 896, 898 (1980).

[21] IRC § 7502.

[22] IRC § 6213(f)(1) ("the running of the time prescribed by subsection (a) for filing a petition in the Tax Court with respect to any deficiency shall be suspended for the period during which the debtor is prohibited by reason of such case from filing a petition in the Tax Court with respect to such deficiency, and for sixty days thereafter").

[23] Levy v. Commissioner, 76 T.C. 228 (1981).

F. Issuance of Additional Deficiency Notices

The Service normally issues only one statutory notice of deficiency. However, it can issue another notice, if necessary, under certain circumstances. If the taxpayer did *not* file a petition with the Tax Court in response to the first notice of deficiency and if the statute of limitations on assessment has not expired, the IRS may issue a valid second notice of deficiency for the same taxpayer, tax, and period covered by the first deficiency notice. If the taxpayer petitions the Tax Court within ninety days of the second notice, the issues raised in both notices are properly before the court.

On the other hand, if the taxpayer timely petitioned the Tax Court in response to the first deficiency letter, section 6212(c)(1) precludes the Commissioner from determining an additional deficiency. The only way the government can raise a new issue would be if the court were satisfied that the taxpayer was not unduly prejudiced and granted the government's motion to amend its pleadings. The IRS normally bears the burden of proof on new issues.[24]

The prohibition against a second notice of deficiency only applies if the second notice is for the same tax and taxable year and is with respect to the same taxpayer as the first notice. A second notice issued to the same taxpayer for another taxable year but the same tax, or for another tax but the same taxable period as covered by the first notice is not a prohibited second deficiency notice under section 6212(c)(1). The limitations also do not prevent the IRS from asserting an additional deficiency in the case of fraud or jeopardy.[25]

G. Tax Court's Exclusive Jurisdiction

The Tax Court has priority to hear tax deficiency cases. Once it acquires proper jurisdiction by the taxpayer filing a timely adequate petition, no other court may consider the case. A taxpayer may not get the case dismissed without prejudice once the Tax Court has acquired jurisdiction.[26]

In addition, section 7422(e) provides that if the taxpayer already has a refund action before a District Court or the Court of Federal Claims and, prior to the hearing of the suit, the IRS mails a notice of deficiency, the refund action is stayed to give the taxpayer time to decide whether to petition the Tax Court. If the taxpayer does so, the District Court or the Court of Federal Claims loses jurisdiction and the Tax Court will hear the case. If the taxpayer does not file

---

[24] IRC § 6214(a); Tax Ct. R. 41.

[25] IRC § 6212(c); Zackim v. Commissioner, 887 F.2d 455 (3d Cir. 1989), *rev'g* 91 T.C. 1001 (1988) (the court held that, despite the doctrine of res judicata, the fraud exception prevails even if the Tax Court already decided the matters before it arising from the first notice of deficiency).

[26] Estate of Ming v. Commissioner, 62 T.C. 519 (1974) (denying taxpayer's motion to dismiss his Tax Court case without prejudice to filing a refund action).

a petition with the Tax Court for a redetermination of the asserted deficiency, the United States may counterclaim in the taxpayer's suit and bring the issues in the notice before the court.

III. OVERVIEW OF A TAX COURT CASE

A. Pleadings

In a deficiency redetermination matter, the taxpayer initiates a case by filing a petition with the court within ninety days of the mailing of the notice of deficiency. Along with the petition, the taxpayer, now known as the petitioner, designates a place for the trial and remits $60.[27] Where the amount of tax and penalty at issue does not exceed $50,000,[28] the taxpayer may request, as part of the petition, that the court hear the case under the simplified procedures associated with "S" cases.

Upon receipt of the petition, the Tax Court serves a copy of it on the Commissioner, the respondent. Within sixty days of service, an attorney in IRS Chief Counsel's office files an answer. The answer must respond to each material allegation in the petition.[29] Failure to challenge a material allegation is deemed a concession on that issue. A reply by the petitioner to the government's answer is not required, unless the Court orders otherwise, or the IRS moves that the affirmative allegations in the answer be deemed admitted.[30]

B. Discovery

After the pleading stage is complete, the parties may begin discovery. Unlike many other courts, the Tax Court requires that the parties exchange information informally to the extent possible before resorting to the more formal methods of discovery, like interrogatories, depositions, requests for production of documents and things, and requests for admissions.[31] In "S" cases, formal discovery is rare since there is such a short time between when the case is petitioned and when it is tried.

---

[27] The filing fee can be waived for indigent taxpayers. In non-deficiency cases, such as a CDP case, the pleadings are similar to those that must be filed in deficiency cases though the time limits for doing so may be different.

[28] Currently, this option is only available with respect to deficiency and employment classification cases; innocent spouse and collection due process cases can only be heard as regular cases.

[29] Until recently, if the case was petitioned as an "S" case, no answer was required, unless the IRS raised an issue with respect to which it bore the burden of proof. However, for petitions filed after March 13, 2007, the government must file an answer regardless whether it is an "S" case or not. Tax Ct. R. 173(b).

[30] Tax Ct. R. 37.

[31] Branerton v. Commissioner, 61 T.C. 691 (1974).

On motion of a party, the court can limit discovery where: (1) the discovery demands are unreasonably cumulative or duplicative, (2) the information sought is obtainable from a more convenient source, (3) the demands are unduly burdensome or expensive, or (4) the party had ample opportunity to obtain the information from other sources. While the information sought via discovery must be relevant to the subject matter of the case at hand, it does not need to be admissible. Instead, as is true in other American courts as well, all that is necessary is that the requested information be reasonably calculated to lead to the discovery of admissible evidence.

C. Settlement

During or after discovery, the parties normally begin to discuss settlement. The vast majority of cases are settled rather than litigated. If the Appeals Office has not already considered the case, negotiations will occur with an Appeals Officer rather than an attorney for the IRS. If the taxpayer already had a "bite at the Appeals' apple," a second conference generally is not made available, unless the parties believe there is settlement potential. If the taxpayer is unsuccessful in reaching a settlement with Appeals, the Area Counsel attorney will begin to prepare the case for trial. Settlement is still possible once the attorney takes over the case as the facts become better developed and each side can better evaluate the likely success of trying the case.

Settlements reached between the representatives for the taxpayer and the government are subject to the approval and concurrence of the taxpayer and the managers of the government person. This was made clear in *Keil v. Commissioner*, T.C. Memo 2005-76, in which the Tax Court set aside a settlement because the attorney for the taxpayers was not authorized by them to agree to settle on their behalf without their prior concurrence. Taxpayers specifically had told their attorney at the time of his retention that he could not accept any settlement that affected their liability without their consideration and approval of it. Despite this and unbeknownst to the taxpayers, the attorney caused to be filed with the Court a settlement stipulation that showed their liability computed on the basis of the settlements. The Court entered a stipulated decision that reflected the amounts shown therein. A month later, the taxpayers moved the Court to vacate the stipulated decision and to set aside the related stipulations of settlement. The court granted the taxpayers' motion.

D. Stipulations

A defining characteristic of Tax Court practice is emphasis on the stipulation process. Tax Court Rule 91(a)(1) mandates that the parties stipulate to "the fullest extent to which complete or qualified agreement can or fairly should be reached . . . all evidence which fairly should not be in dispute." The parties must stipulate to those facts, conclusions, and documents whose truth is not disputed. The parties are required to stipulate to as much as possible to minimize trial time. If a party does not stipulate to certain evidence, the other party can file a motion to compel that party to show cause why the matters covered by the motion should not be deemed admitted.[32] In egregious situations, the Tax Court may dismiss the case.[33]

E. Notice of Calendared Case and Pretrial Orders

At some point after the case has been petitioned, the parties get a notice from the Tax Court that the case has been calendared for trial for a specific date. Along with this notice, the parties receive a pretrial order from the judge assigned to the case. The pretrial order requires a status report from each party forty-five days prior to the assigned trial date indicating whether the case has been settled and, if not, the likelihood it will be litigated and the anticipated length of the trial.

The pretrial order requires the parties to prepare pretrial memoranda. The memorandum should give each party's version of the facts and law and identify whom the party plans to call as witnesses and to what the witnesses are likely to testify. Failure to list a proposed witness may result in that person being precluded from testifying at trial.

If a party intends to call an expert witness, the party must submit to the court and the other party a copy of the expert's report. This serves as the witness' direct testimony. The report must be submitted not less than thirty days before trial. The expert is not normally entitled to testify unless the report is submitted timely.[34]

F. Calendar Call, Trial, and Briefs

The date and time specified on the pretrial notice as the trial date is usually a Monday morning. The time mentioned signals what is referred to as the "calendar call," rather than the trial date. The parties are required to be present at calendar call to inform the judge of the status of the case.

If trial is required, the judge will want to know when the best time is to hear the case during the week or two that the judge is "sitting" in the particular city. Factors the judge will consider in deciding when to schedule a trial are the availability of the parties and witnesses and whether the taxpayer will incur additional costs if the case is not heard until later in the session. Especially in low dollar cases, judges normally give out-of-town petitioners preference to have their trials on the same day as the calendar call so that their incon-

---

[32] Tax Ct. R. 91(f).

[33] Williams v. Commissioner, 13 F.3d 1095 (9th Cir. 1993).

[34] Tax Ct. R. 143(f).

venience and costs are minimized. It is sometimes possible to arrange a "date and time certain" for trial before the calendar call. This normally requires both parties arranging a conference call with the judge or the judge's clerk.

All proceedings before the Tax Court are recorded on audiotape by an independent court reporting service that has a contract with the Tax Court. Transcripts of proceedings can be ordered from the reporting service for a per-page fee. There is a court reporter in the courtroom who can assist taxpayers who want to order a transcript.

At the conclusion of the presentation of the case, the parties are required to file post-trial briefs, unless the trial judge specifies otherwise. In "S cases," the pretrial memorandum is usually sufficient for this purpose. A post-trial brief is a summary of the facts and the law raised in the trial. Tax Court Rule 151 details the requirements of post-trial briefs.

The trial judge may require the parties to file simultaneous briefs or seriatim briefs. If the judge requires simultaneous briefs, both parties must file opening briefs within seventy-five days after the conclusion of the trial. The parties file reply briefs forty-five days thereafter. If the judge requires seriatim briefs, the party designated by the judge files its opening brief within seventy-five days after the trial, the other party files its reply brief within forty-five days thereafter and the first party files its reply brief within thirty days after that. Each brief is expected to be a response to the previous brief. Upon request of a party, the judge may enlarge any of the periods.

G. Decision

After the parties present their cases and file briefs, the judge reviews all the evidence and drafts a report. This may take months or even years. The trial judge forwards his or her report to the Chief Judge.[35] The report of the trial judge becomes the opinion of the court unless, within thirty days of the date the

---

[35] IRC § 7459. In many cases, Special Trial Judges act as the trial judges. They hear the evidence and prepare a report of recommended findings of fact and conclusions of law. The report is reviewed by the Chief Judge. If the case is either a "S" case, a case in which the amount of the deficiency placed in dispute is under $50,000 or a lien or levy action, the Chief Judge may authorize the Special Trial Judge to issue the report as the opinion of the court. Tax. Ct. Rul. 182(b).

If the case involves a deficiency greater than $50,000, the Special Trial Judge's report of recommended findings of fact and conclusions of law gets served on the parties. The parties may object to the recommendation in which case the Chief Judge has several options. If the Chief Judge agrees with the objections raised, he may require additional briefing, hearings or the like. If he does not agree with the objections, he may adopt the recommendations as the opinion of the court. Tax Ct. Rul. 183. Rule 183 notes that the Tax Court judge must give due regard to the special trial judge's findings of fact "shall be presumed to be correct." These requirements with respect to larger cases were added to the Tax Court's rules in response to Ballard v. Commissioner, 544 U.S. 40 (2005), in which the U.S. Supreme Court said that the previous practice of withholding such reports failed to disclose how much the judges modified or diverged from the Special Trial Judge's findings as part of its collaborative process.

report is submitted to the Chief Judge, the Chief Judge refers the case for review by the nineteen presidentially appointed judges.[36]

Eventually, the court issues its report, or opinion. Under section 7460, the Chief Judge classifies opinions in regular cases.[37] Court review is directed if the report proposes to invalidate a Regulation, overrule a published Tax Court case, or reconsider, in a circuit that has not addressed it, an issue on which the Tax Court has been reversed by a court of appeals.[38] Court review is also directed in cases of widespread application where the result may be controversial, where the Chief Judge is made aware of differences in opinion among the judges before the opinion is released, or, occasionally, where a procedural issue suggests the desirability of obtaining a consensus of the judges.

The opinion is different from the decision. The opinion states how the court decides the issues presented to it. It does not inform the parties of the dollar amount resulting therefrom. That is the role of the decision. All decisions of the Tax Court, except those dismissing a case for lack of jurisdiction, must specify the dollar amount of the deficiency, liability or overpayment determined by the court. Unless the court finds entirely in favor of either the taxpayer or the government, the parties must prepare a Tax Court Rule 155 computation. There are two types of Tax Court Rule 155 computations: agreed and unagreed.

If the parties agree on the dollar amount of the deficiency, liability or overpayment, an original and two copies of the agreed computation, reflecting such dollar amount, are filed with the Tax Court. When the parties are unable to agree on the appropriate computation of the deficiency, liability or overpayment, either party, or both parties, may file a computation it believes is consistent with the court's findings of fact and opinion. The court will then decide which computation to accept and issue its decision.

The date of entry of the decision is important in terms of fixing the time at which the appeal period begins to run. It is also important because the restrictions on assessing deficiencies imposed on the IRS end on this date.

The losing side has two separate post-trial motions to file with the Tax Court requesting another hearing or reconsideration of the opinion or decision.[39] Parties rarely file these, and the court even more rarely grants those filed.

---

[36] IRC § 7460(b).

[37] "[Some opinions are released as memorandum opinions] instead of a published Tax Court opinion, or division opinion. IRC §§ 7459, 7460. Division opinions officially published by the court are those in which a legal issue of first impression is decided, a legal principle is applied or extended to a recurring factual pattern, a significant exception to a previously announced general rule is created, or there are similarly significant and precedentially valuable cases. On the other hand, cases involving application of familiar legal principles to routine factual situations, nonrecurring or enormously complicated factual situations, obsolete statutes or regulations, straightforward factual determinations, or arguments patently lacking in merit will be classified as memorandum opinions." Mary Ann Cohen, *How to Read Tax Court Opinions*, 1 Hous. Bus. & Tax. L.J. 1 (2001)

[38] Golsen v. Commissioner, 54 T.C. 742 (1970), *aff'd*, 445 F.2d 985 (10th Cir. 1971).

[39] Tax Ct. Rs. 161 (Motion for Reconsideration of Findings or Opinion), 162 (Motion To Vacate or Revise Decisions).

H. Finality of Tax Court Decision

Unless a notice of appeal is filed within ninety days after the entry of the Tax Court decision, the decision becomes final on the ninetieth day after such entry.[40] Decisions that are appealed do not become final during the pendency of the appeal and thereafter until the time for filing a petition for certiorari expires. If a petition for certiorari is filed, the decision becomes final when the petition is denied or, if the Supreme Court accepts review of the case, thirty days after the date of issuance of the Supreme Court's decision.

I. Appeal

In a regular case, the losing party can file an appeal with the appropriate federal circuit court of appeals within ninety days after the decision is entered. Neither party may appeals an "S" case. Filing a notice of appeal with the Clerk of the Tax Court and paying a filing fee of $100 is necessary in order to perfect the appeal.

Venue for appellate review of a Tax Court decision, in the case of an individual taxpayer, typically lies in the judicial circuit where the taxpayer resides. In the case of a corporate taxpayer, venue is in the circuit in which the taxpayer has its principal place of business or principal office at the time of filing the petition.[41]

J. Assessment of Deficiency After Decision

The IRS is restricted from making an assessment after it sends a statutory notice of deficiency for the period during which the taxpayer may file a petition in the Tax Court and, if the taxpayer does so, until the Tax Court's decision becomes final. The prohibition on assessment remains in effect during the ninety-day period after entry of the Tax Court's decision. If the taxpayer does not file an appeal within the ninety-day period, the Tax Court decision becomes final ninety days later and the prohibition on assessment (and collection thereon) expires.[42] However, even if the taxpayer files a timely notice of appeal within the ninety-day period, the prohibition on assessment (and collection thereon) terminates with the filing of the notice. From that point on, the IRS will try to collect in the normal way, as described in Chapter 13. To stay assessment and collection of any deficiency determined by the Tax Court, the taxpayer must file an appeal bond.[43]

---

[40] IRC § 7481.

[41] IRC § 7482.

[42] IRC § 7481.

[43] IRC § 7485. *Kanter v. Commissioner*, T.C. Memo 2006-46, demonstrates the need to post bond after an adverse Tax Court decision if one wishes to avoid assessment of the tax deficiency while the case is on appeal.

IV. SMALL TAX CASES ("S" CASES)

A taxpayer challenging an IRS determination in Tax Court must consider whether to elect that the case be treated as a small tax case, generally referred to as an "S" case. This is important, as the rules of procedure and review are quite different between "S" cases and regular cases.

The main reason for allowing "S" designation is to allow easier access to the court for taxpayers with relatively small amounts in controversy where it is not economically feasible to retain an attorney. The "S" procedures provide an expedited, less expensive way to resolve tax cases than is normally the case. "S" cases are in the tax world what small claims cases are in the non-tax world.

Generally, if a taxpayer is not familiar with courtroom procedures or the rules of evidence, and especially if he or she will be self-represented (pro se), it is wise to elect small tax designation in situations where it is available. One can designate a case as an "S" case where the amount of deficiency, including penalties but excluding interest, placed in dispute does not exceed $50,000 for any one taxable year.[44] The key to eligibility for "S" case status is the amount "placed in dispute." Thus, if the notice of deficiency determines a deficiency in income tax of $47,000 and an addition to tax of $6,000, and the taxpayer concedes $5,000 of the deficiency in the petition, the case is eligible for "S" case status ($47,000 + $6,000 − $5,000 = $48,000).[45]

The decision of the trial court in an "S" case is final and cannot be appealed. Both the taxpayer and the IRS have only one shot at the case.[46] In addition, the decision has no precedential value. Though the Tax Court usually operates under the Federal Rules of Evidence, these rules are applied less rigidly in "S" cases. Other courtroom procedures and rules are also relaxed in "S" cases to make it easier for laypersons to represent themselves.[47] Opening arguments and briefs are not required. Knowledge of procedure and evidence is not necessary. In fact, the judges frequently assist taxpayers to develop the facts by asking questions of the taxpayer and other witnesses. Ordinarily, Special Trial Judges hear and decide "S" cases.

Normally, the taxpayer is the party that seeks "S" designation. However, either party may do so. The parties can make the request at any time up to and including the time the trial begins.[48] If the taxpayer has sought or seeks "S" status and the IRS opposes it, the court will generally allow the designation. Exceptions to this occur when the case has a set of facts or legal principles common to other cases before the court or involves an issue that has significance to the taxpayer over a series of years, such as the basis of depreciable property.[49]

---

[44] IRC § 7463(a)(1).

[45] Kallich v. Commissioner, 89 T.C. 676 (1987).

[46] IRC § 7463(b).

[47] Tax Ct. R. 174.

[48] Tax Ct. R. 171.

[49] Page v. Commissioner, 86 T.C. 1 (1986); IRM 35.8.5.3.

V. BURDEN OF PROOF IN TAX COURT

The burden of proof on most matters raised in the ninety-day letter is on the petitioner. (Fraud determinations are the most common exception.) This is so because the notice of deficiency is presumptively correct. "[The Commissioner's] ruling has the support of a presumption of correctness and the petitioner has the burden of proving it to be wrong."[50] The standard of proof is usually by a preponderance of the evidence.[51] The burden of proof is substantially the same in all three forums.

In certain situations, the burden of proof shifts to the IRS. These situations include: (1) where the IRS raises a matter not presented in the notice of deficiency and (2) with respect to all affirmative defenses raised in the government's answer, such as res judicata, collateral estoppel, waiver, duress, transferee liability, fraud, and statute of limitations.[52] In the case of fraud, the government has to prove its case by clear and convincing evidence.[53]

The Code also places the burden of proof on the IRS if the taxpayer "introduces credible evidence with respect to any factual issue relevant to ascertaining the liability of the taxpayer," (sometimes referred to as the "burden of going forward").[54] This rule is irrelevant, however, with respect to legal issues.[55]

---

[50] Welch v. Helvering, 290 U.S. 111, 115 (1933).

[51] *See* Tax Ct. R. 142.

[52] *See* Tax Ct. R. 142(a), 39.

[53] *See* IRC §§ 6902, 7454; Tax Ct. R. 142.

[54] IRC § 7491; Tax Ct. R. 142(a)(2); Griffen v. Commissioner, 315 F.3d 1017 (8th Cir. 2003) ("credible evidence," for purposes of interpreting and applying section 7491, is "the quality of evidence which, after critical analysis, the court would find sufficient upon which to base a decision on the issue if no contrary evidence were submitted (without regard to the judicial presumption of IRS correctness)"). For this provision to apply, the taxpayer must have complied with all substantiation requirements in the Code. This includes, where applicable, the requirement that an item be substantiated to the satisfaction of the IRS, like travel and entertainment in section 274(d). In addition, the taxpayer must have retained all records required by the Code and, within a reasonable time, cooperated with reasonable requests by the IRS for (access to) witnesses, information, documents, meetings, and interviews. Cooperation includes not only providing reasonable assistance to the IRS in obtaining access to and inspection of the such persons and items not within the control of the taxpayer but also exhausting one's administrative remedies, such as Appeal rights (short of being required to consent to extend the statute of limitations).

The burden of proof really has two separate components. There is the burden of going forward with the evidence (sometimes referred to as the burden of production) and the burden of ultimate persuasion. In nearly all non-fraud matters, the latter burden requires that the weight of the evidence is more than fifty percent on your side, i.e., the scales tip (even if ever so slightly) in your favor. Because the taxpayer must first introduce credible evidence in order to shift the burden of ultimate persuasion, the taxpayer continues to bear the burden of going forward with the evidence. Since very few, if any, cases after trial are a perfect draw, most practitioners believe there is more rhetoric than substance in the burden of proof shift. For excellent discussions, see Nathan Clukey, *Benefits of Shifting the Burden of Proof to the IRS Are Limited*, 1999 Tax Notes Today 20-136 (Feb. 1, 1999); Steve R. Johnson, *The Danger of Symbolic Legislation: Perceptions and Realities of the New Burden-of-Proof Rules*, 84 Iowa L. Rev. 413 (1999).

[55] Nis Family Trust v. Commissioner, 115 T.C. 523 (2000).

In unreported income cases, the taxpayer might be able to shift the burden of proof to the IRS by showing that the IRS' determination of unreported income was arbitrary. One court stated that: "[w]here it lacks a rational basis the presumption [of correctness] evaporates. Otherwise the Commissioner could, merely by arbitrarily issuing a naked assessment, place upon the taxpayer the unfair . . . burden of proving a negative, that he or she did not receive the illegal income assessed against him."[56]

Res judicata and collateral estoppel sometimes play a role in tax cases. These related doctrines are discussed at length in Chapter 5.

VI. CHOICE OF FORUM

There are three routes available to taxpayers to get judicial review of a proposed deficiency.[57] The route that is the focus of this chapter is the "deficiency route," by which the Tax Court's jurisdiction is invoked to redetermine the amount proposed by the IRS *before* the deficiency is assessed and payment required. The Tax Court hears about 85%-90% of all tax cases in which a deficiency was involved.

The second route arises when the taxpayer bypasses Tax Court review, permits the IRS to assess the deficiency, makes payment, and then sues in the District Court or Court of Federal Claims for a refund of all or a portion of the tax paid. Taxpayers seek review in this manner in only a small percentage of deficiency cases. However, litigation of certain tax controversies is available only by paying the disputed amount and seeking a refund. The "refund route" is discussed in Chapter 9.

The third route is "bankruptcy." For this avenue to apply, the taxpayer/debtor has to have filed a bankruptcy petition and a deficiency determination must have been made by the IRS either before, or as a consequence of, the filing. Bankruptcy courts decide a small percentage of tax deficiency cases.

---

[56] Llorente v. Commissioner, 649 F.2d 152, 156 (2d Cir. 1981). *See also* Portillo v. Commissioner, 932 F.2d 1128 (5th Cir. 1991); Weimerskirch v. Commissioner, 596 F.2d 358 (9th Cir. 1979), *rev'g* 67 T.C. 672 (1977).

[57] While the three routes are different procedurally, the bottom line should be the same if the courts reach the same conclusion. For example, assume the IRS asserts two adjustments to taxable income. The total tax deficiency is $30,000, $20,000 of which is attributable to the first adjustment and $10,000 of which is attributable to the second. Assume further that each court would agree with the taxpayer on issue #1 and with the IRS on issue #2. Thus, the bottom line would be that the taxpayer owes $10,000 tax.

Under the deficiency route, the taxpayer would have to pay $10,000 (plus interest) only after the Tax Court's decision becomes final and the tax is assessed. A somewhat similar result would follow from a bankruptcy situation. By contrast, if the taxpayer chooses to litigate in refund status, he or she would have to first pay the entire $30,000 (plus interest) and then sue for its refund. After the decision in favor of the taxpayer on issue #1, the taxpayer would be entitled to a refund of $20,000 (plus interest) with respect to issue #2.

Tax cases are unique in the fact that there are many ways to proceed to litigate a proposed tax deficiency. This gives taxpayers the opportunity to "forum shop" for the best trial court. Some of the more important factors that go into determining which court to choose are discussed below.

A. Breadth of Jurisdiction

The Tax Court has limited jurisdiction and can only hear certain types of tax cases. The Tax Court's principal area of jurisdiction is over cases in which the IRS determines a deficiency[58] in income, estate or gift taxes. Other matters over which the Tax Court has jurisdiction include (i) determinations made in collection due process (CDP) hearings and (ii) denials of relief from joint and several liability with respect to a joint income tax return. Normally, the scope of the court's review of CDP determinations is limited to whether the collection action proposed by the Service is appropriate. However, the Tax Court can consider "challenges to the existence or amount of the underlying tax liability for any tax period if the person did not receive any statutory notice of deficiency for such tax liability or did not otherwise have an opportunity to dispute such tax liability."[59]

By contrast, District Courts and the Court of Federal Claims can hear almost all kinds of tax cases. These courts may, like the Tax Court, resolve disputes that originally gave rise to a deficiency in income, estate, and gift taxes. More often, however, these courts are called upon to resolve disputes affecting other taxes and penalties, such as employment and excise taxes, and disputes initiated by the taxpayer, such as where the taxpayer requests a refund on an amended return.

---

[58] Even when a Tax Court case begins as a deficiency matter, the taxpayer could end up with a refund due. This is because of the court's jurisdiction to decide all issues associated with the year before it. IRC § 6512(b) (granting Tax Court jurisdiction to determine overpayments).

[59] IRC § 6330(c)(2)(B).

[60] Bankruptcy Court is only available to those taxpayers involved with bankruptcy proceedings. In a sense, it is not an "optional" choice like the other forums.

The Bankruptcy Court can determine the tax liability or overpayment of a taxpayer. 11 U.S.C § 505. Furthermore, the Bankruptcy Court can discharge tax liabilities. 11 U.S.C § 523. Decisions of the Bankruptcy Court are appealable to the District Court.

If the taxpayer petitioned the Tax Court before filing a petition in bankruptcy, the Tax Court proceeding is automatically stayed, unless there was a binding decree. 11 U.S.C § 362(a)(1). The Bankruptcy Court can allow the tax issue to be decided by the Tax Court or decide it itself. If the matter is complex, such that the specialization of the Tax Court is highly beneficial to the resolution, the Bankruptcy Court may defer jurisdiction over the deficiency to the Tax Court. In addition, the District Court sometimes withdraws a tax issue from the Bankruptcy Court in order to decide the issue itself.

While the Bankruptcy Court also has very broad jurisdiction, it can only review the propriety of tax debts when a debtor is engaged in a bankruptcy proceeding under Title 11 of the U.S. Code.[60]

B. Payment Considerations

The most significant *practical* reason the vast majority of taxpayers go to the Tax Court for review of deficiency determinations is that one does not have to pay the disputed amount for the court to have jurisdiction. Instead, the Tax Court decides the amount of the liability and only then does the taxpayer have to pay it.

By contrast, in order to take a non-CDP case to the District Court or the Court of Federal Claims, one must pay the *entire* amount asserted by the government *before* suing for a refund of the disputed amount.[61] Prepayment may not be possible for the taxpayer, mooting all other considerations.

C. Precedent

The most important *legal* factor to consider when choosing a forum is the precedent the court will follow in deciding a case. For example, it would make no sense for the taxpayer to take a case to the Tax Court if the court has already addressed the issue and held in favor of the government. Instead, one should review the decisions of other courts and choose the most favorable forum.

To make this judgment, one must know which decisions each trial court is obligated to follow. Under our system of common law and stare decisis, each court will follow its own opinions. Thus, the Tax Court will follow prior Tax Court cases (including cases decided by the Tax Court's ancestor: the Board of Tax Appeals), and the Court of Federal Claims will follow decisions of the Court of Federal Claims and its predecessors—the Court of Claims and the Claims Court. Since it is unusual for a District Court to hear enough tax cases to build a body of decisional law on a given issue, precedent within a particular district is not usually important.

Each trial-level court will also follow the decisions of the Circuit Court of Appeals to which the case is appealable and of the Supreme Court. As discussed in Chapter 1, Tax Court cases and District Court cases are appealable to the circuit court responsible for the location in which the taxpayer resides. Court of Federal Claims' cases are appealable to the Circuit Court of Appeals for the Federal Circuit.

Example (1): The IRS disallowed a deduction for points on mortgage refinancing for a taxpayer who resides in Denver, Colorado. The Tax

---

[61] Flora v. United States, 362 U.S. 145 (1960).

Court has decided this issue favorably to taxpayers in previous cases. The Court of Federal Claims has not. The Tenth Circuit, to which appeals in Denver are filed, has not addressed the issue in the past. Other circuits that have considered the issue have uniformly held in favor of the IRS. All other factors being equal, the taxpayer should take the case to the Tax Court. The taxpayer is sure to win at the trial level. If the IRS appeals the loss to the Tenth Circuit, the court will decide the case as one of first impression. While the Tenth Circuit may look to the opinions of other circuits for guidance, it is not bound by them.

Example (2): Same as example (1) above except that the Tenth Circuit has held for the IRS in the past and the Federal Circuit Court of Appeals has held in favor of the taxpayer. The taxpayer should avoid the Tax Court since it will follow the precedent established in the Tenth Circuit, even though contrary to its own decisional law.[62] Instead, assuming the taxpayer can pay the entire asserted tax, he or she should take the case to the Court of Federal Claims, as it is obligated to follow the decisions of the Federal Circuit Court of Appeals.

D. Judge vs. Jury and Legal Argument vs. Equitable Considerations

Because the District Court is the only forum in which a jury is available, it is the best court in which to bring a case that relies heavily on equitable considerations by the trier of fact that might be lost if examined under the microscope of the law. While taxpayers have faired well in Tax Court on this issue, innocent spouse cases fit this description. This might also be the best forum if the case involves a very complex provision of the tax law that most people cannot understand and with respect to which the taxpayer honestly sought to comply.

By contrast, cases in the Tax Court are heard by judges who have significant backgrounds in tax law. They are tax specialists who understand the nuances of complex tax provisions. If one is trying to advance a logical but novel position, the Tax Court may be the best place to litigate. If one is interested in equity, the Tax Court is not the court to petition.[63]

The Bankruptcy Court is specifically designed to do equity and to help debtors emerge from bankruptcy with a "fresh start." For this reason, the ability to litigate a tax controversy in Bankruptcy Court might be one of a number of factors to consider when determining whether to file for bankruptcy.

---

[62] Golsen v. Commissioner, 54 T.C. 742 (1970).

[63] The Pension Protection Act of 2006, P.L. 109-280, Title VIII, Subtitle E, § 85(a) amended IRC § 6214(b) to permit the Tax Court to apply the doctrine of equitable recoupment in the same manner as other courts may in civil tax cases.

E. Concerns About New Issues

A final decision on the merits is res judicata as to all issues that were raised or could have been raised for the year. Issues raised thereafter are barred, no matter their validity. On the other hand, issues raised before the court renders its final decision normally are not precluded. If it is the IRS that raises a new issue, dramatically different results can come about depending on the route taken and whether the IRS raises the issue before the statute of limitations on assessment expires.

In Tax Court, the IRS can raise the new issue in its answer. If it failed to do so, the IRS can ask the court's leave to raise a new issue by amending its answer and seeking a greater deficiency.[64] Since the statute of limitations on assessment is stayed until the decision of the court becomes final,[65] a successfully argued new issue can result in an increased deficiency. A dramatic example of this occurred in *Raskob v. Commissioner*.[66] *Raskob* petitioned the Tax Court with respect to a deficiency of only $16,000, but the IRS successfully argued a new issue and the taxpayer left the Tax Court with a tax liability of $1,025,000!

By contrast, refund actions do not suspend the running of the statute of limitations on assessment. If the taxpayer brings the refund action after the statute of limitations on assessment has expired,[67] the IRS would be time-barred from assessing amounts the court found in its favor attributable to a new issue. If a refund would otherwise be due the taxpayer for the same year, the best the government can do is offset or reduce the amount of the refund by the amount that cannot be assessed.[68]

> **Example:** In a notice of deficiency mailed April 15, 2006, the IRS claims that Bill Wilson omitted income in the year 2002 by treating compensation as a loan. The resulting proposed deficiency in tax is $15,000

---

[64] With respect to the new issue, the IRS automatically has the burden of proof. The presumption of correctness that applies to the original assessment does not apply to new issues. *See* Abatti v. Commissioner, 644 F.2d 1385 (9th Cir. 1981). The burden of proof and presumption of correctness matters are still important even after the 1998 Reform Act's shift of the burden to the IRS in tax litigation. This is because the new rules require certain prelitigation action by the taxpayer before the shift occurs, whereas with respect to a new issue, the burden shift to the IRS occurs whether or not the taxpayer has met the prelitigation requirement. *See* IRC § 7491.

[65] IRC § 6503.

[66] 37 B.T.A. 1283 (1938), *aff'd sub nom.* Dupont v. Commissioner, 118 F.2d 544 (3d Cir. 1941).

[67] If the refund action is brought when the statute of limitations on assessment is still open, the IRS will try to issue a timely notice of deficiency. If the government does so, the result would be the same as that demonstrated in *Raskob*.

[68] Lewis v. Reynolds, 284 U.S. 281, 283 (1932) ("An overpayment must appear before refund is authorized. Although the statute of limitations may have barred the assessment and collection of any additional sum, it does not obliterate the right of the United States to retain payments already received when they do not exceed the amount which might have been properly assessed and demanded").

(issue #1). The IRS wishes to raise a new issue disallowing tax shelter deductions, the impact of which would be an additional $100,000 deficiency (issue #2). Assume that Bill prevails on issue #1 and the IRS prevails on issue #2. The litigation takes place during December 2007, more than three years after the tax return was filed.

If Bill litigated the deficiency in Tax Court, he would emerge owing $100,000 (having won on issue #1 but having lost on issue #2). The IRS could assess the $100,000 because section 6503(a) suspends the statute of limitations on assessment for the entire period the case is in Tax Court.

If Bill paid the $15,000 deficiency and waited until after September 12, 2006 (the date the statute of limitations on assessment would have run after considering section 6503) to sue for a refund, the result would be quite different. Although while the IRS would be time-barred from assessing and collecting the $100,000 associated with the tax shelter, it could retain the $15,000 to offset against the $100,000.

F. Accruing of Interest

Interest normally accrues on an outstanding tax liability from the due date of the return until the taxpayer pays it. In refund litigation, the continued accruing of interest while the court reviews the determination is not a problem since the taxpayer has to make full payment of the balance to invoke the jurisdiction of the refund courts.

By contrast, continuing accrual of interest is a significant problem when one seeks Tax Court review of a proposed deficiency. As a result, taxpayers wishing to litigate in Tax Court look for ways to stop the interest from accruing.

- The taxpayer can make full payment of an expected deficiency prior to the IRS issuing a ninety-day letter. For example, one might pay the amount on the thirty-day letter. However, since doing so eliminates the deficiency, the government no longer has a basis for issuing a notice of deficiency. Without a notice of deficiency, the taxpayer cannot seek a hearing in the Tax Court.

- The taxpayer can make partial payment of an expected deficiency prior to the IRS issuing a ninety-day letter. This would leave a balance due, thus preserving Tax Court jurisdiction. By doing so, the interest stops running to the extent of the amount paid. If it turns out that the tax was overpaid, the IRS will send a refund for the overpayment, with interest from the date of payment.

- The taxpayer can make full or partial payment of a deficiency *after* the IRS mails the ninety-day letter. Tax Court jurisdiction is not adversely affected by payment at this time since all that is required

is issuance of a ninety-day letter. It is not necessary that the deficiency continue to exist throughout the proceedings. Interest on the
deficiency stops accruing to the extent of the payment and, if it is
later determined that the taxpayer overpaid, a refund with interest
will be sent.

• The taxpayer can designate a remittance as a "deposit in the nature
of a cash bond."[69] Since remittance in this manner is *not* treated as
a payment, it does not pay down the deficiency, thus preserving Tax
Court jurisdiction. Interest stops accruing against the taxpayer to the
extent of the deposit.

G. Costs of Litigation

Although the Tax Court is physically located in Washington, D.C., the judges
travel nationwide to conduct trials in various cities. The District Court and the
Bankruptcy Court are local forums. The Court of Federal Claims is located in
Washington, D.C. Its trials typically occur there, even though the court will
travel, depending on the circumstances. Because of the costs associated with
having counsel and witnesses fly to, and lodge in, Washington, D.C., litigation
in the Court of Federal Claims can be significantly more expensive than in
other courts.

The Tax Court is less expensive than the other courts for other reasons also.
The Tax Court requires informal discovery discussions between the parties
prior to expensive formal discovery. The other courts do not. The Tax Court
also requires the parties to stipulate to as much as possible rather than requiring the parties to prove every fact in a time consuming and expensive trial. In
addition, the representative of the government in Tax Court is an attorney in
a local office of Area Counsel rather than an attorney with the Department of
Justice located in Washington, D.C., which helps keep attorney travel costs
down.

H. Other Factors

1. Publicity

If publicity is a concern, the District Court should be avoided. While it is common for reporters to cover litigation in the local District Court, it is rare for them
to report on litigation in Tax Court, Bankruptcy Court, or the Court of Federal
Claims.

---

[69] IRC § 6603 (discussed in Chapter 12); Rev. Proc. 2005-18, 2005-13 I.R.B. 798.

2. State Law

The District Court is significantly more familiar with state law issues since it is a local court, rather than a national court. Thus, if the case involves complicated issues regarding state law that favor the client, it may be desirable to litigate in District Court.

3. Speed of Disposition

The District Court is a court with broad jurisdiction and its caseload is considerable. It may take anywhere between several months and several years before the case comes to trial. The Tax Court normally resolves cases more quickly.

4. Nationwide Jurisdiction

The Tax Court, Bankruptcy Court, and Court of Federal Claims are "national" courts and their power is nationwide. They can serve process on and subpoena anyone within the country. The District Court, by comparison, is a regional court and can only serve process on and subpoena people within its jurisdiction.

5. Tax Court's Exclusive Jurisdiction

As discussed in section II.G. infra, once the Tax Court acquires proper jurisdiction over a case by the taxpayer filing a timely petition, no other court may consider the case. Therefore, decisions on the best forum in which to litigate a tax case should be made before a petition is filed with the Tax Court.

VII. ATTORNEY'S FEES AND COSTS

Under section 7430, a taxpayer who prevails in proceedings with the IRS or in litigation involving a tax matter may be able to recover costs incurred in the proceedings, including attorney's fees. Before 1982, attorney's fees were recoverable by a prevailing taxpayer under the Equal Access to Justice Act ("EAJA")[70]—but only where the taxpayer prevailed in a suit in federal District Court. The EAJA did not provide for attorney's fees and costs incurred in Tax Court proceedings.[71]

---

[70] 28 U.S.C. § 2412 (1988).

[71] Smith v. Brady, 972 F.2d 1095 (9th Cir. 1992).

In 1982, Congress remedied this glitch by enacting section 7430. Several times since 1982, Congress has expanded the scope of section 7430. The most significant changes include: (1) shifting the burden of proof from the taxpayer (to establish that the government's position was unreasonable) to the government (to prove that its position was substantially justified);[72] (2) allowing taxpayers to recover costs incurred during administrative proceedings as well as during litigation;[73] and (3) establishing clearer guidelines and presumptions for when the government's position is not substantially justified or the taxpayer is deemed to be the prevailing party.[74] Today, to recover costs under section 7430, a taxpayer must satisfy the following requirements:

- The costs must be incurred either in an administrative or court proceeding in connection with the determination, collection, or refund of tax, interest, or penalties or in the case deciding the taxpayer's right to attorney's fees and costs, i.e., fees for fees.[75]

- The taxpayer must exhaust all administrative remedies with the IRS.

- The taxpayer must not unreasonably protract the proceedings.

- The taxpayer must be the prevailing party with respect to the amount in controversy, or the most significant issue or set of issues presented. In order for the taxpayer to be the prevailing party, the government must not be able to establish its position in the proceeding was substantially justified. (Only costs incurred during the time the government's position was unjustified are recoverable under section 7430. Interest does not accrue on section 7430 awards.)[76]

- The taxpayer must satisfy certain net worth requirements.

A particularly interesting provision—the Qualified Settlement Offer rule—was added in the 1998 Reform Act. If the judgment in the court proceedings is in an amount that is equal to or less than the amount of the taxpayer's last offer (the "qualified offer"), the taxpayer is treated as the prevailing party for costs and fees incurred thereafter.

The taxpayer is not required to use any specific form for requesting administrative costs from the IRS. However, the request must be in writing and contain the information specified in Regulation section 301.7430-2(c)(3). The taxpayer must file the request with the IRS for administrative costs within ninety days of the final decision of the IRS regarding the underlying tax, addi-

---

[72] IRC § 7430(c)(4).

[73] IRC § 7430(a)(1).

[74] IRC § 7430(c)(4)(B), (E).

[75] Huffman v. Commissioner, 978 F.2d 1139, 1149 (9th Cir. 1992); Powell v. Commissioner, 891 F.2d 1167 (5th Cir. 1990).

[76] Miller v. Alamo, 992 F.2d 766 (8th Cir. 1993).

tion to tax, and penalties.[77] The request should be filed with the IRS office that has jurisdiction over the underlying tax matter.

If a taxpayer's request for a section 7430 award of administrative costs is denied in whole or in part by the IRS, the taxpayer may appeal to the Tax Court.[78] If the IRS sends its notice of denial to the taxpayer by certified or registered mail, the taxpayer has ninety days from the date of the notice to file a Tax Court petition appealing the denial.

The Tax Court, District Court, and the Court of Federal Claims may all grant section 7430 awards.[79] If the IRS and the taxpayer settle the case, including issues relating to recovery of costs, any section 7430 award must be included in the stipulation agreement. Otherwise, the taxpayer must make a separate written motion for a section 7430 award. Any evidence pertaining only to the section 7430 motion should not be presented in the main case.

The Tax Court will include its decision regarding recovery of fees and costs under section 7430 with its decision in the case. If the taxpayer loses and it is determined that the section 7430 request was frivolous, the taxpayer could be subject to sanctions under section 6673(a)(2).[80]

A court order granting or denying all or part of an award for reasonable litigation costs is subject to appeal in the same manner as the court's decision or judgment.[81] In order for the reviewing court to determine whether the denial was appropriate, the trial court must include a statement of reasons, not merely a conclusory statement.[82] The standard of review is "abuse of discretion" and the appellate court will "reverse only if [it has] a definite and firm conviction that the [trial] court committed a clear error of judgment in the conclusion it reached upon weighing the relevant factors."[83]

PROBLEM

Spencer Richards and Georgia Britton are your clients. They have come to see you on September 22, 2007. He is 30 years old; she is 31 years old. They married six years ago. They have two children—Hans and Sara.

Spencer and Georgia have separate sources of income. Spencer is employed by Ajax Plumbing Corp. as a salesperson. He earns about $75,000, mostly from commissions. He has significant travel and entertainment expenses. Georgia has

---

[77] Reg. § 301.7430-2(c)(5).

[78] IRC § 7430(f)(2).

[79] IRC § 7430(c)(6).

[80] Bragg v. Commissioner, 102 T.C. 715, 720-21 (1994).

[81] IRC § 7430(f)(1).

[82] Liti v. Commissioner, 289 F.3d 1103 (9th Cir. 2002).

[83] Id. at 1104-1105.

her own bookkeeping practice ("Georgia's Books") that she operates from her home. She bills and collects about $100,000 annually and incurs about $20,000 in business expenses, including those associated with an office in home. They individually own stocks and bonds, on which they separately collect dividends and interest.

About four years ago, Spencer began to go into a severe depression and resorted to alcohol. While he is able to "fake it" at work, Spencer has been having a very difficult time being responsible outside of work, especially during 2005 and early 2006. He cannot admit he has a problem and will not seek counseling. This has taken a toll on their marriage and Spencer and Georgia stay together now primarily for the sake of the kids.

For the first four years of their marriage, Spencer and Georgia filed joint Form 1040 income tax returns. During 2005 and 2006, Spencer has not been able to "get his act together" to prepare his tax returns. Georgia did not wait and filed a separate Form 1040 for herself.

On January 25, 2007, Spencer received several letters from the IRS asking him to file a return for 2005. He did not respond to them, hoping the government would just go away. The IRS sent him a notice, dated August 1, 2007, indicating that it had prepared a tax return for him for 2003 from payee information (meaning from W-2s and 1099s). According to IRS calculations, which include all the income but allow him no deductions other than his personal exemption, he owes $15,000 tax and $3,750 in late filing penalty. The notice indicated he could dispute the determination by filing a protest with the Appeals Office of the Service. Of course, until now, he ignored this notice also. To date, he has not heard anything more from the government.

After reviewing the adjustments, it is your belief that the IRS is correct about the income they attributed to him but that there are about $15,000 in various deductions not accounted for to which he is entitled. If these were allowed, his taxes would be reduced by $4,000. In addition, this would decrease the late filing penalty, since it is calculated at 25% of the tax due, per section 6651(a)(1). However, you believe the penalty should not be asserted at all since Spencer's alcoholism and depression gave him reasonable cause for not filing.

Questions:

1. What kind of notice do you believe Spencer received on August 1, 2007? What can Spencer do if he wishes to dispute the determination that he owes additional tax? What is likely to happen if he does not?

2. Does Spencer need to pay the $18,750 to get an administrative hearing with the IRS? With a court?

3. Spencer is concerned that this matter might go on for a long time, with interest accruing. Is there anything he can do to stop or minimize the interest?

4. For reasons not relevant here, Spencer does not do anything in response to the August 1, 2007, letter. Soon thereafter, he receives a certified letter from the IRS, dated October 17, 2007. The body of the letter says it is a notice of deficiency for the year 2005, and informs him of his right to file a petition with the Tax Court within ninety days if he wishes to have the court redetermine the tax liability.

a. Based on the facts presented, what would you advise Spencer about whether to petition the Tax Court or resort to one of the other trial courts instead? What additional information would you want from him before making a final recommendation?

b. If Spencer wishes to get the Tax Court to review the determination of deficiency, by what date must he do so? (Check actual 2007 and 2008 calendars!) What happens if you are late?

c. If you are busy and cannot get to it in time, can you get an extension to file it one week late?

d. What method of mailing would you use and why?

e. After Spencer files his Tax Court petition, the Court of Federal Claims decides the same issue very favorably to taxpayers. Can you get the Tax Court case dismissed without prejudice so a complaint can be filed in the Court of Federal Claims?

f. Based on the petition you would likely draft for the Tax Court, will the case be heard as a regular case or a small tax ("S") case? Explain to Spencer the advantages and disadvantages of one versus the other. What would you have to do to have it heard as one or the other and what will the court likely do if the IRS opposes your request?

5. Assume the following for purposes of this question only. In response to the January 25, 2007, letter from the IRS that asked him to file his 2005 return, Spencer wrote that he was making every effort to do so. He also stated in bold letters: "As of April 1, 2007, my family is moving to 8651 E. Stetson Rd., Parker, CO 80134. Please update your records accordingly and please send all future correspondence to this address." He completed a change of address with the Post Office on April 1, 2007. When he filed the 2005 return on April 5, 2007, he used the Parker address. He did not hear anything more from the Service regarding 2005 until February 22, 2008, when he received a collection notice. What would you do?

6. What are the issues in the notice of deficiency? As between Spencer and the IRS, who has the burden of proof in the Tax Court on the issues in the notice of deficiency? What is the standard of proof required?

a. Will the court consider Spencer's evidence on the $15,000 itemized deductions or must he do that through a subsequent refund action? Who has the burden of proof, and what is the standard of proof?

   b. If, in the notice of deficiency, the government had asserted that Spencer's failure to file was fraudulent and it asserted a fraud penalty under section 6663 of 75% in each year, how is the burden of proof allocated and what is the standard of proof?

   c. After Spencer files the petition, the IRS attorney believes he failed to report $10,000 of kickbacks he received "under the table" from a customer. Can the government now assert this and, if so, how is that done and who has the burden of proof?

7. As Spencer's representative, you receive the following correspondence. How do you respond to each?

   a. The government's answer to your petition.

   b. A letter from the Appeals Office suggesting a conference to try to settle the case.

   c. A letter from the attorney for the IRS for an informal (Branerton) conference.

   d. A letter from the attorney for the IRS suggesting the two of you meet to stipulate to the facts in the case.

   e. The notice from the Tax Court indicating the date the case is calendared for trial.

   f. The pretrial orders from the judge who will hear the case.

   g. The opinion of the Tax Court.

   h. A Rule 155 computation prepared by IRS Counsel's office.

   i. The decision of the Tax Court.

8. Though unlikely on the facts presented, assume the court holds entirely in favor of Spencer. Are attorney's fees and costs available?

Chapter 9

OVERPAYMENTS—CLAIMS FOR REFUND

IRC:	§§ 6072(a); skim 6164(a)-(f); 6401(a), (b)(1), (c); 6402(a), (b), (c), skim (e), (f), (k); 6404; 6405(a), (b); 6406; 6407; 6411(a), (b); 6511(a)-(d)(2)(A), -(h)(2)(A); 6512; 6513(a)-(d); 6514; 6532(a)(1)-(4), (b), (c); 6611(a); 6621(a)(1); 7422(a), (e), (f)(1); 7502
Regs.:	§§ 301.6401-1(a); 301.6402-1; 301.6402-2(a)(1), (b), (d); 301.6402-3(a); 301.6402-4
Forms:	Skim 843; 870; 870-AD; 872; 1040X; 2848; 8379

I. INTRODUCTION

Taxpayers sometimes find that they have paid more than the amount of tax that is due. The Code contains an extensive set of rules that, if followed, permit taxpayers to obtain refunds of the amount overpaid. The most often encountered refund occurs when a taxpayer's federal income tax return shows that the tax withheld on wages,[1] the amount of any estimated taxes paid,[2] and overpayments from a prior year applied to the current year, exceeds the liability reported on the taxpayer's return. The excess is considered an overpayment. In this case, the income tax return serves as a claim for refund and normally the taxpayer will receive a check for the amount of the overpayment. However, if the taxpayer elects, the amount of the overpayment will be applied to the next year's estimated tax liability.[3] Rarely do these overpayments or refund claims present problems for the taxpayer since the IRS refunds (or applies) the overpayment as part of its normal processing.

Difficulties arise more often when the taxpayer becomes aware that the liability was overstated on a filed return and, as a consequence, the tax was overpaid. An overpayment can also arise if, at the conclusion of an audit of a return, the taxpayer pays a deficiency proposed by the IRS. Whether the taxpayer mistakenly overpaid his tax upon filing the return, or paid a disputed deficiency at

---

[1] Technically, the tax withheld on wages under sections 3401–3406, is treated as a refundable credit under section 31. Refundable credits are credited against the taxpayer's income tax liability, and any excess is refunded to the taxpayer. IRC § 36. If the taxpayer is also entitled to nonrefundable credits, those credits are applied first to the tax liability, thereby preserving for the taxpayer the maximum amount that can be received from the refundable credits. IRC § 6401(b).

[2] Payments of estimated income tax are considered payment on account of the taxpayer's income tax for the year. IRC § 6315.

[3] IRC § 6402(b).

the conclusion of an audit, the traditional approach to establishing the right to refund of the overpayment is filing a claim for refund.

The basic procedural structure for obtaining a refund is simple: (1) there must be an overpayment; (2) a claim for refund must be filed in a timely manner; and (3) the amount of the claim must be tested against certain limitations. However, the law is infused with numerous exceptions and rules that deal with specific circumstances. For instance, although the basic statute of limitations on filing a claim for refund is the later of three years from the time the return is filed or two years from the time the tax is paid,[4] under various circumstances the statute of limitations on claiming a refund is longer than the three-year/two-year periods,[5] or is extended,[6] suspended,[7] or re-opened.[8]

If a refund claim is filed within the applicable statute of limitations, the IRS has the discretion to accept and pay the claim, to deny part or all of it, or to simply ignore it. If the IRS denies part or all of the claim, or fails to respond to it, the taxpayer can file a refund suit in either a United States District Court or the Court of Federal Claims. The Tax Court does not have general jurisdiction to determine the validity of refund claims. Its principal role is as a forum for taxpayers to seek a redetermination of a deficiency proposed by the IRS. However the Tax Court does have jurisdiction to determine the amount of an overpayment if, in a deficiency proceeding, it finds that an overpayment has been made.[9]

Added to the procedural maze created by special rules is the fact that a taxpayer may have an overpayment, may have filed a timely claim for refund, may have avoided the limitations on the amount of the refund, and still may not receive the refund. This is because there are several circumstances in which an otherwise valid refund will be diverted to another use. For instance, the statute authorizing the IRS to refund overpayments also authorizes the IRS to first apply a refund against any other tax liability owed to the federal government by the taxpayer, and then directs the IRS to use the balance of the refund, to the extent necessary, to satisfy certain other debts of the taxpayer to federal and state agencies.[10] Any such diversion of an otherwise proper refund reduces the amount refunded to the taxpayer.

An alternate approach to asserting an overpayment was created by the 1998 Reform Act. The legislation gave taxpayers the right to Collection Due Process hearings under sections 6320 and 6330. If the IRS files a notice of lien or

---

[4] IRC § 6511(a).

[5] IRC § 6511(d).

[6] IRC § 6511(c).

[7] IRC § 6511(h).

[8] IRC §§ 1311–1314. *See* Chapter 10.

[9] IRC § 6512(b).

[10] IRC § 6402.

intends to levy on a taxpayer's assets to pay a tax liability, the IRS is required to offer the taxpayer the opportunity for a hearing. These hearings are discussed in Chapter 13. For claim for refund purposes, it is important to note that at such hearings, the taxpayer is entitled, among other things, to "raise . . . challenges to the existence or amount of the underlying tax liability. . . ."[11] Any such challenge is available only if the taxpayer either did not receive a notice of deficiency or otherwise did not have an opportunity to contest the liability.[12]

Finally, to further complicate matters, claims for refund attributable to "partnership items" are excluded from the general refund rules, and are dealt with under the TEFRA partnership provisions adopted in 1982.[13] Section 6227 establishes a separate procedure for claiming such refunds through "administrative adjustment requests."

The general procedure for correcting an overpayment error requires consideration of three questions. First, is there an "overpayment"? Second, can the taxpayer establish the right to a refund? And, third, can an otherwise valid refund be diverted to another use? After considering these questions, the refund jurisdiction of the Tax Court, administrative adjustment requests in the partnership context, and tentative carryback and refund adjustments are discussed. Finally, the procedure for responding to denied claims for refund is discussed. Although many of the procedures mentioned in this chapter apply to other taxes as well, unless otherwise noted, the discussion pertains to federal income taxes.

II. IS THERE AN OVERPAYMENT?

Neither the Code nor the Regulations contains a comprehensive definition of an overpayment.[14] The Supreme Court has defined the term "in its usual sense, as meaning any payment in excess of that which is properly due."[15] This defi-

---

[11] IRC § 6330(c)(2)(B) (as to any proposed levy). Challenges to the existence or amount of the asserted liability may also be raised in a collection due process hearing under section 6320. *See* § 6320(c).

[12] IRC § 6330(c)(2)(B).

[13] IRC §§ 6221–6234. *See* Chapter 6.

[14] Section 6401 describes certain things included in the term "overpayment," such as any amount assessed or collected after the applicable statute of limitations, but neither that section nor its related Regulations purports to define the term comprehensively. In *Williams-Russell & Johnson v. United States*, 371 F.3d 1350 (11th Cir. 2004), the Eleventh Circuit Court of Appeals was faced with the question of whether payments actually owed and made in a timely fashion but assessed after the expiration of the of the statute of limitations should be refunded. The taxpayer argued that any such payments, are by definition in "overpayments" under section 6401(a) and that overpayments are expressly required to be refunded under section 6402(a). The Court, citing "the principles established in Lewis v. Reynolds, 284 U.S. 281 (1932), concluded that for this purpose the term "overpayment" does not include taxes due and paid notwithstanding the fact that they were not assessed in a timely manner.

[15] Jones v. Liberty City Glass Co., 332 U.S. 524, 531 (1947).

nition invites consideration of what constitutes "payment" and how the amount "properly due" is determined.

A. What Constitutes Payment?

Just as the amount of an overpayment is determined "in its usual sense," so is the amount paid as tax determined in its usual sense. Thus, taxes paid with the return or with a request for extension of time to file, taxes reported on the return but paid later, taxes paid in response to a notice of deficiency, and taxes paid in installments are all payments. Likewise prepayments, such as estimated taxes[16] and taxes withheld on wages are considered payment of the taxpayer's income tax liability.

Under section 6603 deposits made to suspend the running of interest are specifically treated as payment at the time of the deposit for purposes of interest computation. If the deposit is applied against a subsequently assessed liability, interest on the underpayment (to the extent of the deposit) stops at the time the deposit is made. If the taxpayer prevails in the dispute over the asserted tax liability or withdraws the deposit, the government pays interest on the deposit at the Federal short-term rate from the time of the deposit to a day not more than thirty days preceding the refund.[17] For purposes other than interest determinations, deposits under section 6603 are treated as payments of tax only at the time they are applied against a tax liability. Treating the payment as having been made as late as possible has the effect of maximizing the amount available for refund under the two-year look-back limitation on refunds.

Section 6603, enacted in the American Jobs Creation Act of 2004, is the statutory version of Revenue Procedure 84-58 which provides for "deposits in the nature of cash bonds" as a means for suspending the running of interest.[18] Under Revenue Procedure 84-58, no interest is paid on either the portion of any deposit withdrawn or on the excess of any deposit over the amount of tax and interest ultimately determined to be due. Revenue Procedure 2005-18[19] supersedes Revenue Procedure 84-58 and provides rules for making and withdrawing deposits under section 6603. Revenue Procedure 2005-18 provides transition rules relating to deposits made under Revenue Procedure 84-58, under which taxpayers are permitted to redesignate their deposits under Revenue Procedure 84-58 as deposits under section 6603.[20] Such redesignation permits the accrual

---

[16] IRC § 6315.

[17] IRC §§ 6603(d)(1), 6611(b)(2).

[18] Rev. Proc. 84-58, 1984-2 C.B. 501.

[19] 2005-13 I.R.B. 1.

[20] *Id.* at § 5. However, to protect against taxpayers purposefully depositing more than the anticipated liability in order to earn interest, section 7 of Revenue Procedure 2005-18 limits the amount of the deposit on which interest will be paid to the amount "attributable to a disputable tax." Taxpayers are required to identify the amount and nature of the disputable tax (determined by any "reasonable method") at the time the deposit is made or, in the case of redesignation of deposits in the nature of a cash bond, at the time of the redesignation.

of interest on deposits even if they are withdrawn or exceed the ultimately determined liability.

B. The Tax Properly Due

The tax properly due is sometimes described as the "theoretically correct" tax liability or "the amount of tax finally determined to be legally due by a court."[21] However, in practice, few claims for refund are actually determined by reference to the theoretically correct tax liability or by a decision of a court.

For refund claim purposes, the amount of tax properly due is normally determined in the first instance by the taxpayer filing a federal income tax return (Form 1040 for individuals and Form 1120 for corporations) that claims an overpayment, or by the taxpayer filing an amended income tax return (Form 1040X for individuals and Form 1120X for corporations) that claims an overpayment. Claims for refund of estate tax, gift tax, employment tax, assessable penalties, and certain excise taxes, as well as claims for refund or abatement of interest, are filed on Form 843. In most cases, the amount claimed on the original income tax return, and consequently the amounts of the tax properly due and the overpayment, are accepted without an audit by the IRS. All claims for refund are reviewed, which may lead to an audit. If the claim for refund triggers an audit, the most likely outcome is that the taxpayer and the IRS will reach an agreement as to the amount to be refunded before a court renders a decision as to the proper amount of tax due. Regardless of the route by which a final decision is reached, the decision may not reflect the theoretically correct amount of tax due.

In 1932 the United States Supreme Court decided *Lewis v. Reynolds,*[22] a significant case relating to the tax properly due for refund claim purposes. In response to an estate's claim for refund of income taxes, the IRS audited the return. The IRS accepted the position taken in the claim for refund, but also disallowed a deduction originally taken on the return. The net result of conceding the taxpayer's position on the refund claim and disallowing the item originally deducted was that the taxpayer owed more tax than was shown on the return.

Because the IRS's determination in response to the refund claim occurred after the statute of limitations on assessing additional tax expired, the IRS made no attempt to assess and collect the additional tax. However, the taxpayer asserted that, because the statute of limitations on assessment had expired, the IRS was precluded from disallowing the deduction and recalculating the entire tax liability. The taxpayer argued that the only change the IRS could make at that time was the adjustment requested in the timely filed claim for refund.

21 Michael I. Saltzman, IRS Practice and Procedure, ¶ 11.02[1] (rev. 2d ed. 2002, 2003).

22 284 U.S. 281 (1932).

The Supreme Court had no trouble in agreeing with the IRS's conclusion that no refund was allowed. The Court said that even though the statute of limitations on assessment had expired, and therefore the IRS could not require the taxpayer to pay more tax, the government has the right "to retain payments already received when they do not exceed the amount which might have been properly assessed and demanded."[23] Since both adjustments were properly made, the net result was that there was no overpayment entitling the taxpayer to a refund.

Lewis v. Reynolds suggests that when a claim for refund is filed consideration should be given to whether, and to what extent, there are offsetting items that the IRS might raise to reduce or eliminate the claimed refund. This is particularly important if, when the claim is filed, the IRS has time to audit the return and perhaps assess and collect a deficiency. In this connection, it should be noted that a claim for refund does not extend the statute of limitations on assessment. As is discussed in Chapter 5, filing a timely claim for refund near the end of the statute of limitations on assessment preserves the claim for refund and provides some protection against exposure to deficiency assessments.

III. CAN THE TAXPAYER ESTABLISH THE RIGHT TO A REFUND?

A. The Requirement of a "Claim"

A taxpayer's right to a refund of an overpayment may ultimately have to be determined in a civil action initiated by the taxpayer against the federal government. Since section 7422(a) provides that no such action may be filed "until a claim for refund . . . has been duly filed with the Secretary" it is important to know what qualifies as an effective claim. First, to be effective, a claim for refund must be in writing and it must be filed "within 3 years from the time the return was filed or 2 years from the time the tax was paid, whichever of such periods expires the later. . . ."[24] Unless a claim is filed in a timely manner, no refund is allowed. Furthermore, any refund made (or credit given) after the expiration of the statute of limitations on filing a claim is considered void and is recoverable by the government. Likewise, if a timely claim is filed and part or all of the claim is disallowed, any refund made (or credit given) with respect to the disallowed portion after the period for filing suit has expired is considered void.[25]

---

[23] *Id.* at 283.

[24] IRC § 6511(a).

[25] IRC § 6514(a). Section 7405(a) authorizes the United States to bring a civil action to recover any erroneously made refund, and section 6532(b) requires such an action to commence within two years of the erroneous refund or, if "the refund was induced by fraud or misrepresentation of a material fact," then within four years. The Supreme Court has held that the limitations period begins to run on the receipt of "payment." O'Gilvie v. United States, 117 U.S. 452, 458 (1996). For this pur-

Second, Regulation section 301.6402-2(b)(1) establishes the standard for an effective claim. "The claim must set forth in detail each ground upon which a credit or refund is claimed and facts sufficient to apprise the Commissioner of the exact basis thereof." After a valid claim is filed, newly discovered items can be raised by filing additional claims so long as the statute of limitations on filing a claim for refund is open.

After the statute of limitations on filing a claim has expired, the IRS will generally consider additional information supplied by the taxpayer in an amended claim. However, under the "variance doctrine," after the statute of limitations has expired, the IRS will not consider either new claims or new legal theories in support of the original claim.[26] The variance doctrine is based on long-standing requirements that the claim must be timely and must set forth both the facts and law that support the requested refund.

There is a significant body of case law dealing with taxpayers who have failed to file formal claims within the statute of limitations, but who, to some extent, have informed the IRS that they believe they are entitled to a refund. Such "informal claims" have been recognized provided that: (1) the IRS was put on notice that the taxpayer was actually asking for a refund for the year in question; (2) the taxpayer makes clear both the factual and the legal basis for the claim; and (3) there is a written document relating to the claim.[27]

As a practical matter, it is almost always the taxpayer who realizes first that an overpayment has been made. The only way the overpayment can effectively be brought to the attention of the IRS is through the filing of a timely claim for refund. However, in the event that the IRS commences an audit of a return, it is possible that the IRS will agree to a refund at the conclusion of the audit, or at the appeals level. Finally, it is also possible that the Tax Court, upon a petition by the taxpayer in response to a notice of deficiency, will determine that there was an overpayment.

---

pose, receipt of payment of the erroneous refund has been held to be either the date the check cleared, United States v. Greener Thapedi, 398 F.3d 635 (7th Cir. 2005), United States v. Commonwealth Energy, 235 F.3d 11 (1st Cir. 2000), or the date of receipt of the check, Paulson v. United States, 78 F.2d 97 (10th Cir. 1935). In a related matter, the IRS has announced in AOD 2006-02 that it does not acquiesce in *Pacific Gas and Electric Co. v. United States*, 417 F.3d 1375 (Fed. Cir. 2005). That case held that the IRS could not offset a refund of taxes and interest due for 1982 by an erroneous refund of interest for that year because the offset was made after expiration of the section 6532(b) limitations period for the government to file suit for the erroneous refund. For a comprehensive analysis of procedures relating to erroneous refunds, see Bryan T. Camp, *The Mysteries of Erroneous Refunds*, Tax Notes, Jan. 15, 2007, at 231.

[26] Mobil Corp. v. United States, 52 Fed. Cl. 327 (2002).

[27] *See, e.g.*, Mobil Corp. v. United States, 67 Fed. Cl. 708 (2005); Wall Industries v. United States, 10 Cl. Ct. 82 (1986); American Radiator & Standard Sanitary Corp. v. United States, 318 F.2d 915 (Cl. Ct. 1963). An application for an automatic extension of time to file an amended return on Form 4868 can constitute an informal claim for refund. Kaffenberger v. United States, 314 F.3d 944 (8th Cir. 2003), acquiesced AOD CC-2004-04, 2004 Lexis 4 (I.R.S. 2004).

B. Who Qualifies as a "Taxpayer"?

Generally persons who are liable for the tax are taxpayers and, as such, are entitled to file claims for refund. In *United States v. Williams*,[28] the Supreme Court was asked to decide whether Williams, who was not personally liable for the tax but who paid it under protest on behalf of another taxpayer, could file a suit in District Court to recover the tax after the IRS denied her claim for refund. Williams had paid the tax in order to remove a tax lien on her property. The government took its long-held position that the refund procedures were only available to "taxpayers"—people against whom the tax could be assessed.[29] According to the government, since the tax in question could not be assessed against Williams, she was not a taxpayer and thus could not avail herself of the refund procedures.

The Court focused primarily on whether the government had waived its sovereign immunity from suit under these facts. Section 1346(a)(1) of Title 28 grants concurrent jurisdiction to the District Courts and the Court of Federal Claims for "[a]ny civil action against the United States for the recovery of any internal-revenue tax alleged to have been erroneously or illegally assessed or collected. . . ." The Court held for Williams, saying that she fell squarely within this waiver of sovereign immunity. In reaching this result, however, the Court expressly withheld decision as to whether "a party who volunteers to pay a tax assessed against someone else [rather than pays the tax under protest to release a lien] may seek a refund under 28 U.S.C. § 1346(a)."[30]

C. The Timely Filing Requirement

When a taxpayer files a claim for refund there are always two questions that must be answered to determine whether the taxpayer is entitled to a refund. The first question, addressed in this section, is whether the claim was filed within the statute of limitations set forth in section 6511(a)? The second question, addressed in the next section, is whether the amount that can be refunded is limited under section 6511(b)(2)?

1. The Statute of Limitations

A claim for refund must be filed in a timely manner. The basic statute of limitations on claiming a refund is the *later* of three years from the time the return

---

[28] 514 U.S. 527 (1995).

[29] *Compare* Snodgrass v. United States, 834 F.2d 537 (5th Cir. 1987), *and* Busse v. United States, 542 F.2d 421 (7th Cir. 1976) (holding that only the person against whom the tax was assessed has the right to maintain a refund suit), *with* Martin v. United States, 895 F.2d 992 (4th Cir. 1990) (allowing the wife who voluntarily paid her former husband's liability to maintain a refund suit).

[30] 514 U.S. at 540.

is filed or two years from the time the tax is paid. Under the "timely mailing is timely filing" rule in section 7502, a properly addressed claim that is received by the IRS after the due date, but which is postmarked (or recorded or marked by a designated private delivery service) on or before the due date, is deemed to be delivered on the date of the postmark. Also, under section 7503, if the last day of the period within which a claim can be filed falls on a Saturday, Sunday, or legal holiday, then a claim filed on the next succeeding day (which is not a Saturday, Sunday, or legal holiday) is considered timely filed.[31]

Applying the basic statute, if a taxpayer pays all tax shown as due on the return before or at the time of filing the return, a claim for refund of tax for the year filed within the next three years will be timely. If additional tax is paid after the return is filed, but within one year of filing, the three-year rule still establishes the last day for which a timely claim can be filed. The two-year rule is relevant only when additional tax for a given year is paid more than one year after the return was filed. In that situation, the two-year rule will always apply, because it will be later than the date computed using the three-year rule.

For example, if the taxpayer files the calendar year 2001 return on April 15, 2002, and pays no additional tax after the return is filed, the general rule requires that the claim for refund be filed on or before April 15, 2005. If the taxpayer files the 2001 return on April 15, 2002, and pays additional tax for the year on June 30, 2004 (usually as the result of a deficiency assessment), then the two-year rule applies and a claim filed on or before June 30, 2006 will be timely.

2. Extension of the Statute of Limitations on Filing a Claim for Refund

The statutes of limitations relating to the government's ability to assess additional tax[32] and the taxpayer's ability to claim a refund are, in a sense, related. In the case of a taxpayer who files a timely return and pays the tax shown on the return in a timely manner, the government can assess additional tax, and the taxpayer can file a claim for refund, within the same three-year period. If the IRS and the taxpayer agree, in a timely manner, to an extension of the statute of limitations on assessment, then the statute of limitations on filing a claim for refund also is extended, to the day that is six months after the

---

[31] If no return is filed, the claim for refund must be filed within two years from the time the tax was paid. IRC § 6511(a). However, in the case of income taxes, a return that is filed claiming an overpayment serves as both a return and a claim for refund. If such a return is filed late, it is always a timely claim for refund because a claim, made on the return itself, is clearly filed within three years of the time the return was filed. See Weisbart v. United States, 222 F.3d (2d Cir. 2000) *and* Rev. Rul. 1976-511, 1976-2 C.B. 428. *See also* Rev. Rul. 2003-41, 2003-1 C.B. 814 (containing examples of the impact of the Saturday, Sunday, legal holiday rule on claims for refund.

[32] IRC § 6501(a).

end of the extended statute of limitations for assessing tax.[33] This preserves a degree of parity in the treatment of assessments and claims for refund.

However, there is no comparable provision in the Code that authorizes the Service and the taxpayer to agree to extend the statute of limitations on filing a claim for refund. Although the statute of limitations on claims for refund is extended, suspended, or re-opened in certain circumstances, in the absence of such circumstances, taxpayers must file claims for refund within the basic three-year/two-year period to preserve their positions.

For instance, if the IRS asserts that a deduction taken in year one should have been taken in year two, the taxpayer must make sure that the year-two statute of limitations on claims for refund does not expire while the issue of the correct year is being resolved. Similarly, if the IRS asserts that an item of income included in year one should have been included in year two, the taxpayer must make sure that the year-one statute of limitations on claims for refund does not expire while the issue of the correct year is being resolved.

The same issue arises if the IRS takes the position during an audit that an item should have been deducted or included by a different taxpayer. If the IRS is proposing to move a deduction from one taxpayer to another taxpayer, the other taxpayer must make sure that the statute of limitations on claims for refund for the year of deduction does not expire while the issue of the correct taxpayer is being resolved. If the IRS is proposing to move an item of income from one taxpayer to another taxpayer, the taxpayer who originally included the item in income must make sure that the statute of limitations on claims for refund for the year of inclusion does not expire while the issue of the correct taxpayer is being resolved.

In each of these cases, because the IRS and the taxpayer cannot agree to extend the statute of limitations on filing a claim for refund, the taxpayer must file a "protective claim" before the statute of limitations expires. The protective claim is different than a regular claim only in that the words "Protective Claim for Refund" are written on the top of the first page. The IRS understands that a timing or proper taxpayer issue is being resolved and it places the protective claim in suspense pending resolution of the underlying issue.[34]

---

[33] IRC § 6511(c).

[34] Protective claims may also be used when taxpayers are paying taxes in installments. Generally, claims for refund may not be filed until the entire tax liability is paid. Flora v. United States, 362 U.S. 145 (1960). The IRS may permit protective claims to be filed while the installments are being paid and not act on the claims until the tax liability is paid in full. *See* Gen. Couns. Mem. 38786 (Aug. 13, 1981). *See* Burgess J.W. Raby & William L. Raby, *Protecting the Protective Refund Claim*, Tax Notes, Apr. 28, 2003, at 529.

3. Special Rules Relating to Income Taxes

Under certain circumstances, the three-year/two-year period for filing a claim for refund is too short. For instance, because determining the year that a debt or security becomes worthless is often difficult, an extended statute of limitations is needed where a taxpayer's choice of timing, if wrong, could result in the correct year being barred. Thus, in lieu of the basic rule, a "seven years from the due date of the return for which the claim for refund was filed" rule applies with respect to the deductibility of a worthless debt or security.[35]

Extension of the statute of limitations on claims for refund is also necessary in order to implement the statutorily authorized carryback of net operating losses[36] and capital losses.[37] In this case, the statute of limitations with respect to the years to which a net operating loss or a capital loss can be carried remains open until the later of (i) three years after the due date (including extensions) of the return for the year which gave rise to the loss or (ii) if there has been an agreement extending the statute of limitations on assessment with respect to the year which gave rise to the loss, six months after the expiration of the period within which assessment may be made pursuant to the agreement.[38]

Another situation warranting a modification of the statute of limitations on claims for refund arises when an individual taxpayer is physically or mentally unable to file timely refund claims.[39] By the time a guardian is appointed to act

---

[35] IRC § 6511(d)(1).

[36] Section 172 permits carryback of a net operating loss (NOL) to the two years immediately preceding the year in which the loss occurred. Section 6164 permits a corporation that expects a NOL for the current year to defer, for a certain period of time, paying a portion, or perhaps all, of the tax owed for the immediately preceding year.

[37] IRC § 1212.

[38] IRC §§ 6511(c)(1), 6511(d)(2)(A).

[39] *See, e.g.,* United States v. Brockamp, 519 U.S. 347 (1997). In *Webb v. United States,* 850 F. Supp. 489 (E.D.Va. 1994), the government prevailed on its motion to dismiss a refund suit because the underlying claim for refund was filed after the statute of limitations on filing the claim expired. The facts alleged by the taxpayer and treated as true by the court in considering the motion to dismiss were as follows:

> By virtue of Parsons' advanced age, trusting nature, emotional vulnerability, declining health and drug dependence, she became a victim of the fraud and undue influence and control of her doctor, Alvin Q. Jarrett, and her lawyer B. Roland Freasier, Jr. As Parsons' fiduciaries, Jarrett and Freasier took over her personal and business affairs so totally that they were able to transfer to themselves substantially all of her stock holdings in 1980. Thereafter, and during the relevant period of 1980 to July 1987, Jarrett and Freasier limited Parsons' contact with friends, and Jarrett regularly administered pain-killing drugs, sleeping pills and tranquilizers. Parsons was confined to her bed in Virginia and was given inadequate medical care while her household staff was cut back and her contacts with the outside world were limited still further. Parsons was totally dependent on Jarrett to manage all of her physical, emotional, and financial needs, and she was neither aware of, nor able to inform herself about, the fraud and self-dealing of her fiduciaries.

Id. at 490. The total gift tax paid was $10,862,876.88. Of this amount, $7,038,054.34 was paid within two year of filing the claim for refund. The refund suit was brought to recover the balance of gift

on behalf of the taxpayer, the statute of limitations on filing a claim may have expired. Section 6511(h) suspends the running of the statute of limitations during the period that the taxpayer is "financially disabled," until a guardian or other person authorized to act on behalf of the taxpayer is appointed. Financially disabled does not refer to limited income or assets. Instead, in order for the statute of limitations on filing a claim to be suspended under this provision, it must be established that the taxpayer has a medically determinable disability "which can be expected to result in death" or "to last for a continuous period of not less than 12 months."[40]

Finally, even if the statute of limitations on filing a claim for refund has expired, under certain circumstances, the barred year may be re-opened under the mitigation provisions.[41] The mitigation provisions are discussed in Chapter 10.

D. The Section 6511(b)(2) Limitation

Even if an otherwise valid claim for refund is filed timely, the taxpayer may not be eligible for refund of the entire underpayment. This is because the amount the government may refund is limited to amounts paid within a specified "look-back" period.[42] If a claim for refund is filed within the statute of limitations, the look-back period runs from the date the claim is filed, back for a period of three years plus any extension of time originally granted for filing the return. In the simplest case, if a calendar year individual's 2001 return is filed on or before April 15, 2002, without an extension,[43] the three-year look-back period for a refund claim filed no later than April 15, 2005 runs back to and includes April 15, 2002. The amount recoverable through a claim for refund in that case is limited to tax paid or *deemed paid* during that three-year look-back period.[44] Tax deemed paid on April 15, 2002 includes any tax for 2001 pre-paid through withholding or estimated tax payments or through application of a prior year's refund to the current year.[45] They also include amounts that are

---

tax paid. Section 6511(h), enacted in the IRS Restructuring and Reform Act of 1998, P.L. 105-206, § 3202(a), was a response to *Webb* and several other cases.

[40] Two statements must accompany a claim for relief under section 6511(h). One is a statement by the person signing the claim that no one was authorized to act for the person during the period that the taxpayer was unable to manage his financial affairs. The other is a certified statement by the taxpayer's physician containing certain representations about the taxpayer's physical or mental impairment. Rev. Proc. 99-21, 1999-1 C.B. 960.

[41] IRC §§ 1311–14.

[42] IRC § 6511(b).

[43] For this purpose, returns filed before the due date are deemed to have been filed on the due date. IRC § 6513(a).

[44] If a return is mailed on April 17th (a Monday) of year one and a claim for refund is mailed on April 16th in year four, the IRS accepts that the date of deemed filing, April 15th of year one, will be included in the look-back period. AOD 2000-09, 2000 AOD Lexis 7.

[45] IRC § 6513(b).

refundable by operation of the earned income credit.[46] Because such payments made before the last day for filling the return, determined without regard to extensions, are deemed paid on that day, usually it is important for the look-back period to include that day.

If a return claiming a refund is filed after the original due date, but within the extended due date, the look-back period with respect to a claim for refund, three years plus any extension of time to file, includes the original due date. Again, this permits recovery not only of tax actually paid on the original due date but also of withholding and estimated tax payments deemed paid on the original due date. It also includes payments made during the extension period. In the case of a refund claim filed more than three years after the return was filed, the amount that can be refunded is limited to the tax paid within two years of the date the claim was filed.[47] In the case of a return, claiming a refund and filed within the third year after the due date, the look-back period is three years. This result was mandated in 1997 when Congress enacted the last sentence of section 6513(b)(3). This sentence was added to change the holding of the Supreme Court, in Commissioner v. Lundy, 516 U.S. 235 (1996), that under these facts the look-back period would be only two years.[48]

IV. CAN A VALID REFUND BE DIVERTED TO ANOTHER USE?

Section 6402(a) authorizes the IRS to apply any overpayment (and accrued interest) otherwise payable to a taxpayer, against any current or future liability of the taxpayer for any internal revenue tax.[49] This "refund offset program" has proven to be an efficient and effective way of collecting tax liabilities. For example, if a taxpayer owes taxes for 2003 and files a 2005 return reflecting an

---

[46] Israel v. United States, 356 F.3d 221 (2d Cir. 2004).

[47] IRC § 6511(b)(2)(B). In *Baral v. United States*, 528 U.S. 431 (2000), the Supreme Court rejected the taxpayer's contention that estimated taxes and withholding taxes could only be considered "paid" when the income tax return was filed and the tax shown thereon assessed. The taxpayer's income tax return, on which he claimed a refund, was filed several years late. If the estimated taxes and withholding taxes were not "paid" until the income tax shown on his late filed return was assessed, then they were "paid" within the two year look-back period. The Court agreed with the IRS that sections 6513(b)(1) and (2) "settle the matter." Those sections provide that withheld and estimated taxes are "deemed" to have been paid of the due date of the return determined without regard to extensions. That being the case, even though the claim was considered timely, the two year look-back period was not long enough to make the withheld and estimated tax payments available for the claimed refund.

[48] 516 U.S. 235 (1996). *See* Leandra Lederman, *Delinquent Returns and Credit-Elect Overpayments: A Procedural Tangle*, Tax Notes, Aug. 23, 2004, at 831 (discussing continuing "confusion" in connection with crediting overpayments against the next year's tax liability and critizing the District Court's opinion in *Harrigrill v. United States*, 297 F. Supp. 2d 909 (S.D. Miss. 2004)).

[49] The general rules and procedures applicable to the collection, through the Treasury Offset Program (TOP), of delinquent, nontax debts owed to federal agencies are contained in 31 CFR part 285.

overpayment, the IRS may intercept the refund and apply it against the 2003 balance due. Congress has tapped into the refund stream three additional times to achieve collection from taxpayers by offsetting refunds to pay: (1) certain past-due support payments,[50] (2) debts owed to federal agencies,[51] and (3) past-due state income tax obligations.[52]

Increasing the number of creditors who have access to any given refund required Congress to establish the order in which the several creditors are accommodated. Interestingly, Congress chose to subordinate some of the Treasury Department's interest in applying refunds to the taxpayer's future tax liability to the interests of the other three classes of beneficiaries of the offset program. Thus, any refund that would otherwise be paid to a taxpayer is instead applied to the taxpayer's debts in the following order:

1. Any existing liability in respect of an internal revenue tax.

2. Any past-due support of which the Secretary has been duly notified by a state.[53]

3. Any past-due, legally enforceable debt owed to a federal agency of which the IRS has been duly notified by the agency.[54] For this purpose, a debt owed to a federal agency includes "any overpayment of benefits made to an individual under title II of the Social Security Act."[55]

4. Any past-due, legally enforceable, state income tax obligation of which the Secretary has been duly notified by the state.

5. Any future liability in respect of an internal revenue tax.

A refund due with respect to a joint return presents the question of to whom the refund is to be paid. Courts have determined that refunds should be paid to

---

[50] IRC § 6402(c) (added by the Omnibus Budget Reconciliation Act of 1981, Pub. L. No. 97-35, § 2331(c)(2), 95 Stat. 357).

[51] IRC § 6402(d) (added by the Deficit Reduction Act of 1984, Pub. L. No. 98-369, § 2653(b)(1), 98 Stat. 494).

[52] IRC § 6402(e) (added by the Personal Responsibility and Work Opportunity Reconciliation Act of 1996, Pub. L. No. 104-193, § 110(I)(7)(B)-(C), 110 Stat. 2105).

[53] Section 6305 requires the Secretary to assess and collect the amount of certain delinquent amounts payable under court order or state administrative process for child and spousal support. This approach is different than the section 6402 offset approach. The two approaches "may be used separately or they may be used in conjunction with each other." Reg. § 301.6402-5(a)(1).

[54] In *Bosarge v. United States Dept. of Educ.*, 5 F.3d 1414 (11th Cir. 1993), the taxpayer, who had defaulted on a student loan, sought to enjoin application of the refund offset procedure which, if implemented, would have resulted in the refund to which he was otherwise entitled being offset against the unpaid student loan debt. Bosarge claimed that Alabama state law exempted $3,000 of personal property from levy or sale for the collection of debts. The court found that neither Alabama law nor the Federal Debt Collection Procedures Act of 1990 (which incorporates state law exemptions) demonstrated that Congress intended the offset procedure to be subject to state law exemptions.

[55] IRC § 6402(d)(3)(D).

the spouses in proportion to their respective contributions to the overpayment.[56] A spouse whose interest in a refund relating to a joint return has been or is expected to be offset under section 6402 can file Form 8379, entitled "Injured Spouse Claim and Allocation." This form requires a proposed allocation of items on the joint return and related documentation. The form may be filed with the joint return or filed separately if the joint return has already been filed.

V. THE REFUND JURISDICTION OF THE TAX COURT

In response to a deficiency notice, if a taxpayer files a timely petition in the Tax Court, the Court has jurisdiction to determine not only whether there is a deficiency and the amount thereof, but also whether there has been an overpayment and the amount.[57] In essence, the Tax Court is responsible for determining the correct tax liability for the year regardless of whether its determination results in a deficiency or refund. An overpayment in a Tax Court case might arise if the taxpayer discovers previously unclaimed deductions, or if the IRS agrees with the taxpayer that one or more items of income were overstated or belonged in another year. An overpayment might also occur if the taxpayer petitions the Tax Court for a redetermination of liability but, in an effort to minimize accrual of interest, pays the asserted tax liability.

If the Tax Court finds an overpayment but the IRS files a notice of appeal, the IRS is authorized to refund or credit the uncontested portion of the overpayment. In any event, once the Tax Court's decision becomes final, the IRS must refund or credit the amount of the overpayment, or so much of the overpayment as has not already been refunded or credited. If the IRS fails to refund or credit the overpayment within 120 days after the Tax Court decision becomes final, the taxpayer can file a motion with the court for an order directing the IRS to refund the overpayment.[58]

VI. THE REFUND JURISDICTION OF THE FEDERAL DISTRICT COURTS AND THE COURT OF FEDERAL CLAIMS

Both the federal District Courts and the Court of Federal Claims have jurisdiction to hear claims for refund of overpaid federal taxes. A lawsuit for the recovery of an overpayment cannot be filed until the taxpayer has filed a claim,[59] and then only after the IRS has had at least six months within which to respond unless the IRS disallows the claim earlier.[60] Furthermore, the fed-

---

[56] Saltzman, note 21, *supra*, at ¶ 11.07[1].

[57] IRC § 6512.

[58] IRC § 6512(b)(2).

[59] IRC § 7422(a).

[60] IRC § 6532(a)(1).

eral District Courts and the Court of Federal Claims have jurisdiction only if the full amount of the assessed tax is first paid.[61] The full-payment rule does apply to penalties but, according to *Flora*, not to interest.[62]

The full-payment rule does not apply to all assessments, some of which can be divided into many parts. These "divisible" taxes include those that involve separate transactions, such as withholding taxes or the trust fund penalty tax under section 6672. A taxpayer facing a trust fund penalty,[63] can obtain judicial review by paying the amount involved for one employee for each calendar quarter in question and posting a bond.[64] The IRS will then counterclaim for the amount involved for the rest of the employees.[65]

If the IRS mails a notice of disallowance in response to a claim for refund, the lawsuit must be filed within two years from the date of mailing of the notice. Taxpayers are permitted to waive the notice of disallowance requirement, in which event the two-year statute of limitations on commencing suit begins on the date the waiver is filed. Also, taxpayers and the IRS are permitted to extend the two-year statute of limitations on filing a suit.[66] Form 907 is used for this purpose.

VII. ADMINISTRATIVE ADJUSTMENT REQUESTS

As indicated in Chapter 6, Congress withdrew error correction in the partnership context from the established deficiency notice and claim for refund procedures. Congress replaced deficiency notice procedures with final partnership administrative adjustment ("FPAA") procedures, and replaced taxpayer initiated amended returns and claims for refund procedures with administrative adjustment request procedures. Thus, any partner who believes that there was an error on the partnership's return may file an administrative adjustment request asking the IRS to correct the error.[67]

Whether made by the Tax Matters Partner ("TMP") on behalf of the partnership, or by any partner on the partner's own behalf, administrative adjustment requests must be filed within three years after the *later* of (i) the due date

---

[61] Flora v. United States, 362 U.S. 145 (1960), *aff'd on reh'g*, 357 U.S. 63 (1958).

[62] *See, e.g., id.* at 175, n.37(d). *But see* DiNatale v. United States, 12 Ct Cl. 72,74 (1987) (holding that "[f]ull payment of the tax liability, penalties, and interest is thus a prerequisite to maintaining a tax refund action in the Claims Court") (citations omitted).

[63] This penalty is really a collection device. It is imposed on control persons of an employer who willfully fail to collect or pay over to the IRS the employee's share of FICA and withholding taxes. *See* Chapter 14.

[64] IRC § 6672(c).

[65] IRC § 6672(c).

[66] IRC § 6532(a)(2).

[67] IRC § 6227(a).

of the partnership return determined without extensions, or (ii) the date the partnership return for the year was actually filed.[68] Additionally, if the IRS has initiated a partnership proceeding, the request must be filed before the notice of FPAA is mailed to the TMP.

When an administrative adjustment request is filed, the IRS has four main options. The Service can: (1) accept and make the proposed adjustments, (2) conduct a partnership proceeding, (3) ignore the request, or (4) disallow the request in whole or in part.[69]

Procedurally, the simplest response is for the IRS to agree to make the requested adjustments.[70] Thus, the IRS can treat a request by the TMP on behalf of the partnership as a substituted return.[71] In this case, the requested changes are deemed "mathematical or clerical errors." As such, the resulting refunds are paid or the deficiencies are assessed under section 6213(b)(1) without further proceedings.[72] If the administrative adjustment request is filed by a partner on the partner's own behalf, the IRS can: (1) treat the request as if it were a claim for refund by that partner with respect to non-partnership items, (2) assess the tax resulting from the requested adjustment, (3) notify the partner that all the partner's partnership items will be treated as non-partnership items, or (4) conduct a partnership proceeding.[73]

If the IRS responds to a request for administrative adjustment by initiating a partnership proceeding, the issues raised in the request are resolved in the course of that proceeding.[74] Once the IRS mails its notice of the beginning of an administrative proceeding, the TMP may no longer petition a court for judicial review of the disallowed administrative request.[75]

The IRS is not required to respond to a request for administrative adjustment.[76] If the IRS does not respond to a request made by the TMP on behalf of the partnership, or responds but disallows any part of the request, the TMP can seek judicial review by filing a petition in the Tax Court, a District Court, or the Court of Federal Claims.[77] The petition must be filed before the IRS mails a

---

[68] IRC § 6226(a)(1).

[69] IRC § 6227(c)(2)(A).

[70] IRC § 6227(c).

[71] IRC § 6227(c)(1).

[72] IRC §§ 6227(c)(1), 6230(b)(1). A partner who does not agree with any such error correction may, by notice to the IRS, not accept the proposed changes. The notice must be filed by the partner within sixty days after the day the IRS mails a notice of correction of the error to the partner. IRC § 6230(b)(2).

[73] IRC § 6227(d)(2).

[74] IRC §§ 6227(c)(2)(A)(ii) (with respect to requests filed by the TMP on behalf of the partnership), 6227(d)(4) (with respect to requests filed by a partner on the partner's behalf).

[75] IRC § 6228(a)(1)(B).

[76] IRC § 6227(c)(2)(A)(iii).

[77] IRC § 6228(a)(1).

notice of beginning of an administrative proceeding and during the period beginning after the request has been on file for six months and ending "before the date which is 2 years after the date of [the] request."[78] If the IRS either does not respond to an administrative adjustment request, or responds by disallowing any part of the request, and the TMP seeks judicial review, all persons who were partners in the partnership at any time during the partnership's year in question are treated as parties and permitted to participate in the proceedings.[79]

VIII. TENTATIVE CARRYBACK AND REFUND ADJUSTMENTS

Section 6411 permits taxpayers to apply for a quick, tentative refund of taxes for a prior taxable year affected by a carryback of a net operating loss, a net capital loss, or an unused general business credit. The quick refund procedure is also available for an overpayment of tax resulting from a claim of right adjustment under section 1341(d). Application for the tentative refund must be made within one year after the year in which the net operating loss, net capital loss, unused business credit, or claim of right adjustment arose, but it may not be filed before the return for that year is filed.

Although the taxpayer could file normal refund claims for the amounts subject to the tentative carryback and refund adjustments, the "quick refund" procedure is preferred by taxpayers. This is because the IRS must respond to the tentative carryback and refund adjustment procedure within ninety days of the later of the date the application is filed or the due date of the return for the year in which the loss, unused credit, or claim of right adjustment occurred. No such accelerated response is required in the case of a normal claim for refund.

The quick refund procedure is tentative in the sense that if the IRS ultimately determines that the amount refunded is excessive it will treat the excess as a mathematical or clerical error. As such, the IRS is permitted to assess and collect the excess, without giving the taxpayer the benefit of either a notice of deficiency or the right, normally available in the case of mathematical or clerical errors, to request abatement.

---

[78] IRC § 6228(a)(2).

[79] IRC § 6228(a)(4).

PROBLEM

Facts

Gordon Mordon, a resident of Gainesville, Florida, an author by vocation and botanist by avocation, made estimated tax payments for his 2001 calendar year in the following amounts on the days indicated.

April 15, 2001	$5,000
June 15, 2001	$5,000
September 15, 2001	$5,000
January 15, 2002	$5,000

He received a four-month extension of time (to August 15, 2002) to file his 2001 income tax return. He actually filed the return on June 30, 2002. It showed a tax of $30,000, which amount was paid in part by the $20,000 of estimated payments and in part by a check for $4,000 which was mailed with the return. The remaining $6,000 was paid by check mailed on August 15, 2002.

For several years up to and including 2001, Mr. Mordon had been selling surplus plants from his extensive collection which consisted of several thousand varieties of cacti. From January 1, 2001, to September 1, 2001, aided by a modest advertising campaign, his sales grew to $12,000. He had always considered his collection to be a hobby. He had never reported any of the income or taken any deductions with respect to his collection. In fact, he had never calculated his "profit" from the sales because he knew there was none and he did not really want to know how much maintaining the collection actually cost him.

As it happened, on September 1, 2001, a hurricane roared ashore at Cedar Key, and the eye passed right over Mr. Mordon's greenhouses. The uninsured damages to the greenhouses and collection approached $50,000. He was quoted as saying, "I never thought this would happen to me." Consistent with his prior practice of ignoring his activities with respect to the collection when he prepared his tax return, he reflected no income, deductions, or losses with respect to the collection on his 2001 return.

a. It is now July 31, 2005. Mr. Mordon has consulted you on another matter, but in the course of the conversation he told you the foregoing story. You are convinced that Mr. Mordon was actually engaged in business with respect to the collection (and for the purposes of this problem we will assume that you are correct) and that Mr. Mordon could have taken an ordinary deduction of $50,000 on his 2001 return. By taking such a deduction (and, of course, including all income and other deductions from the cactus business), Mr. Mordon's income tax liability for 2001 would have been reduced to $12,000. If Mr. Mordon filed a claim for refund of the 2001 tax on

July 31, 2005, how much tax can he expect to recover? Would your answer change if the claim were filed on Monday, July 2, 2005?

b. Suppose that Mr. Mordon had filed an amended return on August 1, 2002. Would his July 31, 2005, claim have been honored?

c. How much tax could he recover if he had filed his return late and paid the additional $10,000 on September 1, 2002, and then filed his claim for refund on August 27, 2005?

d. Assume that Mr. Mordon's 2001 return had been audited and that on May 1, 2003, he received a statutory notice indicating a proposed deficiency of $10,000, all of which was attributed to disallowed travel expenses. The expenses were in fact directly related to speaking arrangements and writing, the primary sources of Mr. Mordon's income. The expenses were, therefore, clearly deductible. However, Mr. Mordon, concerned about certain other aspects of his return, decided to pay the deficiency and not contest it. He paid the deficiency on September 1, 2003. It is now August 27, 2005. If Mr. Mordon files a claim for refund of tax on August 27, 2005, arguing both the losses from the hurricane and the travel expenses, what is the maximum tax he can expect to recover if he is successful?

e. Assume the basic facts and that Mr. Mordon filed a timely claim for refund based on the theory that he was entitled to a $50,000 deduction for a business loss with respect to the collection. Also assume that it is now January 10, 2006, and that the IRS would refund the $18,000 of tax erroneously paid for 2001 if it were not for the fact that upon considering the refund claim, it uncovered an item of income ($15,000) from a speaking engagement in 2001 that had been erroneously excluded from the 2001 income. Can the IRS (on January 10, 2006) reduce the otherwise properly claimed refund of $18,000 by the additional tax due in 2001 ($6,000) attributable to the omitted honorarium?

f. Assume the basic facts (i.e., the return was filed on June 30, 2002), except that there was no hurricane loss. Upon audit of Mr. Mordon's return, the revenue agent raised two issues. The first was inclusion of $3,000 taxable income from the cactus business. The second was the erroneously omitted honorarium of $15,000, received by Mr. Mordon in 2001. These items were raised in informal discussions with the agent during the audit on October 1, 2003. On October 15, 2003, Mr. Mordon made a deposit of $5,000 in the nature of a cash bond pursuant to Revenue Procedure 84-58, in order to stop the running of interest on the deficiency he knew would ultimately be assessed with respect to these two items. As it happened, the agent completed his audit and in fact proposed a $5,000 deficiency based on the two items. Mr. Mordon ignored the thirty-day letter and as a result received a notice of deficiency dated January 20, 2004. Mr. Mordon also ignored the notice of deficiency (after all, he had already deposited the exact amount due) and on April 22, 2004, the deposit in the nature of a cash bond was posted as payment of the tax.

It is now December 15, 2005, and in the course of reviewing Mr. Mordon's estate plan, among other things, you have correctly determined that the $15,000 honorarium was in fact an award received by Mr. Mordon in 2001, which, pursuant to § 74(b) of the Code, was not taxable income.

    i.   Will a claim for refund of $3,500 of tax paid with respect to the award, filed by Mr. Mordon on December 15, 2005, be timely? If timely, how much will he recover?

    ii.   Would section 6603, the new statutory version of Revenue Procedure 84-58, be available to Mr. Mordon? Also, assume that you determine that section 6603 is available; what difference would its application make?

    iii.   Assume that instead of paying the $5,000 as a deposit in the nature of a cash bond, Mr. Mordon had paid the $5,000 asserted tax liability on December 10, 2003, after receiving a statutory notice dated December 1, 2003. Will a claim for refund of the $3,500 of tax paid with respect to the award, dated December 16, 2005, be timely? If timely, how much will he recover?

g.   Assume, as often happens, that the IRS requested that Mr. Mordon sign a one-year extension of the statute of limitations on assessment for his 2001 taxable year. Under the normal rule of section 6501(a), the statute of limitations on assessment would have expired on June 30, 2005, three years after the return was filed. Thus, the requested extension was to June 30, 2006. Mr. Mordon signed the extension (Form 872) on May 2, 2005. What would be the last day Mr. Mordon could file a claim for refund relating to his estimated tax payments for 2001? Assume that the only tax payments he made were the four estimated tax payments.

h.   Assume that Mr. Mordon filed his return for 2001 in a timely manner (on June 30, 2002, pursuant to an extension) and that he paid (through estimated payments of $20,000 and payment with his return of $10,000) the correct tax for the year. The hurricane veered off and first hit land in Galveston, Texas. Assume also that his cactus business flourished until 2004 when, through sophisticated computer analysis and triangulation procedures, the USDA determined that it was his cactus collection that was the host of all of the citrus canker that had devastated the Florida citrus crop. He was forced to destroy his entire collection. This resulted in an operating loss of several hundred thousand dollars for 2004, and not only offset his other income for 2004, but also covered all of his income for 2001 and 2002. His return for 2004, showing no tax and a substantial operating loss, was filed, pursuant to extensions, on September 15, 2005. On that date, is he barred from claiming a refund of 2001 taxes paid based on the otherwise available net operating, loss carryback?

i. Assume that Mr. Mordon filed a timely claim for refund for 2001.

    i. If the IRS did not mail either a refund or a notice of disallowance of the claim, by when must he begin a lawsuit to recover the claimed amount?

    ii. If the IRS mailed a notice of disallowance on February 10, 2004, but Mordon did not receive it, by when must he begin a lawsuit to recover the claimed amount?

j. Leave Mr. Mordon for this problem. If a calendar year corporation experiences a capital loss in 2005, and if it is entitled to a carry back loss under § 1212(a)(1), what is the earliest day it can expect a refund under § 1212(a)(1)? What would be the latest day?

Chapter 10

JUDICIAL AND STATUTORY RULES THAT OVERRIDE THE STATUTES OF LIMITATION

IRC:	§§ 1311-1314; 6407; skim §§ 7121-7122; § 7481
Regs.:	§§ 1.1311(a)-1 through 1.1314(c)-1
Forms:	2259

I. INTRODUCTION

Normally, errors in overpaying or underpaying federal income taxes must be corrected within a specified period of time. In the case of overpayments, taxpayers must file a claim for refund "within three years from the time the return was filed or two years from the time the tax was paid, whichever of such periods expires the later, or if no return was filed by the taxpayer, within two years from the time the tax was paid."[1] This period is extended if the taxpayer and the IRS agree to an extension of time for assessing additional tax.[2] It is also extended in certain special situations, such as overpayments triggered by bad debts or worthless securities,[3] or by net operating or capital loss carrybacks.[4]

In the case of underpayments, the IRS generally must assess additional tax within three years after the return is due or was filed, whichever is later.[5] In some circumstances, the period of limitations on assessment may be longer than three years. For instance, it may be extended by agreement between the taxpayer and the IRS[6] and is extended to six years in the case of a "substantial omission of items."[7] Also, the period of limitations on assessment is suspended upon issuance of a notice of deficiency and, if a petition for redetermination of the deficiency is filed in the Tax Court, it is further extended until sixty days after the Court's decision becomes final.[8] If the taxpayer does not file a return or files a false or fraudulent return, the tax can be assessed "at any time."[9]

---

[1] IRC § 6511(a). For this purpose, returns filed before their original due date are deemed to have been filed on that due date. IRC § 6513(a). *See* Chapter 9.

[2] IRC § 6511(c).

[3] IRC § 6511(d)(1).

[4] IRC § 6511(d)(2). *See* Chapter 9.

[5] IRC § 6501(a). For this purpose, returns filed before their original due date are deemed to have been filed on that due date. IRC § 6501(b)(1).

[6] IRC § 6501(c)(4).

[7] IRC § 6501(e).

[8] IRC § 6503(a).

[9] IRC § 6501(c)(1), (3). *See* Chapter 5.

There is a related, but separate, set of rules applicable to the assessment of tax or the filing of a claim for refund relating to "partnership items." Partnership items are items that the IRS determines should first be accounted for at the partnership level.[10]

If the taxpayer fails to correct an overpayment or the IRS fails to correct an underpayment within the applicable limitations period, correction of the error is normally not possible. In such cases the IRS raises the statute of limitations as a defense against a late filed claim for refund, or the taxpayer raises the defense against a late filed deficiency notice.

In certain situations, application of the statute of limitations results in particularly harsh consequences to a taxpayer attempting to get a refund, or to the IRS attempting to assess a deficiency. These situations usually arise when an item of income or deduction is reported in the wrong taxable year by the taxpayer or in any year by the wrong, related taxpayer. In either case, the facts relating to the treatment of the item in the open year are considered in a timely fashion, and resolution of the matter in the open year reveals an erroneous treatment of the item in a barred year.

For example, assume that John, a calendar year, accrual basis, sole proprietor and manufacturer of hunting arrows, ships an order to a customer on September 15, 2000. He encloses a bill for $5,000 with the shipment. He receives payment on January 15, 2001. As an accrual basis taxpayer, John should include the $5,000 in his income for the year 2000, but he mistakenly includes the payment in his income in 2001, the year in which he is paid. Realizing his error, on July 15, 2004, John files a timely claim for refund with respect to 2001. The IRS accepts John's position and sends him a check for the refund.

At this point, John has not paid tax on the $5,000 income item in either 2000 or 2001. However, the statute of limitations on assessment of additional tax for the correct year, 2000, expired on April 15, 2004. Since John recovered the tax erroneously paid with his 2001 return on this item of income, it would be inequitable to permit him to use the statute of limitations defense to avoid paying tax with respect to the item for the correct year, 2000.

There are both judicial doctrines and statutory provisions that open otherwise barred years to permit correction of errors of this kind where strict application of the statute of limitations would produce inequitable results. In addition, under certain circumstances, the judicially created "duty of consistency" requires that an error in a barred year be corrected in an open year. This chapter deals first with the judicial doctrines and then the statutory provisions that mitigate the sometimes harsh consequences of the applicable statutes of limitations.

---

[10] IRC § 6231(a)(3). *See* Chapter 6.

II. JUDICIAL DOCTRINES

The judicial doctrines of equitable recoupment, setoff, and the duty of consistency, are founded on equitable principles and have their origin in three Supreme Court cases decided in the 1930s.[11] Equitable recoupment was first incorporated into federal tax law by the Supreme Court in *Bull v. United States*.[12] In that case, for estate tax purposes, the value of a partnership interest owned by the decedent was determined by a provision in the partnership agreement. Under the agreement, in exchange for the partnership interest, the estate received its proportionate interest in partnership profits for one year after the decedent's death.

Initially, IRS required the estate to include the amount so determined in the decedent's gross estate for estate tax purposes. Because estate tax was paid on that amount, the executor did not include that amount in the estate's income tax returns. Several years later, the IRS notified the executor that the estate had an income tax deficiency because the profits received from the partnership were not reported as income on the estate's income tax return.

The Board of Tax Appeals sustained the IRS's position that the profits interest was properly includible in the estate's income. The executor then paid the income tax deficiency and filed a claim for refund. The executor's position was that the decedent's partnership interest was either property of the estate and thus includible in the decedent's estate for estate tax purposes, or income of the estate and thus includible in the estate's income tax return, but the partnership interest could not be both property and income. The Court of Claims held that the payment was properly treated as income but declined to address the resulting estate tax overpayment because, by that time, the statute of limitations for filing a claim for refund of estate taxes had expired.[13]

The Supreme Court agreed with the Court of Claims that the post-death profits share was income to the estate. But because the business of the partnership was providing services, and the partners had not contributed any capital to the partnership and the partnership had no tangible assets, the Court said that nothing relating to the partnership should have been included in the estate for estate tax purposes.[14] This left the Court with the question of whether the estate could recover the overpayment in estate tax when the statute of limitations on filing a claim for refund had expired.

The Supreme Court said that under existing law if the Commissioner brought suit against the estate for the income tax deficiency, the estate could raise the

---

[11] Stone v. White, 301 U.S. 532 (1937); Bull v. United States, 295 U.S. 247 (1935); Lewis v. Reynolds, 284 U.S. 281 (1932), *modified by* 284 U.S. 599 (1932).

[12] 295 U.S. 247, 259-63 (1935).

[13] *Id.* at 254.

[14] *Id.*

overpayment of the estate tax related to that same item as a defense. In that case, the estate could "equitably recoup" the overpaid estate tax by, in effect, requiring the IRS to apply the estate tax overpayment against the income tax liability. This defense would be available despite expiration of the statute of limitations on filing a claim for refund of the overpaid estate tax.

The Court acknowledged that in this case the estate was the plaintiff seeking a refund of income taxes and, as plaintiff, technically the estate was not in a position to raise equitable recoupment of the overpaid estate tax as a defense. However, the Court found that equitable recoupment is available even though the taxpayer pays the asserted income tax deficiency, files a claim for refund, and then pursues the matter as a plaintiff in suit to recover the overpayment. Even as a plaintiff in a refund suit, the taxpayer is clearly challenging the IRS's determination and the procedural posture of the case should not affect the availability of equitable relief. Consequently, the estate could recoup the time-barred estate tax overpayment against the income tax liability.

Subsequent cases have limited application of the doctrine of equitable recoupment to situations in which a single item is involved, as was the case in *Bull*. The doctrine has also been applied to permit the IRS to apply an income tax refund due to one taxpayer against an otherwise time-barred income tax deficiency of an economically related taxpayer.[15]

In *Estate of Buder v. Commissioner*,[16] an estate planning attorney died. His estate deducted as QTIP property a trust for his wife's benefit. When his wife later died, her estate included the trust in her gross estate. Later, her estate brought a refund action. The IRS and the estate agreed that the QTIP election had been improper. Thus, the trust should have been taxed in the husband's estate, not in the wife's estate. However, the Government argued, under the doctrine of equitable recoupment, that the refund due the wife's estate should be reduced by the tax improperly avoided by the husband's estate and also by interest thereon. The District Court (1) agreed that equitable recoupment applied but (2) denied recovery of the interest. The Circuit Court affirmed in

[15] Stone v. White, 301 U.S. 532 (1937). In *Stone*, the decedent created a testamentary trust leaving his wife the net income of the trust. She accepted the interest in the trust rather than electing against the will to take her statutory allowance. The trustees paid tax on the trust's income. Although Mrs. Stone received the income, she did not report it on her income tax return based on several circuit court cases holding that the income was not taxable until the value equaled that of the statutory allowance she would have been entitled to receive. The Supreme Court later held such income fully taxable to the beneficiary. The trustees then filed a calm for refund of the taxes they had erroneously paid on the income in question. At that time, the IRS could not assert a deficiency against the wife because the statute of limitations on assessing additional tax had expired. The Supreme Court allowed the IRS to recoup Mrs. Stone's otherwise barred income tax liability by applying against that liability the income tax refund to which the trust was otherwise entitled. *See also* IES Industries Inc. v. United States, 349 F.3d 574 (2003) (government was allowed to equitably recoup underpayment in one year from overpayments made in prior, different years).

[16] 372 F. Supp. 2d 1145 (E.D. Mo. 2005), *aff'd*, 436 F.3d 936 (8th Cir. 2006).

both respects. As to the interest issue, it held that the District Court had not abused its discretion "given the countervailing equitable considerations."[17]

There has been considerable discussion over the years as to whether the Tax Court, as an Article I court of limited jurisdiction, may apply equitable principles. The Court of Appeals for the Sixth and Ninth Circuits were at odds on this question as it relates to the application of equitable recoupment.[18] In the Pension Protection Act of 2006, Congress resolved the matter, at least as it relates to equitable recoupment, by adding a sentence to section 6214(b), confirming that the Tax Court can apply the doctrine "to the same extent that it is available in civil tax cases before the district courts . . . and the . . . Court of Federal Claims."

Setoff is another of the equitable doctrines that, in effect, permits opening an otherwise barred year. It comes up in situations in which a taxpayer files a claim for refund. The IRS may use the occasion to audit the return for the taxable year of the claim to see if there are any other errors. If the IRS discovers omitted income or improper deductions, the Supreme Court has held that even though the statute of limitations on assessing additional tax with respect to the newly discovered items has expired, the IRS can use the new items to reduce the amount of the refund otherwise due to the taxpayer.[19]

Finally, the duty of consistency is an equitable doctrine that found its first clear expression in *R. H. Stearns Co. v. United States*[20] and *Alamo Nat'l Bank of San Antonio v. Commissioner*.[21] The duty of consistency requires that a taxpayer taking a favorable, though incorrect, position with respect to an item in a barred year, report the item in later years consistently with the manner of reporting in the earlier, barred year.[22] For example, if for estate tax purposes the estate uses a low value for an office building owned by the decedent, the duty of consistency would require the estate to use that value as the basis of the property on a subsequent sale after the statute of limitations on assessing additional estate tax expired. Consistent reporting would be required even though the

---

[17] *See* Wendy C. Gerzog, Bruder*: The Extent of Equitable Recoupment*, Tax Notes, Mar. 20, 2006, at 1361.

[18] *See* Estate of Mueller v. Commissioner, 153 F.3d 302 (6th Cir. 1998) (denying the Tax Court's jurisdiction to apply equitable recoupment); Branson v. Commissioner, 264 F.3d 904 (9th Cir. 2001) (recognizing the Tax Court's jurisdiction to apply equitable recoupment).

[19] *Lewis*, 284 U.S. at 283. *See* Burgess J.W. Raby & William L. Raby, *The IRS's Ability to Reduce Refunds by Amount Owed*, Tax Notes, Sept. 26, 2005, at 1547.

[20] 291 U.S. 54 (1934).

[21] 95 F.2d 622 (5th Cir. 1938).

[22] For a detailed discussion of the duty of consistency, see Steve R. Johnson, *The Taxpayer's Duty of Consistency*, 46 Tax L. Rev. 537 (1991).

estate could establish that the value of the office building had been understated for estate tax purposes.[23]

The statutory mitigation provisions, discussed below, also deal with inconsistent reporting. However, unlike the duty of consistency, which corrects the barred year error by imposing incorrect reporting of the item in an open year, the mitigation approach permits correction of the error in the otherwise barred year. The duty of consistency doctrine also differs from mitigation in that the mitigation provisions are limited to inconsistencies in reporting of an item for income tax purposes, whereas the duty of consistency can apply to deal with inconsistent reporting involving different kinds of tax.

Courts have taken different positions on the duty of consistency. The majority of the courts follow the standard set forth in *McMillan v. United States*,[24] articulating three elements necessary for application of duty. Those elements are: (1) the taxpayer makes a representation or reports an item for tax purposes in one tax year; (2) the IRS acquiesces in or relies on that fact for the year; and (3) the taxpayer wishes to change the representation of the item after the statute of limitations for the year has expired.[25] While most cases adopting the duty of consistency generally apply these three elements, some courts have added additional elements in determining whether to apply the duty of consistency.[26] Moreover, a minority of courts has refused to recognize the duty of consistency, preferring to rely on common law estoppel principles.[27]

III. MITIGATION

The statutory rules, known as the "mitigation provisions,"[28] were first adopted in 1938 in response to the Supreme Court's judicial doctrines, and were expanded in scope in 1953. The mitigation provisions extend to a number of situations that the equitable doctrines might also cover. Courts have held

---

[23] A representation by one taxpayer can be binding on another taxpayer when the two taxpayers are in privity. In *Janis v. Commissioner*, T.C. Memo, 2004-117 (2004), taxpayers who were co-executors and beneficiaries of their father's estate and co-trustees and beneficiaries of a testamentary trust were held to be in privity with the estate. In Tech. Adv. Mem. 200407018 (Feb. 13, 2004), the decedent's estate was determined to be in privity with the estate of the decedent's spouse. In *Estate of Posner v. Commissioner*, T.C. Memo. 2004-112 (2004), the court assumed *arguendo* that the decedent's estate was in privity with the estate of the decedent's spouse but rejected application of the duty of consistency because other elements were not satisfied.

[24] 64-2 U.S.Tax Cas. (CCH) ¶ 9720, 14 A.F.T.R. 2d (P-H) 5704 (S.D. W. Va. 1964).

[25] *Id.* (citing *Alamo Nat'l Bank*, 956 F.2d at 623).

[26] *See* Shook v. United States, 713 F.2d 662 (11th Cir. 1983); Garner v. Commissioner, 42 T.C. Memo. (CCH) 1181, T.C. Memo (P-H) ¶ 81,542 (1981).

[27] *See* Crosley Corp. v. United States, 229 F.2d 376 (6th Cir. 1956); Commissioner v. Union Pac. R. Co., 86 F.2d 637 (2d Cir. 1936); Marco v. Commissioner, 25 T.C. 544 (1955).

[28] IRC §§ 1311–14.

that, when applicable, the mitigation provisions preempt the equitable doctrines.[29]

Congress enacted the first part of the mitigation provisions in 1938. The original "circumstances of adjustment," i.e., the original set of factual situations to which the mitigation provisions apply, were limited to the following:

(a) section 1312(1)—double inclusion of an item of gross income;

(b) section 1312(2)—double allowance of a deduction or credit;

(c) section 1312(3)(A)—double exclusion of an item of gross income where the item was included in the return or the tax paid with respect to the item;

(d) section 1312(5)—inconsistent correlative deductions and inclusions for trusts or estates and legatees, beneficiaries, or heirs;

(e) section 1312(6)—inconsistent correlative deductions and credits for certain related corporations; and

(f) section 1312(7)—basis of property corrected after erroneous treatment of a prior transaction.

The fact that the mitigation provisions are founded in principles of equity is apparent from the circumstances to which the provisions apply. For example, if a taxpayer is successful in obtaining a refund with respect to an item erroneously included in income for an open year, it would be unfair if the statute of limitations barred collection of tax on the item in the earlier, correct year. The mitigation provisions open the otherwise barred year and permit the IRS to send the taxpayer a notice of deficiency with respect to the omitted item.[30] As is the case with normal deficiency notices, the taxpayer is free to contest the deficiency by either petitioning the Tax Court or paying the tax and filing a claim for refund.

In 1953, Congress expanded the mitigation provisions to include two additional circumstances deemed to warrant adjustment in an otherwise barred year. In one of these circumstances, the taxpayer had a choice of year in which to take a deduction.[31] In the other, the IRS had a choice of year in which to assert that an item not included by the taxpayer in income for any taxable year should have been included.[32] In each case the wrong year is chosen, but by the time the mistake is discovered, the correct year is closed. As is discussed below, a prerequisite for adjustment in these "choice of year" cases is that when

---

[29] Benenson v. United States, 385 F.2d 26 (2d Cir. 1967); Gooding v. United States, 326 F.2d 988 (Ct. Cl. 1964).

[30] IRC § 1314(b).

[31] IRC § 1312(4).

[32] IRC § 1312(3)(B).

the wrong year was chosen, the statute of limitations for both the wrong year and the correct year were open.[33]

Whether dealing with the original "inconsistent position" circumstances of adjustment, or the later "choice of year" circumstances of adjustment, the following five elements define the right to use one of the mitigation provisions and make an adjustment in a closed year.

1. Correction in the error year is barred by a law or rule of law. Section 1311(a).

2. There is a determination. Sections 1311(a) and 1313(a).

3. There is a circumstance of adjustment. Section 1312.

4. There is a condition necessary for adjustment. Section 1311.

5. If present, the two "related taxpayer" issues are addressed. Sections 1313(c) and 1311(b)(3).

The following is a brief overview of these five elements with emphasis on several aspects of mitigation that are not apparent from the language of the Code or the Regulations. The mitigation Regulations are particularly helpful in explaining the statutory provisions and demonstrating their application through examples. Consequently, careful study of the assigned statutory provisions and Regulations is required to gain a working knowledge of these complicated provisions.

A. Error Year Barred by Law or Rule of Law

If correction of the error is not barred by the statute of limitations on assessment or on filing a claim for refund, or by some other law or rule of law, then there is no need for mitigation. Consequently, the first requisite for application of the mitigation provisions is that a law or rule of law bars correction of the error. While the statutes of limitations on assessment and on claims for refund[34] are most often involved, they are not the only laws that may prevent correction of an error. The Regulations provide other examples of laws that can have the effect of preventing correction of an error and that, like the statutes of limitations, can be mitigated.[35] They include: (i) section 6212(c), which limits the IRS's ability to determine another deficiency if a notice of deficiency has already been sent to the taxpayer and the taxpayer has filed a petition with the Tax Court and (ii) section 6512, which limits the Service's authority to issue refunds if the taxpayer has filed a petition in the Tax Court.

---

[33] IRC § 1311(b)(2).

[34] IRC §§ 6501, 6511.

[35] Reg. § 1.1311(a)-2(a).

B. Determinations

An error in a barred year can be corrected under the mitigation provisions only if there has been a "determination."[36] For this purpose, a determination is a judicial or administrative decision or an agreement as to the proper treatment of the item in an open year. The presence of a determination is critical to application of the mitigation rules because without a judicial or administrative decision, or an agreement, on the proper treatment of an item in the open year, there is no basis for changing the treatment of the item in the barred year.

Thus, a decision of the Tax Court, federal District Court, Bankruptcy Court, or Court of Federal Claims that an item is deductible or includible in an open year becomes a "determination" if no notice of appeal is filed and the time for filing such an appeal expires.[37] If the trial court decision is appealed, the decision becomes final once the Court of Appeal's or Supreme Court's decision becomes final.[38] In the case of a judicial decision that has become final, the proper treatment of the item in the open is conclusively determined. If the same item was erroneously treated in a barred year and if the other requirements of the mitigation provisions are present, the statute of limitations for the barred year is opened for the limited purpose of correcting the error.

Administrative determinations include: (i) a closing agreement made under section 7121, (ii) a final disposition of a claim for refund, and (iii) a formal agreement with the Secretary memorialized on Form 2259.[39] These administrative determinations provide a degree of finality as to the proper treatment of the item in the open year because, in effect, the parties have agreed to the proper treatment of the item. This is clear in the case of closing agreements which, in the absence of "fraud or malfeasance, or misrepresentation of a material fact," may not be reopened or modified by the taxpayer or the IRS. Closing agreements become final for this purpose upon approval by the Commissioner.[40]

Claims for refund also can provide the requisite determination about the proper treatment of an item in the open year. Thus, if a taxpayer files a claim for refund based on his failure to take a deduction for the year and the IRS allows the claim, there is agreement as to the proper treatment of the item in

---

[36] IRC §§ 1311(a), 1313(a).

[37] IRC § 7481(a) (as to Tax Court); Fed. R. App. P. 4(a) (as to District Court); Ct. Fed. Cl. R. 58.1 (as to the Court of Federal Claims). Section 7481(a)(2) provides that if the Tax Court decision is appealed, it will become final if the decision is affirmed or the appeal dismissed and no petition for certiorari has been filed within the allowed time. Tax Court cases handled under the small case procedures are not appealable. Decisions in such cases become final ninety days after the decision is entered. IRC § 7481(b).

[38] Fruit of the Loom, Inc. v. Commissioner, 68 T.C. Memo. (CCH) 867, T.C. Memo (RIA) ¶ 94,492 (1994), aff'd, 72 F.3d 1338 (7th Cir. 1996).

[39] IRC § 1313(a)(2)-(4).

[40] IRC § 7121(b); Reg. § 1.1313(a)-2.

that year. If the other requisites are present, the mitigation provisions then open the barred year in which the taxpayer erroneously deducted the same item and permit the IRS to assert a deficiency with respect to that item.

If a claim for refund is filed the IRS may audit a return and discover one or more omitted items of income or improper deductions. Section 1313(a)(3) and the related Regulations[41] explain that the refund claim filed by the taxpayer may be the basis not only for a determination as to each item raised in the refund claim, but also as to each new item raised by the IRS as an offset to the claimed items. The Code and Regulations describe the time when a determination arises with respect to the new items.[42]

A determination as to the proper treatment of the item is also present in the case of a section 1313(a)(4) agreement with the IRS. This is a formal agreement between the taxpayer and the IRS. If a related party is involved, that person must also be a party to the agreement. The terms and conditions of the agreement are spelled out in Form 2259 entitled "Agreement as a Determination Pursuant to § 1313(a)(4) of the Code."

The section 1313(a)(4) agreement is a reasonably quick way of obtaining a determination. For instance, it can be used when a claim for refund is disallowed in whole or in part. In such case, the taxpayer has two years from the date of mailing of the notice of disallowance to commence an action to recover the claimed overpayment. Until that two-year period expires, the claim for refund cannot be the source of a "determination." Rather than waiting two years, the IRS and the taxpayer can create a determination by entering into a section 1313(a)(4) agreement. The section 1313(a)(4) agreement would trigger application of the mitigation provisions and permit the taxpayer to immediately file a claim for refund with respect to the item in the otherwise barred year.

Section 1313(a)(4) agreements, however, are less "final" than the other administrative or judicial determinations. Thus, if after an audit, the taxpayer and the IRS enter into a section 1313(a)(4) agreement, the Regulations say that until the tax liability for the open year becomes final, the taxpayer can still file a claim for refund and the IRS can still assert a deficiency with respect to the open year.[43] Any section 1313(a)(4) agreement with respect to the open year that is changed by any such claim for refund or asserted deficiency will result in a further change in the tax liability for the barred year.

Disagreements about tax liabilities are often resolved when the IRS and taxpayers enter into compromises.[44] Because a compromise or settlement is a result of give and take between the parties whose shared goal is to agree on an appropriate dollar amount to settle the open issues and not necessarily to deter-

---

[41] Reg. § 1.1313(a)-(3)(b).

[42] IRC § 1313(a)(3); Reg. § 1.1313(a)-3(d).

[43] Reg. § 1.1313(a)-4(d).

[44] IRC § 7122.

mine the correct treatment of any item in question, compromises in the open year cannot serve as a determination. For the same reason, section 1311(a) expressly prohibits use of the mitigation provisions to open any barred year to alter any item that was a subject of a compromise. Thus, a compromise in either the open or the barred year in question precludes application of the mitigation provisions.

C. Circumstances of Adjustment

The original circumstances of adjustment and the later "choice of year" circumstances of adjustment are dealt with separately here because the two are treated differently as they relate to the section 1311(b) condition necessary for adjustment requirement. As a preliminary matter, however, it is helpful to understand the equitable thread that connects all seven circumstances of adjustment to which mitigation applies.

1. The Equitable Basis for Mitigation

The circumstances that warrant breaching the bar of the statute of limitations all involve an inconsistency between the way an item is treated in an open year and the way it was (or should have been) treated in a barred year. For instance, the circumstance described in section 1312(1), entitled "Double inclusion of an item of gross income," is one in which the taxpayer is required to include an item in income for an open year even though the same item was previously included in income for a barred year. The circumstance described in section 1312(2), entitled "Double allowance of a deduction or credit," is one in which a taxpayer correctly deducts an item in an open year even though the taxpayer previously deducted the same item in a barred year. The double inclusion of an item of income is unfair to the taxpayer and the double deduction of an item is unfair to the IRS. These inequities are most accurately corrected by opening the otherwise barred year and treating the item in that year consistently with the correct treatment of the item as determined with respect to the open year.

There is another consideration, beyond fairness, that supports opening barred years under these circumstances. An important reason underlying statutes of limitations—fear that memories may fail and documentation may be lost with the passing years—has little force with respect to circumstances of adjustment involving inconsistent positions. The process of determining the correct treatment of an item in the open year necessarily presents the parties, or the court, with sufficient facts to determine the proper treatment of the same item in the barred year. This suggests that the prevailing party in the open year should not be able to raise the "memories fail" statute of limitations policy when the party that lost in the open year attempts to correct the erroneous treatment of the same item in a barred year. Similarly, the generally sound principle of finality has little to do with these circumstances of adjustment. In each case, the same factual issues are raised to get the determination of the correct treatment of the item in the open year as would be raised to correct the erroneous treatment of the item in the barred year.

2. The Original Circumstances of Adjustment

Each of the original circumstances of adjustment permits either a refund or an assessment of additional tax in the barred year. These circumstances are relatively straightforward and, with the help of the applicable Regulations, their application can be understood. However, a few comments about the sections 1312(3) and 1312(7) may help clarify their application.

The section 1312(3) circumstance of adjustment, entitled "Double exclusion of an item of gross income," has two parts. The first part, section 1312(3)(A), deals with items either included in income in the open year, or originally excluded from income in the open year but with respect to which the tax was subsequently paid (normally following an audit). In both cases, the determination is that the item was erroneously included in the open year and should have been included in a barred year. Circumstances falling within section 1312(3)(A) are referred to as "payment double exclusions."

The second part, section 1312(3)(B), deals with items neither originally nor subsequently included in income for the open year which are determined not to be includible in the open year. The basis for the determination is that they should have been included in another year. But, at the time of the determination, the other, correct, year is barred. This might occur when the IRS does not prevail in its assertion that an item of income should have been included in a particular year and by the time that determination is made, the correct year of inclusion is barred. This circumstance of adjustment is referred to as a "nonpayment double exclusion."

As will be seen in section D below, for mitigation to apply, there must be not only a determination and a circumstance of adjustment, but also a condition necessary for adjustment as described in section 1311(b). The condition necessary for adjustment for the section 1312(3)(A) payment double exclusion is generally described as "maintenance of an inconsistent position." The condition necessary for adjustment for the section 1312(3)(B) nonpayment double exclusion (and for a section 1312(4) double disallowance of a deduction or credit) is that both the open and the barred year must be open at the time either the IRS or the taxpayer first selects the year in which to assert that an item of income should have been included (or a deduction or credit taken). The different conditions necessary for adjustment for payment double exclusions and nonpayment double exclusions can produce different outcomes for a taxpayer and can present a trap for the unwary. This difference is elaborated on in subsection D.

The section 1312(7) circumstance of adjustment involves an open-year determination of the basis of property in connection with which there was a prior transaction that either determined or affected the basis of the property. Also, in respect of that transaction there occurred with respect to a taxpayer described in section 1312(7)(B) one of the errors described in section 1312(7)(C). For example, assume that John Thatcher acquired a parcel of commercial property ten years ago in a transaction that he thought qualified for tax-free treatment under the exchange rules in section 1031. Assume also that last year he sold the property at a substantial gain which he reported on his return. John now understands that he should have recognized a gain when he acquired the property because the tax-free exchange attempted at that time failed a critical part of section 1031. Therefore, he files a claim for refund with respect to the gain on the recent sale, using the increased basis he would have if he had properly recognized the gain at the time he acquired the property. The IRS agrees with his position, accepts the higher basis, and allows the requested refund. The question is whether the IRS can now go back through the bar of the statute of limitations and collect the tax due on the previously unreported gain on the exchange of property now known to be a taxable?

On these facts, there is a determination (the allowed claim for refund). There is a section 1312(7)(A) circumstance of adjustment. John is the taxpayer with respect to whom the determination was made, and his error is non-recognition of gain on a prior exchange of property. The statute of limitations on assessing any additional tax with respect to the acquisition year expired long ago. And, the section 1311(b) condition necessary for adjustment is present. Finally, under section 1311(b)(1)(B), the determination adopted a position maintained by the taxpayer (the stepped-up basis) that is inconsistent with the taxpayer's erroneous non-recognition of gain at the time he acquired the property. Since all of the elements necessary for invocation of the mitigation provisions are satisfied, the IRS may open John's closed year for the sole purpose of collecting tax due on the gain realized on the acquisition of the property.

3. The Choice of Year Circumstances of Adjustment

In 1953, Congress expanded the mitigation provisions to include two additional circumstances that warrant adjustment notwithstanding the fact that the statute of limitation on assessment barred correction of the error. Under one of these circumstances of adjustment, the taxpayer chose the wrong year in which to take a deduction. By the time the IRS obtained a determination disallowing the deduction for the open year, the statute of limitations for the correct year expired. Under the normal statute of limitations rules, this results in disallowance of the deduction in the open year with no way to correct the error in the closed year—a double disallowance of the deduction. Under the mitigation provisions, so long as both years were open when the taxpayer selected the erroneous year for the deduction, the otherwise barred, correct year of deduction is opened for one year after the determination to allow the taxpayer to claim the deduction.[45]

Under the second 1953 circumstance of adjustment, a nonpayment double exclusion, upon audit of a taxpayer's return, the IRS chose the wrong year in which to include an otherwise omitted item of income. By the time the taxpayer, who did not pay the proposed deficiency, prevailed in excluding the item of income from the open year, the statute of limitations for the correct year of inclusion expired. Under the normal statute of limitations rules, this would result in exclusion of the item in the open year and no way to correct the erroneous exclusion in the barred year—a nonpayment, double exclusion. As in the case of the double disallowance of a deduction, so long as both years were open when the IRS selected the erroneous year of inclusion, the barred, correct year is opened for one year to allow the IRS to assert the tax.

As in the case of the circumstances of adjustment based on inconsistent positions, the circumstances of adjustment based on choice of year produce unfair results (double disallowance of a deduction or double exclusion of an item of gross income) in situations that do not necessarily deserve statute of limitations protection. Issues relating to the item in the open year are resolved on the basis of the same facts necessary to determine the proper treatment of the item in the barred year.

D. Conditions Necessary for Adjustment

Section 1311(b) establishes "conditions necessary for adjustment" that are different with respect to each of the two broad categories of circumstance of adjustment—the original circumstances of adjustment based on inconsistent positions and those based on choice of year.

1. Section 1311(b)(1): The Original Circumstances of Adjustment

In the case of the original "inconsistent position" circumstances of adjustment, the condition necessary for adjustment is that the position maintained by the prevailing party in the determination "is inconsistent with the erroneous inclusion, exclusion, omission, allowance, disallowance, recognition, or nonrecognition" in the barred year.[46] The determination-year prevailing position could be one maintained by the IRS (disallowance of a deduction or inclusion of an item of income) or by the taxpayer (allowance of a deduction or exclusion of an item of income). In either case, the barred-year inconsistent position is

---

[45] IRC § 1314(b).

[46] IRC § 1311(b)(1).

taken either by the taxpayer who obtained the determination or, as is explained in section E below, by a related taxpayer.

The courts disagree as to the manner in which an inconsistent position must be maintained. Some courts (following a Senate Finance Committee report) require that the inconsistency must be actively maintained.[47] Other courts have reached different results even on similar facts because they hold that the requisite inconsistency may be maintained either actively or passively.[48]The divergent positions among the courts are illustrated in the following example.

Gus is a partner in XYZ partnership. He contributes a portion of his partnership interest to two trusts, one created for the benefit of his wife and the other for the benefit of his son. Gus and each of the trusts report their respective shares of the partnership's income on their income tax returns for 1995. In 1998, the IRS audits Gus' return, refuses to recognize the two trusts as bona fide partners, and treats the trusts' shares of the partnership income as income to Gus. This results in Gus having a deficiency of $10,000. He pays the deficiency in full in 1998 (in part by a credit of the tax erroneously paid on the income by the two trusts). In 1999, Gus files a timely claim for refund based of the $10,000 deficiency he paid. The Commissioner disallows the claim. Gus then petitions the District Court seeking a refund of the tax he paid, taking the position that the two trusts should be recognized. The District Court agrees with Gus and in 2001 enters a decision that becomes final, recognizing the two trusts as partners and allowing the claim for refund (which included the amount of tax originally paid by the trusts and credited to Gus' liability). The IRS sends Gus a check for $10,000 plus interest, and then sends notices of deficiency to the two trusts for tax they should have paid as partners in 1995. However, by that time, the statute of limitations on assessing additional tax against the trusts has expired.

In the Second Circuit this would be an inconsistent position.[49] The determination by the District Court adopted a position maintained by Gus that the two trusts were partners in XYZ and should therefore have included their respective shares of the partnership's income in their returns. This is inconsistent with the IRS's erroneous exclusion of the respective shares of the partnership's income from the trusts' returns. The statutory requirements for application of the mitigation provisions, particularly the inconsistent position requirement, are satisfied and mitigation would apply to allow the IRS to collect tax on the income for the otherwise barred year.

However, courts requiring that the inconsistent position be actively maintained would *not* find an inconsistent position under these facts because the trusts did not actively seek to avoid tax by asserting the statute of limitations.

---

[47] *See, e.g.*, Commissioner v. Estate of Weinreich, 316 F.2d 97 (9th Cir. 1963); Glatt v. United States, 470 F.2d 596 (Ct. Cl. 1972).

[48] *See, e.g.*, Chertkof v. Commissioner, 649 F.2d 264 (4th Cir. 1981); Yagoda v. Commissioner, 331 F.2d 485 (2d Cir. 1964).

[49] *See Yagoda*, 331 F.2d at 490-91.

Here, the trusts had maintained a correct position on the original return and the IRS made the incorrect determination that the trusts were not partners. The equitable underpinning for application of the mitigation provisions by the IRS is not present here when the trusts filed their original returns correctly. The IRS cannot rely on its error in disregarding the trusts as the basis for establishing the inconsistent position element necessary for application of the mitigation provisions.

2. Section 1311(b)(2): The "Choice of Year" Circumstances of Adjustment

In the case of "choice of year" circumstances of adjustment, section 1312(3)(B) nonpayment double exclusion and section 1312(4) double disallowance of a deduction, the condition necessary for adjustment is that at the time the decision is made (by the IRS or the taxpayer) to account for the item in the wrong year the correct year is still open. For example, assume that the IRS identifies an item of income that the taxpayer received but never reported and includes the item in a deficiency notice relating to year two. Also assume that the taxpayer prevails in Tax Court on his theory that the item of income should not be reported in year two because it was actually income in year one, but that by the time the Tax Court opinion becomes final, year one is barred by the statute of limitations. If at the time the IRS asserted that the item was includible in year two, the Service could have asserted that the item was includible in year one, then a condition necessary for adjustment with respect to that item exists. Thus, if both year one and year two were open when the IRS selected one of the years as the year of inclusion, then the IRS is not penalized for selecting the wrong year.[50]

The double disallowance of a deduction circumstance of adjustment, section 1312(4), has a similar condition necessary for adjustment requirement.[51] If a taxpayer reports an item as deductible in year two, and the IRS later obtains a determination that the item was properly deductible in year one, a condition necessary for adjustment is present if, at the time the taxpayer first maintained in writing that he was entitled to the deduction in year two, he was not barred from taking the deduction in year one. Again, it is not intended that the taxpayer be penalized for initially selecting the wrong year at a time when both years are open.

There is a compelling reason why the condition necessary for adjustment for the two choice of year circumstances of adjustments is relatively restrictive. If the section 1311(b)(1) "inconsistent position" condition necessary for adjustment were applicable to the two choice of year circumstances of adjustment

---

[50] IRC § 1311(b)(2)(A).

[51] IRC § 1311(b)(2)(B).

then, in effect, there would be no statute of limitations with respect to these circumstances of adjustment. Assume that the IRS discovers an item of income that a taxpayer should have included in a now barred year. Without section 1311(b)(2), in order to open the barred year for mitigation purposes, all the IRS would have to do is assert that the item is properly includible in *any* open year. Ultimately, the taxpayer would likely get a final decision of the Tax Court that the item was not includible in the open year. The position maintained by the taxpayer in Tax Court would be inconsistent with the taxpayer's erroneous exclusion of the item in the barred year, thereby providing the IRS with a section 1311(b)(1) condition necessary for adjustment. In such case, all the elements for application of the mitigation provisions to open the barred year are present—the correct year is closed, there is a final decision of the Tax Court (a determination), there is a section 1312(3)(B) nonpayment double exclusion circumstance of adjustment, and an inconsistent position condition necessary for adjustment.

Thus, in connection with a nonpayment double exclusion, if all that is required to have a condition necessary for adjustment is that the taxpayer prevail in the open year, the IRS could use the mitigation provisions to open any barred year in which there was an omitted item of income. Such inappropriate use of the mitigation provisions is precluded by operation of the section 1311(b)(2) condition necessary for adjustment. It requires that the correct year be open at the time the IRS first asserts in a deficiency notice that the item should be included in another (as it turns out, incorrect) open year. A similar analysis with respect to the section 1312(4) double disallowance of a deduction will demonstrate that, in effect, there would be no statute of limitations in the double disallowance of a deduction case if all that is necessary is that the prevailing party in the open year take an inconsistent position.

E. Related Parties

It is possible under the mitigation provisions for a determination obtained by a taxpayer to open a barred year with respect to a "related" taxpayer. Assume that the IRS asserts a deficiency against a husband for an item of income omitted from his return. Assume also that the deficiency is sustained by the Tax Court and that the Tax Court's opinion is now final. Finally, assume that the husband's wife erroneously included the same item in income in her separate return for the same year and that by the time of the Tax Court judgment relating to the treatment of the item by her husband is final, the taxable year in which she erroneously included the item is barred. The erroneous inclusion of the item by the wife, who is a "related party," can be corrected through the mitigation provisions even though the necessary determination was obtained in a judicial proceeding between the husband and the IRS.

For purposes of this example, a related taxpayer is a taxpayer who, during the taxable year in which the error occurred, stood in one of the relationships specified in section 1313(c) with the taxpayer who obtained the determination.

It is not necessary that the relationship exist throughout the error year—that it exists "at some time" during the year is sufficient.[52] The specified relationships include that of husband and wife.

Two points about related taxpayers deserve mention. First, the concept of related taxpayers applies only to the first six of the circumstances of adjustment set forth in section 1312. It does not apply to the section 1312(7) circumstance of adjustment relating to the erroneous determination of basis. It is possible that an error in determining basis in a barred year can be corrected with respect to a taxpayer other than the one who obtained the determination, but the section 1313(c) related-party concept is not applicable. Section 1312(7) contains its own related-taxpayer rule.

Second, if the IRS is using mitigation to assess tax against a related taxpayer in an otherwise barred year, there is an additional timing rule. Under section 1311(b)(3), the relationship must have existed at the time the taxpayer who obtained the determination:

> first maintains the inconsistent position in a return, claim for refund, or petition (or amended petition) to the Tax Court for the taxable year with respect to which the determination is made, or if such position is not so maintained, then at the time of the determination.[53]

F. Amount and Method of Adjustment

When mitigation is available, the error in the otherwise barred year is corrected by the taxpayer filing a claim for refund (if correction of the error results in an overpayment), or by the IRS issuing a notice of deficiency (if correction of the error results in a deficiency). In either case, the amount of the adjustment is determined by correcting only the "treatment of the item which was the subject of the error."[54] If correction of the error and the resulting change in gross or taxable income affects other items relating to the computation of tax (such as the limitation on charitable deductions), then those other items must be taken into consideration in determining the amount of the adjustment.[55] Also, penalties and interest "wrongfully collected" and traced to the error are included in the amount of the adjustment.[56] However, neither the taxpayer nor the IRS can raise any other issue in connection with the computation of the amount of the adjustment or as a set-off against the adjustment.[57]

---

[52] Reg. § 1.1313(c)-1.

[53] IRC § 1311(b)(3).

[54] IRC § 1314(a).

[55] Cory v. Commissioner, 261 F.2d 702 (2d Cir. 1958).

[56] *Id.*

[57] *See Lewis*, 284 U.S. 281; Reg. § 1.1314(c)-1(a).

If the adjustment causes an increase in tax liability, the deficiency is collected under the normal deficiency procedures including the issuance of a notice of deficiency. The notice must be issued within one year from the date of the determination. Similarly, if the adjustment results in a decrease in tax liability, the refund is obtained under the normal procedures applicable to obtaining a refund. In this case, the claim for refund must be filed within one year from the date of the determination.

PROBLEM 1

T, an attorney, had lunch with his most important client on December 31, 1997. At the lunch the client said, "Here's a check for your last invoice, $38,000." T replied, "Do me a favor, drop the check in the mail this afternoon. You will still get a deduction, but I won't have to include the amount in income until next year." T actually received the check in the mail in 1998 and reported it on her timely filed return for that year. In December 2000, the Commissioner asserted that the $38,000 was properly includible in T's income in 1997. In 2001, T petitioned the Tax Court for a redetermination of the deficiency. The Tax Court ruled for the Commissioner in a decision that became final on July 15, 2004. Can T now (February 12, 2005) obtain a refund of the tax erroneously paid with respect to the fee in 1998?

<u>Time Line</u>

December 31, 1997	Lunch; payment of fee tendered but rejected by T
1998	Fee received
1999	1998 return filed April 15, 1999
2000	IRS asserted a deficiency for 1997 based on including fee in income
2001	T petitioned the Tax Court for redetermination of 1997 tax liability
2002	April 15, 2002, 3-year period for refunds (§ 6511) of tax paid with respect to 1998 expired
July 15, 2004	Tax Court's decision for IRS became final
February 12, 2005	T filed claim for refund of tax erroneously paid in 1998 on fee

PROBLEM 2

Assume that a claim for refund has been filed with respect to three items. Those items can be allowed or disallowed by the IRS. Also, the IRS can audit and find new items that increase tax liability. Under the following facts, determine the date as of which there is a determination and the applicable Code and Regulation section.

IRS Action	Date	Code and Reg Section
a. All items allowed		
b. Some items allowed other items disallowed		
c. An item is allowed in part and disallowed in part		
d. An item is allowed but offset in part by a new item		
(i) as to allowed item		
(ii) as to offsetting item		
e. An item is allowed but offset entirely by a new item thereby normally producing a deficiency		
(i) as to allowed item		
(ii) as to offsetting item		
(a) if offsetting item <u>does not</u> result in a deficiency		
(b) if offsetting item <u>does</u> result in a deficiency		
f. All items disallowed		

PROBLEM 3

In their calendar year 1997 income tax return, filed April 15, 1998, taxpayers, husband and wife, reported $20,000 of income with respect to a particular contract which they were reporting under a completed-contract method of accounting.

After an audit of their 1999 return, and in January 2003, the taxpayers received a timely notice of deficiency from the Service. The Service took the position that the $20,000 was properly includible in the taxpayers' 1999 income because that was in fact the year the contract was completed. Other issues were also raised, and the total additional tax for 1999 was $35,000.

In March 2003, the taxpayers paid the additional tax, filed a refund claim with the IRS which was immediately denied, and filed a timely suit for refund in the District Court.

In February 2005, taxpayers, through their attorney, forwarded a letter to the attorney in the Department of Justice who was handling their case in which they proposed a settlement along the lines that the $20,000 would be treated as income in 1999 but that the other proposed adjustments would be resolved in the taxpayers' favor. In June 2005, the government accepted the proposal and in July 2005, the parties filed a stipulation voluntarily dismissing the District Court suit with prejudice.

The period of time within which a claim for refund of tax for 1997 can be filed has passed. Can the error (double inclusion of the $20,000) nonetheless be corrected today (September 21, 2005) under the mitigation provisions?

PROBLEM 4

Part A: Taxpayer realized in May 2005, that a $10,000 item of gross income included in his timely filed calendar year 2001 return should have been included in his calendar year 2003 return. He filed an amended return for 2003 on June 1, 2005, and paid the additional tax and interest. Will his November 2005 claim for refund of taxes paid with his 2001 return with respect to that item be honored?

Part B: Assume that the taxpayer included the same income item in both his 2001 and 2003 returns. The correct year was 2003. On January 15, 2005, when both years are open, the taxpayer asks you what to do.

One option is to file a claim for refund for 2001. The other option is to file a claim for refund for 2003, expecting it to be disallowed, after which you would wait two years for the time to file suit to expire thereby getting the necessary "determination." All other elements of mitigation would then be present and the taxpayer would be entitled to a refund for 2001.

What would be the advantage of filing the claim for refund for 2003?

PROBLEM 5

Taxpayer ("T") owned and operated an apartment complex that was next to a major limited-access highway. In 1997, the State instituted condemnation proceedings to acquire a portion of T's land and buildings in order to construct an entrance to and exit from the highway. Though T could litigate the value of the condemned land and buildings, the State was required to deposit in court its estimate of the value of the condemned portion of T's property and T was able to withdraw that amount.

T did not withdraw the amount deposited in Court, and he in fact litigated not only the question of value but also whether the State had the right to take the land and whether it could take only a portion of the land. The litigation was resolved in the State's favor in 2002. T included his gain on the transaction in his 2002 return, but because of other items T paid no tax on the gain.

On November 12, 2002, the IRS took the timely position that the entire gain was taxable in 1997 (the year of condemnation). After T failed to file a Tax Court petition challenging the statutory notice issued by the IRS, the IRS assessed a deficiency for 1997 of $100,000. T paid the tax and sued for a refund. T said that the item was not income until 2002 but that even if it was income for an earlier year, it wasn't income in 1997 because the critical documents weren't signed until 1998.

In 2005, the District Court held that the IRS was right that the income was recognized at the time of the condemnation but that the condemnation was not completed in 1997 because the critical documents were not actually signed until 1998. Thus the District Court determined that the income was reportable in 1998, and T was entitled to a refund of the tax paid for 1997.

The IRS refunded the tax for 1997, but in December 2005, after the time to appeal the District Court order expired, the Commissioner issued a determination letter with respect to 1998 (a then barred year) in which he proposed to assess the tax due from the condemnation.

Will T's defense that the statute of limitations barred the proposed assessment be sustained? Assume that § 1033 was not applicable.

PROBLEM 6

On December 31, 1999, William Robert Chadd, a highly successful businessman and cattle rancher who was affectionately known by his friends as "Billy-Bob," made the fateful mistake of getting between his 1,800-pound, prize-winning, registered Brahman bull, known as "Big Daddy," and the then object of Big Daddy's affection, an unnamed, but apparently to Big Daddy's discerning eye, quite attractive, heifer. Billy-Bob's funeral a few days later was the social event of the year for the town of Alachua, Florida.

Billy-Bob's wife, Lila-Mae, became the personal representative of Billy-Bob's estate. Like Billy-Bob, the Estate adopted a calendar year for federal income tax purposes, and all of the estate's returns were filed in a timely manner without extensions. All went well until June 2002, when the IRS began auditing Billy-Bob's federal income tax return for 1999. That return had been filed on April 15, 2000 (separately from Lila-Mae's return). On January 15, 2003, the agent asserted in a thirty-day letter that the $1,000,000 lump sum payment Billy-Bob had received in 1999 for allowing a lime rock mining operation on a section of land he owned in western Alachua County, was properly treated as ordinary income and not as a non-reportable return of capital.

On February 1, 2003, you (as attorney for the taxpayer) filed a timely protest in response to the thirty-day letter. At the ensuing Appeals Office conference, among other things, you mentioned for the first time that, even if the revenue agent were right that the $1,000,000 lump sum payment constituted ordinary income, Billy-Bob had a previously unreported, offsetting, ordinary loss of $1,000,000 in a business venture that failed in 1999.

It seems that Billy-Bob had tried to combine muck, being removed from several local lakes to improve the bass fishery, with cow manure, for sale to gardeners at Wal-Mart. In addition to a court challenge to the name adopted for the product, "M&M's" (for muck and manure), purchasers complained loudly because when spread out and dried, the material formed a granite-like barrier that could be penetrated only by a pick-axe. This feature made the product useless for gardeners.

At the same time you filed the protest, February 1, 2003, and at the revenue agent's request, you extended the statute of limitations on assessment with respect to Billy-Bob's 1999 income tax return until December 31, 2003, in order to permit time for reflective consideration by the Appeals Officer.

However, discussions with the Appeals Officer were to no avail and on November 21, 2003, the Appeals Officer issued a timely ninety-day letter. On December 12, 2003, and on behalf of Lila-Mae in her capacity as personal representative of Billy-Bob's estate, you filed a timely petition in the Tax Court with respect to Billy-Bob's 1999 return. In your petition to the Tax Court, you asked that the $1,000,000 loss on the business venture be taken into consideration in redetermining Billy-Bob's 1999 income tax liability.

The Court rendered its opinion on March 19, 2005. As to the lump-sum payment, there was not much that the Tax Court could do. The lump-sum payment was clearly income to Billy-Bob and should have been reported on his 1999 return. Also, the Court concluded that the M&M business loss was an ordinary loss on a transaction entered into for profit. However, because the estate continued the business by shipping some of the product to Wal-Mart in January, February, and March 2000, and because the letter from Wal-Mart canceling the contract and demanding reimbursement for all amounts paid by Wal-Mart both for the product and to its customers who demanded refunds, did not come until April 31, 2000, the Tax Court agreed with the IRS that the loss did not occur in 1999, but in 2000.

It is now April 1, 2005. You are meeting with your client this afternoon to discuss options. What do you plan to tell your client?

PLEASE NOTE THERE IS NO NEED TO DISCUSS ANY SUBSTANTIVE INCOME OR ESTATE TAX ISSUES THAT MIGHT BE PRESENT UNDER THESE FACTS. YOU ARE TO ASSUME THAT THE ESTATE WOULD BE ENTITLED TO THE SAME $1,000,000 ORDINARY LOSS THAT YOU TRIED TO GET FOR BILLY-BOB'S 1999 RETURN.

PROBLEM 7

Don Trump, a real estate developer, owned a parcel of real property located on Lake Santa Fe in Alachua County, Florida. He had paid $1,000,000 for the property in 1991, with the intention of putting in roads and utilities and selling lots. On June 30, 1998, Don exchanged the property for five acres of waterfront property in Key Largo, Florida. The Key Largo property was worth $2,250,000.

Don believed that his development activities with respect to the Alachua County property had not gone so far as to preclude § 1031 tax-free exchange treatment, so he treated the exchange as tax free on his 1998 return. That return was filed on April 15, 1999, separately from that of his wife Joan. That return showed only $100,000 of salary and $24,000 of tax liability. It made no reference to the exchange.

Don had planned to build a home on the Key Largo property for himself, Joan, and their dog "Izzy." However, things were not going so well in the Trump household. On March 31, 2003, Don and Joan divorced. As part of the property settlement, Don gave the Key Largo property to Joan. She also got Izzy, which upset Don more than losing the Key Largo property.

Joan sold the Key Largo property for $3,000,000 on July 14, 2003. Her basis in the property was the same as Don's under the provisions of section 1041(b). So, she reported a $2,000,000 gain on the sale ($3,000,000 amount realized less Don's original cost of $1,000,000). Her 2003 return was filed on April 15, 2004.

All of these facts were revealed to you in a meeting with Joan in your office on January 15, 2005. You are convinced that the Alachua County-Key Largo property exchange was taxable and that Don's basis in the Key Largo property at the time of the property settlement was actually $2,250,000.

At your suggestion, and on January 15, 2005, Joan filed a claim for refund for 2003 in which the only change she requested was the increased basis in the Key Largo property and the consequent reduction in realized and recognized gain on the sale.

In response to the claim, the IRS audited Joan's 2003 return and found several significant changes that entirely offset the refund relating to the Key Largo property sale. Thus, although the IRS agreed that the Alachua County-Key Largo property exchange had been taxable and therefore Don's (and therefore Joan's) basis in the Key Largo property was in fact $2,250,000, Joan's claim for refund for 2003 was denied by notice of disallowance mailed to Joan on Monday, November 2, 2005.

Part A: Under these facts, can the Commissioner now (December 1, 2005) collect from Don the tax that Don should have paid because the 1998 Alachua County-Key Largo property exchange did not qualify under section 1031 and was in fact taxable?

Part B: Briefly explain why determinations described in sections 1312(3)(B) and 1312(4) have different "conditions necessary for adjustment" under section 1311(b) than are required with respect to other determinations described in section 1312.

PROBLEM 8

Roz Miller is, and for many years has been, a successful real estate broker engaged in brokering both residential and commercial real estate. In October 1996, Roz found a buyer for one of the most prestigious Morgan horse farms in the United States that is located in Ocala, Florida. The purchase price, including the "farm house," out buildings, equipment, and horses was $7,250,000. Roz's commission was $275,000. The closing went smoothly and was accomplished on December 23, 1996. However, as was customary in the community, the sales proceeds (including, of course, Roz's commission) were held in escrow pending recording of the various documents and making a final check to determine that there were no previously undiscovered liens on the farm.

On the afternoon of the closing (December 23, 1996), the parties recorded the documents and checked for liens. They in fact found a new lien filed by a workman who had been fired a few weeks earlier. The lien was not cleared until December 27, 1996, at which time the escrow was terminated and all the funds distributed except for Roz's commission. The reason Roz's commission wasn't distributed to her was that she was in Vail, Colorado, enjoying a long-planned ski trip. She had remained in touch with the escrow agent by phone and learned on December 27, 1996, that the escrow had terminated. She declined the escrow agent's offer to transfer her commission to her account, saying that she would be back on January 2, 1997, and would pick up her check at that time. She, in fact, returned on January 2, 1997, and on that day picked up the check for the commission from the escrow agent and deposited it in her checking account.

Roz's federal income tax return for 1996 was timely filed on April 15, 1997, and it reflected $100,000 of gross income. She did not include the commission because, as a cash-basis taxpayer, she thought it would be includible in her 1997 return.

Roz brokered sale of several other large-dollar properties in 1997, which indicated that she was going to have a banner year. Consequently, in September 1997, Roz approached you for tax planning advice. Upon learning all of the foregoing facts, you advised Roz that the $275,000 commission should have been reported on her 1996 federal income tax return. Your theory was that taxpayers are not permitted to reject income proffered to them (the constructive receipt doctrine), that the escrow had terminated on December 27, 1996, and that the $275,000 held by the escrow agent became hers at the time even though it had not been deposited in her account. On this basis, you advised Roz that she should not report the $275,000 on her 1997 return and that she should, but was not legally obligated to, file an amended return for 1996. Roz chose not to file an amended return for 1996 and did not include the commission in her 1997 return. The gross income actually stated on her 1997 return was $200,000.

In May 2003, the IRS began an audit of Roz's returns for the open years. Being unable to reconcile Roz's income with her rather high standard of living and accumulated wealth, the agent asked for and was given copies of the past six years' returns—1997 through 2002. Further inquiry by the agent led to the disclosure of the $275,000 commission that was deposited in Roz's account in January 1997. The agent concluded that the commission should have been reported in 1997. He issued a thirty-day letter indicating that he intended to assert a deficiency for 1997 in connection with the commission. Roz filed a protest and was given an Appeals conference. Roz's position at the conference, which you asserted on her behalf, was that the $275,000 commission was actually income in 1996. The Appeals officer did not agree with you and on December 14, 2003, a deficiency notice (ninety-day letter) was issued with respect to 1997. The only issue was the includibility of the $275,000 commission. On December 20, 2003, Roz petitioned the Tax Court for a redetermination of her 1997 tax liability. However, in an effort to avoid the accrual of additional interest with respect to the proposed 1997 deficiency, and on your advice, Roz paid the tax and accrued interest on December 23, 2003.

In due course, and on June 12, 2005, the Tax Court's decision in favor of Roz became final. The Tax Court agreed with you that the commission was actually income in 1996. Pursuant to section 6512(b) of the Code, the Court also determined that Roz was entitled to a refund of the tax she paid in response to the deficiency notice as well as to interest thereon.

On July 1, 2005, the IRS sent Roz a deficiency notice with respect to 1996, claiming that the $275,000 commission was income in that year. Upon receipt (on July 5, 2005) of the notice of deficiency for 1996, Roz asks you whether she will have to pay the proposed deficiency. Answer her question and explain your answer.

PROBLEM 9

George was married to Barbara, and they had two adult children, Jim and Bill. George died on January 15, 1997. His estate filed a timely estate tax return on October 15, 1997. The coexecutors of George's will were his wife and two sons. They were also the beneficiaries of the will. In part, the will provided that a trust should be created to benefit Barbara for her life with the corpus of the trust being terminable interest property in the amount of $5,000,000. The will provided that a "qualified terminable interest property" (QTIP) election could be made by the executor which would have allowed the property to qualify for the marital deduction and not be taxed in George's estate; otherwise the value of the trust would be includible in George's estate. The QTIP election was not made. However, the $5,000,000 was excluded from George's estate tax return. Barbara died on November 1, 2003. Her will devised her entire estate to her sons, Jim and Bill. Barbara's estate tax return was timely filed on August 1, 2004. The return did not include the value of the trust created by George's will (which is now valued at $4,500,000) on the grounds that the QTIP election was not made with respect to George's estate. Under these facts, can the IRS collect any tax with respect to the trust created by George's will?

Chapter 11

PENALTIES

IRC:	§§ 6012; 6081; 6151(a); 6161; 6166(a), (g)(3); 6651, 6654(a)–(e), (g), (h); 7491(c); review §§ 7502, 7503
Regs.:	§§ 1.6081-3, -4; 1.6161-1; 301.6651-1
Cases:	Crocker v. Commissioner, 92 T.C. 899 (1989) Estate of La Meres, 98 T.C. 294 (1992)
Forms:	Skim 1127; 2210; 2220; 2688; 4768; 4868; 7004; 9465

PART A:
PENALTIES FOR FAILURE TO FILE OR PAY TIMELY

I. GENERAL

The Code imposes upon taxpayers a variety of due dates for filing tax returns and paying tax. To encourage taxpayers to meet the deadlines, the law establishes an array of penalties, some civil and some criminal.[1] The most significant of the civil sanctions that address these failures are penalties for not prepaying the required amount of tax liability (the "estimated tax penalty"), for not filing returns timely (the "late filing penalty"), and for not paying taxes timely (the "late payment penalty"). For taxpayers already in difficult financial straits, these penalties, plus interest on the outstanding balance, may be particularly burdensome.

In order to fully appreciate the subject of this chapter, students should review the portions of Chapter 2 that discuss what constitutes a return for filing pur-

---

[1] Penalty Policy Statement P-1-18 (IRM 1.2.1.2.3) states:

> **Penalties are used to enhance voluntary compliance:** Penalties constitute one important tool of the Internal Revenue Service in pursuing its mission of collecting the proper amount of tax revenue at the least cost. Penalties support the Service's mission only if penalties enhance voluntary compliance. Even though other results such as raising of revenue, punishment, or reimbursement of the costs of enforcement may also arise when penalties are asserted, the Service will design, administer and evaluate penalty programs solely on the basis of whether they do the best possible job of encouraging compliant conduct.

> In the interest of an effective tax system, the Service uses penalties to encourage voluntary compliance by: (1) helping taxpayers understand that compliant conduct is appropriate and that noncompliant conduct is not; (2) deterring noncompliance by imposing costs on it; and (3) establishing the fairness of the tax system by justly penalizing the noncompliant taxpayer.

poses, what the due dates are for filing returns and making payments, and how one can get extensions when timely filing or payment is not possible.

II. PREPAYING TAX LIABILITY

Congress requires taxpayers to pay almost their entire tax liability during the year it is earned rather than wait until the return is filed in March or April of the next year. One of the reasons for this requirement is the government's need for continuous infusions of operating revenue. However, the obligation to prepay also protects taxpayers from getting to the date payment is due and finding they did not set aside enough money to meet the obligation.

Section 6654 does two things: it establishes for individual taxpayers[2] the guidelines for how much of their income tax and self-employment tax needs to be paid during the year on a "pay-as-you-go" (PAYGO) basis,[3] and it imposes a penalty for underpaying the required amount. Subject to various exceptions to be discussed later, the rule is that individuals must prepay 90% of their current year's liability. If the taxpayer does not adequately prepay the liability, a penalty is imposed by applying the underpayment rate to the amount of the underpayment of estimated tax for the period of underpayment.

PAYGO is most often accomplished by having the taxpayer's employer withhold income tax from wages. It is also frequently satisfied by the taxpayer making quarterly estimated payments or by the taxpayer requesting that one year's overpayment be applied to the following year's liability.

Taxpayers whose only source of income is wages and who properly complete Form W-4[4] usually satisfy the 90% requirement. This is because Circular E, the government-created tables used by employers to determine the amount to be withheld from wages, provides a reasonable estimate of the employee's tax liability for the year from that source. However, if the Form W-4 overstates the number of allowances or dependents, the amount withheld may be inadequate, forcing the taxpayer to make quarterly estimated tax payments to avoid the section 6654 penalty.

---

[2] Although the focus of this chapter is on individuals and on Form 1040, the late filing and late payment penalties also apply to the filing of most other tax returns and the payment of most other taxes. The rules for corporations are similar but not identical. *See* IRC § 6655.

[3] IRC § 6654(d)(1)(B)(i).

[4] The Form W-4 informs a person's employer of his or her filing status and number of dependents. This provides the employer with a basis to determine the amount of federal income tax to withhold from the person's earnings. The filing status and the number of dependents claimed on the W-4 do not have to be the same as that claimed on the Form 1040. The Form W-4 is meant to estimate the person's full-year tax liability. If a person will claim more deductions on his or her Form 1040 than the standard deduction, extra dependents may be claimed on the Form W-4. In this manner, less tax is withheld.

Example (1): Karin is a single person with no children. Her only source of income during 2004 is from her job at ABC Company. She plans to take the standard deduction rather than itemize deductions when she files her Form 1040. On the Form W-4 she submits to ABC, she reports herself as single with one allowance. From each weekly paycheck of $1,000, ABC Company withholds $160 per Circular E. When she files her Form 1040 in early 2005, she will have prepaid $8,320 ($160 × 52 weeks) toward her income tax liability. Since her tax liability will be about $7,800, she will be adequately prepaid and, in fact, entitled to a refund of $520.

Example (2): Same facts as example (1), except that Karin plans to itemize her deductions when she files her Form 1040. She estimates her itemized deductions at $14,150. Using the W-4 worksheet, she reports that she is entitled to four allowances. As a result, ABC withholds $117 for income taxes from each paycheck. When she prepares her Form 1040, she will have had $6,084 prepaid through withholding. Assuming she claims $14,150 as itemized deductions, her tax liability for 2004 will be about $5,400 and she will be entitled to a refund of $684. On the other hand, if she does not itemize and uses the standard deduction when filing her Form 1040, she would be underwithheld by $1,716 ($7,800 less $6,084). Since $6,084 is less than 90% of $7,800 (her tax liability using the standard deduction), she would be subject to the section 6654 penalty.

Taxpayers who have significant sources of income other than wages, such as dividends, interest, gains, rents, and royalties, or who have income from a sole proprietorship or partnership, are the most likely candidates for having to make estimated quarterly tax payments.[5] For calendar year taxpayers, quarterly estimated tax payments are due on the 15th of April, June, and September of the current tax year and the 15th of January of the following tax year. Taxpayers are generally required to pay 25% of their annual estimated tax on or before each installment payment due date.

Example: Margo is a self-employed graphics designer. Her net earnings from self-employment for 2004 are $52,000. She is a single person and has no dependents. Her itemized deductions are $14,150. Her income tax liability for 2004, based on the first example above, will be about $7,800. However, she must also pay Social Security and Medicare taxes at 15.3% of her net earnings from self-employment. This amounts to approximately $7,950. Margo would have to make quarterly estimated

---

[5] Taxpayers who have significant income that is not subject to withholding must be financially self-disciplined. If they failed to pay estimated taxes on a quarterly basis, they not only will find themselves liable for the penalty under section 6654 but they will also find themselves burdened with a large tax liability. This is especially true for self-employed individuals, as they have to PAYGO not only for income taxes but also for the 15.3% self employment tax.

tax payments of 90% of $15,750 ($7,800 + $7,950), or $14,175, to satisfy her estimated tax liability.

A. Calculating the Penalty

Section 6654(a)(1) sets the penalty rate at the underpayment rate established under section 6621.[6] For purposes of the penalty, the underpayment rate is a simple interest rate; it is not compounded daily.[7]

The penalty is calculated based on the "underpayment period," which is the number of days from the payment due date to the earlier of (a) the date the payment is received, or (b) the 15th day of the fourth month following the close of the taxable year, which is the due date of the return without regard to extensions, usually April 15 of the following year. Each underpaid installment period must be computed separately. The length of an underpayment period is not reduced by an extension of time to pay the tax.

The amount of the underpayment of estimated tax is defined as the excess of (1) the required installment over (2) the amount, if any, of the installment paid on or before its due date. Payments of estimated tax are credited against the unpaid portion of the required installment that is most overdue at the time of the payment, unless the taxpayer elects otherwise. By contrast, withheld taxes are divided evenly among all four installments,[8] unless the taxpayer completes and attaches Form 2210 to the return indicating a choice to apply the withholding to the period in which it was actually withheld.

Whether one has met the 90% requirement is determined based on the amount of tax reported on the original return. Even if the tax is later adjusted because of an audit or the filing of an amended return, the amount of the underpayment remains the same. An exception exists when an amended joint return is filed after separate returns, in which case the penalty is based on the joint return.

B. Defenses to the Estimated Tax Penalty

If the taxpayer has not met the 90% requirement, the IRS automatically assesses the penalty and sends the taxpayer a notice and demand for payment. The section 6654 penalty is not entitled to deficiency procedures. Most available

---

[6] Taxpayers are not subject to estimated tax penalties if their tax liability is less than $1,000, after subtracting amounts withheld from wages and other payments/credits during the year. Further, no estimated tax penalty will be imposed on taxpayers who had no liability for the preceding (12-month) tax year and who were U.S. citizens or residents throughout the preceding tax year. IRC § 6654(e).

[7] IRC § 6622(b).

[8] IRC § 6654(g).

defenses are presented to the Service by individuals completing a Form 2210.[9] Taxpayers may attach the completed forms to their tax returns, seeking non-assessment in the first place. Alternatively, if the IRS assesses the penalty automatically, one can request its abatement by sending in the form after the balance due notice is received.

As was true for the initial determination of whether the taxpayer failed to prepay 90% of the current year's liability, most of the defenses to the penalty are mathematical. The most frequently employed exception allows the taxpayer to demonstrate that the amount paid during the year equals or exceeds 100% of the tax shown on the preceding year's return.[10] The purpose of this exception is to make it possible for taxpayers to estimate the amount they must prepay based solely on the tax paid in the previous year, thus avoiding having to frequently update estimated tax calculations for changing circumstances.

> **Example:** Robert is a single individual whose tax liability for year #1 was $15,000. He changes jobs in year #2 and receives a 100% increase in salary. Even though Robert's income tax liability may more than double in year #2, he can still pay only $15,000 in estimated taxes and avoid the section 6654 penalty. (If his adjusted gross income in year #1 was over $150,000, he would be required to prepay $16,500 (110% of $15,000)). He does not need to go to an accountant during year #2 to estimate his tax liability for the year.

A less frequently used defense to the estimated tax penalty is established in section 6654(d)(2). Under this method, the amount that must be prepaid is determined under a method that annualizes income. This method allows estimated tax payments to be made as income is earned. The annualized installment method works best for taxpayers who receive the greater portion of their income late in the year and, therefore, did not have a duty to prepay earlier in the year.

There exist two subjective defenses to the section 6654 penalty. Under section 6654(e)(3)(A), the IRS may waive the estimated tax penalty if it determines that the imposition of the penalty would "be against equity and good conscience" because of a casualty, disaster, or other unusual circumstances. This is not necessarily equivalent to reasonable cause. Requests for such a waiver must be submitted in writing and signed by the taxpayer.

Finally, a taxpayer may be eligible for a waiver of the penalty under section 6654(e)(3)(B), if in the tax year in which the payments came due, or in the pre-

---

9 Similar exceptions apply to corporations and are presented on Form 2220.

10 IRC § 6654(d)(1)(B)(ii). In the case of a taxpayer with adjusted gross income over $150,000 ($75,000 for married filing separately) in the preceding year, the required amount is 110% of the prior year's liability.

According to IRM 20.1.3.2.1.1, last year's tax, for these purposes, is determined exclusive of tax resulting from a deficiency or an amended return filed after the due date of the current year's return.

ceding tax year, the taxpayer either retired after having attained the age of 62 or became disabled[11] and the underpayment is due to reasonable cause and not willful neglect. There is no established procedure to raise these defenses, but a letter should suffice.[12]

III. FAILURE TO FILE RETURNS TIMELY

A. Due Dates, Extensions, and Substitutes for Return

As more fully discussed in Chapter 2, the Code establishes due dates for all returns that must be filed with the Service. If a taxpayer does not have the information needed to complete the return by its due date, an extension of time to file can be requested. Extensions are taken into account in determining whether the return filing is timely and whether assessing the late filing penalty is appropriate.[13]

Taxpayers who fail to file returns by the extended due date are at risk of being targeted by the IRS. Once a nonfiling situation is identified, the Internal Revenue Manual directs the assigned agent to review the situation for fraud.[14] If there appear to be indications of fraud, the agent is instructed to prepare a referral to the Criminal Investigation Division.

If there are no apparent indications of fraud, the agent contacts the nonfiler to request that all delinquent returns be filed.[15] If the taxpayer still fails to do so, the Service will prepare a Substitute for Return (SFR) for the taxpayer from the information in its computer under the authority of section 6020(b).[16]

B. Failure to File Penalty

When a return is not timely filed, the government automatically asserts a late filing penalty under section 6651(a)(1). The taxpayer can avoid the penalty if the

---

[11] *See* IRM 20.1.3.4.1.5.

[12] *See* note 25, *infra*.

[13] An extension to file only extends the time to file. It does not extend the date for payment. Although an extension to file is automatic, an extension to pay is difficult to obtain. IRM 20.1.2.1.2.1. *See* Chapter 2.

[14] IRM 4.12.1.4, 5.1.11.6.

[15] IRM 5.1.11.1.1, 5.19.2.3.

[16] IRM 4.12.1.13, 5.1.11.8. When the IRS prepares SFRs, it is likely that the tax liability will be greater than what it would have been if the taxpayer filed the return. This is so because the IRS generally prepares SFRs in a manner that tends to artificially increase the tax liability. For example, the IRS includes as income the gross proceeds of a sale rather than the gain after reduction for basis, allows the taxpayer only one exemption and the standard deduction rather than itemizing deductions, and utilizes a filing status of married filing separately if the taxpayer is married rather than married filing jointly. *See, e.g.*, IRM 5.18.1.7.26, 5.19.2.6.4.5.1(3).

failure to file timely was due to "reasonable cause and not willful neglect."[17] The amount of the late filing penalty (also referred to as the failure to file penalty) is the product of three variables:

- The Penalty Rate,

- The Penalty Period, and

- The Net Amount of Tax Due.

The rate of the penalty is generally 5% of the amount of tax due for each month or fraction of a month that the return is late, up to a maximum of 25%.[18] The maximum rate is reached after only four months and one day. If the failure to file is fraudulent, the penalty is increased to 15% per month, up to a maximum of 75%. If a taxpayer does not owe anything or is due a refund, there is no penalty.

The failure to file (FTF) penalty accrues from the due date of the tax return to the date the IRS actually *receives* the return. If an extension to file is granted, the extended due date is the date on which late filing penalties begin to accrue.[19] If the return is received after the due date or the extended due date but mailed before it, section 7502 applies. *See* Chapter 2. The FTF penalty is imposed based on the number of months, including any fraction of a month, during which the failure to file continues.

> **Example:** Assume Allison got a valid extension to October 15, 2006, relative to her 2005 tax return. She mails the return on November 14, 2006, and the IRS receives it on November 17, 2006. The return is two months late as the valid extension period is given full weight in determining the number of months the return is late.

The FTF penalty is calculated as a percentage of "net amount due,"[20] which is the amount of tax required to be shown on the return, reduced by any tax payments made, or credits allowed, *on or before* the prescribed due date of the return.[21] If there is no net amount due, such as where there is an overpayment, there is no late filing penalty.

While extensions to file affect the number of months that a return is late, they are disregarded for purposes of determining the amount of the underpayment. Thus, payments made after the prescribed due date and before the extended due

---

[17] *See* IRM 20.1.2.1.

[18] Where a tax return showing a balance due is more than sixty days late, taking into account any extensions of time to file, the minimum failure to file penalty is not less than the lesser of $100 or 100% of the net tax required to be shown on the return, unless the failure is due to reasonable cause and not willful neglect. IRC § 6651(a)(1); IRM 20.1.2.2.

[19] See IRM 20.1.2.1.2.1 for rules where extensions were not granted or were voided.

[20] See heading of IRC section 6651(b).

[21] IRC § 6651(b)(1).

date do not reduce the net tax amount. Net operating losses or credit carrybacks similarly do not reduce the base upon which the penalty is computed.

> **Example:** Robert is required to file his 2005 income tax return on April 15, 2006. During the year, Robert made $11,000 of estimated tax payments and paid an additional $4,000 on April 15, 2006, with his application for an automatic extension of time to file the return. Robert filed his return late on October 30, 2006, reflecting an $18,000 income tax liability. He paid $3,000 ($18,000 - $11,000 - $4,000) with the return. For the tax year 2007, Robert incurred a loss, which he carried back to reduce his 2005 tax liability from $18,000 to $16,000. For purposes of section 6651(a)(1), the net amount of tax due is $3,000—i.e., $18,000 (tax required to be shown on the return not reduced by the carryback) minus $15,000 (payments made on or before the due date of the return).

The "tax required to be shown on the return" includes not only the tax shown as due on the return as filed but also tax later determined to be due as the result of an examination.

> **Example:** Tony files her return two months late showing tax liability of $60,000 and payments of $45,000. The original penalty amount is computed as 10% (two months at 5% per month) of the $15,000 as yet unpaid tax shown as due on the return, or $1,500.

> Tony's return is examined one year later. Tony and the IRS agree that Tony's correct tax should have been $80,000, thus giving rise to a tax deficiency of $20,000. A penalty of $2,000 ($20,000 times 10%, due to the return being filed two months late) will be assessed along with the deficiency in tax. Thus, in total, the taxpayer's late filing penalty is $3,500 ($1,500 + $2,000, or 10% × $35,000 [the difference between the $80,000 tax required to be shown on the return and the $45,000 tax paid on or before the due date]).

C. Fraudulent Failure to File

Section 6651(f) provides for an increased civil penalty (15% per month, up to 75%) where the failure to file a return is fraudulent.[22] The civil fraud penalty under section 6663, only applies when a return is filed. When no return is filed, the fraudulent failure to file penalty imposes a similar sanction.

Fraudulent failure to file generally involves evidence of intentional wrongdoing on the part of the taxpayer with the specific purpose of evading a tax known, or believed, to be owed. The IRS bears the burden of proving fraud by

---

[22] *See* IRM 20.1.2.7. Both the fraudulent failure to file penalty and the 75% accuracy-related fraud penalty under section 6663 can apply if the taxpayer originally failed to file for fraudulent reasons but, when filed, did so fraudulently.

clear and convincing evidence.[23] If the IRS is unable to sustain its burden of proof on the fraud issue, the basic failure to file penalty, 5% a month, up to a maximum of 25%, may still be imposed.

The IRS considers the following factors, among others, to be indicators of fraud:

- The taxpayer refuses, or is unable to, explain his failure to file;

- The taxpayer's statements do not comport with the facts of the case;

- The taxpayer has a history of failing to file timely, but an apparent ability to pay;

- The taxpayer fails to reveal or tries to conceal assets;

- The taxpayer either pays personal and business expenses in cash, when cash payments are not usual, or cashes, rather than deposits, checks which are business receipts; and

- The taxpayer's occupation shows he should be aware of the obligation to pay tax, regardless of the amount due (i.e., lawyers, teachers, accountants, real estate brokers, and public officials).[24]

IV. FAILURE TO PAY TAX TIMELY

Section 6151 establishes the due dates for paying tax. Generally, it is the same as the date for filing the associated return. Extensions to pay may be requested but, in the case of income taxes, they are difficult to secure. In order to get an extension to pay, the taxpayer must establish that paying timely would create an undue hardship. If granted, an extension to pay is normally for no longer than six months. An extension of time to pay the tax does not affect the accruing of interest, which runs from the original due date.

If a taxpayer does not pay taxes by the due date, as extended, a failure to pay (FTP) penalty will be imposed. There are two distinct FTP penalties: the failure to pay the tax shown as due on the return (section 6651(a)(2)) and the failure to pay an assessed deficiency (section 6651(a)(3)).[25]

---

[23] IRC § 7454.

[24] IRM 20.1.2.7.

[25] When a taxpayer has filed a petition in bankruptcy, section 6658 may provide relief from late payment penalties. Section 6658(a) provides, in part, that "[n]o addition to the tax shall be made under section 6651, 6654, or 6655 for failure to make timely payment of tax with respect to a period during which a case is pending under title 11 of the United States Code. . . ." Section 6658 applies to tax arising before the taxpayer files a bankruptcy petition if (1) the petition was filed before the due date of the return or (2) the date for making the addition to the tax occurs on or after the day on which the petition was filed. Section 6651 imposes penalties for failure to file a return or pay a tax, and sections 6654 and 6655 impose penalties for failure to pay estimated taxes. The term "pending" is not defined in section 6658.

In Rev. Rul. 2005-9, 2005-6 I.R.B. 470, the IRS sought to clarify when a bankruptcy case is pending. A bankruptcy case is commenced by filing a petition with the bankruptcy court pursuant

A. Failure to Pay the Tax Shown as Due on the Return

While the estimated tax payment requirement in section 6654 requires taxpayers to prepay their tax liabilities, section 6651(a)(2) imposes a penalty on those who fail to pay the balance by the due date, unless the failure is due to reasonable cause and not willful neglect. The late payment penalty is generally 0.5% (1/2%) of the unpaid tax for each month, or fraction thereof, that the payment is late, up to a maximum of 25% (fifty months).

To encourage taxpayers to address their obligation to pay, the penalty is reduced to 0.25% (1/4%) per month during periods the taxpayer is making payments pursuant to a section 6159 installment agreement.[26] Conversely, the penalty rate increases from 1/2% to 1% during certain "advanced" collection proceedings, i.e., on the earlier of (i) the eleventh day after a notice of intent to levy is issued under section 6331(d), or (ii) the date notice and demand for immediate payment is given on a jeopardy assessment under section 6331(a).[27]

This penalty applies to all individual, corporate, trust, and estate income tax returns, employment tax returns, estate and gift tax returns, and certain excise tax returns. A substitute for return (SFR) completed by the IRS is treated as a "real" return for purposes of determining the failure to pay penalties.[28]

As with the failure to file penalty, the failure to pay penalty is a percentage of the "net amount [of tax] due." If that amount is not paid, the penalty is imposed on the net tax amount after subtracting amounts that have been withheld, estimated tax payments, partial payments, and other applicable credits. For purposes of computing the late payment penalty for any month, the tax liability is reduced by any payments of tax made on or before the beginning of each month.

The failure to pay penalty runs for the number of months, or part thereof, from the payment's due date through the date on which the IRS receives pay-

---

to sections 301 through 304 of the Bankruptcy Code. A case is "pending" for purposes of section 6658 after the debtor files a petition with the bankruptcy court. A bankruptcy case is no longer pending for purposes of section 6658 when it is closed or dismissed. *See* Carey v. Saffold, 536 U.S. 214, 219-20 (2002) (consulting Webster's Third International Dictionary for the ordinary meaning of the word "pending," the Court determined that a state court application for collateral review remains pending "until the application has achieved final resolution").

[26] IRC § 6651(h); IRM 20.1.2.8; SCA 200135025 (reduction in rate takes place when the installment agreement is accepted by the IRS, not when it is submitted by the taxpayer).

[27] IRC § 6651(d). Once the penalty rate is increased, it applies for all subsequent months for that particular assessment, subject to the same maximum of 25%.

[28] *But see* Cabirac v. Commissioner, 120 T.C. 163 (2003). The penalty is entitled to deficiency procedures. *See* CCN(35)000-169. Prior to July 30, 1996, there was no failure to pay penalty imposed if a return was not filed or if the IRS prepared an SFR. This, however, was not a benefit, since the failure to file penalty applied anyway and without the pro rata reduction by the amount of any failure to pay penalty for any month in which both penalties apply.

ment. The due date of a tax payment is generally the date on which the return is required to be filed, determined with regard to extensions of time *to pay*, but without regard of extension of time *to file*. A "month" is measured from the date in a calendar month to the date numerically corresponding to it in the succeeding calendar month.[29]

B. Failure to Pay Tax Deficiency

Recall that when the IRS examines the taxpayer's return and determines a deficiency, that amount is not assessed until the deficiency procedures have run their course. Once the deficiency is assessed, the IRS issues a notice and demand for payment. If the additional amount owed is not paid within twenty-one days of notice and demand (ten days in the case of tax liabilities over $100,000), the failure to pay penalty imposed each month or fraction thereof is a percentage of the deficiency amount outstanding until the tax is paid.

With minor variations discussed below, the section 6651(a)(3) failure to pay penalty is calculated in the same manner as the section 6651(a)(2) penalty. And like the other failure to timely act penalties, the section 6651(a)(3) penalty does not apply if the taxpayer shows that the failure was due to reasonable cause and not willful neglect. The total section 6651(a)(3) penalty cannot exceed 25%.

The penalty imposed is computed based on the deficiency amount stated in the notice, less the amount of any partial payments made on the deficiency. Thus, the monthly penalty is computed on the net deficiency as of the beginning of each month.

C. Combined Late Filing and Late Payment Penalties

Taxpayers who file late often also pay late. If the section 6651(a)(1) failure to file penalty and the section 6651(a)(2) failure to pay penalty apply for the same month, or fraction of a month, the amount of the failure to file penalty is reduced by the amount of the failure to pay penalty for that month.[30]

For this purpose, it is important to note that the base of the failure to file penalty is different than the base for the failure to pay penalty. The base for the failure to file penalty is the correct amount of the tax liability (i.e., "the amount required to be shown as tax on [the] return") reduced by the portion of the tax

---

[29] Since, in calculating a late payment penalty, the payment is per se late and has passed "the last day . . . for performing [an] act," the "timely mailed is timely paid" rule of section 7502 and the weekend/holiday rule of section 7503 do not affect the determination of the number of months a payment is late. Reg. §§ 301.6651-1(b)(3), 301.7502-1(a).

[30] IRC § 6651(c)(1).

"paid on or before the date prescribed for payment. . . ."[31] Because the failure to file penalty is based on "the amount *required to be shown* as tax on [the] return," the amount of the penalty will be increased in the event that the return understated the actual tax liability. Also, note that the base is not reduced by any amount that is paid late. Thus, late payment, even of the entire amount of the tax "required to be shown," will not stop the accrual of the penalty unless the return is filed at that time.

The base for the failure to pay penalty is determined monthly and is the amount of the tax actually shown on the return, reduced by "the tax which is paid on or before the beginning of [the] month."[32] In this case, late payments made before filing the late return will reduce both the late payment penalty and the offset of the failure to file penalty. Because the base of the failure to pay penalty, the amount shown on the return reduced by the amount paid, cannot exceed the amount shown on the return, subsequently determined deficiencies will not increase the base for the penalty. However, the section 6651(a)(3) penalty applies when a deficiency is not paid within 21 days from the date of the IRS's notice of tax due and demand for payment.

V. THE REASONABLE CAUSE DEFENSE

The late filing and late payment penalties are avoided if the taxpayer establishes that there was reasonable cause for the lateness and that it was not due to willful neglect. Reasonable cause is defined as an inability to file or to pay, which arises despite one's exercise of ordinary business care and prudence that is due to circumstances beyond the control of the taxpayer.[33] Willful neglect is defined as a conscious, intentional failure to do what is required or a reckless indifference to the requirement. Since the requirement for reasonable cause tends to encompass a concurrent showing of the absence of willful neglect, courts and the IRS generally discuss both exceptions under the heading of "reasonable cause" alone.

Reasonable cause determinations are based on the facts and circumstances of each case. The burden of proving reasonable cause is on the taxpayer, but in a court proceeding the IRS has the burden of producing evidence that it is appropriate to apply the penalty to the taxpayer in the first place.[34] In making a determination whether there is reasonable cause, the IRS considers the following, among other factors:[35]

---

[31] IRC § 6651(a)(1), (b)(1).

[32] IRC § 6651(a)(2), (b)(2).

[33] Reg. § 301.6651-1(c); IRM 20.1.1.3.1.

[34] IRC § 7491(c).

[35] Reg. § 301.6651-1(c); IRM 20.1.1.3.1.2.

- Whether the taxpayer's reasons address the penalty imposed;

- The taxpayer's payment and penalty history;

- The length of time between the event cited as a reason for noncompliance and the subsequent compliance;

- Whether the event that caused the taxpayer's noncompliance could have reasonably been anticipated; and

- Whether the taxpayer exercised ordinary business care and prudence to meet the requirement as soon as possible, even if late.

A. Situations That Might, Depending on the Circumstances, Qualify as Reasonable Cause

1. Reliance on a Tax Advisor or Other Third Person

Normally, a taxpayer cannot shift blame for his or her late filing or payment to another, such as to one's tax advisor, employee, or spouse. Everyone is deemed to know of their obligation to file and pay and is expected to learn when these obligations are due. Case law, however, distinguishes between those situations where a tax advisor or third person has the ministerial duty to file or pay on the taxpayer's behalf, and those situations where a tax advisor gave substantive advice regarding the requirements.[36] Reasonable cause may exist in the latter situation.

2. Death, Serious Illness, or Unavoidable Absence

The death, serious illness, or unavoidable absence of the taxpayer, or the death or serious illness of a member of the taxpayer's family, may constitute reasonable cause.[37] In the case of an entity, the incapacity must relate to either the individual having the sole authority to take the action required of the entity, or to a member of that individual's family.

In making the determination as to whether an illness constitutes reasonable cause, courts focus on the severity and duration of the illness. The incapacity must be so severe that the taxpayer cannot function during the period, and so sudden that the taxpayer could not reasonably make plans for handling his or her financial affairs during the illness. Mental illness, drug or alcohol dependency, battered spouse situations, issues of old age, infirmity, and mental incapacity may also provide a basis for reasonable cause.

---

[36] *E.g.,* United States v. Boyle, 469 U.S. 241 (1985). *See* IRM 20.1.1.3.2.4.

[37] IRM 20.1.1.3.1.2.4.

Though one may have reasonable cause for late action because of death or illness for some period, the waiver does not apply forever. At some point, the IRS will expect the taxpayer to file or pay. Too great a delay might vitiate the earlier reasonable cause. Where the taxpayer continues to work or take care of other normal business matters during his or her alleged incapacity, reasonable cause generally does not exist.[38]

3. Erroneous Advice From the IRS

Pursuant to Regulation section 301.6404-3, the IRS must abate the portion of any penalty attributable to *written* erroneous advice furnished to the taxpayer by an IRS employee if: (1) the advice is reasonably relied on by the taxpayer; (2) the advice is issued in response to a specific written request for advice by the taxpayer; and (3) the taxpayer provided adequate and accurate information in connection with the request. Reasonable reliance does not continue after the taxpayer is put on notice that the prior written advice no longer represents the IRS's position.

The IRS may abate a penalty for reasonable cause where the taxpayer relies on *oral* advice from an IRS employee.[39] To claim the waiver, the taxpayer must show that the IRS was supplied with complete and accurate information and that he or she exercised ordinary business care and prudence in relying on that advice. Meeting this burden of proof may be extremely difficult relative to oral advice, unless the taxpayer kept a written record of all dealings with the IRS, including meetings, telephone calls, correspondence, and the name of the IRS representative involved.

4. Fire, Casualty, Natural Disaster, or Other Disturbance

A fire, casualty, natural disaster, or other disturbance may constitute reasonable cause if the taxpayer exercised ordinary business care and prudence but was unable to comply with tax obligations due to circumstances beyond his or her control.[40] Good recordkeeping and contemporaneously filed claims with the police and insurance company help establish the truth of the defense. In the case of a significant disaster affecting numerous taxpayers, the IRS generally provides special guidance for penalty relief.

---

[38] Barber v. Commissioner, T.C. Memo 1997-206.
[39] IRM 20.1.1.3.2.4.2.
[40] IRM 20.1.1.3.2.5.

5. Service in a Combat Zone

An individual serving in the U.S. Armed Forces, or in support thereof, in an area designated by the President as a "combat zone" has until 180 days after the "period of combatant activities" or period of continuous qualified hospitalization attributable to an injury received while serving in such combat zone, to file a return and pay the tax.[41] This extension also applies to the taxpayer's spouse.

6. Automatic Reasonable Cause for Late Payment if Payment within 90% of Tax Liability

Under Regulation section 301.6651-1(c)(3), if there is an extension of time to file, and payment of the tax balance due is made with a timely filed extended return, the taxpayer is deemed to have acted reasonably if the amount shown as due on the filed return is less than 10% of the taxpayer's total tax liability. If the balance due is more than 10% of the total tax or if it is not paid with the return, the penalty applies to the total balance due from the original due date.[42]

> **Example (1):** Meg obtained an automatic extension of time to file her 2005 tax return from April 15, 2006, until October 15, 2006. She files her return on October 9, 2006, reflecting a tax liability of $30,000 and a credit for withholding of $20,000. She pays the $10,000 balance due when she files. Meg is liable for a late payment penalty of $200.00 (0.5% $\times$ 4 months $\times$ $10,000). Even though Meg had a four-month extension of time to file her return, she did not have an extension of time to pay.

> **Example (2):** Assume in example (1) above, Meg paid $8,000 on April 15, 2006, when the automatic extension form was filed. When she files her return on October 9, 2006, she pays the additional balance due of $2,000. Meg qualifies for the reasonable cause safe harbor since 90% of the liability was paid by the due date.

B. Situations That Generally Do Not Qualify as Reasonable Cause

1. Mistake or Forgetfulness

A taxpayer's or a subordinate's mistake as to the proper treatment of a particular item[43] generally does not demonstrate ordinary business care and prudence and therefore is not a basis of reasonable cause. The same is true for one's

---

[41] IRC § 7508.

[42] Reg. § 301.6651-1(c)(3).

[43] IRM 20.1.1.3.1.2.2.

forgetfulness[44] or carelessness. Absent affirmative reliance on erroneous advice of counsel, a good faith, mistaken belief will not relieve a taxpayer from the penalty.

2. Time and Business Pressures

The taxpayer's heavy workload does not constitute reasonable cause for failure to perform a required act. People exercising ordinary business care and prudence do not take on assignments that prohibit them from fulfilling their legal obligations within prescribed times. Similarly, the time pressure of a taxpayer's agent (e.g., a return preparer) cannot excuse a taxpayer's failure to file a return.

3. Invalid Extension

A return that is filed, or a payment that is made, within the period of an invalid extension is still late. Even an automatic extension can be voided, for example, if the taxpayer fails to estimate the tax properly. A voided automatic extension is not reasonable cause for failing to file a timely return. Similarly, filing within an extension period that is requested but not granted does not constitute reasonable cause. A taxpayer cannot presume that the request for an extension of time will be granted. Accordingly, the mere request for an extension does not eliminate the penalty when the extension is denied.

4. Records Unavailable

Unavailability of records is generally not considered reasonable cause for a taxpayer's failure to file a return. Rather, the taxpayer must estimate the tax liability based on the best information available and, where necessary, obtain an extension of time to file. However, if a proper return cannot be filed because information remains unavailable despite ordinary business care and prudence by the taxpayer, there is reasonable cause. For example, in *Dejoy v. Commissioner*,[45] the court held there was reasonable cause where the principals in an accounting firm that provided services to the taxpayer ceased practice and disappeared, taking many of the taxpayer's business and financial records with them.

---

[44] IRM 20.1.1.3.1.2.3.

[45] T.C. Memo 2000-162.

5. Ignorance of the Law

Ignorance of the law, in and of itself, does not constitute reasonable cause.[46] This includes, for example, a taxpayer's erroneous belief (not based on advice of counsel) that no return is required, a lack of knowledge as to the correct due date, or an erroneous belief that the proceeds of a transaction were not taxable. Ordinary business care and prudence requires that all taxpayers be aware of their tax obligations.

On the other hand, ignorance of the law in conjunction with other facts and circumstances, such as one's limited education or lack of experience with taxes and penalties, may support a claim of reasonable cause. For example, where the IRS has not provided any guidance as to difficult and complex issues, reasonable cause may exist for a position taken in good faith. Similarly, a taxpayer may have reasonable cause if there is a recent change in the tax law or forms of which the taxpayer could not reasonably be expected to know.

6. Constitutional Objections and Religious Beliefs

Neither constitutional objections nor religious beliefs are valid reasons for failing to file a return or failing to pay the required tax. The Fifth Amendment privilege against self-incrimination extends only to a taxpayer's refusal to answer specific questions on the return and does not constitute reasonable cause sufficient to justify a taxpayer's complete refusal to act at all.

7. Lack of Funds

A claim of insufficient funds is never reasonable cause for failing *to file* a return. Lack of funds, however, may be an acceptable reason for failure to pay a tax if the taxpayer can demonstrate that, despite the exercise of ordinary business care and prudence, the taxpayer either lacked the funds to pay the tax or would experience an "undue hardship" if paid on time.[47]

In determining whether a taxpayer lacked funds, all of the facts and circumstances of the taxpayer's financial situation are considered, including the amount and nature of one's expenditures in light of assets, the funds one could reasonably expect to receive, and one's investment practices.[48] Insolvency before

---

[46] IRM 20.1.1.3.1.2.1.

[47] *See* Reg. § 301.6651-1(c); IRM 20.1.1.3.2.3. *Compare* Fran Corp. v. United States, 164 F.3d 814 (2d Cir. 1999) (financial difficulties as a defense is a facts and circumstances determination in all late payment situations), *with* Brewery, Inc. v. United States, 33 F.3d 589 (6th Cir. 1994) (financial difficulties may be a reason for not paying income taxes timely but never is it a "reasonable cause" with respect to depositing employment taxes).

[48] *See* In re Arthur's Indus. Maint., Inc., 92-1 U.S.T.C. (CCH) ¶50,242 (Bankr. W.D. Va. 1992).

the tax payment date, leading to a petition in bankruptcy, is significant evidence of an inability to pay. Inability to pay due to the embezzlement by employees, however, indicates a lack of ordinary business care and prudence.[49] A taxpayer who cannot claim "lack of funds" may still qualify for the reasonable cause exception for late payment if he or she would suffer "undue hardship" if the tax is paid when due.[50]

VI. HOW AND WHEN TO DISPUTE "LATE" PENALTIES

A. Some Filing and Payment Penalties May Be Automatically Assessed and Others Are Entitled to Deficiency Procedures

When a taxpayer files a return or makes a payment, sections 6201(a)(1) and 6213(b)(4) authorize the IRS to automatically assess the tax shown on the return or the amount paid, respectively. If the return or payment of tax shown on the return is late, the IRS may automatically (summarily) assess appropriate penalties. Since the penalties are computed based on the information on the self-assessing return, they too are treated as self-assessing.[51] As a result, taxpayers normally learn that the IRS assessed a penalty when they receive a notice and demand for its payment.[52]

By contrast, if the IRS determines a deficiency in tax, a late filing penalty attributable to, and calculated as a percentage of, the deficiency will be added to the deficiency amount. It cannot be assessed automatically because the amount is not known until a deficiency is finally determined. The penalty, as part of the overall deficiency, is entitled to the same deficiency procedures as the underlying tax.[53]

1. General

A taxpayer believing good reason for filing or paying late exists can seek to avoid the automatically assessed portion of the penalty by writing an explanation of the circumstances either when filing the return, or after the IRS sends a notice of the assessment of the penalty. If the Service persists in assessing the penalty despite the explanation, the taxpayer may seek administrative review

---

[49] Conklin Bros. of Santa Rosa, Inc. v. United States, 986 F.2d 315 (9th Cir. 1993).

[50] See Regulation section 1.6161-1(b), which discusses "undue hardship" in the context of getting an extension of time to pay.

[51] IRC § 6665(b).

[52] See IRM 20.1.1.4.2.

[53] IRC § 6665(b)(1); IRM 20.1.1.4.2.

of the determination by filing a protest with the Appeals Office. This can be done either before or after paying the assessment.[54]

If the taxpayer and the Appeals Office cannot reach a settlement, the taxpayer may seek judicial review. If the penalty was automatically assessed, review is with the District Court or Court of Federal Claims. If the penalty was part of a deficiency, review is available in all courts hearing tax matters.[55]

> **Example (1):** Rochelle files her 2004 tax return on December 23, 2005, after having received extensions of six months using Forms 4868 and 2688. The return reflects a tax liability of $50,000, the entire amount of which is paid with the return. Since the return is treated as three months late (from October 15, 2005), a penalty of 15% will be assessed summarily, unless a letter is sent with the return explaining the reason for the lateness and the IRS accepts the explanation. Interest for the period April 15, 2005 to December 23, 2005 will also be assessed.[56]
>
> If no letter of explanation accompanies the return or the IRS did not accept the position advanced, the IRS will send Rochelle a notice of the assessment and a demand for payment. As there is no tax due, the notice would be only for the penalty in the amount of $3,500 (15% x $50,000) and interest. At this point, Rochelle may request waiver (or abatement) of the penalty on the basis of reasonable cause. If the IRS denies the request, Rochelle can protest the determination to the Appeals Office. If the appeal is denied, her principal avenue for challenging the assessment in court is to pay the full amount, file a claim for refund (Form 843), and then file a complaint in District Court or the Court of Federal Claims.
>
> **Example (2):** Some time after Rochelle files her 2004 return, the IRS examines it. In a notice of deficiency, the IRS asserts a deficiency in tax of $80,000. Due to the fact that the return was filed three months late, the notice of deficiency would include a deficiency associated with the late filing penalty of $12,000 (15% of $80,000). Being deficiencies, both the $80,000 tax and the $12,000 penalty would normally receive pre-assessment/pre-payment administrative review and Tax Court review. If Rochelle convinces the IRS or the Tax Court of the reasonableness of the late filing, not only will she not owe the $12,000 penalty attributable to the deficiency, but she is also entitled to a refund of the $3,500 she

---

[54] Except to the extent taxpayers are entitled to the Collection Due Process (CDP) procedures in sections 6320 and 6330, there is no *statutory right* to an administrative hearing or judicial review before the self-assessing variety of late filing or late payment penalties must be paid.

[55] In addition to the more traditional methods for presenting a "reasonable cause" defense, discussed in the text, one may (i) file an offer in compromise based on doubt as to liability, (ii) request a Collection Due Process hearing, or (iii) submit an Application for a Taxpayer Assistance Order.

[56] Interest runs on the penalty amount from the date the return was due until the date the IRS receives payment. IRC § 6601.

paid earlier for the late filing and payment penalties assessed on her 2004 return.

2. What to Include in the Presentation

The late filing and late payment penalties can be avoided only upon a showing that the lateness for the filing or payment was due to reasonable cause and not due to willful neglect. By requiring the penalty to be imposed "unless" the failure is due to reasonable cause, the statute precludes any partial waiver of the penalty. The IRS must either waive or impose the penalty in full. Despite this, the Appeals Office can settle a penalty for any amount if there are hazards to the government that would occur by litigating the issue.

A request for non-assertion or abatement should be accompanied by supporting documentary evidence and legal authority whenever possible. This might include death certificates, doctor's statements, insurance statements, police or fire reports, etc. The IRS may request additional information if it is needed to make a determination.

3. Burden of Proof and Burden of Production in Court Proceedings

If settlement with the IRS is not possible and the matter has to be tried, Section 7491(c) applies and creates a labyrinth with respect to which party has the various burdens.[57] Section 7491(c) provides:

> Notwithstanding any other provision of this title, the Secretary shall have the burden of production in any court proceeding with respect to the liability of any individual for any penalty, addition to tax, or additional amount imposed by this title.

If the taxpayer assigns error to the Commissioner's penalty determination in the petition, the challenge generally will succeed unless the Commissioner produces evidence that the penalty is appropriate. If the taxpayer does not challenge a penalty by assigning error to it (and is, therefore, deemed to concede the penalty), the Commissioner need not plead the penalty and has no obligation under section 7491(c) to produce evidence that the penalty is appropriate.[58]

Assuming the penalty determination is put in issue by the taxpayer, section 7491(c) requires the Commissioner to produce evidence that it is appropriate to impose the relevant penalty, addition to tax, or additional amount (collectively,

---

[57] See Wheeler v. Commissioner, 127 T.C. 200 (2006).

[58] Swain v. Commissioner, 118 T.C. 358 (2002) (a taxpayer who fails to assign error to a penalty is deemed under Rule 34(b)(4) to have conceded the penalty, notwithstanding that the Commissioner failed to produce evidence that the imposition of the penalty is appropriate).

penalty). However, the Commissioner is not required to introduce evidence regarding reasonable cause, substantial authority, or similar provisions. The conference report explains the respective obligations of the Commissioner and a taxpayer under section 7491(c) as follows:

> Further, the provision provides that, in any court proceeding, the Secretary must initially come forward with evidence that it is appropriate to apply a particular penalty to the taxpayer before the court can impose the penalty. This provision is not intended to require the Secretary to introduce evidence of elements such as reasonable cause or substantial authority. Rather, the Secretary must come forward initially with evidence regarding the appropriateness of applying a particular penalty to the taxpayer; if the taxpayer believes that, because of reasonable cause, substantial authority, or a similar provision, it is inappropriate to impose the penalty, it is the taxpayer's responsibility (and not the Secretary's obligation) to raise those issues.[59]

VII. CONCLUSION

The penalties discussed in this part of the chapter pertain when returns or taxes are not filed or paid in a manner prescribed by the Code. The penalties discussed in the next part of the chapter concern situations where the return contains errors in the treatment of the items constituting taxable income.

---

[59] H. Conf. Rpt. 105-599 at 241, 1998-3 C.B. at 995.

PROBLEM

Filing no extension, Dylan mailed his 2006 Form 1040 on 8/13/07 to the Ogden Service Center and it was received 8/16/07. (In 2007, assume April 15th was a Saturday). The tax return reflected the following:

Total tax liability		$50,000
Less: withholding	$26,000	
Less: estimated tax	17,000	43,000
Tax Due		$7,000

The tax due of $7,000 was paid on 9/20/07.

a. Will Dylan owe late filing and late payment penalties? Assume the IRS sends Dylan a bill for $1,785 for such penalties; what is the procedure to avoid the penalties?

b. On the assumption Dylan is liable for the section 6651(a) penalties, how much are they?

c. Is Dylan liable for the section 6654 estimated tax penalty?

d. If Dylan's 2005 tax return was as follows, would he be excused from the section 6654 penalty? How does Dylan's adjusted gross income affect your answer?

Total tax liability		$42,000
Less: withholding	$12,000	
Less: estimated tax	17,000	29,000
Tax Due and paid with return		$13,000

PART B:
ACCURACY-RELATED AND FRAUD PENALTIES

IRC:	§§ 6404(f), (g); 6662; 6663; 6664(a)–(c); 6665; 6751; 7491(c)
Regs.:	§§ 1.6662-1, -2, -3(a)–(c), -4 (all except (c), (g)), -7; 1.6664-1, -2 (all except (d)–(f)), -3, -4 (a), (b), (c), (h))
Rulings:	Rev. Proc. 2004-73, 2004-51 I.R.B. 999
Forms:	8275, 8275R

I. INTRODUCTION

Many taxpayers facing the prospect of proposed adjustments to taxable income must also confront the imposition of a group of penalties codified in sections 6662-6664 that are commonly known as the "accuracy-related penalties." The term "accuracy-related penalties" encompasses several separate and distinct penalties, including those imposed for reporting positions that were (i) negligent, (ii) not adequately disclosed and lacked substantial authority, (iii) substantially misvalued, or (iv) fraudulent.

Prior to 1989, the Code contained over 160 provisions that imposed penalties for various transgressions associated with return positions. Each of these could be applied independently of the others, with the result that a single "behavioral" misstep could produce duplication and "stacking" of penalties. In 1989, Congress passed the Improved Penalty Administration & Compliance Tax Act ("IMPACT"),[60] which overhauled the penalty regime. IMPACT addressed the problems by eliminating many of the penalties and consolidating others.

A. Procedures Regarding Assessment

The accuracy-related penalties are calculated as a percentage of the deficiency owed by the taxpayer. They are assessed and collected in the same manner as deficiencies in tax, meaning the taxpayer is entitled to certain procedural rights before they are assessed.[61] Specifically, a taxpayer can challenge the proposed penalties first by filing a protest with the Appeals Office and, if necessary, by filing a petition in the Tax Court.[62]

---

[60] Pub. L. No. 101-239, 103 Stat. 2106 (1989).

[61] IRC § 6665. These rights, generally known as "deficiency procedures," are discussed in Chapters 3, 6, and 8.

[62] Many times taxpayers and their advisors do not focus on the penalty during the examination phase, and even fail to address the issue at Appeals or in court. This is a mistake. If the IRS prevails on the deficiency, the taxpayer can still significantly reduce the liability by defeating the penalty asserted by the IRS. The taxpayer must be prepared to present evidence and the legal basis as to why the penalty should not apply.

B. IRS' Burden of Production Relative to the Penalty

In the past, when a section 6662 penalty was proposed against a taxpayer in the thirty-day letter or notice of deficiency, the Service usually provided an open-ended pro forma catch-all statement that did little to describe which inappropriate conduct was being penalized. Such generic statements left it to the taxpayer to determine what he or she did wrong. Thus, deciding what evidence to produce to refute the assertion of the penalty was difficult and costly.

But now, under section 7491(c), the IRS has the burden of production in any court proceeding[63] with respect to a taxpayer's liability for a penalty. The IRS must come forward with specific evidence supporting the application of a particular penalty to the taxpayer. If the IRS fails to meet its burden, the penalty is denied. If the IRS sustains its burden, the taxpayer has the burden to produce evidence to defend against the penalty, such as establishing substantial authority, reasonable reliance on a professional advisor, or the like.

II. CALCULATING THE PENALTY

The accuracy-related penalties in section 6662 are imposed at the rate of 20% of that portion of an underpayment of tax attributable to any of the following:

- Negligence or disregard of rules and regulations (section 6662(b)(1));

- Substantial understatement of income tax (section 6662(b)(2));

- Substantial valuation misstatement (section 6662(b)(3));

- Substantial overstatement of pension liabilities (section 6662(b)(4));

- Substantial estate or gift tax valuation understatement (section 6662(b)(5)).

The rate for section 6662(b)(3)–(5) penalties increases to 40% on any portion of an underpayment attributable to a "gross" valuation misstatement. A gross valuation misstatement is one that is twice as large as the misstatements that give rise to the 20% penalty.

The fraud penalty of section 6663 is equal to 75% of the portion of the underpayment which is attributable to fraud. If the government proves that any portion of an underpayment is attributable to fraud, section 6663(b) says the *entire* underpayment shall be treated as attributable to fraud, except with respect to any portion of the underpayment that the taxpayer establishes (by a preponderance of the evidence) is not attributable to fraud.

---

[63] The new statute, added by the 1998 Reform Act, does not affect the taxpayer's burden during administrative proceedings before the IRS. However, it is safe to assume that once the matter is before the Appeals Office, the Service's new burden of production will be considered a possible "hazard of litigation."

A. Stacking of Penalties

Prior to IMPACT, penalties were applied to the entire underpayment. Now, the accuracy-related penalties are applied only to that portion of the underpayment attributable to the particular type of behavioral transgression involved. Stacking is no longer permitted.[64] That is, only 20% (or 40% in the case of gross valuation misstatements) may be imposed against any portion of a tax underpayment, even if more than one of the section 6662 misconduct bases is present. For instance, a taxpayer may be subject to the negligence penalty and the valuation misstatement penalty with respect to overvalued art that was contributed to a charitable organization. However, only a single 20% penalty can be asserted on the portion of the underpayment attributable to this item.[65]

While stacking is prohibited, the Regulations establish a series of "ordering" rules in the event different elements of the section 6662 penalty apply to different portions of an underpayment.[66] Normally, the order is not significant since the 20% rate of the penalty is the same regardless of which penalty applies. However, where fraud (75%) or a gross valuation misstatement (40%) is asserted on some of the adjustments and the 20% accuracy-related penalty is asserted on others, the ordering rules are important.

The Regulations specify that, in determining the amount of tax on which the penalties are calculated, taxable income is increased first by adjustments on which no penalties are asserted, then by adjustments on which the 20% penalty is asserted, followed by the 40% and 75% penalties.[67] The effect of this is to calculate the more significant penalties at the highest marginal rates, thus increasing the cost of the penalties.

> **Example:** Sigmund's taxable income for 2005 as reflected on the filed return is $100,000 and the tax liability is $21,000. The Service examines the return and makes three adjustments to taxable income in the amounts of $20,000, $30,000 and $40,000, claiming a total understatement in tax of $27,000. The IRS asserts no penalty with respect to the $20,000 adjustment, a 20% negligence penalty on the $30,000 adjustment, and a 40% gross valuation penalty on the $40,000 adjustment.
>
> The ordering rules dictate that the $20,000 item be given effect first in determining what portion of the $27,000 understatement is free of misconduct. To do this, one would add $20,000 to the $100,000 on the

---

[64] Reg. § 1.6662-2(c).

[65] IRM 20.1.5.2.1. The prohibition against "stacking" of penalties does not preclude the Service from alleging penalties in the alternative. For example, the IRS can assert that the taxpayer was negligent or met the conditions for imposition of the substantial understatement penalty. This alternative allegation approach is quite common in statutory notices of deficiency where the Service wants to insure that every conceivable basis for the application of the penalty is raised.

[66] Reg. § 1.6664-3.

[67] Reg. § 1.6664-3(b).

return, calculate the tax on $120,000 and subtract the $21,000 tax previously paid. The result is the deficiency on the $20,000 adjustment. On these facts, no penalty would be charged against this portion of the understatement.

After that, one would add the $30,000 adjustment to the $120,000 amount, calculate the tax on the $150,000, subtract the tax from the previous step, and apply a 20% penalty to the difference.

Finally, one would add the $40,000 adjustment to $150,000 ($100,000 income on return plus the first two levels of adjustment), calculate the tax attributable to it, subtract the tax from the previous steps, and apply a 40% penalty to the difference.

In keeping with IMPACT's anti-stacking focus, the section 6662 penalty can only be applied to a filed return.[68] If no return is filed, other penalties, such as the failure to file penalty, may be applicable, but section 6662 and section 6663 do not impose additional layers of sanction.[69]

B. What is an Underpayment?

Since the section 6662 penalty can only be imposed on that portion of the tax underpayment attributable to the proscribed conduct, one must understand what constitutes an underpayment. Broadly speaking, section 6664 defines "underpayment" as the amount by which the tax imposed by the Code exceeds the tax shown on the original return.[70] Normally, an underpayment for section 6662 purposes is the same as the deficiency in tax. The definitions part company, however, where a qualified amended return was filed (see discussion next) or, with respect to the substantial understatement penalty, where the taxpayer either had substantial authority for the reporting position or disclosed the relevant facts affecting the item's tax treatment (see discussion in section III below). If either of these two situations applies, the amount of the underpayment will be less than the amount of the deficiency by the tax attributable thereto.

C. Impact of Filing a "Qualified Amended Return"

As stated, an amended return that meets the definition of a "qualified amended return" may limit one's exposure to accuracy-related penalties. This is so because the adjustments to taxable income shown on a qualified amended return are treated as if they were reflected correctly on the originally filed return.[71]

---

[68] Reg. § 1.6662-2(a).

[69] *Id.* A late filed return that also contains an understatement of tax, however, will be subject to both the late filing penalty and an accuracy-related penalty.

[70] IRC § 6664(a); Reg. § 1.6664-2(a).

In order for an amended return to be considered a qualified amended return, it must be "voluntary." This means that the amended return must be filed before the earliest of:

- The date the taxpayer is first contacted by the IRS concerning any examination (including a criminal investigation) with respect to the return;

- The date a promoter of an abusive tax shelter is first contacted by the IRS concerning an examination of that person for an activity with respect to which the taxpayer claimed any tax benefit on the return directly or indirectly through the entity, plan or arrangement;

- In the case of an investor in a pass-through item (such as a partnership or S corp.), the date the pass-through entity is first contacted by the IRS in connection with an examination of the return to which the pass-through item relates;

- The date on which the IRS serves a "John Doe" summons relating to the tax liability of a person, group, or class that includes the taxpayer with respect to an activity for which the taxpayer claimed any tax benefit on the return directly or indirectly; or

- The date on which the Commissioner announces, by revenue ruling, revenue procedure, notice, or announcement, a settlement initiative to compromise or waive penalties, in whole or in part, with respect to a listed transaction.[72]

An amended return satisfies the definition of a qualified amended return even if it is filed *solely* to make a disclosure to avoid the substantial understatement penalty. This might happen, for example, where the amended return does not report additional tax due but includes a Form 8275 disclosing an aggressive reporting position.[73]

III. THE NEGLIGENCE PENALTY

The section 6662(b)(1) penalty applies to any portion of an underpayment attributable to negligence or disregard of rules or regulations. It is useful to think of this section as having two separate components—negligence and the disregard of rules or regulations. As compared to the more mechanical bases for the other accuracy-related penalties, the negligence penalty is determined only after all the facts and circumstances are considered. In addition, although the IMPACT-created penalties are new, the negligence penalty has been part of the tax laws from time immemorial. As a result, there is a significant body of

---

[71] Reg. § 1.6664-2(c).

[73] Reg. § 1.6664-2(c)(3).

[73] Reg. §1.6664-4(f)(2).

case law one can consult to "put flesh on the bones" of what constitutes negligence.

A. Negligence

"Negligence" is a failure to make a reasonable attempt to comply with the tax laws.[74] It includes failure to exercise ordinary and reasonable care in the preparation of a tax return, as well as failure to keep adequate books and records or substantiate items properly.[75] Regulation section 1.6662-3(b)(1) gives several examples of what constitutes negligence.

With respect to return reporting positions, one is negligent if the position taken lacks a reasonable basis,[76] a standard of tax reporting significantly higher than "not frivolous" or merely arguable.[77] Regulation section 1.6662-3(b)(3) says that the *process* employed in evaluating whether a reporting position is reasonable is the same as that employed in deciding whether a reporting position has substantial authority for the section 6662(b)(2) penalty, even though the *standards* for determining exposure to each are different. The negligence regulations do not place a percentage on the level of confidence one must have in the reporting position for it to be deemed reasonable. However, practitioners generally place it at somewhere between a 15% and 20% chance of success on the merits if the position were litigated.[78]

As in other areas of the law, negligence is defined in the tax content as the failure to do what a reasonable and prudent person would do under the circumstances.[79] Indicators of negligence run the gamut. The Internal Revenue Manual instructs agents to consider the following when deciding whether to assert the negligence penalty:

- Have previous returns been filed timely?

- Have penalties been assessed in other years?

- Did the taxpayer fail to keep adequate and accurate books and records?

- Did the taxpayer fail to maintain adequate internal controls for processing and reporting business transactions?

---

[74] IRC § 6662(b)(1); IRM 20.1.5.7.

[75] Reg. § 1.6662-3(b)(1).

[76] Reg. § 1.6662-3(b)(1) (for tax returns due after December 31, 1993). Prior to this date, the return position merely had to be "not frivolous," a relatively low standard easily satisfied as long as the position was not "patently improper."

[77] Reg. § 1.6662-3(b)(3).

[78] Burgess W. Raby & William L. Raby, *Reasonable Basis vs. Other Tax Opinion Standards*, Tax Notes, Dec. 9, 1996, at 1209.

[79] *See, e.g.*, Neely v. Commissioner, 85 T.C. 934 (1985).

- Did the taxpayer fail to report all income accurately, and was he or she unable to offer a reasonable explanation for the error?

- Did the taxpayer overstate deductions or credits, including claiming clearly improper or exaggerated amounts, unsubstantiated by facts or documentation?

- Did the taxpayer use descriptions for deductions that were meant to conceal the true nature of the item in question?

- Did the taxpayer fail to explain items questioned by the Service?

- Did the taxpayer take actions to ensure that the return preparer did not have all the necessary and appropriate information to prepare a correct and/or timely return?[80]

A penalty is not appropriate if the law was unsettled or if a taxpayer, acting in good faith, made a mistake of law or fact. Reliance on a professional advisor can absolve the taxpayer of liability for the penalty.[81]

B. Disregard of Rules and Regulations

The disregard element of the section 6662(b) penalty base "includes any careless, reckless or intentional disregard of rules and regulations."[82] The rules and regulations to which one must adhere to avoid the penalty include the Code, temporary and final Regulations, revenue rulings, and notices issued by the Internal Revenue Service and published in the Internal Revenue Bulletin.[83]

"Careless" disregard occurs when a taxpayer fails to exercise reasonable diligence to determine the correctness of a return position that is contrary to a rule or regulation.[84] The disregard becomes "reckless" if the taxpayer makes little or no effort to ascertain whether a rule or regulation exists, under circumstances that are a substantial deviation from the conduct expected from a reasonable person.[85] An "intentional" disregard is one in which the taxpayer is aware of the rule or regulation being disregarded.[86]

---

[80] IRM 4.10.6.2.1.

[81] *See* Henry v. Commissioner, 170 F.3d 1217 (9th Cir. 1999) (taxpayer had no obligation to independently verify his tax liability after advice given by accountant); Chamberlin v. Commissioner, 66 F.3d 729 (5th Cir. 1995); Sim-Air, USA, Ltd v. Commissioner, 98 T.C. 187 (1992).

[82] IRC § 6662(c); Reg. § 1.6662-3(b)(2).

[83] See IRC sections 6034A(c)(5), 6037(c)(5), and 6222(d) for situations where inconsistent reporting of information provided the taxpayer on Forms K-1 would likely be considered "disregard."

[84] Reg. § 1.6662-3(b)(2).

[85] *Id.*

[86] *Id.*

Imposing the penalty for disregard of the rules and regulations is inappropriate even if the taxpayer's position is contrary to a revenue ruling or an IRS notice, if the taxpayer's position has a "realistic possibility of being sustained on its merits."[87] The "realistic possibility" standard is also found under section 6694, and is interpreted to require a showing that there is a better than one-in-three chance of prevailing on the merits of the position.[88]

C. Impact of Disclosure on the Section 6662 Negligence or Disregard of the Rules and Regulations Penalty

While Regulation section 1.6662-3(c)(1) states: "[n]o penalty under section 6662(b)(1) may be imposed on any portion of an underpayment that is attributable to a position contrary to a rule or regulation if the position is disclosed . . . and, in case of a position contrary to a regulation, the position represents a good faith challenge to the validity of the regulation," the scope of this exception is narrowed in Regulation section 1.6662-7. Only the penalty for disregarding rules or regulations, but not the penalty for negligence, may be avoided by adequate disclosure of a return position and then only so long as the position has at least a reasonable basis. The exception was designed to make it possible for taxpayers to challenge rules and regulations without incurring a penalty. Disclosure gives the IRS notice of, and an opportunity to respond to, the challenge. As a general rule, disclosure for these purposes must be made on Form 8275 (or Form 8275-R for positions inconsistent with a Regulation), which should be attached to the taxpayer's return or qualified amended return.[89]

IV. THE SUBSTANTIAL UNDERSTATEMENT PENALTY

Congress added the substantial understatement penalty to discourage taxpayers from attempting to take advantage of the low audit rate by taking aggressive tax return positions unsupported by significant authority. The penalty applies when the IRS asserts a "substantial understatement" of income tax in situations where the taxpayer did not have substantial authority for a tax return position and failed to disclose the relevant facts affecting the item's tax treatment.

---

[87] Reg. § 1.6662-3(b)(2).

[88] Reg. § 1.6694-2(b)(1).

[89] Reg. § 1.6662-3(c)(2). From a practical perspective, if one is contemplating taking a position contrary to a revenue ruling or notice, one must weigh whether disclosure is the best way to avoid the penalty. One can avoid the penalty either by disclosing the position or meeting the reasonable basis standard. Accordingly, disclosure makes sense only if the merits of the position do not meet the reasonable basis standard.

The provisions of Regulation section 1.6662-4(f)(2), which permit disclosure in accordance with an annual revenue procedure for purposes of the substantial understatement penalty, do not apply for purposes of this section. See the text accompanying Section III.

Compared with the facts and circumstances analysis associated with the negligence and fraud penalties, this penalty is more mechanically determined. The only issues that require analysis are whether the taxpayer consulted the appropriate authority, what weight should have been placed on the supporting and opposing authorities, and whether there was adequate disclosure of positions that lacked substantial authority.

The following is a brief overview of the substantial understatement penalty with emphasis on several aspects that are not apparent from the language of the Code and the Regulations. Regulation section 1.6662-4 is particularly helpful in explaining the law and its application. Consequently, the assigned statutory provisions, Regulations, and revenue procedure should be carefully studied.

An understatement is defined as the excess of the amount of tax required to be shown on the return for a taxable year over the amount of tax shown on the return.[90] An understatement is substantial if it exceeds the greater of 10% of the tax required to be shown, or $5,000.[91] The penalty applies to any tax imposed by Subtitle A, i.e., income, self-employment, and withholding tax on nonresident aliens and foreign corporations.

> **Example:** Johnny Rose files his 2005 income tax return showing taxable income of $50,000 and a corresponding tax liability of $8,000. A subsequent IRS examination determines that Johnny's taxable income is $70,000 with a corresponding tax liability of $14,000. There is no substantial authority for Johnny's tax reporting positions and no qualifying disclosures, so the entire $6,000 increase in tax liability is treated as an understatement. Because the $6,000 understatement exceeds the greater of (i) 10% of the tax required to be shown on the return (i.e., 10% of $14,000, or $1,400) or (ii) $5,000, the understatement is considered substantial. Accordingly, assuming the good faith/reasonable cause exception of section 6664 does not apply, an accuracy-related penalty equal to 20% penalty of the $6,000 understatement ($1,200) will apply.

In order to encourage taxpayers to take responsible reporting positions or to disclose those positions that were more aggressive, Congress provided that an understatement is reduced to the extent (i) there is substantial authority for the taxpayer's treatment of a questionable item[92] or (ii) the relevant facts affecting

---

[90] IRC § 6662(d)(2)(A). This is reduced by any rebates.

[91] IRC § 6662(d)(1)(A); Reg. § 1.6662-4(b). In the case of a corporation other than an S corporation or a personal holding company (as defined in section 542), there is a substantial understatement of income tax for any taxable year if the amount of the understatement for the taxable year exceeds the lesser of 10% of the tax required to be shown on the return for the taxable year (or, if greater, $10,000), or $10,000,000. IRC § 6662(d)(1)(B).

[92] Reg. § 1.6662-4(b)(4). The taxpayer must have substantial authority at the end of the tax year or when the return is filed.

the item's tax treatment are sufficiently disclosed on the return.[93] In essence, if there is appropriate authority for a position or there is adequate disclosure, the item is treated as if it were initially reported on the income tax return properly.

> **Example:** Assume all the facts in the previous example except that on the 2005 return, Johnny adequately disclosed the facts giving rise to $11,000 of the adjustment to income and has a reasonable basis for his position. The tax on the disclosed item is removed from the understatement for purposes of the penalty. The tax on the $9,000 remaining portion of the understatement would be less than $5,000. Therefore, Johnny's understatement for the year is not "substantial" and the substantial understatement penalty is avoided.

"Substantial authority" for a reporting position is met only after reviewing many types of authority, such as the Code, Regulations, IRS pronouncements, decisions of the courts, and legislative history, and objectively concluding that the weight of authorities in support of the treatment is substantial in relation to those supporting a contrary position. The weight of authority in favor of a position is likely substantial if there is at least a one in three chance of succeeding on the merits if the case were litigated.[94] If the reporting position is attributable to a tax-shelter item,[95] the understatement is reduced for substantial authority only if the taxpayer reasonably believed that the tax treatment of the items was more-likely-than-not the proper tax treatment.

As in the case of disclosure with respect to the disregard penalty, for purposes of the substantial understatement penalty, disclosure is accomplished either by attaching a disclosure statement (Form 8275 or Form 8275-R) to the tax return or qualified amended tax return[96] or by complying with the dictates of annual revenue procedures issued by the Service for this purpose.[97] If the reporting

---

[93] For tax returns due after December 31, 1993, disclosure does not reduce the understatement unless the item or position on the return has a reasonable basis and is properly substantiated, or the taxpayer has kept adequate books and records with respect to the item or position. Reg. § 1.6662-4(e)(2).

[94] While the accuracy-related penalty regulations do not quantify what is meant by "substantial," Regulation section 1.6694-2(b)(1) quantifies the perhaps similar term "realistic possibility" (the standard required of a practitioner to sign a tax return as a preparer) as a position that has approximately a one in three, or greater, likelihood of being sustained on its merits.

[95] See IRC section 6662(d)(2)(C)(ii) for a definition of a tax shelter item.

[96] Courts have also held that a disclosure statement is adequate if it reasonably apprises the Service of the nature and amount of the potential controversy. *See* Schirmer v. Commissioner, 89 T.C. 277, 285–86 (1977); Dibsy v. Commissioner, T.C. Memo. 1995-477. If the disclosure statement fails to include all of the above, misrepresents the facts, or is too general to reasonably apprise the Service of the potential controversy, the disclosure exception does not apply. *See also* IRM 20.1.5.8.4.2.

[97] Reg. § 1.6662-4(f)(2); Rev. Proc. 2006-48, 2006-47 I.R.B. 934 (for 2006 returns). By and large, the revenue procedure does not require the taxpayer to do anything more than complete the designated schedules as fully as one would expect to do anyway and attach whatever documentation might be required by the instructions for the schedule.

position is attributable to a tax shelter item, disclosure has no effect on the amount of the understatement.[98]

V. SUBSTANTIAL VALUATION MISSTATEMENTS

The substantial valuation misstatement component of the accuracy-related penalty applies if the value of property (or its adjusted basis) is substantially in error.[99] It applies to overvaluations, in the case of income tax (section 6662(e)),[100] or undervaluations, in the case of estate or gift taxes (section 6662(g)).[101]

A. Substantial Income Tax Overvaluations

There is a substantial valuation misstatement for income tax purposes if the value or adjusted basis of property on a return is 200% or more of the correct value or adjusted basis.[102] The penalty amount on substantial valuation misstatements is 20% of the underpayment attributable to the substantial valuation misstatement. Under section 6662(h), a special 40% penalty applies to gross valuation misstatements, i.e., where the value or basis of any property claimed on an income tax return is 400% or more of the correct amount.[103]

With the exception of the possible application of the section 6664 reasonable cause exception, the application of this penalty is purely mechanical. If an underpayment is attributable to a valuation misstatement of 200% or more and if it exceeds the threshold amount of $5,000 for individuals and $10,000 for corporations (other than S corporations or personal service corporations), the penalty applies.

> **Example (1):** Ms. Philanthropic donated a painting to the local art museum. She took a deduction of $46,000, which she believed was the painting's fair market value based on a qualified appraisal she obtained.[104] The IRS examined her return and valued the painting at

---

[98] Reg. § 1.6662-4(g)(1)(iii).

[99] It may also apply with respect to a section 482 transaction. However, the discussion will only consider value and basis issues outside the section 482 context. *See* Reg. § 1.6662-6.

[100] Reg. § 1.6662-5.

[101] If one of the valuation misstatement penalties applies to the taxpayer, the person who prepared the appraisal may be subject to a penalty under section 6695A.

[102] IRC § 6662(e)(1).

[103] Regardless of the amount of overvaluation, if the property's correct value or basis is determined to be zero, the 40% gross valuation penalty will apply. Reg. § 1.6662-5(g).

[104] A taxpayer will not be considered to have reasonably relied in good faith on advice unless the requirements of Regulation section 1.6664-4(b) and (c) are met. This may require more than merely obtaining a qualified appraisal. In addition, when charitable deduction property is involved, the taxpayer must meet the requirements in Regulation section 1.6664-4(h).

$20,000. Ms. Philanthropic's underpayment resulting from the $26,000 valuation adjustment is $7,000. Since the reported valuation is 230% of the final valuation, the 200% threshold is satisfied. In addition, since the underpayment of $7,000 attributable to the misstatement of $26,000 exceeds $5,000, the dollar limitation is met. Thus, the IRS will assert the 20% penalty and Ms. Philanthropic will have to establish that she qualifies for relief under section 6664(c).

Example (2): If the final adjusted value in example (1) above were $10,000, the amount reported of $46,000 would then exceed the final adjusted amount ($10,000) by more than 400% ($46,000 divided by $10,000 = 460%). The 40% gross valuation misstatement penalty would apply to the applicable underpayment.

The Regulations provide important rules to implement the provision and should be consulted by the student. For example, the determination as to whether there is a valuation misstatement is done on a property-by-property basis.[105] Also, Regulation section 1.6662-5(a) does not allow a taxpayer to avoid this penalty by disclosing that the valuation might be too high. And finally, with respect to pass-through entities, the determination of whether there is a substantial or gross valuation misstatement is made at the entity level, while the dollar limitation ($5,000 or $10,000, as the case may be) is calculated at the investor level.

B. Substantial Estate and Gift Tax Undervaluations

The accuracy-related penalty also applies to substantial estate or gift tax valuation understatements. If the property's value claimed on the estate or gift tax return is 50% or less of the correct value, there is a substantial understatement. The 20% penalty applies to the underpayment attributable to the substantial understatement, although no penalty applies if the underpayment attributable to the substantial understatement is $5,000 or less.

Under section 6662(h), the penalty increases to 40% if the property's value is grossly understated, i.e., the value claimed on the return is 25% or less of the property's correct value. As with the valuation misstatement penalty, disclosure on the return does not avoid this penalty.

VI. THE FRAUD PENALTY

Section 6663(a) states, "[i]f any part of any underpayment of tax required to be shown on a return is due to fraud, there shall be added to the tax an amount equal to 75 percent of the portion of the underpayment which is attributable to fraud." As compared to the other accuracy-related penalties where the burden

---

[105] Reg. § 1.6662-5(f)(1).

is by a preponderance of the evidence and the government merely has the burden of production in court proceedings, the entire burden of proof with respect to fraud is on the government[106] by the "clear and convincing" standard.[107] If the government proves that any portion of an underpayment is attributable to fraud, section 6663(b) says that the *entire* underpayment shall be treated as attributable to fraud, except with respect to any portion of the underpayment which the taxpayer establishes, by a preponderance of the evidence, is not attributable to fraud.

Tax fraud is often defined as an intentional wrongdoing on the part of a taxpayer with the specific purpose of evading a tax known or believed to be owing.[108] Evasion involves some affirmative act to evade or defeat a tax, or payment of tax. A good list of examples of affirmative acts is found in the Internal Revenue Manual, where agents are instructed to look for "badges of fraud."[109] These badges of fraud include, but are not limited to:

- Understatement of income, e.g., by omissions of specific items or entire sources of income, failure to report substantial amounts of income received;

- Fictitious or improper deductions, e.g., overstatement of deductions, personal items deducted as business expenses;

- Accounting irregularities, e.g., two sets of books, false entries on documents;

- Acts of the taxpayer evidencing an intention to evade tax, e.g., false statements, destruction of records, transfer of assets;

- A consistent pattern over several years of underreporting taxable income;

- Implausible or inconsistent explanations of behavior;

- Failure to cooperate with the examining agent;

- Concealment of assets;

- Engaging in illegal activities (e.g., drug dealing) or attempting to conceal illegal activities;

- Inadequate records; and

- Dealing in cash.

---

[106] IRC § 7454.

[107] Tax Ct. R. 142(b). The government may be able to meet its burden utilizing res judicata and collateral estoppel. See Chapter 5 for a detailed discussion of this.

[108] Tax evasion is to be contrasted with tax avoidance. The former is illegal; the latter is not. Taxpayers have the right to reduce, avoid, or minimize their taxes by legitimate means. One who avoids tax does not conceal or misrepresent, but shapes and preplans events to reduce or eliminate tax liability within the perimeters of the law.

[109] IRM 20.1.5.12.1.

Where one intentionally understates income or overstates deductions with the intent to evade tax, that person is potentially liable for both criminal and civil tax penalties. The elements constituting fraud are substantially the same for both civil and criminal purposes. Civil fraud penalties are in addition to any criminal fine imposed under section 7201 et seq.[110] It is difficult to state with specificity what makes an underreporting or a non-filing subject to criminal sanction rather than merely to civil penalty. One factor is whether the IRS can meet its burden of proving willfulness beyond a reasonable doubt.[111] Other factors include whether prosecution of the target has sufficient publicity value to justify expanding on a criminal investigation and prosecution the limited resources of the IRS and the Department of Justice and whether there are mitigating circumstances that diminish the case's jury appeal, such as the target's extreme ill health.

In order to prove its case that the taxpayer fraudulently attempted to evade taxes, the government utilizes either the direct (or specific items) method of proof or one of several indirect methods. When direct proof does not exist to reconstruct a taxpayer's financial transactions, indirect methods of proof,[112] such as the expenditures method or the bank deposits method, are used. The government tends to use indirect methods when the defendant deals in cash and has not maintained adequate records from which to reconstruct income. The indirect methods rely primarily on circumstantial evidence. It is common for the government to use more than one method in proving its case.

A. Statute of Limitations and Fraud

The statute of limitations for assessing a deficiency in tax and associated penalties is generally three years from the due date of the return or its filing date, whichever is later. Where civil fraud is established, the statute of limitations on assessment is unlimited. By contrast, under section 6531(a), a criminal indictment or information for fraud must occur within six years of the commission of the offense, usually the due date of the return.

---

[110] Schachter v. Commissioner, 113 T.C. 192 (1999). Applying both civil and criminal penalties is not a violation of the Double Jeopardy Clause of the Constitution. Helvering v. Mitchell, 303 U.S. 391, 299 (1938); Grimes v. Commissioner, 82 F.3d 286 (9th Cir. 1997).

[111] This typically requires proof that the person knew of the duty to file, understood it, and yet affirmatively chose to underreport or to not file.

[112] See, e.g., Holland v. United States, 348 U.S. 121 (1954) (net worth analysis); United States v. Johnson, 319 U.S. 503 (1943) (expenditures method); United States v. Soulard, 730 F.2d 1292 (9th Cir. 1984) (bank deposits method). A discussion of these methods is beyond the scope of this book. Good explanations and examples can be found at IRM 9.5.9.

When the government decides to pursue a criminal investigation, it usually suspends all action on the civil case.[113] The principal reason for doing so is a concern that the taxpayer might utilize the rules of discovery in the civil case to discover evidence involved in the criminal investigation. Other reasons include fear that the IRS and the Department of Justice might take inconsistent positions in the parallel cases and the desire to avoid placing excessive demands on the witnesses. However, especially in many recent tax shelter investigations, the government has been proceeding civilly and criminally simultaneously.

Because criminal cases can take years to work their way to resolution, the normal three-year civil statute of limitations on assessment usually will have expired by the time the civil case is resuscitated. If the government cannot prove fraud or a greater than 25% omission of gross income,[114] the taxpayer escapes liability. However, if the IRS successfully proves that the return was prepared fraudulently, not only has the government met its burden for purposes of the fraud penalty but it has also satisfied the conditions necessary to extend the statute of limitations on assessment.

B. Res Judicata and Collateral Estoppel

Rather than being put to the task of proving fraud in the civil phase of the controversy, the government may be able to take advantage of the collateral estoppel doctrine to prove its case. If the government earned a conviction under section 7201 for evasion, the collateral estoppel doctrine spares it the burden of proving fraud a second time for assessment purposes in the civil case. This is because the government must prove guilt beyond a reasonable doubt to gain a criminal conviction while in a civil tax fraud case, the government is only required to prove fraud by clear and convincing evidence.

On the other hand, if the government was not successful in the criminal evasion case or if the taxpayer was convicted of some other offense, such as section 7206(1) perjury, collateral estoppel does not apply and the IRS is obligated to prove fraud in the civil case to get an extended civil statute of limitations and to carry the section 6663 penalty.[115]

---

[113] *See* Taylor v. Commissioner, 113 T.C. 206 (1999) (the decision to suspend the civil examination is not a purely "ministerial act" and a taxpayer is not entitled to suspension of interest under IRC section 6404(e)); IRM 9.5.13.2; ILM 200250001 (CDP hearing postponed while criminal investigation is pending).

[114] IRC § 6501(e).

[115] *See* Wright v. Commissioner, 84 T.C. 636 (1985); DelVecchio v. Commissioner, T.C. Memo. 2001-130. An extended discussion of the topic is in Chapter 5.

VII. THE REASONABLE CAUSE EXCEPTION

Section 6664 provides that the accuracy-related penalty does not apply to any portion of an underpayment if it is established that there was reasonable cause for the position and the taxpayer acted in good faith.[116] Regulation section 1.6664-4(b)(1) provides that this determination is made on a case-by-case basis, taking into account all facts and circumstances. The Regulations state that the "most important factor is the extent of the taxpayer's effort to assess the taxpayer's proper tax liability."[117]

Reasonable cause relief is generally granted when the taxpayer exercises ordinary business care and prudence in determining his or her tax obligations. "[E]xperience, knowledge and education of the taxpayer" are factors to be considered in determining if an honest misunderstanding of fact or law constitutes reasonable cause and good faith.[118] An isolated computational or transcriptional error generally is consistent with reasonable cause and good faith.

A. Reliance on Advice of Tax Professionals

A taxpayer's good faith and reasonable reliance on a professional tax advisor will normally insulate the taxpayer from the imposition of the accuracy-related penalties where the advisor was provided with all the information needed to render a well-informed opinion.[119] In addition, the taxpayer must prove that he or she actually relied on professional advice,[120] and that the reliance was both reasonable and in good faith.[121] The sophistication or expertise of the taxpayer is relevant in determining whether a taxpayer's reliance is in good faith or reasonable.[122] Reliance may not be reasonable or in good faith if the taxpayer

---

[116] Reg. § 1.6664-4(a). See IRM 20.1.5.6.

[117] See Regulation section 1.6664-4(f) for special rules applicable to corporate tax shelter items.

[118] Reg. § 1.6664-4(b)(1).

[119] *See* United States v. Boyle, 469 U.S. 241, 246 (1985) ("When an accountant or attorney advises a taxpayer on a matter of tax law, such as whether a liability exists, it is reasonable for the taxpayer to rely on that advice."); Reser v. Commissioner, 112 F.3d 1258 (5th Cir. 1997); Reg. § 1.6664-4(b), (c). In *Henry v. Commissioner*, 34 Fed. Appx. 342 (9th Cir. 2002), the Ninth Circuit not only held that the IRS' assertion of a negligence penalty when the taxpayer relied on the advice of counsel was wrong, but also found it was not substantially justified and awarded attorney's fees and costs. (Note: Since the Ninth Circuit did not select *Henry* for publication, one should check the applicable court rules to determine whether such unpublished cases can be cited.)

[120] Regulation section 1.6664-4(c)(2) identifies "advice" as any communication setting forth the analysis or conclusion of a person (including a professional tax advisor), other than the taxpayer, provided to or for the benefit of the taxpayer and on which the taxpayer relies, directly or indirectly, with respect to the imposition of the IRC section 6662 penalty.

[121] *See* DeCleene v. Commissioner, 115 T.C. 457 (2000) (taxpayer's reliance on counsel with respect to a complex IRC section 1031 exchange was justified).

[122] *See* Cramer v. Commissioner, 64 F.3d 1406 (9th Cir. 1995) (accuracy-related penalties upheld on sophisticated taxpayers); Heasley v. Commissioner, 902 F.2d 380, 383 (5th Cir. 1990) (unsophisticated moderate-income taxpayers held to a more forgiving standard).

knew, or reasonably should have known, that the advisor lacked knowledge in the relevant aspects of tax law.[123]

Appraisals may provide insulation from the accuracy-related penalties as to a valuation error. To test the taxpayer's supposedly good faith and reasonable reliance on the appraisal, the IRS and the courts consider factors such as the appraisal's underlying assumptions, the appraiser's relation to the taxpayer or to the activity in which the property is used, and the circumstances under which the taxpayer obtained the appraisal.

B. Special Rules Apply to Charitable Deductions

Special reasonable cause/good faith rules apply to valuation misstatements attributable to charitable deduction property.[124] These rules provide generally that a taxpayer may demonstrate reasonable cause and good faith only if the taxpayer obtains a "qualified appraisal" from a specially defined qualified appraiser, and if the taxpayer made a good faith investigation of the value of the contributed property. A qualified appraisal must be made not earlier than sixty days before the date of contribution and not later than due date of the return (or the filing date of an amended return) on which the donation is first claimed.[125] The appraisal must contain specific information and the appraisal fee cannot be based on a percentage of the appraised value.[126]

VIII. CONCLUSION

Taxpayers must treat the imposition of the accuracy-related penalties as a separate issue from the underlying adjustments. From the earliest stage of a tax controversy, they must consider evidence and arguments with respect to the penalties, even if they believe they have a strong position on the underlying tax adjustment. It is a mistake to ignore these penalties, as the amounts at stake can be substantial, and interest runs on the accuracy-related penalties from the due date of the original return. An understanding of how the accuracy-related penalty and the fraud penalty operate, and the available defenses to the penalties, is essential. While the IRS is saddled with the burden of production with respect to penalties, a taxpayer must always be prepared to show why a penalty is inappropriate for the specific behavior attributable to him or her.

---

[123] The Regulations provide fairly detailed minimum requirements, which must be satisfied in order to justify a finding that the taxpayer's reliance on the advice of a professional was in good faith or reasonable. Reg. § 1.6664-3.

[124] Reg. § 1.6664-4(h)(1).

[125] IRC § 6664(c)(3)(C); Reg. § 1.170A-13(c)(5).

[126] Reg. § 1.170A-13(c)(3).

PROBLEM

Pablo Gonzales, a traveling salesman, came to you with respect to a notice of deficiency he just received. Your review of the notice shows the following adjustments and penalties are being asserted by the government:

Business expenses disallowed for lack of substantiation	$15,000 (1)
Travel to Florida disallowed as a personal expense	10,000 (2)
Unreported income	25,000 (3)
Gain recognized on exchange of property	100,000 (4)
Charitable contribution disallowed	30,000 (5)
Total adjustments	180,000
Taxable income as reported	100,000
Corrected taxable income	280,000
Corrected tax	100,000
Tax per return	25,000
Deficiency in tax	75,000

(1) Adjustment subject to penalty under section 6662(b)(1).

(2) Adjustment subject to penalty under section 6662(b)(1).

(3) Adjustment subject to penalty under section 6663.

(4) Adjustment subject to penalty under section 6662(b)(2).

(5) Adjustment subject to penalty under section 6662(b)(3).

Your discussions with Pablo and research of the law indicate the following:

- Pablo did not keep all the substantiating documentation required by section 274(d). He estimated their total to be $15,000. He tells you that similarly unsubstantiated expenses were the subject of an IRS exam three years ago, and he was able to satisfy the examiner as to 75% of the items.

- Pablo incurred expenditures of $10,000 in travel to Miami Beach where he owns a condo that is rented out all but the six weeks a year he vacations there. He deducted the $10,000 per section 212. Your research indicates that the only support for this position are a couple of District Court cases and that the great weight of authority is otherwise. If forced to quantify, you would say that there is a 10-15% chance of succeeding on the merits if the matter is litigated.

- Pablo says he received $25,000 from doing odd jobs as a carpenter. Since he did not receive 1099 forms, he truly did not think he had to report the income. He tells you he's done this for several years.

- Pablo engaged in a very complicated like-kind exchange involving five parties. The replacement property was identified thirty days after the transaction and the deed was executed on the 180th day but not delivered and filed until the 182nd day. Section 1031(b)(3) is unclear as to the proper treatment of this transaction. You have researched the Code, proposed and temporary Regulations, revenue rulings and procedures, other IRS pronouncements, and decisions in litigated cases. There are authorities that deal with issues tangentially related to the one involved in Pablo's case that support the reporting position taken. Some are old, but there is a fairly recent decision from the circuit court of appeals to which Pablo has a right of appeal that is also supportive, though it too does not deal with the exact situation that Pablo experienced. While helpful, they do not give you an absolute answer to what should have been done on the return. Besides, there is some recent authority in other circuits that appears to be more directly related to the issues in Pablo's case and that are not supportive of his reporting position. On the whole, your research indicates that the way it was reported on the return has a 25-40% chance of being sustained.

- Pablo contributed a painting by his neighbor to the local art museum. He bought the painting a year earlier for $10,000, and though his neighbor has not become any better known, took a deduction for $40,000. He obtained an appraisal in that amount from a qualified art appraiser and attached it to the return. He tells you he was surprised the valuation was greater than $15,000.

Questions:

1. What could you argue on Pablo's behalf either as a defense to each asserted penalty, or as a means of reducing its size?

2. Had Pablo come to you earlier, what would you have recommended as precautions against the assertion of the penalties?

3. How might the IRS prove its case that Pablo fraudulently omitted the $25,000 in carpentry income? What types of additional facts and circumstances might be relevant to ascertaining whether fraud existed? Consider the interplay of proving fraud for penalty and statute of limitations purposes.

4. How would your answer to question 1 above differ had the adjustments been the result of a tax shelter in which Pablo invested?

Chapter 12
INTEREST

IRC:	§§ 172(a), (b)(1)(A); 1274(d)(1)(C)(i); 6072(a), (b); 6151(a), (c); 6211(a); 6213(a), (b)(4), (d); 6215(a); 6404(a), (b), (c), (e), (f), (g), (h); 6407; 6601(a), (b)(1)–(3), (c), (d)(1), (e)(1)–(3); 6603; 6611(a), (b), (d), (e), (f)(1), (4)(A), (g); 6621(a), (b)(1), (b)(2)(A), (b)(3), (c)(1); 6622; 6631; 6651(a)(1); 6662 (skim); 7481(c)(1); 7502; 7503; 7508(a) (skim); 7508A (skim)
Rulings:	Rev. Rul. 2004-56; Rev. Proc. 2005-18; Rev. Rul. 88-97
Forms:	Skim 843; 870

I. INTRODUCTION

Generally, a taxpayer who pays all or part of his tax liability after the last date prescribed for payment is required to pay interest on the amount of the underpayment from the last date to the date it is paid.[1] Similarly, a taxpayer who pays more than his tax liability is entitled to receive interest on the amount of the overpayment from the date of the overpayment to a date "preceding the date of the refund check by not more than 30 days. . . ."[2] Determining the amount of the underpayment or overpayment, the beginning and ending dates of the period for which interest is paid, and the applicable interest rate is relatively straightforward. A degree of complexity is introduced by provisions designed:

    (a)   to ease administration of the interest requirements, such as stopping the accrual of interest on refunds for a period up to thirty days prior to the issuance of a refund check;

    (b)   to accommodate items affecting income tax liabilities that have a multi-year impact, such as loss carrybacks;[3]

    (c)   to encourage certain conduct by taxpayers, such as prohibiting interest on refunds until the return is in "processible form";[4]

---

[1] IRC § 6601(a). A notable exception is contained in section 6205 which, under specified circumstances, permits interest-free correction of underpayments of certain employment taxes.

[2] IRC § 6611(b)(2).

[3] IRC § 6611(f).

[4] IRC § 6611(g).

(d) to encourage certain conduct by the IRS, such as suspending interest on underpayments if the IRS fails to send a notice and demand for payment within thirty days after the taxpayer files, under section 6213(d), a waiver of restrictions on assessment;[5] and

(e) to reduce or increase the otherwise applicable interest rate on certain taxpayers, such as the favorable 2% rate imposed on certain estates which, under the provisions of section 6166, defer paying estate tax with respect to interests in closely held businesses.[6]

The basic rules and the complicating modifications to those rules are discussed below, first with respect to underpayments and then with respect to overpayments. Finally, the scope of the Tax Court's jurisdiction to determine the interest due with respect to underpayments and overpayments over which the Tax Court has jurisdiction is discussed.[7]

II. INTEREST ON UNDERPAYMENTS

A. The Basic Rules

Interest must be paid on the amount of any tax (other than estimated tax payable under sections 6654 and 6655) not paid before the last date prescribed for payment, from the last date to the date payment is received by the IRS.[8] With respect to any tax for which a return is required, the tax is to be paid on or before the due date of the return, determined without regard to extensions.[9] Income tax returns of individuals are due on the fifteenth day of the fourth month (typically April 15) following the close of the taxable year.[10] Income tax returns of corporations are due on the fifteenth day of the third month (typically March 15) following the close of the taxable year.[11] Interest accrues from those

---

[5] IRC § 6601(c).

[6] IRC § 6601(j).

[7] Software is available for the computation of deficiency and overpayment interest. See, for instance, the website of Decision Modeling, Inc., www.dmitax.com.

[8] Reg. § 301.6601-1. The additions to tax set forth in sections 6654 and 6655 for failure to pay estimated tax in a timely manner are, in effect, interest and are therefore excluded from the normal interest rules. IRC § 6601(h). Interest is also not payable with respect to underpayments of federal unemployment tax for a calendar quarter (or other period) required to be paid under section 6157. IRC § 6601(i). Also, in the case of jeopardy assessments under Chapter 70 (sections 6851-6873), if a notice and demand is made before the last date prescribed for payment, then no interest accrues between the date of the notice and demand and the last date prescribed for payment. IRC § 6601(b)(3); Reg. § 301.6601-1(c)(3).

[9] IRC § 6151(a).

[10] IRC § 6072(a). These and related rules are discussed in Chapter 2.

[11] IRC § 6072(b).

original return due dates whether or not the taxpayer has obtained an extension of time to file the return[12] or to pay the tax.[13]

The interest rate on underpayments (as well as on overpayments for taxpayers other than corporations) is now 3% over the federal short-term rate.[14] The federal short-term rate is determined for the first month in each calendar quarter and applies during the next calendar quarter.[15] The federal short-term rate, in turn, is defined as "the average market yield (during any 1-month period selected by the Secretary and ending in the calendar month in which the determination is made) on outstanding marketable obligations of the United States with remaining periods to maturity of three years or less."[16] Interest is compounded daily.[17] Interest on tax underpayments paid by noncorporate taxpayers is not deductible; however, interest on tax underpayments paid by corporations is deductible.

"C" corporations that experience a "large corporate underpayment" are entitled to the 3% over the federal short-term rate interest rate but only up to the thirtieth day after the earlier of: (i) the date of the first letter of proposed deficiency with respect to which the corporation can obtain administrative review; or (ii) the date a notice of deficiency is sent.[18] After that date, the rate on large corporate underpayments increases from the federal short-term rate plus 3% to the federal short-term rate plus 5%. A large corporate underpayment is any underpayment that exceeds $100,000.[19]

A separate, favorable, rate of interest is imposed on qualifying estates that elect, under the provisions of section 6166, to pay the estate tax attributable to interests in closely held businesses in from two up to ten annual installments. The first installment can be deferred up to five years from the original due date of the tax. In the case of any such election, interest is 2% for the "2% portion" of the deferred estate tax and 45% of the normal section 6601(a) rate (currently the federal short-term rate plus 3%) for the excess over the 2% portion.[20]

---

[12] IRC §§ 6081, 6601(b)(1).

[13] IRC §§ 6161, 6601(b)(1).

[14] IRC § 6621(a). From 1987 to 1998, the underpayment rate for individuals was one percentage point higher for underpayments than for overpayments.

[15] IRC § 6621(b).

[16] IRC §§ 1274(d)(1)(c)(i), 6621(b)(3).

[17] IRC § 6622. However, interest is not compounded daily with respect to the estimated tax penalties under sections 6654 and 6655. IRC § 6622(b).

[18] IRC § 6621(c).

[19] IRC § 6621(c)(3)(A).

[20] IRC § 6601(j). The 2% portion is the lesser of (i) the tentative tax on the sum of $1,140,000 (for 2004, which amount is annually adjusted for inflation) plus the section 2010(c) applicable exclusion amount reduced by the applicable credit amount under section 2010(c), or (ii) the amount of estate tax that is deferred under section 6166.

For the calendar quarter beginning January 1, 2007, the interest rate for underpayment by a corporation is 8% if the underpayment for the year is $100,000 or less and 10% if the underpayment for the year exceeds $100,000. Rev. Rul. 2006-63, IRB 2006-52 (Dec. 26, 2006) IRC § 6221(c).

During the period from 1987 through 1998, the basic underpayment rate was 1% higher than the basic overpayment rate for both corporate and noncorporate taxpayers. If a taxpayer had an outstanding overpayment for one year and an outstanding underpayment for another year, the IRS would normally offset them and apply the appropriate rate to the net amount. However, if either the overpayment had been refunded or the underpayment had been paid, the IRS would calculate the interest separately on the two obligations for any period that the two overlapped and find interest due even though the net amount of tax owed, at least to the extent the underpayment and overpayment overlapped, was zero. In 1998, the Senate Finance Committee Report on the Reform Act expressed its view that taxpayers "should be charged interest only on the amount they actually owe, taking into account overpayments and underpayments from all open years."[21]

Congress addressed this problem in two ways in the 1998 Reform Act. First, the Act removed the rate differential for all noncorporate taxpayers for all periods beginning as of January 1, 1999. Second, the Act adopted "global interest netting." Under section 6621(d), to the extent that any interest is payable on an underpayment and allowable on an overpayment for the same period and amount and for the same taxpayer, the interest rate is zero for the period.[22] This rule applies even if different kinds of taxes are involved and even if the rates on the underpayment and overpayment are different.[23] However, interest netting does not apply if one of the periods in question is barred by the statute of limitations.[24]

Within sixty days after the IRS assesses a tax, it is required to provide the taxpayer a notice of tax due and demand for payment.[25] Although interest normally accrues until the underpayment is paid, if the taxpayer pays the amount

---

[21] S. Rep. No. 105-174, § 3301, at 61 (1998), reprinted at 1998-3 C.B. 537, 597-98.

[22] The IRS has dealt with several variations on this theme to which the statute does not necessarily apply. For instance, if the taxpayer reports an overpayment for a given year and receives a refund without interest and it is subsequently determined that there was an underpayment for the year, then interest will be assessed on the portion of the underpayment covered by the amount refunded from the date of the refund. If the underpayment exceeds the amount refunded, interest on the excess will accrue from the due date of the return on which the overpayment was reported. Rev. Rul. 99-40, 1999-2 C.B. 441.

[23] The rates might be different because of the increased rates on large corporate underpayments and the reduced rates on corporate overpayments in excess of $10,000.

[24] Although section 6621(d) refers to interest "payable" and "allowable," which seems to be limited to outstanding underpayments and overpayments, the Conference Committee Report made it clear that netting was to occur "without regard to whether the underpayment or overpayments are currently outstanding." H.R. Conf. Rep. No. 105-599, § 3301, at 256 (1998), reprinted at 1998-3 C.B. 747, 1010-11. This is consistent with the fact that in the same Act, Congress amended § 6601(f), which deals with a similar issue involving the satisfaction of any tax by a credit, to make § 6621(d) apply where the two sections would otherwise overlap. *See also* Federal National Mortgage Association v. United States, 69 Fed. Cl. 89 (2005) (discussing an uncodified provision which allows taxpayers to request the Service to apply section 6621(d) to periods predating its enactment).

[25] IRC § 6303.

due within twenty-one calendar days (ten business days if the amount equals or exceeds $100,000) after the date of notice and demand for payment, then no interest is due for the period after the date of the notice. Both the "timely mailing is timely filing" rule in section 7502 and the "Saturday, Sunday, legal holiday" rule in section 7503 apply to the twenty-one/ten day time periods. For those taxpayers that pay within the twenty-one/ten day period, this rule avoids the necessity for successive interest computations and notices to collect the amount of interest due up to the actual date the tax is paid.

According to the Senate Finance Committee's Report accompanying the 1998 Reform Act, "[t]he computation of interest is a complex calculation, often involving multiple interest rates."[26] For that reason, the 1998 Reform Act added new section 6631, which, with respect to individual taxpayers, requires the IRS to include in its notices of tax and interest due "information with respect to the section of [the Code] under which the interest is imposed and a computation of the interest." This was a long overdue service to taxpayers who owe interest on underpayments of tax. Without this information, confirming the IRS's interest computation can be a challenge.

B. Modifications to the Basic Rules

1. Carrybacks

Net operating loss, net capital loss, and certain tax credit carrybacks may have the effect of reducing the amount of an income tax liability for a carryback year.[27] If there was an underpayment of tax in the carryback year, the loss or credit carryback would, in effect, reduce the amount of the underpayment. However, the carryback loss or credit does not reduce the underpayment (or penalty, additional amount, or addition to tax relating to the underpayment) for purposes of determining the interest due with respect to the carryback year's tax until the period beginning after the due date of the return for the year in which the net operating loss, net capital loss, or credit carryback occurs.[28] Similarly, a foreign tax credit carried back "shall not affect the computation of interest . . . for the period ending on the filing date for the taxable year in which such taxes were in fact paid or accrued. . . ."[29]

---

[26] S. Rep. No. 105-174, note 20, *supra*, § 3308, at 66, 1998-3 C.B. at 602.

[27] According to section 6601(d)(3)(B), tax credit carryback is defined in section 6511(d)(4)(C), which, in turn, defines credit carryback as "any business carryback under section 39."

[28] IRC § 6601(d)(1), (3).

[29] IRC § 6601(d)(2).

2. Suspension of Interest on Underpayments

a. Suspension in case of delayed issuance of notice of tax due

If within thirty days after a taxpayer waives the restrictions under section 6213(a) on assessment of a deficiency in income, gift, estate, or generation-skipping taxes (or certain excise taxes), the IRS has not sent the taxpayer a notice of tax due and demand for payment, then interest is suspended beginning on the thirty-first day.[30] The suspension lasts until the date of the notice and demand. Additionally, during the suspension period, no interest is imposed on interest accrued prior to the suspension period. This thirty-day rule also applies to suspend the accrual of interest if a partner enters into a settlement agreement (under section 6224(c)) that results in the conversion of partnership items into nonpartnership items. In such case, the settlement serves as a waiver and interest is suspended with respect to the resulting computational adjustment if the IRS does not send the partner a notice of tax due and demand for payment within thirty days of the settlement.[31]

b. Suspension in case of failure to contact the taxpayer in a timely manner

Section 6404(g) suspends interest, certain penalties, additions to tax, and additional amounts, if the IRS does not notify an individual taxpayer, who filed his return on time, of both the amount of his liability and the basis therefore within eighteen months after the later of the date on which the return is filed or the due date of the return without regard to extensions.[32] Any such suspension ends on the twenty-first day after "the date on which notice . . . is provided by the Secretary." In this context, both the Senate and the Conference Committee Reports say that "[i]nterest and penalties resume 21 days after the IRS sends [the notice] to the taxpayer."[33]

"For purposes of section 6404(g), the Service provides notice . . . to the taxpayer if it sends a writing to the taxpayer at his or her last known address and that writing includes the amount of the liability, the basis for that liability, and sufficient information or explanation regarding the adjustment to enable the

---

[30] IRC § 6601(c).

[31] *Id.*

[32] A provision under newly signed hurricane relief legislation (H.R. 4440) retroactively does away with the 18 month interest suspension for abusive transactions. If taxpayers take advantage of the recent settlement offer under Notice 2005-80, they will not have to face retroactively imposed interest. Alison Bennett, *Taxpayers with Abusive Shelters Facing Higher Interest Under New Law, IRS Says*, 246 DTR G-5 (2005).

[33] S. Rep. No. 105-174, note 20, *supra*, § 3305, at 64, 1998-3 C.B. at 600-01; H.R. Conf. Rep. No. 105-599, note 23, *supra*, 1998-3 C.B. 747, 1013-14.

taxpayer to challenge the adjustment."[34] Examples of valid notice include: notices of math errors, Underreporter Program notices, revenue agent reports, and notices of deficiency with an accompanying Explanation of Items.[35] In addition, the service of a pleading alleging an increased deficiency in a Tax Court proceeding will be sufficient notice.[36] Presumably, the date of mailing of the notice establishes the time that the notice is "provided" to the taxpayer.[37]

In Revenue Ruling 2005-4, 2005-4 I.R.B. 366, the Service addressed the application of section 6404(g) to an amended return which reports additional tax liability. If an amended return is filed within 18 months of the original filing, then interest accrues on the additional tax liability from the due date of the original return. If an amended return is filed more than 18 months after the original return is filed, then interest on the additional tax liability is suspended for the period beginning with the expiration of the notification period and ending with the filing of the amended return. Notice is unnecessary when a taxpayer files an amended return because the taxpayer knows the basis and amount of the additional tax liability. If payment is not included with the amended return, interest on the additional tax liability begins accruing on the date that is twenty-one days after the date of filing the amended return.

The Senate Committee Report explained the reasoning behind this provision as follows.

> The Committee believes that the IRS should promptly inform taxpayers of their obligations with respect to tax deficiencies and amounts due. In addition, the Committee is concerned that accrual of interest and penalties absent prompt resolution of tax deficiencies may lead to the perception that the IRS is more concerned about collecting revenue than in resolving taxpayer's problems.[38]

While promptly providing taxpayers notice of the nature and extent of their liability is an admirable goal, providing noncompliant taxpayers an interest and penalty holiday if they are not quickly notified of their noncompliant behavior is difficult to justify. In fact, the effect of this rule is to reduce the cost of noncompliance. And it does so with the unrealistic expectation that the IRS can and should process more than one hundred million income tax returns, select those

---

[34] Chief Counsel Notice N(35)000-172 (2000 ARD 959-3), 2000 IRS Chief Counsel Notice Lexis 11 *3.

[35] *Id.*

[36] *Id.* at *4. However, if the parties agree to an increased deficiency in a stipulated decision, "the stipulated decision and a letter transmitting such decision to the petitioner for signature will constitute notice of the liability." *Id.*

[37] *See id.* at *5 (examples suggest, although do not state directly, that the time of mailing will be the time that notice is "provided").

[38] S. Rep. No. 105-174, note 20, *supra*, at § 3305.

that need to be audited, distribute them throughout the country, and complete the audits, within eighteen months after receipt of the returns.

That having been said, Congress did limit the scope of this concession to noncompliant taxpayers. As originally enacted in 1998, it did not (and still does not) apply to:

(a) penalties under section 6651;[39]

(b) interest, penalties, additions to tax, or additional amounts in a case involving fraud;

(c) tax liabilities reported on the return; or

(d) any criminal penalty.

In the American Jobs Creation Act of 2004 ("Jobs Act"), Congress further narrowed the scope of the interest and penalty holiday. First, as originally enacted, the eighteen-month period before the start of the holiday was to be reduced to one year for taxable years beginning on or after January 1, 2004. The Jobs Act eliminated the drop-down to one year and, for all purposes, retained the original eighteen-month period.[40]

Second, the Jobs Act added two additional situations to which the favorable treatment is denied. Favorable treatment will not apply to any interest, penalty, addition to tax, or additional amount with respect to any:

(a) gross misstatement, or

(b) reportable transaction with respect to which the facts are not adequately disclosed (under section 6664(d)(2)(A)) or to any listed transaction as defined in section 6707A(c).[41]

Gross misstatements for this purpose include any substantial omission of gross income that triggers the six-year statute of limitations under section 6501(e) as well as any gross valuation misstatements as defined in section 6662(h).[42] Reportable and listed transactions are both generally defined in section 6707(c) as transactions that the Secretary determines to involve tax avoidance or tax evasion.[43]

---

[39] It is not clear why this exception is necessary. Interest suspension only applies to timely filed returns. If the return is timely, there can be no section 6501(a)(1) penalty. Also, interest suspension is expressly not applicable to "any tax liability shown on the return." IRC § 6404(g)(2)(C). This covers the section 6651(a)(2) penalty. Thus, to that extent making the general statutory exception of penalties under section 6651 redundant..

[40] American Jobs Creation Act of 2004, Pub. L. No. 108-357, § 903(a), 118 Stat. 1418 (2004).

[41] *Id.* at § 903(b).

[42] H.R. Conf. Rep. No. 108-755, § 903, at 770 (2004), *reprinted in* 2005 U.S.C.C.A.N. 1341, 1822.

[43] In section 303 of the Gulf Opportunity Zone Act, Congress modified section 6404(g) of the Code to extend interest suspension taxpayers who agreed to participate in the IRS's settlement initiative set forth in Announcement 2005-80. For a discussion of this modification see Lee Shepherd, *Two Minutes to Midnight: Settle your Shelter Case*, 110 Tax Notes, Feb. 2, 2006, at 814.

c. Suspension in the case of a presidentially declared disaster or terroristic or military action

The IRS also has the authority, under section 7508(A), to suspend the accrual of interest (as well as any penalty, additional amount, or addition to tax) for a period of up to one year if the taxpayer is "affected by a Presidentially declared disaster . . . or a terroristic or military action. . . ."

3. Abatement of Interest Attributable to Unreasonable Errors and Delays by the IRS

Section 6404(e)(1) authorizes the IRS, in its discretion, to abate all or any part of any assessed interest "for any period" in two circumstances. First, abatement is appropriate if the interest is on a *deficiency* "attributable in whole or in part to an unreasonable error or delay by an officer or employee of the Internal Revenue Service . . . in performing a ministerial or managerial act." Second, abatement is appropriate if the interest is on a *payment* of any income, estate, gift, or generation-skipping tax or certain excise taxes "to the extent that any unreasonable error or delay in such payment is attributable to such officer or employee being erroneous or dilatory in performing a ministerial or managerial act. . . ."[44] Generally, requests for abatement of interest are made by filing Form 843.

Section 6404(e)(1) points out that an error or delay, any "significant aspect" of which is attributable to the taxpayer, will not be taken into account for abatement purposes. The Regulations, somewhat aggressively, expand the scope of this exception to abatement by concluding that abatement is not available if any significant aspect of the error or delay is attributable to a person related to the taxpayer under sections 267(b) or 707(b)(1).[45]

Another constraint is that abatement is available only for interest accruing after the IRS "has contacted the taxpayer in writing with respect to [the] deficiency or payment."[46] Thus interest cannot be abated during the period from the filing of the return to either the beginning of an audit or, in case the return was filed but all of the tax shown as due was not paid, the demand for payment.

Whether the interest is on a deficiency or payment resulting from the IRS's conduct, two additional criteria severely limit the scope of the IRS's authority. The conduct in question must relate to the performance of a "ministerial or man-

---

[44] *See* Richard A. Levine & Carlton M. Smith, *Interest Abatement Actions—An Important New Avenue for Taxpayer Relief*, 86 J. of Tax'n 5 (Jan. 1997). *See also* White v. Commissioner (holding that interest abatement is not available with respect to interest paid on employment taxes because such taxes do not require a section 6212 notice of deficiency—a condition for abatement set forth in section 6404(e)).

[45] Reg. § 301.6404-2(a)(2).

[46] IRC § 6404(e)(1).

agerial act" and the error or delay in performing that act must be "unreasonable."

Regulation section 301.6404-2(b) and (c) contains brief definitions of both ministerial and managerial acts and provides thirteen examples that give substance to the definitions. The Regulations define ministerial acts as acts which do not involve the exercise of discretion or judgment and that occur "after all prerequisites to the act, such as conferences and review by supervisors have taken place."[47] Managerial acts take place during the processing of a case and involve "the temporary or permanent loss of records or the exercise of judgment or discretion relating to management of personnel." The determination of the proper application of state or federal law is neither a ministerial nor managerial act. The Regulations do not attempt to define acts that are "unreasonable" although some understanding of the IRS's view of the term can be gleaned from the examples.[48]

A taxpayer's right to abatement of interest under this section is conditioned on conduct by IRS personnel that is deemed to be undesirable. For that reason, persons representing clients during audits should be careful to document throughout the audit the apparent errors or delays caused by IRS personnel with a view to being able to justify application of the abatement rules.

The Taxpayer Bill of Rights 2[49] added what is now section 6404(h) to permit certain taxpayers whose request for abatement of interest has been denied by the IRS to petition the Tax Court to determine whether the denial was an abuse of discretion.[50] The taxpayers entitled to such judicial review are limited to those whose net worth does not exceed the section 7430(c)(4)(ii) caps applicable to parties seeking reimbursement of administrative and litigation costs incurred in successfully contesting their liability for any tax, interest, and penalties. Under this rule, the maximum net worth an individual can have and be eligible for judicial review of an IRS denial of interest abatement is $2 million. For corporations, the cap is $7 million.

The Tax Court has adopted Rules 280-84 relating to actions for review of the IRS's failure to abate interest. The action is commenced by filing a petition

---

[47] *See* Taylor v. Commissioner, 113 T.C. 206, *aff'd*, 87 A.F.T.R.2d. 2001-1, U.S.T.C. ¶ 50,441 (9th Cir. 2000) (holding that suspension of civil action against the taxpayer pending the outcome of the criminal trial was not a ministerial act).

[48] *See* Nelson v. Commissioner, 87 T.C. Memo. (CCH) 958 (2003) (holding that incorrect advice given by the IRS did not constitute ministerial acts for purposes of abating interest).

[49] Pub. L. No. 104-168, § 302(a), 110 Stat. 1452 (1966).

[50] *Id.* at 1457. On May 21, 2007, the Supreme Court resolved a conflict between the Federal Circuit and the Fifth Circuit on the question of whether the Tax Court has exclusive jurisdiction under section 6404(h) to consider IRS denials of interest abatement claims made under section 6404(e). Hinck v. United States, 550 U.S. ___, 127 S. Ct. 2011 (2007). The Court agreed with the Federal Circuit's opinion in *Hinck v. United States*, 446 F.3d 1307 (Fed. Cir. 2006), that Congress had granted exclusive jurisdiction to the Tax Court and rejected the Fifth Circuit's opinion in *Beall v. United States*, 336 F.3d 419 (5th Cir. 2003), that the district courts can also hear such cases.

entitled: "Petition for Review of Failure To Abate Interest Under Code Section 6404." Rule 281 describes the required content of the Petition and establishes a sixty-dollar filing fee.[51]

Taxpayers must petition the Tax Court "within 180 days after the date of the mailing of the Secretary's final determination not to abate [the] interest,"[52] and they are required to plead and prove that they qualify for judicial review under the applicable net worth cap.[53] Decisions of the Tax Court relating to abatement of interest may be appealed in the same manner as other decisions of the court.[54]

Section 6404(e)(2) *requires* the IRS to abate interest imposed by section 6602 on any erroneous refund if neither the taxpayer nor a related party caused the refund, and if the refund amount does not exceed $50,000. Interest will accrue on such a refund only after the IRS makes a demand for repayment.

Section 6404(f) *authorizes* the IRS to abate any penalty or addition to tax attributable to erroneous written advice by the IRS. Abatement under this provision is conditioned on the taxpayer having: (i) requested the advice in writing,[55] (ii) reasonably relied on the advice, and (iii) provided the IRS adequate and accurate information about matter. The Regulations make clear that when a penalty or addition to tax is abated, any related interest will also be abated.[56]

4. Interest on Penalties, Additional Amounts, and Additions to Tax

Section 6601(e)(2) divides penalties, additional amounts, and additions to tax into two categories for purposes of determining the period over which interest accrues. Generally speaking, penalties that the taxpayer could have anticipated at the time the return was filed bear interest from the date, including extensions, that the return is required to be filed.[57] This category includes the additions to tax under sections 6651(a)(1) for failure to file a return on time, 6653 for failure to pay stamp tax, 6662 for accuracy-related penalties, and 6663

---

[51] The Court of Federal Claims lacks jurisdiction to review interest abatement claims. Hinck v. United States, 95 A.F.T.R.2d 2005-873 (Cl. Ct. 2005).

[52] Nothing in the Code or Regulations requires the IRS to issue a final determination denying a claim for abatement of interest.

[53] Estate of Edward J. Kunze v. Commissioner, T.C. Memo. (CCH) 1999-344 (1999), *aff'd*, 233 F.3d 948 (7th Cir. 2000).

[54] IRC § 6404(h)(2)(c).

[55] Reg. § 301.6404-3(b)(1)(ii).

[56] Reg. § 301.6404-(3).

[57] The beginning date of interest for these additions to tax (the date the return was required to be filed including extensions (section 6601(e)(2)(B)) is different from the beginning date of interest on underpayments of tax (the last date prescribed for payment excluding extensions). IRC § 6601(a) & (b)(1).

for fraud.[58] Although these additions to tax are not limited to noncompliance with the income tax provisions, their impact is almost certainly felt most often in the income tax context. Interest accrues on these additions to tax until they are paid, but taxpayers have an interest-free period of twenty-one calendar days after the date of the notice and demand for payment, if the additions to tax are paid within that period.[59]

The second category consists of all other penalties, additional amounts, and additions to tax. Amounts in this category are interest-free if they are paid within twenty-one calendar days of the date of the notice and demand for payment.[60] If they are not paid within that period, interest accrues from the date of the notice and demand for payment to the date of payment.[61]

III. INTEREST ON OVERPAYMENTS

A. The Basic Rules

A refund attributable to overpayment of taxes bears interest from the date of the overpayment to a date preceding the date of the refund check by not more than thirty days.[62] Generally, advance payments of tax through withholding, estimated tax payments, and application of prior years' overpayment to the current year's estimated tax payments are deemed paid on the due date (determined without extensions) of the return for the year for which the amounts were withheld or paid.[63] The Regulations make it clear that all payments of tax are first applied to the tax liability, and only when and if tax payments in excess of that liability are made does an overpayment occur.[64]

For taxpayers other than corporations, the interest rate on overpayments is the same as the interest rate on underpayments—three percentage points over the federal short-term rate. For corporations, the interest rate on overpayments is two percentage points over the federal short-term rate for the portion of the overpayment up to and including $10,000, and one-half percentage point over the federal short-term rate for the portion, if any, of the overpayment that

---

[58] This category also includes the 50% penalty imposed on any person who willfully fails to pay any stamp tax or who willfully attempts to evade or defeat such tax. IRC § 6653.

[59] The twenty-one day period is shortened to ten business days if the amount for which the notice and demand is made equals or exceeds $100,000. IRC § 6601(e)(3).

[60] *Id.*

[61] IRC § 6601(e)(2)(A).

[62] IRC § 6611(b)(2). Any refund check "tendered" will stop the running of interest. Therefore, taxpayers who receive a refund check in an amount less than they think is correct should deposit the check rather than rejecting it and requesting a check in the amount they think is correct. Accepting the check will not preclude the taxpayer from claiming the additional tax and interest believed to be due. *Id.*

[63] IRC § 6611(d).

[64] Reg. § 301.6611-1(b).

exceeds $10,000.[65] In the case of overpayment of tax on a built-in gain by an S corporation, the Tax Court has held that the higher rate of interest paid to noncorporate taxpayers, rather than the lower rate paid to corporations, is applicable.[66] Interest is recoverable against the government only when specifically provided for by statute because only by statute can the government waive its sovereign immunity.[67]

B. Modifications to the Basic Rules

1. Rules Affecting the Period Over Which Interest Is Paid

There are four important exceptions to the general rule that the government must pay interest with respect to overpayments from the date of the overpayment. First, no interest is due on an overpayment if the amount claimed on a timely filed return is refunded within forty-five days after the last day prescribed for filing the return (determined without regard to extensions of time to file). In the case of a return filed after the last day prescribed for filing the return (determined without regard to extensions of time to file), no interest is due if the overpayment amount is refunded within forty-five days after the return is filed.[68] Second, if the taxpayer files a claim for refund, no interest is paid for the period after the claim is filed if the refund is paid within forty-five days after the claim is filed.[69] Third, no interest is paid with respect to an overpayment reported on a return filed after its due date (determined with regard to extensions) for the period ending on the day before the day the return is filed.[70] Fourth, no interest is paid with respect to any return that is not in processible form when filed.[71]

---

[65] For the calendar quarter beginning January 1, 2007, the interest rate for an overpayment by a corporation is 7% for the first $10,000 and 5.5% for the excess of the overpayment over $10,000. For taxpayers other than corporations, the interest rate for overpayments is 8%. IRC § 6621(a)(1); Rev. Rul. 2006-63, 2006-52 I.R.B. 1143.

[66] Garwood Irrigation Co. v. Commissioner, 126 T.C. 223 (2006).

[67] *See* Gandy Nursery Inc. v. United States, 412 F.3d 602 (5th Cir. 2005) (taxpayer not entitled to post-judgment interest on damages awarded under section 7432).

[68] IRC § 6611(e)(1). In C.C.A. 200441002, the IRS examined when the forty-five day period starts when an income tax return reflecting an overpayment is postmarked on the extended due date for filing the return. The Service adopted a taxpayer friendly interpretation, finding that the forty-five day period starts on the date of the United States postmark.

[69] IRC § 6611(e)(2).

[70] IRC § 6611(b)(3).

[71] IRC § 6611(g).

2. Carrybacks

Net operating loss, net capital loss, and certain tax credit carrybacks may have the effect of reducing the amount of income tax liability for a carryback year. This, in turn, entitles the taxpayer to a refund for that year. For purposes of determining the amount of interest the taxpayer receives with respect to such a refund, however, the resulting overpayment is deemed not to have occurred before the filing date (determined without regard to extensions) for the year in which the loss or credit giving rise to the carryback occurred.[72] The forty-five-day period within which the IRS can refund any overpayment without paying interest thereon applies to any refund generated by a carryback.[73] Thus, if the refund is paid within the later of forty-five days after the due date of the return for the loss year (determined without regard to extensions) or forty-five days after the date the return is filed, then no interest must be paid with respect to any refund generated by the carryback.

IV. TAX COURT JURISDICTION OVER INTEREST DETERMINATIONS

The principal role of the Tax Court in the federal tax system is to provide taxpayers an opportunity for judicial review of determinations by the IRS that income, estate, gift, or generation-skipping taxes have been underpaid. Upon the filing of a petition in Tax Court, the court acquires "jurisdiction to redetermine the correct amount of the deficiency. . . ."[74] However, if the court finds that the taxpayer actually made an overpayment, it also has jurisdiction to determine the amount of the overpayment.[75]

Whether the Tax Court finds that the taxpayer underpaid or overpaid the tax, the IRS will neither collect the additional tax and interest, nor pay the refund and interest, until the decision of the Tax Court becomes final. Generally Tax Court decisions become final if neither the taxpayer nor the government files an

---

[72] IRC § 6611(f).

[73] IRC § 6611(f)(4)(B).

[74] IRC § 6214(a). The Tax Court's jurisdiction includes the right to increase the deficiency beyond that set forth in the notice of deficiency. If a petition is filed in the Tax Court in response to a deficiency notice then no assessment and no collection efforts may be made until the decision of the Tax Court becomes final. IRC § 6213(a). Notwithstanding this seemingly broad taxpayer protection, section 7485 makes it clear that assessment or collection of the amount determined by the Tax Court to be due is not stayed by the filing of an appeal unless the taxpayer also files a bond with the Tax Court. The amount of the bond is to be determined by the Tax Court and is to secure payment of the deficiency, interest, additional amounts, and additions to tax. IRC § 7485(a).

[75] IRC § 6512(b)(1). The taxpayer may request that the Tax Court treat his case under the "Small Tax Case" procedures under section 7463. Procedures in such cases are different from those in regular cases. Among other things, the scope of the court's jurisdiction in Small Tax Cases is limited and the court's decisions are not subject to any appellate review. *See* Chapter 8.

appeal within ninety days after the Tax Court enters its decision.[76] If an appeal is filed within the ninety-day period, the decision becomes final when the time for obtaining additional judicial review expires.[77]

If the Tax Court determines that there was an underpayment of tax, when the Court's decision becomes final, the IRS will assess[78] the tax determined to be due and send the taxpayer a notice of the amount and demand for payment.[79] At the same time, the IRS will calculate the interest due on the underpayment and will include the interest in the notice and demand for payment.

Although interest is assessed and collected in the same manner as taxes, the deficiency procedures expressly do not apply to interest.[80] This is because once the amount of tax due has been determined, the amount of interest due is purely a mathematical computation.

If the Tax Court determines that the taxpayer actually overpaid the tax, after the Court's decision becomes final, the IRS will normally refund the amount of the overpayment and pay any accrued interest to the taxpayer. If the IRS does not refund the overpayment and pay interest within 120 days after the Court's decision becomes final, upon the taxpayer's motion, the Court may order the IRS to make the refund and pay interest. Tax Court Rule 260 establishes procedures to be followed in connection with such motions.

Whether interest is accrued with respect to an underpayment or an overpayment of tax, as finally determined by the Tax Court, computation of its amount is initially done by the IRS. In 1988, the Tax Court first acquired jurisdiction to redetermine the correct amount of interest arising out of its determinations. Under section 7481(c), the taxpayer has a period of one year after a Tax Court decision becomes final within which to file a motion with the Tax Court for a redetermination of the amount of either the interest to be paid in the case of a deficiency or the interest due the taxpayer in the case of an overpayment. In the case of interest on a deficiency, the right to a redetermination is conditioned on the taxpayer first paying the full amount of the deficiency and of the interest as computed by the IRS.[81]

---

[76] IRC §§ 7481(a)(1), 7483.

[77] IRC § 7481.

[78] IRC § 6215.

[79] IRC § 6303(a).

[80] IRC § 6601(e).

[81] IRC § 7481(c)(2)(A)(ii). Section 6404(h)(2)(A) contains a curious cross-reference to section 6213 "for purposes of determining the date of the mailing" of the claim for abatement. But, nothing in section 6213 deals with the date of mailing.

PROBLEM

Bill and Brenda Jordan (cash-basis Taxpayers) filed their joint federal income tax return for calendar year 2000 in a timely manner, pursuant to a four-month extension of time to file, on July 15, 2001. The tax liability shown on the return was $100,000, of which $45,000 had been paid by withholding and $15,000 had been paid through timely estimated tax payments. The balance due, $40,000, was paid with the return. On October 1, 2003, the Jordans received a statutory notice (ninety-day letter), dated September 30, 2003, in which the IRS asserted an additional liability of $30,000 of tax for 2000. Litigation in the Tax Court ensued, and the Court ultimately determined that $20,000 of additional tax was in fact due. The Jordans decided not to appeal. They received a timely notice, dated October 15, 2005, demanding payment of the $20,000 plus all interest due with respect to 2000 under these facts.

a. It is now October 22, 2005, and the Jordans have asked you to determine the amounts subject to interest, the applicable interest rates, and the period for which interest is due with respect to their 2000 return.

b. Suppose that market interest rates have fallen to 4% and that the aggregate interest due seems disproportionately large in relation to the tax due. In the course of settlement discussion before the Tax Court trial, Bill asks the IRS for some relief, by way of reduced interest, to avoid what appears to him to be almost a penalty. In the interest of settling the case can the IRS agree to take less than the full amount of interest due?

c. Suppose that after a conference with the Revenue Agent, Bill and Brenda and the agent agreed that $20,000 was due. Bill and Brenda signed and gave to the agent a Form 870 waiver of restrictions on assessment. That was accomplished on May 31, 2002. In September 2002, Bill and Brenda received a notice of tax and interest due dated September 15, 2002. Through what date is interest due on the $20,000 underpayment?

d. Under the facts of (c) above, assume that the $20,000 underpayment was due to a settlement agreement executed for the purpose of concluding a partnership audit conducted under the TEFRA partnership audit procedures. In the agreement, the Jordans expressly waived the restrictions on assessment and collection of the deficiency pursuant to § 6225. Through what date is interest due on the $20,000 underpayment?

e. Assume that $5,000 of the $20,000 ultimately determined by the Tax Court to be due for 2000 actually was a penalty imposed under § 6673 because of the Jordan's bad conduct. How, if at all, would your answer in (a) above change?

f. Upon receipt of the statutory notice on October 1, 2003, Bill and Brenda decided to minimize any obligation for interest they might incur by paying the proposed $30,000 tax adjustment. They therefore sent a check for $30,000 to the IRS on October 31, 2003.

    i)   If the notice had been sent by regular mail (not certified or registered) would it be valid?

    ii)   By paying the tax, and eliminating the deficiency, have Bill and Brenda lost the right to have their case decided by the Tax Court?

    iii) Have Bill and Brenda effectively stopped the running of interest?

    iv) Will Bill and Brenda receive interest with respect to their $10,000 overpayment when it is ultimately determined that their liability for tax is limited to $20,000?

g. As it happened, Bill and Brenda suffered a loss in their business during 2002 which was properly carried back under § 172 to 2000. In fact, by a coincidence, the 2002 loss (reported on their 2000 return which was filed on April 15, 2003) reduced the tax liability for 2000 by exactly $120,000. How, if at all, would their liability for interest on their 2000 tax liability be affected by this fact?

h. Assume that Bill and Brenda filed their return for 2000 late, without an extension, on July 1, 2001. Also assume that the actual liability was only $40,000. They requested that the extra $20,000 that they had paid, through withholding and estimated payments, be refunded to them. How much interest would the IRS have to pay Bill and Brenda if it mailed them a check for $20,000 on August 15, 2001?

Chapter 13

COLLECTION OF TAX

IRC:	§§ 6159, 6201(a)(1) & (d), 6303, 6304, 6320, 6321, 6322, 6323 (skip subsection (e), skim the remaining subsections), 6325, 6326, 6330, 6331(a)-(f) & (k), 6332(a), (c) & (d), 6334(a)-(e), 6337, 6343(a) & (b), 6502, 6503(b)-(h), 6532 (b) & (c), 7122, 7403, 7421, 7425, 7426, 7432(a) & (b), 7433
Regs.:	§§ 301.6203-1, 301.6204-1, 301.6320-1, 301.6330-1, 301.7122-1, 301.7122-1T
Forms:	Skim 23C; 433-D; 433-A; 656; 668-A(c)(Do); 668-B; 668-Y; 911; 2261; 6338; 12153

I. INTRODUCTION

"[T]axes are the life-blood of government, and their prompt and certain availability an imperious need."[1] The overwhelming majority of taxes collected by the IRS are self-reported and paid "voluntarily" by taxpayers. Nonetheless, the enforced collection mechanisms in the Code are of crucial significance. The money they collect, though small relatively, is substantial in absolute terms (usually around $40 billion a year). More importantly, the possibility of enforced collection encourages taxpayers to pay "voluntarily."

The Code rules governing collection are extensive and complex. The Code equips the IRS with a formidable arsenal of collection devices, stronger than those available to private creditors.[2] Yet, the very power of these devices inspires concern about the possibility of their abuse. Thus, the Code also contains substantial protections for taxpayers and third parties adversely affected by IRS collection activities. This chapter describes the administrative structure through which collection is effected. It then examines key collection devices available to the IRS, administrative and judicial protections available to taxpayers and third parties, statute of limitations considerations, and new rules permitting the IRS to contract with private companies to collect federal taxes.

---

[1] Bull v. United States, 295 U.S. 247 (1935). As Edmund Burke said: "The revenue of the state is the state." *Quoted in* State Tax Notes, Jan. 15, 2007, at 149.

[2] *See, e.g.,* United States v. Whiting Pools, Inc., 462 U.S. 198, 209-10 (1983).

II. COLLECTION STRUCTURE

The collection process typically begins at an IRS service center. Usually, the initial steps are assessment, followed by the issuance by the service center of the first of a series of letters to the taxpayer. The first letter notifies the taxpayer of the nature, amount, and date of the assessment and demands payment. If payment is not made, as many as three more letters may be issued, each spaced about four to five weeks apart. The last of the letters is sent by certified mail and states the IRS's intent to locate assets, levy on them, and perhaps to file notice of the tax lien.

The letters have the effect of satisfying statutory requirements, including the section 6303(a) requirement of notice and demand for payment and the section 6331(d) requirement of notice before levy. Although the letters have this effect, the Code does not require a series of letters.[3] Thus, the series is a matter of policy with the IRS. As such, the IRS can truncate the accustomed series if it concludes that circumstances so warrant.

The letters are designed to induce payment or, at least, to prompt the taxpayer to contact the IRS. If neither payment nor contact ensues, the service center will transfer the case to the Automated Collection System ("ACS") or, less commonly and usually only in large-dollar cases, to a collection specialist known as a revenue officer.

ACS relies on telephone contacts. If the ACS employee assigned to the case succeeds in contacting the taxpayer, the employee will seek financial information in order to facilitate levy. If the taxpayer is represented pursuant to a proper power-of-attorney (Form 2848) filed with the IRS, ACS ordinarily must deal with the representative, not the taxpayer.[4] ACS will attempt to obtain immediate full payment, but it is empowered to accept payments over time.

If ACS fails to collect or to establish an agreement for collection, the case will be transferred to a revenue officer in the field, under the rubric of a Taxpayer Delinquent Account ("TDA").[5] The revenue officer is supposed to contact the taxpayer promptly,[6] but the reality of heavy case loads sometimes thwarts this command. Once again, the attempt will be to secure full payment or its best feasible alternative. If the revenue officer concludes that there is no worthwhile col-

---

[3] Indeed, the section 6303(a) notice and demand need not even be in writing; oral communication can suffice. *See, e.g.,* Hahn v. United States, 77-1 U.S. Tax Cas. (CCH) ¶ 9334 (C.D. Cal. 1977). The section 6331(d) notice preceding levy, however, must be in writing. If the taxpayer's contact with the IRS is extensive, the taxpayer may be held to have waived receipt of notice and demand. *See, e.g.,* In re Baltimore Pearl Hominy Co., 5 F.2d 553 (4th Cir. 1925).

[4] *See* IRC § 7521(b)(2), (c).

[5] TDA should not be confused with Taxpayer Delinquency Investigation ("TDI"). In a TDI, a revenue officer is assigned to investigate a taxpayer's failure to file a required return and to procure the missing return.

[6] *See* IRM 5.1.10.3.

lection potential, the case will be assigned to Currently Not Collectible ("CNC") status.[7] CNC cases are periodically reviewed and will be returned to active status if new information suggesting collection potential develops. The IRS eventually collects only about 2% of the amounts due on accounts that are designated with CNC status.[8]

Other IRS functions provide support to revenue officers in certain categories of cases. After many years, such work was centralized in the Special Procedures Function ("SPF"). As a result of reorganizations, SPF was abolished and its work transferred to other units. SPF's former role as to bankruptcies now is played by the Insolvency Unit. SPF's former role as to collection suits, liens, and levies now is played by Compliance Field Operations or Compliance Technical Services. Additional reorganizations and name changes are probable. These offices are distributed throughout the country.

III. ASSESSMENT

Assessment pursuant to section 6201 is the first stage of the collection process. It is key because the IRS cannot legally collect any tax until it has been properly assessed. Assessment must be made within the statute of limitations period, as described in Chapter 5. The assessment itself is a purely mechanical act: the recordation of the liability on the books of the IRS.[9] If the IRS determines that the initial assessment was imperfect or incomplete, it may make supplemental assessments as long as the limitations period remains open.[10]

To protect taxpayers, the Code imposes prerequisites to assessment in some situations. These are the deficiency procedures of sections 6211 through 6215 detailed in Chapter 8. Briefly, the IRS may not assess deficiencies in income, gift, estate, and certain excise taxes until it has issued a statutory notice of deficiency to the taxpayer who then has an opportunity to petition the Tax Court for redetermination of the adjustments in that notice.

Certain kinds of taxes—employment taxes and most excise taxes, for instance—are wholly outside the deficiency procedure. Moreover, even taxes generally subject to the deficiency procedures sometimes can be assessed without going through those procedures. For instance, all of the following can be directly assessed: amounts shown on a return but not paid with it, erroneous income tax prepayment credits, mathematical errors, clerical errors, amounts arising out of tentative carryback or refund adjustments, and amounts paid by the taxpayer.[11] In addition, as described in Chapter 7, the deficiency procedures do not apply when jeopardy to collection makes expedited assessment appropriate.

---

[7] In the jargon of tax practice, putting a case into CNC status is often called "53 ing" the case (after IRS Form 53 used for this purpose).

[8] IRS News Release IR-2007-04 (Jan. 9, 2007).

[9] The recordation procedures are described in Regulation section 301.6203-1.

[10] IRC § 6204(a).

[11] IRC §§ 6201(a), 6213(b).

Penalties are assessed and collected in the same manner as the taxes to which they relate.[12] Thus, the accuracy-related penalties and the section 6651 "timeliness" penalties usually can be assessed only after the issuance of a notice of deficiency. However, section 6651 penalties not attributable to a deficiency can be assessed without the issuance of a notice of deficiency. Interest on assessed taxes may be assessed at any time within the limitations period for collection of the underlying taxes.[13] Section 73 provides that amounts received in respect of the services of a child are included in the child's gross income, not his or her parents' income, even if the amounts are not received by the child. Any such amounts assessed against the child "shall, if not paid by the child, for all purposes be considered as having also been properly assessed against the parent."[14]

In general, the IRS is given substantial latitude in estimating the amount to be assessed when taxpayer records and other evidence do not admit of precision,[15] leaving it up to the taxpayer to establish in litigation what the true liability is. However, if the IRS's determination is based on an information return filed by a third party and if the taxpayer has cooperated with the IRS, section 6201(d) imposes on the IRS "the burden of producing reasonable and probative information" beyond the information return in order to support its determination.

Under section 6404, the IRS has authority to abate unpaid assessments of taxes, other than income, estate, and gift taxes, and in some cases unpaid assessments of interest. Abatement is authorized under various circumstances, including: assessments excessive in amount, made after expiration of the limitations period, or otherwise erroneously or illegally made; small balances that would be uneconomic to collect; amounts attributable to mathematical errors by the IRS; interest attributable to unreasonable errors, delays, or incorrect written advice by the IRS; interest and penalties when the IRS fails to contact the taxpayer; and interest in presidentially declared disaster areas.

IV. LIENS

A. Creation and Extent

The assessment begins the collection process. The next step is the IRS notifying the taxpayer of the assessment and demanding payment. Notice and demand are to be made "as soon as practicable, and within 60 days," after the assessment.[16] The notice is to be left at the taxpayer's dwelling or usual place

---

[12] IRC §§ 6665(a)(1), 6671(a).

[13] IRC § 6601(g).

[14] IRC § 6201(c). "Parent" includes any person "entitled to the services of a child by reason of having parental rights and duties in respect of the child." IRC § 73(c).

[15] *See, e.g.*, United States v. Fior D'Italia, Inc., 536 U.S. 238, 243-44 (2002).

[16] "The failure to give such notice within 60 days does not invalidate the notice." Reg. § 301.6303-1(a).

of business or mailed to the taxpayer's last known address.[17]

If the taxpayer neglects or refuses to pay after notice and demand, the general federal tax lien automatically arises under section 6321. The amount of the lien equals the unpaid tax plus any interest, penalties, and costs with respect to it. Section 6322 provides that the general tax lien, once it arises, relates back to the date of assessment and continues until it is satisfied by payment or becomes unenforceable because of expiration of the statute of limitations on collection. In general, under section 6502(a), the collection statute of limitations expires ten years after the date of the assessment. However, under certain circumstances, that period may be extended either generally or as to specific assets. The collection statute of limitations is discussed further in Section IX of this chapter.

Taxpayers sometimes argue that the IRS failed to make notice and demand, thus that no tax lien came into existence. These arguments rarely succeed. The courts have been liberal in the kinds of proof of notice and demand they have deemed acceptable.[18]

The section 6321 lien attaches to "all property and rights to property, whether real or personal" of the taxpayer's. The Supreme Court has repeatedly emphasized that this statutory language, and thus the reach of the general lien, is extremely broad.[19] Case law applying the tax lien to particular types of assets and interests underlines this broad reach.[20] Obviously, the lien attaches to property solely owned by the taxpayer in fee simple absolute, but it attaches as well to lesser or weaker interests. For example, it attaches to the taxpayer's interest in jointly owned property,[21] executory contracts,[22] spendthrift trusts,[23] future or contingent property interests,[24] and to property acquired by the taxpayer after the date on which the tax lien came into existence.[25]

For decades, a vexing question was the relationship of state law and federal law in tax lien controversies. However, the following rule is now settled law. In

---

[17] IRC § 6303(a).

[18] *See, e.g.*, United States v. Dixon, 672 F. Supp. 503 (M.D. Fla. 1987) (IRS certificate of assessments and payments constitutes proof of assessment). Third parties may not assert that the lien is invalid because of absence of notice and demand. *See, e.g.*, United States v. Lorson Elec., 72-2 U.S. Tax Cas. (CCH) ¶ 9614 (S.D.N.Y. 1972), *aff'd per curiam*, 480 F.2d 554 (2d Cir. 1973).

[19] *See, e.g.*, Glass City Bank v. United States, 326 U.S. 265 (1945) ("Stronger language could hardly have been selected to reveal a purpose to assure the collection of taxes").

[20] For discussion of case law applying the tax lien in context of numerous types of property interests, see William D. Elliott, Federal Tax Collection, Liens, and Levies ¶ 9.09 (2d ed. 2003).

[21] *See, e.g.*, United States v. Trilling, 328 F.2d 699 (7th Cir. 1964).

[22] *See, e.g.*, Randall v. H. Nakashima & Co., Ltd., 542 F.2d 270 (5th Cir. 1976).

[23] *See, e.g.*, Magavern v. United States, 550 F.2d 797 (2d Cir. 1977).

[24] *See, e.g.*, United States v. Solheim, 91-1 U.S. Tax Cas. (CCH) ¶ 50,108 (D. Neb. 1990), *aff'd on other grounds*, 953 F.2d 379 (8th Cir. 1992); Bigheart Pipeline Corp. v. United States, 600 F. Supp. 50, 53 (N.D. Okla. 1984), *aff'd*, 835 F.2d 766 (10th Cir. 1987).

[25] *See, e.g.*, Glass City Bank v. United States, 326 U.S. 265 (1945).

the first stage, one identifies the powers, strings, or controls that the taxpayer has over the asset in question. In the second stage, one decides whether those powers, strings, or controls rise to the level of being "property or rights to property" within the intendment of section 6321, in which case the lien attaches to the taxpayer's interest in the asset. The first stage is a matter of state law (or of whatever other law created the interest or asset). The second stage is a matter purely of federal law. In addition, all post-lien-attachment consequences depend on federal law (except when federal law incorporates state law).[26]

The fact that the second stage is a matter of exclusively federal law means that state law characterizations as "property" or "not property" are irrelevant. For example, state law often declares that liquor licenses are privileges, not property. Since state law characterizations are irrelevant, the federal tax lien attaches to a liquor license held by a delinquent taxpayer. State debtor-creditor restrictions also are irrelevant. For example, state law often shields homestead interests or tenancy-by-the-entireties interests from claims of separate creditors of one of the spouses. Yet the federal tax lien attaches to any homestead or entireties interests of the delinquent taxpayer even if his or her spouse owes no tax.[27]

Thus, determining whether the powers the taxpayer has as to the underlying asset are section 6321 property or property rights or not, is an exercise in federal law. There is no bright line or single criterion for making this decision. Given the numerous forms that property interests take, there couldn't be. Among the relevant factors are whether the interest is protected by law, has value, is beneficial (as opposed to mere legal title), and is transferable—although not all factors must be present in order to permit an affirmative characterization. The most important consideration may be the extent of control the taxpayer can exercise over the assets.[28]

The general lien under section 6321 is by far the most important federal tax lien. To supplement it, a number of special tax, liens exist. For instance, the Code creates special liens as to estate taxes,[29] gift taxes,[30] estate taxes deferred under section 6166,[31] and additional estate tax attributable to property qualifying for special valuation under section 2032A.[32]

---

[26] *See, e.g.,* United States v. Craft, 535 U.S. 274 (2002); Drye v. United States, 528 U.S. 49 (1999); United States v. Rodgers, 461 U.S. 677 (1983).

[27] For description of the voluminous case law as to these and other examples, see Steve R. Johnson, *Why* Craft *Isn't Scary,* 37 Real Prop., Probate & Trust J. 439 (2002).

[28] *See* Steve R. Johnson, *The Good, the Bad, and the Ugly in Post-*Drye *Tax Lien Analysis,* 5 Fla. Tax Rev. 415 (2002).

[29] IRC § 6324(a).

[30] IRC § 6324(b).

[31] IRC § 6324A.

[32] IRC § 6324B. For other special tax liens, see sections 4081, 4901, 5004, and 6311.

Often, the special liens will involve variations from normal lien rules. For instance, the special estate tax lien is imposed, on property in the gross estate, for ten years from the decedent's death and the special gift tax lien is imposed, on gifted property, for ten years from the date of the gift. These periods contrast with the normal lifespan of the section 6321 lien: ten years from the date of the assessment.

When a special lien applies, typically the general lien does as well. In such cases, the two liens are independent. If one of the liens terminates, the other does not automatically terminate. The continued applicability of the second lien will depend on its own terms.

The IRS also uses nominee liens and alter ego liens. These are broader applications of the normal lien, not special liens. When an individual or entity is holding the taxpayer's property as a subterfuge, the IRS may proceed against the property. It need not make a new assessment against the holder or possessor; its lien against the taxpayer is the basis on which the IRS can file a lien against the nominee or alter ego. For example, assume the IRS has a lien against John Smith and that some of his property is being held by Smith Co., a shell entity under whose name John sometimes acts. The IRS might assert its claim against that property by filing a lien against "Smith Co., as nominee or alter ego of John Smith."[33]

B. Notice of Lien

The IRS is not required to make known the existence of the lien. Often, the IRS does not publicly file or record its lien.[34] When it doesn't, the lien is called a "secret" lien. The lien nonetheless is in force and effect and can serve as the basis of enforced collection against the taxpayer's property and property rights.

When the IRS does decide to file its lien, section 6323(f) directs that it do so in the proper place pursuant to state law. As to real property, the notice must be duly filed and recorded in the public index of the local office designated by the law of the state in which the property is situated.[35]

---

[33] For additional discussion of nominee liens, alter ego liens, and related devices, see Chapter 7.

[34] Whether to file notice of the tax lien is a business decision for the IRS: will filing promote collection of the liability? A filed notice of tax lien can negatively affect the taxpayer's ability to borrow or the willingness of others to do business with the taxpayer, reducing the prospect that the taxpayer's future business activities will generate funds to pay the tax liability. On the other hand, the filing of the notice could apply the pressure needed to motivate the taxpayer to find a way to pay. Filing also protects the IRS's interest against certain persons who might otherwise acquire a higher priority interest in the property. *See generally* IRS Policy Statement P-5-47.

[35] If that state's law fails to designate any local office or if it designates more than one office, the notice is to be filed with the clerk of the federal District Court for the district where the property is located.

As to personalty (whether tangible or intangible), section 6323(f) again provides that the place of filing is the office designated by the law of the state in which the property is situated.[36] Taxpayers not residing in the United States are deemed to reside in the District of Columbia. Business entities are deemed to "reside" where their main executive offices are. This means where major decisions are made, not simply where the bricks and mortar are located.[37]

The personalty/realty distinction is unproblematic in most cases, but special situations occasion special rules. When it is arguable into which category a particular asset falls, the classification is made using state law.[38] Sometimes, assets may change in character. For instance, natural resources may be realty before extraction but personalty after. Although there is not a great deal of law on the point, it is likely that the character of the property at the time of lien filing would control. If the notice had been filed with the right office based on the property's character, then refiling in another office probably would not be necessary simply on account of subsequent change in the property's character. Still, an abundance of caution might prompt the IRS to make such a secondary filing should it become aware of the transmutation.

Section 6323(f) also governs the form and contents of the notice. A filing satisfying that section's requirements is valid even if it fails to satisfy some requisite under state law. This follows from the fact that federal, not state, law controls all post-lien-attachment consequences. The IRS has developed forms to meet the section 6323(f) requirements.[39]

Inevitably, given the volume of notices filed, some filings contain errors: misspellings, misnumerations, incorrect or incomplete addresses, etc. Many cases have considered whether such errors invalidate the notices. The decisions are not always reconcilable, but the courts usually take a functional approach. Typically, the notice will be invalidated only if the error is such that it would defeat discovery of the lien by a reasonably diligent search.[40] If the taxpayer changes his or her name after the notice filed, the policy of the IRS is to file another notice reflecting the taxpayer's new name as well as his or her "formerly known as" name. When a taxpayer against whom a tax lien is in place moves, the IRS is compelled to use the new address in the filing or refiling of a notice only if the taxpayer timely informs the IRS of the new address.[41]

---

[36] If that state's law fails to designate, the personalty is deemed situated where the taxpayer resides when the notice of tax lien is filed.

[37] Rev. Rul. 74-571, 1974-2 C.B. 398.

[38] *See, e.g.,* Brooks v. United States, 833 F.2d 1136 (4th Cir. 1987).

[39] *See also* Reg. §§ 301.6323(f)-1 (place for filing notice and form of notice), 301.6323(g)-1 (refiling of notice).

[40] *See, e.g.,* Richter's Loan Co. v. United States, 235 F.2d 753 (5th Cir. 1956).

[41] Reg. § 301.6323(g)-1(b)(2).

The normal life of a general tax lien is the ten-year collection limitations period, and initial notices cease to be effective at the end of this time. If the limitations period is extended, the IRS must refile the notice under section 6323(g). The notice will remain continuous if refiled within the "required refiling period," which is "the one-year period ending thirty days after the expiration of 10 years after the date of the assessment of the tax, and . . . the one-year period ending with the expiration of 10 years after the close of the preceding required refiling period for [the] notice."

C. Priorities

A federal tax lien does not directly compel payment. Sometimes, the existence or, especially, the filing of the lien does induce payment—in order to remove cloud on title, perhaps, to render the property more readily saleable. Yet there is no assurance that this will happen.

Thus, the real significance of a tax lien is that it serves as a security device. Those who owe money to the IRS usually owe others as well. Often there aren't enough assets to satisfy all of the creditors' claims. The tax lien is a means by which the IRS protects its position relative to the positions of competing creditors. How successful the lien is in that regard depends on the priorities rules described below.

The current priorities scheme has its roots in the Federal Tax Lien Act of 1966. But, of course, priorities disputes long preceded that legislation. The common law rule—"first in time, first in right"—helped shape the current regime and still governs when no statute applies. Under the common law rule, the claim of the competing creditor would have priority over the tax lien only if that creditor's claim was choate before the assessment date. A claim is not choate until three items have been established: the identity of the creditor, the amount of the debt, and the identity of the property to which the claim attaches.[42] In the tax area, the main purpose of the choateness requirement is to prevent the tax lien from being subordinated to mere contingencies.

In important instances, the common law rule has been modified or displaced by statutes. The most frequently applicable priority statute is section 6323.[43] The section was given its modern form by the Federal Tax Lien Act of 1966 and subsequent amendments. Subsections (a) (b), and (c) of section 6323 protect different sets of third-party creditors. Specifically,

---

[42] *See, e.g.*, United States v. McDermott, 507 U.S. 447 (1993); United States v. City of New Britain, 347 U.S. 81 (1954).

[43] Two other specialized sets of rules sometimes come into play. First, 31 U.S.C. sections 191 and 192 involve tax claims against an insolvent estate of a decedent or against a fiduciary in possession of property of an insolvent taxpayer (though one not in bankruptcy). Second, 11 U.S.C. section 507 involves priorities of tax and other claims in bankruptcy cases.

• Section 6323(a) pertains to four categories of third-party creditors: (1) purchasers of property from the taxpayer, (2) holders of security interests in the taxpayer's property, (3) mechanic's lienors, and (4) judgment lien creditors. Under the subsection, the IRS lien yields to the claims of these four groups until notice of the tax lien is filed. Thus, interests of the four groups arising after the tax lien comes into existence but before notice of the tax lien is filed have priority over the tax lien.[44]

An increasingly common situation involves IRS-filed notices of tax lien bearing taxpayer names slightly different from the exact name of the taxpayer. When a third party, such as a potential lender to the taxpayer, searches the public records using only the taxpayer's exact name, the third party does not discover the tax liens, and extends credit to the taxpayer which it would not have done had it been aware of the tax liens. Whether the filing gives the IRS lien priority over the third party's claim depends on whether the court concludes that the third party's search was reasonable and diligent.[45]

• Section 6323(b) creates ten so-called superpriorities, that is, types of interests which "prime" or trump the IRS lien even if the interest arises after notice of the tax lien was filed. Several of the categories are further defined by section 6323(h). There is no single theme that explains the ten superpriorities, but some strands wind through several of the superpriorities. For instance, several appear to be explained by the infeasibility or unlikelihood of the third party's checking for federal tax liens in light of the nature of the transaction. Several others are explained by the fact that the transaction increases the value of the taxpayer's property. The IRS is not hurt when the third party is protected to the extent of new money or value made available to the taxpayers. Indeed, the IRS's chance collecting may be enhanced in the long run. Many of the superpriorities are defeated if the third party had actual notice of the tax lien, and one is defeated if the transaction was intended to hinder tax collection. Thus, some patterns exist, but they are hardly intuitively obvious. Tax lawyers dealing with priorities issues would be unwise to rely on general principles. The specific provisions of section 6323 and its Regulations must be reviewed in each case, to identify the peculiarities of the applicable measure(s).[46]

• Finally, section 6323(c) creates another superpriority, this one to protect some security interests arising as a result of commercial financing transactions. A number of pre-1966 cases had held that liens arising from loan agreements providing for future advances did not become choate until the advances actually were made. As a consequence, tax liens filed after the agreement was entered into but before the advance later was made, were held to have priority.

---

[44] *See, e.g.*, Rev. Rul. 2003-108, 2003-2 C.B. 963 (ruling that section 6323(a) priorities are not affected by actual knowledge of the existence of unfilled tax liens).

[45] *E.g.*, In re Spearing Tool & Mfg. Co., 412 F.3d 653 (6th Cir. 2005).

[46] For an illustration, see Rev. Rul. 2006-42, 2006-2 C.B. 337 (discussing the procedures a bank should use in asserting the superpriority under section 6323(b)(10)).

Section 6323(c) addresses this and other situations by according priority to security interests in some common commercial financing situations. Section 6323(d) provides implementing rules for one of those situations.

V. ENFORCED COLLECTION

Unless it engenders "voluntary" payment, the tax lien itself puts no money in federal coffers.[47] The IRS thus will be compelled to engage in enforced collection. The two techniques most frequently used by the IRS are (1) administrative levy and sale[48] and (2) judicial sale with distribution of proceeds.

A. Administrative Levy

The IRS's normal approach to enforced collection involves levying on the taxpayer's property, then, in the case of non-cash property, selling it. First, the IRS gains possession of the property through the related measures of levy, seizure, and distraint. These terms are not always given consistent meaning. Sometimes, "levy" is used broadly to encompass seizure and distraint as well.[49] Other times, the terms are used more narrowly, levy referring to taking the taxpayer's property which is in the custody or possession of a third party, seizure or distraint referring to taking property directly from the taxpayer. We will follow the first locution, using "levy" encompassingly.

Levy is a provisional remedy only.[50] The levy does not change ownership of the property, only its possession. The IRS becomes the custodian of the property. Thus, the IRS has a duty to protect the property, and the taxpayer generally is entitled to a credit against her liability for the extent to which the property deteriorates in value after levy but before sale.[51] A taxpayer who attempts to forcibly regain possession of the property levied upon, or who corruptly or forcibly attempts to interfere with collection by other means, is guilty of a crime.[52]

---

[47] The IRS distinguishes between voluntary payments and involuntary payments. The latter are amounts received as a result of judicial action or administrative levy. *See, e.g.*, Muntwyler v. United States, 703 F.2d 1030, 1033 (7th Cir. 1983). Taxpayers may designate to which of their outstanding liabilities a voluntary payment will be applied, but the IRS asserts the right to allocate involuntary payments as it wishes. *See, e.g.*, O'Dell v. United States, 326 U.S. 451 (10th Cir. 1964); Rev. Rul. 73-305, 1973-2 C.B. 43.

[48] These devices are called "administrative" because the IRS uses them purely on its own. With only a few exceptions, court approval is not required before the IRS levies on or sells property. Nonetheless, the constitutionality of such levy and sale "has long been settled." Phillips v. Commissioner, 283 U.S. 589, 595 (1931).

[49] IRC § 7701(a)(21) ("The term 'levy' includes the power of distraint and seizure by any means").

[50] *See, e.g.*, United States v. National Bank of Commerce, 472 U.S. 713, 721 (1985).

[51] *See, e.g.*, United States v. Pittman, 449 F.2d 623 (7th Cir. 1971).

[52] IRC § 7212.

The language of section 6331 as to the reach of levy is similar to the language of section 6321 as to the reach of the tax lien. Under section 6331(a), the IRS may "levy upon all property and rights to property [of the taxpayer] or on which there is a lien . . . for the payment of such tax." In general, under section 6331(b), a levy extends "only to property possessed and obligations existing at the time [the levy is made]." However, continuing levies—which are effective as well for rights coming into existence after the levy is served—may be made on salaries, wages, and certain other rights to payments.[53] Some types of property are exempt from levy under section 6334. However, the exemptions are generally of limited value. They are designed to avert penury but may be too limited to achieve even that modest objective.[54]

In general, the IRS must notify the taxpayer in writing of its intent to levy at least thirty days before it actually levies, but this requirement does not operate in cases of jeopardy to collection. Section 6331(d) describes the contents of the required notice and the manner in which it must be given.

Levy is prohibited during certain periods. Subject to certain exceptions, levy may not be made (i) during the pendency of proceedings for the refund of divisible taxes (such as employment taxes), (ii) before the IRS has investigated the status of the property in question, (iii) during the pendency of an offer-in-compromise, or (iv) during the term of an installment agreement provided that the taxpayer is living up to the terms of the agreement.[55] Uneconomic levies—those as to which the expenses of levy and sale would exceed the value of the property—are prohibited.[56] Special approvals are required for levies on principal residences (*ex parte* district court approval) or on certain business assets (higher-level IRS approval).

Studies have concluded that the IRS does not always follow all safeguards applicable to levies.[57] The Treasury and IRS have issued revised final regulations reflecting the 1998 Reform Act and providing guidance as to (1) obtaining judicial approval of levies on residences, (2) exemption from levy for certain residences and business assets, and (3) applicable dollar amounts for certain exemptions.[58]

---

[53] IRC § 6331(e), (h). *See* Scott A. Schumacher, *Unnecessary Harm: IRS Levies on Social Security Benefits*, Tax Notes, Oct. 16, 2006, at 265.

[54] The items listed in section 6334 are exempt from levy but not from the tax lien. *E.g.*, In re Voelker, 42 F.3d 1050, 1051 (7th Cir. 1994).

[55] IRC § 6331(i)-(k).

[56] IRC § 6331(f). Whether this is a direction purely to the IRS or a judicially operable defense for taxpayers is not yet clear.

[57] Treasury Inspector General for Tax Administration, Fiscal Year 2006 Review of Compliance with Legal Guidelines when Conducting Seizures of Taxpayers' Property (2006-30-113) (Aug. 9, 2006); Treasury Inspector General for Tax Administration, Fiscal Year 2006 Statutory Review of Compliance with Legal Guidelines when Issuing Levies (2006-30-101) (Aug. 4, 2006).

[58] Treas. Reg. § 301.6334-1. *See* T.D. 9189, 2005-1 C.B. 788.

When the property is in the taxpayer's possession, the IRS levies on it simply by taking it or (if the property is immovable) by providing notice that the property is now in the custody of the IRS. If the taxpayer's property is in the possession of a third party (such as a bank or brokerage house at which the taxpayer has an account), the IRS issues a written notice of levy to the third party. Such notice creates a custodial relationship between the third party and the IRS. The IRS constructively possesses the property until the third party turns it over to the IRS.[59]

There are only two admissible defenses on the basis of which the third party can resist the levy: (1) that the third party neither possesses nor is obligated with respect to any property of the taxpayer or (2) that the property is subject to prior judicial execution or attachment.[60] A third party who improperly fails to honor a levy becomes personally liable in the amount of the property's value (or the amount of the tax liability, if lower) and becomes liable as well for a 50% penalty.[61] A third party who honors the levy is "discharged from any obligation or liability to the delinquent taxpayer and to any other person with respect to such property or rights to property arising from such surrender or payment."[62]

Banks are directed to surrender property "only after 21 days after service of levy."[63] During this period, the taxpayer's account is frozen. The idea is to give the taxpayer and the IRS time to resolve the matter and correct any mistakes before potentially harmful action is taken.

B. Administrative Sale

If what was levied on was money, the IRS will remit it to the Treasury and will credit the taxpayer's account for the payment. If what was levied on was other property, the IRS will need to reduce it to cash by selling it.[64] Alternatively, the IRS may choose to lease levied-on real property, realizing rents therefrom, but this route is not commonly followed.

The principal section governing administrative sale is section 6335. Subsections (a) and (b) require the IRS to give the taxpayer notice of the fact that

---

[59] *See, e.g.*, Phelps v. United States, 421 U.S. 330, 334 (1975).

[60] *National Bank of Commerce, supra*, 472 U.S. at 721-22.

[61] IRC § 6332(d). *See* Danielle M. Smith, *Bank Levies: Proper Compliance Prevents Hefty Penalties*, Tax Notes, April 17, 2006, at 311.

[62] IRC § 6332(e).

[63] IRC § 6332(c). For implementing rules, see Reg. § 301.6332-3.

[64] If the IRS levies on property but for some reason does not sell it, the taxpayer's account must be credited for the value of the property. *See, e.g.*, United States v. Pittman, 449 F.2d 623, 627-28 (7th Cir. 1971). *But see* McCorkle v. Commissioner, 124 T.C. 56 (2005) (taxpayer made $2 million income tax remittance, but the IRS paid it over to the U.S. Marshals Service pursuant to a court forfeiture order entered in a non-tax case; held: the $2 million payment is not applied to the tax liability).

seizure has been made and of the IRS's intent to sell. Both required notices are to be made "as soon as practicable," and the subsections prescribe the manner in which the notices must be given.[65] The IRS typically issues the notice of sale within thirty days after the notice of seizure, but the two notices may be given simultaneously.

A fairly recent Supreme Court case involving state tax sales may eventually affect federal tax sales.[66] In that case, a homeowner failed to pay property taxes. The state taxing authority sent a letter by certified mail, addressed to the property address, stating the authority's intention to sell the property for non-payment of taxes. The owner had not lived there for years, however, and the letter was returned to the state marked "unclaimed." Notice of tax sale was published in the local newspaper, and the property was sold. The Court held the sale to be constitutionally defective. It held that more process was due than was provided. Although declining to prescribe universally applicable procedures, the Court remarked that the state has a duty to do what a person who actually desired to inform a property owner of an impending tax sale of his house would do.[67]

Section 6335 prescribes when ("not . . . less than 10 days nor more than 40 days from the time of giving of [notice of sale]") and where sale may occur. Subsection (e) sets out the manner and conditions of sale, including the minimum sale price (usually at least 80% of the property's forced sale value after subtracting liens on the property superior to the IRS's lien).

If more than one bid meets or exceeds the minimum sale price set by the IRS, the IRS will sell the taxpayer's interest in the property to the highest bidder. Payment must be made via certified or cashier's check. The sale proceeds will be applied first to pay the expenses of sale, then to any specific tax liability on the property, then to the liability on account of which the property was levied on and sold. Should there be any surplus proceeds, they will be credited or refunded to the taxpayer (or other person if legally entitled thereto).[68] If the taxpayer intends to contest the validity of the sale, the taxpayer should not accept any check tendered by the IRS since such acceptance may be viewed as ratification of the sale.[69]

It is important to appreciate that the buyer from the IRS does not necessarily acquire full, free-and-clear ownership of the property. All the IRS can sell is

---

[65] If the IRS fails to give proper notice, the sale may be invalidated. *See, e.g.*, Reece v. Scoggins, 506 F.2d 967, 971 (5th Cir. 1975). However, courts sometimes excuse minor notice defects. *See, e.g.*, Westaire Properties, Inc. v. Tucker, 89-2 U.S. Tax Cas. (CCH) ¶ 9473 (S.D. Cal. 1989).

[66] Jones v. Flowers, 547 U.S. 220, 126 S. Ct. 1708 (2006).

[67] *Id.* at 1716.

[68] IRC § 6342.

[69] *See, e.g.*, Johnson v. Gartlan, 470 F.2d 1104, 1106 (4th Cir. 1973) (IRS did not comply with rules governing sale but the sale was held valid since the taxpayer cashed the proceeds check).

whatever right, title, and interest the taxpayer had in the property.[70] Moreover, the IRS does not warrant the validity of the title or the quality of the property. As a result, a disappointed purchaser has no recourse against the IRS.[71]

Sale extinguishes junior liens (liens with lower priority than the tax lien) on the property as long as the IRS had notified the lienholder of the sale (giving the lienholder the chance to bid at the sale), but the junior lienor has the right to redeem real property within 180 days after the IRS sells it.[72] As a matter of law, senior liens on the property are not affected by an IRS sale,[73] but elimination of the taxpayer's interest may create practical difficulties for senior lienholders.

The taxpayer has several rights and protections in the sale context, some of them significant. For example, (1) the taxpayer may request the IRS to sell the property within sixty days after the request.[74] (2) Sale of seized property may be stayed during pendency of a Tax Court case as to the merits of the liability.[75] (3) Special rules apply if the IRS determines that seized property is likely to perish or decline greatly in value, or cannot be kept without great expense. If the IRS wishes to sell such property, it must (if practicable) give the taxpayer an appraisal of the property. The taxpayer can get the property back by tendering the appraised price or can stop the sale by posting bond for the amount.[76] (4) Both before sale and, as to real property, for up to 180 days after sale, the taxpayer can redeem levied-on property.[77]

C. Judicial Sale

Administrative levy and sale will not always be practicable. The taxpayer's title may be cloudy, or the property may have multiple owners. As a result, there may be few, if any, potential buyers for administrative sale. In such cases, the IRS may resort to judicial sale under section 7403.

Here are the steps. The IRS, through IRS Counsel's office, authorizes the Department of Justice to bring an action in federal District Court.[78] The action

---

[70] *See, e.g.*, National Bank & Trust Co. v. United States, 589 F.2d 1298, 1302 (7th Cir. 1978).

[71] Reg. § 301.6335-1(c)(4)(iii).

[72] IRC § 6337(b)(1).

[73] *See, e.g.*, Pargament v. Fitzgerald, 272 F. Supp. 553 (S.D.N.Y. 1967), *aff'd per curiam*, 391 F.2d 934 (2d Cir. 1968).

[74] IRC § 6335(f).

[75] IRC § 6863(b)(3). This situation can arise when the IRS makes jeopardy assessment and levy, and wishes to sell the levied property, before conclusion of Tax Court review of the notice of deficiency. *See* Chapter 7.

[76] IRC § 6336.

[77] IRC § 6337.

[78] *See* IRC § 7401. As described in Chapter 1, the Department of Justice represents the IRS in all courts except the Tax Court. Since nearly all collection cases—both offensive (the Government brings suit) and defensive (the Government is sued by the taxpayer or a third party)—are tried in District Court, the Department of Justice will represent the IRS. Under section 7401, Justice can bring suit in a tax case only if authorized by the IRS.

usually is called a lien foreclosure suit although the section is styled "Action To Enforce Lien or To Subject Property to Payment of Tax." Under section 7403(b), all persons having liens upon or claiming interests in the property are joined as parties. Under section 7403(c), the District Court determines the merits of all claims.[79] If the tax lien is found meritorious, the court may effect sale of the whole of the property. The net proceeds of sale are divided among the interestholders in proportion to their interests, with the IRS standing in the shoes of the taxpayer to the extent of the taxpayer's interest in the property or, if less, to the extent of the unpaid tax liabilities.[80]

The District Court is not compelled to grant the Government's request to sell the property. Section 7403(c) is phrased permissively: the court "may" decree sale, not "shall" decree it. Thus, District Courts have some equitable discretion to deny sale. However, that discretion is limited.[81]

Once a District Court has granted the IRS's request for judicial sale, taxpayers sometimes request that the sale be stayed pending appeal. Invoking familiar factors, one recent case denied a stay because (1) the taxpayer was unlikely to prevail on the merits on appeal; (2) the taxpayer would not suffer irreparable injury; (3) other parties would be injured by granting the motion; and (4) a significant public interest existed in prompt enforcement of the revenue laws.[82]

VI. ANCILLARY PROCEDURES

Numerous additional mechanisms are available to the IRS to assist in tax collection, either to back-stop the devices described above or as alternatives to them. Some of the additional mechanisms are addressed in other chapters, such as jeopardy and termination assessments and levies (Chapter 7), the trust fund recovery tax of section 6672 (Chapter 14), and transferee and fiduciary liability (Chapter 15). Other mechanisms are described below.

Section 7402(a) is a flexible source of options independent of those provided for in other sections. It grants the District Courts, at the behest of the government, the power to issue "writs . . . and such other orders and processes, and to render such judgments and decrees as may be necessary or appropriate to the enforcement of the internal revenue laws." The subsection mentions injunctions, writs of *ne exeat republica*, and orders appointing receivers. In addition to sec-

---

[79] There is no right to a jury in a section 7403 proceeding. *See, e.g.*, Hyde Properties v. McCoy, 507 F.2d 301 (6th Cir. 1974).

[80] If the proceeds allocated to the taxpayer's interest exceed the tax liability, the excess is paid to the taxpayer.

[81] *See* United States v. Rodgers, 461 U.S. 677, 703-11 (1983) (setting forth factors to guide the exercise of such discretion).

[82] Grass Lake All Seasons Resort, Inc. v. United States, 2005 U.S. Dist. LEXIS 36708 (E.D. Mich. Dec. 15, 2005).

tion 7402, the All Writs Act, 28 U.S.C. section 1651, provides additional authority for issuance of writs by the district courts.

An important type of suit under section 7402 is an action to reduce the tax liability to judgment. The principal significance of this approach is that it extends the life of the lien. Under section 6322, the general federal tax lien continues until the liability is paid "or becomes unenforceable by reason of lapse of time." When a suit to reduce the liability to judgment is begun during the limitations period and such judgment ultimately is obtained, the tax lien remains enforceable during the life of the judgment.[83] As a practical matter, this eliminates any statute of limitations barrier to tax collection. The government typically uses this device only when the outstanding tax liability is large or the IRS believes that assets to pay the liability will be available after the normal ten-year collection window closes. The government often combines in one action demands to reduce the liability to judgment and to foreclose on the tax lien.

Other types of suits in aid of collection, whether under section 7402 or other sections, include: suits to recover refunds made erroneously by the IRS,[84] suits to impose receiverships,[85] suits to open safe deposit boxes, and actions to quiet title.[86] The government also has the ability to intervene in a suit between others that might have the effect of impairing the IRS's interest in the taxpayer's property.[87]

Sometimes, another creditor of the taxpayer may foreclose on or cause sale of property to which the tax lien attaches. If the tax lien is senior, it will remain on the property despite the foreclosure or sale. If the other creditor's claim is senior, the tax lien is terminated if the senior lienor either joins the IRS in a judicial sale or notifies the IRS of its nonjudicial sale.[88] However, if real property of the taxpayer's is subjected to nonjudicial sale, the IRS has the right to redeem the property within 120 days after the sale.[89]

In some instances, the IRS may need or want more information in order to pursue collection. Administratively, the IRS may use summonses in aid of collection under rules largely similar to those governing examination summonses

---

[83] *See, e.g.*, United States v. Hodes, 355 F.2d 746 (2d Cir. 1966).

[84] IRC § 7405. See Section III.A. of Chapter 9.

[85] IRC § 7403(d).

[86] IRC § 7402(e).

[87] IRC § 7424. If the suit is in state court, the government can and usually does remove it to federal District Court under 28 U.S.C. section 1444.

[88] IRC § 7425(a), (b). Section 7425(c) contains special rules as to sales and notices. The courts tend to read the section 7425 rules strictly. *See, e.g.*, Alt & RS Coal Corp. v. United States, 461 F. Supp. 752 (W.D. Pa. 1978).

[89] IRC § 7425(d). The amount the IRS must pay the purchaser of the property is determined under 28 U.S.C. section 2410(d).

described in Chapter 4.[90] In addition, section 6333 provides that, if levy has been made or is about to be made, the IRS may demand that any person having custody or control of books or records relating to the property, show them to the IRS.

Other procedures also may be invoked. For instance, the Government may petition a District Court for a writ of entry, allowing the IRS to enter premises to obtain either information or property. Seizure of property on private property raises constitutional, principally Fourth Amendment, issues. Tax law enforcement is not an exception to constitutional requirements.[91] Accordingly, IRS collection procedures are structured to conform to Fourth Amendment dictates. The IRS typically first seeks consent of the property owner to entry onto the property. If consent is not forthcoming, the government will seek to obtain a writ of entry from the federal District Court, usually from a U.S. Magistrate Judge.

VII. ADMINISTRATIVE AND HYBRID PROTECTIONS FOR TAXPAYERS AND THIRD PARTIES

The collection arsenal available to the IRS is formidable. To avert or to mitigate the possible misuse of weapons in that arsenal (and to cushion the blows of even proper use of such weapons), Congress and the IRS have crafted an array of relief devices for taxpayers and third parties harmed by tax collection. These include administrative mechanisms and hybrid (combination of administrative and judicial) mechanisms described in this Section VII and judicial mechanisms described in Section VIII.

A. Relief From Tax Liens

Section 6325 is an important source of relief options. It allows the IRS, typically upon request by the taxpayer or another affected person, to release the tax lien, discharge property from the lien, subordinate the lien to other interests in or claims upon the property, or issue a certificate stating that the lien does not attach to particular property. A release ends the entire lien. The other actions affect the relationship of the lien to particular assets but have no effect on the lien's relationship to other assets.[92]

---

[90] There are some differences. For instance, the section 7609 special procedures as to third-party summonses apply to examination summonses but not to summonses in aid of collection. IRC § 7609(c)(2)(D).

[91] G.M. Leasing Corp. v. United States, 429 U.S. 338, 358-59 (1977).

[92] The Treasury and the IRS have proposed regulations to update procedures for release of liens and discharge of property under sections 6325, 6503, and 7426. REG-159444-04, 72 Fed. Reg. 1301 (January 11, 2007). See also Rev. Rul. 2005-50, 2005-2 C.B. 124 (ruling that no judicial remedy is available to a third party who seeks a certificate of discharge under section 6325(b)(2)).

Substitution agreements often make sense for taxpayers. Measured by the prices actually realized, administrative sales by the IRS do not have an impressive history. The taxpayer often will be able to obtain a higher price by selling the property herself. Thus, a common type of substitution agreement removes the tax lien from property (so that the taxpayer can convey clear title) and imposes the lien instead on the proceeds obtained from the sale. Other types of substitutions are possible but less common.

Each of the types of actions described under section 6325 is largely independent of the other types. Each type differs as to conditions that trigger relief. In addition, some actions require the IRS to grant the relief if the stated conditions exist while other types give the IRS some discretion as to whether to grant the relief.[93] Accordingly, in each case, the taxpayer's representative must focus on the specific relief desired and the particular rules governing that type of relief.

Other remedies aim not at the lien and its scope but at the filing of the notice of tax lien. The taxpayer and the IRS may enter into a collateral agreement in which the IRS gains security as to payment of the tax liability in return for which the IRS agrees not to file notice of the lien. Acceptable forms of security include, among others, mortgages, letters of credit, and bonds.[94]

Section 6323(j) authorizes the IRS to withdraw a filed notice of tax lien if (1) the IRS determines that the notice was filed prematurely; (2) the IRS and the taxpayer enter into an installment agreement; (3) withdrawal will facilitate collection; or (4) the IRS and the National Taxpayer Advocate agree that withdrawal is in the best interests of the taxpayer and the IRS. A withdrawn lien is treated as if it never had been filed.

In 2005, the IRS consolidated thirty-three formerly geographically dispersed lien units into a single Centralized Case Processing Lien Unit ("CCP-LU") at the IRS's Cincinnati campus. The objectives included providing more timely notice of appeal rights to taxpayers and releasing inappropriate liens in a more timely fashion. These objectives do not appear to have been realized yet. Taxpayers and even IRS employees have experienced difficulties in reaching CCP-LU to initiate contact about particular liens. The National Taxpayer Advocate has urged the IRS to reevaluate this centralization.[95]

---

[93] This difference comes from Congress' use of "shall" in some of the provisions but "may" in others.

[94] For rules governing the use of bonds in this and other collection contexts, see sections 7101-7104.

[95] National Taxpayer Advocate 2006 Annual Report to Congress, Executive Summary I-3 (January 2007).

B. Relief From Levies

Section 6343 creates authority for the release of a levy and notice of levy and for the return of property that has been levied on. As is true of section 6325 as well, a variety of relief triggers exist under section 6343. Some types of relief are mandatory under stated conditions while other types are subject to the discretion of the IRS.[96]

C. Taxpayer Assistance Orders

Considering the size of the IRS and the volume and complexity of its work, it is inevitable that some cases will be handled badly. Sometimes clear procedures for handling a type of situation do not exist; sometimes good procedures do exist but they are not followed because of staff shortage, human error, or other causes. In 1988, Congress established what has evolved into the current Taxpayer Advocate function to cut across bureaucratic obstacles in IRS operations, including collection.

The Taxpayer Advocate's Office is described in Chapter 1. As relevant here, the office is empowered, under section 7811, to issue a Taxpayer Assistance Order ("TAO") if it determines that the taxpayer is suffering or is about to suffer significant hardship because of the way in which the IRS is administering the law. The TAO operates, in effect, as an administrative injunction, halting the IRS action in question. Taxpayers request TAO's by submitting Form 911.

The Taxpayer Advocate's Office does not review substantive decisions by the IRS. A TAO, however, can be a useful option when the problem is the failure of the IRS to follow established procedures.

D. Installment Agreements

Section 6159 authorizes the IRS to enter into written agreements with taxpayers allowing them to pay their liabilities over time. Formerly, the agreement had to provide for eventual full payment of the liability. As a result of 2004 amendment, the IRS now may enter into partial payment installment agreements.

Installment agreements often are useful options, but there are features that need to be considered. Interest continues to accrue as to the deferred amounts.[97] Thus, if the taxpayer can raise money from other sources at no or low interest (for example, by borrowing from a friend or relative), full immediate payment may be less expensive than an installment agreement.

---

[96] The Treasury and the IRS have promulgated revised final regulations under section 6343 relating to return of property after levy in some cases. Reg. § 301.6343-3, T.D. 9213, 2005-2 C.B. 440.

[97] See IRC § 6601(b)(1), (2).

In addition, the IRS usually will not entertain an installment agreement offer unless the taxpayer has filed her return and paid her tax for the current year. Section 6159(c) requires the IRS to accept installment agreements under some circumstances. In other circumstances, when acceptance is discretionary with the IRS, the IRS will require the taxpayer to demonstrate his inability to fully pay immediately. The vehicle for this demonstration is a financial statement setting forth in detail the taxpayer's non-tax debts, his assets, and his future income prospects.[98] The IRS may also demand follow-up information if the term of the agreement exceeds a year, and it may modify or terminate the agreement if the taxpayer's financial status improves enough that full payment becomes feasible. The IRS may insist on further conditions memoralized in collateral agreements.

Under recently revised final regulations, individuals wishing to enter into an installment payment agreement must pay the IRS a user fee of $105 ($43 for low-income individuals).[99] The IRS recently launched a new system that will allow many individuals to apply online for a payment agreement.[100]

E. Offer-in-Compromise

For generations, section 7122 and its predecessors have given the Government the authority to compromise tax liabilities.[101] The liberality of the IRS in entering into compromises has varied over time and by geographical area, prompting frequent criticisms in Congress and by practitioners. Congress has urged the IRS to accept more offers.[102] Responding to complaints about inconsistent decisionmaking as to offers, the IRS has centralized into one office the processing of all offers.

The taxpayer can submit an offer-in-compromise at virtually any stage of the tax process, including during audit, administrative appeal, and litigation. However, by far the majority of offers are submitted during the collection phase. The offer is submitted on IRS Form 656.[103] The IRS usually suspends collection while it is processing the offer.[104] The IRS may accept the offer as made, may reject it outright, or may negotiate with the taxpayer for better terms. Some-

---

[98] IRS Forms 433-A (Collection Information Statement for Individuals), 433-B (Collection Information Statement for Businesses).

[99] T.D. 9306, 71 Fed. Reg. 78074 (Dec. 28, 2006).

[100] IR-2006-119 (July 31, 2006).

[101] The IRS has the power to compromise before the time it refers the case to the Justice Department for prosecution or defense. Justice has that power after such referral. IRC § 7122(a). See section 7122(b) for review by IRS Counsel.

[102] *See, e.g.*, IRC § 7122(d) (requiring the IRS to establish procedures to review rejected offers).

[103] See Rev. Proc. 2003-71, 2003-2 C.B. 517, for procedures for submitting and processing offers.

[104] IRM 5.8.3.7. Revenue Procedure 2003-71, 2003-2 C.B. 517, explains procedures for submitting an offer-in-compromise and the procedures used by the IRS in processing an offer.

times, as a condition for accepting the offer, the IRS will require the taxpayer to enter into collateral agreements. The most common of them deal with future income, reduction of the taxpayer's basis in assets, and waiver of loss carryovers and other deductions.

The pre-printed language on the Form sets out numerous conditions the taxpayer will be expected to honor. Breach of those conditions can lead to revocation of the compromise. Apart from such breach, the compromise is binding on both parties from the point at which the IRS notifies the taxpayer in writing of the offer's acceptance. However, the agreement may be voided under the conditions described in Regulation section 301.7122-1(d)(5). Contract law principles govern interpretation of an accepted compromise.[105]

There are three bases on which an offer can be accepted: doubt as to liability, doubt as to collectability, and effective tax administration. Doubt as to liability has been a basis for many years, but it is not frequently asserted. Presumably, this is because of the availability of both pre-assessment and post-assessment channels (such as the Appeals Office, Tax Court review, and refund suits) for challenging the merits of IRS determinations. Nonetheless, an offer based on doubt as to liability may be useful if the taxpayer failed to take advantage of such alternative channels.

Doubt as to collectability is overwhelmingly the most frequent basis for offers. The notion is that, although the taxpayer owes the tax, not even the IRS can "get blood from a stone." The taxpayer will assert that he is now, and foreseeably will remain, unable to pay the entire liability. The taxpayer will offer an amount that represents the present value of the taxpayer's ability to pay. If the IRS accepts the offer, it will take the amount and cancel the remainder of the liabilities.

The IRS will accept an offer based on doubt as to collectability when it is unlikely that the tax liability can be collected in full and the amount offered reasonably reflects collection potential. The IRS's objective is to collect what is collectible as early as possible and at the least cost.[106] Offers are viewed as an alternative to putting a case in CNC (currently not collectible) status. A further objective is to give taxpayers a "fresh start" to help them to voluntarily comply with their obligations under the tax system.

The key in doubt-as-to-collectability offers is determining what amount constitutes an adequate offer. Offers may not be rejected solely because the amount of the offer is low.[107] Rather, what matters is whether the offer reasonably reflects collection potential.[108]

---

[105] Reg. § 301.7122-1(c).

[106] IRS Policy Statement P-5-100.

[107] IRC § 7122(c)(3)(A).

[108] IRM 57.10.10.1(1).

Reasonable collection potential reflects at least[109] (i) the quick sale value of the taxpayer's assets plus (ii) the present value of the taxpayer's future income minus necessary living expenses. The taxpayer must provide detailed information in support of these amounts. An offer that fails to do so (or that fails to conform to the other technical conditions set out for the Form 656) will be returned by the IRS as "not processable." About 45% of submitted offers have returned to taxpayers without being considered, because they are deemed to be "not processable."

The "present value" component in the prior paragraph adverts to the taxpayer's projected income and expenses over the next forty-eight months (for offers as to which the offered amount is to be fully paid in cash within ninety days after acceptance of the offer by the IRS) or the next sixty months (for offers involving payments deferred for a longer period). Under section 7122(c)(2), necessary living expenses are determined by reference to "schedules of national and local allowances" developed by the IRS.[110]

The third basis for accepting an offer—effective tax administration—was added as a result of congressional prompting as part of the process during consideration of the 1998 Reform Act. It is meant to be a flexible category, and insufficient experience exists to evaluate how significant this basis ultimately will be.[111] The key authority is Regulation section 301.7122-1(b)(3) and (c)(3).

There is a $150 user fee with respect to most offers-in-compromise. The fee does not apply to offers based on doubt as to liability or offers submitted by low-income taxpayers. The fee may be applied against the offered amount in some situations.[112]

IRS policy has been not to consider offers-in-compromise while the taxpayer/debtor is in bankruptcy. After prodding from bankruptcy courts,[113] the IRS announced that, instead of considering offers from debtors, the IRS will con-

---

[109] The IRS sometimes also considers amounts that could be collected from third parties (such as transferees) and the amount the taxpayer should be able to raise from assets which may be beyond the effective reach of the IRS (such as property located outside the United States).

[110] *See* Temp. Reg. § 301.7122-1T(b)(2)(ii). Nonetheless, interesting disputes can occur as to whether particular expenses are necessary. *See, e.g.*, Pixley v. Commissioner, 123 T.C. 269 (2004) (considering whether tithes should be taken into account in determining the taxpayer's ability to pay for offer-in-compromise purposes); Fowler v. Commissioner, T.C. Memo. 2004-163 (CCH) (2004) (IRS's use of national statistical amount as estimate of taxpayers' expenses, rather than expense figures provided by taxpayers held to be arbitrary and capricious). *Cf.* Sarasota, Inc. v. Weaver, 2004 U.S. Dist. LEXIS 22515 (E.D. Pa. 2004) (upholding $200 per month cigarette expenses as reasonably necessary for debtor's support and maintenance in Chapter 13 bankruptcy case).

[111] *See* Speltz v. Commissioner, 124 T.C. 165 (2005) (holding that the IRS did not abuse its discretion by rejecting an "effective tax administration" offer based on unfair consequences of the alternative minimum tax), *aff'd*, 454 F.3d 782 (8th Cir. 2006); David M. Fogel, *The "Effective Tax Administration" Offer in Compromise*, Tax Notes, Aug. 29, 2005, at 1015.

[112] Treas. Reg. § 300.3(b). *See* T.D. 9086, 2003-2 C.B. 817.

[113] *E.g.*, In re Peterson, 317 B.R. 532 (Bankr. D. Neb. 2004).

sider payment proposals made by debtors as part of review of proposed bankruptcy plans.[114]

The Tax Increase Prevention and Reconciliation Act of 2005 ("TIPRA") makes important changes to the offer-in-compromise program. A taxpayer making a lump-sum offer (defined as payable in five or fewer installments) must submit, along with the offer, a payment of 20% of the offered amount, in addition to the $150 user fee. Offers not accompanied by the payment will be returned as non-processable. If the taxpayer submits a periodic payment offer (consisting of more than five installments), the first proposed installment must be included with the offer.[115]

The IRS has revised Form 656 and issued guidance on the TIPRA changes.[116] There are concerns that participation in the offer-in-compromise program has declined since imposition of user fees and that TIPRA changes will further reduce such participation.[117] More favorably, TIPRA also provides that if the IRS fails to act on an offer within twenty-four months, the offer will be deemed accepted.[118]

F. Collection Due Process

The controversial set of remedies, known as the Collection Due Process ("CDP") rights, is contained in sections 6320 and 6330, added by the 1998 Reform Act. These rights are triggered when the IRS files a notice of tax lien against the taxpayer or before the IRS levies on the taxpayer's property. The taxpayer has a right to hearings on these occasions. The two hearings may be consolidated for efficiency. If two hearings are held, the taxpayer may not raise at the second hearing issues raised at the prior hearing.[119]

The IRS is required to inform the taxpayer of the CDP rights. The statutes describe the manner and contents of such notice. The taxpayer requests CDP hearing by filing Form 12153. If the taxpayer timely files the Form, collection activity and the collection statute of limitations usually are suspended during the CDP process. However, on motion and for good cause shown, the IRS may be allowed to pursue collection even after a CDP appeal has been filed.[120] Tax-

---

[114] Chief Counsel Notice CC-2004-025 (July 12, 2004).

[115] IRC § 7122(c)(1)(A), (B).

[116] IRS Notice 2006-68, 2006-31 I.R.B. 1; IR-2006-106 (July 11, 2006); FS-2006-22 (July 2006).

[117] *See, e.g.,* Richard L. Alltizer & Jeffrey L. Bryant, *TIPRA Further Compromises a Taxpayer's Ability to Compromise,* Taxes, Nov. 2006, at 23; Joseph DiSciullo, *ABA Tax Section Analyzes Offer in Compromise Amendments,* Tax Notes, Oct. 30, 2006, at 451; National Taxpayer Advocate's 2007 Objectives Report to Congress 3-4 (June 30, 2006).

[118] IRC § 7122(f).

[119] Reg. §§ 301.6320-1(e), 301.6330-1(e).

[120] *E.g.,* Burke v. Commissioner, 124 T.C. 189 (2005); CC-2005-007, CC-2005-009 (May 20, 2005).

payers subject to jeopardy collection proceedings are entitled only to post-levy, not pre-levy, CDP hearing.[121]

A taxpayer who timely invokes his CDP rights is entitled to both administrative and judicial consideration. First, an IRS Appeals Officer who has not previously been involved with the case will meet with the taxpayer. The Appeals Officer must confirm that the IRS has taken the required steps in the collection process. In addition, the taxpayer may raise at the hearing any proper defenses to the lien or levy, spousal defenses, and alternatives (such as an offer-in-compromise or an installment agreement) which the taxpayer may propose to the collection action contemplated by the IRS. The taxpayer can contest her substantive liability for the tax only if she did not receive a notice of deficiency or otherwise have opportunity to challenge the asserted liability.[122]

The Appeals Officer's decision after the hearing is set forth in a Notice of Determination sent to the taxpayer. If the determination is adverse to the taxpayer, he may request judicial review on an abuse-of-discretion standard.[123] Originally, the case would be brought in either the Tax Court or District Court, depending on which court had jurisdiction over the type of tax involved. The Tax Court heard principally income tax cases, while the District Court handled mainly cases involving employment taxes, the section 6672 trust fund recovery "penalty," and the section 6702 frivolous return penalty. However, many cases were filed in the wrong court. Accordingly, the Pension Protection Act of 2006 amended section 6330(d)(1) to give the Tax Court exclusive jurisdiction to review all CDP determinations after October 17, 2006, regardless of the type of tax liability involved.[124]

A taxpayer who fails to timely request CDP review may request an "equivalent hearing." An equivalent hearing takes place in the Appeals Office under largely the same ground rules as govern CDP hearings. However, collection activity will not be suspended, and judicial review of Appeals' decision letter after the equivalent hearing is not available.[125]

There have been many studies of IRS collection performance and the effect of the CDP regime on it.[126] The benefits and costs of CDP have been widely debated. What cannot be doubted is that CDP has consumed substantial admin-

---

[121] IRC § 6330(f).

[122] IRC § 6330(c)(2). Liabilities that the taxpayer self-reported on his or her returns may be so contested. Montgomery v. Commissioner, 122 T.C. 1 (2004), *acq.*, AOD 2005-03 (Dec. 19, 2005).

[123] *See, e.g.*, Goza v. Commissioner, 114 T.C. 176 (2000).

[124] The IRS Chief Counsel's Office has issued guidance as to the new jurisdictional rules. CC-2007-001 (Oct. 17, 2006).

[125] *See, e.g.*, Herrick v. Commissioner, 85 T.C. Memo. (CCH) 1467 (2003).

[126] *E.g.*, Government Accountability Office, Little Evidence of Procedural Errors in Collection Due Process Appeal Cases, but Opportunities Exist to Improve the Program (GAO-07-112) (Oct. 2006); Treasury Inspector General for Tax Administration, Fiscal Year 2006 Statutory Review of Compliance with Lien Due Process Procedures (2006-30-094) (June 2006), *available at* www.tigta.gov.

istrative and judicial resources. By 2005, CDP cases represented about one-quarter of the workload of the Appeals Office. Over a six-year period, more than 92,000 CDP hearings and more than 30,000 equivalent hearings were held.[127]

In addition, CDP is perennially the most frequently litigated class of tax issue.[128] Numerous important CDP issues are decided each year. In recent years, questions involving jurisdiction,[129] record-for-review,[130] and recording of the appeals hearing[131] have been particularly prominent.

Most CDP petitioners appear *pro se*, and some are tax protesters or others interested in obstruction. As a result, section 6673 damages and similar sanctions have often been imposed on CDP taxpayers asserting frivolous issues or using the process for delay.[132] They have not proved sufficient, however. Accordingly, the Treasury and IRS have finalized revised CDP regulations designed to curb frivolous challenges and delay tactics.[133] The IRS Chief Counsel's CDP "Handbook" is an excellent resource.[134]

G. Collection Appeals Program

Section 7123(a) directs the IRS to prescribe procedures for early Appeals Office consideration of both examination and collection issues. In response, Appeals operates its Collection Appeals Program ("CAP"). CAP is independent of CDP, and the two sets of procedures differ in material ways.

An attractive feature of CAP is that it is available under more circumstances than is CDP. The taxpayer can invoke CAP (1) before or after the IRS files notice of tax lien, (2) to challenge IRS decisions not to withdraw a notice of lien or not to issue certificates of discharge, subordination, or non-attachment of the lien, (3) before or after the IRS levies on or seizes property, and (4) to contest an

---

[127] Carol M. Luttati, *Final Regulations Make Significant Changes to the Collection Due Process Procedures*, J. Tax Prac. & Proc., Oct.-Nov. 2006, at 9.

[128] *See, e.g.,* National Taxpayer Advocate 2006 Annual Report to Congress, Executive Summary III-1 (Jan. 2007).

[129] Boyd v. Commissioner, 451 F.3d 8 (1st Cir. 2006); Greene-Thapedi v. Commissioner, 126 T.C. 1 (2006); Smith v. Commissioner, 124 T.C. 36 (2005).

[130] *E.g.,* Murphy v. Commissioner, 469 F.3d 27 (1st Cir. 2006); Robinette v. Commissioner, 439 F.3d 455 (8th Cir. 2006); Chief Counsel Notice CC-2006-008 (Dec. 27, 2005) (describing procedures for submitting standard, comprehensive CDP records for review).

[131] *E.g.,* Calafati v. Commissioner, 127 T.C. 219 (2006).

[132] *See* IRS Information Release IR-2005-64 (June 2, 2005) (listing over two dozen such cases in 2004 and 2005).

[133] T.D. 9290, 2006-2 C.B. 879 (amending Treas. Reg. § 301.6320-1); T.D. 9291, 2006-2 C.B. 887 (amending Treas. Reg. § 301.6330-1).

[134] Chief Counsel Notice CC-2006-019 (Aug. 18, 2006).

IRS decision to deny or to terminate an installment agreement. An unattractive feature is that the Appeals Officer's decision is not subject to judicial review.[135]

VIII. JUDICIAL PROTECTIONS FOR TAXPAYERS AND THIRD PARTIES

There also are purely judicial remedies available to taxpayers and third parties aggrieved by overly zealous tax collection. Because of the doctrine of sovereign immunity, the government can be sued only when it has consented to the type of action being brought against it. Some waivers of sovereign immunity are contained in the Code; others are in different statutes.

A. Judicial Remedies in the Code

Subchapter B of Chapter 76 of the Code (sections 7421-7437) provides for suits by taxpayers and third parties against the IRS. We already have discussed some of suits, such as refund suits under section 7422 (Chapter 9),[136] actions to review jeopardy and termination assessments under section 7429 (Chapter 7), and recovery of administrative and litigation costs and fees under section 7430 (Chapter 8).

Another significant provision is section 7426. Section 7426(a) authorizes four types of suit against the United States.[137] These are suits for (1) determination that the levy was wrongful, (2) return of surplus proceeds (amounts raised by sale of the property to the extent they exceed the tax liability), (3) funds held as substituted sale proceeds under an agreement to discharge property from the lien to allow its sale, and (4) determination that the interest of the IRS is less than the IRS asserts when, under section 6325(b), other property has been substituted for the taxpayer's property subject to the tax lien.

As to some of these categories, only a third party, not the taxpayer, may bring the suit. Additionally, as to wrongful levy suits, the third party must have an ownership, possessory, or security interest. An unsecured creditor lacks standing to sue.[138]

---

[135] *See* Rev. Proc. 99-28, 1999-2 C.B. 109.

[136] Amounts recovered by the IRS as a result of enforced collection can constitute payments, giving rise to the refund remedy as long as the requirements described in Chapter 9 have been satisfied. A third party who paid the taxpayer's liability also may pursue the refund remedy. United States v. Williams, 514 U.S. 527 (1995). Subsequently, the Supreme Court held that suit under section 7426(a) provides the exclusive remedy for wrongful levies. Effectively, this limits the *Williams* refund suit to wrongful liens as to the property of third practices. EC Term of Years Trust v. United States, 127 S. Ct. 1763 (2007). *See* Steve R. Johnson, *Recent Supreme Court Cases Read Remedies Restrictively*, 2614 ABA Sec. of Tax'n News Quarterly 17 (Summer 2007).

[137] Suit cannot be brought against IRS officers or employees individually. IRC § 7426(d). If it is, the United States is substituted as the defendant for the officer or employee. IRC § 7426(e).

[138] *See, e.g.*, Aspinall v. United States, 984 F.2d 355 (10th Cir. 1993).

A number of sections authorize damages suits by taxpayers or third parties aggrieved by improper IRS collection actions. Recovery of damages is authorized under section 7426(h) for IRS violation of any Code provision, under section 7431 for unauthorized inspection or disclosure of tax returns and return information, under section 7432 for improper failure to release a tax lien, under section 7433 for unauthorized collection actions, and under section 7435 for unauthorized enticement of information disclosure.

The sections typically require that the IRS's improper action or failure was intentional, knowing, or reckless. The amount of damages recoverable typically is capped at stated levels. Frequently, a precondition of recovery is that the taxpayer or other party have exhausted her administrative remedies as to the failure before bringing suit. Damages suits are brought in federal District Court.[139]

B. Judicial Remedies Under Other Statutes

Many types of suits as to property allegedly subject to the tax lien are allowed by 28 U.S.C. section 2410(a). The United States can be made a party to actions as to the property commenced in federal District Court or state court (although the government typically will remove state cases to federal court). The suits may be to (1) quiet title as to the property, (2) foreclose on the property (action brought by third-party creditor), (3) partition the property (action brought by non-debtor co-owner), (4) condemn the property (eminent domain action brought by governmental unit), and (5) interplead funds (action brought by third party holding property when faced with conflicting claims by IRS and others). Those seeking relief under 28 U.S.C. section 2410 should scrupulously comply with its requirements.[140]

Filing a bankruptcy petition is a major defensive option for taxpayers confronting serious tax collection. Chapter 1 briefly described the role of the bankruptcy court in tax controversies. For a variety of reasons—including client reluctance or failure to meet eligibility criteria under particular chapters of the Bankruptcy Code—bankruptcy sometimes will not be an option. However, when it is available, bankruptcy always should be compared to more traditional remedies and defensive measures.

Detailed discussion of bankruptcy is beyond the scope of this course, but we will note some salient features. When a taxpayer files a bankruptcy petition, a bankruptcy estate comes into being. All of the taxpayer's assets, except those

---

[139] *See* Steve R. Johnson, *Code Sec. 7433: Damages Against the IRS for Wrongful Collection Actions*, J. Tax Prac. & Proc., Dec.-Jan. 2007, at 27.

[140] *See, e.g.*, United States v. Aultman, 2006 Dist. LEXIS 11984 (W.D. Pa. 2006) (holding that federal tax liens remained on the property because of failure to comply with formal notice requirements under 28 U.S.C. § 2410(b) and IRC § 7425(a)(1)).

which are exempt from bankruptcy administration,[141] become the property of the bankruptcy estate, which is directed by a bankruptcy trustee. Depending on when the IRS acquired the assets, the IRS may be required to turn over to the trustee assets of the taxpayer's which the IRS had acquired by levy or otherwise.[142]

Some aspects of the bankruptcy process relate to determination of the extent of liability,[143] but there are at least four significant aspects of bankruptcy bearing on collection. (1) Under 11 U.S.C. section 362(a), an automatic stay comes into existence when the bankruptcy petition is filed. The stay halts or delays creditor action against property of the debtor's or the estate's. Because of faulty internal controls, the IRS sometimes violates the automatic stay. When it does, the debtor may be able to recover damages under IRC section 7433(e) or 11 U.S.C. section 362(h).

(2) Along with the bankruptcy petition, the debtor must file extensive schedules of assets and liabilities, and further discovery opportunities exist later. These features may provide the IRS with valuable information to assist future collection. Under 18 U.S.C. section 152, lying as to the information constitutes a crime: bankruptcy fraud.

(3) The various claims against the estate, including tax claims, are paid in a prescribed order. In general, the order is: administrative expenses (such as taxes arising after the petition is filed), secured claims, priority unsecured claims, and general unsecured claims.[144]

(4) Some taxes and other debts are dischargeable. The IRS is prohibited from trying to collect discharged taxes not paid in the bankruptcy process. However, if the tax lien exists, it survives bankruptcy.

Also relevant to insolvencies is 31 U.S.C. section 3713(a), a superpriority statute. It provides that claims of the United States, including tax claims, are to be paid before the claims of other creditors. This priority attaches upon insolvency and is indefeasible.[145]

---

[141] For exemption rules, see 11 U.S.C. section 522. Bankruptcy exemptions and tax exemptions (such as assets exempt from levy under IRC section 6344) are wholly independent. Thus, the IRS may eventually proceed against bankruptcy-exempt property.

[142] In return, the IRS is entitled to "adequate protection." *See, e.g.*, United States v. Whiting Pools, Inc., 462 U.S. 198 (1983).

[143] For example, the IRS will be compelled to submit claims for the taxes it believes to be owed, and the taxpayer and other creditors can challenge those claims. In addition, the trustee can request prompt determination of new tax liabilities. 11 U.S.C. § 505(b).

[144] The filing of notice of the tax lien gives the IRS a secured claim to the extent of its interest in the value of the taxpayer's property. 11 U.S.C. § 506. Some unassessed tax liabilities are entitled to eighth priority status under 11 U.S.C. section 507.

[145] *See, e.g.*, Greene v. United States, 440 F.2d 1304 (Fed. Cir. 2006).

C. The Anti-Injunction Act

Section 7421(a) provides that "no suit for the purpose of restraining the assessment or collection of any tax shall be maintained in any court by any person." "The purpose . . . is to permit the [IRS] to assess and collect taxes without judicial interference and to require that disputes be determined in a suit for refund."[146]

However, the prohibition is not absolute. The statute itself contains a number of express exceptions. In addition, a very limited judicially created exception exists. It is available only when the taxpayer establishes both that (1) under the most liberal view of the law and the facts, it is clear that the Government cannot prevail on the merits and (2) the taxpayer will suffer irreparable harm for which no adequate remedy at law exists.[147]

D. Non-Starters

Forgoing, or ineligible for, the available judicial remedies, some taxpayers have attempted to avail themselves of other remedies—without success. The Federal Tort Claims Act ("FTCA") is a major waiver of sovereign immunity. However, the FTCA does not apply to claims "arising in respect of the assessment or collection of any tax."[148] Similarly, damages suits based on state law also are barred by sovereign immunity and, in some cases, qualified immunity.[149]

In *Bivens*, the Supreme Court created a damages remedy with respect to constitutional violations by government officials and employees.[150] However, a *Bivens* action will not lie if Congress intended to provide an exclusive remedy or if Congress created a statutory scheme that it sees as an adequate substitute for *Bivens*. Accordingly, because of the existence of section 7433 and other Code damages sections, the majority view is that a *Bivens* suit is unavailable with respect to IRS actions.[151]

---

[146] Powers v. Gibbs, 1989 U.S. Dist LEXIS 12302 (D.D.C. 1989). Section 7421 (the Anti-Injunction Act) and 28 U.S.C. sections 2201-02 (the Declaratory Judgment Act) are coextensive in practical effect. *E.g.*, Ambort v. United States, 392 F.3d 1138, 1140 (10th Cir. 2004).

[147] Enochs v. Williams Packing & Navigation Co., 370 U.S. 1, 6-7 (1962).

[148] 28 U.S.C. § 2680(c). *See, e.g.*, Miklautsch v. Gibbs, 90-2 USTC ¶ 50,587 (D. Alas. 1990) (taxpayer unable to recover under FTCA, RICO, or *Bivens*).

[149] *E.g.*, Kyler v. Everson, 442 F.3d 1251 (10th Cir. 2006) (also requiring the taxpayer to pay $8,000 in costs as a sanction for filing a frivolous appeal).

[150] Bivens v. Six Unknown Named Agents, 403 U.S. 388 (1971).

[151] *See, e.g.*, Adams v. Johnson, 355 F.3d 1179 (9th Cir. 2004); Christopher M. Pietruszkiewicz, *A Constitutional Cause of Action and the Internal Revenue Code: Can You Shoot (Sue) the Messenger?*, 54 Syracuse L. Rev. 1 (2004).

IX. STATUTE OF LIMITATIONS

The IRS can collect only within the statute of limitations ("SOL") period. As previously noted, under section 6502(a)(1), the normal SOL period ends ten years after the date on which the liability was assessed. The IRS calls the collection statute expiration date the "CSED."

Many events can extend or suspend the running of the ten-year period. Some of the more important are: the filing of a bankruptcy petition,[152] submission of an offer-in-compromise ("OIC"),[153] filing a request for a CDP hearing or seeking judicial review of the results of a CDP hearing,[154] requesting spousal relief from a joint income tax liability,[155] requesting an installment agreement or appealing the IRS's rejection of an installment agreement,[156] judicial control over or custody of the taxpayer's assets,[157] continuous absence of the taxpayer from the United States for at least six months,[158] and extension of time to pay estate tax under sections 6161(a) or 6166.[159] Many other conditions suspending the SOL are described in section 6501, section 6503, and other sections.

The collection limitations period may be extended via a consent duly executed by the taxpayer and the IRS.[160] The IRS uses Form 900 for this purpose.[161] To be valid, the Form 900 must be executed on or before the CSED. In a Supreme Court case, the IRS had properly assessed unpaid employment taxes against a partnership. The Court held that such assessment suffices to extend the statute of limitations to collect tax in judicial proceedings from general partners liable for payment of the partnership's debts.[162]

Fairly recent legislation altered the SOL rules. First, the 1998 Reform Act amended section 6502(a) to prohibit the IRS from seeking taxpayer consents to extend the collection SOL except in conjunction with an installment agreement or a release of levy.[163]

---

[152] IRC § 6503(h).

[153] IRC §§ 6331(i)(5), 6331(k)(1).

[154] IRC §§ 6320(e)(1), 6330(e)(1).

[155] IRC § 6015(e)(2).

[156] IRC § 6331(k)(2).

[157] IRC § 6503(b).

[158] IRC § 6503(c).

[159] IRC § 6503(d).

[160] For principles governing consents, see Chapter 5.

[161] The IRS prefers to obtain the taxpayer's original signature on the Form 900. In some cases, however, it will accept a Form 900 received by facsimile transmission thus bearing only a fax signature. *See* SCA 200504033, 2005 WL 190327 (Jan. 28, 2005).

[162] United States v. Galletti, 541 U.S. 114 (2004).

[163] The 1998 Reform Act, section 3461(c)(2), also contained a provision dealing with waivers secured by the IRS in connection with an OIC before December 31, 1999. It provided that any such waiver would expire on the later of December 31, 2003, or on the expiration of the ten-year SOL period.

Second, before the 1998 Reform Act, the Form 656 for OIC contained a condition whereby the taxpayer consented to suspension of the SOL while the offer was being considered by the IRS plus an additional year. The 1998 Act amended sections 6331(i)(5) and 6331(k)(1) to provide, for offers submitted or pending on January 1, 2000, that the suspension period ended thirty days after the IRS ceases its consideration of the offer.[164] However, legislation in 2000 changed the rule. It provided that the SOL period was not suspended while offers were pending or in effect.[165] In 2002, Congress changed the rule again, to reapply the suspension during the pendency of offers.[166] These changes greatly complicate the task of computing the CSED when years between 1998 and 2002 are involved. The risk of error here is high.[167]

The IRS sometimes erroneously calculates the CSED. This can adversely affect the IRS because the Service may halt collection in the mistaken belief that the SOL has expired or it may defer collection in the mistaken belief that time remains on the SOL. The taxpayer also can be hurt by being subjected to collection efforts beyond the time for which the taxpayer legally was at hazard.

Sometimes the IRS calculates the CSED automatically by computer; other times, IRS personnel calculate it manually. Unfortunately, the IRS uses multiple computers, not all of which are correctly updated when some of the many events occur which suspend or extend the SOL. In addition, IRS personnel are not always promptly trained as to statutory changes to the suspension or extension conditions or may misinterpret the effects of the statutes when applied to complex facts.[168]

The IRS is attempting to address the problems of inaccurately calculated CSEDs. Nonetheless, the wise practitioner will not simply rely on whatever the IRS asserts the CSED to be in a particular case. Instead, the practitioner should independently calculate the CSED whenever relevant in a collection case.[169]

---

[164] The Treasury and the IRS have promulgated final regulations amending Treas. Reg. § 301.6502-1 to reflect these provisions of the 1998 Reform Act. T.D. 9284, 2006-2 C.B. 582, *corrected by* 71 Fed. Reg. 56225-04 (Sept. 26, 2006).

[165] Community Renewal Tax Relief Act, Pub. L. No. 106-554, 114 Stat. 2763A-589 (amending section 6331(i); effective December 20, 2000).

[166] Job Creation and Worker Assistance Act, Pub. L. No. 107-147, 116 Stat. 21 (amending section 6331(k); effective March 9, 2002). There is no statutory suspension of the SOL period as to installment agreements. Instead, the IRS secures written waiver agreements from the taxpayer(s) in case of installment agreements.

[167] For a good example of the application of these complex rules, see United States v. Ryals, 96 AFTR 2d 2005-7344 (N.D. Fla. 2005), *aff'd*, 480 F.3d 1101 (11th Cir. 2007).

[168] For example, not surprisingly, the effects of the 1998, 2000, and 2004 changes described above have caused confusion in many collection cases.

[169] These problems are discussed at length in 1 Annual Report to Congress of National Taxpayer Advocate 183-192 (2004).

The common law doctrine of laches denies relief to parties who "sleep on their rights." However, "[i]t is well settled that the United States is not . . . subject to the defense of laches in enforcing its rights."[170] Thus, IRS collection action which is timely under section 6502 cannot be challenged as untimely under the doctrine of laches.

X. TAX COLLECTION BY PRIVATE COMPANIES

The collection structure described thus far focuses on the IRS as the body charged with collecting federal taxes. Legislation in 2004 made a conceptually dramatic change. It authorized the IRS to enter into contracts with private companies to collect assessed but unpaid federal taxes.[171]

It is too early to judge the significance of this new option. Proponents stress the revenue potential, pointing to the growing amounts of assessed but uncollected taxes. Opponents fear loss of privacy, harassment of taxpayers, and consequent erosion of support for the tax system. The IRS has announced detailed program safeguards designed to assuage such concerns.[172] Actual collection began in fall 2006 with about 19,000 accounts being given to three firms, which collected slightly over $8,000,000. Nonetheless, substantial and growing opposition may lead to curtailment or repeal of the private collection program.[173]

Here are the major features of the initiative. The private companies would be allowed, under contract with the IRS, to locate and contact taxpayers with outstanding liabilities for any type of tax. The company will not be permitted to perform acts that IRS employees could not legally perform. Indeed, the private collectors' range of permissible action is more circumscribed. If they cannot secure full payment immediately, private collectors' main option would be to offer the taxpayer an installment agreement providing for full payment in up to five years. If the taxpayer cannot fully pay over five years, the financial information the company obtains with respect to the taxpayer is to be provided to the IRS for further action.

To prevent or to remedy abuse, a taxpayer aggrieved by the actions of a private collector may (1) ask the Taxpayer Advocate's Office to intervene to halt the actions and (2) under section 7433A, sue the private contractor for damages to

---

[170] United States v. Summerlin, 310 U.S. 414, 416 (1940); *see, e.g.,* Lucia v. United States, 474 F.2d 565, 570, n.13 (5th Cir. 1973).

[171] American Jobs Creation Act of 2004, § 881, Pub. L. No. 108-357, 118 Stat. 1586 (creating new Code sections 6306 and 7433A and amending Code sections 7809 and 7811) (effective October 22, 2004).

[172] *See* IRS Information Release IR-2006-42 (Mar. 9, 2006) (and accompanying fact sheet FS-2006-18).

[173] *See, e.g.,* Dustin Stamper, *Twelve Senators Seeking to Kill IRS Private Debt Collection,* Tax Notes, Jan. 22, 2007, at 286; *Dorgan, Murray Introduce New Legislation to Halt IRS Use of Private Debt Collectors,* Bankr. L. Rep., Jan. 25, 2007, at 78.

the same extent that the IRS could have been sued had the IRS taken the actions in questions. The IRS is allowed to compensate a private contractor up to 25% of the amounts collected.[174]

PROBLEM

The Church of Redemption by Faith has relatively few members, but they are noted for the strength of their commitment to the Church's teachings. Alana and Bob Plumb met as members of one of the Church's congregations. They married in 1995. They remain married and also remain strong supporters of the Church. Alana and Bob had one child. Bob is employed as a computer software specialist. Alana is a homemaker. They file joint federal income tax returns.

In 1995, Bob's employer was extremely profitable and it projected continuing robust growth for the years ahead. As part of its employee reward-and-incentive program that year, the company granted Bob a substantial amount of incentive stock options ("ISOs"). Bob exercised the ISOs in 1998, receiving the stock. He consulted his certified public accountant as to the proper tax treatment of these transactions. The C.P.A. told Bob that there would be no tax until Bob sold the stock. This advice was correct as to the regular income tax. However, the C.P.A. neglected to inform Bob that alternative minimum tax liability arises in the year ISOs are exercised. Relying on their C.P.A.'s erroneous advice, Bob and Alana filed their 1998 income tax return without reporting any income (for either regular tax or AMT purposes) with respect to the ISOs and the stock.

In 2000, the IRS audited the Plumbs' 1998 return. The IRS revenue agent raised the AMT issue. In 2000, after unsuccessful Appeals Office discussion, the IRS issued a statutory notice of deficiency containing the AMT adjustments and determining that a deficiency of over $100,000 existed as to the Plumbs' 1998 return.[175]

Between 1998 and 2000, the Plumbs suffered both personal tragedy and economic misfortune. First, as part of a sharp downturn in the technology sector of the economy, Bob's company collapsed. Bob lost his job, and the stock in the company that Bob had received from exercising the ISOs became worthless.

Second, the Plumbs' child was diagnosed with a virulent disease. The Plumbs exhausted their savings and went into substantial debt because of the resultant medical bills. The Plumbs had no health insurance because a fundamental tenet of their Church is that buying insurance demonstrates a lack of faith in the benevolence of the Creator. Despite the expensive medical care, the Plumbs' child died in 2000.

---

[174] *See generally* IRS Pub. 4518 What You Can Expect When the IRS Assigns Your Account to a Private Collection Agency (Aug. 2006).

[175] For purposes of this Problem, assume that the IRS's adjustment is legally correct. In fact, many taxpayers were hit by this tax "trap." *See* Warren Rojas, *Outdated AMT Claims First Victims of the 21st Century*, Tax Notes, Apr. 30, 2001, at 691.

As part of their efforts to raise money to pay for their child's medical care, the Plumbs sold their home and moved into a smaller, less expensive home. They sold the old home to Bob's sister, Alicia, who promptly moved into that home. The sale was for an amount slightly under the fair market value of the home. These events happened in 1999 while Bob was still employed. To maximize their cash on hand, the Plumbs bought the new house through mortgage financing from the Eighth National Bank. Home prices in the area have been rising sharply, so the Plumbs already have some equity in their home (i.e., the value of the home exceeds the mortgage on it).

The IRS sent the statutory notice of deficiency for the 1998 tax year to the Plumbs' last known address. The Plumbs did not receive the notice, however, because they had moved from their old house to their new house and because Alicia, who received the IRS's letter at the house, lost the letter and forgot to tell Bob and Alana about it. Preoccupied with other cares, Bob and Alana neglected to submit a change-of-address form to the Post Office and neglected to inform the IRS of their change of address. Because they did not receive the notice of deficiency, the Plumbs did not file a Tax Court petition. As a consequence, in March 2001, the IRS assessed the 1998 deficiency plus interest.

In January 2001, Bob found a new job with another company, although he received a lower salary than he had received at his previous employment. The Plumbs started paying off some of their debts, and they established a modest checking account at the Eighth National Bank. In addition, both Alana and Bob are listed with Alana's mother as co-holders of a savings account at the Eighth National Bank. It is not clear who made which deposits into the account, but each co-holder has the right to withdraw any amounts in the account.

The IRS sent the Plumbs the usual series of post-assessment letters. These reached the Plumbs since the IRS had learned of their new address from the Plumbs' 1999 income tax return (which the Plumbs had filed late, on January 2, 2001). The Plumbs did not respond to any of these letters.

A day after receiving the last of these letters, Bob heard of the death of his Aunt Elvira and learned that she had left him some property in the mountains on which stands a small, partly completed vacation chalet that Elvira had been building. Elvira's will has not yet been probated, so Bob has not yet received a deed to the property. Bob and Alana have no desire to use the property, and they intend to dispose of it.

Bob has retained an attorney who has brought a malpractice suit against the C.P.A. who gave Bob the bad tax advice as to the 1998 return. The suit is beset with uncertainties, though, including whether the suit had been timely brought under the applicable state statute of limitations.

In searching the public records, the IRS discovered an automobile registered to "Ms. A. Plumb" at the address at which Alana and Bob had resided before they sold the home to Bob's sister, Alicia. An IRS revenue agent levied on the automobile, which he found in the driveway at the address. No one was home at that address when the levy was effected. In fact, the car was Alicia's, not Alana's.

1. The IRS letters got the Plumbs' attention. They retain you to represent them with respect to the IRS's collection activities. Develop a plan of defense. As part of your plan, discuss what actions the IRS might take, how likely the various possibilities are, and what countermeasures are available to the Plumbs.

2. Change the client. You do not represent the Plumbs. Instead, you represent Alana's mother. She is concerned that the IRS might proceed against the savings account she has jointly with Alana and Bob. Assess the reality of your client's concern and describe measures she might take.

3. Change the client again. Now, you represent the Eighth National Bank.

a. The bank is concerned that the IRS might try to levy on the checking account or the savings account. That would weaken the Plumbs' financial position, decreasing their ability to pay the mortgage the bank holds. Also, the bank is concerned about being "put between a rock and a hard place." That is, the bank fears that its failure to honor such a levy would create problems with the IRS while its honoring the levy would cause the Plumbs to sue the bank. Assess the reality of the bank's concerns and describe measures the bank might take.

b. The bank also is concerned that the IRS might try to levy on the Plumbs' house, impairing the bank's mortgage. Assess the reality of the bank's concern and describe measures the bank might take.

4. Change the client again. Now, you represent Alicia Plumb, Bob's sister. Advise her with respect to the IRS's seizure of her automobile. In addition, she fears that the IRS "might try to do something" with respect to her house. Assess the reality of that concern and describe measures she might take.

Chapter 14

THE SECTION 6672 "TRUST FUND RECOVERY PENALTY"

IRC:	§§ 3505; 3509; 6205; 6302(c), (g); 6501(b)(2); 6521; 6601(e)(2)(B); 6651(a)(1), (2); 6656(a); 6671; 6672; 7202; 7215; 7436; 7501
Cases, etc.:	Rev. Proc. 2005-34, 2005-24 I.R.B. 1233 Rev. Proc. 2002-26, 2002-15 C.B. 746 Wetzel v. United States, 802 F. Supp 1451 (S.D. Miss. 1992)
IRS Forms:	Skim 940; 941; 2750; 2751; 2751-AD; 4180

I. INTRODUCTION

Owners of failing businesses, confronted with creditors who have already terminated the extension of further credit and who demand payment cash on delivery (C.O.D.), are usually desperate to find funds to keep operating. A ready source within their control is the checking account holding the taxes withheld from employees that are due to be paid over to the IRS.[1] On the belief the business will turn around and they will be able to remedy the situation later, the owners do not make the required payment to the government and instead preserve the money for suppliers and other creditors. This frequently goes on for quite a few months, with the amount borrowed from the IRS "pyramiding" one quarter on top of the other to a sizeable amount. Sadly, many of these businesses fail leaving the withheld taxes unpaid.[2]

For businesses that operate as sole proprietorships or general partnerships,[3] any unpaid debts of the business, including the unpaid withheld taxes, are the

---

[1] While the discussion in this chapter focuses on the most common situation that causes section 6672 to arise, i.e., employment-related "trust fund" taxes, it is broader than this. Other taxes, such as certain excise taxes, are also collected from third parties and held in "trust" for the government. Their nonpayment likewise brings section 6672 into play. Also, though this chapter focuses on federal tax withheld and owing to the IRS, most, if not all, states have similar procedures they can employ. *See, e.g.*, C.R.S. § 39-21-116.5; Rock v. Dep't of Taxes, 742 A.2d 1211 (Vt. 1999).

[2] While the failure of the business is the most common scenario causing a trust fund violation, there are others, such as when the employer's accounting system or bookkeeping personnel are unsophisticated and fail to assure that the filing and deposit requirements are met or when someone embezzles the funds that were to have been used to pay the employment taxes.

[3] United States v. Galletti, 541 U.S. 114 (2004) (proper tax assessment against partnership sufficed to extend the statute of limitations to collect tax in judicial proceeding from general partners who were liable for payment of partnership's debts).

personal liability of the sole proprietor or general partners.[4] The owners of corporations and multi-member limited liability companies, on the other hand, normally are protected from personal liability for the debts of the business.[5] This protection does not apply, however, with respect to withheld employment taxes that were not paid over to the government. Instead, section 6672 allows the Service to pierce the limited liability veil and demand payment from all individuals who were responsible for the default.[6]

Section 6672, often referred to as either the "trust fund recovery penalty (TFRP)," the "civil penalty" or the "100% penalty,"[7] is a powerful tool in the hands of the government. It creates a unique vehicle for the collection of "trust fund" taxes, i.e., those taxes collected from employees and "held to be a special fund in trust for the United States."[8] Section 6672(a) imposes the penalty on "[a]ny person required to collect, truthfully account for, and pay over any tax . . . who willfully fails to collect such tax, or truthfully account for, and pay over any tax, or willfully attempts in any manner to evade or defeat any such tax or the payment thereof. . . ."

The Service usually asserts the penalty against everyone who *might be* liable.[9] The government's motto seems to be: "When in doubt, assert the penalty and let

---

[4] The IRS takes the position that this is true with respect to single-member limited liability companies that did not elect to be taxed as a corporation. Notice 99-6, 1999-1 C.B. 321; CCA 200235023; Reg. § 301.7701-3; United States v. Galletti, 541 U.S. 114 (2004) (the Supreme Court held that a timely assessment of a partnership's employment tax liability permits the Service to collect the liability in a bankruptcy case filed by the general partners who were derivatively liable for the taxes under state law).

[5] In Rev. Rul. 2004-41, 2004-18 I.R.B. 845, the IRS held, citing *United States v. Galletti*, 541 U.S. 114 (2004), that state law determines whether owners of a business can be held liable for unpaid employment taxes of the entity. Since state law generally provides that general partners of a general or limited partnership are jointly and severally liable derivatively for the partnership's obligations, the Service may seek to collect federal tax liabilities incurred by a partnership, such as federal employment taxes, from the general partners. *See also* Chief Counsel Notice 2005-003 (Jan. 19, 2005). However, a limited liability company (LLC) taxed as a partnership is different. Since state law affords members protection from the debts of the LLC, the IRS may not pursue the members individually except to the extent they might be liable under section 6672.

[6] If a corporation is unable to pay its trust fund taxes, the United States Treasury suffers the loss because the employees from whose wages the taxes are withheld are still credited with the withheld amounts as if they had been paid to the government. IRC § 31.

[7] The provision is presently referred to as the "trust fund recovery penalty." Policy Statement P-5-60, IRM 1.2.1.5.14. Prior to February 1993, section 6672 was commonly referred to as the "100% Penalty." The name was changed since taxpayers (and some practitioners) seemed perpetually confused by the title, often believing that those found liable owed a certain amount of tax and an equal amount, i.e., 100%, as a penalty. In fact, the penalty aspects of the provision are that (i) one is not shielded by the limited liability doctrine, (ii) the penalty is not deductible, and (iii) the penalty is not dischargeable in bankruptcy.

[8] IRC § 7501.

[9] Regardless of the number of persons against whom the liability is assessed, the IRS cannot collect more trust fund taxes than are owed by the business. Thus, even though the IRS might assess the penalty against three persons and so appear to be seeking 300% of the tax, the government can only eventually collect 100% of that which is owed.

those pursued fight it out among themselves." This policy inevitably leads to a frantic call from someone who says, "I was vice-president of XYZ Corporation until about six months ago. I just got a notice from the IRS saying I owe $125,000 for unpaid employment taxes for 2004 and 2005. That isn't possible, is it?"

This chapter attempts to familiarize the student with the law, procedures, and strategies associated with representing someone against whom the IRS is asserting the section 6672 penalty.[10]

II. THE EMPLOYER'S COMPLIANCE DUTIES: WITHHOLDING TAXES, MAKING PAYMENT, AND FILING RETURNS

To understand what the IRS can assess and collect using section 6672, an understanding of the three types of federal employment taxes is necessary. The first type is income tax. This is collected by the employer through withholding pursuant to section 3402. The amount withheld is determined by schedules created by the IRS based on an employee's Form W-4, which lists marital status and number of personal exemptions.

The second type of employment tax is Federal Insurance Contribution Act (FICA), which funds Social Security and Medicare. For wages paid up to a certain amount ($97,500 in 2007), the total FICA contribution is 15.3% of wages. For wages paid above the annual limit, the contribution drops to 2.9% and is for Medicare only. The burden for FICA taxes, whether at 15.3% or 2.9%, is divided equally between the employee and the employer. The half that represents the employee's portion is collected from the employee by the employer through withholding pursuant to section 3121(a). The other half—the employer's portion—is solely the employer's responsibility and is *not* withheld from the employee.

The third type of employment tax is referred to as Federal Unemployment Tax Act (FUTA). This tax is exclusively the responsibility of the employer; no portion of it is withheld from the employee.

Employers are regularly required to pay over to, or deposit with, certain designated depository institutions both the employees' and employer's portions of federal income tax and FICA tax.[11] In addition, a business' FUTA tax liability

---

[10] Section 3505 may also create personal liability for trust fund taxes for persons or businesses that are not employers of the workers. Specifically, section 3505(a) imposes liability on lenders, sureties, and other persons who directly pay the wages of another and fail to withhold the appropriate taxes. Section 3505(b) establishes a penalty of 25% where funds have been supplied to pay wages. In contrast to the penalty under section 6672, which can be assessed and collected administratively, the government must institute legal proceedings in order to collect under section 3505.

[11] The frequency of the required deposits is dictated by the amount of employment taxes incurred during certain periods. Periods may be as short as one business day or as long as quarterly.

must normally be deposited by the end of the month following each calendar quarter.

Non-agricultural employers are required to file a Form 941 ("Employer's Quarterly Federal Tax Return") on a quarterly basis. The Form 941 return is due on or before the last day of the month following the close of each calendar quarter; in other words, on April 30, July 31, October 31, and January 31. The Form 941 reports the quarterly wages paid, the federal income tax withheld, the sum of the employer's and employees' FICA tax liability and the deposits paid. Any taxes still owed after the deposits are accounted for must be paid with the return. In addition to the quarterly Form 941, the employer is required to annually file a Form 940 ("Employer's Annual Federal Unemployment [FUTA] Tax Return") and to pay the balance due after taking deposits into account.

In the context of employment taxes, the term "trust fund" taxes, i.e., those to which section 6672 applies, refers *only* to taxes that are withheld from employees—federal income tax and one-half of the FICA tax. It does not refer to employment taxes, penalties, and interest that the employer itself owes, such as its one-half share of the FICA tax and all the FUTA tax.[12]

III. LIABILITY FOR TRUST FUND TAXES PURSUANT TO SECTION 6672

For an individual to be liable under section 6672, it must be determined that he or she (1) was a *responsible person* (2) who *willfully* failed to collect, truthfully account for, and pay over "trust fund" taxes. One can escape liability by proving that either of these elements does not apply. As determinations of the Service are entitled to a presumption of correctness, the taxpayer has the burden of proof and must satisfy it by a preponderance of the evidence.[13]

Though not a separate element, the Internal Revenue Manual (IRM) states that collectibility should be a factor in determining whether the penalty is asserted against an individual. Since the penalty is a derivative liability and its assessment is discretionary, the IRM directs IRS employees not to assess the section 6672 penalty at all if "the likelihood of successful collection [now or in the future] is minimal."[14]

---

[12] In most situations that are the focus of this chapter, the business has failed to file the returns and pay and deposit the taxes timely. Thus, many penalties will have accrued against the business. The section 6672 penalty cannot be applied to impose liability for the late filing or late payment penalties or interest assessed against the employer that relate to employment taxes. *See, e.g.,* Williams v. United States, 939 F.2d 915 (11th Cir. 1991). However, once the section 6672 penalty is assessed against a responsible person, that person will have interest accruing on his or her own penalty balance. IRC § 6601(e)(2)(A).

[13] *See, e.g.,* Calderone v. United States, 799 F.2d 254 (6th Cir. 1986).

[14] IRM 5.7.5.1.

A. The "Responsible Person" Element

Interestingly, the Code never defines the term "responsible person."[15] That task has been left to administrative rulings and case law. The touchstones for determining whether one is a "responsible person" are the person's "status, duty and authority" within the organization.[16] Knowledge that the taxes are unpaid, while relevant for the *willfulness* factor, is not germane to a determination of the person's status, duty, and authority.

Most commonly, responsibility attaches when a person has the authority to decide which creditors to pay and when to pay them. In short, one is considered responsible if one has the ability to control the purse strings of the business.[17] It is not necessary that the individual have the final word, however.[18] For example, one can be liable if he or she has the authority to pay the IRS but fails to assert that authority when directed by more senior officers to pay other creditors instead.[19]

The determination whether an individual has the status, duty, and authority is a factual question.[20] A person's title is not controlling. Nevertheless, acts performed, and positions held, by an individual within the organizational structure tend to indicate "responsibility."[21] Responsibility is indicated if one has:

- The authority to sign checks.

- Control of the financial affairs of the business.

- Served as an officer, director, or shareholder of the corporation.

- Such duties and responsibilities in the corporate by-laws.

- The ability to hire and fire employees.

- The authority to borrow money for the company.

- The authority to sign and file federal tax returns, particularly the Form 941s, and exercises the authority possessed.

---

[15] The Code defines the term "person" in both sections 6671(b) and 7701(a)(1). Section 6671(b) states that "[t]he term 'person' . . . includes an officer or employee of a corporation, or a member or employee of a partnership, who as such officer, employee, or member is under a duty to perform the act in respect of which the violation occurs" and section 7701(a)(1) states, more broadly, that "[t]he term 'person' shall be construed to mean and include an individual, a trust, estate, partnership, association, company or corporation."

[16] Mazo v. United States, 591 F.2d 1151, 1153 (5th Cir. 1979). *See also* IRM 5.7.3.3.

[17] Purcell v. United States, 1 F.3d 932 (9th Cir. 1993). *See also* IRM 5.7.3.3.1.

[18] *See, e.g.*, Hochstein v. United States, 900 F.2d 543 (2d Cir. 1990); Neckles v. United States, 579 F.2d 938, 940 (5th Cir. 1978).

[19] *See* Caterino v. United States, 794 F.2d 1, 5 (1st Cir. 1986).

[20] *See* IRS Policy Statement P-5-60 (IRM 1.2.1.5.14); IRM 5.7.3.3.

[21] *See* IRM 5.7.3.3.1.1.

- Dealt with customers and creditors.
- Control over payroll disbursements.
- The ability to direct payments to creditors.
- The final word as to which bills are paid and when.
- Control of the corporation's voting stock.
- Responsibility for making the federal tax deposits.

1. Defense Strategies With Respect to the Responsible Person Element

a. Establish that individual did not have status, auty, or authority

The most obvious strategy associated with proving one is not a responsible person is proving that the person in question lacked the actual status, duty, or authority to direct the collecting of, accounting for, and paying over of trust fund taxes. This burden is not met merely by proving that someone else had greater power, as several persons within an organization may have the requisite status, duty, and authority.[22]

Persons who are officers or stockholders in a corporation often are responsible. However, officer or stockholder status cannot be the sole basis for a responsibility determination.[23] In rare cases, taxpayers have been able to establish that an officer, such as a secretary or treasurer, or someone with the ability to sign checks, did not have the authority to decide which bills got paid.[24] On the other hand, a person who has the ultimate authority to make the financial decisions cannot avoid responsible person status by either being "willfully ignorant" or delegating the authority to someone else.[25] Nevertheless, if the delegation was so complete as to have rendered the delegator powerless to make financial decisions, such person may avoid responsibility.[26]

---

[22] IRM 5.7.3.3; Heimark v. United States, 18 Cl. Ct. 15 (1989). *See* United States v. Stanton, 37 A.F.T.R.2d (RIA) ¶ 76-1427 (S.D. Fla. 1976) (corporation's vice president was foreman and had no control over or participation in business or financial decisions); In re Clifford, 255 B.R. 258 (D. Mass. 2000) (majority owner kept check-signing vice president and shareholder "in the dark" about finances and retained control over payroll payments).

[23] IRM 5.7.3.3.1.1.

[24] Vinick v. Commissioner, 205 F.3d 1 (1st Cir. 2000).

[25] Kinnie v. United States, 994 F.2d 279 (6th Cir. 1993).

[26] IRM 5.7.3.3; Stewart v. United States, 90-1 U.S.T.C. (CCH) ¶ 50,002 (Cl. Ct. 1989).

b. The "I was just following orders" defense

"I was just following orders" is one of the most common defenses raised with respect to the responsible person element. Inequities are particularly likely to occur if the IRS pursues lower-level employees, such as staff bookkeepers or accounts payable clerks, who prepare tax returns or sign checks purely at the direction of someone with decision-making authority.[27] The IRS no longer asserts the penalty against non-owner employees if it can be established that they were "just following orders," and did not exercise independent decision-making authority regarding which creditors got paid.[28]

c. Not a responsible person at the time taxes withheld

To be subject to liability, a person must be responsible at the time the wages were paid and the taxes withheld; the date the employment tax return was filed is not the critical date.[29] Resignation after the liability arose but before the tax returns were due does not avoid responsible person status.[30] On the other hand, resignation before or during the accruing of liability not only mitigates the exposure but also goes a long way to establishing lack of willfulness, especially if the person quit because of the defalcation.

Conversely, one who assumes control of a business (or attains the status, duty, and authority) after taxes have accrued and gone unpaid can unwittingly become a responsible person to the extent of the unencumbered funds of the business at the time control of the business is acquired.[31] Exposure is particularly likely if the person merely moved from one position in the company to another position in the company, rather than being newly hired.[32]

---

[27] *Compare* Howard v. United States, 711 F.2d 729 (5th Cir. 1983), *and* Roth v. United States, 779 F.2d 1567 (11th Cir. 1986), *with* Jay v. United States, 865 F.2d 1175 (10th Cir. 1989).

[28] Policy Statement P-5-60 (IRM 1.2.1.5.14); IRM 5.7.3.3.1.2. One important caveat is that the government's position appears to be limited to non-owners and those who would not otherwise be responsible persons. If one is a responsible person, such as a treasurer, one cannot avoid liability simply because of a superior's orders not to pay the tax. Roth v. United States, 779 F.2d 1567 (11th Cir. 1986). *See also* United States v. Rem, 38 F.3d 634 (2d Cir. 1994) (the controlling questions are (1) whether the individual firmly believed that his actual authority was limited to following another's orders; and if so (2) whether such belief was reasonable under the circumstances).

[29] Davis v. United States, 961 F.2d 867 (9th Cir. 1992); Vinick v. United States, 205 F.3d 1 (1st Cir. 2000).

[30] Long v. Bacon, 239 F. Supp. 911 (S.D. Iowa 1965).

[31] Slodov v. United States, 436 U.S. 238 (1978) (dictum).

[32] Davis v. United States, 961 F.2d 867 (9th Cir. 1992).

B. The "Willfulness" Element

The trust fund penalty applies only if the person who failed to collect, truthfully account for, and pay over the tax did so "willfully." Willfulness, for these purposes, is not defined in the Code[33] and its scope can only be determined by reference to case law. For example, the Tenth Circuit defined willfulness as follows:

> Willfulness in the context of Section 6672, means a voluntary, conscious, and intentional decision to prefer other creditors over the government. . . .Willfulness is present whenever a responsible person acts or fails to act consciously and voluntarily and with knowledge or intent that as a result of his actions or inaction trust funds belonging to the government will not be paid over but will be used for other purposes. . . . Proof of willfulness does not require proof of bad motive. . . . It is the burden of the responsible person to show that he did not willfully fail to remit taxes.[34]

Willfulness is present (1) if the responsible person was aware that the taxes were unpaid and, possessing the power to pay them with funds of the taxpayer entity, decided to pay other creditors, or as some cases have held, (2) the responsible person was "grossly negligent" or acted in "reckless disregard" of the fact that the taxes were due and would not be paid.[35] The latter scenario would arise, for example, if the responsible person was on notice that taxes were past due and, while knowing the business was in financial distress, made no effort to deal with the situation.[36]

---

[33] It is important to understand that there are different willfulness standards applied in criminal tax cases and in section 6672 cases. The standard in criminal cases is "a voluntary, intentional violation of a known legal duty." Cheek v. United States, 498 U.S. 192 (1991). By contrast, willful conduct for section 6672 purposes merely requires a "voluntary, conscious, and intentional—as opposed to accidental—decision not to remit funds properly withheld to the government." Kalb v. United States, 505 F.2d 506, 511 (2d Cir. 1974) (quoting Monday v. United States, 421 F.2d 1210, 1216 (7th Cir. 1970)). Neither requires bad faith or evil intent, though clearly the former suggests more purposeful conduct. Caterino v. United States, 794 F.2d 1 (1st Cir. 1986) (the presence of an improper motive or specific intent to deprive the U.S. of revenue is not required to demonstrate willfulness). See also IRM 5.7.3.3.2(1), 8.11.1.8.2.

[34] Muck v. United States, 3 F.3d 1378, 1381 (10th Cir. 1993). See also Denbo v. United States, 988 F.2d 1029 (10th Cir. 1993).

[35] IRS v. Blais, 612 F. Supp. 700 (D. Mass. 1985). See also Caterino v. United States, 794 F.2d 1 (1st Cir. 1986); Kalb v. United States, 505 F.2d 506, 511 (2d Cir. 1974); Kinnie v. United States, 771 F. Supp. 842, 851 (E.D. Mich. 1991) (" 'willfully' does not mean that the responsible person acted by virtue of a bad motive or the specific intent to defraud the government or to deprive it of revenue. . . . 'Willfully' means merely that the responsible person had knowledge of the tax delinquency and knowingly failed to rectify it when there were available funds to pay the government"); United States v. Macagnone, 86 AFTR2d ¶ 5307 (M.D. Fla. 2000) (holding that the president's failure to inquire about the status of taxes, absent a history of delinquency that would put him on notice to establish a known or obvious risk, did not equal reckless disregard.)

[36] Denbo v. United States, 988 F.2d 1029 (10th Cir. 1993); Mazo v. United States, 591 F.2d 1151 (5th Cir. 1979); Kalb v. United States, 505 F.2d 506, 511 (2d Cir. 1974).

1. Defense Strategies With Respect to the Willfulness Element

a. Establish that the responsible person did not act "willfully"

While acting either "willfully," in a "grossly negligent" manner, or in "reckless disregard of the facts" may cause liability, being careless does not.[37] If a person's conduct was merely negligent and not willful, the person should not be held liable for the penalty. Numerous courts have found that a taxpayer who lacked actual knowledge that the liability existed or lacked actual knowledge that the trust fund taxes had not been paid did not act willfully.[38] For example, an attorney acting on behalf of the corporation, signed checks for employment taxes and entrusted them to the corporate president for delivery. The president failed to deliver the checks. The court held that even though the attorney may have been a responsible person and his failure to ascertain whether the checks were deposited may have constituted negligence, his action or inaction was not willful.[39]

b. Establish reasonable cause

Responsible persons may also be able to avoid liability if they had reasonable cause for not acting. "Reasonable cause" is a term of art in certain areas of the Code providing a defense to the assertion of a penalty.[40] In the context of the section 6672 penalty, reasonable cause is not explicitly stated as a defense. However, the Second, Third, Fifth, and Tenth Circuits, and the Court of Federal Claims, have held that willfulness is mitigated if the taxpayer can show reasonable cause for the failure to pay.[41] For example, one would have reasonable cause if he or she had been advised by counsel that no tax was due,[42] that the tax did not need to be paid,[43] or if others assured the individual that the tax had already been paid.[44]

---

[37] Godfrey v. United States, 748 F.2d 1568 (Fed. Cir. 1984); Kalb v. United States, 505 F.2d 506, 511 (2d Cir. 1974).

[38] *See, e.g.*, Gustin v. United States, 876 F.2d 485 (5th Cir. 1989); Dudley v. United States, 428 F.2d 1196 (9th Cir. 1970).

[39] Markewich v. United States, 61-1 U.S.T.C. (CCH) ¶ 9241 (S.D.N.Y. 1961).

[40] *See, e.g.*, IRC §§ 6651(a), 6656.

[41] *See, e.g.*, Winter v. United States, 196 F.3d 339 (2d Cir. 1999); Finley v. United States, 123 F.3d 1342 (10th Cir. 1997); McCarty v. United States, 437 F.2d 961 (Ct. Cl. 1971); United States v. Slattery, 333 F.2d 844 (3d Cir 1964); Frazier v. United States, 304 F.2d 528 (5th Cir. 1962).

[42] Cross v. United States, 204 F. Supp. 644 (E.D. Va. 1962).

[43] Cash v. Campbell, 346 F.2d 670 (5th Cir. 1965).

[44] Richard v. United States, 72-1 U.S.T.C. (CCH) ¶ 9267 (C.D. Cal. 1972).

The Tenth Circuit held that the question of liability was for a jury to determine in view of all relevant evidence.[45] The court held that recognizing reasonable cause as a defense avoids a "strict liability" interpretation of the penalty. It noted that certain factual situations are paradigms that "create an expansive web of liability 'as a matter of law' and significantly ease the government's burden." The court indicated that since willfulness in the section 6672 context requires "scienter" on the taxpayer's part, all the facts and circumstances should be considered. However, the court limited the reasonable cause defense to those situations where the jury concludes (1) the taxpayer made reasonable efforts to protect the trust funds but (2) those efforts were frustrated by circumstances beyond the taxpayer's control.

The First, Seventh, Eighth, and Ninth Circuits,[46] have explicitly rejected the notion that reasonable cause or a justifiable excuse negates willfulness under section 6672. Accordingly, these circuits hold that a taxpayer's intentional actions are willful regardless of whether he or she can provide justification for the action. The reasonable cause defense has been rejected by these courts in situations similar to those in which it has been accepted by the other circuits.

c. Establish there were no funds available at the time the person became a responsible person

A particularly troubling situation arises when someone is employed by a company that already owes significant trust fund taxes. In *Slodov v. United States*,[47] the Supreme Court held that a person who took control of a business became a responsible person with respect to existing tax obligations to the extent the business had unencumbered funds at that time available to pay the government. If the business did not possess such funds, or possessed only a limited amount of such funds, the use of subsequently generated money to pay other creditors would not violate the willfulness standard, except to the extent of the then-existing unencumbered funds.[48] This doctrine holds whether the after-acquired money is raised by a contribution to capital or through earnings.

Subsequent decisions have limited *Slodov* to a narrow window. These cases have established that the *Slodov* doctrine does not provide relief if either the person was already a responsible person when the liability arose[49] or the busi-

---

[45] Finley v. United States, 123 F.3d 1342 (10th Cir. 1997).

[46] Olsen v. United States, 952 F.2d 236 (8th Cir. 1991); Harrington v. United States, 504 F.2d 1306 (1st Cir. 1974); Monday v. United States, 421 F.2d 1210 (7th Cir. 1970); Pacific Nat'l Ins. Co. v. United States, 422 F.2d 26 (9th Cir. 1970). *But see* Gray Line Co. v. Granquist, 237 F. 2d 390 (9th Cir. 1956).

[47] 436 U.S. 238 (1978).

[48] Davis v. United States, 961 F.2d 867 (9th Cir. 1992); Kenagy v. United States, 942 F.2d 459 (8th Cir. 1991).

[49] Davis v. United States, 961 F.2d 867 (9th Cir. 1992); Honey v. United States, 963 F.2d 1083 (8th Cir. 1992).

ness possessed funds which were not encumbered at that time.[50] Thus, to fully utilize *Slodov*, the person must be a newly responsible person and the business must not have *any* encumbered funds at that time.[51]

IV. PROCEDURES FOR DETERMINING LIABILITY FOR THE PENALTY

Section 6672 cases are investigated and proposed by Revenue Officers in the IRS Compliance Collection function. Standard IRS procedures, discussed below, include some combination of the following: (1) proposal of the penalty by the Compliance Collection function, (2) assessment of the tax by the IRS, (3) paying a portion of the tax, (4) filing appropriate documents to seek review of the matter by the local office and, if necessary, the Appeals Division, and (5) filing a refund action in federal court.

The IRS identifies late paying employers by means of an IRS program called "FTD (Federal Tax Deposit) Alert." Once a late paying employer is identified, the IRS local office will forward an "FTD Alert Notice" to the employer. If the explanation received from the employer is not acceptable, a Revenue Officer will be assigned the case to conduct a "full compliance check."

The Revenue Officer normally tries to bring the employer into full compliance with all past and current filing and payment requirements. If the employer is unable to comply, the Revenue Officer has several options, including requiring monthly filing of employment tax returns, requiring the employer to set up a "Special Trust Account" for deposit of employment taxes and, in egregious situations, preparing a criminal referral.[52] The most common procedure is to initiate a TFRP investigation.

As part of the TFRP investigation, the Revenue Officer will examine the business' records, such as tax returns, bank records and signature cards, Articles of Incorporation and Bylaws, canceled checks and corporate minutes and resolutions. If necessary, the Revenue Officer may utilize the IRS's administrative summons power under section 7602 to obtain this information.

The Revenue Officer will also attempt to interview all individuals who might have knowledge of (1) how decisions were made within the organization, (2) who had decision-making authority to control which creditors were paid, and (3) who was familiar with the company's financial condition and the status of outstanding tax debts.[53]

---

[50] Kenagy v. United States, 942 F.2d 459 (8th Cir. 1991); Honey v. United States, 963 F.2d 1083 (8th Cir. 1992); Huizinga v. United States, 68 F.3d 139 (6th Cir. 1995).

[51] In re Bewley, 191 B.R. 459 (Bankr. Okla. 1996). *See* Michaud v. United States, 40 Fed. Cl. 1 (1997).

[52] IRM 5.7.2.6. *See* CCA 200133042.

[53] In conducting interviews, the Revenue Officer will question potential targets by completing a Form 4180 (Report of Interview with Individual Relative to 100-Percent Penalty Recommenda-

At the conclusion of the investigation, the Revenue Officer will decide against whom to propose the penalty. It is almost a certainty that officers and others whose names appear on business documents will be targets if the documentation indicates some level of responsibility for financial matters. For each individual identified, the Revenue Officer will prepare a Form 4183 (Recommendation re: Trust Fund Recovery Penalty Assessment) for review by the Revenue Officer's group manager.

The penalty is assessable and does not require a deficiency notice.[54] Nevertheless, the Code requires the Service to hand-deliver or mail to the taxpayer at his or her last known address by certified mail a "sixty-day letter" (Letter 1153(DO)), specifying the amount of the penalty and the periods at issue.[55] In addition to the sixty-day letter, the IRS encloses a Form 2751 that provides the specifics of the proposed assessments, and allows the taxpayer may to consent to the penalty assessment. Neither the accuracy-related nor civil fraud penalty can be imposed for any noncompliance covered by section 6672.[56]

A. Protesting the Proposed Penalty to the Appeals Division

After receiving a sixty-day letter, a taxpayer can seek Appeals Office review. This can be done before the penalty is assessed. Upon receiving the letter proposing the penalty, the taxpayer has sixty days to file a protest with the Revenue Officer who, after reviewing and commenting on the protest, will forward it to the Appeals Office.[57]

If the sixty-day period expires without a response by the taxpayer, the Revenue Officer will assess the penalty. The government will then send the taxpayer a notice of assessment and a demand for payment. The taxpayer may obtain post-assessment review in Appeals by paying a portion of the penalty, filing a claim for refund, and protesting the likely disallowance.[58] Procedurally, this is normally accomplished in the following manner:[59]

---

tion). For non-targets, the Revenue Officer will either interview the person and take notes or send the witness a Form 4181 (Questionnaire Relating to Federal Trust Fund Tax Matters of Employer), asking the person to complete and return it. IRM 5.7.4.2.2.

[54] *See* IRC § 6671(a).

[55] IRC § 6672(b)(1); IRM 5.7.4.7. An important advantage to protesting the penalty before it is assessed is that by doing so, assessment of the penalty and, correspondingly, accrual of interest on the penalty, is stayed. IRC § 6601(e)(2); CCA 200235028.

[56] IRC § 6672(a) (last sentence).

[57] *See generally* Rev. 2005-34, 2005-24 I.R.B. 1233; IRM 5.7.6.1.3.

[58] If the taxpayer wishes to suspend collection of the balance of the assessment, he or she must take this action within thirty days and also post a bond in an amount equal to 150% of the amount by which the penalty assessed exceeds the amount of the payment made. IRC § 6672(c).

[59] IRM 5.7.7.6.

1. The taxpayer pays the amount of withholding attributable to at least one employee for each quarter in issue.[60]

2. Either concurrently with payment or subsequent thereto, the taxpayer files a Form 843 ("Claim for Refund and Request for Abatement") for each such quarter[61] and attaches an explanation of all factual and legal bases upon which the claim is predicated.[62]

3. An IRS unit, currently called Technical Support, normally works the claim.

4. If the IRS disallows the claim or does nothing,[63] the taxpayer can pursue the matter within the IRS by filing a protest with the Appeals Office.

In order to properly protest a TFRP assessment when the amount at issue is less than $25,000, the taxpayer must complete a small case appeal request. If the amount proposed for any tax period exceeds $25,000, the taxpayer may appeal the proposed assessment by submitting a formal written protest.[64] In preparation for filing the protest and meeting with an Appeals Officer, one should conduct a thorough review of all records, documents, and files relating to the taxpayer and the business. Likely sources of information include the taxpayer, third parties and, via disclosure requests, the IRS. One should attach to the protest any supporting documents, evidence, and affidavits tending to prove that the taxpayer was not a "responsible person" or that he or she did not act "willfully."

Thoughtful legal analysis is also critical. There are literally thousands of cases in this area. Each is very fact-specific, and many of the outcomes are contradictory or, at least, in tension. Consequently, one may be able to find cases to cite with facts and law favorable to the taxpayer's position. In addition, the portions of the IRM that support the proposed theory need to be examined.

---

[60] Payment of the withholding tax with respect to one employee is sufficient to begin review of the proposed penalty because employment taxes are considered divisible taxes.

[61] The relief sought is a refund of the taxes paid within the two years prior to the filing of the claim plus abatement of the balance of the assessment. *See* Chapter 9.

[62] Because the arguments made in the claim for refund and the protest are the only ones subject to court review, it is critical that an attorney be involved at this stage to avoid jeopardizing the lawsuit. *See* Chapter 9.

[63] Once the Form 843 is filed, the IRS has six months within which to respond. During this six month period, the IRS will do one of several things: (1) agree with the taxpayer that a refund is warranted; (2) send a certified letter, referred to as the Notice of Disallowance, rejecting the claim in whole or in part; (3) send a letter requesting more information; or (4) do nothing. Unless the taxpayer can provide something new that was not considered by the IRS when the Revenue Officer did the examination, it is likely the government will disallow the claim summarily.

[64] IRM 5.7.6.1.5.

One should use the protest to challenge the Revenue Officer with respect to any inaccurate findings of fact and any incorrect legal assumptions or precedent.

Even though filed with Appeals, the protest is first reviewed by the Revenue Officer. In instances where the Service has made an obvious mistake, the Revenue Officer may concede the case and not send it on to Appeals. However, if the Revenue Officer does not agree with the taxpayer's position, the Revenue Officer will prepare his or her responses in a memorandum and forward the case to Appeals.[65]

Once the taxpayer and the Appeals Officer have exchanged their views on the evidence and applicable law, they normally attempt to reach a settlement. Any reasonable approach can be the basis of a settlement. This may include liability for certain periods and not for others or liability for a specified percentage or dollar amount of that which was proposed. If the IRS has asserted the same penalty against several persons, it might benefit all or some of the targets to meet and work out a settlement among themselves, propose it to the IRS, and sign Forms 2751-AD to memorialize it. Alternatively, one might negotiate a pro rata settlement with the IRS.[66]

If the Appeals Officer and the taxpayer do not reach agreement, Appeals will send the case forward. If the case was in sixty-day status, it will be sent to the Service Center, where the tax will be assessed. If the case was already in collection and the taxpayer previously filed a refund claim or offer in compromise, the file will be returned to the Collection function for further collection activity.

B. Judicially Appealing an Adverse Determination

Trust fund penalty cases may be litigated in the U.S. District Court, the Court of Federal Claims, or the Bankruptcy Court.[67] Unless it is in connection with a collection due process (CDP) hearing,[68] the Tax Court is not available because the section 6672 penalty is an assessable penalty—a penalty not subject to deficiency procedures. The District Court is the only court in which one can obtain a jury trial. The taxpayer's burden to prove that at least one of the two elements for imposition of the penalty is lacking is the same in all courts.[69]

---

[65] IRM 5.7.6.1.8.

[66] IRM 8.11.1.8.9.

[67] Since the trust fund penalty is not a dischargeable debt, a bankruptcy action is of little value if discharge is the sole purpose of the petition. 11 U.S.C. § 523.

[68] The Pension Protection Act of 2006, P.L. 109-280, Title VIII, Subtitle E, § 3, amended section 6330(d) to confer jurisdiction on the Tax Court to hear all collection due process cases regardless of the type of tax owed. However, the merits of the assessment are rarely in issue in CDP cases because the taxpayer normally would have had an opportunity for a hearing on the underlying liability, a fact which precludes its being raised n a CDP hearing. IRC § 6330.

[69] Raleigh v. Illinois Dept. of Revenue, 530 U.S. 15 (2000).

For the District Courts and the Court of Federal Claims, full payment of the tax liability is a jurisdictional prerequisite.[70] However, because the "divisible tax" doctrine applies to employment taxes, a taxpayer need only pay the tax associated with one employee for each of the quarters in dispute in order to place the issues associated with the trust fund liability before the court.[71] Thus, as compared to income or estate tax refund cases in which full payment of the tax may be onerous, the tax cost to litigate the trust fund penalty is not prohibitive. In Bankruptcy Court, of course, prepayment of the tax is not a jurisdictional prerequisite.

A complaint cannot be filed in District Court or the Court of Federal Claims *earlier* than six months after the claim for refund is filed, unless within that six-month period, the IRS mailed a Notice of Disallowance. A complaint cannot be filed *later* than two years from the date the IRS mailed the Notice of Disallowance by certified mail. If no Notice of Disallowance is mailed, the time for filing suit is unlimited. These time limitations do not apply to a bankruptcy petition.[72]

Normally, if an action is brought in District Court or the Court of Federal Claims by one of the responsible persons, the IRS will join the others by means of a third-party complaint, so all persons are before the court.[73] Joinder is not possible in a bankruptcy action, though a proof of claim can be equivalent to a counterclaim.

Unless appealed, the decision of the trial court is final regarding the issues of responsible person status and willfulness with respect to each quarter before the court. At that point, the IRS will move to collect or abate the section 6672 penalty.

V. PROCEDURES FOR COLLECTING THE PENALTY

Collection procedures associated with the section 6672 penalty are both similar to and different from those respecting other taxes. With respect to the responsible person individually, the similarities lie primarily in the series of collection notices the responsible person will receive, the opportunity to seek an installment agreement or an offer in compromise or be placed in "currently not

---

[70] *See* Chapter 9.

[71] *See, e.g.*, Steele v. United States, 280 F.2d 89 (8th Cir. 1960); IRM 5.7.7.6(2). As a shorthand approach to this, some practitioners say that the taxpayer should pay $100 and designate the payment as being for the particular taxes and quarters. In order to suspend collection activity on the unpaid balance while the claim is considered administratively, the taxpayer must first have complied with section 6672(c)(1) by paying the required minimal amount, filing the refund claim, and posting 150% bond within thirty days of having received the notice of assessment and demand for payment. In order to continue the stay during the judicial phase of the case, the taxpayer must begin a proceeding in the appropriate U.S. District Court (or in the Court of Federal Claims) within thirty days after the day on which his claim for refund is denied.

[72] IRC § 6532.

[73] *See* Rev. Proc. 84-78, 1984-2 C.B. 754.

collectible" status and the right to a collection due process hearing before the IRS. These steps in the collection process are discussed in detail in Chapter 13.

The Code creates one significant difference, though. As discussed above, the only payment required before a judicial decision becomes final is the tax on one employee for each quarter involved. However, to take advantage of this benefit, the taxpayer must act promptly. Section 6672(c) suspends collection activity against those responsible persons who have, within thirty days of having received the notice of assessment and demand for payment, timely paid the minimum amount to file a refund suit, posted bond for 150% of the unpaid balance, filed a claim for refund, and, if the claim is disallowed, filed a lawsuit within thirty days thereafter. Absent jeopardy circumstances, collection is suspended until the matter is finally resolved. The 1998 Reform Act added a new section (i) to section 6331 to state that no levy may be made on the responsible person's assets during the pendency of refund litigation regardless whether collection activity is suspended under section 6672(c), unless the taxpayer waives this restriction or there is a jeopardy.

Other differences result primarily from the fact that since the trust fund liability is derivative of the business' tax liability, there are two levels of taxpayers involved—the business and the individuals. So long as the business remains operating and is a viable collection source, it may be possible to shift the focus of the government's collection efforts from the responsible person to the business.

If the client or another responsible person can influence the actions of the business, assuming the business is still operating, it behooves all the responsible persons for the business to enter into an installment payment plan to pay the trust fund taxes.[74] Within the discretion of the Revenue Officer, assessment of the section 6672 penalty against the responsible persons may be deferred if the business has entered into an installment agreement to pay past due payroll taxes.[75] This normally will be done only if the business is paying its payroll taxes on a current basis and is not pyramiding its delinquencies. Even if collection is withheld, the government will likely file a Notice of Federal Tax Lien against the responsible persons who have been assessed the penalty.

---

[74] Alternatively, the business can seek an offer in compromise. However, an offer in compromise at the business level for an ongoing business does not do the individual client much good, as the IRS will require the compromise amount to be the sum of what can be collected from the business and all responsible persons. IRM 5.7.4.8.2.

[75] IRM 5.7.4.8, 5.7.8.3, 5.8.4.10, 5.14.7. (The business will have to complete a Form 433-B to prove it cannot afford to pay immediately.) Persuading the IRS to accept an offer in compromise in this area is made more difficult by the fact that the trust fund penalty is not dischargeable in bankruptcy. Nevertheless, if the IRS becomes too aggressive toward either the business or an individual, filing a petition in bankruptcy invokes the automatic stay provisions to stop the government and, under Chapters 11 or 13 bankruptcies, the taxpayer may be able to force the IRS to accept the taxpayer's payment plan.

VI. MONITORING THE STATUTE OF LIMITATIONS

A defense based on the expiration of the statutes of limitations (SOL) on assessment or collection can be a wholesale victory for the taxpayer. For this reason, one should consider the SOL in all cases.[76] The SOL for *assessing*[77] the section 6672 penalty is three years from the later of April 15th following the year in issue, or from the date the return was actually filed.[78] April 15th following the year in issue is the starting point for all quarters of the year, as the quarterly returns are deemed "early filed."[79] The SOL *on collection* is ten years from the date of assessment.[80]

There are many exceptions to the rules that are likely to apply in section 6672 cases. It is important to recognize that the exceptions that might apply to extend the SOL on assessment or collection with respect to the employment taxes of the business do not normally affect the SOL on assessment or collection of the TFRP against responsible persons.[81] The business and the responsible person are two separate taxpayers.

The most likely exception with respect to the three-year TFRP assessment statute is section 6672(b)(3). It provides that once the sixty-day letter is mailed, the SOL shall not expire less than ninety days after the letter was mailed or, if a protest is filed with the Appeals Office, not less than thirty days after an administrative determination is rendered. The SOL on assessment may also be extended by timely agreement on Form 2750.[82]

In addition to extensions described in section 6502, extension of the ten-year SOL on collection occurs when the individual (i) submits an offer in compromise

---

[76] *See* IRM 5.7.3.5 et seq.

[77] The TFRP is assessed as the "civil penalty" on the IRS's computer. Normally, there is one assessment posted for the entire period for which liability is asserted, rather than separate assessments for each quarter. Taylor v. IRS, 69 F.3d 411, 418-19 (10th Cir. 1995); Stallard v. United States, 12 F.3d 489, 495-96 (5th Cir. 1994). The quarterly details of these "lump sum assessments" are available upon request. Obtaining the detail may be particularly important for SOL purposes, since the assessment may be late for some earlier quarters.

[78] Lauckner v. United States, 68 F.3d 69 (3d Cir. 1995); AOD 1996-006, 1996-2 C.B. 1. *See also* IRC § 6672(b)(3); United States v. Jones, 60 F.3d 584 (9th Cir. 1995); Stallard v. United States, 12 F.3d 489 (5th Cir. 1994).

[79] IRC § 6501(b)(2).

[80] IRC § 6502.

[81] In Chief Counsel Advice 200532046, the IRS took the position that the unlimited SOL on assessment with respect to the employment tax return of the business attributable to its fraud also resulted in an unlimited SOL for assessing the TFRP against the responsible person. The IRS cited to Lauckner, supra, footnote 76, for the proposition that the SOL for the two are linked since the court had held that the SOL begins to run with respect to the responsible person when the employment tax return of the business is filed.

[82] IRC § 6501(c)(4).

or a request for an installment agreement,[83] (ii) requests a collection due process hearing,[84] or (iii) institutes a refund suit.[85]

Just as the failure of the IRS to comply with the SOL can be a victory for the taxpayer, a missed deadline by the taxpayer can be a "win" for the IRS. Generally, for purposes of section 6672, the SOL for filing an administrative claim for refund is two years from the date of the last payment.[86] However, the statute limits the maximum refund to the amount paid in the two years prior to filing the claim for refund. Once the administrative claim for refund has been filed, the filing of a lawsuit has its own time periods.

VII. GENERAL STRATEGIES IN SECTION 6672 CASES

Whether or not the matter is going to be pursued on the merits, there are many strategies to defend against or minimize the impact of section 6672. The following are the most useful.

A. Try to Shift Blame to Others

With respect to liability under section 6672, the taxpayer's best defense often involves trying to shift blame, i.e., helping the government establish the facts and evidence that another individual had the status, duty, and authority to control the purse strings of the company and acted willfully. Even when doing so does not result in an abrogation of liability, shifting blame to others may enlarge the pool of persons and assets available to pay the tax.

In a practical sense, shifting blame means assisting case development against others by providing evidence pertaining to who the corporate officers were, who had check signing authority, who prepared payroll tax returns, who hired and fired employees, who controlled the corporate finances, and who, in any measure, controlled, or otherwise directed or managed corporate affairs.

B. Act to Gain More Time

Another effective tactic is to try to gain more time for the taxpayer in the hope that, in the meantime, another target or the business will pay the employment taxes first. This approach is particularly effective if the other targets have "deep pockets." Extra time is gained when the taxpayer exhausts his or her

---

[83] IRC § 6331(k)(3).

[84] IRC § 6330(e)(1).

[85] IRC §§ 6331(i)(5), 6672(c)(4).

[86] Though a three-year SOL (from the date the return was filed) normally exists for filing refund claims, it does not apply in IRC section 6672 cases because the taxpayer (the "responsible person") never filed a tax return, the Form 941 is filed by the corporate taxpayer. *See* Kuznitsky v. United States, 17 F.3d 1029 (7th Cir. 1994).

administrative and judicial procedures to challenge the government's determination that he or she is liable for the penalty under section 6672. The taxpayer also achieves extra time when he or she enters into an installment agreement, files an offer in compromise, or requests a collection due process hearing.

C. Evaluate Bringing a Suit for Contribution Against Other Potentially Liable Persons

While the government will not collect more than the amount of the penalty due, the amount paid by any particular responsible person may be disproportionate to their culpability. This is due to the fact that the section 6672 penalty is joint and several and the IRS seeks payment from whomever it can. Because this is a penalty, most states don't enforce or recognize a right of contribution, even if in writing.

Section 6672(d) was added to remedy this. It provides that if more than one person is liable for the 100% penalty, each person who paid the penalty shall be entitled to recover from the other persons who are liable for such penalty an amount equal to the excess of the amount paid by such persons over their proportionate share of the penalty.[87] An action under section 6672(d) is separate from, and may not be joined or consolidated with, litigation on the merits of the section 6672 liability.

D. Designate Payments to Trust Fund Portion of Assessments

If a taxpayer submits a payment to the government *involuntarily*, such as by levy or when the taxpayer is in bankruptcy[88] or when payment is made pursuant to an installment agreement or offer in compromise, the IRS applies it in a manner that is in the Service's best interests.[89] For example, if it is a business that is submitting payment, the IRS will apply the payment to accounts with respect to which the SOL is about to expire, to non-trust fund tax liabilities and to penalties and interest incurred at the corporate level before applying it elsewhere.[90] Applying payments in this manner leaves the "trust fund" taxes still

---

[87] Even though the right exists, one should consider (i) the likelihood of being able to prove the other persons were responsible persons and (ii) whether it would be financially worthwhile to pursue the other persons recognizing that the IRS may have been, or determined that it would be, unsuccessful in collecting from them.

[88] In *United States v. Energy Resources Co., Inc.*, 495 U.S. 545 (1990), the Supreme Court held that even if a payment is not voluntary because the business is in a Chapter 11 bankruptcy reorganization, the IRS is obligated to follow the direction of the debtor-in-possession corporation if the debtor can establish that payment in that manner is necessary to the success of the reorganization. For example, this burden can be met if designation to the trust fund portion of the business' liability would encourage the responsible persons to stay with the business while it reorganizes.

[89] IRM 5.1.2.3; Rev. Proc. 2002-26, 2002-1 C.B. 746.

[90] IRM 5.7.7.1.

owing and collectible from either the business or the personal assets of the responsible persons while minimizing the risk to the IRS that taxes will be lost to the SOL, discharged in bankruptcy, or become effectively non-collectible due to the collapse of the business. The IRS handles payments made *voluntarily* by the taxpayer in a manner similarly advantageous to the government when payment is submitted without clear instruction as to which liabilities should be credited.

By contrast, if one makes a payment voluntarily *and*, in writing, instructs the Service against which tax debts to apply the payment, the Service is obligated to follow these instructions.[91] Specifically, one may direct (1) how much should be applied, (2) to what periods, and (3) for which outstanding taxes.

Designation is very important in the case of trust fund taxes. If the business is still in existence and if one can influence its decisions, it behooves all involved for the business (or the other targets, for that matter) to pay the business' trust fund taxes first. This reduces the outstanding employment tax balance for both the business and all responsible persons alike. Designation is accomplished by transmitting a cover letter instructing that the payment be applied only to trust fund taxes, for all quarters, until they have been fully satisfied.

If the business is considering bankruptcy, a 1990 Supreme Court case can be of great help. In *Begier v. IRS*,[92] the court held that trust fund taxes are not the property of the business but are always the property of the government. Consequently, designated payments of trust fund taxes are not preferential transfers even if made within the ninety-day window prior to filing the petition in bankruptcy.[93] This means that pre-bankruptcy payments of trust fund taxes, even if done solely for the purpose of reducing the liability of responsible persons, cannot be avoided by the trustee and drawn back into the estate as a preference.

E. Try to Settle the Case Among the Targets

If there are multiple responsible persons, it may be in everyone's best interest to work together to settle with the IRS, based on some division of the liability, rather than risk the possibility that the IRS may come after one person for the full amount. Clearly, this is of greatest concern for those persons with "deep pockets." But even for shallower-pocketed persons, this method avoids the filing of a Notice of Federal Tax Lien and damage to one's creditworthiness. In exchange for working with the parties, the IRS demands full payment and that each signatory agree not to file a claim for refund.

---

[91] IRM 5.1.2.3; Rev. Proc. 2002-26, 2002-1 C.B. 746.

[92] 496 U.S. 53 (1990).

[93] 11 U.S.C. § 547.

PROBLEM

Jeff Rosen and Howard Ducat formed a corporation, Eastern Truck Sales, Inc. ("ETS"), in 1982. The business purpose of the corporation was to lease and service new and used trucks. The corporation operated under franchise or dealer agreements with Mercedes-Benz, Freightliner, Inc., and later with Isuzu Trucks. Ducat was president and Rosen was vice-president. Lee Flaishman was later hired by Ducat as secretary and treasurer. Ducat and Rosen, investing equal amounts of money, were each 50% owners. Ducat, as general manager, ran the company on a day-to-day basis. Rosen contends that he was only an investor and that as such his only interest in the corporation was to get the return on his investment.

Beginning in 2004, ETS prepared but stopped filing employment tax returns. The delinquencies appeared on both the year-end financial reports and the monthly financial reports sent to Mercedes-Benz, copies of which were provided to Ducat. According to Ducat, he stopped filing payroll tax returns and making payments so that the business might continue operations, and it was anticipated that sufficient funds would be available in the future to pay the tax liability.

The outstanding liabilities, as reflected on the prepared but unfiled returns, for all delinquent quarters is as follows:

- Federal income tax withheld from employees $125,000

- Social Security/Medicare (FICA) withheld from employees   50,000

- Social Security/Medicare (FICA)—employer's share   50,000

- State income tax withheld from employees   20,000

- Unemployment Compensation Tax   15,000

Rosen says that he first learned of the unpaid payroll taxes in August or September 2005. As of September 2005, ETS had unencumbered assets of $27,601.86. Rosen admits that he knew the corporation was required to pay withholding taxes, but he assumed that Ducat was taking care of the taxes. He states that when he learned that ETS had not paid the taxes nor filed employment tax returns, he requested that Ducat and the corporation's accountant, Howard Lucker, meet with the IRS. In a November 2005 meeting with the IRS, Rosen personally guaranteed a loan for $100,000 to pay the delinquent taxes. Accountant Lucker says that he orally directed the IRS to apply 100% of the $100,000 to the trust fund portion of the delinquent taxes.

In late 2005, Rosen hired an outside accountant to review the corporate records for possible diversion of corporate funds by Ducat for personal and other improper use and directed Flaishman to make the corporate records available to the accountant. In February 2006, the $100,000 was paid to the IRS that the corporation borrowed from Rosen from his personal funds.

However, the IRS applied only 50% to the trust fund portion of the back taxes instead of 100% as orally directed by Lucker and applied 50% to the non-trust fund portion of the back taxes owed.

In March 2006, Rosen forced Ducat out of the corporation (though Ducat still retained a 50% interest), allegedly because lenders refused to provide capital to ETS as long as Ducat was associated with ETS. After Ducat left, Rosen authorized each check that was made by ETS to its creditors. Rosen used his personal funds to pay creditors, payroll, and, at times, the IRS. He also obtained personal loans to pay creditors and payroll. Rosen closed ETS in May 2004 because Mercedes-Benz and Freightliner refused to continue their dealerships with ETS or any entity associated with Ducat.

Subsequently, Rosen began a new corporation by the name of Lakes Freightliner, Inc. ("Lakes") which operated for the same business purpose, at the same address, with virtually the same employees and customers as that of ETS. Lakes operated as a franchise or dealer for Mercedes-Benz and Freightliner. Rosen was the sole owner of Lakes. The assets of ETS, including its inventory, were taken over by Lakes, and before ETS ceased to exist, it paid Lakes over $78,000. (Rosen and Ducat each received $39,000 in redemption of their stock.) Lakes also used ETS' Visa and MasterCard credit cards until it received cards issued in its name. In addition, Rosen personally borrowed $100,000, which he used in incorporating Lakes; however, none of those borrowed funds were used to pay the tax liability. Lakes paid creditors, suppliers, and its payroll rather than the trust fund portion of taxes owed by ETS. Rosen knew of and allowed the payments to other creditors.

Between August 2005 and July 2006 more than $500,000, an amount three times the funds necessary to pay the entire trust fund liability, passed through ETS' and Lakes' bank accounts.

Questions:

1. Rosen and Ducat have each received letters from the IRS requesting an interview in regard to the employment tax issues. An accountant has referred them to you knowing you are well-versed in tax procedure matters. You have had no contact with either them or the corporations in the past. If Rosen and Ducat came to you to represent them concerning exposure they might have for the unpaid employment taxes, what would you discuss with them?

2. What exposure do the companies have for unpaid employment taxes?

3. Discuss the merits of the government's case against Rosen. What defenses would you advance on Rosen's behalf? How do you think the case would be resolved?

4. Should the IRS propose the assessment of the trust fund recovery penalty against Rosen, explain what opportunities he will have to administratively and judicially contest this and how this is accomplished procedurally.

5. Tactically, what might you do to lessen the financial impact on Rosen?

Chapter 15
TRANSFEREE AND FIDUCIARY LIABILITY

IRC:	§§ 6901-05; 7421(b); 7701(a)(6)
Regs.:	§ 301.6901-1
Other:	Title XXXVI, Crime Control Act of 1990, Pub. L. No. 101-647, 104 Stat. 4789, 4933

I. INTRODUCTION

Transferee and fiduciary liability are not penalty devices. Instead, they are techniques by which the IRS can collect from secondary persons the taxes that it cannot collect from the primarily liable taxpayer. The core idea behind the mechanisms is easily grasped, but many sharp reefs lurk near the apparently placid surface.

The difficulties in the area come from three tensions. First, many cases require the application of state law as well as federal law. Second, both procedural and substantive principles must be consulted, and they arise from different sources or bodies of law. Third, while it is essential to the fisc that techniques of secondary liability exist, their exercise must be balanced with fairness to the parties. The core ideas behind the devices of transferee and fiduciary liability are discussed below, after which the applicable rules and their sources are described.

II. CORE IDEA OF NEXUS

In the first instance, of course, payment of tax is the responsibility of the taxpayer who incurred the liability. When payment from that taxpayer is not forthcoming, however, and enforced collection against the taxpayer is unlikely to prove availing, the IRS may pursue secondary persons.

The concept of nexus is central to secondary collection. It would be fundamentally unfair, indeed it likely would violate due process,[1] to seek collection from a person unconnected to the liability or to its non-payment. Secondary liability is appropriate only when the person to be held secondarily liable either participated in the non-payment or benefitted from it in a meaningful way.

---

[1] The Supreme Court has upheld the constitutionality of the transferee liability mechanism. Phillips v. Commissioner, 283 U.S. 589 (1931).

Other chapters already have illustrated this and related ideas. For instance, Chapter 3 discussed spousal relief. The Code permits collection from a spouse who knew of the tax understatement or to whom assets were transferred in order to defeat payment of the tax.[2] Chapter 14 discussed the Trust Fund Recovery Penalty. Persons responsible for the payment of trust fund taxes who willfully fail to provide for their payment become secondarily liable for them.[3] The conditions of knowledge, responsibility, or participation in improper transfers in these situations constitute sufficient nexus to visit liability on others. Transferee liability and fiduciary liability also involve the idea of nexus. Consider these scenarios.

Scenario 1: Jesse owes federal income taxes. He has assets sufficient to pay some or all of the taxes, but it's not hard for him to think of friends or relatives whom he would rather endow than the IRS. Specifically, Jesse transfers all his assets to his brother Frank.

If the law allowed this transfer to stand, a valid tax debt would be uncollectible and Frank would have received a windfall. Assuming conditions described later are satisfied, Frank is liable as a transferee for some or all of the unpaid taxes. The nexus that makes this result fair is that Frank's receipt of the assets deprived the IRS of the ability to collect the taxes from Jesse, the primary taxpayer. A legitimate creditor should prevail over a windfall recipient.

Scenario 2: Martha dies. Her children—Carol, Carl, and Clark—are the beneficiaries under Martha's will. Carol also is the executrix of Martha's estate. The estate owes federal estate taxes. However, Carol empties the estate without having paid or made provision for the payment of the estate taxes. She does so either by distributing the assets to the beneficiaries or by paying creditors of lower priority than the IRS.

For the same reason as in Scenario 1, Carol, Carl, and Clark may be liable as transferees. Carol may also be separately liable in her capacity as executrix. The nexus here is that her prematurely distributing the estate's assets or expending them on lower priority claims prevented the IRS from collecting from the estate, the primary taxpayer. Fiduciary and transferee liability are independent: Carol is liable as a transferee whether or not she is the executrix and liable as a fiduciary whether or not she is a beneficiary. However, the IRS will not collect the unpaid taxes twice, once from transferees and again from fiduciaries. Transferee and fiduciary liability are collection devices, not penalties.

---

[2] IRC § 6015(b)(1)(C), (c)(3)(A)(ii), (c)(3)(C), (c)(4).

[3] IRC § 6672(a).

III. SECTION 6901 AND RELATED SECTIONS

The starting point in understanding transferee and fiduciary liability is section 6901. Evidencing early awareness of the importance of a secondary liability remedy for the government, section 6901 or its predecessors have been in the law since 1926.[4]

Section 6901(a) provides that certain secondary liabilities generally shall "be assessed, paid, and collected in the same manner . . . as in the case of the taxes with respect to which the liabilities were incurred." Thus, the procedures for transferees and fiduciaries are similar to those for primary taxpayers.

The liabilities covered are (i) the liabilities of transferees for federal income, estate, or gift tax, (ii) the liabilities of transferees for other federal taxes "but only if such liability arises on the liquidation of a partnership or corporation, or on a reorganization within the meaning of section 368(a)," and (iii) the liabilities of fiduciaries for federal income, gift, and estate taxes. Pursuant to section 6901(b), such liabilities may be either tax shown on a return or deficiencies.

Subsections (c) through (f) of section 6901 address limitations periods. They incorporate many concepts familiar from Chapter 5 as to tax statutes of limitations generally, with adaptations appropriate to the secondary liability context.

In some situations (mainly involving income, gift, and estate taxes), the IRS is required to assert transferee liability through procedures similar to the deficiency procedures described in Chapter 8. A notice of transferee or fiduciary liability replaces the notice of deficiency. It contains many of the same elements, adapted to the secondary liability context. Section 6901(g) prescribes rules governing such notices. In general, a notice of transferee or fiduciary liability must be sent to the secondary taxpayer's last known address, a concept having the same meaning for section 6901 purposes as for section 6212(b) purposes.[5] A properly addressed notice is valid under section 6901(g) "even if such person is deceased, or is under a legal disability, or, in the case of a corporation, has terminated its existence."

Section 6901(h) defines "transferee."[6] It provides that the term "includes donee, heir, legatee, devisee, and distributee, and with respect to estate tax, also includes any person who, under section 6324(a)(2), is personally liable for any part of such tax." Regulation section 301.6901-1(b) adds a number of other categories, including a shareholder of a dissolved corporation, an assignee of an insolvent person, a successor to a corporation,[7] and a party to a reorganization described in section 368.

---

[4] *See* Revenue Act of 1926, § 280(a)(1).

[5] For discussion of section 6212(b), see Chapter 8.

[6] *See* Jerome Borison, Comment, *Section 6901; Transferee Liability*, 30 Tax Law. 433 (1977).

[7] For a fairly recent case upholding the transferee liability of a successor corporation, see *Self Heating and Cooling, Inc. v. Commissioner*, T.C. Memo. (CCH) 2004-85.

Case law has developed as to transferee status in a variety of contexts, including life insurance beneficiaries, partners, and surviving joint tenants and tenants by the entireties. However, the law is not settled in some areas. For instance, as to surviving tenants by the entireties, the traditional view was that they are not transferees for section 6901 purposes from their deceased co-tenants.[8] It is unclear whether this traditional view will survive the Supreme Court's 2002 *Craft* decision.[9]

"Fiduciary" is defined in section 7701(a)(6). The term means "a guardian, trustee, executor, administrator, receiver, conservator, or any person acting in any fiduciary capacity for any person." This concluding "catch all" language contemplates a person acting in a representative capacity for another, not one acting on one's own behalf.[10]

Section 6901 is supported by the remaining sections in chapter 71 of the Code. Specifically, section 6902(a) allocates the burden of proof in transferee liability cases. Section 6902(b) creates special discovery options for transferees in Tax Court cases. Section 6903 provides for the filing with the IRS of notice that a person is acting in a fiduciary capacity. Section 6904 prohibits suits to restrain enforcement of transferee or fiduciary liability, via cross-reference to section 7421. Sections 6904 and 7421(b) make the Anti-Injunction Act[11] applicable to transferee and fiduciary liabilities.

Finally, provisions exist for the relief of liability of executors and other fiduciaries under some circumstances and upon written application. This is provided for estate taxes under section 2204(a) for executors and section 2204(b) for other fiduciaries, and for income and gift taxes under section 6905 for executors. "Executor" is defined slightly differently for the two contexts. For section 6905 purposes, "executor" is defined as "the executor or administrator of the decedent appointed, qualified, and acting within the United States."[12] The term for section 2204 purposes includes such persons plus, if there is no executor or administrator, "any person in actual or constructive possession of any property of the decedent."[13] The executor or other fiduciary can be discharged from liabilities determined by the IRS more than nine months after the written application (or the return, if filed later) was submitted to the IRS, so the practical effect of submitting the application is to accelerate an examination.

The above rules are procedural in nature. Section 6901(a) describes how transferee and fiduciary liabilities are asserted and collected, but it does not

---

[8] *See, e.g.*, Tooley v. Commissioner, 121 F.2d 350 (9th Cir. 1941); Rev. Rul. 78-299, 1978-2 C.B. 304.

[9] United States v. Craft, 535 U.S. 274 (2002) (holding that the federal tax lien attaches to the tax debtor-spouse's interest in entireties property even when the other spouse doesn't owe tax).

[10] Grieb v. Commissioner, 36 T.C. 156 (1961), *acq.* 1961-2 C.B. 3.

[11] See Chapter 13 for discussion of the Anti-Injunction Act.

[12] IRC § 6905(b). *See* Reg. § 301.6905-1.

[13] IRC § 2203. *See* Reg. § 20.2203-1.

itself create or impose liability on any secondary party. The Supreme Court confirmed that in 1958 in the *Stern* case,[14] involving the immediate predecessor of section 6901. The Court held that no federal common law of substantive liability existed, thus that the substantive source for transferee liability could be found, if at all, only in state law.

This statement was somewhat imprecise even in 1958. By now, it is clearly outdated, especially given the creation of a federal fraudulent conveyance statute in 1990, as described in subpart IIIC below. Thus, the real teaching of *Stern* is that section 6901 is a purely procedural section. The substantive source of liability—the rule that *does* create or impose liability on the transferee or fiduciary—lies outside section 6901. To successfully assert transferee or fiduciary liability, the IRS must both identify a substantive basis or source of liability outside section 6901 and assert that liability via the procedures mandated by section 6901 and related sections.[15]

IV. SUBSTANTIVE BASES OF LIABILITY

A. Fiduciary Liability

As will be seen, there are many possible substantive bases of transferee liability. In contrast, there is only one substantive basis of fiduciary liability: 31 U.S.C. section 3713(b). This section provides: "A representative of a person or an estate (except a [bankruptcy] trustee . . .) paying any part of a debt of the person or estate before paying a claim of the Government is liable to the extent of the payment for unpaid claims of the Government."[16] This language appears to create strict liability. However, as described below, the courts have not interpreted the statute in that fashion.

When such liability attaches, the fiduciary may be liable for the entire amount that he or she paid out (up to the amount of the tax debts)—even if the fiduciary received no personal benefit from the payments. Because of this potential rigor, it has been said that fiduciary liability should attach only when required under "the clearest and most unmistakable reading of [the statute's] precise terms."[17]

---

[14] Commissioner v. Stern, 357 U.S. 39 (1958).

[15] The purely procedural nature of section 6901 is explained by history. Before 1926, the government had only a cumbersome response to transfers to defeat tax collection. The government first had to bring suit against the primary taxpayer, then—when that judgment was returned unsatisfied because the transfer had left the primary taxpayer unable to pay—file a bill in equity to set aside the transfer as a fraudulent conveyance. Because of the separation of law and equity, the two actions could not be combined. Moreover, without obtaining the judgment against the primary taxpayer and taking out an execution that was returned unsatisfied, the fraudulent conveyance suit would not lie, because it had not been shown that no adequate remedy existed at law.

[16] For this purpose, the tax claims are taken into account whether or not they have yet been assessed. *See, e.g.*, Viles v. Commissioner, 233 F.2d 376 (6th Cir. 1956).

[17] Fitzgerald v. Commissioner, 4 T.C. 494 (1944).

In this spirit, a number of defenses have been recognized. For instance, liability will not be imposed when the fiduciary was relying on advice of counsel or when the fiduciary lacked actual or constructive knowledge of the claims of the government.[18] Also, liability will not be imposed if the debts paid by the fiduciary had higher priority than the government's tax claims.[19]

Fiduciary liability is not avoided by the executor obtaining a discharge from the local probate court.[20] The executor may consider obtaining a discharge from the IRS under section 6905, requesting prompt assessment of taxes under section 6501(d). Alternatively, as a condition of making distributions to them, the executor might obtain a bond from the distributees.

B. Transferee Liability at Law

Section 6901 refers to the liability of a transferee "at law or in equity." Those words relate to the substantive bases of liability. The substantive basis of transferee liability "at law" is either (i) a contract under which the person to be held secondarily liable assumes the obligation of the primary taxpayer or (ii) a federal or state statute other than a fraudulent conveyance statute.

1. Contract

"At law" liability exists if the person to be held liable assumed the primary taxpayer's tax liabilities *and* received assets of the primary taxpayer. Absent a transfer of assets, assumption of the liabilities alone will not suffice to impose transferee liability.[21]

The transfer requirement usually doesn't matter much in this context, however. First, while some assets must be transferred, the IRS is not required to prove their value.[22] Second, it is rare for one to assume liabilities without getting anything in return. The typical context of assumption occurs when a purchaser buys the assets of a going concern and assumes its liabilities—a situation which features a transfer of assets. Third, the IRS often would have an alternative remedy in assumption-without-transfer situations since the IRS might be viewed as a third-party beneficiary under state contract law.

Thus, the other requirement—that there was an assumption of the tax liability—is the more important element. Courts typically hold that an assumption of "all the liabilities" of a transferor includes assumption of tax debts,[23] but only

---

[18] McCourt v. Commissioner, 15 T.C. 734 (1950).

[19] *See* United States v. Weisburn, 48 F. Supp. 393 (E.D. Pa. 1943).

[20] *See, e.g.*, Viles v. Commissioner, 233 F.2d 376 (6th Cir. 1956).

[21] Denton v. Commissioner, 21 T.C. 295 (1953).

[22] *See, e.g.*, Bos Lines, Inc. v. Commissioner, 354 F.2d 830 (8th Cir. 1965).

[23] *See, e.g.*, California Iron Yards Corp. v. Commissioner, 82 F.2d 776 (9th Cir. 1936).

those that are valid and enforceable at the time of the assumption.[24] Courts have disagreed as to whether assumption of liabilities includes tax liabilities arising from the sale itself.[25]

Not strictly a contract, but akin to one, is an agreement between the transferee and the IRS consenting to transferee liability. Under section 6213(d), a primary taxpayer may consent to assessment in lieu of receiving a notice of deficiency. A similar option exists for secondary taxpayers. A transferee may execute IRS Form 2045 "Transferee Agreement" admitting to transferee liability in return for the IRS not making an assessment against the transferor. Although Form 2045 is an agreement, it differs in several respects from a contractual basis of "at law" liability. First, the form is rendered legally operable through the doctrine of estoppel, not contract. A party who executes a Form 2045 will be estopped from subsequently contesting liability as a transferee.[26] Second, a Form 2045 provides more than just a substantive basis of liability; it resolves all potential issues—procedural as well as substantive—in the IRS's favor.

2. Federal Non-fraudulent-conveyance Statute

The most frequently asserted federal "at law" basis of substantive liability is section 6324. Under section 6324(a)(2), transferees from the decedent's estate are personally liable for unpaid estate tax. Under section 6324(b), donees are personally liable for their donor's unpaid gift taxes. These sections constitute a substantive basis of liability, and the persons identified in sections 6324(a)(2) and 6324(b) are within the definition of "transferee" in section 6901(h).

3. State Non-fraudulent-conveyance Statute

The principal state non-fraudulent conveyance statutes are (i) laws as to distribution of assets of an estate, (ii) laws prescribing treatment of corporate liabilities in the event of organic changes such as mergers, consolidations, and liquidations, and (iii) Bulk Sales Acts.

States typically have statutes that address distribution of probate assets of an estate before claims against the estate have been fully satisfied. Although such statutes theoretically are available to the IRS as a substantive basis of liability, they rarely are used in transferee liability cases. Code section 6324 is a familiar and comprehensive basis of liability, covering non-probate as well as probate assets. Thus, the IRS prefers section 6324 as the basis of liability in estate situations.

---

[24] *See, e.g.*, Diamond Gardner Corp. v. Commissioner, 38 T.C. 875 (1962), *acq.*, 1963-2 C.B. 4.

[25] *Compare* Reid Ice Cream Corp. v. Commissioner, 59 F.2d 189 (2d Cir. 1932) (no), *with* Shepard v. Commissioner, 101 F.2d 595 (7th Cir. 1939) (yes).

[26] *See, e.g.*, Bellin v. Commissioner, 65 T.C. 676 (1975).

Commonly, state corporate laws make the survivor of a merger or a consolidation liable for the debts of the merged or consolidated entities. Such liability sometimes is conceived of as primary, but the laws can serve as the substantive basis of transferee liability. In addition, state laws prescribe who shall be responsible for any unpaid debts of a dissolved or liquidated corporation. Frequently, distributee shareholders of the corporation are rendered responsible. Again, the state laws are available as the foundation for transferee liability.

A "bulk sale" entails the transfer as an aggregate, and other than in the ordinary course of the business, of a major portion of the inventory or other assets of the business. A bulk sale can imperil the position of creditors of the transferor business. To guard against this, many states have enacted creditor protections in their bulk sale statutes. Article 6 of the Uniform Commercial Code is a model for such laws. Such statutes provide that a bulk sale is ineffective against creditors of the transferor unless the transferor is required to give the transferee schedules of property and creditors and the transferee notifies creditors of the transfer. If a transferee fails in this duty, there is a substantive "at law" basis of transferee liability against it as to unpaid tax debts of the transferor.[27]

C. Transferee Liability in Equity

A substantive basis of transferee liability exists if the transfer from the primary taxpayer to the person sought to be held liable constitutes a fraudulent conveyance. Fraudulent conveyance is an equitable remedy with deep roots in Anglo-American law. A fraudulent conveyance statute was enacted in England in 1571.[28] All states in the United States have had fraudulent conveyance regimes, whether based on the statute of 1571, another statute, or the common law.

There was (and, to a lesser extent, remains today) great confusion and variation among state fraudulent conveyance laws. As a result, work was begun in 1915 which led to promulgation of the Uniform Fraudulent Conveyance Act (the "UFCA"). Some version of it was adopted by 25 American jurisdictions. A major review in the 1980s led to the Uniform Fraudulent Transfer Act (the "UFTA"). Many states that had adopted the UFCA switched to the UFTA. Currently, about a half dozen U.S. jurisdictions continue to use the UFCA in part or whole, and over 40 use the UFTA in part or whole.

Before 1990, the federal government had no comprehensive fraudulent conveyance statute of its own, so it generally had to rely on state laws when seeking collection from transferees. This changed with the adoption of the Federal

---

[27] The schemes that prompted states originally to enact bulk sales acts are less dangerous today because of changes in business practices, commercial law, and civil procedure. Accordingly, the National Conference of Commissioners of Uniform State Laws and the American Law Institute recommend that states repeal their bulk sales statutes as unnecessary. A revised Article 6 is still published, however, for states choosing not to repeal.

[28] Statute of 13 Elizabeth, ch. 5 (1571).

Debt Collection Procedures Act of 1990.[29] Subpart D of the Act (entitled "Fraudulent Transfers Involving Debts") is a federal fraudulent conveyance statute.

Accordingly, today, the government has available to it, as a substantive source of transferee liability in equity, either the 1990 federal fraudulent conveyance statute or the applicable state fraudulent conveyance statute.[30] The government can choose which source to proceed under. In cases in which the IRS is represented by the Chief Counsel's Office, the IRS rarely has asserted the 1990 federal statute as the basis of substantive liability. It has been more frequently asserted in cases in which the IRS is represented by the Department of Justice.

Some of the salient features common to fraudulent conveyance statutes are described below. However, generalization will not do for the attorney in practice. In each transferee liability case, the attorney must advert to the precise fraudulent conveyance statute on which the government is relying or may rely. The attorney must consider the particular—sometimes peculiar—terms of that statute. Typically, a transfer will be deemed within the statute if it is either actually or constructively fraudulent.

1. Actual Fraud

A transfer is actually fraudulent if, in making it, the transferor had a definite purpose of defeating creditors. This adverts to the mental state of the transferor. In many states, it is irrelevant whether the transferee knew of or colluded in the transferor's intent. However, there are differences among the states on this point, as on many other points as to fraudulent conveyance. Direct proof of actual fraudulent intent seldom is available. Thus, the common approach is that such intent may be inferred from the surrounding circumstances, from so-called "badges of fraud." Such badges include that:

- the transfer was to a relative, close friend, corporate insider, or entity under common control;

- the transferor retained some possession, control, or use of the property even after its transfer;

- the transfer was concealed;

- before the transfer was made, the creditor had initiated or threatened to initiate legal action against the transferor to collect the debt;

- all or most of the transferor's assets were conveyed;

---

[29] This Act became effective on May 20, 1991. It constitutes Title XXXVI of the Crime Control Act of 1990, Pub. L. 101-647, 104 Stat. 4789, 4933.

[30] The "applicable" statute is the one of the state in which the transfers occurred. *See, e.g.,* Fibel v. Commissioner, 44 T.C. 647 (1965). In theory, this could present choice-of-law issues in cases with complicated facts as to multistate activities. In practice, though, such controversies have been rare.

- the transferor absconded;

- the transferor removed or concealed assets;

- the consideration given by the transferee was less than reasonably equivalent to the value of the assets conveyed;

- the transferor was insolvent at the time of the conveyance or was rendered insolvent by the transfer or the series of transfers of which it is a part;[31] and

- the transfer occurred shortly before or shortly after a substantial debt was incurred.

There is no formula for the application of the badges of fraud. Obviously, the more badges that are present, the better the IRS's chance of prevailing. Still, the IRS may prevail even if only some of the badges are present, as long as they are clear. The question always is the general impression that emerges as to the character of the transaction in the mind of the judge from the totality of the circumstances.[32]

2. Constructive Fraud

Constructive fraud can be established without any showing of intent or purpose. A conveyance is constructively fraudulent as long as it had the *effect* of hindering or impeding the creditor in collecting the debt. Typically, this effect will exist when both (i) the transferee rendered inadequate consideration (usually, in money or money's worth) and (ii) the transferor was insolvent at the time of the conveyance or was rendered insolvent by it.[33]

A requirement common to both the actual and constructive fraud theories is that the IRS has exhausted its remedies against the primary taxpayer before proceeding against the putative transferee. This is inherent in the theory that transferee liability is *secondary* liability. However, the requirement is applied pragmatically. Equity does not require performing a futile act.[34] The IRS need not, as a condition of pursuing the putative transferee, first issue a notice of deficiency or take other action against the transferor if the transferor is insolvent[35] or, if an entity, has been dissolved.[36]

---

[31] As to the "series of transfers" idea, see, e.g., *Drew v. United States*, 367 F.2d 828 (Ct. Cl. 1966).

[32] *E.g.*, McGraw v. Commissioner, 384 F.3d 965 (8th Cir. 2004) (upholding transferee liability based on actual fraud).

[33] *E.g.*, Suchar v. Commissioner, T.C. Memo. (CCH) 2005-23 (2005).

[34] *See, e.g.*, Benoit v. Commissioner, 238 F.2d 485 (1st Cir. 1956).

[35] *See, e.g.*, Coca-Cola Bottling Co. of Tucson, Inc. v. Commissioner, 37 T.C. 1006 (1962), *aff'd*, 334 F.2d 875 (9th Cir. 1964).

[36] *See, e.g.*, Dillman v. Commissioner, 64 T.C. 797 (1975).

V. PROCEDURAL ASPECTS

Once a substantive theory of liability exists, that theory is applied through the procedures established by section 6901 and related sections. State rules matter insofar as they affect the substantive source of liability but are irrelevant as to procedure. Procedure is controlled by the federal rules. For example, assume the IRS is relying on a state fraudulent conveyance statute which contains a shorter statute of limitations than section 6901 establishes for transferee liability. The state limitations period will not limit the IRS's remedy. That period is procedural, and transferee liability procedures are provided by federal, not state, law.[37]

A. Incorporated Procedures

Section 6901 provides that transferee liabilities are "assessed, paid, and collected in the same manner and subject to the same provisions and limitations as" the underlying taxes. Non-exclusively, the Regulations provide that the rules so made applicable include those related to:

    (i)   Delinquency in payment after notice and demand and the amount of interest attaching because of such delinquency;

    (ii)   The authorization of distraint and proceedings in court for collection;

    (iii) The prohibition of claims and suits for refund; and

    (iv) In [income, gift, or estate tax cases], the filing of a petition with the Tax Court of the United States and the filing of a petition for review of the Tax Court's decision.[38]

A number of unfortunate decisions have identified what they call "the procedural elements" of transferee liability that the IRS must establish in addition to the basis of substantive liability. These elements are said to be (1) that the transferee received property of the transferor; (2) that the transfer was for inadequate consideration; (3) that the transfer was made during or after the period for which the transferor's liabilities accrued; (4) that the transferor was insolvent before or because of the transfer, or the transfer was one of a series of property distributions that rendered the transferor insolvent; (5) that the IRS made all reasonable efforts to collect from the transferor and further efforts would be futile; and (6) the value of the transferred property.[39]

---

37 *See, e.g.,* Bresson v. Commissioner, 111 T.C. 172 (1998), *aff'd*, 213 F.3d 1173 (9th Cir. 2000).

38 Reg. § 301.6901-1(a)(3).

39 *See, e.g.,* Gumm v. Commissioner, 93 T.C. 475 (1989), *aff'd without opinion*, 933 F.2d 1014 (9th Cir. 1991).

These decisions misconstrue the nature of transferee liability. First, most of the identified elements are substantive in nature and cannot be rendered procedural merely by the wave of the judicial wand. Second, the enumeration mixes discrete bases of substantive liability. The enumeration most closely reflects constructive fraud in equity, and is overly restrictive or simply wrong if the asserted substantive theory is either actual fraud in equity or fraud at law.

These decisions seem to be an attempt to create what the Supreme Court said in *Stern* did not exist: a federal common law of transferee liability. Recourse, in different cases, to fifty state fraudulent conveyance statutes, a federal statute, contracts, and the array of state and federal non-fraudulent-conveyance laws is messy, so the temptation to create a federal common law of transferee liability is understandable.[40] Yielding to the temptation, though, is wrong. The cases asserting the above six so-called "procedural elements" of transferee liability ignore both the Supreme Court's teaching in *Stern* and the multiplicity of the sources of substantive liability.

B. Statute of Limitations

Section 6901 contains detailed limitations rules, which control over any conflicting limitations rules governing the substantive basis of liability. In fiduciary liability cases, the limitations period extends until the later of (i) one year after the liability arises or (ii) the expiration of the period for collection of the tax.[41]

In transferee liability cases, section 6901(c) directs that the starting point is the limitations period against the transferor, as measured under the 6501 rules described in Chapter 5. That period is unaffected by the subsequent death or dissolution of the transferor.[42] To the limitations period against the transferor is added an additional period. That period is one year as to an initial transferee plus an additional year as to each later-stage transferee (i.e., a transferee receiving from a prior transferee, rather than from the primary taxpayer/transferor), with the additional period capped at three years.[43]

Assessment or non-assessment against the transferor is irrelevant for this purpose. Assessing against the transferor before the limitations period has run does not contract the limitations period with respect to the transferee, nor does omitting assessment against the transferor have this effect. However, if the limitations period to assess against the transferor expires before the conveyance of

---

[40] Presumably, the temptation would lose some allure were the IRS to routinely rely on the federal fraudulent conveyance statute in preference to state fraudulent conveyance statutes in "in equity" cases.

[41] IRC § 6901(c)(3).

[42] IRC § 6901(e).

[43] IRC § 6901(c)(1), (2).

assets to the transferee occurs, the transferor's tax liability is extinguished and there can be no transferee liability.[44]

Under section 6901(c), the limitations period with respect to an initial transferee is four years from the due date or filing date of the transferor's return,[45] whichever is later. However, the period may be longer. The limitations period as to the transferor may be expanded by conditions stated in sections 6501 and 6503. Moreover, the additional period with respect to the transferee(s) may be expanded by a number of events, including transfers by one transferee to another,[46] consents to extend,[47] issuance of a notice of transferee liability,[48] and armed service by the transferee in a combat zone.[49]

C. Burden of Proof

Most transferee liability cases are tried in the Tax Court. Section 6902(a) creates a split burden of proof in Tax Court cases. The petitioner bears the burden as to whether the transferor owes tax while the IRS bears the burden as to whether the petitioner is liable as a transferee for the transferor's unpaid tax. Section 7491 does not affect this allocation since, under section 7491(a)(3), the general provision of section 7491(a)(1) yields to other, more specific burden-of-proof rules—like section 6902(a). The applicable standard of proof typically is preponderance of the evidence.

"Burden of proof" for this purpose means the risk of nonpersuasion.[50] Within the overall allocation of that risk, the burden on specific issues may vary. The notion that specific rules control over general ones will sometimes put the burden of proof on the IRS on particular issues. For instance, if the IRS were to raise a new issue, not contained in the notice of transferee liability, increasing the transferor's alleged liabilities, the IRS typically would bear the burden on that issue.[51] Also, if the IRS were to assert fraud penalties against the transferor, the IRS likely would bear the burden as to them.[52]

Although the risk of nonpersuasion does not shift, the burden of going forward on particular issues can shift between the parties. In general, once the IRS has established a *prima facie* case on the "petitioner liable as transferee" issue,

---

[44] *See, e.g.*, Illinois Masonic Home v. Commissioner, 93 T.C. 145 (1989).

[45] The normal three-year period against the transferor under section 6501(a) plus an additional year under section 6901(c)(1).

[46] IRC § 6901(c)(2).

[47] IRC § 6901(d).

[48] IRC § 6901(f) (suspending the running of the limitations period).

[49] IRC §§ 6901(i), 7508.

[50] See Chapter 8 for more detailed discussion of the burden of proof.

[51] *See* Tax Ct. R. 142(a).

[52] *Cf.* IRC § 7454(a).

the burden of going forward on it shifts to the petitioner.[53] For instance, once the IRS shows that there was a transfer of valuable assets, the burden shifts to the petitioner to establish the value of any consideration he or she alleges to have given to the transferor in return.[54]

The allocation of burdens between the IRS and the putative secondary tax-payer is somewhat surprising. Commonly, the law puts the burden of proof on the party closest to the transactions, thus best able to adduce in court the relevant facts. But a transferee may not know much about the transactions that gave rise to the transferor's tax liabilities (as to which issue the transferee does have the burden under section 6902), while the transferee was involved in the transactions (the transfers) on which liability as a transferee will hinge (as to which issue the transferee does not have the burden under section 6902).

Yet, there are some counters to these anomalies. As to the "transferor's liability" issue, transferors and transferees often are closely related, perhaps giving the transferee some opportunity to know or find out about the transferor's transactions. Moreover, as described below, section 6902(b) gives the petitioner special discovery options to facilitate shouldering the burden. As to the "transferee's liability" issue, allocation of the burden to the IRS likely reflects concern about trying to collect one person's liability from another person. Before the system will permit that, the IRS will have to convince a court that it's really necessary.

The foregoing section 6902 rules apply only in the Tax Court. When transferee liability cases are tried in a refund forum, the normal refund action burden of proof rules discussed in Chapter 9 apply. The plaintiff must establish his or her entitlement to a return of funds, and thus bears the burden on the "transferee's liability" issue as well as the "transferor's liability" issue.[55]

D. Discovery

Both the IRS and the party to be held secondarily liable are entitled to whatever discovery is available under the rules of the court in which the case is tried. But a putative transferee may need discovery not only from the IRS but also, on the issue on which he or she bears the burden of proof, from the transferor as well. Responding to this need, section 6902(b) creates special discovery opportunities, but only in the Tax Court—a fact which may influence the forum in which the putative transferee chooses to bring the case.

Under section 6902(b), the putative transferee/petitioner shall, upon application to the Tax Court, be entitled "to a preliminary examination of books,

---

[53] *See, e.g.,* Noell v. Commissioner, 22 T.C. 1035 (1954).

[54] *See, e.g.,* Alonso v. Commissioner, 78 T.C. 577 (1982).

[55] *See, e.g.,* Wehby v. Patterson, 60-2 U.S. Tax Cas. (CCH) ¶ 9611 (N.D. Ala. 1960).

papers, documents, correspondence, and other evidence of the taxpayer or a preceding transferee of the taxpayer's property." That court

> may require by subpoena . . . the production of all such books, papers, documents, correspondence, and other evidence within the United States the production of which . . . is necessary to enable the transferee to ascertain the liability of the taxpayer or preceding transferee and will not result in undue hardship to the taxpayer or preceding transferee.

What if a putative transferee is denied such discovery because the transferor's books and records were lost or destroyed? This denial does not require that the case be resolved in the putative transferee's favor, particularly when there exists secondary evidence or sources of information.[56]

E. Privity

Transferors and their transferees are deemed to be in privity.[57] This has various consequences. For example, an admission by the transferor may be viewed as a vicarious admission by the transferee. Also, if the IRS and the transferor litigated, the result thereof may have res judicata or collateral estoppel effect.

F. Right to Contribution

Transferees are severally liable. When there are multiple transferees, the IRS may proceed disproportionately, or even exclusively, against one or some of them.[58] For example, assume the transferor owes $50,000 in taxes and gave $50,000 on the same day to each of his three children: Agnes, Bill, and Clara. The IRS could choose to go against only Agnes, leaving Bill and Clara alone.

As described in Chapter 14, when there are multiple responsible persons as to the unpaid trust fund taxes of a business, section 6672(d) creates a cause of action whereby a responsible person disproportionately burdened by IRS collection can obtain contribution from the less burdened or unburdened responsible persons. There is no comparable rule in section 6901 or allied sections. Arguably, rights to contribution may exist under state law, but the law in this regard is not well developed.[59]

---

[56] Kreps v. Commissioner, 42 T.C. 660 (1964), *aff'd*, 351 F.2d 1 (2d Cir. 1965).

[57] *See, e.g.*, Estate of Egan v. Commissioner, 28 T.C. 998 (1957), *aff'd*, 260 F.2d 779 (8th Cir. 1958).

[58] *See, e.g.*, Phillips-Jones Corp. v. Parmley, 302 U.S. 233 (1937).

[59] *See* Steve R. Johnson, *Unfinished Business on the Taxpayer Rights Agenda: Achieving Fairness in Transferee Liability Cases*, 19 Va. Tax Rev. 403 (2000).

VI. EXTENT OF LIABILITY

A fiduciary is liable for the lesser of the primary taxpayer's liabilities (including interest and penalties) or the amount that the fiduciary wrongly paid out. A transferee is liable for the transferor's unpaid taxes (including interest and penalties) for the year in which the transfer occurred and prior years.[60] A transferee is not liable for the transferor's liabilities for years after the transfer took place.

In "in equity" transferee cases, the transferee's liability is capped at the value of the assets transferred, plus interest if allowed under the rule providing the basis of substantive liability in the case.[61] For this reason, proof of the value of the transferred assets is part of the IRS's *prima facie* case. "Value" for this purpose means the date-of-transfer fair market value of the transferred assets minus any consideration given by the transferee. Consideration includes any debt assumed by the transferee which burdens the transferred assets. If, incident to the transfer, the transferee pays other debts of the transferor, that counts as consideration only if those other debts had priority over the tax debts. Any assets that the transferee reconveys to the transferor before receiving the notice of transferee liability are disregarded; they cannot form a basis of liability.

In "at law" transferee cases, the transferee's liability usually is not capped. That is, the extent of that liability may exceed the value of the assets received by the transferee. However, this depends upon the contents of the rule of law which provides the basis of substantive liability. That rule may impose a cap reflecting the value of the transferred assets or some alternative measure.

Interest can be tricky in transferee liability cases.[62] There are three stages at which interest may come into play. First, the transferor's liability will include interest computed pursuant to the normal rules of sections 6601 and 6621.[63] Second, interest on what liability the transferee is determined to bear accrues (again at the IRC rates) from the date of issuance of the notice of transferee liability until the date the transferee pays those liabilities.[64] Third, interest also may run for the period between the transfer and the issuance of the notice. However, the IRC is not the source of this third-stage interest. Third-stage interest

---

[60] *See, e.g.*, Papineau v. Commissioner, 28 T.C. 54 (1957).

[61] *See, e.g.*, Yagoda v. Commissioner, 39 T.C. 170 (1962), *aff'd*, 331 F.2d 485 (2d Cir. 1964).

[62] *Compare* Baptiste v. Commissioner, 29 F.3d 1533 (11th Cir. 1994), *with* Baptiste v. Commissioner, 29 F.3d 433 (8th Cir. 1994) (two brothers were transferees of their deceased father's estate and were substantively liable under section 6324(a). The circuits disagreed as to whether the transferees' liability for interest was capped by the value of the assets transferred to them).

[63] *See* Chapter 12.

[64] *See, e.g.*, Mysse v. Commissioner, 57 T.C. 680 (1972).

is available only if authorized by the body of law that provides the basis of substantive liability, and only at the rate prescribed by that body of law.[65]

As stated in Chapter 13, tax liabilities sometimes are dischargeable in bankruptcy. A relatively rarely litigated issue is whether transferee liabilities can be discharged incident to the transferee's bankruptcy. Construing conflicting statutes, the Tenth Circuit has held that the dischargeability of transferee liabilities should turn on the dischargeability of the underlying tax.[66]

VII. ALTERNATIVES TO TRANSFEREE AND FIDUCIARY LIABILITY

The mechanisms of transferee and fiduciary liability are non-exclusive or cumulative remedies. That is, they are among the remedies available to the IRS but are far from the only ones. The IRS may choose to pursue transferee or fiduciary liability or, in preference to them, any other remedy which may be better in the given situation.[67]

For example, the government sometimes (practices vary among IRS field offices) may prefer to bring a fraudulent conveyance action in federal District Court instead of issuing a notice of transferee liability asserting a fraudulent conveyance statute as the source of substantive "in equity" liability. A principal difference is what the government gets if it wins. If the government prevails in a fraudulent conveyance action, the result is the reconveyance to the transferor of legal title to the assets. Then, the IRS will levy against those assets in the transferor's (primary taxpayer's) hands pursuant to the assessments made and liens existing against him or her. In contrast, if the IRS prevails in a transferee liability case, the result is a money judgment against the transferee, which the IRS will assess and collect from the transferee.

The Uniform Fraudulent Transfer Act—which has been substantially adopted by a number of states—allows a creditor to, among other remedies, recover a money judgment against a transferee.[68] Accordingly, in appropriate cases, the IRS might obtain a money judgment against a transferee via the transferee liability procedures (including possible Tax Court proceedings) or the Department of Justice might obtain a money judgment on the IRS's behalf against the transferee via a fraudulent transfer suit in District Court.

---

[65] *See, e.g.*, Stansbury v. Commissioner, 104 T.C. 486 (1995), *aff'd*, 102 F.3d 1088 (10th Cir. 1996).

[66] McKowen v. IRS, 370 F.3d 1023 (10th Cir. 2004) (holding the transferee liability to be nondischargeable because the underlying income tax was nondischargeable).

[67] *See, e.g.*, United States v. Chrein, 368 F. Supp. 2d 278, 283 (S.D.N.Y. 2005) (holding that the IRS may pursue its remedies against the transferor and need not assert transferee liability against a transferee).

[68] *See* United States v. Verduchi, 434 F.3d 17 (1st Cir. 2006); Steve R. Johnson, *Using State Fraudulent Transfer Law To Collect Federal Taxes*, Nevada Lawyer, June 2006, p. 14.

Transferee liability and fraudulent conveyance theories also should be distinguished from nominee and alter ego liens and levies. Nominee and alter ego mechanisms are availed of when the IRS already has assessments against the primary taxpayer and that taxpayer's property is being held by another, without a formal conveyance of legal title to the property to that other. They also may be used when the transferee really has no identity and existence separate from the transferor, such as when a sole shareholder routinely ignores corporate formalities, hopelessly blurring any line between the two. In such cases, the property remains the taxpayer's, and the IRS can levy on it directly, without the necessity of either bringing a fraudulent conveyance suit or issuing a notice of transferee liability.[69]

Other possibilities exist as well. For instance, as noted earlier, section 6901 was enacted to give the IRS a more expeditious procedure than the original trust fund doctrine. But that doctrine survived enactment of section 6901. Thus, although it doesn't happen often, the IRS may still rely on that doctrine in appropriate cases.[70]

PROBLEM

Rhonda and Paul Spear were married on May 20, 1994. They were divorced on July 2, 2001. They were residents of the State of Utopia (not a community property state) throughout their marriage.

Rhonda filed individual federal income tax returns for 1997 through 2001. Despite the fact that Paul had substantial taxable income for 1997 through 2001, he did not file federal income tax returns for those years. The likely source of Paul's unreported income was illegal drug trafficking.

In April 2001, the IRS began an examination of Paul's income tax liabilities for 1997, 1998, and 1999. Paul was represented during the examination by his accountant, E.M. Peoples. By May 27, 2001, Mr. Peoples had been informed of the IRS revenue agent's belief that Paul would owe a substantial amount of taxes for 1997, 1998, and 1999. By September 2001, Mr. Peoples and the IRS agent had discussed Paul's tax liabilities on six occasions.

A hearing incident to Mr. and Mrs. Spear's divorce was held on July 2, 2001. Rhonda and her counsel were present at the divorce hearing. Paul was not present. However, he filed an answer and waiver. Neither Rhonda nor Paul requested a division of property at the hearing or in papers filed incident to the divorce action. Rhonda maintains that she and Paul had discussed a property division before the divorce hearing but had not reached agreement as of the date of the hearing. The divorce court declared the marriage irretrievably broken, and the marriage was dissolved.

---

[60] *E.g.*, Grass Lake All Seasons Resort, Inc. v. United States, 96 AFTR 2d ¶ 2005-6072 (E.D. Mich. 2005), *judgment entered*, 96 AFTR 2d ¶ 2005-6548 (E.D. Mich. 2005).

[70] *See, e.g.*, Leighton v. United States, 289 U.S. 506 (1933).

On September 27, 2001, Paul transferred to Rhonda various assets in which he had an ownership interest. During a later interview with an IRS agent, Rhonda characterized the transfer of assets as follows: "Paul had been drinking a lot, and one night he just called me and told me that he couldn't deal with the property anymore and I could have it."

Indentures transferring Paul's interest in several parcels of real estate were prepared by Rhonda's daughter, an attorney. The indentures contain the sentence: "THIS CONVEYANCE IS PURSUANT TO PROPERTY SETTLEMENT AGREEMENT AND DISSOLUTION OF MARRIAGE."

The market values (net of liabilities) of Paul's interests in the assets he transferred to Rhonda totalled $193,193 on the date of transfer. Immediately after the transfer, the value of the assets Paul retained totalled approximately $404,000. At the same time, his liabilities, including the tax liabilities the IRS believes to exist for 1997 through 1999, totalled approximately $486,000. That amount consisted of $200,000 of tax liabilities (including interest and fraud and other penalties), and $286,000 of debts to creditors other than the IRS. About a month before he made the transfers to Rhonda, Paul gave $100,000 in cash to Wanda Brill, a long-time friend.

In 2005, Paul was tried on criminal tax charges for 1997, 1998, and 1999. He was convicted of violating I.R.C. § 7201 for 1998 and 1999. He was acquitted of criminal tax charges for 1997. As a result of the convictions, Paul was incarcerated for 18 months.

In a notice of deficiency dated March 15, 2005, the IRS determined deficiencies in Paul's income tax and determined fraud penalties for 1997, 1998, and 1999. Paul did not file a Tax Court petition challenging the IRS's determinations. Accordingly, the deficiencies, interest, and penalties were assessed. To date, Paul has not paid the assessed liabilities.

What, if any, potential may the IRS have to collect from Rhonda the unpaid liabilities of Paul? Consider in depth all mechanisms available to the IRS, possible problems with application of those mechanisms and defenses against them, and the steps that would have to be taken to invoke those mechanisms. Also, identify factual ambiguities and indicate why each would be relevant.

Table of Cases

References are to pages and notes.

Table of Statutes

References are to pages and notes.

UNIFORM COMMERCIAL CODE

Table of Secondary Authorities

References are to pages and notes.

INTERNAL LEGAL MEMORANDA (ILM)

Memo.

INTERNAL REVENUE MANUAL

I.R.M.

I.R.S. ANNOUNCEMENTS
Ann.

IRS CUMULATIVE BULLETIN

I.R.S. FORMS
Name

Number/Letter

IRS INFORMATION/NEWS RELEASES

I.R.S. NOTICES

I.R.S. POLICY STATEMENTS

I.R.S. PUBLICATIONS

SENATE REPORTS
Report

REVENUE RULINGS
Rev. Rul.

SERVICE CENTER ADVICE
S.C.A.

STAFF OF JOINT COMM. ON TAXATION

Index

References are to pages.

Private Letter Rulings (See PRIVATE
    LETTER RULINGS)
Regulations (See REGULATIONS)
Revenue Procedures . . . 20
Revenue Rulings (See REVENUE
    RULINGS)
Small Business and Self-Employed
    Division . . . 8–9
Special Procedures Function . . . 349
Sub-regulation IRS pronouncements . . .
    28–29
Tax Exempt and Governmental Entities
    Division . . . 8
Taxpayer Advocate Service . . . 10
Technical Advice Memoranda . . . 23–24
Technological modernization initiatives
    . . . 8
Wage and Investment Division . . . 8

IRS (See INTERNAL REVENUE
    SERVICE)

J

**JEOPARDY/TERMINATION
    ASSESSMENTS**
Generally . . . 139–140; 202–203
Abatement . . . 195–196
Bond in lieu of collection . . . 196
Conditions justifying . . . 186–187
Consequences of
    Jeopardy assessment . . . 210
    Termination assessment . . .
        187–189
Judicial review
    Intended sale of seized property . . .
        196–197
    Section 7429 review, *below*
Section 7429 review
    Generally . . . 191–192
    Administrative phase . . . 192
    Post-trial phase . . . 195
    Trial phase . . . 192–194
Stay of sale . . . 196–197
Taxpayer options and protections
    Abatement . . . 195–196
    Bond in lieu of collection . . . 196
    Section 7429 review, *above*
    Stay of sale . . . 196–197
When used . . . 184–186

JOINT COMMITTEE ON TAXATION
Congress of the United States . . . 3

JOINT INCOME TAX RETURNS
Generally . . . 48–49
Assessment statute of limitations . . .
    157–158
Signatures . . . 55–56
Spousal relief (See SPOUSAL RELIEF)

JUDICIAL BRANCH
Generally . . . 12
Appeals (See APPEALS)
Courts (See SPECIFIC COURT)
Tax cases, types of . . . 13–14

JUDICIAL REVIEW
Generally . . . 17
Deficiency determinations
    Choice of forum (See DEFICIENCY
        DETERMINATIONS)
    Tax Court redeterminations (See
        TAX COURT)
FPAAs . . . 172–174
Jeopardy assessments (See
    JEOPARDY/TERMINATION
    ASSESSMENTS)
Spousal relief determinations . . . 84
Tax Court deficiency redeterminations
    . . . 221
Termination assessments (See
    JEOPARDY/TERMINATION
    ASSESSMENTS)
Trust fund recovery penalty . . . 396–397

JUDICIAL SALES
Collection of taxes . . . 361–362

JURISDICTION
Court of Federal Claims
    Generally . . . 225
    Refund claims . . . 251–252
District Courts
    Generally . . . 225
    Refund claims . . . 251–252
Refund claims
    Court of Federal Claims . . .
        251–252
    District Courts . . . 251–252
    Tax Court . . . 251
Tax Court (See TAX COURT)

L

LEGAL MEMORANDA
Internal Revenue Service . . . 25

LEVIES
Administrative levies . . . 357–359
Relief from . . . 366
Sale of property
    Administrative sales . . . 359–361
    Judicial sales . . . 361–362

LIENS
Creation . . . 350–351
Enforcement
    Administrative levy . . . 357–359
    Administrative sale . . . 359–361
    Judicial sale . . . 361–362
Extent . . . 351–353
Notice of lien . . . 353–355
Priorities . . . 331–333
Relief from . . . 364–365

LIMITATION OF ACTIONS (See STATUTE OF LIMITATIONS)

LIMITED ISSUE FOCUSED EXAMINATIONS
Audits . . . 100

LITIGATION
Generally (See TAX CASES)
Costs (See COSTS)

LITIGATION GUIDELINE MEMORANDA
Internal Revenue Service . . . 24

M

MANUALS
Government manuals . . . 24–25

N

NATIONAL TAXPAYER ADVOCATE
Generally . . . 10

NEGLIGENCE PENALTY
Generally . . . 313–314
Disregard of rules or regulations . . . 314–315

"Negligence" element . . . 314–315

NOTICE OF DEFICIENCY
Additional notices, issuance of . . . 215
Assessment statute of limitations,
    suspension of . . . 150–151
Form and content . . . 210–211
Mailing to taxpayer . . . 211–213
Tax Court jurisdiction and . . . 208–216

NOTICE OF LIEN
Generally . . . 355–357

NOTICE(S)
Advanced Notice of Proposed Rulemaking
    . . . 18
Deficiency, of (See NOTICE OF DEFICIENCY)
Disbarment notices . . . 21
FTD Alert Notice . . . 393
IRS notices . . . 21
Partnership administrative proceeding,
    beginning of
    Generally . . . 167–168
    Period for mailing . . . 168–169
Tax Court deficiency redetermination
    proceedings . . . 218

O

OFFICE AUDITS
Generally . . . 99

OFFICE OF GENERAL COUNSEL
Internal Revenue Service . . . 6

OFFICE OF TAX ANALYSIS
Generally . . . 5–6

OFFICE OF TAX LEGISLATIVE COUNSEL
Generally . . . 6

OFFICE OF TREASURY INSPECTOR GENERAL FOR TAX ADMINISTRATION
Generally . . . 6

OVERPAYMENTS
Generally . . . 237–239
Interest